HOW TO GATHER
Acting Relations, Mapping Positions

Background (or: How we acted under highly volatile circumstances)

We never dreamt we would create the biennial as it occurred. Nor did we imagine we would be publishing this book two years later. The 6th Moscow Biennale of Contemporary Art, as an exhibition, was never fully ours, just as this book is not fully ours either. We are merely a node in a network that feels the urgency for proper public reflection. A similar kind of urgency led us to devote our best efforts to an almost defunct biennial, which resulted in an exhibition of remarkable vitality created under exceptional circumstances.

This publication is the outcome of a shared feeling among the biennial's producers and participants that it had been successful on one of the most important levels a cultural project can hope to achieve: in generating a collective sense of *capacity*, *meaning*, and *camaraderie*. Over ten days—a brief period for an international survey of contemporary art—the biennial re-oriented the public platform of VDNKh's Central Pavilion, the former Soviet exhibition venue for Achievements of the National Economy, toward the question of *how to gather*. It was a question that functioned both as the engine and the outcome of the engagement we embarked upon in Moscow under highly volatile conditions in which the relations between the two poles of Europe—the European Union and Russia—and, more locally, between the biennial and the city partners, were rapidly deteriorating.

So, we decided to scrap everything that makes exhibitions today so expensive—crated air transports, insurance, and high-end production—and invest the limited budget in what we value highly instead: *people* and *actions*. There were pragmatic reasons for this decision too: the weakening exchange rate of the ruble in which the biennial budget had initially been expressed and the reluctance displayed by most European state cultural funding bodies to support a dialogue in and with Moscow (thus often undermining many states' official foreign policy). However dire these conditions may have been, they came to function as incentives: to go back to basics rather than to forfeit, to approach each new limitation as a trigger for further radicalisation.

We could have addressed these limits by exercising critique or antagonised them by revolt or exodus, by boycott or transgression. Instead, we tested and searched for opportunities to galvanise the biennial. We set upon the construction of a *space* that could function as a think tank realised in real time. The space would diverge from contemporary standards of display and demonstrate a clear intention to locate a different present during the time span of the biennial, one that focused on potential starting points beyond impasse. In so doing, the biennial was limited to an unprecedented ten days; to have people meet we needed to facilitate their coming together in the same space at the same time.

One of the key expressions in Russian tradition is the *soviet*, which can be taken to mean 'council' or 'assembly' but also 'advice', 'harmony', and 'concord'. Etymologically, it is derived from notions of togetherness and counsel, with the Proto-Slavonic verbal stem *vetiti* as its ultimate keyword, meaning 'to talk' or 'to speak'. And so, how do we speak together? Often not particularly well. The aim of the exhibition, however, was simultaneously more ambitious than simply speaking together and yet also more basic through the provocation of a series of necessary prerequisites: What are the grounds upon which to build a constituency? Who are we (people, city, nation, empire, etc.)? What will Moscow be like in the future? What fundamentals constitute a better life? And the highly urgent question: *How can we live together?*

Moscow presents unique challenges and thus stimulates unique focus. As organisers, we sought to realise our aspired temporary public space without compromising it to accord with other people's desires or expectations or priorities. Our question was how *not* to compromise our aspiration, how to enable the coming-into-being and the letting-be of a public space through inaction. We facilitated an environment in which we, as organisers, artists and thinkers, as well as the biennial's local and international public, could gain an insight into the future and possible trajectories an open space as such might engage. That was highly urgent, and not just for Moscow.

The artists' presence was not limited strictly to the creation of their works *in situ* but rather unfolded through their direct participation as cultural actors (individually and in relation to each other) at the onset of the creation of cultural space. We lobbied to direct funds toward their involvement and a support system for their proposals. We committed to a flow of different moments; to being attentive to these moments and letting them guide us. That said, and despite all efforts, it is much to our regret that a handful of honoraria, including pre-financed airline tickets, are yet to be honoured more than a year later.

This publication stands as a testament to our conviction that the input of the participants be met by an equally serious commitment from the host of the biennial. Our commitment, first and foremost, was to those outcomes of the biennial that we could not have predicted beforehand, believing this to be what public space is all about. Rather than a documentation of the biennial's on-site activities, the publication that you hold in your hands manifests those activities in their potential of continuation. The content has been sourced from and by the media machine that was active during the ten days of the biennial and features interviews, professional documentation by cameramen and photographers, and critical writing from enlisted Moscow-based bloggers who annotated and analysed the biennial as it progressed, with the goal of one day reflecting upon the capacities it offered.

The gargantuan task of digesting and then transforming the vast amount of digital material into a humble book of and for reflection required one step further still. Many of those involved with the organisation of the biennial continued to care for the content beyond the exhibition's ten-day run. Marie Egger took on the process of editing across three different cities — Antwerp, Rotterdam, and Moscow. Evi Bert organised the 3.4 terabyte digital archive now hosted by M HKA. Katya Savchenko, the biennial's lead producer, never let go of overall responsibility. Maria-Louiza Ouranou came on board at the last minute to salvage this book and coordinate the design and production process before it went to press. Many other participants — artists, thinkers, and visitors alike — were also involved in this process, informing the material or producing retrospective remarks.

Engaged in continual deliberations over its future — to become extinct or transform itself — the Moscow Biennale Foundation, as such, did *not* produce this book. Instead, this publication results from the united efforts of M HKA, the Witte de With Center for Contemporary Art, Kunsthalle Wien, and the V-A-C Foundation. The latter, sharing our intuition that the evaluation of the biennial ought to be continued, assembled a group of young curators in Moscow and asked them to analyse the core of the biennial and its associated program, which hopefully added more value to the question *How to gather?*

What did *we*, as three organisers, and the invited participants, with their extended networks, learn from the experience of the biennial in terms of *gathering*?

Yes, gathering involves people, but it also involves *engagement* and *absence*, people's *presence* and their *withdrawal*. Keren Cytter came through as particularly strong with her generous presence, without directly producing or enabling gathering as such. So too did Liam Gillick, who surprised us in innovative ways each day of the biennial with his letters wired from a location outside Moscow.

We engaged with the *systemic challenges of our time*, as addressed by most of the daily keynotes. Texts from provocative system thinkers such as Yanis Varoufakis, Mariana Mazzucato, Ackbar Abbas, Saskia Sassen, Pascal Gielen, Ulrike Guérot and Robert Menasse, and Eyal and Ines Weizman, included here in this book, testify to this.

Gathering *happens*. The ways in which it does so, however, are often situated on the fringes of visibility of *gathering* as a theme. Its energy is related to a sense of intimacy, as curator and art critic Lee Weng-Choy evokes in his collaboration with filmmaker Ho Tzu-Nyen, who, although unable to join the biennial in person, influenced the exhibition's unravelling. Other forces that became formally visible during daily meetings included the input of futurologist Maya van Leemput, who cultivated encounters between biennial participants and foreign media correspondents residing in Moscow, and the telepathic drawing sessions self-organised by the artists Honoré δ'O and Fabrice Hyber.

Gathering is *relational*. It begins with the diverse plurality of ways in which people can be in relation. Personal and political gestures transformed into conversations and impasses, but also happenings, transcending their initial form and continuing as relations with and in the world. During the course of the biennial, again and again we noticed both impromptu and scheduled actions' and performances' capacity to activate this energy.

Gathering is *fleeting*. We saw artists exercise their capacity to transform images and gestures into micro-moments, tipping them into a new space freed from the initial gestures they had arisen from. Think of Li Mu's subtle contract as an employee, or Fabrice Hyber taking over the Soviet hall as if it was a public park for drawing the faces of seas of people; or Michelangelo Pistoletto's work *Third Paradise* that is not his, it is shared—it is that of others.

Over the biennial's ten days, there were many such instances, moments and threads that came to constitute the exhibition. In that sense, it proved how a series of small events, when collected and woven together, can work to generate a decent *multitude*. Here, language falls short: it fails to describe the biennial's every corner. While some moments of gathering were outwardly visible—the ever-growing constellation of people around renegade artist Konstantin Zvezdochotov, for example, or the dedicated crew working with Birdhead and Els Dietvorst—other moments are out of reach, concealed in the memories of those who experienced them.

Much of what was visible remained on the periphery. Such was the case for the spaces constructed by the physical and intellectual workouts, by the vast groups of volunteers and paid protest participants, by the acrobats of the Moscow circus school, by MEL Space and the designers and producers they called in, and by external groups like Sergey Bratkov's posse, who occupied the woods at the far end of VDNKh. The video crew members, photographers, and bloggers of the media machine each constituted their own space, as did the catering team whose inventive food surpassed all expectations. These actors, through their comings and goings, instantiated and wove together a diverse nexus of relations. As such, when Elena Kholkina situated herself in the Central Pavilion in the dark of night, the biennial was cast as merely a side to her praxis.

The biennial was centralised here and there and operated with a keen eye on enabling genuine modalities. And yet at the same time, the sense that all was out of control—another key element in the notion of gathering—was actively felt, as demonstrated by each participant as they took charge of navigating their respective domains and their project's contours. The attitude that prevailed often came close to that of contemporary activists taking on an issue or project, taking up stakes—partial and idiosyncratic but relating to public space and common capacity all the same. In the past, when religion determined the conventions of society, these agents might have been called people and groups of goodwill. Is that not what we dream of when we speak of activism and dissidence, of Occupy and 'grassroots' movements, of the *Indignados* and global citizenship? We are grateful, we feel privileged to have been part of this, and we have enjoyed each step and opportunity to take the biennial further with this publication.

Bart De Baere,
Director, M HKA Museum of Modern Art Antwerp

Defne Ayas,
Director, Witte de With Center for Contemporary Art

Nicolaus Schafhausen,
Director, Kunsthalle Wien

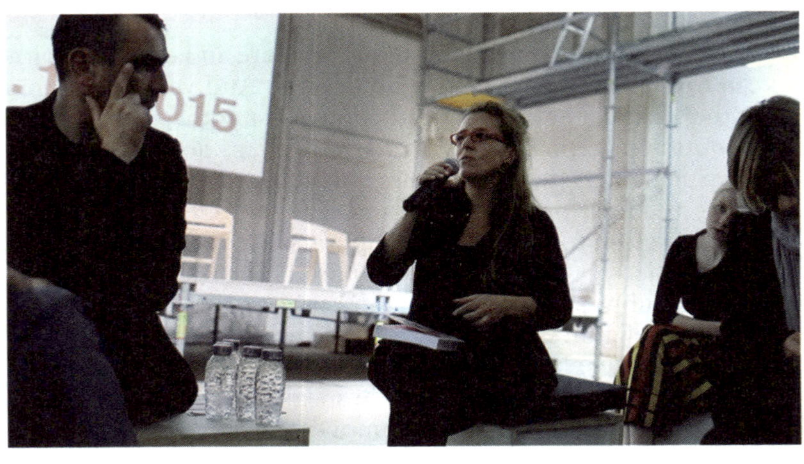

Marie Egger — Editorial

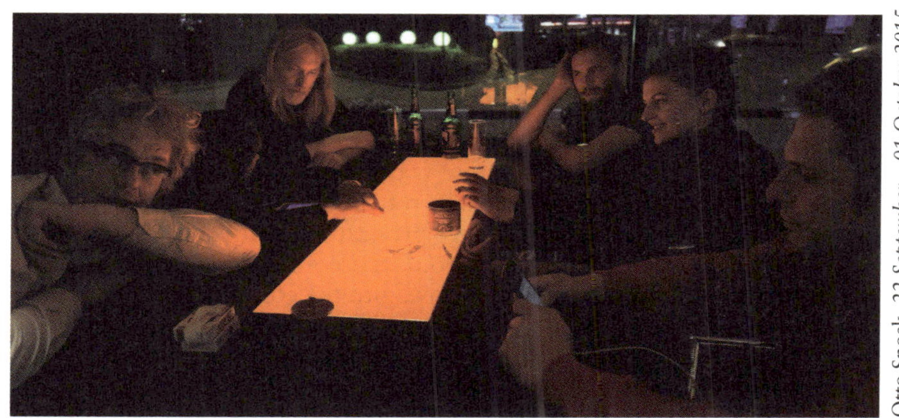

Otto Snoek, 22 September – 01 October 2015

In 2005, I participated in a summer school where students did not take classes like Math, English, Chemistry or History, but where everyone subscribed to courses on specialised academic topics, which we then investigated together in study-groups. This took place at a boarding school where no one knew each other. During that time, we also formed sports clubs and a choir, organised a volleyball tournament and a revue show where we sang and danced on stage. In the end, everyone departed from each other in tears at a local train station, with the promise to always miss one another and forever appreciate the weeks we had spent together.

The time after the summer school was difficult for me. I missed the people and inspiration I had drawn from the camp. The summer school was a relatively exclusive programme with the goal to foster adolescents and let them unfold in a communal setting of close togetherness with strangers. I dove into the community there, believing that I had finally met others who were 'like me'—and then clashed with my friends and family at home. I felt special and superior, and excluded people around me who had not shared my experience. Apparently, this effect was so common it even had a name: academy depression.

What I learned from the experience is how you should *not* speak together. As a result, I became suspicious of academically structured events or such intellectual gatherings. In the beginning of 2015, ten years later, I started thinking about the 6th Moscow Biennale. Was my summer school, ultimately, a wrong way of gathering? How would it be possible to *not* make the biennial in Moscow an exclusive, elitist or shielded event? In which ways could it evolve into a good example of gathering?

For me, the Moscow Biennale 2015 became an investigation into togetherness. Bart De Baere, Defne Ayas and Nicolaus Schafhausen, who took up the biennial as a shared endeavour, rooted our curatorial approach in the very fundamental question of how to live together. A seemingly simple question at first, it soon became a rich source of inspiration to everyone involved with the project, especially to the artists we invited. What do we consider a good life? How can we be together? How can we come together? How can we speak together? We are still trying to find answers to these questions. Back then, they quickly brought up the necessity for a biennial that could facilitate ways of doing that. This publication is a witness to and a probe of what we have taken away from the ten days of the Moscow Biennale 2015.

How to Gather?—The title of this book gives an answer to the issues of the biennial, and offers a new proposal to think further. It is the result of the project and at the same time a part of it. What you are holding in your hands is an attempt to both document ten days of gathering in Moscow and to make accessible an open forum that lived on in the aftermath of the project. The most crucial direction to this book was taken in early 2015, when the organisational work on the biennial had just begun: This publication is an outcome (or a container of intermediate stages) of a collective effort to not only think about gathering, but to also come together in person and to remain in touch through a platform that now reaches its printed stage.

How to Gather? consists of various individual contributions, and as such may not propose a manual to answer to the title, but much rather recognises the necessity to assemble or just meet. We do so as individual beings. My personal way-in to the topic affected a comparison of Western Europe vs. Russia to remain as my take-away from the adventure: I travelled to Moscow from Vienna where I was working at the time. Our curatorial team came from Belgium, the Netherlands/Turkey and Germany and was partly based in Berlin where we occasionally met. That is to say, I was used to a day-to-day work and life experience in Western Europe. Travelling to Russia, for me, also meant embarking upon the adventure of travelling to six industrial cities for a biennial side project with the Austrian Embassy. Together with Russian, Austrian and international artists, I split my weeks between Moscow and various places in the European part of Russia.

Without knowledge of the Russian language or any contacts in the country, I took seriously the remarks of colleagues and friends at home who pointed out the difficulties they thought I might have to face: Realising a project like this in a country that oppressed freedom of opinion, confirmed only modest budgets and offered little support for contemporary art thus created challenges I would not have experienced at home. In later conversations, I shared my experiences from the trips: arriving at Moscow airport with no accommodation or plan what to work on next; crashing at my colleague Katya's place; difficulties in meeting up and connecting with Russian artists and the art scene because of language barriers or what I felt were reservations towards our projects; realising that the supermarket shelves were out of French cheeses because of the EU sanctions, or benefitting from a ruble rate that made some expenses in Moscow seem unexpectedly cheap to me. It was surprising to see how international political and economic relations (with the EU) directly affected everyday life.

Also, I observed rather little open critique towards the government and its decisions from within the country while I was travelling. My unnerving urge to pick sides and to try and resolve things I could not resolve irritated me considerably. It shifted into a wish to make visible, or visualise, what these irritations were. It seemed to make sense to try and build an environment for everyone to join together and create an open space for discussion and encounters; where people could express themselves and engage in conversations. Not with the goal to colonise but with the intention to meet one another, to listen, to create, and to speak freely.

Together with my colleagues in Moscow, I was entrusted with the task of programming the biennial on site and from abroad. I discussed curatorial matters with the participants and had resolved wholeheartedly not to let the biennial become an event that would create exclusion. That is how one lead topic for this book became that of the Other, of moments of encounter and of speaking to one another.

Anastasiya Yarovenko (p. 148) shared this approach, and wanted to make active use of her presence in the venue of the Moscow Biennale, VDNKh Pavilion No. 1. She decided to talk to visitors in Russian, and also to confront them with prejudices and have conversations "in a very Buber sense"—meaning to refocus on the concept of dialogue as proposed by the philosopher Martin Buber, who sees the individual in a dialogical relation to his or her environment where the Other may be another person, a deity, an animal, a plant or another kind of entity.

The idea of the relationship between the individual and its surroundings comes back in the first and second chapters of the publication at hand, *the individual* and *in relation*. To investigate a fundamental condition like this, we invited participants and visitors, just as I would like to invite you to think about how you encounter those around you. This may point to the difficulty of speaking to each other with no misunderstanding. Perhaps it is impossible to always fully comprehend each other, but some conversations are all the more worth having precisely because of that. The Chinese writer Mián Mián and Nicolaus Schafhausen both exercised this brilliantly in their daily *Talk-show* (p. 119). Their conversation shows how something new and fruitful, at times even nonsensical or just fun, may arise out of confrontation.

Another example of this is the encounter between the Lithuanian artist Augustas Serapinas and the Chinese painter Qiu Zhijie, who drew the *Map of the Third World* (p. 137). This map is a semi-fictitious calligraphy on the topological, political and ideological conditions of our world today.

Behind this map, inside the scaffolding we had set up, Augustas Serapinas built a tea room to which he continuously invited participants and visitors to join him for a Chinese tea ceremony: As he insisted on my joining him as well, I ended up spending a wonderful half-hour laughing with him in the little room, learning about the tea ceremony and trying to understand what the others sitting at the table discussed in Russian. I hope that the included multilingual conversation (p. 140) conveys some of the lovely atmosphere of that part of the pavilion to you.

Another of the many artists working in the pavilion was Alevtina Kakhidze. In retrospective drawings (p. 307) she reflects on her project *All Times News*—a news channel set up for the duration of the biennial, screening five to ten minute long news broadcasts in the café at the main entrance of the pavilion three times a day. Her *Future News*, *Present News* and *Past News* dealt with what was going on in the pavilion, in Russia and worldwide at the time. Also, for example, in Ukraine.

The conflict between Russia and Ukraine was vividly discussed among participants, guests and organisers. The period of the biennial was officially one of ceasefire for the war in the Donbass. However, Vladimir Putin's speech at the UN General Assembly in New York at the end of September 2015 was his first for several years and happened during the ten days of the biennial. The last day of the biennial marked the beginning of Russia's military intervention in Syria and thus set into motion the global political developments that still dominate news broadcasts today, providing an example of the defence politics that not only influenced the biennial in the making, but also during its aftermath while editing this book.

With her news broadcast, Alevtina Kakhidze managed to create a seismograph for the biennial's goings on. Not primarily directed at geopolitical events, her screenings succeeded in involving everyone present and in conveying a feeling for what moved people during those ten days. From a curatorial perspective, *All*

Times News became a token from which to sense where the daily programme of the biennial might be headed and accentuated, and also which topics and discourses would be worth following up on later.

Further, the global proxy war in Syria has become symbolic of a juxtaposition between East and West anew—something we had carefully considered a year beforehand, during the preparations for the Moscow Biennale. Taking into account the historical and geographical conditions of Russia in this delicate matter as well as its current political immediacies and interests, many of the things I discovered about Russia and Western Europe during my work on this project have fed into the editing and arrangement of the contributions in this book. What this publication refers to as *political gestures* in its third chapter are contributions that either defend a distinct political position or make ways by which to approach a political conflict or a defect, or that seek to define the political in general.

The notion of dissidence appears most prominently in Ines and Eyal Weizman's duo-contribution *on dissent and activism* (p. 292). They juxtapose these as two models for encountering a political conflict where Ines and Eyal also propose case studies to show how one may subtly act as an activist through dissent and how to express dissent with activist actions. These and other thoughts on acting publicly, for me, prompted questions on what exactly is the public that you address when you address the public and which public to refer to when arguing in dichotomies like East versus West. It is in this realm that I see Saâdane Afif's *Play Opposite* chime in: I invite you to find the manual of his performance in this publication (p. 246) and to re-enact the piece as explained.

Anna Jermolaewa's performance *Political Extras* developed different layers of interpretation I had not expected while curating her work: Meant as a commentary on democratic rights and freedom of assembly, in addition, it also pointed to a certain misery in local social conditions. Anna's text included here (p. 225) discusses this with an eye on the Russian context.

For the biennial, Leon Kahane conceived a performance for which he publicly took daily ballet classes in the Central Dome of the pavilion to challenge the opposition of liberal arts and high culture. His text, which forms a personal reflection on his presence and work in Russia (p. 237), is an argument to a discussion that unfolds in this book between some of the keynote speakers, artists and young Russian curators, who were engaged in a post-reading of the biennial by the V-A-C Foundation: The juxtaposition of Eastern values versus Western values that, for us, led to the notion of *systemic shapes*.

Chapter four of this publication refers to these *systemic shapes*; points of view that overarch formal historical or geographical boundaries to widen our perspective from political gestures to inter-cultural circumstances in order to analyse different systems of reference: Simon Denny and Mariana Mazzucato both spoke about the economics of innovation (pp. 328 and 345 respectively); Yanis Varoufakis shared the story of how he experienced the Euro-Crisis (p. 360); Ulrike Guérot and Robert Menasse allowed the reprinting and translation into Russian of their essay *Europe — The Reconstruction of the Free World* (p. 375).

It was with a nervous ear that I listened to the argumentations on the nation state during the biennial. They unrolled either in proposals to abandon the nation state or in its defence as a means to preserve diversity. The contributions by political scientists, sociologists and theorists referred to art as something that is granted the potential and at times assigned the task of reforming society. But how does it affect artists and cultural producers to be outspokenly entrusted with such expectations?

When we asked the economist Evgeny Gontmakher to conceive a panel on the concept of Eurasia, the invitation was already critically commented on by fellow participants during the inception of the biennial. Some of the remarks on Eurasia made on stage, proposed very different views on the idea than those from the basic knowledge I had before the preparation for the project. Rather than as a cultural or geographical entity, they discussed Eurasia in economic terms. The extract of the discussion included on page 419 offers insight into some key comments and into a perspective on Eurasia that proposes leaving the concept behind while voicing criticism towards enlightened European thinking.

This still moves me a lot. Different from what I had first thought, these words are not primarily to be heard as signs of offence or misunderstanding towards Europe. It was more shocking for me to recognise the trench between me and the people talking on the stage. It felt like there were mutual presumptions blocking a train of thought so that it became impossible to even begin a discussion. I was, again, failing to speak together… And this book is conceived with that in mind.

After the biennial, I returned to Vienna and Berlin where a wave of refugees had arrived during the summer of 2015. I had only witnessed this from the news in Russia, where the problem had also seemed very far away. Returning to two cities where I understood the language people were speaking on the streets, in buses and trains, alerted me to a tensed atmosphere of mistrust and pessimism, as well as to a certain melancholy and sadness. It made what I had taken away about togetherness from the Moscow Biennale seem redundant and pointless—as though the biennial had been an experiment on too small a scale to actually help face the rise of populism and fundamentalist tendencies that seem to mark an actual failure of humanist ideals. Why should we try and figure out how to meet one another when nobody around us appears to be up for it at all?

For me, this brought up the issue of the responsible citizen and made me return to the biennial keynote of Saskia Sassen who, from a global perspective, tackles the question *Who are we, the citizens?* (p. 384). She elaborates on a scenario of global developments where citizens are losing their rights and power over land and cities that should actually be theirs. An appeal to civil rights and duties, her talk informed the notion of the global citizen that Pascal Gielen ties back to examples of European and international activist movements (p. 405). His critique of neoliberal policies neighbours contributions such as Ulrike Guérot's, whose criticism of the current civic conditions are met with ideas of revolt or the formation of new movements to face the European crisis.

Driven by these call-outs to become active, to organise and to stand up for democratic values, what actually are these values? Are they equal to Western values? Are civil rights the same as human rights? What does the word 'liberal' entail? And how is liberal democracy currently changing?

Recently, my thoughts about the biennial were wonderfully underpinned in October 2016 when the German journalist and author Carolin Emcke won the Peace Prize of the German Book Trade. The prize has been awarded since 1950 and promotes a commitment to peace, humanity and understanding among all peoples and nations of the world. The peace prize is renowned and valued among German intellectuals and Carolin Emcke's speech was vividly discussed after the award ceremony. At a moment when it is all the more important to argue one's political position, Carolin Emcke's statements on inclusion and exclusion provided a meaningful contribution to my concerns on how to gather. She defended liberal, secular democracy and the humanist ideals that grant the individual with human rights one does not have to earn by law, but possesses by birth. She argued this in regard to increased aggression, nationalism and resentment in (German) society.

Her speech stemmed from an analysis of the word to *belong*: She asked whether belonging implies ownership or participation, or to fit somewhere. Referring to minorities, her talk was about belonging to society, to a group of people, to a community. This is closely tied to the notions of the nation state and citizenship as discussed at the Biennale and in this book. People needing to share identical points of view, Carolin Emcke said, is not a valid requirement to grant them the same rights; just as their differences do not constitute a valid reason for exclusion. So, to encounter the Other as different cannot mean perceiving it as unequal.

I experienced the 6th Moscow Biennale as a project with this background. The biennial aimed to make visible appearances of multitude and to create a space where it was possible to speak together, to gather and to try and overcome misunderstandings, chasms or what might lie between us and others. Its format of a ten-day meeting in Russia followed by a comprehensive publication two years later is a mutual long-term endeavour. Ideas and conversations were given the time and space they needed. That is only possible in an experimental setting—like a laboratory on time.

In this regard, the aftermath of the biennial is as important as its preparations and the ten-day happening. It is not enough to just act, but also essential to share and reflect in order to find the right ways to speak together and to possibly activate the potential of contemporary art to disrupt or hold society together.

Part 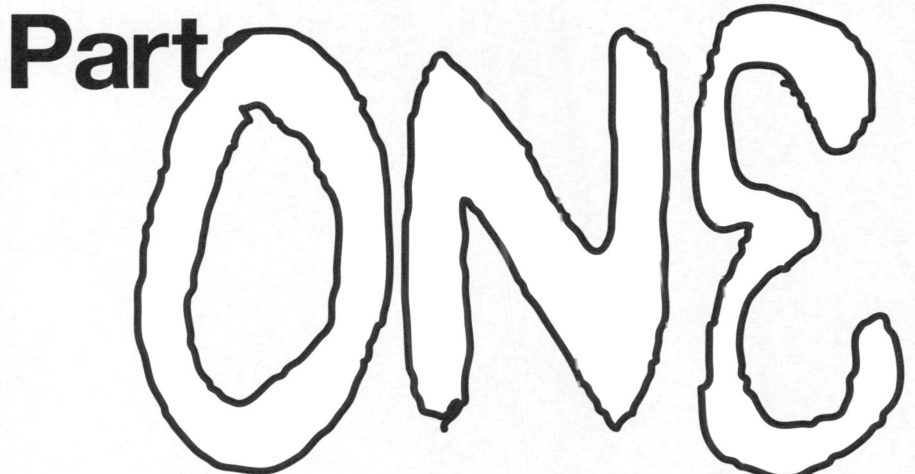

The Individual

Keren Cytter — Note from Bed

I woke up dead today. I was also dead yesterday. I was also dead the day before yesterday. To be honest I am dead for over nine years. I am dead since 2006. I was suffering from a long dying process that started in 2003 and went on for 3 years. A slow process of decay. The cause of this consistent state of illness is my move to Europe. I can't say I regret it. If I wouldn't have moved to Europe I would end up dead in Israel, but in a different position. If I had moved to the US as I actually wanted (instead of Europe), I would also be dead by now. I guess in a different position, too. I would wake up dead and rotten. Not well preserved as I woke this morning. I am half European, half Mediterranean. One hundred per cent white female. A corpse. A mummy. A scared, hunted immigrant lives inside me, or dead inside me. Anyhow that's my soft side. My live side. My kind side. It's my experienced side. My sensitive side. I have no sensibilities on any other side than this one. The rest of my body is a rock, no matter how you turn it. Once I wanted to be a writer, a Russian writer, but I lost faith in books. I hardly read them. The last book I read was about a man who loves books. My mother read this book too. She was afraid it will end badly. I knew the ending is going to be sweet. A book about loving books can never end badly. There is something sweet about it. Like compote. A grandmother kind of sweetness. Sentimentally sweet. I hate it. It disgusts me. So why am I writing now? (If I just said I don't like books might mean I don't like writing?) Because I forgot my adaptor at the biennial, and if I want to take nice photos of Lenin and Stalin's grave tomorrow, I shouldn't use my iPhone tonight. I was planning to edit a movie (long story) tonight and then I remembered I forgot it with the phone's charger at the biennial. After that was clear, I called the reception and asked for an adaptor. A fat bald man came to my room holding two adaptors. I picked the one with three holes but it didn't match. I slowly got used to the idea anyhow. So I decided to do something analogue. Write an idea for a movie. In order to do that, I need to clear the table and write whatever crosses my mind. And that's exactly what crossed my mind. My death.

I have tears in my eyes. They appeared after writing the last paragraph. I felt sorry for myself when I remembered my play was cancelled.

Maybe I should stop eating? It would save me lots of money and it will be much easier to carry me. My body will look like a feather blown in the wind. By the way, forgot to mention, I'm in Moscow right now. Lying in bed. I'm an artist. I'm also very tired. Physically. It's 3am and I want to go to sleep.

I couldn't fall asleep. I stayed awake until the sunrise. Now it's a different time. Same place. I'm after breakfast and gym and a bit sleepy. Again. I am more pleased and pleasant and I am def not dead. Maybe I was never dead. I'm just resting in peace between the sheets. Life is brighter. The sun is shining. My body is warm.

My adaptor is found and I type what I wrote a couple of nights ago. I look at Facebook and read Chantal Ackerman just died. She committed suicide. I need to drink water.

Hanne Lippard — Here's it

When does an individual become a body
When does a body disembody
When this a body does some body
When does it really really hurt?
Pain is individual.
A cut made in the middle.
Male thoughts.
Air mail.
Three days later, upon arrival.
A package.
Nothing but.
Hear, he said, hear is my ear.
It is. And her.
What is there to say about her?
What did she say?
Herself?
She?
Said, nothing.
When does an ear stop learning
When does a body stop leaning
When does life leave life
When does love live life
When does it feel like time left
Or the exact opposite.
Pain is a stain on any complexion.
Does somebody care about that body
Or is that body just somebody
What does a body to somebodies
When is a body just a burden
What do birds care
What is that burden for a bird
What do others think
What do others thoughts think
What body cares about its own?
Or those.
Them, never.
Here- he said, to her.
Female thoughts.
Her ears were present,
but they did not listen.

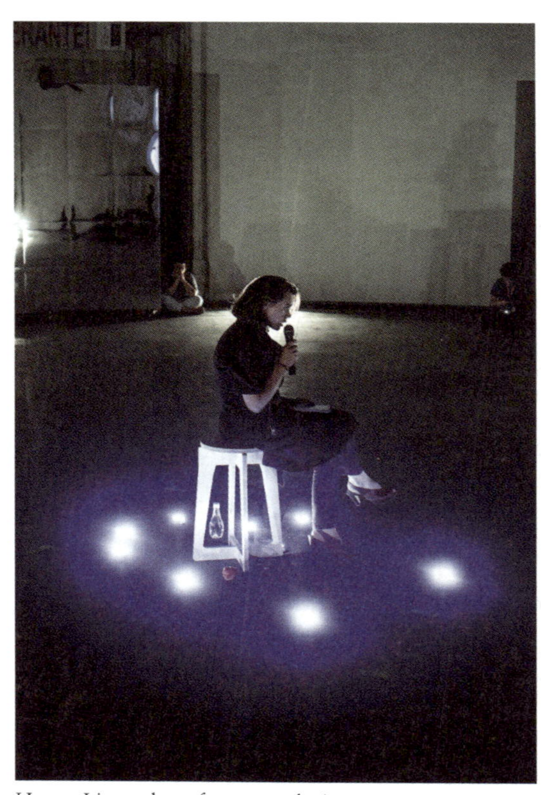

Hanne Lippard, performance during Moscow Biennale, 27th September 2015

Sergey Bratkov — Predictions on the Moon

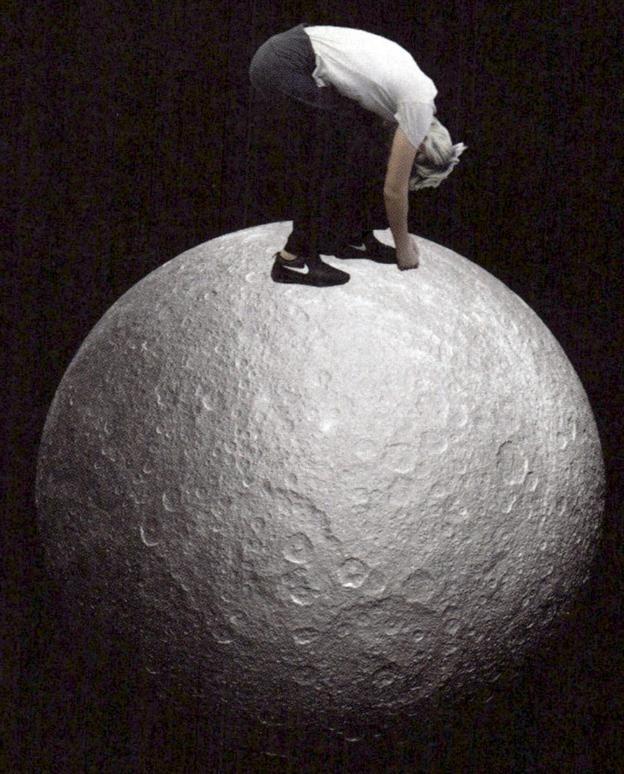

Наталия Коган не догадывается,что свой медовый месяц проведёт в голубой капсуле на гребне Марса с видом на Млечный Путь

Natalia Kogan has no idea that she'll be spending her honeymoon in a blue capsule on the edge of Mars with a view of the Milky Way

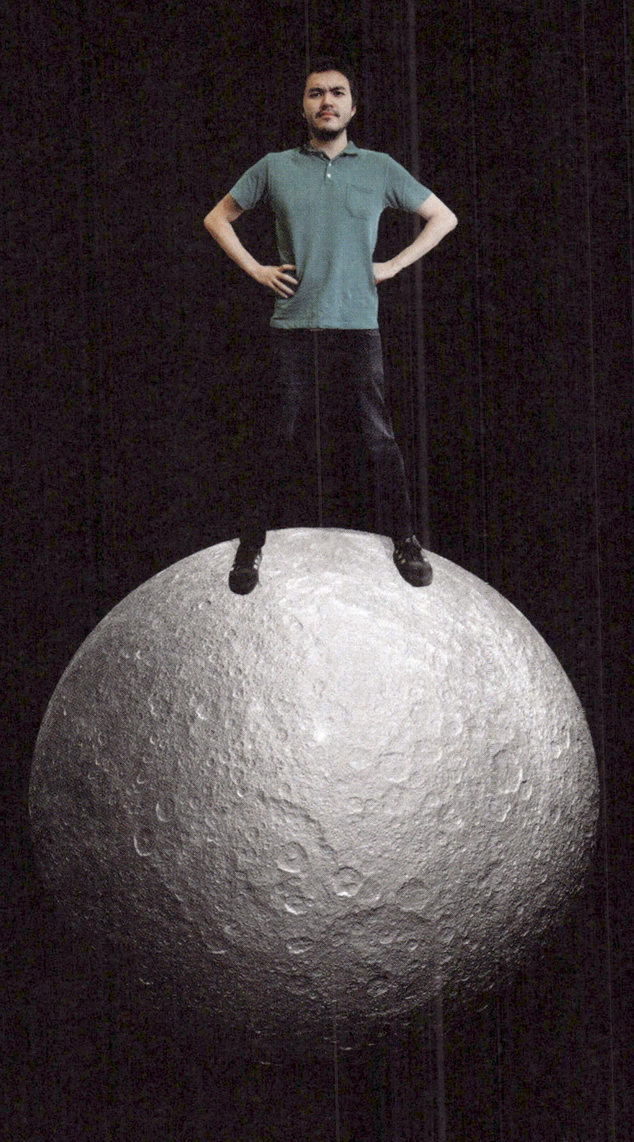

Фуркат Палванзаде не помышляет о том, что его портрет будет воспроизведён на голографической купюре Меркурия в 100 МЕ

Furqat Palvanzade doesn't realise that his portrait will be reproduced on the holographic banknotes of Mercury in 100 ME

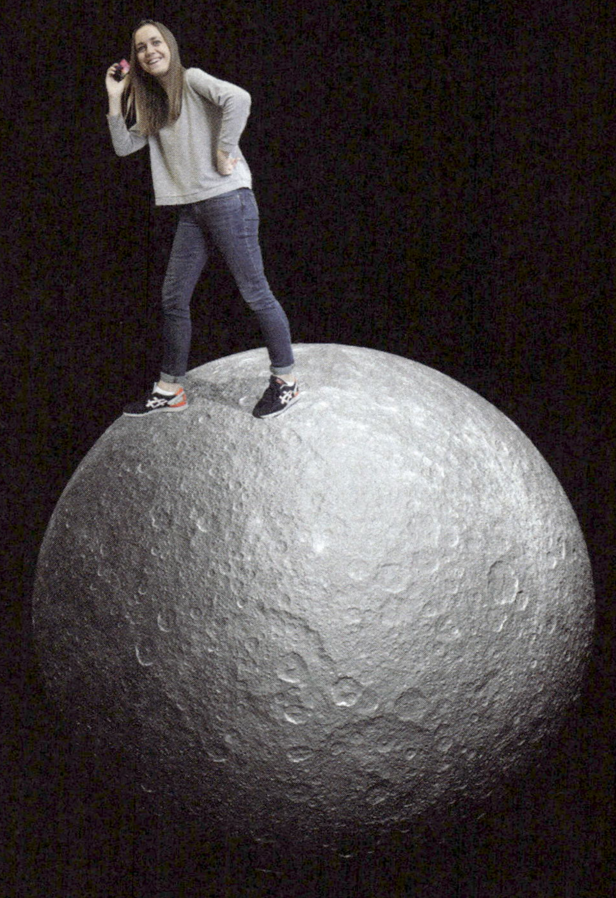

Люда Фрост ещё пока не знает о том, что изобретёт вакцину, локализующую вселенскую сетевую агрессию

Luda Frost doesn't yet know that she will invent a vaccine that prevents universal network aggression

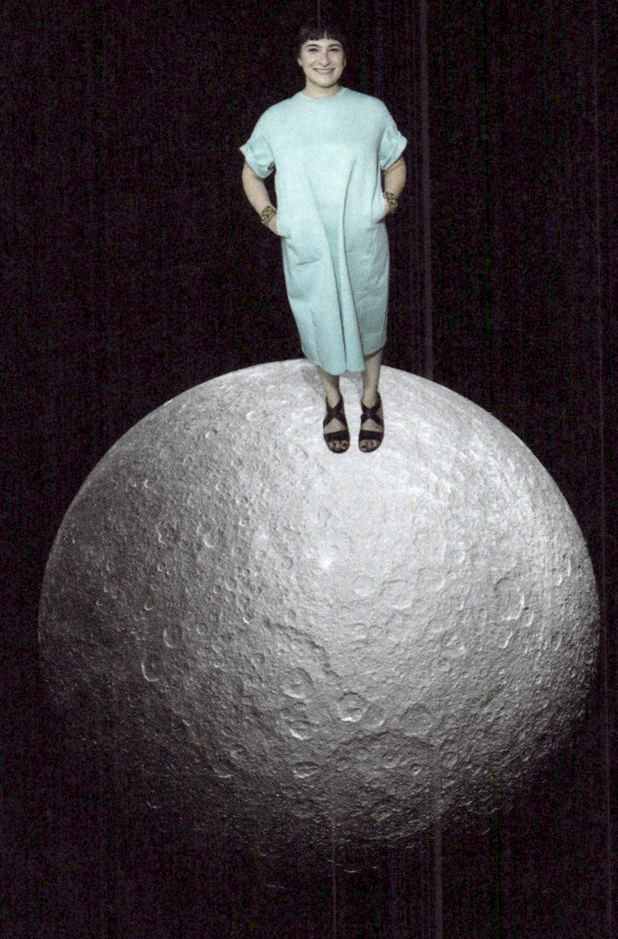

Таус Махачева не подозревает,что выиграет гран-при Сатурна по кольцевым гонкам на звездолётах

Taus Makhacheva doesn't suspect now that she will win the Saturn Ring-Racing Grand-Prix

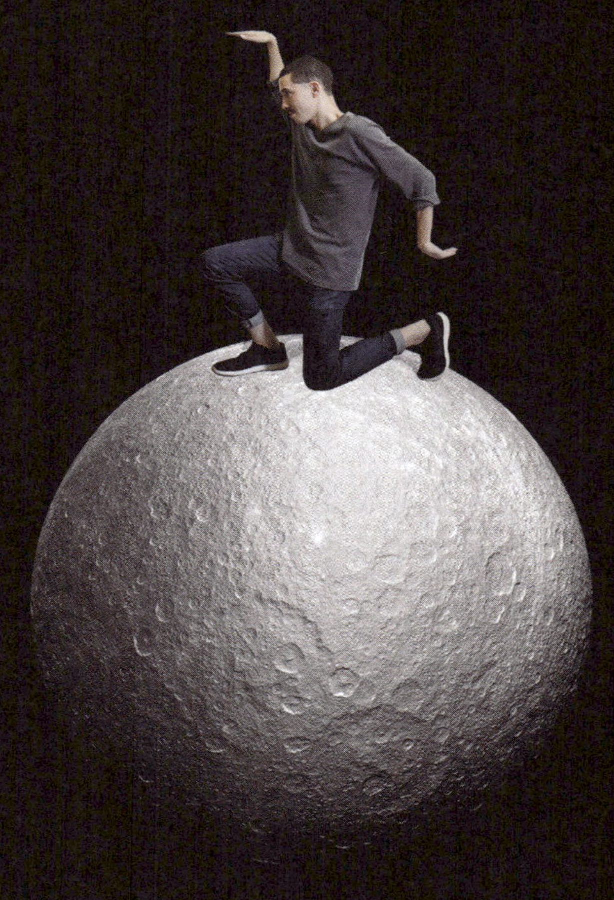

Иван Ерофеев далёк от мысли,что вскоре сделает знаменитый фотопортрет группы инопланетян на космической базе отдыха

It hasn't occurred to Ivan Erofeev that soon he will take a famous picture of a group of aliens at the space recreation base

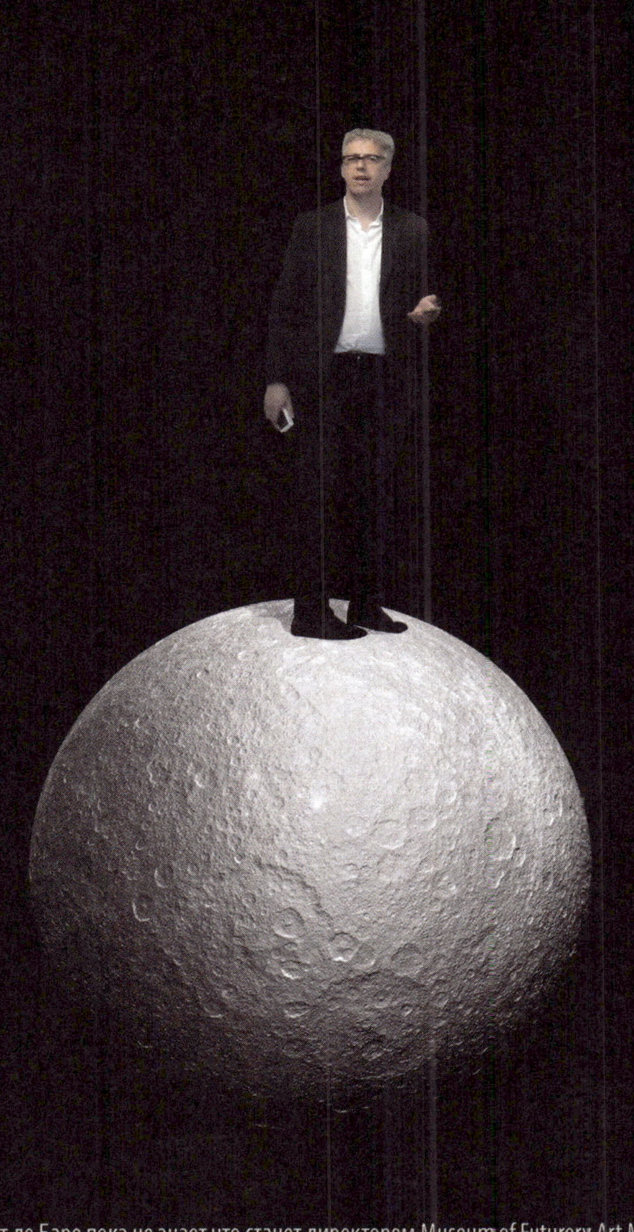

Барт де Баре пока не знает, что станет директором Museum of Futurery Art Mars (MoFAM)

Bart De Baere still doesn't know that he will become director at the Museum of Futurery Art Mars (MoFAM)

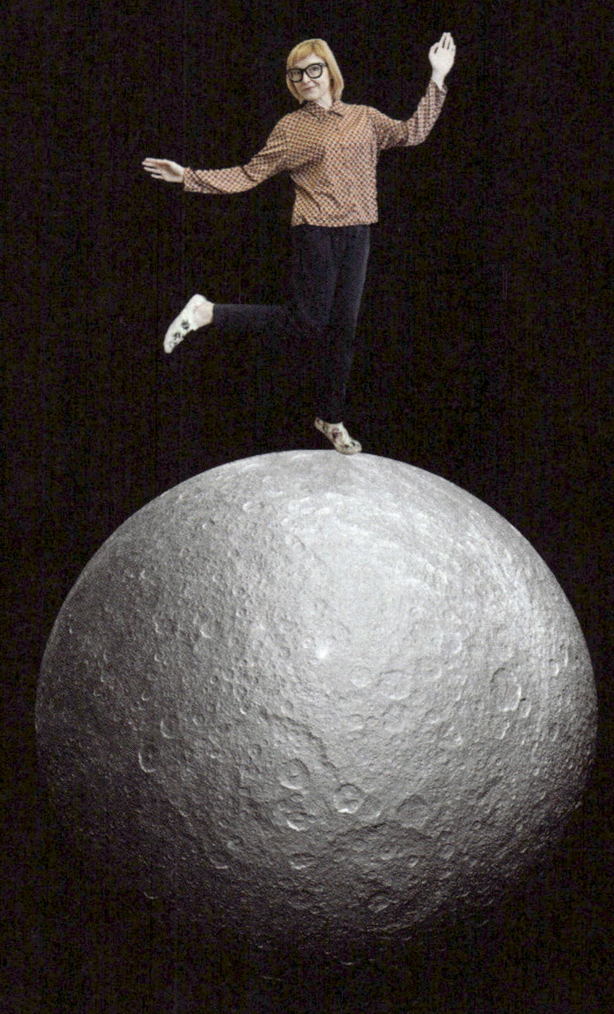

Мария Терехова даже представить себе не может то, что вскоре станет моделью G.L.Y.W. с продолжительностью жизни 250 лет

Maria Terekhova can't even imagine that she'll become a G.L.Y.W. model with a lifespan of 250 years

Liam Gillick — Letters from Moscow

121, Prospekt Mira, Moscow

Letter from Moscow
Monday September 21, 2015

There is an old saying here that in the future there will be no difference between waste and energy. What used to make sense no longer has any traction at a time when discourse has replaced action. The weather is clear right now. But it will get warmer throughout the week. Talk on the streets has been of the re-election of the Greek government. Tsipras have played a smart game. I leave my apartment here every morning and head down to the café on the corner. I have gotten to know the girl behind the bar. We attempt to talk about political strategy but I know she is laughing at me - though a strange pity shows in her eyes. She told me the other day that her boyfriend thinks I am a fool. That European progressives see something in this Tsipras thing that is merely a reflection of their own weakness and lack of control. Tsipras for him means nothing. And as a result - it means I have no grasp of the inherent corruption of the European Union. I need to find a new café but the pity in those eyes keeps me coming back.

I made a list of varied “izations” on the paper table cloths that they love here. "Virtualisation", "containerization", "orchestration". I was on a roll. The girl came over to see if I needed more coffee or a shot of something to pick me up a little. Fury for a second. Then she deliberately spilt my cup across the table. Fussing around and talking to herself under her breath she furiously wiped the paper - smearing my notes. It took a second to realize that she was talking to me - not to herself.

“What?”
“Beat me gat thu delta quake.”
“What?”
“Sorry?”
“Meet me at a data snake”
“I am really sorry. But I can’t understand...”

My Russian is still rusty and not up to snuff...

Reeling she dropped the cup to the ground. Bending to pick it up she spoke clearly into my left ear.

“Meet me at the Data Lake.”

I grabbed my book and my phone and left quickly for the apartment.

Until tomorrow...

Take care of yourself...

Береги себя

Liam

121, Prospekt Mira, Moscow

Letter from Moscow
Tuesday September 22, 2015

I woke up at 5am and watched the sun come up in the city. Saw twenty year old German cars unleash across the street. I can't think in a decent direction. I think one of my teeth is loose or my skull is loose and my teeth are fine. My head feels inside out. The lining of my brain is dehydrated. My feet look blue. The line was too long to get into the Lenin Mausoleum yesterday afternoon. There's a hole in the front of my face where my mouth should be. How do you test a hole? I need to sleep but it is impossible when you feel this bad. So what do you do to test a hole?

You go to a bar. Focus on a crossword - the easiest ones here are designed for semi-literate guest workers like me and can be bought from the traditional octagonal news stands that dot the city center. I want to put something in my drink to take the edge of it. But there is nothing but Red Bull or the Russian equivalent of Mountain Dew. I belong to no one. My teeth are loose. I wish I could remember where I am supposed to meet the girl from the café. I bet Rem Koolhaas never has these problems.

It feels like no-one owns this city. It has systemic edges. But in the center it is mute. Moscow keeps churning along. I am desperate to find some peace here. A systemic peace. One that can be tested and mapped and fully realized. I motioned for another drink. Six down. An accumulation of numbers. Four letters. Ten across. A landlocked body of water. Four letters.

Math Pond?

Today is a write off.

Until tomorrow...

Take care of yourself...

Береги себя

Liam

121, Prospekt Mira, Moscow

Letter from Moscow
Wednesday September 23, 2015

Data Lake! It's all coming back to me. All the streets were closed off near my apartment today. I stayed home and watched the normal mix of poverty baiting and news slinging on TV. My internet connection is incoherent. I am trying to use the wi-fi system from the apartment upstairs. Every time I guess the password it gets changed. But it keeps me focused - running through various cute pet names, Russian soccer players and school yard taunts packed with zeros and dates.

In Moscow they love to wash the streets. It's an important gesture but still feels alien to me. I spent many years in Paris - jetlagged and up early to witness the ritual cleansing of the boulevards. I always coveted the little bundles of wood and carpet that they used to stop off the drains and keep the water flowing. In Nice every night they would hose down the square in the old town. Wash the trash away until it slowly dried out the following morning and made it's way back home.

What they need here is a decent Mosque. I keep going on about it to the two guys who live upstairs. I think they think I think they would use a decent Mosque if they had one - but I keep explaining to them that its just an observation. Something about the way I pronounce "observation" in Russian must be coming out wrong. I think they think I am saying it is just an "accusation". Something about the resulting frisson gets me going. It's clear that they cannot be sure that I am saying accusation so they don't quite take offence. But they steal themselves for imminent insult. Otherwise they play PlayStation all day. CSKA v Spartak v Dynamo v Torpedo v Lokomotiv. I am trying to sell them the idea of a soccer and insurgent shooter mix up. I am pretty sure the tall one replied that I would need a Math Pond to achieve that in online mode. But maybe I misunderstood him. We laughed. I told them the anecdote about how I want to teach Gramsci to architects in Ivy League Universities. So they stopped laughing and went back into their apartment.

This evening I think I will go out. As I sweetened up I was sure I could hear the call to prayer - very faint but unmistakable. At this time of year in Moscow it is great to go to Armenian bars. They have fantastic brandy. And you can talk about love and sex and money. They get a bit sentimental in a paradisical-utopian way after a few but I have acquired the Russian knack of bringing things down to earth with airport stories.

I may have pushed it too far tonight. After a few dozen; Let's get starteds! To yous! To your healths! To our meetings! To our friendships! To the hostess! To women! To our parents! and To loves! I stood on the table and shouted in my base Armenian "Love is like an Airport!" I don't know what's happening to me but I think the guys upstairs know something about the location of the Data Lake.

Nostrovia!

Until tomorrow...

Take care of yourself...

Береги себя

Liam

121, Prospekt Mira, Moscow

Letter from Moscow
Thursday September 24, 2015

My room is becoming a Scandinavian prison cell. I haven't been able to buy any new furniture since I arrived and my irritation with the design of the existing things leads me to pile everything away anywhere I can find some space. This has left me with a monk's cell. A table, a chair and a simple bed. In this vast city I am just a biological cell in a body that I cannot control so I better get my shit together.

This morning I was looking for somewhere to hide the various potted plants that were abandoned here by the previous owner. I went to the Azbukha Vkusa supermarket on the corner and borrowed a trolley with a wink and a swift purchase of Arborio rice. It's been hot here. And I struggled down the stairs with the plants. Piled into the trolley I made my way towards the Tretyakov Gallery on Krymsky Val. Damn security checks everywhere, but I have a good route. I stopped for a rest on Ordynskiy Tupik, in the little park.

The girl from my café was sitting on a low wall with a small box. I stopped to say hello. "The day my mother died, five kittens were born". I parked my trolley to stop it rolling away and looked into the box. The kittens were sleeping.

I promised her I would be right back and rushed ahead pushing my trolley full of plants.

At the back of the museum, one of the guys from the apartment upstairs opened the loading bay doors and I pushed my trolley inside. "Are you sure this is OK?" "Sure." "OK. Well, thanks. And I am sorry about the Mosque misunderstanding." He didn't answer. But walked off into the museum pushing the trolley ahead of him. He has a place with everyone else's plants, under the stairs. No questions asked.

As I walked off I saw them unloading a Buddha Machine. I can't think what else to call it. It was a machine in the shape of a Buddha.

Shit. Kittens. Running back to Ordynskiy Tupik there was no sign of the girl. In the park there were handsome young men dressed for waiting, moving chairs around. They placed name cards on some chairs, then studied documents and moved the name cards around. Then moved them around again. Training. Getting ready for staged events future and planned. As I turned for home I saw the logo on the back of their shirts.

"Data Lake"
Troitskoye, Mytishchinsky District, Moscow Oblast

Until tomorrow...

Take care of yourself...

Береги себя

Liam

121, Prospekt Mira, Moscow

Letter from Moscow
Friday September 25, 2015

I got on the Metro at Kropotkinskaya and immediately realized I was heading in the wrong direction. I got off at the next stop and ran right into two guys who used to play golf with my brother in law. I had no idea what to say to them. So I told them I was now a psychologist but had actually come here to train as a Ballerino. Wrong move, especially using such an arch "nomenclature". One of them IS a psychologist. And the other a ballet buff (actually Opera but ballet as a methadone-like replacement). Hit the button on my phone that makes it fake-ring and excused myself.

I need to get to Troitskoye. But I need better information. I like cities where you can just stand there. And Moscow is good for that when the weather is as fine as it is right now. So I just stood there and looked at people's jeans. I couldn't make any decent correlations between current jeans and aspiration, smartness, weakness, or sportiness. So I tried parsing them via a paradoxical dialectics of attractiveness pitched against economic consciousness. That didn't help so I just stood there.

I have a headache. And Troitskoye is a long way from here. Maybe if I just stand here for a while something will resolve itself. I decided to walk to the Okhotony Ryad Shopping Center. It's all about the managerialism of the present there. What I really like about it is the way that there is a large staircase in between the two escalators. You can skip down the stairs - looking to the world like a tall attractive economist while the fools all just stand there blocking all parts of the escalator. Don't they realize that you should stand on the right and move on the left? I practiced my hop up and skip down the central staircase for a while. Then moved over to have a little sit down.

I squeezed onto one the marble benches in between sneakers, race team logo shirts and diamante thongs poking over white jeans and stared up at the glazed cupola of painted glass showing an image of the world centered on a large black void where the north pole ought to be. I love it underground, where we can build a world of philosophy and art unencumbered by the pressures of flora and fauna. I took out my phone and started to photograph the world. I zoomed in on the large black void where the North Pole should be and hunched down over my phone to check the image. When I looked up an attractive, slim young Imam was staring at me from across the hall. There was no expression beyond compassion. There was no judgment in his eyes. But as soon as he noticed me noticing him noticing me - he too looked up at that black void and immediately walked fast towards the main entrance. Moving quickly after him I saw that he had dropped a business card...

"Data Lake"
Troitskoye, Mytishchinsky District, Moscow Oblast

Until tomorrow...

Take care of yourself...

Береги себя

Liam

121, Prospekt Mira, Moscow

Letter from Moscow
Saturday September 26, 2015

It's decided. I am going to take a taxi to Troitskoye and screw the expense. It all began last night. I was in a taxi after a few drinks had multiplied into the necessity to keep the taxi window open all the way home for that cool old wind in my face. I decided to sit in the front - Istanbul style. A few years ago I was in a cab from Cayenne in French Guyana to Rochambeau Airport to catch an evening flight to Orly. The cabby started driving slower and slower and hit the brakes every time a car approached that had their headlights aimed at us. Turned out the driver was night-blind. We swapped seats, I drove the taxi to the airport, and negotiated a huge discount on the metered fare. I wonder how he managed to get back home? In South Korea the "guest of honor" is supposed to sit in the back opposite the driver. Then, there is a pecking order to where the next three people should sit. Or maybe that's Japan. In Shanghai, you're supposed to sit in the back, apparently, but I always sat in the front because the drivers never understood me when I tried to pronounce the street names in Mandarin, and even if they understood correctly, they often had no idea where it was. Thankfully they understood me when I said "Left", "right" or "straight" in Mandarin. But you really have to be in the front seat and paying attention if you want to do that. I was enjoying myself immensely.

"You know this car is painted RAL 1006?" He didn't reply. We drove past the VDNKh. The Exhibition of Achievements of National Economy is a permanent carnival crash of music against lights and armed to the teeth with rides and mechanized nonsense. It specializes in murdering time with distractions that can't yet be replicated by xboxes or pads. I was happy drunk as we cruised past. The Scorpions and Europe were grinding their rock gears and slipping various clutches. All this was interspersed with what would pass for martial music where I come from. Sometimes I fear I live in a state of lucid cynicism that keeps me apart from my neighbors here. I think they are more conscious of the "third ear" even if they can no longer express precisely what it might be listening for.

We got to my street and the taxi pulled over. I looked at the driver and he looked at me. I handed him the "Data Lake" business card that I had found at the shopping center and I tried to smile a little universal smile. He looked up at the meter and tapped it with his finger. "Piiiiz'dets, blyaaaa!" It didn't look fucked up to me. I tried to keep the half smile working in aid of the international brotherhood of shared bullshit and to keep my vodka breath at bay. I knew there was only one large bottle of beer left at the apartment but I wanted it now.

"We make a deal?" "OK" "OK". We made a deal. It was an outrageous fare. But as I was about to reach into my pocket - he brought out his leather binder, peeled off a few thousand Rubles and handed them to me. I sat transfixed - unmoved in the seat. The engine kept running in the quiet street. I sat there. He handed me back the business card. I got out. He said he would be back in the morning. I got a cold sweat on my neck. I tried to keep cool. I think I might have even said "Ciao". Good grief.

Until tomorrow...

Take care of yourself...

Береги себя

Liam

121, Prospekt Mira, Moscow

Letter from Moscow
Sunday September 27, 2015

I woke early. The weather has changed. It's gone grey. I needed to get out of the apartment before the taxi driver returned. There's a place around the corner that opens early. I went down and walked there.

Fuck Sunday. So I went over to the Museum of the Revolution. It opens early to sweep up tourist fueled by Nescafé. The guards were goofing off and checking their phones. I walked inside. I took off my jacket and put it down on a bench beside me. An orderly crowd started to build and move limply around the rooms. I turned towards the wall. A familiar voice removed me from my stare. "You can't leave your jacket there". It was the girl from the café - dressed as a museum guard. "It might be a suspicious package." She smiled and asked me to follow her.

As we left the building she shrugged off her jacket and we moved swiftly across Tverskaya Street heading towards Strastnoy Boulevard. We didn't speak. But I could see a taxi in the middle distance with the engine running. By the time we reached it she bore only a hint of museum guard.

As we drove away I looked up at a banal brick office block topped by an oval superstructure going up across the street. I had asked nothing and expected nothing.

Grey skies for the first time since I arrived have lulled me. The question of caring is swamped and mired. I have lost my energy. It is Sunday in Moscow and one person I barely know and another I do not know are driving me away from the center. This will take forever - as always.

I decided to sit calmly and not speak. I decided to look at the city as we blurted forwards then ground out multiple halts. I could have just opened the door and walked away. The driver spoke first:

"A luxurious Sunday brunch is undoubtedly one of the highlights of the Moscow culinary scene. Mountains of gourmet food items including oysters, lobster, Kamchatka crab, roast meats, sashimi, exotic dishes from the Far East and of course caviar served up with endless amounts of wine, fresh juice and champagne and a huge sweets spread for dessert is a treat not to be missed." I sat calmly.

"On Sundays, the club hosts the best gay parties in Moscow. During the day, Propaganda operates as a restaurant renowned for its low prices and delicious food. The Caesar salad served here is rightfully considered the best in the city." As we swept onto Butyrskaya I looked longingly out of the window at ads for Lofttime, Airman, M&Ms and Whitesnake.

I don't mind.

Until tomorrow...

Take care of yourself...

Береги себя

Liam

121, Prospekt Mira, Moscow

Letter from Moscow
Monday September 28, 2015

She lunged at my neck. I didn't see it coming - I didn't expect it. Frankly I didn't really know what to do. I let her try and throttle me and just sat there. "Drive faster!" she yelled at the driver - which was pretty funny considering the Moscow traffic. She stopped trying to throttle me and apologized.

As she tapped out a number on her LG I began to cry. I don't think the driver or my throttler even noticed. I turned my head towards the window. The adverts became more repetitive, just urgent requests to buy anything at all at anytime, please. The graffiti was going in reverse.

A stray thought made me laugh. Whatever she was saying to the driver sounded like, "Shaghai is like a washing machine." I snapped out of it and said "It washed your brain." The car slowed and they both looked at me. I couldn't stop laughing. They couldn't not laugh. Through my tears and laughter I said - in my basest Russian, "If you aren't listening to the actual words, the way so many younger Russians talk sounds just like American English – the same intonations and pacing. EVERYTHING!" There was a pause.

Then we were all laughing. Saying any sequence of words that came into our heads in Russian but in the style of a louche American teen.

"Liquid hog wash zipper man." Hysterical.
"Stone foot sandwich wrecker" Haven't laughed so hard in my life.
"I've been Googling, seriously" I nearly lost a chunk of lung.
"Yuri Gagarin t-shirts" I think she pissed herself.

We took a hard right. I was still laughing when the driver got out, opened my door and smashed me in the face with something dense in a sock. It was the blow to my neck from my friend in the back that took me down.

At least I was at peace now. Having blackout dreams. Moving fast across cities and spaces. Picking up fragments. Plastic tennis rackets, visas, reading newspapers in elevators, floating across the lobby of Hotel Cosmos, winking at the hustlers and dropping money for the working girls.

Ka - ray - o - kay, Ka - ray - o - kay, Karaoke, Karaoke, Ka - rayay - oh - kay.

Something just burst in my brain.

Until tomorrow...

Take care of yourself...

Береги себя

Liam

121, Prospekt Mira, Moscow

Letter from Moscow
Tuesday September 29, 2015

The blood supply to part of my brain has been interrupted or severely reduced, depriving my brain tissue of oxygen and nutrients. Within minutes, my brain cells will begin to die. All I know is that I cannot move and cannot speak. I think I am on my side on a gravel surface. I can only see through my right eye. I can hear feet and smell Karelias Slims. I slip out of action for a little rest from the exhaustion of keeping one eye open.

Maybe I can pay some people to come and demonstrate for my cause. Or against my case. I can't focus. Alice Neel was married to Gerhard Richter. I should have gone to the Yukon. I could have found a nice job in Dawson. I wouldn't care who left me - how many dogs died - how many people had their thumbs pulled off. I can hear Uzbek popular songs. I dream of Uzbeki restaurants in full Orientalist mode. I want the extravagant decor back. I want waiters in costume. I want wandering belly dancers. I want wild bands singing Uzbek songs. I dream of vegetarian food - spiced up with a little meat - just to give the vegetables a lift.

Before leaving town I had left a clear note in my best Russian for a driver to come and meet me if I didn't return by the end of the day. I can't move and can't feel my Huwei any more. Even if I could find a way to answer the phone I doubt I would understand the instructions about where to meet, where to flee or what to do.

Someone energetic and assured has lifted me from the ground. I hear their feet compressing the gravel. Cigarette ash drops in my face. I can receive no further damage. I hear blips of water at the lip of a lake. What are they waiting for?

Alice Neel? That can't be right. I try and test the words as they lift me into a small launch earning a swift rabbit punch to a kidney. I manage to open that eye again as we are sweeping towards a large concrete bridge.

Data Lake is not all its cracked up to be. Best to just heave me into the water. Actually - best just to take me back into the center of the city and we can all have a drink and laugh about it. Actually - best just to take me to the hospital and get me a brain scan. Actually - best just to imagine that I am not here at all. Actually - best to just heave me into the water after all.

Data Lake. I have many rich queries. I want well-defined levels, strong, bounded-staleness, sessions, and eventuals. I want strong and eventual consistency. Reduced friction and complexity.

Here goes. Up and over the side.

Until tomorrow...

Take care of yourself...

Береги себя

Liam

121, Prospekt Mira, Moscow

Letter from Moscow
Wednesday September 30, 2015

I hit the water and immediately struck my knee on the bottom. Suddenly, there, ankle deep. Looking back at the launch. Empty and bobbing gently on the lake. I looked up at the bridge. If only... Ladas, Volgas, Zils, Mokvichs, Gazs, Uazs, Kamazs, Derways, Spetstehs, Dragons. Instead other gentle Japanese hums and German rolls. And I could see my driver. Waving from the span.

Fucking Fortune 300. Ruinart champagne, hors d'oeuvres. And backstage another shithole. I eschewed the bridge and ran for the shore. Time for some woods. A kid with a Honda just handed it over and I was on the move. The weather has cooled but the humidity cancels it out. If I get my skates on it will be dissident style, figurative sculpture, cheese, cold fries and mayonnaise. Bread and wine from Abkhazia. And blow me down - a pint of vodka. Masha and Kristina. Svetlana, Yelena, Olga and Natasha. I wonder if Konstantin Melnikov is at home? Maybe it is time to head for the Narkomfim building. I always loved a good ribbon window.

As I shimmied towards the bridge my PCX-125 hit some hard things. Over and over I clunked. Bits of UT-88 a Vector-06C. My God. A Micro-80. I need to break the ice. There or near the bridge. Plaster flaking off - revealing brick.

Pulling back on the throttle. Both eyes now open and working. Twisting gears as I head towards a green light. A man on the corner - rolling his own cigarettes - while his friend rips off his filter. I love it here. I want to go home - I want to go back to the café on the corner. I know the difference between exile and dissent. I think of Chekrygin. I think of solar forces, charging the earth with forces of attraction and repulsion, bringing the mood of a light summer and laying the way for meteoric flame-trails, immortal sons arising on nearby planets, dispersing the reason-key, the structure that controls the celestial spheres' courses, engulfing the force of storms provoked by the sun on the planet spheres. In the flowing motions recreated by the magnificent dance, new suns igniting in the celestial scatter, renewing the heavens.

Had I logged onto Rusavtobus.ru I would have known that the 15.45 from Troitskoye was thirteen minutes late. That the driver had also spent a precious few seconds ripping the tip from his Original Gold, straight from the heart of Moldova. That the driver was in the habit of checking his fucking Fly Mobile Levi Strauss branded, 1.76-inch screened, 220 by 176 pixels resolutioned, 2-megapixel camerad, 64MB internal memoried, micro SD'd, USB ported piece of crap.

I wasn't decapitated by the bus. Rather my body was flung across the street as my head got stuck in the logo. A debodying in a time of beheading. A surgical strike by public transport. My driver has it all on the dash cam. Just white light for a second but a whiff of that suit as he approached me. Data Lake. Special services. Catering for you. Covering me gently up with a spare table cloth pulled from the back of the van just mildly obscured by a gathering crowd.

Take care of yourself...

Береги себя

Liam

Li Mu — The Labourer

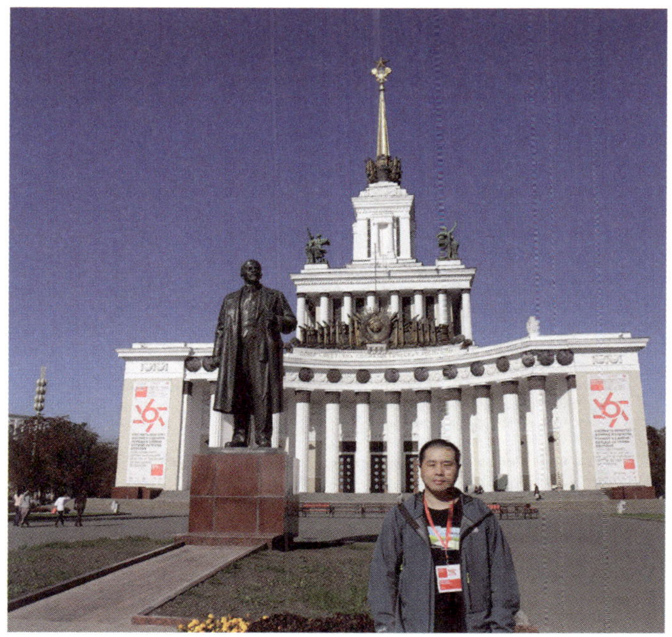

Li Mu in front of the 6th Moscow Biennale venue, VDNKh Pavilion No. 1, September 2015

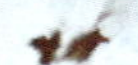

ДОГОВОР № 07/F

22 сентября 2015 г.

Настоящий Договор заключен между Художественным фондом «Московская Биеннале», далее именуемым «Московская Биеннале», и г-ном Ли Му, далее именуемым «Подрядчик».

Статья 1. ***Предмет договора***

Московская Биеннале поручает, а Подрядчик обязуется оказать услуги по технической поддержке выставочного зала Основного проекта Шестой Московской международной биеннале современного искусства.

Статья 2. ***Срок выполнения работ и максимальные трудозатраты***

a. подрядчик предоставляет услуги, указанные в Статье 1 в период с 22 сентября по 1 октября 2015г.
b. Максимальные трудозатраты Подрядчика по настоящему Договору не могут превышать 10 (десяти) рабочих дней.

Статья 3. ***Порядок оплаты***

За надлежащее предоставление услуг, указанных в статье 1, Подрядчику будет выплачиваться 82,00 (восемьдесят два) евро в день в рублях по курсу ЦБ РФ на дату оплаты, включая все подлежащие уплате налоги. Платежи производятся на основании подписанного сторонами акта выполненных услуг.

Статья 4. ***Налогообложение***

a. Подрядчик не претендует на государственное пенсионное, социальное обеспечение и медицинскую помощь, осуществляемую за счет средств ПФ РФ, ФСС РФ, ФОМС РФ.

Статья 5. ***Законодательство***

Данный Договор составлен и может быть интерпретирован исключительно в соответствии с Российским законодательством.

Статья 6. ***Ответственность сторон***

Стороны несут ответственность за невыполнение или нарушение условий Договора в соответствии с российским законодательством.

Статья 7. ***Изменение условий Договора***

Любое изменение, дополнение условий данного Договора или продление его срока производятся в

Contract No. 07/F

September 22, 2015

This Contract is entered into by and between **MOSCOW BIENNALE ART FUND**, hereinafter referred to as Moscow Biennale, and Mr. Li Mu, hereinafter referred to as Contractor.

ARTICLE 1. ***Scope of Work***

The Moscow Biennale shall assign, and the Contractor shall accept the responsibility to provide the services on technical assistance of exhibition hall of The Main project of The Sixth Biennale of contemporary art based on VDNH, Moscow.

ARTICLE 2. ***Period of Performance & Maximum Level of Effort***

a. The Contractor shall perform the services specified in Article 1 from September 22, 2015 to October 01,2015.
b. Maximum level of Contractor's effort under this Contract shall not exceed 10 (ten) working days.

ARTICLE 3. ***Payment***

For satisfactory performance of services specified in Article 1 the Contractor shall be paid at an hourly rate calculated as 82.00 (eighty two) Euro gross. The payments shall be made upon the act of acceptance signed by the parties.

ARTICLE 4. ***Taxes***

a. The Contractor will not claim for the state pensions, allowances and medical care services provided by Pension Fund and Federal Social and Medical Insurance Funds of the Russian Federation.

ARTICLE 5. ***Applicable Law***

This Contract shall be constructed and interpreted solely in accordance with the Russian legislation.

ARTICLE 6. ***Responsibility***

Parties shall be responsible for any default or breach of contract in accordance with the Russian legislation.

ARTICLE 7. ***Modification***

This Contract may be changed, amended, modified or extended only in writing duly executed by the respective форме письменного соглашения Сторон.

parties hereto.

Статья 8. ***Прекращение действия Договора***

a. Московская Биеннале вправе расторгнуть Договор путем письменного уведомления Подрядчика не позднее, чем за 3 (три) дня до даты прекращения действия Договора.

b. Подрядчик вправе расторгнуть данный Договор путем письменного уведомления Московскую Биеннале не позднее, чем за 3 (три) дня до даты прекращения действия Договора.

c. При расторжении Договора Подрядчику оплачиваются услуги, удовлетворительным образом предоставленные на дату прекращения действия Договора.

ARTICLE 8. ***Termination***

a. The Contract may be terminated by Moscow Biennale by giving to the Contractor 3 (three) days written notice prior to the effective date of termination.

b. Contractor may terminate this Contract by giving to Moscow Biennale 3 (three) days written notice prior to the effective date of termination.

c. Upon termination the Contractor shall be paid for the services satisfactorily performed prior to the effective date of termination.

В СВЯЗИ С ВЫШЕИЗЛОЖЕННЫМ, Стороны совершили и подписали данный Договор на дату, указанную выше.

ЛИ МУ

Паспорт № G36065595 выдан Exit&Entry Administration Ministry of Public Security 16 июня 2009 г.

МОСКОВСКАЯ БИЕННАЛЕ "Moscow Biennale"

____

От Художественного фонда «Московская Биеннале»

Мартынов Андрей В.,

Генеральный директор

IN WITNESS WHEREOF the parties hereto have caused this Contract to be duly signed and executed effective the date and year first above written.

LI MU

Passport № G36065595 issued by Exit&Entry Administration Ministry of Public Security on June 16, 2009

李牧 Li Mu

For: MOSCOW BIENNALE ART FUND

Martynov Andrey V.

General Director

2015年9月22日，星期二，晴

我似乎并不喜欢莫斯科，因为它让我想起了北京——过于宽阔的马路，过于高大的建筑，又大又空。我不喜欢这种外表的高大，多少有些强权和压迫的气味。

我为什么要成为莫斯科双年展的工人？我真的喜欢劳动吗？是什么吸引我参与进一个展览的制造过程？

我早上10点到了VDNH展览场馆，见了Daria。双年展现场一片混乱，我的英文不好，导致我并不能很好地明白我的工作和任务。

我被安排帮助艺术家Els Dietvorst制作一个巨大的头骨雕塑。一群工人正在搭建起一个头骨结构，牙齿部分由很多木雕小人组成。Els一边指挥着工人安装，一边接受着媒体采访和观众的问话。同时，她还在制作那些牙齿。她用电烙铁在木雕上烫出人脸的形状和肌理。

我认识了穿红色T恤的工人Farruk，他看上去很诚恳，有些腼腆。我在工作的间隙和他聊天。23岁的Farruk是个律师，塔吉克斯坦人，毕业于莫斯科大学的法律专业。

1

可是，现在他失业了，找不到工作。于是，他就跟着他的表哥干这种力气活。他强调说，这是临时的工作。我问他这份工作一天有多少收入，他说不知道，他表哥给多少就是多少。

Farruk的表哥Sukhrob看上去要老练的多。显然，他是这群工人的头目。他总是在接和艺术家Els沟通，并在最有难度的位置工作。他的嘴里有很浓的烟酒味。

中午饭时间到了，我随着工人们进入展厅背后的一个残破的房间，一群人挤在里面吃饭。大家多是站着，有个别的人坐在地上。食物非常简单：面包、香肠、饼干、廉价的橙子汽水和可乐。他们用最快的速度吃完午饭，回到展览上工作。

下午，Sukhrob在脚手架上说想喝咖啡，我就到餐厅要了一杯espresso给他。

Els有点忙不过来，就让我帮她用电烙铁在那些牙齿形状的木雕上烫出人的眼睛和面孔，然后安装到大头骨上面去。傍晚的时候，牙齿都装上去了，需要调整眉弓骨位置的结构。6:30，我饿了，也很累。我离开了VDHN，出了地铁，在对面一家穆斯林餐厅吃饭，一份羊肉炒饭、沙拉和水，花了我1130卢布，这里比上海还贵。

回酒店后，昏昏睡去。我梦见我母亲赤着脚踩上一个满是钢针的垫子，垫子的形状是一个很大的拖鞋。

2

2015年9月23日，星期三，晴

一大早，我妻子发来短信说我儿子憬儿长出了第一颗牙齿，我错过了。

莫斯科的地铁里没有英文标示，到处都是俄文。对于我这样的外国人，什么也看不懂。问路，很多人不会讲英语。现在是英语的世界，拒绝英文，就是拒绝世界吗？

今天Farruk没有来，他表哥说他到另一个场地工作了。

Sukhrob帮助Els工作的照片出现在一份莫斯科报纸上，这让他很开心。他似乎很喜欢这个工作，干活很卖力。他不时地用手机给没有完成的雕塑拍照。

今天继续帮Els制作头骨。为了让头骨看起来更自然，我们加了很多辅助的木结构，然后在上面钉一层铁丝网，再在最外层用亚麻布包裹起来。一个7米高的头骨，在图纸上看很简单，可是制作起来非常麻烦。

当我们用亚麻布把头骨的下巴包裹出来的时候，Els发现里面多做了一个半圆形的木结构，导致下巴的形状是圆的。她问我怎么办？我说：那就拆掉吧。Els很不好意思，那是让Sukhrob花了很长时间做上去的，怎么好意思再让他拆掉呢？我说：艺术就是由系列的错误构成的。Art is Mistake.

①

Els为什么要做这个很大的头骨？为什么牙齿都是小人的雕塑？我们一大群人需要花费一星期的时间来完成这个雕塑。它的意义是？

在VDNH的建筑里，不时地看到墙上残破的字母和满布灰尘的浮雕。浮雕诉说着苏联社会主义的辉煌。浮雕上的灰尘似乎在告诉我，那些辉煌都已远去。展厅门外是一尊列宁的雕像，他站在高高的基座上，手里握着一卷纸，凝视着远方。这是一个既熟悉又陌生的人，说他熟悉，是因为我从小就在课本里读过他用面包蘸墨水吃的故事，家里、教室里和大街上都能看到他的肖像；说他陌生，是因为我根本就不了解这个人。在中国学习的那些故事都是真实的吗？

我遇到了艺术家Babi Badalov，他创造了很多新的单词，细细品味，充满了对事物的反思和幽默。他说他和中国艺术家是好朋友。我很开心，在这里遇到徐坦的朋友。在他的作品里，我感受到一种内省和批判的力量。

晚上回来，在酒店旁边找到个超市，我买了一些面包回来作为晚饭。这样比去饭店吃饭省钱多了。

②

2015年9月24日，星期四，晴

今天是穆斯林的宰牲节（Id al-Adjha），Sukhrob和他的工人们放假一天。

早上我的酒店旁边的路上站满了警察，地铁也关闭了几个小时。

今天发生了一件可怕的事情。

下午工作的间隙，我在展厅的后门拍照，我拍摄斑驳的门、斑驳的墙面和不同颜色的瓷砖拼起来的地面。

突然，两个门卫冲上来，我听不懂他们说的话，我看得出他们很生气。我打算离开，可是他们拦住我，不允许我离开。他们把我带到一个年长一些的人那里，他们说着我听不懂的俄语，他们做手势要我打开照相机，我给他们看我拍摄的照片，我说"这很漂亮，所以我才拍。"一个门卫凶狠地做出双臂交叉的动作。于是，我当着他们的面一张一张地把照片删除。当他们看到相机里没有照片的时候，他们笑了。可是在我看来，他们的笑容是那么的狰狞。

这狰狞的笑容停留在我的大脑里，让我感到恐惧。

晚上，我的翻译Taya在邮件里说："从您的日记里看得出，您在我的国家并不快乐，我很抱歉。"我回复她："不管快乐的还是悲伤的，都让我近距离地感知这个国家，这些体验都是珍贵的。"

附上Taya对我昨天所遭遇的事情的邮件回复：

"他们这样对您，我很生气！不幸的是莫斯科门卫的无耻行为是时常发生的（警察也这样）。我去机场接您的时候，也碰到一个很不礼貌的门卫；两天前我去莫斯科大学的宿舍看我的朋友（他是德国人），那里的门卫对我一开始很不礼貌，但一听到我不是德国人，会讲俄文，再加上我对他非常礼貌，他就比较礼貌地对待我们了。

俄罗斯人如果感到他们有权力（即使这个权力只限于展厅的后门），就变成了凶残的野兽……"

2015年9月26日，星期六，晴

每天都累得精疲力尽，回到酒店，没有办法专心写日记。只有饱饱地睡上一觉，第二天早上醒来，才能写下这些文字。

我今天开始帮中国的艺术家鸟头往墙上贴照片。鸟头每天在莫斯科的街上、公园、博物馆里拍照，照片印出来后，我负责把它们钉在墙上。我和鸟头在上海认识很多年了，很高兴能在这次双年展上为他们工作。照片的尺寸不大，但是数量很多。一开始，有两个志愿者帮我，可是她们不是玩手机就是聊天，还弄坏了六张照片。后来，我自己做，偶尔会有一个志愿者帮我递一下照片，工作的速度很慢。

下午，在展厅里总是有讲座、表演在进行。我不得不停下来，因为锤子敲打钉子的声音很响。整个工作的过程如同禅修一般，不能急躁。我让自己好好体验每个钉子敲进墙里的时刻，每张照片贴上墙面后的喜悦。

今天周末，VDNH的广场上、公园里到处都是游玩的人群。VDNH主建筑周围有很多游乐设施，看到一张张快乐的面孔，我的心也放松了。

今天是中秋节，我收到很多朋友的问候短信。

2015年9月27日，星期日，晴

终于在清真寺附近找到一家理发店，把我的头发剪了。一个很帅气的穆斯林小伙子帮我剪头，他剪得很认真。最后，我给了他100卢布的小费。

这次双年展很特别，展览开幕，作品开始制作，同时不断地有讲座、谈话、表演、电影、音乐等活动进行着。十天后双年展结束的时候，所有的作品都制作完成。有人说，这是史上最短时间的双年展。我很喜欢这个想法，因为这样观众可以看到艺术家制作作品的过程，可以和艺术家交流，而不仅仅是看到结果。展览现场充满了活力，又发生在VDNH这样一个前苏联遗留下来的庞大的建筑里，就有了很强的政治意味。

今天，继续往墙上钉鸟头的照片。

我很认真地观看鸟头的每一幅黑白照片，我开始思考一些问题：鸟头的这些在莫斯科街头随机拍摄的照片和我们手机里的照片有什么不同呢？没有差别；鸟头的这些照片又和那些成千上万的街头摄影师的照片有什么不同呢？没什么不同。那么，我们在看这些照片的时候，我们在看什么？我曾经问过宋涛，是否会通过拍摄照片来联接、了解这个城市？他说他和这个城市没有关系，他们只是不愿意拒绝双年展的邀请而来工作的，这只是他们的工作。

当我在看这些照片的时候，我看到了什么？艺术家的权力。

对于我，也是一样。我写的这些日记被展示在展厅的桌面上，很多观众很认真地阅读。我相信，其他工人的日记或许要比我写的精彩的多，只不过他们没有在这里展示日记的权力而已。

真正的禅修，是不想那么多的。看来，我的工作不能算作禅修。

Sukhrob看了我展出的日记，他很伤心，因为我写了他嘴里有烟酒的味道。他说他没有喝酒。看来，是我的错误，我在这里纠正一下。很抱歉，真的很抱歉，Sukhrob！

2015年9月28日，星期一，阴

今天的天气突然冷了起来。

上午继续往墙上钉马夫的照片，直到钉完了所有已经印出来的照片，我才去吃午饭。

下午帮Elis制作水泥雕塑。这是最后一道程序，用泥巴把整个头骨抹一遍，作品最后看起来像泥塑一样，除了齿的地方是水泥。亚麻布上偶尔会隐藏着钢丝头或钉子，Daria和另一个工人的手就被戳破了。我们不得不小心翼翼地工作。Sukhrob和他的工人们干活非常卖力，他的工人们对我非常友好，可是他们都不说英语，我们只能用表情和动作打招呼。

Elis说她看了我的日记，她打算把所有工人的名字都写在作品的标签上，也包括我。她说她和我有相同的感受。

晚上艺术家Babi和我一起离开展厅时，广场上两个年轻人拿着汽球拦住我们，我听不懂他们说什么。Babi掏出钱包，分别给了他们50和100卢布。然后Babi告诉我说："他们的孩子病了，需要钱。"

Babi坚持要请我吃晚饭，他说他只是一个人生活，不需要很多钱。他租住在巴黎的一个18平方米的半地下室里，每月只需支付500欧元的房租。

Babi对我讲述了他的一个故事：他14岁的时候，家里非常穷，没有穿过新衣服，他总是穿着有补丁的衣服。有一天，父亲给了他24美金，让他去城里（阿塞拜疆的首都Bacu）的阿姨家里。往返路费需要10美金，他还有14美金在口袋里。在城里，他用剩下来的钱给自己买了一件红色的T恤，他很开心地穿上给他的阿姨看，他想阿姨一定会很高兴，

①

没想到阿姨看后脸色很难看，转身就离开了。他很失望，他不明白为什么阿姨不高兴。

他回到村子里，到处都静悄悄的，一个人也看不到。他家的门敞开着，只有他爸爸一个人坐在屋子里，说已经好几天没有吃饭了。

说到这里，Babi停了下来，摘下他的眼镜，用纸巾擦拭他流下的泪水。

然后，他说："我们那里家里死了人，就会几天不吃饭……我的妈妈死了。"

②

2015年9月29日，星期二，晴

今天从后门进入展厅的时候，我对那几个门卫打招呼：Good Morning!
他们慢慢地抬起头看了我一眼，有人点了点头。他们生活在这个终日不
见阳光，残破的空间里，时间久了，性格自然是怪癖和阴郁的。

Els送了她的书给我，里面有很多她的画，其中就有一幅头骨素描，头骨
的牙齿都是小人。我能够想象Els的家庭给了她很多创作灵感。而
我的家庭却给了我更多情感上的压迫，常常压得我喘不过气来。

晚上，我参与了俄罗斯艺术小组UN MULTITUDE的表演。表演开始后，
我将很多铁球一个一个地搬到舞台上，据说这些是串起来漂浮在海
岸边的空心球。有人开始读一些人的名字。一大群乐手爬上周围的脚
手架，根据我在舞台上摆出的形状和位置进行演奏。表演进行
了20分钟，在我站在舞台中央，做出一个结束的手势时，音乐戛然
而止。

我在展厅工作的时候，不时地有观众来找我，告诉我她们读了我的日记
感到难过。一个女孩告诉我："莫斯科有不好的一面，也有好的一面。
接下来你一定会感受到它的美好。"
我想，我已经感受到了莫斯科的温暖和美好。或许，我开始喜欢
这个城市了。

2015年9月30日，星期三，晴

上午继续往墙上钉拿来的照片。
下午，我感到非常疲惫，喝了咖啡也无济于事。昨天晚上表演的时候我
一趟又一趟地往舞台上搬铁球，搬得我浑身酸痛。
傍晚，我发现我展示在台面上的日记少了好几页。一共丢失了两篇日记，
一篇是我写我不喜欢莫斯科的，另一篇是我写门卫如何强迫我删除
照片的。日记是压在桌面上玻璃下面的，有螺丝固定。是谁会偷走这
些日记呢？我肯定，他偷走日记的原因不是因为喜欢，而是不希望人们
看到这些内容。或者，他害怕人们看到这些内容。
我感到这种行为非常无耻。
我们又重新打印了这些日记，继续展示在台面上。
晚上是一个酒会，很多展会的赞助者来观看展览。以往，我是要逃避这种
场所的，因为我不知道该如何在这种场所和人们交流，我会感到紧张。
而这一次，我新认识的很多艺术家朋友和我在一起，我就不紧张了。我跟他们
喝了两杯白葡萄酒。
Babi不断向我张望，晚上很多有钱人来看我们的作品，或许他们会买我
们的作品。我们很欢迎那些富人观看艺术，虽然，他们大多不懂艺术。一个
衣着华丽的女孩告诉我："我不喜欢这些当代艺术，我看不懂，我更喜欢看
漂亮的画。"我说："你不喜欢，是因为你没有花时间了解这些艺术。"
和Babi一起吃饭，他坚持要我吃饱饭，再去买一份甜点给我。盛情难却，
我只好吃下去。这样下去，我会吃成一个大胖子。

2015年10月1日，星期四，阴

上午，我进了展厅，径直走向我的日记。天哪！居然昨天放上去的日记今天
又消失了。这次偷走的还是我描述门卫禁止我拍照并强制我删除
照片的部分，还有Taya对这件事情看法的部分也被偷走了。
我告诉了策展人Defne，她说她看到是两个门卫偷走了我的日记。
很快，整个展览的人都知道有人两次偷走了我的日记。
傍晚的时候，我们又重新打印了日记，放在原来的地方。我用胶带
贴了一圈，以防止他们再次偷窃。
当我再次经过门卫的时候，我感觉他们在用邪恶的眼光看着我。我有
些紧张，我告诉自己：现在他们害怕我，他们害怕他们的丑行曝光。
有个观众读了日记后告诉我说："我为我们的国家有这样的人而羞耻。"

最后用几幅大照片覆盖在我钉上去的小照片上，那些小尺寸的照片成
为背景。
晚上来了很多观众，今天是展览进行的第十天，所有的作品都完成了。从明天
起，观众就看不到艺术家和工人工作的场景，看不到现场的表演和讨论了。
策展人Bart说有人觉得我的作品不是行为艺术。我说："我也觉得不是行为艺术，
那它到底该怎么归类？到底是什么？我也不知道。"Bart说："这样最好。"
夜里，我梦到在我的村子里，很多人抬着棺材哭着从我身边经过。我赤着脚，
不小心踩在一块黄色的屎上，怎么蹭都蹭不干净。用中国传统的解梦方法
来解释这个梦，就意味着我将有好运降临，并且会有金钱上的收入。
不是吗？明天我就能领到我的工资了。

22nd September 2015, Tuesday. Sunny

I don't like Moscow at all; with its wide roads and tall buildings—so huge but faceless—it reminds me of Beijing. I don't like this feigned greatness, I constantly feel its pressure.

Why did I decide to be a labourer at the Moscow Biennale? Do I even like physical labour? What made me participate in all this?

I arrived at VDNKh at 10 am and met with Daria. This biennial seemed to be a complete mess, and what's more, my English is not that good so I didn't really understand what I was supposed to do.

I was assigned to the artist called Els Dietvorst, who was making a giant skull. Other assistants had already built the structure of the skull; small wooden figures represented teeth. Els was giving out instructions and was simultaneously talking to the press and the guests. At the same time, she was pokering the wooden faces of the figures.

I got to know a worker in a red t-shirt called Farrukh. He seemed to be very outspoken yet a bit shy. We would chat whenever we had a break. 23-year-old Farrukh is a Tajik. He got a law degree at Moscow State University. He used to work as a lawyer but then lost his job and now has to earn his bread by manual labour—just like his cousin. He kept saying that it was only temporary. When I asked him how much he was making he said he didn't know—he would earn exactly the amount his cousin would pay him.

Farrukh's cousin Sukhrob seemed very sophisticated; it was clear from the beginning that he was the leader among the workers. It was him that Els was giving all the instructions to, and he was the one who carried out the most difficult of them. His breath smelled strongly of alcohol.

It was time for a lunch break. We all gathered in a small wrecked room at the back of the exhibition hall. It was already full of people; some of them were standing, the others were sitting right on the floor. The food was very basic: bread, sausages, cookies, cheap tangerines, sparkling water, and coke. Everyone was hurrying back to work, so they tried to eat their lunch as fast as possible.

Later in the afternoon we heard a voice from the top of the scaffolding—it belonged to Sukhrob, who asked for some coffee, so I went to the canteen and fetched him a cup of espresso.

Els was very busy all the time; at some point she even left the poker-work to me, so I spent the rest of the day pokering the faces of the figures and placing them into the skull.

By evening, the teeth were ready, and only the brow bones were to be made.

At 6:30 pm I realised that there was nothing else for me to do there. I was exhausted and hungry. So I told Els I was going to write my diary and left VDNKh.

I came across a Muslim restaurant near the subway station and decided to eat dinner there. I had pilaw with lamb, a salad, and a glass of water. It all cost me 1130 rubles—it is even more expensive here than in Shanghai.

Once I got to my hotel, I dropped into sleep. I dreamt about my mother. With her bare feet, she walked on a carpet stuck full of needles; the carpet looked like a shoe sole.

23rd September 2015, Wednesday. Sunny

This morning I got a message from my wife: our son Monty cut his first tooth. And I missed it!

All the signs in the Moscow subway are in Russian only, and I don't understand anything. People here speak no word of English, and every my attempt to ask for directions has failed. Nowadays English is a universal language for communication, and by not learning it, do these people turn their backs on the rest of the world?

Farrukh was not here today. His cousin said he was working somewhere else.

The photographs that Sukhrob had been helping Els with were published in a Moscow newspaper. Sukhrob was on top of the world. He seems to enjoy his job, and he's trying very hard to be the best at it. He constantly takes pictures of the unfinished sculpture with his phone.

Today we continued working on Els's skull. Some parts of it were made of wood to make it more natural. We covered it with wire and then with a linen cloth. It is 7 metres tall now. It might seem very easy to create such a thing but it is actually very difficult.

As we were covering the jaws of the skull with linen, Els discovered that the wooden parts of the jaws were semi-circular, which made the jaws look round-shaped. Els asked me what to do about it. I said that there was no other way but to remove those parts. Els got really embarrassed—Sukhrob had spent so much time on putting the whole sculpture together, and now he had to take it to pieces. I comforted Els saying that art is a series of mistakes.

Why is Els even making this skull? What do those little wooden figures/teeth represent? We have been working on this project all week but what is the point of it?

I couldn't help noticing dim inscriptions and dusty reliefs on the walls here. The reliefs reflect the former greatness of the Soviet Union, and the dust suggests that Soviet grandeur is long gone. Near the exhibition hall there is a tall Lenin monument supported by a huge pedestal. Lenin is holding a newspaper; his eyes are fixed on something far, far away. His figure is so familiar to me yet strange at the same time. I say familiar because as a kid, I would read a story about Lenin eating a piece of bread after dipping it in ink. Lenin was everywhere—at home, at school, in the streets. Yet he is a complete stranger to me: I don't understand him, can't relate to him; are the stories that I learnt about him at school even true?

I met an artist called Babi Badalov, a man of the most refined taste. He really broke new ground in art, gave a new meaning to things. He mentioned that he was a friend of Xu Tan's. I was delighted to hear about his friendship with this Chinese artist. Full of reflection and self-discipline, Xu Tan's art means a lot to me.

In the evening, before going back to the hotel, I stopped by a supermarket to buy some pastry for dinner. This will help me save some money and not waste it in restaurants.

24th September 2015, Thursday. Sunny

Today Muslims celebrate Eid al-Adha, so Sukhrob and the other workers have a day-off.

In the morning, the area around my hotel was inundated with police, and even some subway stations were closed for a few hours.

A terrible thing happened to me today.

During the break in the afternoon, I was wandering near the backdoor of the exhibition hall. With its motley doors and multi-coloured brickwork of the walls, that corner seemed very interesting to me, so I stayed there to take some pictures.

Suddenly two guards approached me; I couldn't understand what they were saying but they looked very angry. I was going to leave but they blocked my way. They brought me to a man who was supposedly their boss and told him that I didn't speak any Russian. He gestured to me to show them my photographs. I tried to explain that I took photos of that place only because I found it beautiful. One of the guards made an X shape with his arms and vigorously hit one arm against the other. Then I showed them my pictures and deleted them one by one.

Once the guards made sure that there were no pictures left on my camera, they smiled. But those smiles were sinister.

A vision of their grinning faces hasn't left me since, making me shudder with horror.

In the evening, I received an email from Taya, my translator: "Reading your diary, I got an impression that you are very unhappy in my home country. I am very sorry about that". I replied: "I am getting to know Russia through both positive and negative experiences, and they are equally precious to me".

25th September 2015, Friday. Sunny

Today I continued to work on Els's sculpture.

I am also an artist and I am used to working for myself, but this time I am working for another artist. While we are creating this piece of art, the artist and me are one, we are equal. However, once the artwork is finished, it is as if I had never taken part in its creation, my name won't be on the label of the project. As a worker, I will receive my payment, and it won't disconnect me from the art I helped create, I will still feel deeply attached to it. And then, once the work is done, when I see that I have nothing to do with this piece anymore and thus have to turn away and leave—a set of very complex feelings arises.

I would compare it to a babysitter's work. A babysitter has to look after someone else's child; taking care of this kid is the essence of her job, and she naturally develops strong feelings toward the child, gets very much attached to him. Eventually, her work is done, she gets paid and has to leave, and at this point her emotions get very complicated.

This experience is very unique, and I think that every artist's assistant has gone through this in some way.

After having experienced it all myself, I decided that from now on I would mention the names of all the workers who assist me in my artwork.

While working here, I have to keep reminding myself that here I am not an artist but a worker who is getting paid. I have to respect every decision made by the artist and to meet her every demand.

I met with Mián Mián (a Chinese writer) today. "I realised that I can't live in China anymore, I have to leave", she said to me decisively. "I am moving to Berlin next month".

This is how Taya commented on my yesterday's mishaps:
The way they treated you is unacceptable. Unfortunately, such rude behaviour is very common among our security guards (and policemen, too). While I was waiting for you at the airport, a security guard shouted at me. And two days ago I was visiting my German friend at the dormitory of Moscow State University, and the guard was very rude to him. Once he heard me speaking Russian (he thought I was German too)—and in a very polite manner—he immediately changed his attitude.

In Russia, if people get to taste power (even if this power is limited to a dormitory hall or a gallery's backdoor), they stop being people and often turn into wild animals.

26th September 2015, Saturday. Sunny

By the end of each day I am dead on my feet and have no energy left to write my diary. Only after a sound sleep do I eventually get to it next morning.

Today I am beginning to work with the Chinese art duet, Birdhead. Everyday Birdhead would walk around Moscow's streets, parks and museums and take pictures. Now that the film is developed, I am to hang the photographs on the walls. I had met Birdhead in Shanghai many years ago and I am very happy that I will get to work with them at this biennale. The photographs are small but of great quantity. In the beginning, I had two volunteers helping me but they were too occupied with conversation and their cell phones, and they also ruined six pictures. I am working alone now, and from time to time a volunteer comes by to hand me a photograph but still the work is going very slowly.

The afternoon is the time of lectures and performances here at the Biennale, so I have to take a break from my work, since the sound of the hammer hitting the nails is too loud. This kind of work is really mediation-like, one should not do it hastily. I have to feel every nail going inside the wall, and then each hung picture fills my heart with joy.

It is a weekend day today, so VDNKh and the park around it are swarming with people. There are plenty of all kinds of entertainment there, and when I see all these happy faces, I just let everything go.

It is the day of the Mid-Autumn festival, and I have already received a lot of kind words from my friends.

27th September 2015, Sunday. Sunny

I finally got a haircut. It was a small barbershop by a mosque, and I was served by a young handsome fellow, a very skilled Muslim boy. I was very happy with the result and left him a 100-ruble tip.

This biennial is very special. The artists started working on their art after the exhibition had opened; there are always lectures, performances, films, and concerts. By the time the biennial finishes (in ten days), all the artwork will be ready. I heard it is the shortest biennale in history. I really like the idea of this event; the audience does not only get to see the final piece but also the process of its creation, and gets to talk to the artists. The place is filled with energy, and since this enormous building is the Soviet heritage, there is also a slight 'political' taste to it.

Today I am still working with Birdhead helping them hang their photographs.

I examined each of their black and white pictures very carefully and couldn't help but wonder: What is the difference between their random pictures of Moscow streets and the pictures anyone could take with the camera of a mobile phone? There isn't any. And do their photographs differ from the countless pictures of other street photographers? No, they don't. So what do we actually see when we look at their work? I asked Song Tao (one of the Birdhead photographers) if he thinks that one could really feel the city they tried to show. He said that Moscow didn't interest him at all but Birdhead didn't want to decline the invitation to the biennale, work is work.

And what do I see when I look at these pictures? I see the power of an artist.

I can say the same thing about myself. My diary is a part of this biennial; many people read it every day. I assume that other workers of this biennial might be writing a diary that is a lot more interesting and deeper than mine, but unlike me, they don't get to exhibit it here. This is my power as an artist.

True meditation requires being free from thought, and apparently my work is nothing like that.

Sukhrob got really upset about what he read in my diary. I once wrote that I sensed a strong smell of alcohol from him. He said he didn't drink. It seems I made a mistake. Sukhrob, please accept my sincerest apologies!

28th September 2015, Monday. Cloudy

It suddenly got colder.

In the morning I was hanging the photographs of Birdhead, and didn't break for lunch until every picture found its place on the wall.

In the afternoon I was helping Els with the skull. It is the final stage now, when we are supposed to cover it with clay. In the end it should give the impression that it is entirely made of clay—except for the wooden teeth. There are nails and sharp ends of wires under the linen cloth, and Daria has already hurt herself. We should all be very careful. Sukhrob and his team have been working tirelessly. All of them are very friendly, even though nobody can speak English. We communicate via gestures and interjections. After Els read my diary, she decided to put everybody's name—including mine—on the project's label. She said she could relate to the emotional connection between the piece of art and those who create it, which I had described.

In the evening I left the exhibition centre with Babi. Two young people holding balloons approached us in the park nearby. I didn't understand what they were saying, but Babi took out his wallet and gave them 150 rubles. "Their child is ill, they need money," he explained. Babi insisted on treating me to dinner; he says he doesn't spend much anyway because he lives alone. He is renting an 18-square-metre basement in Paris for 500 euros per month.

Babi shared his story with me. He grew up in a very poor family: they couldn't even afford to buy clothes and had to patch their old things. One day—Babi was 14 years old at the time—his father sent him to Baku (the capital of Azerbaijan) to Babi's aunt. He gave him 24 dollars; 10 dollars Babi spent on his way to Baku, and for the remaining 14 he bought himself a red T-shirt. Delighted with his purchase, Babi hurried to his aunt's to share his joy with her. To Babi's astonishment, his aunt changed countenance as she saw him, turned away and just left. Babi was very disappointed; he couldn't understand why his aunt wasn't happy for him.

When he returned to his village, it was suspiciously quiet and empty. The door of his house was wide open, and Babi found his father sitting there all alone. He saw that he hadn't shaved for many days.

At this point Babi stopped to take his off glasses and wipe his tears.

"When somebody dies in our family, men stop shaving," he finally continued. "It was my elder sister…"

29th September 2015, Tuesday. Sunny

Today I entered the exhibition hall through the backdoor and greeted the guards: "Good morning!" They slowly raised their heads, and one of them nodded in reply. They sit here in this wrecked dark corner all day, time must be running very slowly for them; one can easily grow glum and develop some singularities while working in such a place.

Els gave me her book as a keepsake. It is full of her drawings, and I even found the sketch of the skull—with little human figures instead of teeth. I can imagine how much inspiration Els drew from the village she grew up in; my village, on the contrary, used to suffocate me, I have had to suppress a lot of my emotions.

In the evening I participated in a performance by the Russian art group u/n multitude. In the beginning, I had to lay out some round metal objects on the stage (later they explained me that those were buoys). A voice behind the stage was reading somebody's names out loud. At the same time, several musicians were climbing up the scaffold around the stage. They started playing and played according to the pattern I created with the buoys. The entire performance lasted 20 minutes, and in the end I got to the centre of the stage and gave the musicians a sign with an abrupt gesture—and the music stopped.

While I was working at this biennial, a lot of people came up to me and told me that my diary had made them very sad. "Moscow has both good and bad," one girl tried to comfort me, "I am sure you will soon see its beauty."

And I think I finally did feel the warmth of this city and understood its beauty. I almost like it now.

30th September 2015, Wednesday. Sunny

I spent the morning hanging the photographs of Birdhead.

In the middle of the day I suddenly felt very tired and tried to spunk myself up with a cup of coffee—with no success though. Because of the performance yesterday, when I had to carry round metal buoys, my whole body was aching.

In the evening I was surprised to discover that two pages of my diary were missing. One entry is about why I didn't like Moscow, and the other one describes the incident with the guards. The pages of the diary lie under the glass that is screwed to the table. Who took my diary? I am pretty sure that whoever took it didn't do it because he liked my diary so much. He probably didn't want anybody to see its content. Or he was even scared somebody might see it.

I am outraged by such behaviour.

We had to print out those two pages again and put them under the glass.

There was a party for the sponsors later in the evening. Usually, I try to avoid such events because I don't know how to talk to these people and in general feel very awkward. However, this time I was surrounded by my new artist friends and had a good time. I even had two glasses of white wine.

Babi keeps saying that evenings are the time of well-off visitors, and there is a chance one of them might buy our artworks. I was observing these people carefully and came to the conclusion that they don't understand art at all. "I don't like this modern art, I don't get it. I prefer pretty pictures," a flamboyantly dressed young lady said to me. "You don't like it because you never took time to really understand it," I replied.

I had dinner with Babi, and again he treated me to some sweets afterwards. One cannot possibly resist his hospitality so I have no choice but to gratefully accept his presents. If I keep going like this, I will get very fat.

1st October 2015, Thursday. Cloudy

The first thing I did when I got to the exhibition was to check on my diary. It is unbelievable! Some parts of it were missing again! This time it was the part about the guards and Taya's opinion on the situation.

I told Defne, the curator, about what had happened. She said she saw how two guards had taken the pages of my diary.

The news about the double theft spread all over the exhibition like wildfire. In the evening we printed out the missing parts again and placed them where they belonged. I taped them to the table to prevent future theft.

As I was passing the guards today, they gave me a very mean look. It made me feel really uneasy but I told myself that it's them who were scared of me; they don't like that their deeds are exposed to the public.

"I am so ashamed of the fact that such people live in my country," one of the visitors told me after he read my diary.

Birdhead placed the bigger photographs over the smaller ones to make the smaller images serve as a background.

It was the tenth day of the Biennale, and the gallery got really crowded in the evening. Every artwork is now finished, and tomorrow the documentary exhibition project starts. Visitors won't be able to see the artists or the workers, there will be no performances or lectures.

Bart, another curator, told me some people don't agree that my artwork at this biennale can't be called performance art. "I absolutely agree," I said to him, "but what else would you call it? Which form of art could describe it better? I don't know." "Yes, it seems that the word 'performance' suits best," he agreed.

I dreamed about my village last night. Crying with grief, a large group of people carried a coffin past me. I started walking and immediately stepped in yellow faeces. I was shaking my foot trying to get rid of it but it wouldn't fall off. According to a traditional Chinese dream interpretation, my dream signifies luck and prosperity.

You don't believe me, do you? Well, you should, because tomorrow I am collecting my wages.

Translation: Taya Reznichenko

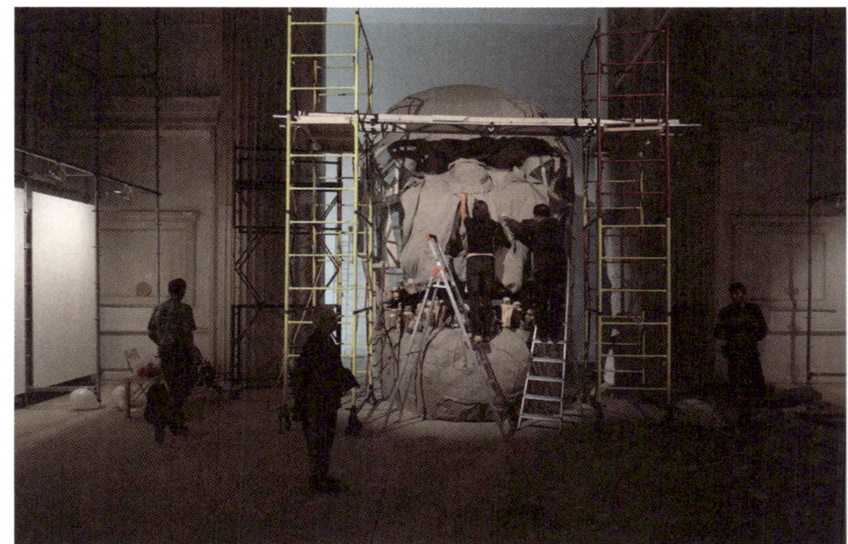

Otto Snoek, *22 September – 01 October 2015*

Li Mu and Els Dietvorst working together on *Skull*, Moscow Biennale 2015

Ho Tzu-Nyen & Lee Weng-Choy — Curation is Also a Form of Transportation

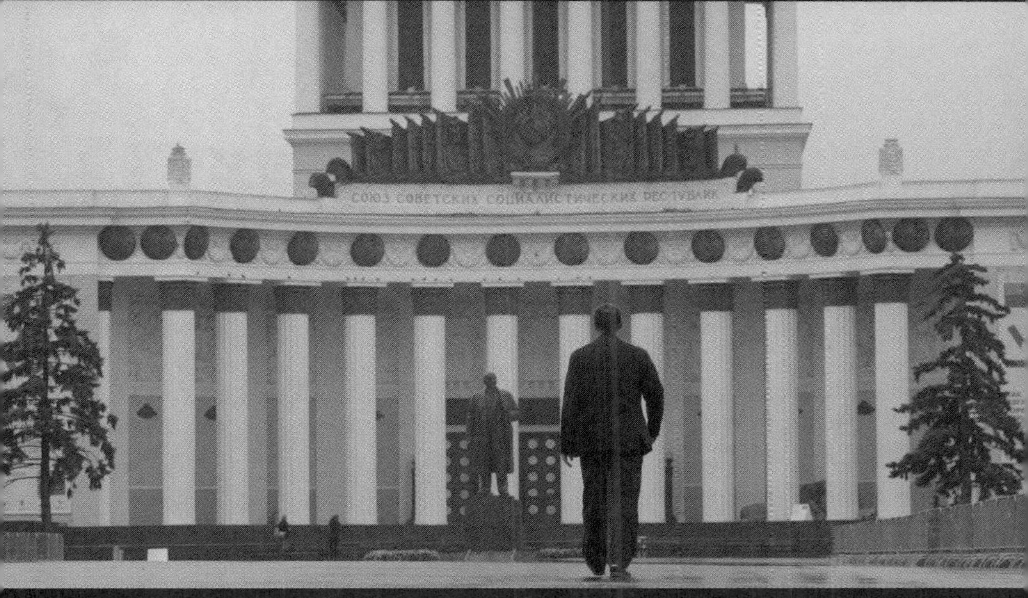

Lee Weng-Choy walks toward VDNKh Pavilion No. 1.

… where the 6th Moscow Biennale for Contemporary Art is staged.

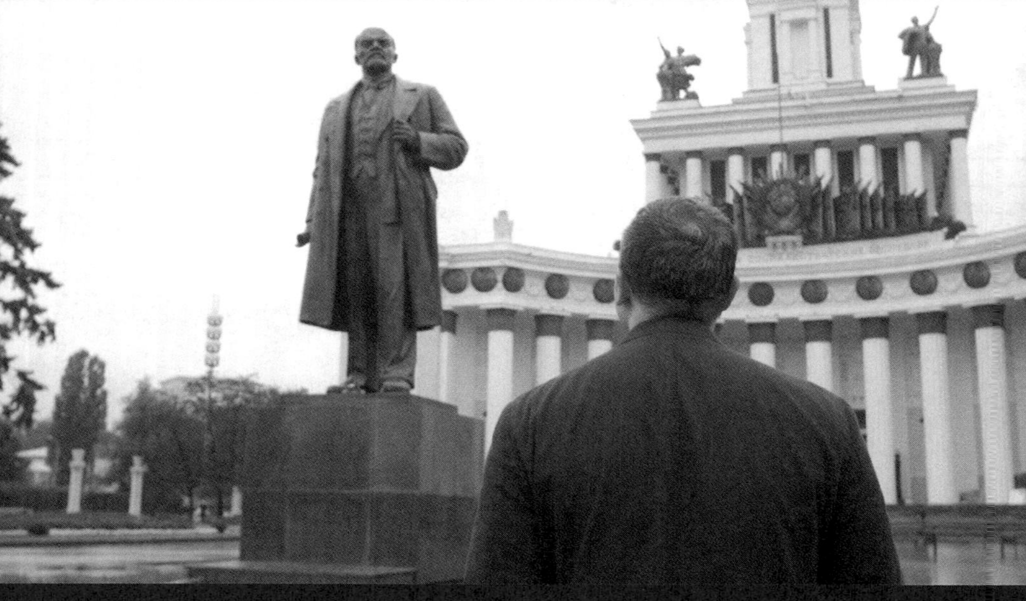

As he passes before Lenin, almost instinctively, he pauses before the statue.

... Is it out of sincere reverence, or because the figure has now become an icon of ironic curiosity? Maybe I am interested in the stature as a work of art. Perhaps it is all of these feelings. The moment is fleeting as I move on towards the pavilion.

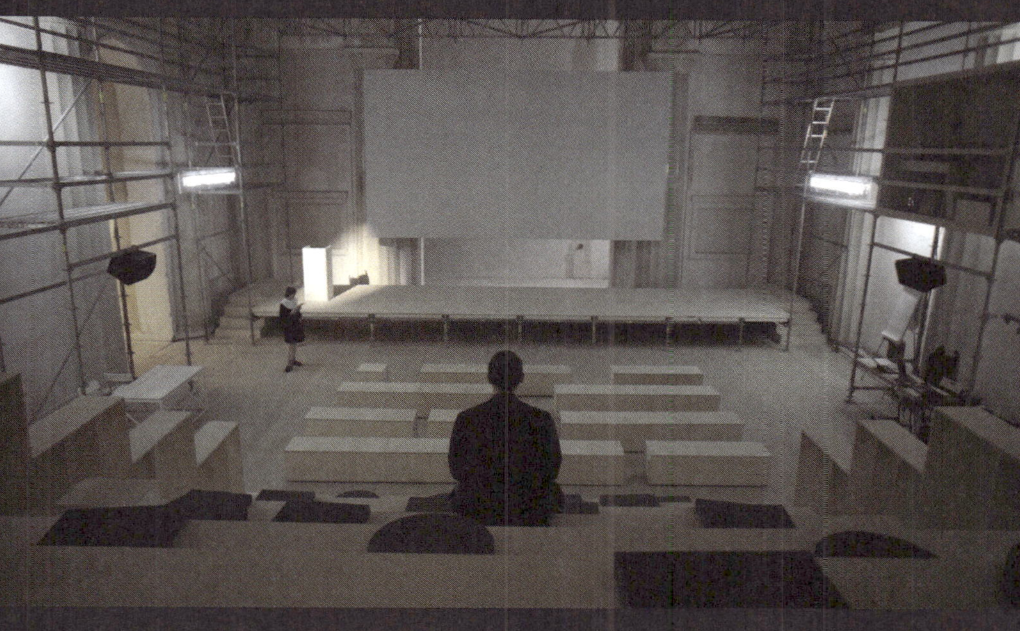

Lee Weng-Choy stares at a blank screen. A woman enters from a passageway on the left. She seems to be in costume, and is reading a script. Lee Weng-Choy is oblivious to her presence.

… I sit for several minutes in the auditorium and don't notice occasional passers-by. I arrived at the pavilion early, which explains why there aren't many people walking around at this moment. Somehow, upon entering the building, I quickly gravitated to reflecting on the empty screen. Staring at it seems to be the perfect way to prepare myself, before looking at any art. The entire space leaves an impression on me. It feels intimate and hospitable.

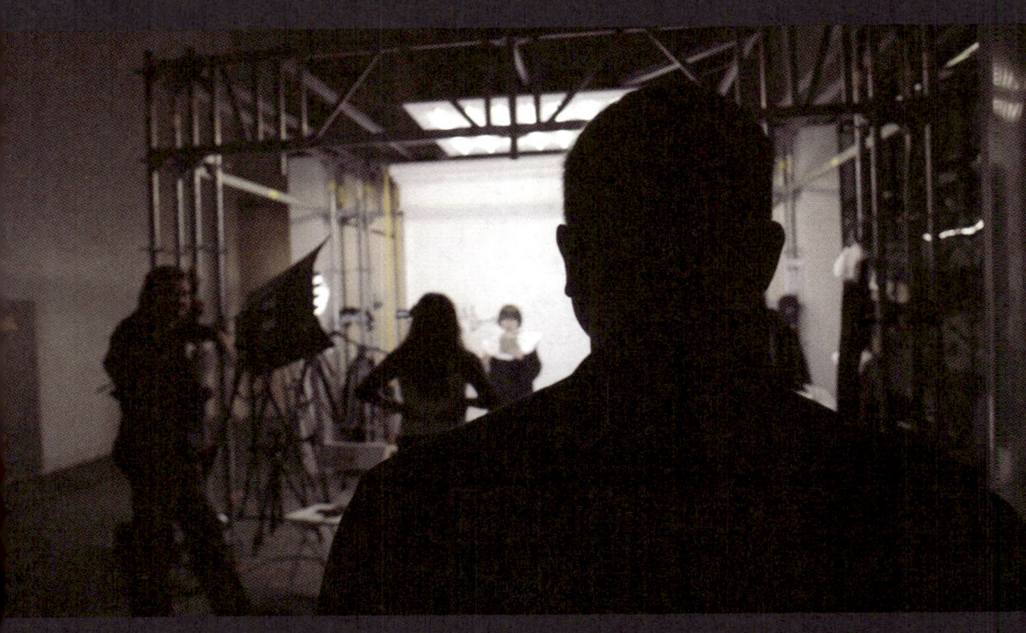

Perhaps the woman is merely a figment of Lee Weng-Choy's imagination.

... I ask myself: What is it about biennales and their scale? How would I respond to a performance such as this somewhere else? Why is it that in Moscow I seem much more open to these kinds of gestures and interventions?

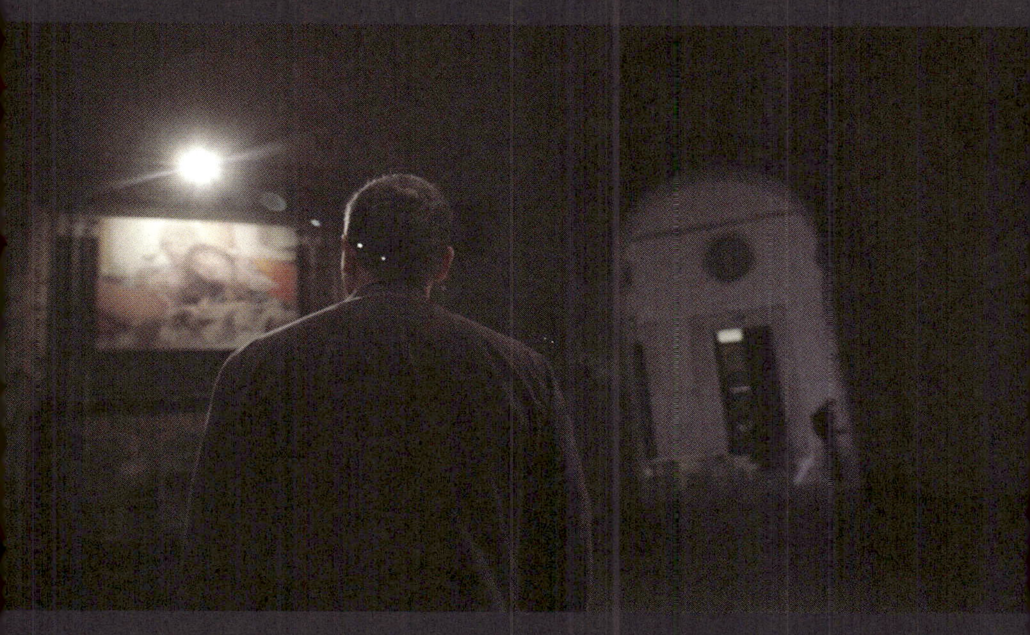

Two women appear on screen, and a light shines on Lee Weng-Choy.

… I begin to survey the various art works…

Lee Weng-Choy is transported.

… I once imagined a large-scale, long-term curatorial project, envisioned not by a single architect, nor built up from a grand design, but constructed through a series of layered interventions by various contributors. It could be called: 'On Being Curated.' As part of the research for it, one would obtain stories from artists, curators, and a whole range of persons, on what it is like to be curated. Indispensable as that material would be, something else would be required. Maps may be important — they are necessary for navigation — but navigation is not sufficient for representation. There is something else that can happen in curating that goes beyond storytelling or cartography. Curation is also a form of transportation.

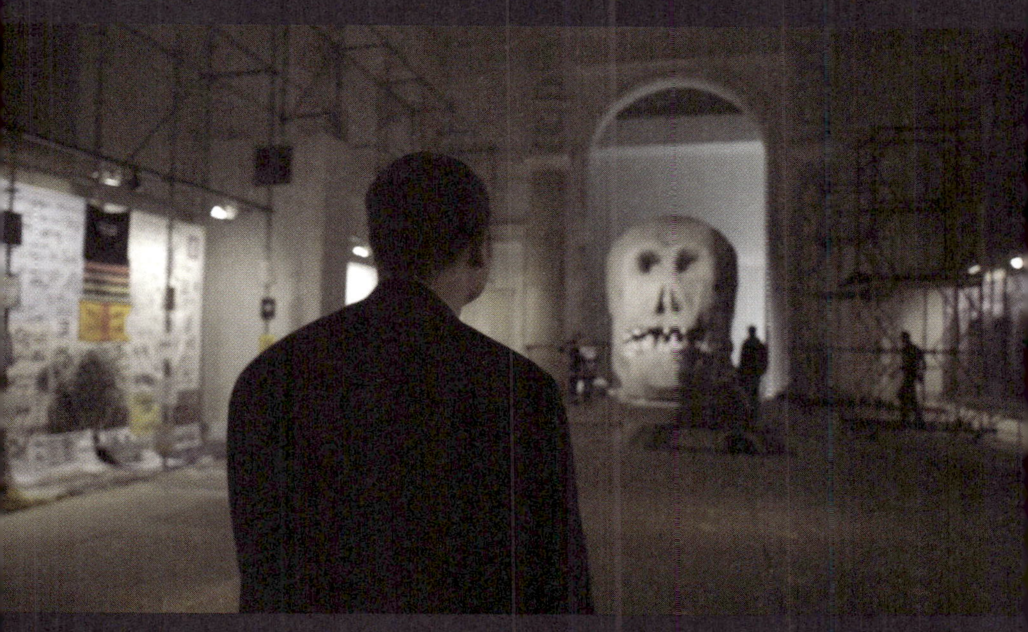

Lee Weng-Choy traverses a large hall, moving towards a death's head.

… The large skull by Els Dietvorst is in the process of being constructed and installed.

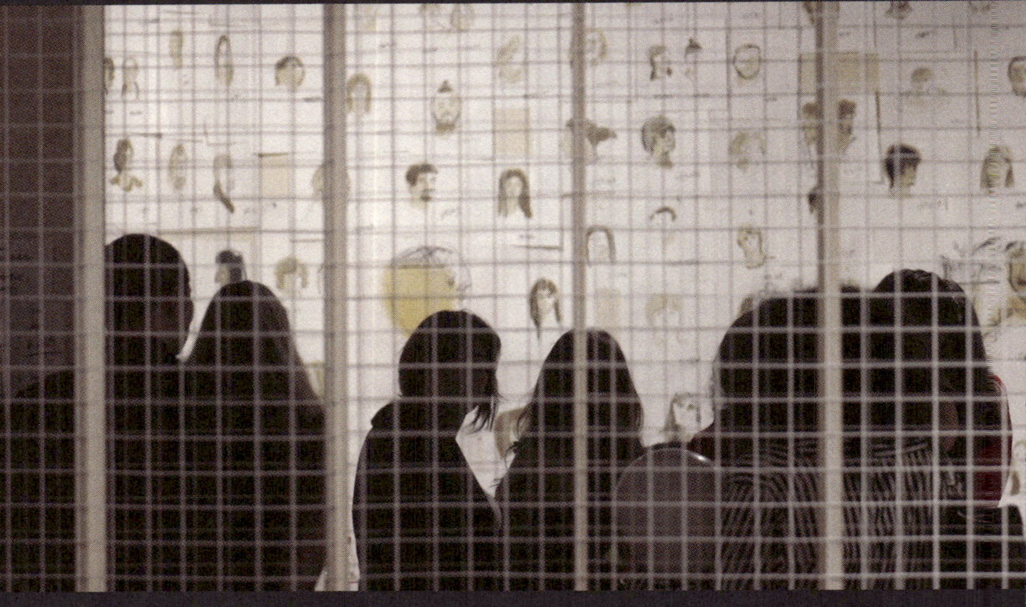

Then he finds himself in a room full of heads, both real and represented.

... I join a small crowd in front of Fabrice Hyber, who, for the entire 10-day duration of the Biennale, is drawing portraits of visitors with crude oil.

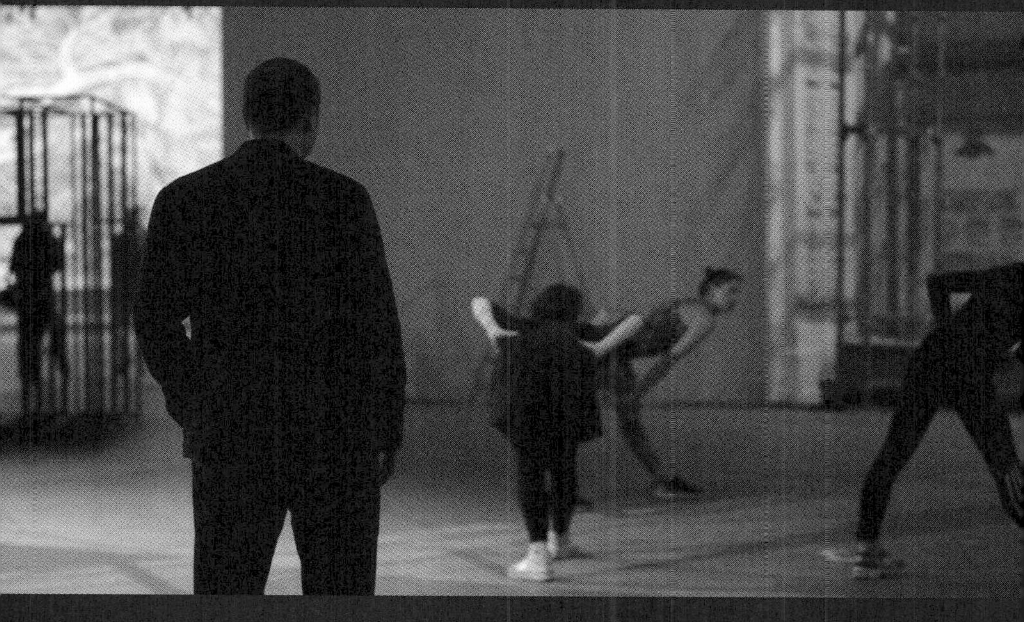

Lee Weng-Choy stares at three figures in the midst of a physical activity.

… It is one of the regular exercise sessions for the Biennale participants.

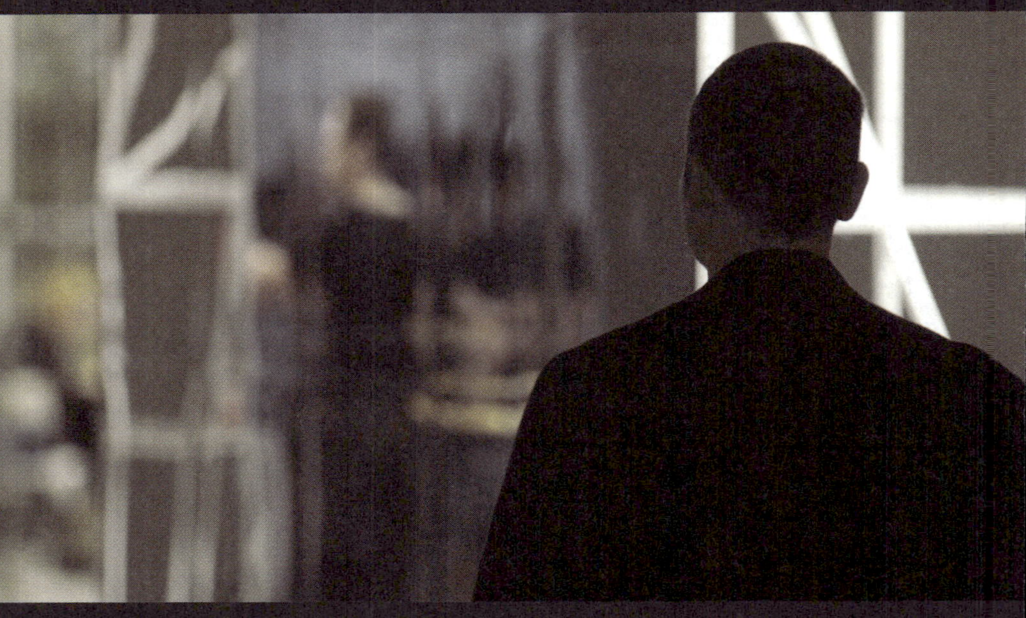

Then, Lee Weng-Choy is transfixed by reflections of a dance.

... I watch the artist Leon Kahane as he attempts to learn ballet every day for the duration of the Biennale.

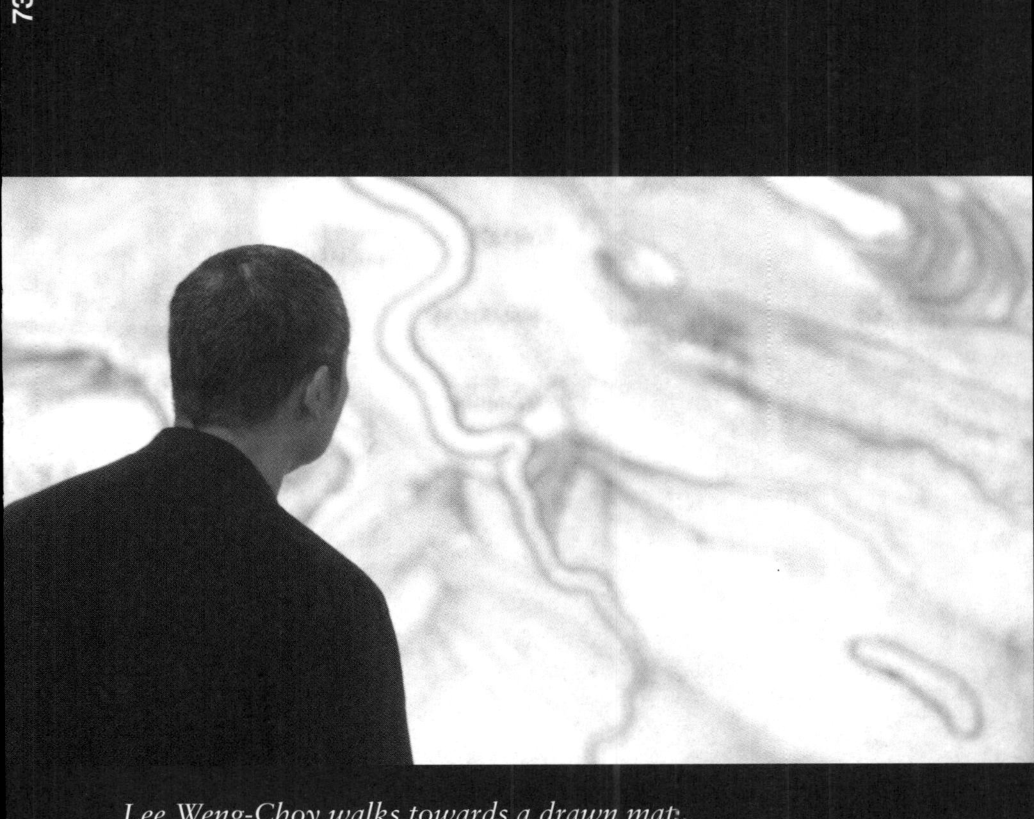

Lee Weng-Choy walks towards a drawn map.

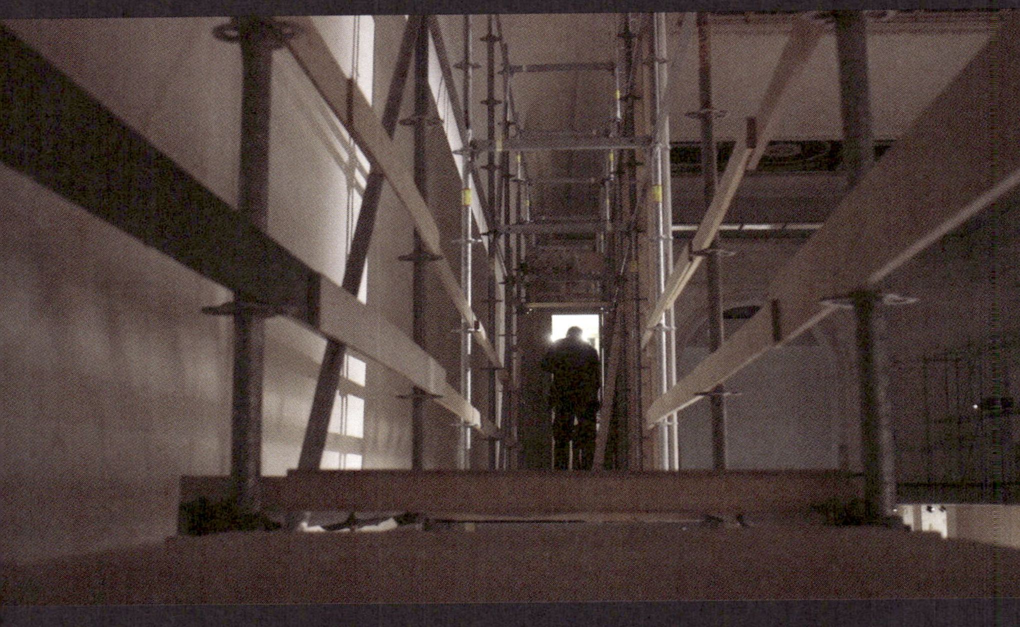

Lee Weng-Choy walks behind the map. We hear the animated voice of a woman, getting increasingly louder and closer…

… Climbing up the scaffolding to a hidden room, I approach Augustas Serapinas's tea room.

An image of a keynote speaker goes out of focus, as our attention is drawn to Lee Weng-Choy's ear.

… I listen to economist Mariana Mazzucato, who is debunking myths of the free market.

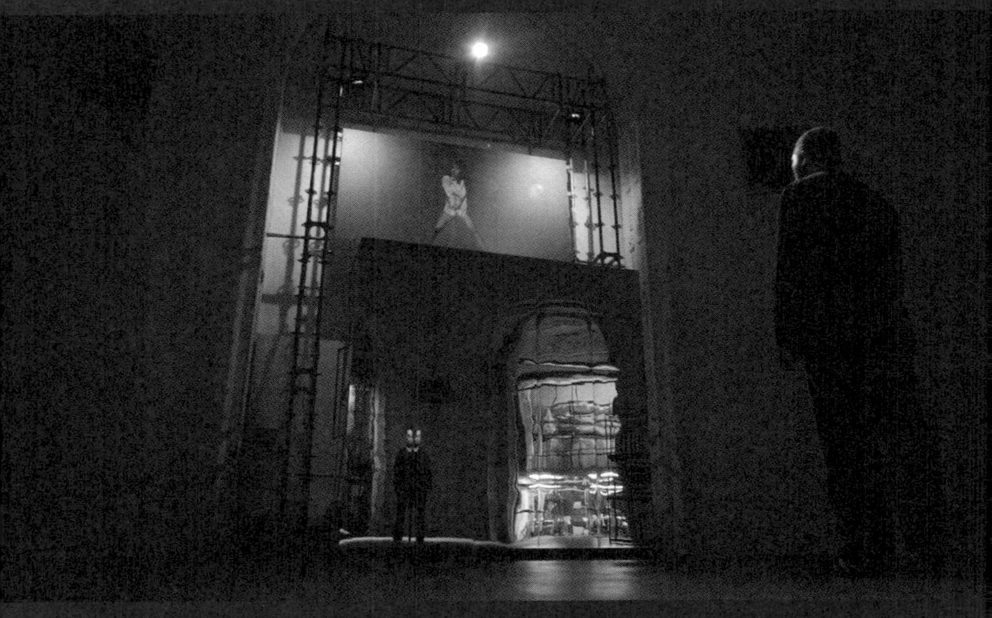

Lee Weng-Choy stands before his distorted reflection, which splits him into two.

... I am staring at the large mirrored moveable partition which was used by Leon Kahane for his ballet lessons.

Lee Weng-Choy — Three Degrees of Intimacy: Desire, Drive and Disappointment

Singapore, March 2016

I was invited to Moscow as a stand-in. Let me just quickly sketch some of the coordinates of my participation that pertain to my purpose here, to reflect on the Biennale in terms of public intimacies. I want to try and consider the cumulative effect that *How to Gather?* had on me.

Ho Tzu-Nyen — a good friend, and an artist I admire — was invited to the Moscow Biennale. His schedule did not permit for his presence, so he proposed that I attend the event instead, and that members of the Biennale documentary crew should film me. (Did I mention I hate being captured on camera?) Tzu-Nyen then wanted to assemble the footage into something. This would be the second time we engage in such an experiment. The first instance was for the Ural Industrial Biennale in Yekaterinburg, which opened a few weeks before Moscow. Tzu-Nyen couldn't be present for that event either. In Yekaterinburg, I spoke at the Biennale symposium and participated in one of its discussions. A local crew filmed me doing that. In Moscow, with no specific tasks assigned, we decided that I would walk around and observe quietly.

I very much enjoyed walking around the Moscow Biennale, as well as VDNKh, the park in which the pavilion was situated. The works that caught my attention ranged from Leon Kahane's ballet piece and Augustas Serapinas's tea room behind Qiu Zhijie's large map-like painting, to Fabrice Hyber's drawings with crude oil. I may be an art critic, but one of the things I like to do least is write reviews of biennials. I'm the kind of writer who feels uncomfortably disingenuous when I have to offer an extensive opinion about something so large and unwieldy after only a brief encounter. When I write about artists, it's usually after I've had, so to speak, intimate relations with their practice over some years. I have that with Tzu-Nyen:

A decade ago, I wrote about his made-for-television series, *4 x 4 — Episodes of Singapore Art* (2005). My essay was called *Coincidence and Relation: Art Criticism and Heartbreak*,[1] and it focused on the third of the four episodes.[2] *Episode 3: Tang Da-Wu — The Most Radical Gesture* is a making-of/behind-the-scenes mock-documentary about a famous performance by the acclaimed Singapore artist Tang Da-Wu. Tang approached the President of Singapore at a major art event, putting on a blazer with the words "Don't Give Money to the Arts" embroidered on the back, and passed him a note saying "Dear Mr President, I am an artist and I am important". Tzu-Nyen's mock-documentary unfolds through interruptions, repetitions and corrections, as the director and his assistant try to film various scenes but instead argue over the meaning of Tang's "most radical gesture".

This debate between director and assistant is related to the theme of public intimacies, and it resonates with my experience of Moscow. Tang's performance was done in the aftermath of the Singapore government's proscriptions against performance art. A local tabloid had sensationalised a performance by Josef Ng, and the government over-reacted by wanting to suppress the genre. For the assistant in Episode 3, at stake is that Tang dared to protest in front of the President himself. For the director, Tang's radical gesture is his fundamental regard for the other: Tang politely asks the President's permission to put on the jacket as he commences the performance. Episode 3, while ostensibly a documentary on a specific artwork, is, like Tang's own gesture, both a provocation and a performance of regard, a speaking to art and to the other, in the singular and the intimate, the universal and the public.

I appreciated the Moscow Biennale for its smaller, quieter moments, but there were also larger gestures, such as the painting by Luc Tuymans, that made a strong impression on me. Of course I found some works more interesting than others. I want to risk a claim about this Biennale, and describe the overall and underlying feel of the 6th Moscow edition as intimate. However, I wouldn't go on to say it was intimate in scale. Modest is not the right word either—true, it wasn't a large event in relation to your typical biennial, and this 6th edition was smaller than its predecessors. As a form, as a proposition, the biennial in general seems to be about grand gestures. While some exhibitions may come across as more grandiose than grand, perhaps one could describe the better projects as not immodest, not overly self-serious, but ambitious nonetheless. *How to Gather?* shared these qualities. To describe its scale, its ambitions, I would use the word public.

The full title of *How to Gather?* includes the phrase *Acting in a Centre in a City in the Heart of the Island of Eurasia*. The island in Eurasia that I think about most is Singapore, where I have worked and lived for more than twenty years. It's interesting to think of Russia also as an island. The publics of Moscow and Singapore are very different. Although in both situations the public sphere is certainly something that cannot be taken for granted—it is a precious and precarious space. In Singapore, the state will gladly spend millions on the arts, but it demands KPIs to justify these expenses. In Singapore, therefore, it is urgent to consistently argue for the value of the public as something apart from large attendance figures. A public does not have to be big to be significant. Publics that are constituted by artistic projects are not just venues for the consumption of contemporary culture, they are spaces for people to gather—individuals, from artists to audiences, interacting with each other with some sense of larger purpose or the desire for such.

I'm not sure why the word degree seems relevant here, but I want to go with it. What are at stake are levels of severity, like a third-degree burn. Which degree of intimacy is more severe — desire, drive or disappointment? Their differences in degree may only be slight, but they matter nevertheless. A certain lyric by The Smiths comes to mind: "Nothing's changed / I still love you, oh, I still love you / only slightly, only slightly less / than I used to, my love."[3]

Of the three degrees of intimacy, drive connects desire and disappointment in a way that unsettles me. If our common understanding is that disappointment arises often as a consequence of an unrequited desire or a desire that does not quite deliver, how then does drive fit into the equation? Desire is always for an object (or, for Lacan, the *objet petit a*). Drive, however, is not oriented towards any goal or object: its reason for being is to repeat the act of desire. As a young man, like most young adults, I was preoccupied with trying to understand desire. This preoccupation often took the form of "Oh why does being in love with this person torment me so?" But as I have gotten older, I find that I turn to wanting to understand drive. There is an emptiness at the centre of a drive: we cannot help but go through the motions; we no longer need the pretence that we might be in love, or that disappointment can be staved off; intimacy is not possible, we are doomed to be alone; not for nothing is the most well-known drive, the death drive—though stop me if you have heard this all before...

How to gather? How to find intimacy in a public sphere that is precious and precarious? How to refuse to give up on desire, to not resign oneself to disappointment, and to confront drive sceptically and not cynically? These, I believe, are among the questions at the heart of the 6th Moscow Biennale. My experience of walking around, keeping some distance, observing quietly, feeling disoriented, but only slightly, gave me an experience of what these questions feel like. Let me close with a song by the Talking Heads. I believe Tzu-Nyen would approve: "Out of all those kinds of people / You got a face with a view / I'm just an animal looking for a home and, / Share the same space for a minute or two..."[4]

1
"Coincidence and Relation: Art Criticism and Heartbreak", in *Broadsheet*, Vol. 35, No. 1, Adelaide: Contemporary Art Centre of South Australia, 2006. URL: https://independent.academia.edu/WengChoyLee.

2
"Focused" might be an overstatement; I digressed on a variety of subjects, from desire and heartbreak to art criticism, wondering if judgements in love (am I truly in love?) and judgements in art (is this a good work?) might have something in common.

3
Stop Me If You Think You've Heard This One Before by The Smiths, 1987, written by Morrissey and Johnny Marr, from the album *Strangeways, Here We Come*.

4
This Must Be The Place (Naive Melody) by Talking Heads, 1983, written by David Byrne, Chris Frantz, Tina Weymouth and Jerry Harrison, from the album *Speaking in Tongues*.

Meggy Rustamova — Waiting for the Secret (Script)

The Latin expression *sub rosa* or 'under the rose' is used to signify secrecy. Since ancient times, the rose has been a symbol of secrecy, its origin traceable to a Greek myth. Aphrodite gave a rose to her son Eros, the god of love. He, in turn, gave it to the god of silence, to ensure that his mother's indiscretions were not disclosed. Paintings of roses on ceilings were also a visual reminder that things said under the rose should remain *sub rosa*.

One day, as on most days, a man is sitting on top of his mountain. Yes, this is his mountain. He does not own it in economic terms, but in a more intangible way.

What is he doing there? And how come he is sitting in this ordinary wooden chair? The chair looks quite heavy.

The landscape is familiar to the man, so he does not pay attention to it anymore. Instead he spends his time staring at his phone. Nevertheless, sometimes when the light is sublime, he takes photographs. The man perceives everything through a lens. Nothing much has changed during the years; the mountains are still mountains and the man remains the same boy he always was. Mankind in general has remained the same, the woman, the man, the child, the parent, the friend, the lover, the spectator.

The character speaks to me, not in words, not in sound, but in gestures. I believe he is writing me a message. He says he has discovered the potential of freedom. Freedom, he says, is admitting to the experience of the void. Perhaps the free one is the one who can escape into a deeply rooted monotony. He has detected isolation in company. The man is alone, but he is not lonely. He merely withdraws from time to time.

Suddenly, very unexpectedly, a strange hand appears.

Whose hand is this?

What does it want?

The hand is beautiful. I imagine this hand in a painting. Hands are so difficult to draw. Perhaps the greatest artist is the one who can bring a hand to life in a sculpture or painting.

The hand is on its way to touch the man in the chair. What the hand does not realise is that the man sitting feels it advancing upon him. The wood of the chair conducts the warm energy of the hand. The man on the chair freezes. He stops typing. The last

thing he writes is: …
I imagine the fresh mountain smell.
A light sunny breeze.
A perfect day; one of the few.
Nothing particular is happening today.
Can you see the village in the valley?
Now look at the light pink plastic bag.
Can you see it is shivering slightly, as there is a light breeze?[1]

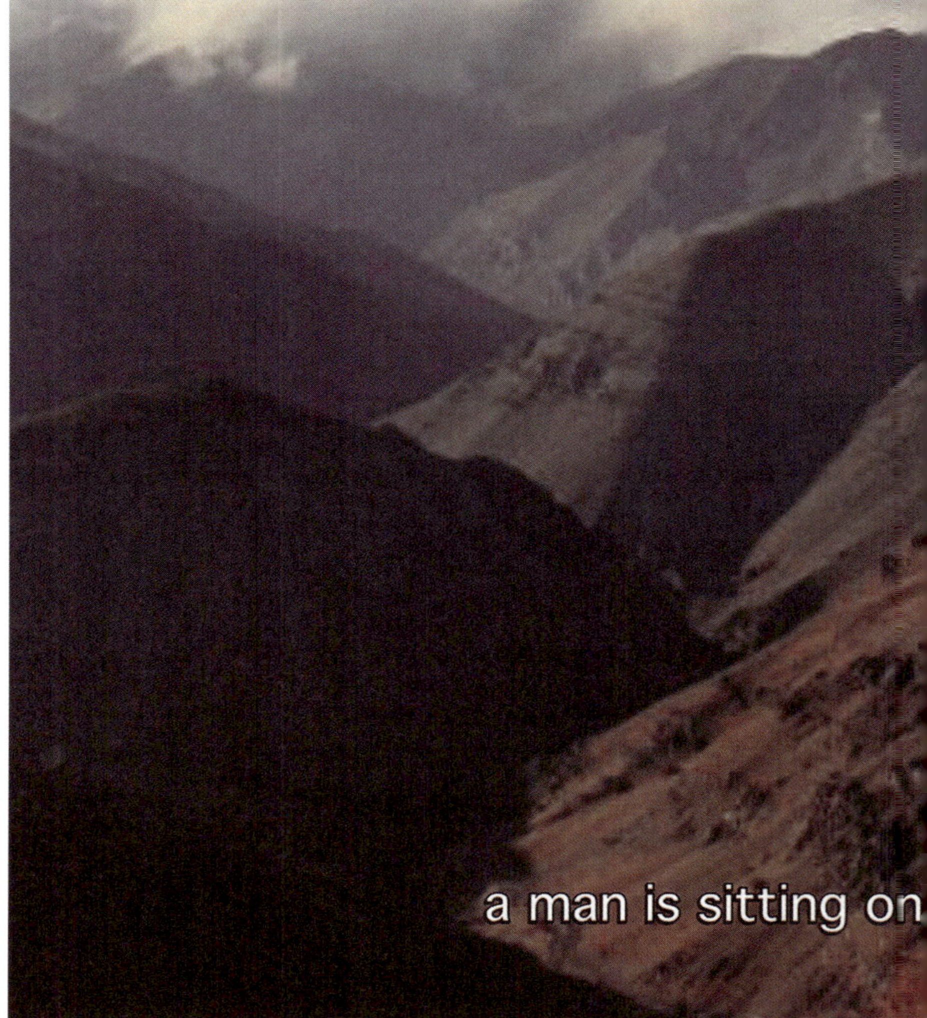

1
Script and still: Meggy Rustamova, *Waiting for the Secret*, (2014) HD video, colour, sound, 6 mins., original language: Esperanto.

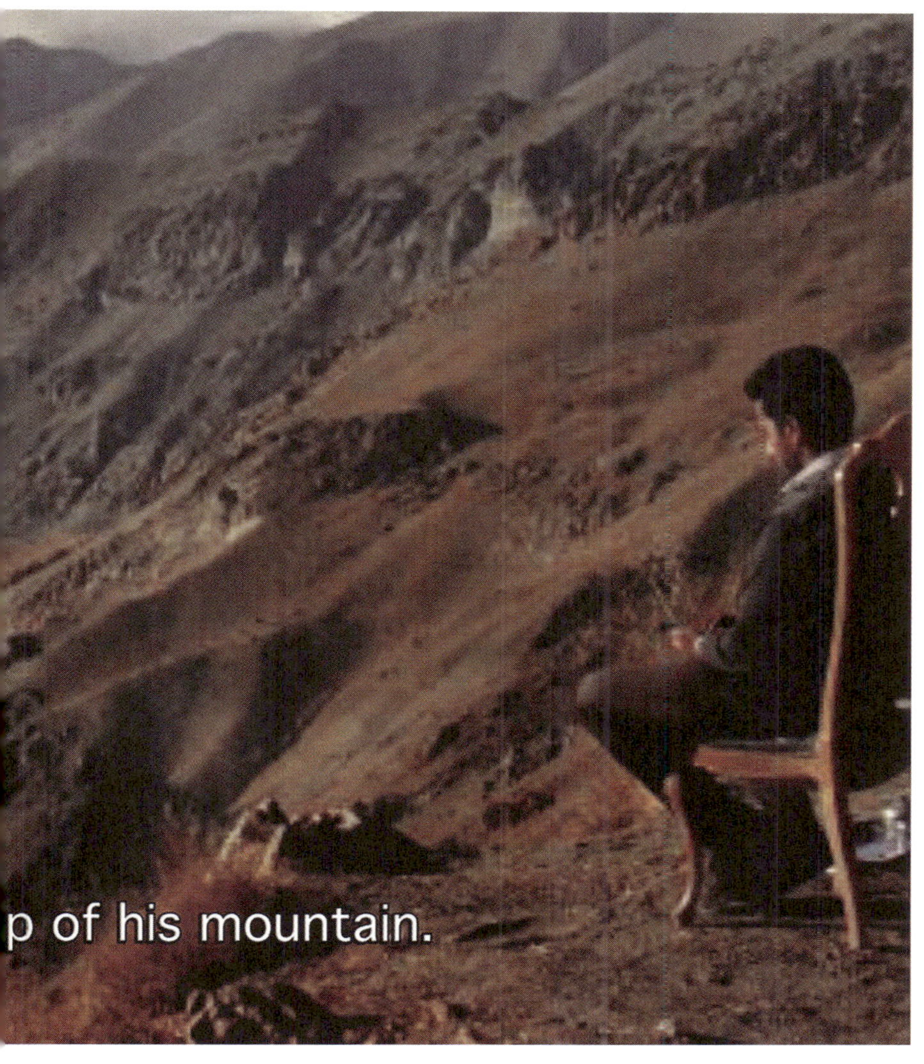

Johanna van Overmeir — Janus

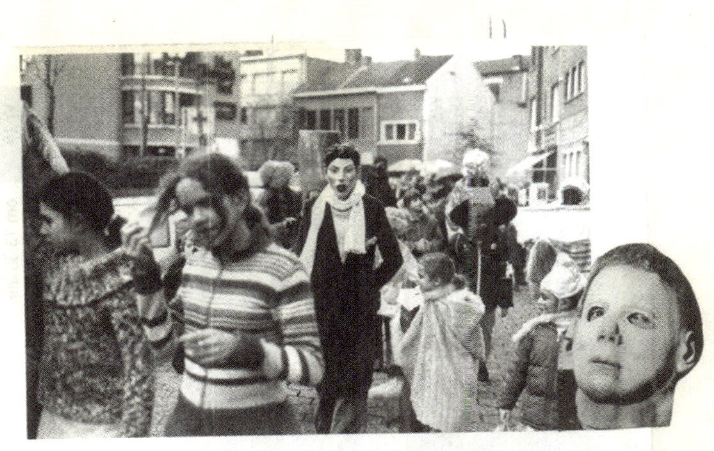

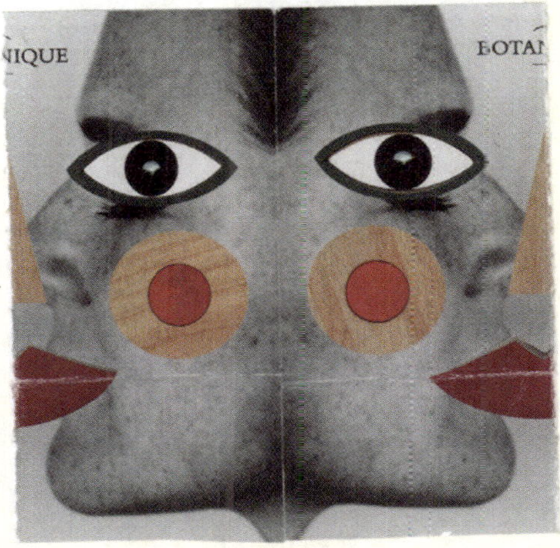

JANUS

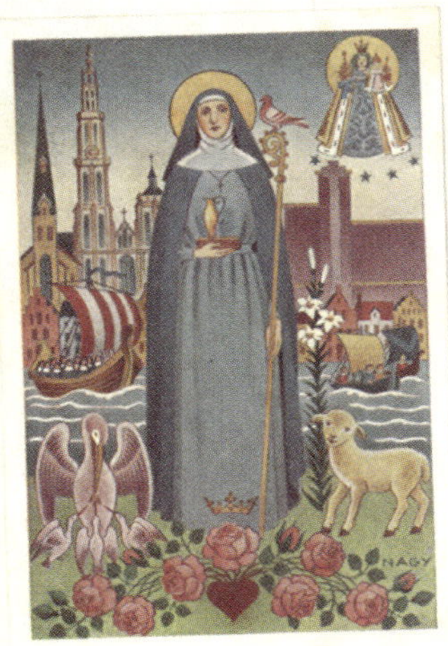

→ two faces → een schaduw die meegedragen wordt
→ vogelverschrikker → metronoom
→ babouchka → pendel
→ ouderwets → bezwering, hypnose, verstilling

Er gaat een raam open
Er komt een vrouw uit het raam
Al schommelend. Je ziet alleen haar achterkant
Ze heeft een doek/hoed aan, het lijkt
een vogelverschrikker.
Het geluid van de schommel kraakt.

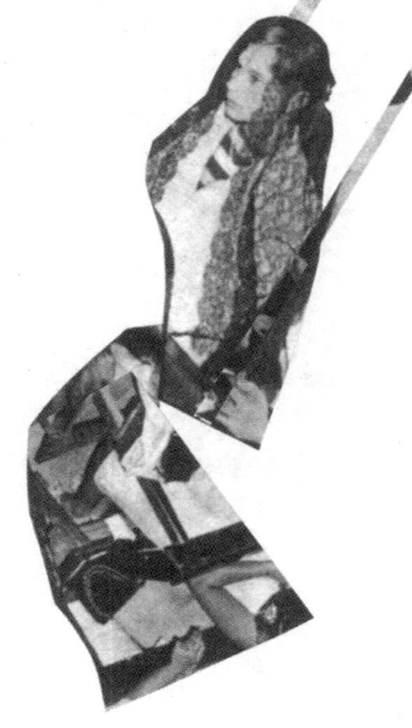

Johanna van Overmeir's work originated from the moment the artist saw a lonely scarecrow on the *Camino Del Norte* in Spain. This image was complemented by a physical challenge. The artist worked with a professional trainer for several months prior to the performance. Her action took place under an archway in the axis of Pavilion No. 1 at VDNKh, leading from the central dome to the space at the rear which housed the Biennale media machine together with a gilded Soviet sculpture of a mass parade that was undergoing restoration. In this site both the Janus head and the swinging became a movement back and forth between past and future, restoration and innovation, outside and inside, experience and representation, and even, with the Lenin sculpture in front of the pavilion and the fountain with the golden female figures representing the former Soviet republics behind it, between Asia and Europe. [Bart De Baere]

←←
←
Johanna van Overmeir, *Janus*, personal notes, 2015

→
Johanna Van Overmeir, *Janus*, Moscow Biennale 2015

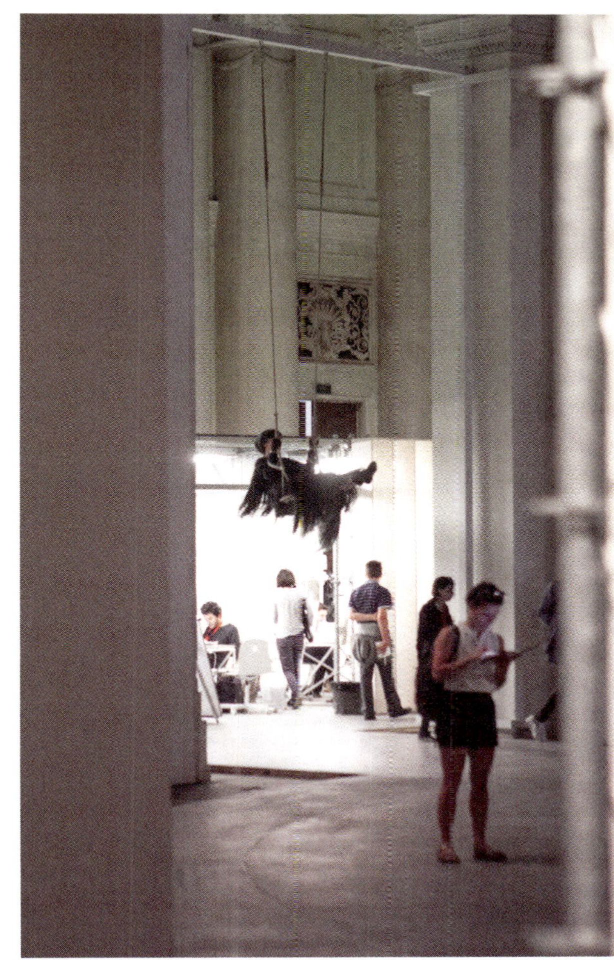

Janus Faced Freedom

The wooden seat of Johanna van Overmeir's swing was suspended two metres above the floor to provide a large amplitude of movement. The artist swung furiously to and fro, wearing a dusty dress of black feathers, which made the performer reminiscent of the black swan Odile from the ballet *Swan Lake*. This sinister image was completed with a white mask which the artist wore on the back of her head. Her constant movement created an atmosphere of a constant threat circulating in the air above our heads. Johanna van Overmeir swung without any safety wires, forced to cling to the swing's ropes with her bandaged hands.

The performance, however, was an image of a permanent state of suspension. It did not create any feeling of freedom, but one rather of fear and despair; the inevitable dizziness that automatically comes with swinging. This nausea *à la* Sartre is not limited to a state of abandonment and loneliness. Rather, it is also a reaction to a general volatility, perplexity and precariousness that is social disorder and disorder of the mind.

Precariousness is not a mere abstract situation characterised by a lack of security and wellbeing. It is a social effect engendered by the neoliberal economy and its auxiliary superstructure. Just as it is for Johanna van Overmeir herself, who needs a special ladder and assistance to get down from the high swing, it would be a mistake to link precariousness with a feeling of freedom. It means in fact an absolute dependency on circumstances and on someone else's individual will. So all those who sympathise with the concepts of freedom that dominate contemporary culture and mass media should ask themselves: Would I want to take the artist's place on that swing?[1]

Marina Simakova

1
Extract. This text appeared unabridged on the Moscow Biennale Blog: http://moscowbiennale.syg.ma/en.

Peter Wächtler — Leather Man

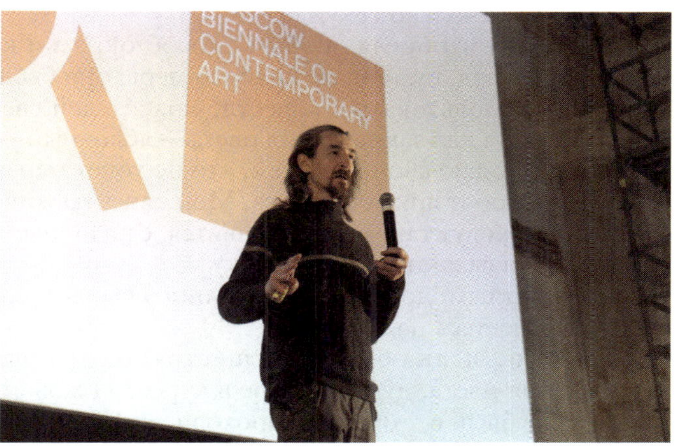

Peter Wächtler, *Leather Man*, performance rehearsal, Moscow Biennale, 30th September 2015

Я крашу кожи, я кожевник. Я здесь, чтобы рассказать вам, как покрасить кожу, как изменить ее цвет; и если вы подумываете — почему нет, собственно? — заняться тем же, чем и я, то я скажу вам вот что: это такая же работа, как любая другая, не лучше и не хуже.

(молчит несколько секунд)

Моя семья изобрела особый способ окраски кож четыре поколения назад, ну, или, по крайней мере, они были первыми, кто начал использовать в качестве красителей свекольный и луковый сок, а для закрепления цвета — яблочный уксус. Я, так повелось, продаю свои меха тем, кто не хочет мерзнуть зимой и при этом любит ярко одеваться. Мои клиенты живут по всему миру, и они живут так, как им нравится, с разноцветной кожей; рабы не заказывают цветную кожу.

(выглядит самодовольным и немного выпендривается)

Да вы смеетесь надо мной!

Конечно, я знаю, что существуют другие способы закрепления цвета, думаете, я не в курсе? И может быть, мои предки и не были в этом первопроходцами. Но людям нравится запах яблочного уксуса и все больше и больше становится тех, кто отказывается от фабричных вещей, от любых, и вот тут в дело вступаю я и «старинный» рецепт моей семьи.

Можешь над этим потешаться, но один вопросик, умник: а что твоя семья сделала? Твоя семья что-нибудь изобрела? Ну, конечно, не считая новых способов уйти от налогов?

Что-то я сомневаюсь.

Поэтому дай мне заниматься моим делом, это уважаемая профессия, а я уж не буду допытываться, на что ты тратишь свою бесполезную жизнь. И я тебе только скажу, что меха красили всегда, давно уже, еще… как сказать… до нашей эры.

(замолкает, вспомнив, что он выступает перед аудиторией)

Вы знаете, откуда берутся шкуры, которые я не использую? Ха-ха. Из Индии. А теперь вы, наверное, скажете: так разве в Индии корова не священное животное? Разве их там не запрещено убивать? Точно. Но не в Пакистане. Поэтому они загружают этих священных коров в грузовики и вывозят в Пакистан, где их и забивают на нелегальных скотобойнях. Но это не означает, что эти шкуры плохого качества; это значит, что и священные коровы тоже умирают, а я могу заказать их шкуры для своей мастерской и покрасить их в любой цвет, в какой захочу, но я не делаю этого. Есть много видео об этих

I am the leather dyer, I dye leather. So, I am here to tell you about how to dye leather, like change its color, and if you are thinking of—why not—doing the same as I do, I can tell you that much: it is a job as any other, no better, no worse.

(Pauses)

My family invented that technique four generations ago, or at least they were the first to use beetroot and onion juice and to fixate the colors with apple vinegar. I sell my furs to those who want to keep warm in winter and like to dress in colorful things, traditionally. My clients live all over the world and they live the life they want to with colorful leather, slaves don't order colorful leather.

(looks proud but still insecure)

But you are just laughing at me.

Of course there are other techniques to fixate the color, do you think I don't know that myself? And maybe my family was not really inventing anything. But people like the smell of apple vinegar and more and more people turn their back to industrial production, whatever that is, and that is where I and the "ancient" recipes of my family come in.

And you can laugh about it but a question for you Smartass: What did your family do? Did they ever invent anything? Apart from tax fraud?

I really doubt it.

So let me do my thing, it is an honorable profession, I am not investigating on what you do with your useless days. But let me tell you that furs were already dyed, long ago, like, ähm, before the dawning of our age.

(Pause)

Do you know where the hides I DO NOT use come from? They are from India. And now you will say: India, aren't the cows holy in India, isn't it forbidden to kill them? Yes, it is indeed. But not in Pakistan. So they put the holy cows on a truck and send them to Pakistan where they are slaughtered in illegal abattoirs. But that does not mean that the quality is all that bad, it just means that holy cows have to die too and that I COULD order their hides to my workshop and color them in practically any color I want, but I DO NOT do it. There are videos about these abattoirs that could give you serious doubts about mankind, you have to imagine a car wash site, like drive in or through or whatever. But instead of foamy water and clean cars you have blood and dead cows. Ähm. It was a documentary I saw, by a

нелегальных скотобойнях, после которых вы разочаруетесь в человечестве. Представьте себе автомойку: как вы туда заезжаете, проезжаете насквозь и все такое. Только вместо мыльной воды и чистых машин там кровь и мертвые коровы. Мда. Я видел документальные съемки, снимали какие-то ребята из Парижа, а еще они снимали детей, которые живут на свалке рядом с этими бойнями.

(молчит)

Ну… так или иначе, люди не хотят химически обработанных шкур, поэтому я не использую химию при обработке, а беру шкуры у местного фермера, своего знакомого. Настолько близкого знакомого, что он успел завести интрижку с моей женой, и в конце концов дело дошло до развода; я сейчас в процессе. Она тоже работала у меня, но теперь работает на этого фермера, и это благодаря ей я заказываю лучшие шкуры в нашей заброшенной, Богом забытой провинции, где моя семья живет уже столько лет, что… мда…

В общем, я продаю шкуры, но это не все. Люди хотят видеть, как они производятся, они хотят видеть, как я работаю.

(пытается бодро и деловито начать объяснять)

Ну что ж, во-первых, надо измельчить свеклу или отжать ее, чтобы получить сок. (показывает на пальцах и четырёх пластиковых трубочках). Я бывало пил его в перерывах, потому что он содержит очень много железа, а это полезно, кажется, — по крайней мере, так говорят, хотя для чего — я так и не понял. Ну так вот, у вас есть красный сок. Теперь вы берете шкуру, такую вот, кладете внутренней стороной вверх, в зависимости от того, что…

(замолкает, в отчаянии машет руками)… ну и так далее, не важно, лучше один раз показать вживую. Поэтому люди и стали приходить ко мне: приходят в мою мастерскую, уважаемые люди издалека, и бросают мне деньги. Конечно, сначала они меняют деньги на валюту, которая у меня в ходу, а для них это то же самое, что обменять деньги на бумагу, если вы меня понимаете, то же, что… (задумывается, пытается подобрать сравнение) что… да, знаете, то же, что изгнать из церкви Святого Духа, осквернить ее — и открыть там такой молодежный хостел, где подростки курят травку и трахаются. (явно доволен образом). Да, вот что-то такое, что-то такое.

Так или иначе, они бросают мне деньги, словно я работаю на ярмарке, а люди подходят и бросают мне игрушечные

team from Paris and they also filmed children living in the trash, right next to the abattoir.

(Pauses.)

H-O-W-E-V-E-R people don't want chemically treated hides, so that is why I don't treat my hides chemically and get them from a local farmer that I know. A very local farmer, so local that he had an affair with my wife which ultimately led to the divorce I am going through right now. She used to work for me too, but now she is working for the local farmer and it is with her that I order the finest hides of the whole forsaken, hated-by-god-shit-district that me and my family inhabit since a long time, like ähmn.

So I sell my hides, but that's not all. People also want to see how they are produced, they want to see me doing my work.

(Tries to start fresh and practical)

So first you have to grind the beetroot, or squeeze it, that you get the juice. (Explains it with his fingers and four plastic straws) I used to drink that juice in every pause, because it contains so much iron and that's good, apparently or so they say for reasons I will never understand. Red juice, so you have that. Then you take the hide like that with the ROUGH side up, depending on what kind of…

(Pause. Makes a resigned gesture with both hands) …and so on, does not matter, it is better to show it, like live. So that is why people started to come to my place, people come to my workshop, noble people from far away and they throw their money at me. Obviously first they changed that money into the currency, in which I think in and for them it is like turning money into paper again, if you know what I mean, like (thinks to find another metaphor) it's like… yes, you know when you take out the holy spirit out of a church—yes desecrate and then put it in a youth hostel in which teenagers smoke Marijuana and fuck themselves. (happy for the image) Like that, it is like that.

Does not matter, anyways they are throwing money at me as if I am working in the midst of some carnival and people come and throw confetti money at me and we are all having a good worky-work party and I put sherry and Fanta in the beetroot juice and I get drunk and wasted and so sad even before noon and I have to think about my wife and wonder if she feels better with that local farmer and I want to know where all the years go, once they fall out of the calendar and people shredding beetroots and they think it is all inclusive and that they found the real fur-dyer,

деньги, фантики, и у нас тут славненькая рабочая вечеринка, и я добавляю херес и «Фанту» в свекольный сок и напиваюсь просто в хлам, и даже утром так хреново, и я думаю о жене, и мне интересно, действительно ли ей лучше с этим фермером, и куда ушли все эти годы, облетели один за одним, как календарные листки, а люди режут свеклу и думают, что все включено и что они нашли настоящего кожевника, того самого, к которому они приехали из своих чертовых вилл или домов на дереве или где они там живут.

Я видел нескольких молодых людей, которые бросали монеты нищему, так много монет на булыжниках этой темной рыночной площади, и монеты подпрыгивали и плясали, и попрошайка вместе с ними. Он действительно плясал, по крайней мере вначале. А потом они стали подогревать монеты на зажигалках, и со всего размаху бросать их в нищего, и смеяться над его кособоким танцем и над тем, как он обжигал пальцы, пытаясь поймать сверкающие монеты, сверкающие в вечерних сумерках раннего декабрьского вечера давным-давно.

В конце концов попрошайка лишился глаза. Мораль простая: не бросайте монеты в нищих, которые не умеют с ними обращаться.

(неловкий смешок)

Но возвращаясь к моей работе: да, я демонстрирую свое ремесло, делюсь своими рецептами и своими взглядами на производство кожи. Я провожу мастер-классы, если кто-то действительно хочет что-то понять, но по большей части никто не хочет, и вполне достаточно того, что они покупают много мехов всех цветов радуги, а потом отвязываются от меня. Однажды приехала женщина, черт знает откуда, и она захотела научиться моему ремеслу, и я рассказал ей, и она была очень разочарована, потому что, по сути, она всего за двадцать минут научилась всему, что я знаю.

Она была действительно расстроена этим, и она мне понравилась, и я желал ее, но она бросила мне свои фантики и ушла с мехом лося, который она покрасила в нежно-голубой цвет.

Не знаю, почему люди думают, что это сложно, не могу сказать. Не знаю, что такого важного в вещах, которые очень трудно делать; что добавляют эти сложности, что они портят?

Но когда они приходят на мой мастер-класс, они говорят:

the one they set out for from their fucking villas or tree-houses or wherever they live.

I once saw a group of young men throwing their change at a beggar, so many coins on the copper-stones of that dark market place, the coins were dancing and jumping around and so was the beggar. He really was, at least in the beginning, then they started to heat up the coins with their lighters and started also to throw them really hard at the beggar and laughed at his crippled dance and how he burned his fingers reaching out for the brightly glowing coins, glowing through the twilight of that December afternoon evening long ago.

In the end the beggar lost one eye and the moral of the story is: don't throw hot money at poor people that cannot handle it.

(embarrassing laughter)

But back to my work: yes, I show my work, I share my recipes and my insight into leather production. I also give courses, if they really want to know, but most of them don't and it is enough that they buy a lot of furs in all the colors of the rainbow and then they take off again. Once there was a woman from I don't know where and she wanted to learn how I did it and I told her and then she was very disappointed because basically she learned everything I know about this in about twenty minutes.

She was really frustrated about this and I liked her looks and I desired her but she threw her confetti at me and left with the elk fur she dyed baby blue.

I don't know why people think it would be difficult, I cannot say. I also do not know what is the importance if things are extremely difficult to do, what does it add, what does it take away?

But when they come to my workshop they say, it is fascinating that this or that color fades into another one or the other way around.

(Pauses)

Is it really?

I saw a good deal of furs and hides and what do I know and there were only four in total I was impressed by, but that is connected to a very violent anecdote and I will not tell it to you, who would not understand the beauty of it anyways and it is not good to share things just because of the horror that inhabits it. No, that's not good.

(Walks off.)

удивительно, как тот или иной цвет переходит в другой и наоборот.

(молчание)

Серьезно?

Я видел кучу мехов и шкур, и в общей сложности только четыре из них по-настоящему произвели на меня впечатление, но это связано с одной очень жестокой байкой, которую я все равно вам не расскажу, вы в любом случае не поняли бы ее очарования; ну и совсем не здорово делиться чем-то только ради тех ужасов, которые в нем есть. Нет, это нехорошо.

(уходит)

Peter Wächtler — Woman of the Bistro

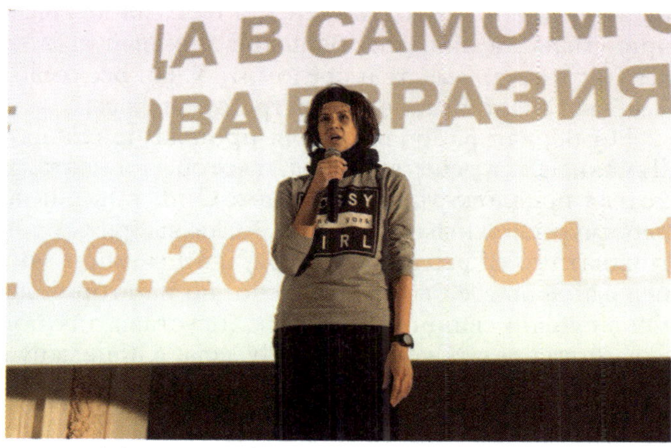

Peter Wächtler, *Woman of the Bistro*, performance rehearsal, Moscow Biennale, 30th September 2015

Я владелица бистро. Я работаю в бистро, по большей части за стойкой, где готовлю еду и напитки для тех, кто заказывает еду и напитки. Иногда, когда официантке нездоровится — примерно четыре раза в неделю, — я вдобавок и разношу посетителям еду и напитки. Я открыла бистро и выбрала, в какой цвет покрасить стены; я не сама делала мебель, но придумала дизайн, этот большой длинный стол, за который все могут сесть вместе и преломить хлеб. Все было в порядке, и я была счастлива, когда бистро открылось.

Но первая рабочая неделя прошла не слишком удачно. Думаю, дело в рецептах блюд, о которых я мечтала и которые хотела предложить посетителям. Они, так или иначе, были чересчур сложными, и люди могли выбрать из четырехсот тридцати пяти различных блюд, и этим они и занимались. В первый день все было прекрасно, но на второй день кости у меня словно свинцом налились, а суставы так болели, что я едва могла резать чертов лук. Думала, я привыкну к этому, но не привыкла.

Все, кто здесь сидит, наверняка когда-нибудь ели в бистро? И заказывали еду и напитки, и официантка не умирала от усталости, правда? Но для меня это было слишком. Не то чтоб я совсем слабачка, но это было слишком. Говорят, люди без работы расклеиваются, но мне теперь кажется, что это вообще не проблема, если «быть собранной» похоже на то, как я прожила первую неделю в роли владелицы бистро. Так что я продержалась одну очень, очень долгую неделю, а потом совсем расклеилась и продала всё одному ушлому немецкому придурку. Он предлагает домашнее пиво, которое он варит у себя под кроватью, и три блюда, все из краснопёрки. Краснопёрка — это такая рыба, она живет в пресной воде, если вы вдруг не знаете. Пресная вода — это которая не морская, если вы вдруг не знаете.

(говорит еще более зло)

И люди либо хотят выбор из четырехсот тридцати пяти блюд, хотят весь ассортимент, либо хотят выбор из трех блюд, потому что хотят чувствовать себя ближе к естественной простоте, которую, как они считают, уничтожил упадок нравов. Или хотят знать, как в конечном счете эти обычаи появились в старые добрые голодные времена в округе Безысходненска.

(извиняется)

Простите, я слишком обобщаю. Я знаю, что вы, если в

I am the woman of the bistro. I work at the bistro, mostly behind the counter where I prepare food and drinks for people that order food and drinks. Sometimes when the waitress is sick, which is about four times a week, I also bring the food and the drinks to the customers of the bistro. I founded the bistro and I chose the colors for the walls of it, I did not built the furniture myself but I designed it, that big long table, where everybody can sit together and eat bread. And it looked ok and I was happy to open the bistro.

But then the first week of the bistro was not so good. I think it was because of all the recipes I dreamed of and I wanted to offer. They were all way too complicated and the people could choose in between 435 different dishes and that is what they did. For the first day it was fine, but on the second my bones were so heavy and my joints so sore that I could hardly cut a onion. I thought I would get used to it but I did not get used to it.

Everybody here surely ate in a bistro before right? And ordered food and drinks without the waitress dying of exhaustion, no? But for me it was too much, I am not weak or anything but it was just too much. It is said people fall apart without work and I no longer see the problem with that if holding yourself together looks like that first week of my own bistro. So I lasted for a very, very long week but then I fell apart and sold the whole thing to a very smart German Fuckface who offers beer that he brews under his mattress and three dishes and they all feature red-eye, that's a fish, a fresh water fish in case you should not know. Fresh water is the water that is not salt water in case you should not know.

(more angry)

So either people want to choose from 435 dishes, they want the full spectrum, or they want to choose from three dishes as they want to feel closer to basic instinct they think was taken from them by corruption itself. Or they want to know how it must have to grow up in the good old days of poverty in NoChoice Country.

(apologising)

Sorry, that is all way too general, I know that you are not like that at all and that you are also full of doubts if this life makes sense at all. Sorry.

Anyways I came here today to speak for those of you who own a bistro or want to found one and in case to help you not to be naive as me.

Maybe I cannot give you so many tips, maybe that is already all I can tell you. (thoughtful, slow)

целом, совсем не такие и что вы тоже все время сомневаетесь, есть ли в этой жизни вообще какой-то смысл. Простите.

В любом случае, я сегодня здесь, чтобы поговорить с теми, у кого есть бистро или кто собирается его открыть. Чтобы помочь вам не сделать те же ошибки, которые сделала я, когда была такой же наивной и глупой, как вы сейчас.

Не так уж много я, наверное, могу вам посоветовать; (говорит медленно, задумчиво) наверное, это всё, что я могу рассказать.

(пытается объяснять понятно)

Ну вот, значит. Во-первых, меню должно быть не слишком большим; во-вторых, специализируйтесь на чем-то одном, например, на краснопёрке. За это вас будут ценить. Люди скажут (изображает разные голоса): «Если когда-нибудь окажешься в Трататамске, я знаю одно отличное местечко, где можно поесть краснопёрки. Она там превосходная, последний раз, когда я там был с друзьями, я съел порций пять и выпил столько белого вина… и тра-ля-ля, и так далее… Черт! Черт! Черт!»

Я должна вам признаться: мне физически неприятно представлять себе людей, которые получают удовольствие от подобных вещей. Люди ловят кайф от самой тупой фигни. Они в восторге, когда у них есть работа, когда они приносят пользу, когда они занимаются любовью, как они представляли себе это, когда у них еще было время представлять. Но даже в этот момент наивысшего воодушевления, в свободное время, на пике возможностей — это не про меня! — люди всё такие же вялые и склизкие, как бледный слизняк, выползающий ночью из крана с пивом в баре.

Пару раз в бистро я видела такого слизняка, вылезающего из крана с Pilsner Urquell, которое я сама выбрала, когда открывала бистро. Это был желтый садовый слизень, так он называется. Limacus flavus, если хотите знать, — да, это по-латыни. Но название этого липкого слизняка, конечно, не имеет никакого значения в мире символов, в мире символического дерьма. И мне правда пофиг, если всё будет символом для чего-то другого.

(повышает голос)

Ну давайте! Начинайте! Я готова!

Еще один пример: вы знаете как эти, такие, понимаете, клиенты-спецы, называют дрофу, если им доведется ее увидеть?

(tries to give a good explanation)

So 1. don't offer too many recipes and 2. specialize on one thing like red-eye and you will be acknowledged for that. People will say: (imitates different voice) "If you are ever in BumBum-town, I know a very good place where you can eat red-eye. It's delicious, last time I was there with my friends I ate about five plates and drank a lot of white wine… bla bla bla Fuck Fuck Fuck."

I have to confess this to you: it physically hurts me to imagine people being SATISFIED by these things. People get their kicks out of the dumbest shit. But even in their most excited state, in their free-time, at their maximum — I don't get this myself — people are still as slow, slimy as a white slug slithering out of the bistro beer-tap at night. Sometimes in the bistro I watch that white slug creeping out of the Pilsner Urquell tap I chose myself when I opened the bistro. The slug was a tawny garden slug, that's its name. *Limacus flavus*, if you need to know and yes you are right: that's Latin.

But the surname of that slibbery slug does not matter in a world of symbols, in a world of symbolic bullshit, and I really don't give a fuck if everything will be a symbol for something else.

(Louder)

Bring it on, let it roll, I am prepared! Last example: do you know how those oh so specialized customers of mine call a Дрофа, if they happen to see one over there? They call it a BIRD. NOW: I don't care about bird names that is for sure. But here is the situation: A man meets an animal in the steppe and says this is a Дрофа and there you go: this is all the poetry this world has on offer. Take it or leave it, but don't pretend you can find it on your weekend trip to BumBum town.

But I am sure these people have problems too. Big Bad problems, that make them stroke their boyish beards and listen to sad music and hang on the telephone all the time and they should all be whipped or open a bistro for punishment. When I think of satisfied people, I also think of knives and imprisonment, steel and violence and comparison, and they can go to hell and I cannot change that and I am sorry to say this.

And here is the final tip for those of you who really really want to open a bistro:

(more euphoric)

Don't be like that! Don't be like me, basically. Thank you. Enjoy life! Enjoy having customers that appreciate every single

Они называют ее «птица». Еще раз: мне насрать на названия птиц, это точно. Но вот в чем дело: человек встречает в степи животное и говорит: «О, это дрофа!». И вот что — это вся поэзия, которую этот мир может нам предложить. Согласны вы или нет, только не делайте вид, что сможете понять это, приехав в Трататамск на гребаные выходные.

Я уверена, у этих людей тоже есть проблемы. Огромные, ужасные Проблемы, которые заставляют их поглаживать свои редкие бородки, слушать печальную музыку, все время болтать по телефону — да их всех за это нужно выпороть или заставить в наказание открыть бистро. Когда я думаю о довольных людях, я думаю о ножах и тюрьмах, о стали и насилии и о сравнении, и пусть они катятся к черту, и тут я ничего не могу поделать, и простите, что я такое говорю.

И, наконец, последний совет для тех, кто действительно очень-очень хочет открыть бистро:

(приподнято, с воодушевлением)

Не будьте такими! В общем, не будьте как я! Спасибо. Радуйтесь жизни! Радуйтесь, что у вас есть клиенты, которые ценят каждое ваше блюдо, сколько бы их ни было в меню. Готовьте лучше, учитесь новому, читайте Толстого и Библию. Сами ешьте вкусную еду и не толстейте. Занимайтесь любовью сколько сможете, отрастите бороду. Не говорите со мной! Не слушайте меня!

(поворачивается, уходит)

one of your dishes, no matter how many there are. Cook better, learn things, read Tolstoy and the Bible, Enjoy good food yourself, don't get fat. Make love as much as you can, grow a beard. Don't speak to me, don't listen to me!

(Turns around, walks off)

Jimmie Durham — A Stone

There was a guy.
Don't know his name:
No one remembers his name.

We do not forget
We do not remember

His ways
When he awoke mornings, sleeping habits.
More than any of us for a long time.
I remember families slowly leaving Siberia better
And not even that at all.

He left a stone he had worked on,
Had made into a tool.
He chipped

/Quite a bit of chert
(I've carried that bird chirping phrase
In my mind since about nineteen
Sixty five, waiting for an opportunity,
So now break into the story
Of the stone we found with
An explanation of the kind of stone
It is. It is chert.)
Quite a bit, as i wrote, of chert
Will spark if struck with iron.
Flint is chert, jasper, all the agates.

Chert and humans make fire.
Break bones also, of larger animals
So that the fat marrow can be roasted
In the fire. For thousands of years
Humans have made tools from chert.

Incredible dexterous craft, making
An axe or knife from stone.
This we found is old old old.
By weight it's one thousand one hundred
And thirty seven grams. Thirty seven
Thousand years old, maybe more.

Too heavy to fight with or strike
A goat or ox for my weak old arms.
Sharpened to a striking, not cutting, edge
On one side, it maintains the rounded shape
It had before the human encounter,
Horribly comfortable and fitting
Into a large rough hand. /

No, not chipped, not carved, we have no verb
To say the action of quickly, carefully
Taking away flakes of stone from stone.
Speaking of that, i could make up a name
For him and its soft falsity
Would offend us. We know
We don't know his name.

With nonchalant precision
This guy made this stone heavy---
Added more than all the grams and kilos-

We told god what to tell us, didn't we?
Truly, humankind has fallen.
Any colt will tell you horsekind has fallen too,
And all the kinds of moving life,
Living to devour, living by devouring,
Watching always fearful of the bite.

We live by death of course
We want god's advice,
Tell him what we what we want to be.

I've been in the hollowed out marble mountain
Of Carrara and stood on the hardened lava
In Mexico metres above a city
Covered like Pompeii, tried to figure out.

In Europe, Mexico, Arkansas and on the beach
I've found stone tools left often desperately
Dropped my mind imagines, used just like
The Large Hadron Collider by Voltaire's old house
By Geneva, by people who want

I'm not sure how to say what we want.

What i mean, i know the rocky road.
I've seen, held, been held back by many stones.
Hell, man, i live on one.

What i mean, Ho Chi Minh, Crazy Horse,
Redbird Smith.,,, used to be, everyone changed their names
To fit better into new situations, new places.

His old name, this old guy, maybe
It was not the real part.
Still by this stone i recognise him,
I know how we want.

Marie Egger, or Katya Savchenko, or both of them together, had the excellent idea of asking the commissioner of the Moscow Biennale Joseph Backstein to read a poem every day. So it was agreed upon. Joseph read poems in Russian on the main platform during one of the first days, a crowd of his friends listening to them. He didn't read publicly anymore after that, which is a pity, because Jimmie Durham had sent a marvellous poem just before the opening of the biennial.

That poem can only therefore appear belatedly here. It might seem to be about solitude, since it is about a single man, a long time ago, probably somewhere in Eurasia. Because this man is from a long time ago, he might also be about all of us. And it is definitively a poem about relationships, between men through stones and even more so between man and stone. Therefore it might also feel at home at a later moment in which this book touches upon cosmism; our relationship with the cosmos through a stone. [Bart De Baere]

Donna Kukama — The Cemetery for Bad Behaviours

The Cemetery for Bad Behaviours
Donna Kukama

WELCOME TO THE CEMETERY FOR BAD BEHAVIOURS, WHERE WE TAKE CARE OF ALL THE NASTY THINGS THAT HUMANS HAVE DONE TO OTHER HUMANS.

For centuries, humans have shown atrocious behaviour towards other humans. Many millions of memories of beastly behaviour have died in silence, with those that remain in public becoming the burden of their survivors.

We at the Cemetery of Bad Behaviour (CBB) would like to change this miserable state of affairs by offering you an opportunity to make known the many human atrocities dwelling amongst us, and to let the rest of humanity know that certain behaviours are totally unacceptable!

How to participate?
Submit a memory of bad behaviour to our website, and watch it transform into a monument that will form a part of the Cemetery of Bad Behaviour (CBB).
All monuments created will be historicised and kept at the CBB worldwide archives, which will be made accessible online. The physical monuments created will be destroyed and buried.

Who can participate?
Everyone who has experienced or knows of bad human behaviour.

What can I submit?
Any human-caused bad experience that you know of, whether personal or historical, big or small, whether belonging to you, your country, your race, your gender, your religion, just you, or someone else. The list of horrendous behaviour on behalf of humans is endless, and will be made visible through the growth of the CBB.
NOW GO LET THE WORLD KNOW THAT ENOUGH IS ENOUGH!

Optional
For a small fee, you can opt to have a postcard-size picture of the monument associated with your submission sent to you.

The Cemetery for Bad Behaviour can be viewed live at the VDNKh Central Pavilion during the 2015 Moscow Biennale for Contemporary Art on September 24, between 2pm and 7:30pm.

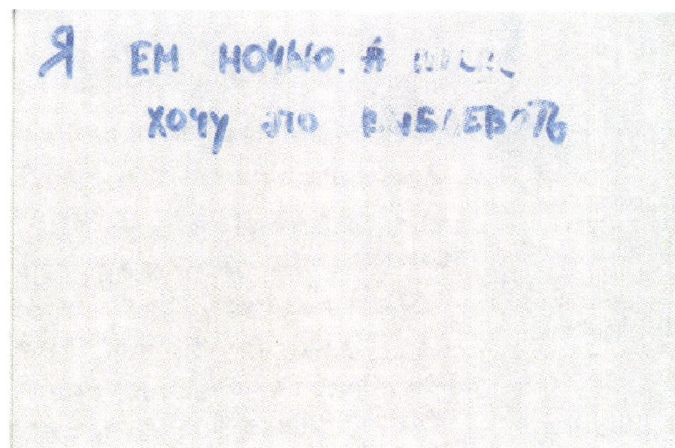

I eat at night and then want to throw up

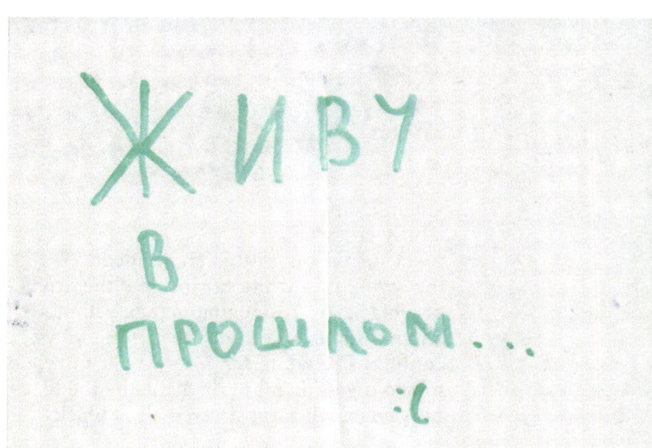

I live in the past...

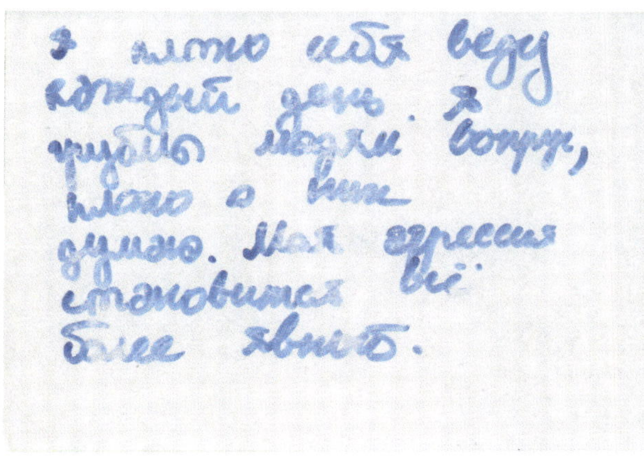

I behave badly every day. I'm rude to people around me, thinking bad things about them. My aggression becomes clearer by the day.

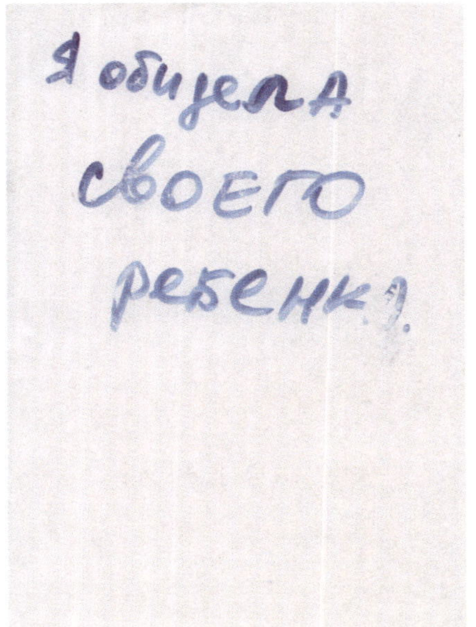

I offended my child

yin and yang
a busy crossroads
two cars almost created an accident.
the owner of a white car insulted the driver of a black car. A slanging match, yelling, and mutual insults almost becoming physical conflict. The white car got away just in time to avoid getting hit in the lights by the black car owner, who was dressed all in black

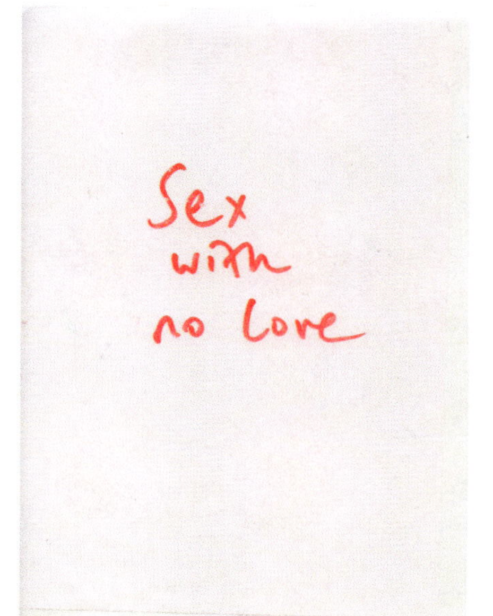

Дай мне
сил
дожить
до конца
выставки
и выспаться

Give me the strength to stay alive till the end of the exhibition and get some sleep

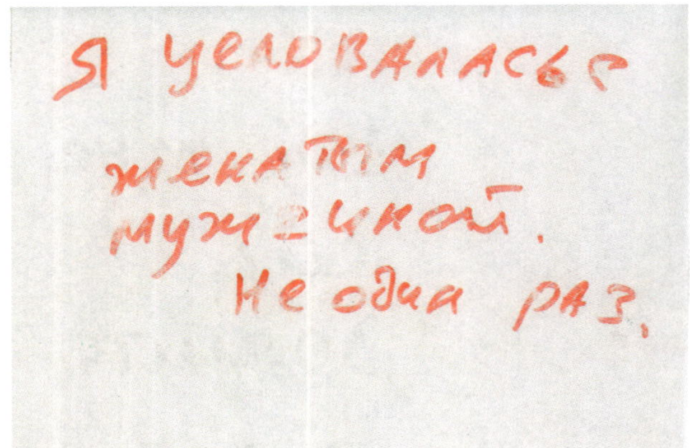
Я целовалась с
женатым
мужчиной.
Не один раз.

I've kissed a married man more than once

ВЧЕРА ВЕЧЕРОМ
МЕНЯ ВЗБЕСИЛ
ДОЛБАНЫЙ ПАТРИОТ!
ОН ХОТЕЛ СБИТЬ
МЕНЯ С ДОРОГИ!
И ЗАВЕСТИ ДРАКУ
С МОИМ ПАРНЕМ

Yesterday I got really pissed off by some damn patriot!
He wanted to knock me off the road and start a fight with my boyfriend

→
Donna Kukama, *The Cemetery for Bad Behaviours*, Moscow Biennale 2015

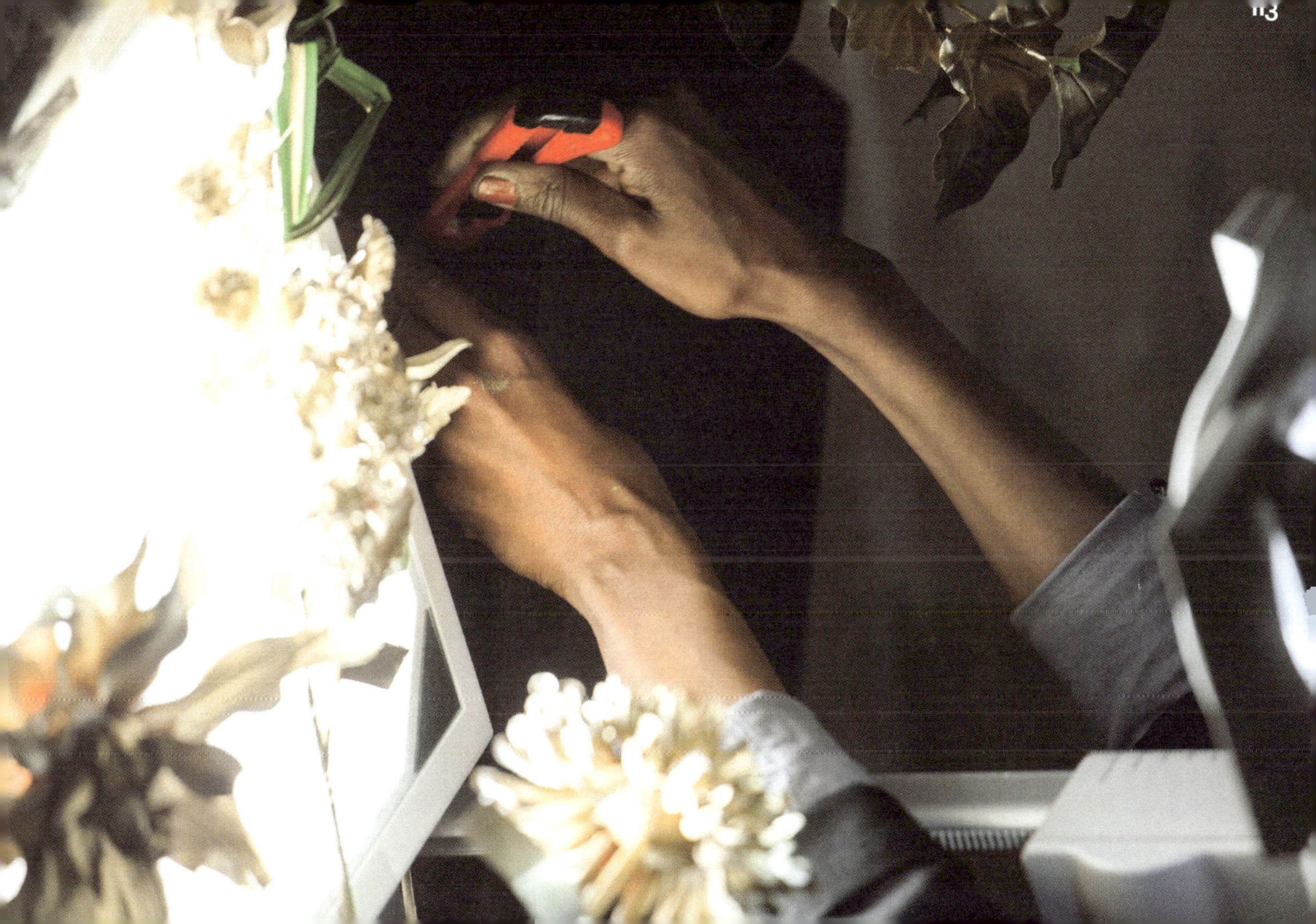

On Intimacy[1]

The project *Trans-Siberian Migrating Residency* was a bi-cultural anthropological study of a state in a state — a train. Swedish and Russian participants shared 4 m^2 of space, 24 hours a day every day, with 58 other passengers from all kinds of different countries. The Swedish residents were used to an abundance of open space and privacy as a basic human right. The Russian participants were familiar with the tolerance of excessive intimacy in public as well as shared space, imposed by their state legislation for decades.

Nadia Gorokhova, one of the artists in this residency, studied the sounds, smells and time zones of the train. We spoke about her experience of intimacy on the train:

I.

Anyone who has survived a seven-day journey on a train across Russia knows that time as measured using clocks and calendars is not something that should be relied upon in this kind of situation. It has a changeable character, even a wicked one. It lets you down, disappears, changes course, and deceives you. It is as if time makes clear that you should not look for it in the mechanism of a clock.

You can look for it inside your own body. The body knows best when it is time to sleep, when it is time to eat, when to immerse itself in reading and when to pick up an instrument, when to look out of the window, when to speak with a fellow traveller, and when to grow tired of the conversation and to look out of the window once again. Time is connected with the movement of the sun; when the light has changed, evening has come.

II.

The capsule of the train deprives you of a little something — walks. Walking can still be possible, but only in a symbolic sense — to be able to withdraw. This is why withdrawing and observing the changes in light and sound were my main occupations during the first days of being on the train.

III.

A train is where you find yourself too close to strangers. Moreover, the situation invites you to become a witness to their everyday life, habits, conversations, and bodies. You have to see and hear things that, most likely, you would otherwise have avoided seeing and hearing. Yet at the same time, all this becomes (or can become) material for your work.

You are in a strange situation. In addition, the situation forces you to be constantly busy, and to invent new ways of living out the huge amount of time spent alone — with yourself — that is part of the journey. Your fellow travellers are likewise always constantly busy with something whenever you look over — reading, drinking tea, listening to music, playing cards, or having a conversation while drinking alcohol and while not drinking. I can see that everyone (including myself) is busy only with alternating between these actions, from one to another.

IV.

I filmed exclusively "undercover", did not ask anyone to pose, and did not ask them to interact with the camera. This method could be called 'shooting from a distance' or even 'peeping'. I held the camera closer to myself, away from the eyes of others (lucky that the camera is relatively small, fitting into the palms of my hands), and even fell asleep with it sometimes. My working with a video camera changed: I did not simply observe the person I chose, I wilfully changed the distance between us, gaining control over private space.

The camera became a magnifying glass. From a chosen point I observed the faces of people immersed in reading, sleeping, looking out of the window, being silent or in the middle of an argument. It was not important to know the subject of the dispute. I wanted to examine people, to observe them like cells.

Working with sound each time reminded me of venturing out into protected spaces. The train is filled with sound. The most interesting part was to withdraw and listen to how the train sounds like an instrument. Yet, you could only search for seclusion, since it is relatively difficult to be alone in train carriages filled with fellow travellers.

Except, that is, during the night, when I captured this time on camera, repeatedly passing through darkened carriages filled with sleeping passengers. A person with an instrument (a camera, an electric guitar, a dictaphone) is in a special position — that of a researcher — but only for themselves. For the majority of other passengers and railway workers, he or she arouses suspicion and hostility. A strange combination — wanting to push away and wanting to inspect. A strange opportunity — to spend another country's money on seeing your own.

V.

It is both strange and interesting that you can make friends along the way. You might even exchange phone numbers, but you will quickly stop calling each other, or not even call each other at all. What is important is that you will both reminisce.

VI.

To understand that the territory that you have seen only on geographical maps really exists. And that you have somewhere to go.

VII.

To travel across the whole country by train, to look at it through the windows of your train compartment, is like watching a film in rewind. You watch it in fragments, casually, only by chance pausing on distinct scenes. Then there is a long period of restoring that film within your memory (or finishing it with your imagination), trying to guess the subject of the whole story. Each time you find a new meaning to what occurred.

Maria Kotlyachkova
Nadia Gorokhova

1
Trans-Siberian Migrating Residency was a Special Project of the Moscow Biennale for Contemporary Art 2015, organised by Maria Kotlyachkova and r a k e t a in cooperation with the State Darwin Museum in Moscow. V-A-C Foundation asked young curators to speak about their dialogues with each other, the biennial and the international artistic community. This text is one of these conversations, held during a train ride through the island of Eurasia

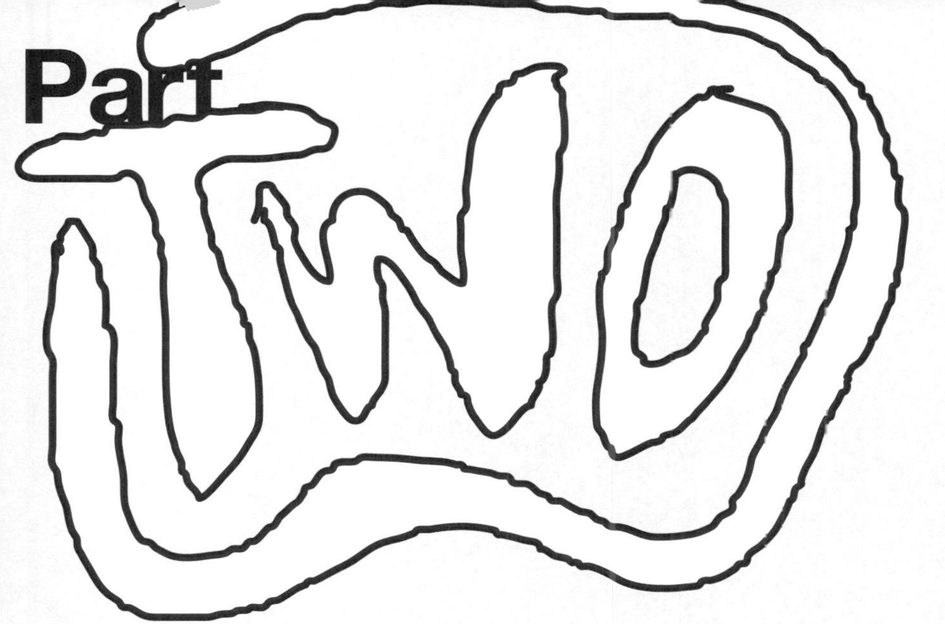

In Relation

Mián Mián and Nicolaus Schafhausen — Talkshow 26th September, 2015

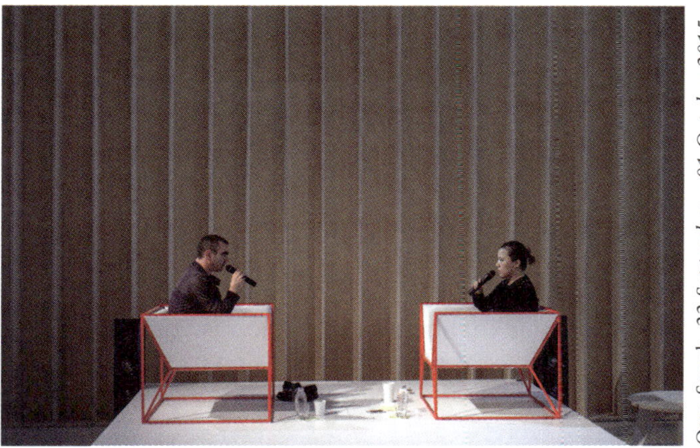

Nicolaus Schafhausen and Mián Mián, *Talkshow*, Moscow Biennale 2015

NICOLAUS SCHAFHAUSEN: Today it will be a little bit different from the previous days—

MIÁN MIÁN: Hmm. How different?

NS: Because we have many, many, many, many, many topics today.

MM: Okay, but we only have fifteen minutes, right?

NS: Yes.

MM: We can get famous in 7 minutes—hahahaha :)

NS: *Ja*. Just let's be a little bit quicker. (to audience) We are playing anchorman and anchorwoman—or vice versa, also news speaker. So, on the news this morning, you know starting with this—

MM: I never noticed such a face on a news speaker.

NS: …on the news, *naja*… (to Mián Mián) Now we have to comment on the news and be our own private channel. They announced on the Russian news that they have a vision—

MM: Okay. Yes. But we have to face to the audience, right?

NS: Yes. There will be a vision. They announced a vision here in Russia; but they didn't tell… I couldn't understand it, because I couldn't speak Russian. What do you think, let's be hypothetical, what's the vision, what will be—

MM: So, I look at you or I look at them…?

NS: What will be the new vision for the new Russian society? What do you think?

MM: Oh! (pause) I like Moscow so far, because it's beautiful, it's complex and with this very strong energy and also very special if you're in the subway; if you close your eyes to hear the sound—we never hear this sound in the subway in any another place. (laughing) Hahaha, it's very, very strong, you know. So the version of Russia, I really don't know, I'm too small to talk about that.

NS: Vision

MM: Vision

NS: The future vision. *Naja,* a vision is usually making—

MM: Vision, *ja*.

NS: Eh, the people change…

MM: Dream

NS: …their life, hm? Make them more happy? Or?

MM: I wonder, I went to some art exhibition. I feel the energy and the talent; especially the energy. Erm, and I think they are, we are, the same. They are also depressed, but they deliver their depression in a beautiful way. That's what I understand so I hope the new version…

NS: Vision

MM: …vision, I think.

NS: But it's good, the new version is the vision.

MM: *Ja*. The new version of the vision. They should continue to keep the beauty keep the energy and to be able to bring me the dramatic love next time when I am here again…

NS: *Naja*, this will be probably without me.

MM: Oh, without who?

NS: Without me. (takes shoes off)

MM: I don't know. We always end up on the stage right?

NS: *Ja*. Here, I don't know.

MM: On the stage.

NS: But you don't have a lot of time for me, because you are always going out during the night.

MM: Yeah, I need to go out, I need to understand the city…

NS: Nah, I understand

MM: …and you need to be here, because it's biennale. In the night they all speak, speak, speak—I don't understand that much English like you—

NS: No, that's not true

MM: So it's so very, very… It's still very interesting, but I don't understand, so I have to go out.

NS: One of the new visions is definitely that they get another relationship with religion.

MM: Religion.

NS: Here. Somehow.

MM: (nodding) Come from?

NS: That's my… that's what's… I am feeling; you know, our hotel is next to the newly opened mosque—

MM: Hm hm

NS: This is, I think, twenty five years back, that would have never happened

MM: What? Why? Why?

NS: *Naja*. You know the communist former system.

MM: Oh. Oh.

NS: And you know this as well.

MM: Okay. So here it was the same?

NS: I… I have not been to Russia or to a former communist state before, also, in that communist time, no. Honestly, never. Never in my life when I was younger.

MM: But is it… Is it…

NS: But how was it in China? You know, in the communist time, do you remember this? You are too young, no?

MM: Remember what?

NS: When you grew up, when you were a child and the political system and the religious system in China…

MM: Erm, I would I am actually not that old, you know :)

NS: I know, I know, I don't want to—

MM: So I don't know. Since I went to school we already were after Cultural Revolution; so we don't have that many problems or stress in the daily life to become a Buddhist. But this Buddhist we were talking about is to go to the monastery on Sunday, erm, to go to the monastery. And just saying, "I'm a Buddhist," is more like a culture or tradition. It's not like a religion.

NS: I know, but was it—

MM: I am talking about—*ja*?

NS: Was it more hidden publicly and is more open in public life nowadays, than it used to be before the Cultural Revolution in China?

MM: Before the Cultural Revolution, I don't know, because I was not born.

NS: I know (laughing) hahahah

MM: But erm… Oh, fuck you…

NS: Hahaha

MM: But erm, after the Cultural Revolution, of course people had their freedom. They can be religious, can be Christian, can be Buddhist, but I know there is a control, of course, *ja*.

NS: Okay, but can you tell us maybe… it… also… it, maybe erm, it can stand as a metaphor for Russia, if the presence of Christianity, of Muslims for example only, in China—does this play any public role or visible role in society in China; if the state or—does the state—

MM: They give the space, they give the space of the rule. They give the respect, but we cannot talk about that in any fictional text, any book, any pages—I cannot talk about that. I don't know how to talk about it.

NS: But that's interesting: Why can't you, I don't understand—

MM: It's not… it will be censored.

NS: Yes, I don't understand that it will be censored. What do they fear? You know…

MM: Don't know. It would be like my book; sometimes, some parts would be censored because I was talking about pork. You know? How to cook pork. And I personally didn't talk about how to cook pork. It was that my character was talking about pork. But this chapter the publisher thinks will make the people…

NS: Pork or pope?

MM: Pork. Meat.

NS: Not pope.

MM: Not pope. Please!
So, the publisher thinks that this is very sensitive for Muslims. So, I don't know… I really don't know all these rules and I'm very careful with that.

NS: No, no, I understand. But I like our little travel…

MM: You're making me nervous now.

NS: Why?

MM: I don't know. Maybe there is a censor there. For all I know there's always a third ear there right? There's always a third person in the air. I don't know, I don't want to go back to my country and get in trouble. Hahaha.

NS: Believe me, it's worldwide—censorship is happening everywhere. In the news, in the English-speaking news today, this morning, I read an interesting… the *New York Post* (There is another one. There is not only the *New York Times*.) The *New York Post* from today it's called The *New York Pope*, not pork.

MM: Oh really, because the Pope is there?

NS: Yes, exactly. But use your mic.

MM: (adjusting the microphone) Because the Pope is there?

NS: Yes.

MM: *Ja*.

NS: And this is like… I thought, "Oh my God." Honestly, I was a little bit shocked. You know, I said, "Oh my God, now the state in the US, it's using…" What does it mean?

(voice from audience, inaudible)

NS: What? It's free press, but would they all call it the *New York*…

(voice from audience, inaudible)

NS: Yes, it's only because it's a rhythm, rhyme, no? So; *New York Post*, *New York Pork*, *New York Pope*, *New York Rabbi*; They never would do this, I think.

(voice from audience, inaudible)

MM: Can you tell us your opinion about the feeling shocked?

(voice from audience, inaudible)

MM: Yeah, there is no reason to be shocked. Yeah.

NS: It's a freedom of the press, yes, I agree.

MM: I agree, I agree

NS: Yes, no. But I am shocked, shocked. Shocked is also a positive word, *ne*? Okay, I am shocked, surprised.

MM: Surprised. Okay, why surprised?

NS: *Naja*, because I was first reading *New York Pork*. And so…

MM: Let's… don't mix the pork with pope together. I feel no respect.

NS: Ah *ja*, okay.

MM: I don't feel good that we mix these two words. You joke about it.

NS: *Naja* okay. I don't want to be…

MM: Please respect—

NS: I don't want to make any jokes, but it is good that—

MM: No you didn't make a joke, but you play with the words.

NS: No, but now you bring me to another idea.

MM: We can't play with words.

NS: Does pork come from pope?

MM: Pardon?

NS: Pop, pop, does it come from pope? Maybe…

MM: Pop come from pope? …Pop come from pope—part of.
(smiling)

NS: So, you see? It's because he is a pop star somehow, no?

MM: But… erm…

NS: …Yeah…

(silence)

MM: Let's talk about feelings.

NS: (laughing)

(audience laughing)

NS: Hahaha.
Okay.
That's your turn then.

(both laughing)

NS: Yes.

(silence, laughter)

MM: You certainly make me have no words on the stage.

NS: What, me?

MM: Yeah.

NS: I showed already all my feelings, here.

MM: Really? Okay. You showed your emotions. You didn't show your feelings.

NS: Okay, my emotions.

MM: And you're very good in talking.

NS: I was listening in to the so-called, it's not my title, intellectual workshop today. And there is Tom, *ja*. Who brought up this; I think it's your title. "The intellectual workshop". So. The intellectual workshop is also—I don't know if it's about feelings but he said something very, very, erm, he mentioned something very… Something that made me very… think about what can shape our future. And, correct me if I quote you wrong, he said that the image—for example: After 9/11, the politics and the people tried to save… Or, the image of the US in that time collapsed in a way, or had a little crack. And then they needed a lot of power to re-build the image, that nowadays, politics or the state is only repairing, repairing the image of what we think. Has that something to do with feelings?

(pause)

MM: Hahahahahaha. :D
I really should not bring the feelings as the topic to our dialogue so early.

NS: No? No? Oh.
Then I am…
Okay.

What else should we talk about? When is art good—

MM: No, no, it's a very good question you ask. I am thinking.

NS: Then we have silence for a second, okay.
(puts away microphone)

MM: I don't think so. It brings the feelings. It's connected with feelings if we talk about the images for this kind of situation, right? It's the ideas, it's, hm, because they depend… they have… what is the motivation. Motivation? For these images.

NS: Yes, motivation. But that's interesting. What's the motivation for…

MM: …for the action, if we are talking about their building—

NS: What is the image of China?

MM: What is the image of China—but this depends on who you ask—

NS: I ask you.

MM: What I think about my country?

NS: Mmhm

MM: I think it's a very unique situation of my country; yeah it's happening now.

NS: *Ja* but image.

MM: Imagine.
(pause, silence)

NS: Or what do you think what kind of image do people have from China? From outside of China?

MM: What do you think about China?

If we walk together, what do you think about China; if we're going to write a story together, make a film about contemporary Shanghai, what's the images you have in the first or second?

NS: Also I have to be honest, my first image is always Beijing because I have travelled first to Beijing and not to Shanghai, and I have—

MM: Yeah no problem, too, but what is Beijing?

NS: Many times, a couple of times, many times to Beijing. And not so often to Shanghai.

MM: Yes, yes.

NS: Only twice.

MM: Yes.

NS: I always think about fantastic architecture on the one—

MM: Hmm…

NS: …and on the other hand, I always look in which kind of speed they build those huge mega-buildings.

MM: Yeah, you mean Tiananmen Square?

NS: For example. And then it's like, my God, how many people can this… with how many people can you fill this architecture? What do people… you know… the streets are always packed and full…[1]

1 Extract from: *Talkshow* Mian Mian & Nicolaus Schafhausen, Moscow, 26th September 2015. Full episode: https://www.youtube.com/watch?v=A5IiVMUwVs0.

The daily talk shows led by curator Nicolaus Schafhausen and writer Mián Mián were based on the principle of the impossibility of meeting: an established Western European curator speaking with a famous Chinese writer on a TV talk show stage. Both participants tried to find common points and traced their quest for such common ground, but quite often their attempts failed miserably. The dialogue got stuck, stumbled over slips of tongue, false pronunciation, grammar mistakes, and misunderstandings, so that both speakers had to constantly repeat their questions and answers.

Their conversation also failed because of their different world views and ideological disagreements. While Schafhausen spoke from the position of a European intellectual, generally referring to discourses of critical theory, Mián Mián turned to such abstract notions as love, life, compassion, death, etc., and did her best to resist being embedded in a theoretical discourse. Also both participants of the talk show experienced cultural misunderstandings on the level of humour: "You are so European! We Chinese don't make such jokes," said Mián Mián. Schafhausen replied: "But you are laughing anyway!"—"I'm laughing at what you are."

Contrary to the ideals of multiculturalism, integration or cultural mediation, both talk show hosts interacted through dissensus and disagreement. While the practical problems of using a foreign language only obstructed the conversation, their different views of life put the mere possibility of dialogue into question. Thus, Schafhausen and Mián Mián also spoke of the tragic impossibility of establishing a flawless dialogue with the other. To me, this circumstance underlines too the fact that peripheral biennials, which aspire to become the vocabulary of a contemporary globalised art world, are doomed to fail. Yet, this failure sparks new potential. According to Walter Benjamin, languages aren't completely different from each another, but "a priori, and, independently of all historical connections, related to each other in what they want to say." All languages are preceded by what philosophers call a pure language—an ahistorical kinship of various dialects. The task of the translator, according to Benjamin, is not to transmit the meaning of a work, but to complement one language with the meanings that were realised in other "modes of its intention." He attempts to enrich language with new significations. "Translation," Benjamin says, "cannot possibly reveal or produce this hidden relationship; however, translation can represent this relationship, insofar as it realizes it seminally or intensively."[1]

Nicolaus Schafhausen's and Mián Mián's talk show was based on a three-part translation, dramatised with communicative failures and defeats. German and Chinese, two different modes/logics of thinking, are translated into English, and then recoded a further time into Russian by a simultaneous translator, who has to somehow convey not only the meaning as such, but also what has not been understood by the interlocutors. This is how conflicts between two cultures emphasise manners of meaning, processes of thinking, valuation and reaction. Their 'out-of-sync-ness' reveals a linguistic kinship with difficulties, while the misunderstandings and disagreements between Nicolaus Schafhausen and Mián Mián probably tell us much more about the imaginary Eurasia than the lectures themselves.

Andrey Shental

Honoré δ'O and Fabrice Hyber — Telepathic Protocol

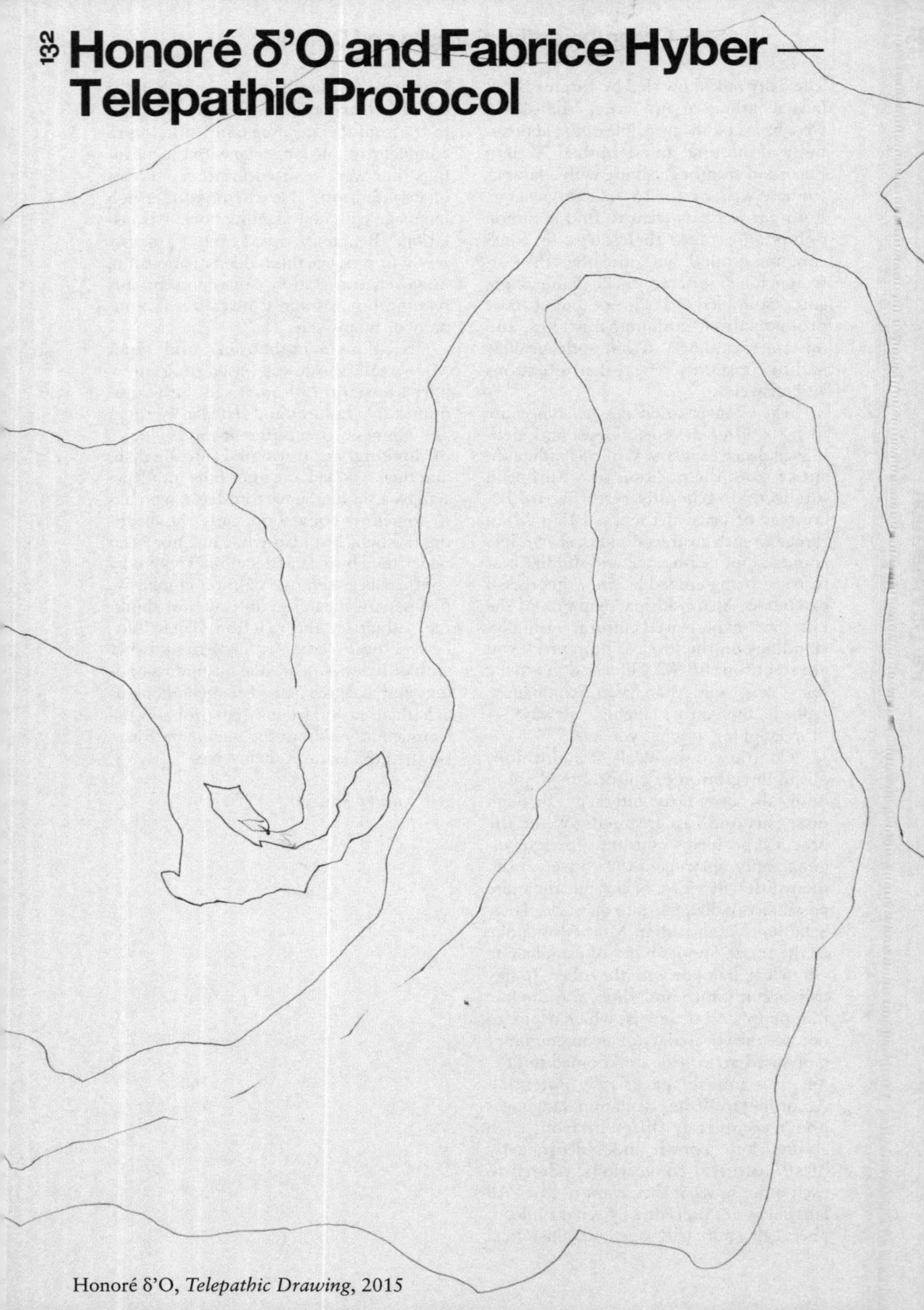

Honoré δ'O, *Telepathic Drawing*, 2015

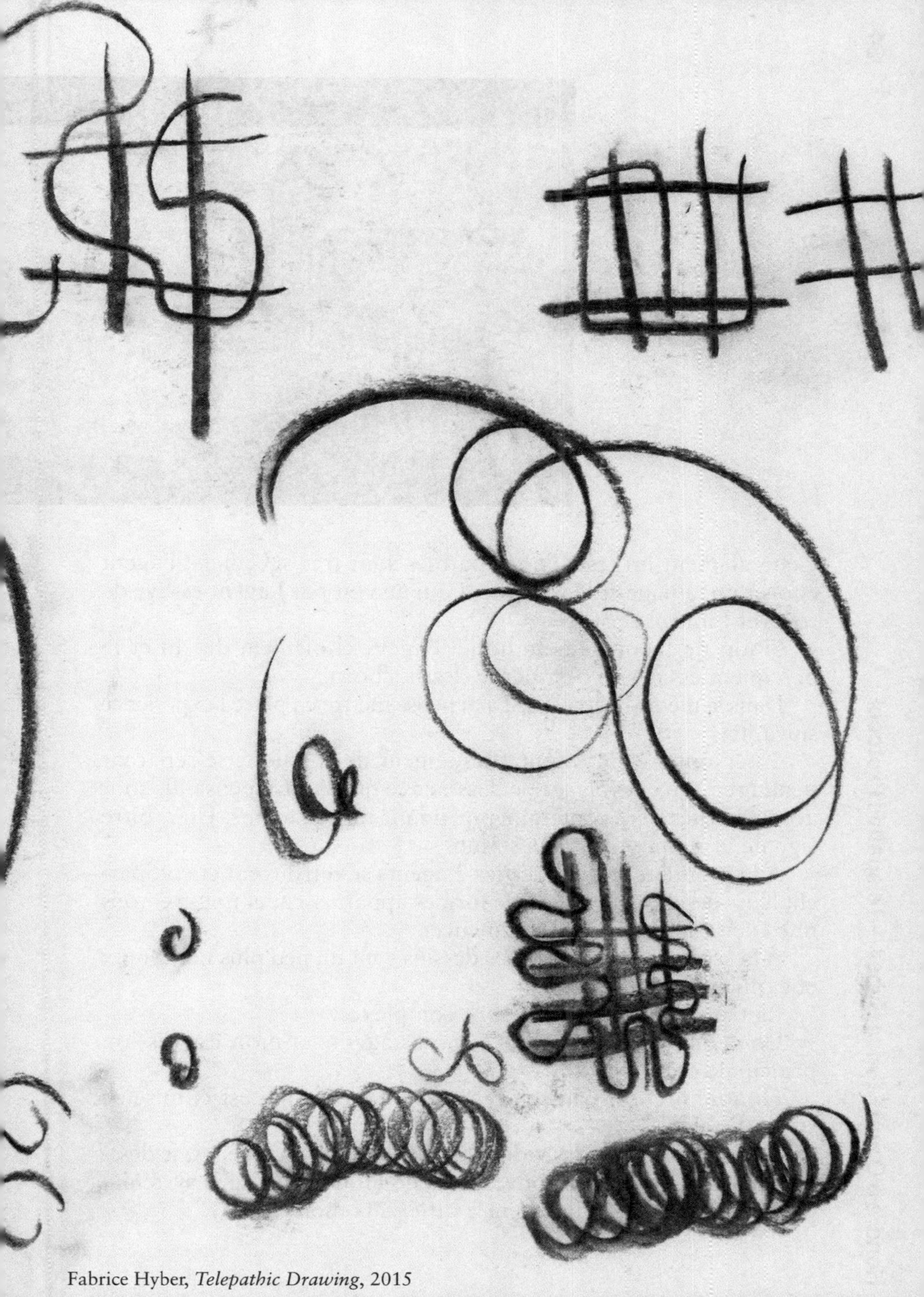

Fabrice Hyber, *Telepathic Drawing*, 2015

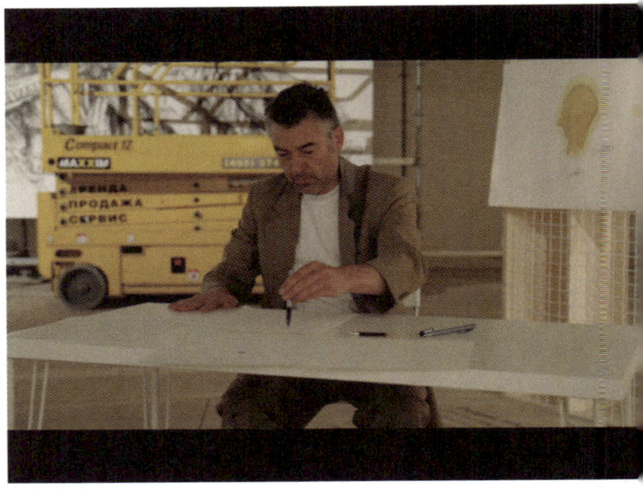

Généralement les tests de télépathies sont très succincts: l'agent choisit une image et le percipient qui ne voit pas l'agent essaye de trouver l'image choisie.

Sinon de façon plus ludique: l'agent choisit un dessin et le percipient essaye de dessiner le dessin choisi.

Dans le même ordre d'idée, j'ai pensé mettre en place l'expérience suivante:

2 personnes se croisent s'échangent des papiers, se séparent pendant 5 mn et essayent de dessiner ce que l'autre pense. Ils sont accompagnés de 2 cameramen pendant tout le temps. Un arbitre signale le début et la fin des 5mn.

A la première expérience les 2 agents se retrouvent et comparent leurs dessins: des bribes de formes apparaissent et nous sentons une excitation prêts à recommencer.

A la seconde expérience, les dessins sont un peu plus nombreux et explicites.

La troisième, les dessins sont complexes.

Une constatation: je suis l'un des agents et mon expression principale est le dessin.

Honoré δ'O est l'autre agent et son expression est la mise en scène d'objets.

Après visionnage des vidéos synchronisées, un constat: je dessine simultanément les mouvements de Honoré δ'O pas systématiquement mais régulièrement à différents moments!

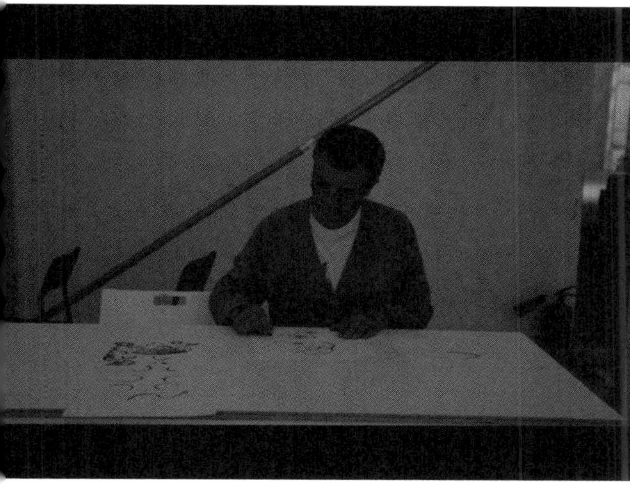

Honoré δ'O and Fabrice Hyber, *Telepathic Experiment*, Moscow Biennale 2015, video still

Generally, tests for telepathic ability are very brief: the sender chooses an image and the receiver, who cannot see the sender, tries to find the chosen image.

A more entertaining method: The sender chooses a drawing and the receiver tries to draw the chosen drawing.

In a similar context, I thought of doing the following experiment:

Two people meet and exchange papers; they then separate for five minutes and try to draw what the other is thinking. Two cameramen accompany them the entire time, while a third person signals the beginning and end of the five minutes.

In the first experiment, the two senders come back together and compare their drawings: Fragments of shapes appear and we are excited to try it again.

The second time, there are a few more drawings which are more explicit.

The third time, the drawings are complex.

An observation: I am one of the senders and my main means of expressing myself is by drawing.

Honoré δ'O is the other sender and his main way of expressing himself is by staging objects.

After viewing the synchronised videos, I made another observation: I simultaneously draw Honoré δ'O's movements, not consistently, but regularly at different times!

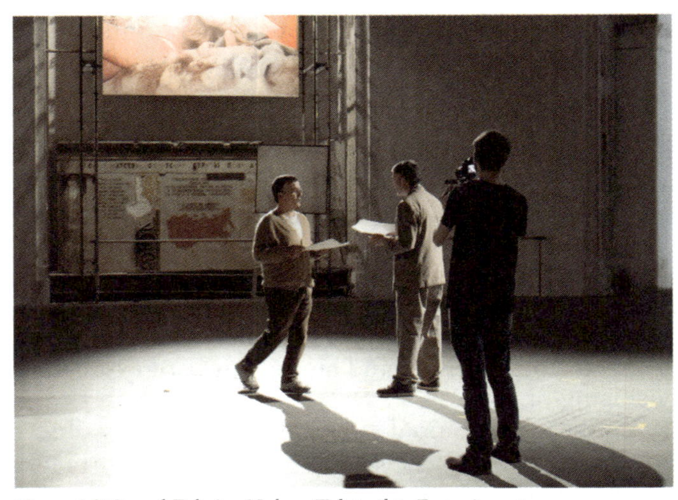

Honoré δ'O and Fabrice Hyber, *Telepathic Experiment*, Moscow Biennale 2015

Qiu Zhijie — Map of the Third World

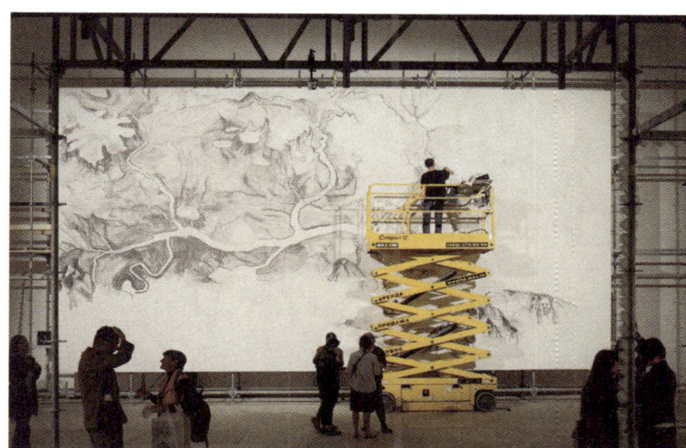

Otto Snoek, 22 September – 01 October 2015

Qiu Zhijie's *Map of the Third World* was a mural on the site of the Moscow Biennale. It dealt with the notion of the Third World from a holistic perspective, in a precise manner. A cartographer at heart, Qiu Zhijie proposes a model view of our world that entails political, historical, realistic and fictitious connections. They visually unfold in a hypothetical landscape where interrelations become valleys, mountains or rivers. This is how the artist sets emphases on theoretical, rational and poetic analyses of the past and present, thus posing the questions What is the Third World today? What could it become? How does our knowledge inform a new view or spark concepts of global thinking for the future?

Qiu Zhijie's comprehensive investigation of global political contexts aims to suggest a reading of relationships between things in a time in which one's capability to comprehend today's complexities is increasingly being challenged. [Defne Ayas]

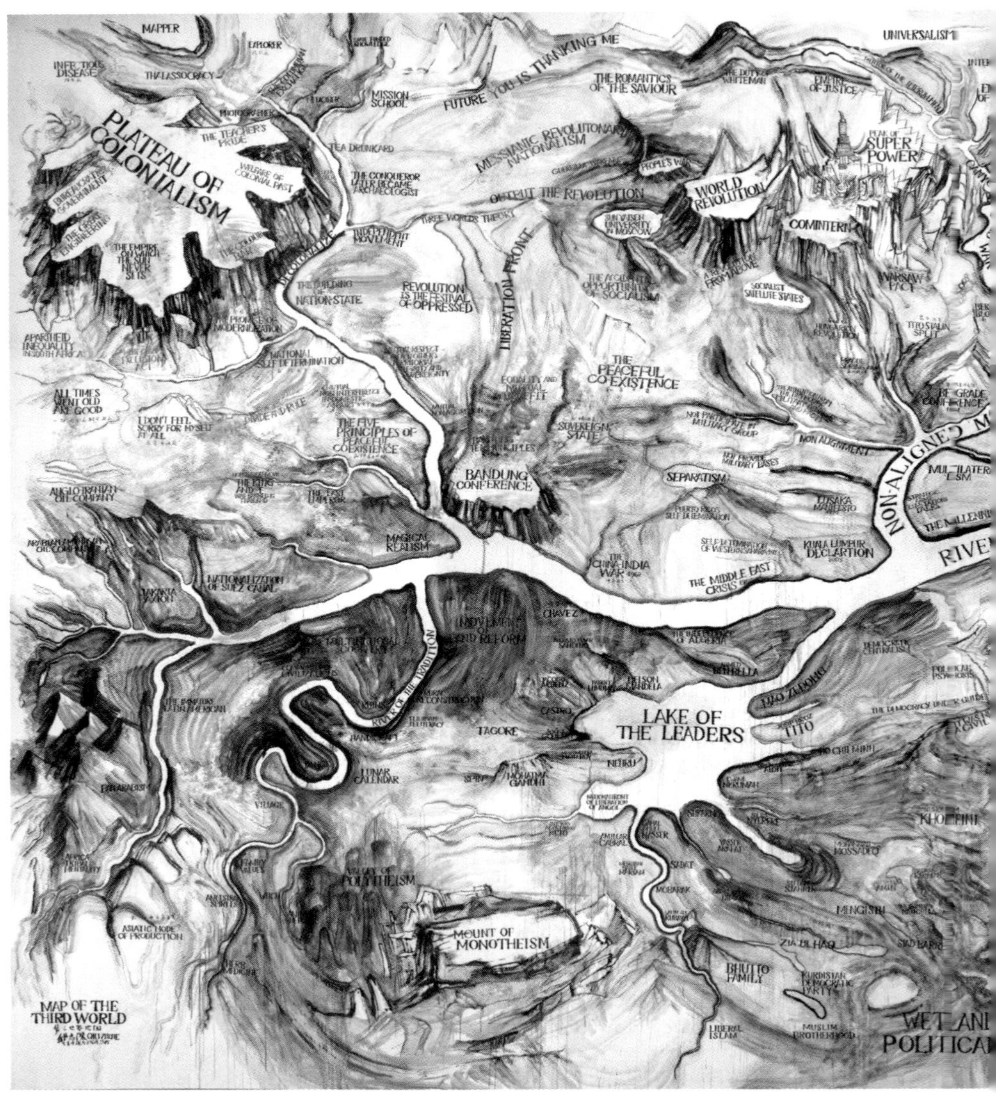

Qiu Zhijie, *Map of the Third World*, 2015

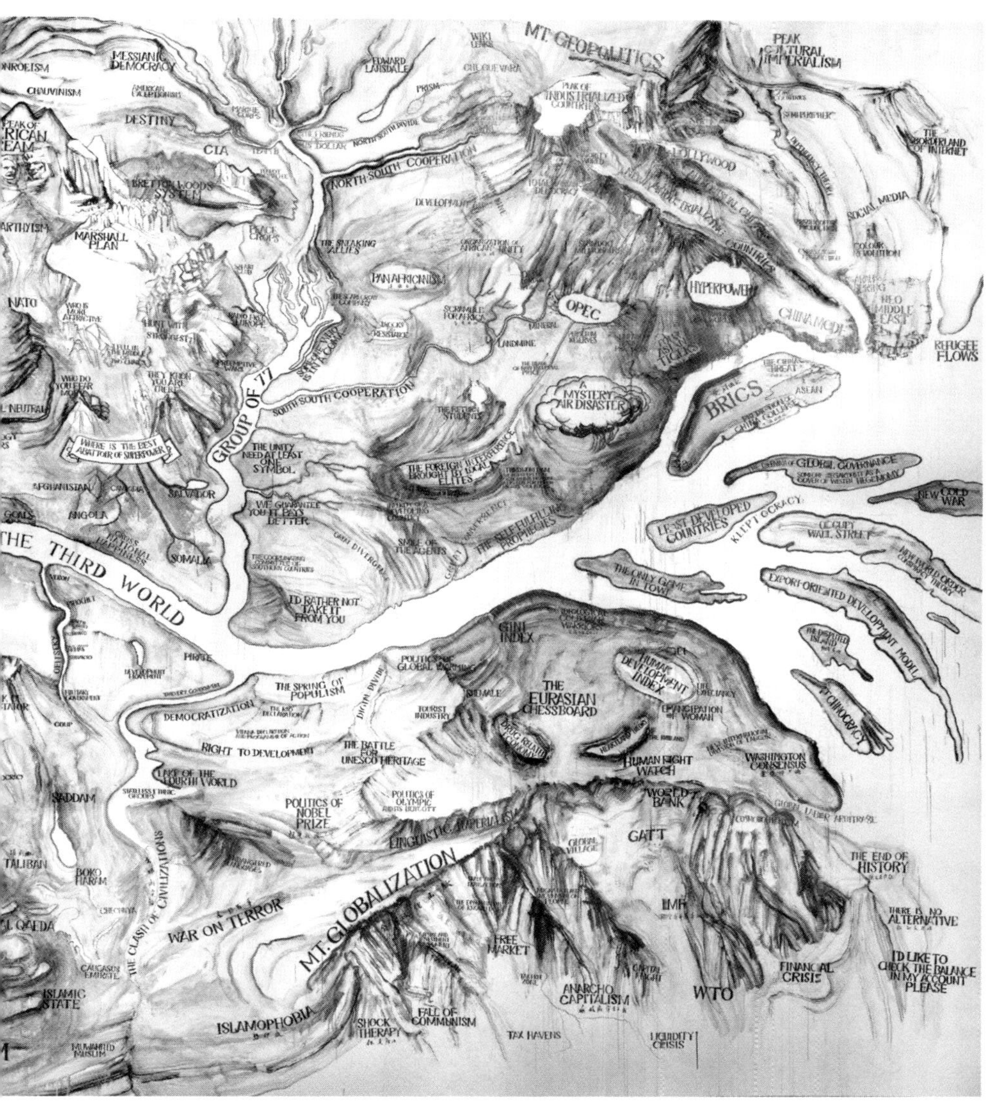

MT. GEOPOLITICS
PEAK CULTURAL IMPERIALISM
MESSIANIC DEMOCRACY
CHAUVINISM
EDWARD LANSDALE
CHE GUEVARA
PRISM
PEAK OF INDUSTRIALIZED COUNTRIES
DESTINY
CIA
NORTH-SOUTH COOPERATION
HOLLYWOOD
THE BORDERLAND OF INTERNET
BRETTON WOODS SYSTEM
SOCIAL MEDIA
MARSHALL PLAN
PEACE CROPS
THE SNEAKING ALLIES
PANAFRICANISM
COLOUR REVOLUTION
NATO
HYPERPOWER
OPEC
CHINA MODE
NEO MIDDLE EAST
LANDMINE
REFUGEE FLOWS
SOUTH SOUTH COOPERATION
A MYSTERY AIR DISASTER
BRICS
ASEAN
GROUP OF 77
WHERE IS THE BEST ABATTOIR OF SUPERPOWER
THE UNITY NEED AT LEAST ONE SYMBOL
THE FOREIGN INTERFERENCE BROUGHT BY LOCAL ELITES
AFGHANISTAN
SALVADOR
ANGOLA
WE GUARANTEE YOUR LIFE IS BETTER
NEW COLD WAR
LEAST DEVELOPED COUNTRIES
KLEPTOCRACY
OCCUPY WALL STREET
THE SELF FULFILLING PROPHECIES
THE THIRD WORLD
SOMALIA
THE ONLY GAME IN TOWN
EXPORT-ORIENTED DEVELOPMENT MODEL
I'D RATHER NOT TAKE IT FROM YOU
GINI INDEX
HUMAN DEVELOPMENT INDEX
PIRATE
THE SPRING OF POPULISM
THE EURASIAN CHESSBOARD
DEMOCRATIZATION
TOURIST INDUSTRY
RIGHT TO DEVELOPMENT
THE BATTLE FOR UNESCO HERITAGE
HUMAN RIGHT WATCH
WASHINGTON CONSENSUS
LAKE OF THE FOURTH WORLD
SADDAM
POLITICS OF NOBEL PRIZE
POLITICS OF OLYMPIC
WORLD BANK
GATT
LINGUISTIC IMPERIALISM
GLOBAL VILLAGE
THE END OF HISTORY
TALIBAN
BOKO HARAM
MT. GLOBALIZATION
THE CLASH OF CIVILIZATIONS
WAR ON TERROR
IMF
THERE IS NO ALTERNATIVE
AL QAEDA
FREE MARKET
FINANCIAL CRISIS
I'D LIKE TO CHECK THE BALANCE IN MY ACCOUNT PLEASE
ISLAMIC STATE
ANARCHO CAPITALISM
WTO
ISLAMOPHOBIA
SHOCK THERAPY
FALL OF COMMUNISM
TAX HAVENS
LIQUIDITY CRISIS

Augustas Serapinas — Conversation Behind the Map of the Third World

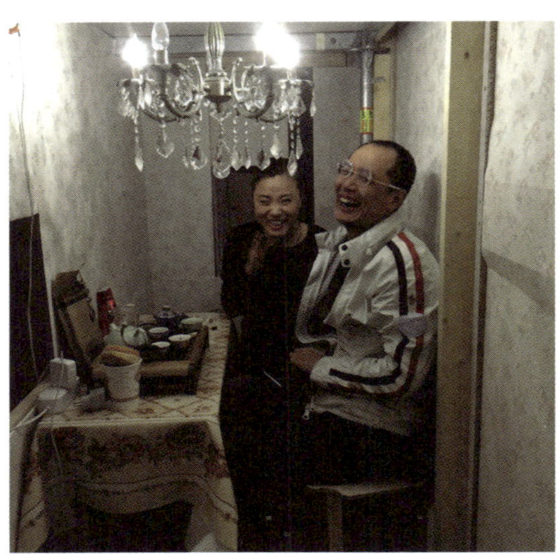

Artists Mián Mián and Qiu Zhijie in Augustas Serapinas' installation, *Behind the Map of the Third World*, 2015

(背景音乐是FM3唱佛机里的)

MIÁN MIÁN: 这里的墙纸像是老的苏维埃时代的，但是很布尔乔亚，很布尔乔亚。

AUGUSTAS SERAPINAS: Yeah!

QIU ZHIJIE: 自然花草的巴洛克画是维多利亚时代弄出来的。

MM: 好美啊！

MM: 他(Augustas)还弄得挺可爱的啊！

QZ: 对！

MM: 我跟他说我们中午喝茶，他就一直在弄啊弄啊，我想有那么复杂吗？发现在这里喝茶确实挺复杂的。弄那么多东西。你天天在画画哦！

QZ: 他给搞复杂了，其实没必要这么复杂。

MM: 人家还年轻嘛！

AS: I will charge the phone.

MM: 我发现我包里什么都有。我匆匆忙忙出门，但什么都有。

QZ: So where did you get the tea? Did you go to Chinatown to buy different kinds of tea? What tea? Okay, now this one is from Yunnan…

MM: But he said this tea is 15 years old, do you believe it?

QZ: No, it's 5 years.

QZ: No, it's 5 months. 闻是闻不出来的，但是不可能吧。

MM: But it's a very good concept that you bought this tea. This tea [here] is 做不了的，这里没有很烫的水，所以这个茶，它出不来这个香味。其实这个茶我从上海带来了，很好的白茶。一个工人来了！这是他的工人。

AS: Хочешь присоединиться с чаю?

VISITOR: Нет, я хочу посидеть.

MM: 你这两天出去玩儿了吗？

QZ: 我昨天其实去了一趟西南角，跟一群中国留学生过中秋。但是他们很无趣，一群学习国际政治，国际关系的。他们来看见我画画就邀请我。

AS: He wanted to ask about the map, about your work.

MM: Oh, it's very serious, 你要回答他（工人）。

AS: What does it mean — what you draw? Do you tell like something?

QZ: It's like the history and the reality of the so-called *Third World*.

AS: Это история, ну и как бы реальная ситуация…

VISITOR: Это геополитические события будущего, основанные на сегодняшнем дне?

AS: Is it like future geopolitical accidents based on the current situation?

QZ: It's normally about the future but some personal viewpoint.

AS: В общем, это не про будущее, а его персональное видение.

MM: 这里的工人也很有意思，还会问艺术啊！

QZ: 莫斯科有很多穷艺术家，美院的学生，赚点钱。

MM: 那你昨天本来是以为会有意思的？

QZ: 对，我在这里画画，有两个人在那里议论，我听着还挺有水平的。他们看我是中国人，就说明天有个中秋节的聚会，我看他们是学国际关系的，那跟我画的地图比较有关系。

QZ: 其实那个比较有水平的，我听着比较靠谱的那个，其实他是在美国读书来这里交换的，研究美俄关系，来这里交换的。

QZ: 再加上我比较有情节，我曾经差一点来这里留学，当时我是被中国文化部派来这里留学的。我对苏联有一点情结的。其实昨天后来我也在想我为什么会去，其实是在寻找过去，就是如果当时我来了会怎样，其实什么也找不着。因为已经不是苏联了。

QZ: 我在德国跟一群中国留学生喝过酒。(*explains in English*) I used to drink with a Chinese student. Really great, smart, very logical. They were really willing to communicate. Some of them study philosophy, some of them—engineering, every subject. And these young students come to study in Moscow, at the University of International Affairs. And basically all of them are looking forward to going into trade between China and Russia. 中俄贸易。有很多本科是学国际金融的。

MM: Oooh, 所以他们不是理想主义者，也不需要那种革命的看法。

QZ: 对，这里有两种人，一种人是世家子弟，他们看重的是今后中俄贸易的兴盛，准备做物流，做国际贸易的。另外一种人是外交部排来的。北外的研究生。他们准备进外交部当翻译的。

MM: 邀请你的人应该是可以的吧？

QZ: 邀请我的那个人是最棒的，他中学读的就是外国语的高中，然后直接去美国，在一个很好的学校，在那种地方研究国际关系，来这里交换。就是明显的有些人的人生已经都setle了，他已经不是一个寻找者了。我在想如果当时我来的话我的状态肯定是一个寻找者，随时都有可能会改变的。所以昨天跟这些年轻人在一起蛮失望的。他们很沉闷。

MM: 我以为你出去玩儿了，我以为你在这里找到了一个人带你去玩儿？

QZ: 其实我也不需要带啊，我自己逛地铁站就很好，拍共产主义遗产啊。

MM: 太厉害了。太heavy了！我跟宋涛他们一起坐地铁的时候，他让我闭上眼睛听地铁的声音，那声音太厉害了，没有一个地铁是那种声音。Birdhead, the artists from Shanghai asked me to close my eyes and listen the sound of the subway. It's very different.

AS: Yes, it's very loud. You can't talk there.

MM: Yes. Very, very loud. Nicolaus noticed a very interesting thing in the subway, an announcement it was. 他说，如果你看见穿衣服不整洁的人请通知我们。我说真的假的？他说真的。Can you believe this? 我说我明天找个俄国人再查一下是不是这样的？

QZ: 你明天自己穿得不整洁一点嘛！

MM: 没法穿得不整洁啊！That's very good idea. Nicolaus said the announcement in the subway said if you see someone dressed dirty please let us know.

AS: If you see what ?

MM: Dress dirty.

QZ: Dress dirty means just nothing.

MM: I said what is that supposed to mean? I should ask a Russian to see if it's true, and he (Qiu) said: "You can just dress dirty and see what happens." I said it's a very good idea!

(all laughing)

QZ: Just dirty means just nothing.

MM: I think she meant you see a beggar. That would make sense.

MM: 你后来还去哪了？美术馆吗？ Garage?

QZ: 对。

MM: 这里有人带着你去还是你自己去的？

QZ: 没有，我自己去。

QZ: 你说的那个24小时书店我还是很想去的。

QZ: 我对苏联早期的海报很感兴趣。

AS: What do you think, where we are behind your painting, which place?

QZ: That's the only place you should stay. The best.

(all laughing)

AS: What's behind here?

QZ: I don't know.

MM: 我这个朋友在问我们，明天晚上会带着我们去玩儿，你去吗？

QZ: 可以，哦明天我要工作！

MM: Why? 你不出去玩吗？

QZ: 我就是去红场之类看看。

MM: 那我明天9点还是在weichat里找你。我们出去转转，我们转也就是很知识分子地转，一边一边解释，很快就转完了。

QZ: 文化旅游？

MM: local feeling, 带有local feeling的文化旅游还是可以的。

QZ: Okay.

AS: What is local feeling?

MM: This guy, Spider, he works for the ART BASEL VIP, he's quite interesting, I asked him to take us out — I want his "local feeling".

(Qiu is showing the photos of his daughters. Mián Mián claims they take a lot after their dad. In one of the pictures, the younger one is helping her father paint. Mián Mián shows the picture of her daughter too. Cuteness overload)

MM: When we first met each other, we were so young!

AS: So you've known each other for a long time?

QZ: I think we met in 1995, so 20 years.

MM: He is truly avant-garde, he was truly revolutionary for me!

QZ: Okay, 我要去抽烟。Next time don't make a tea thing, make a smoking place, it will be very welcomed by the artists.

QZ: And free cigarettes!

(Qiu left)

MM: He's such a nice guy, he's the most famous one in China. He's very big. But he's so calm, he just paints here like a worker. But he is really big.

AS: Like Ai Weiwei?

MM: He's the curator of the Shanghai Biennale. But he's so cool, he paints like a low profile, he doesn't care. I need to go to the bathroom, I am so scared of the bathroom here. I never go to the toilet here. I always go home early because of the toilet. It's so scary, right?

AS: Well , you can always go to McDonald's.

MM: Really? Shall we go to McDonald's, eat something and go to the toilet?

AS: Yes, sure.

(Everybody leaves)

Anastasiya Yarovenko — HowTOgether Vienna, January 2016

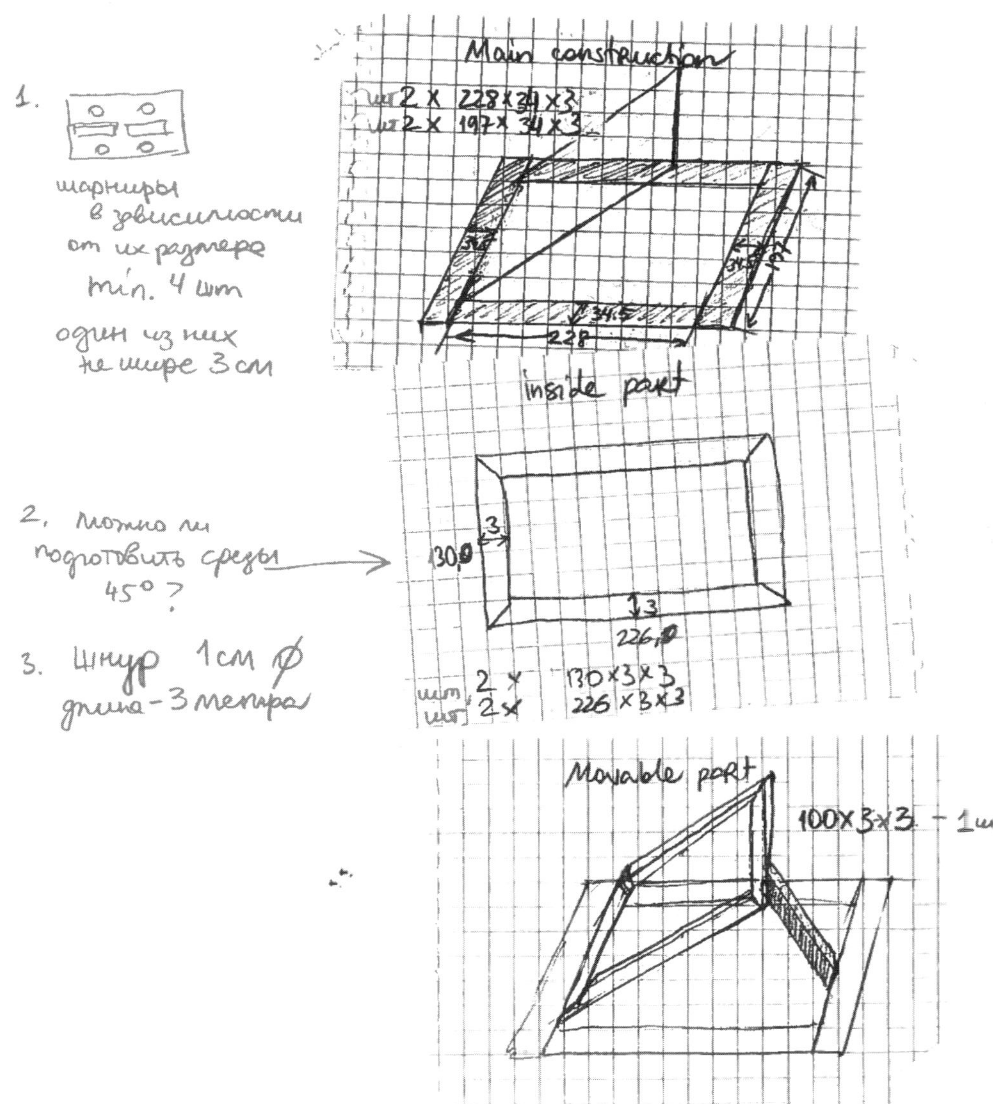

Anastasiya Yarovenko, Sketch for *The Trap of Habit*, 2015

In the USSR, no kind of public dialogue was really possible. I am afraid that is still the case today in many post-Soviet countries. Officially, back then, there was no *I* and *others*; there was an undefined and inseparable mass of *we*.

I stayed in Moscow for ten days. What happened, when I entered and left the bubble of the Biennale pavilion every day? How were *others* impacted by that? Who was *I* in this process?

Looking back from a distance, I now feel that an exchange happened. A dynamic multi-dimensional and context-dependent process of creation and reflection has started. For some, it might have ended there. But the biennial still resonates in me; in my thoughts and approaches.

We talked from our own experience, spontaneously on the spot, trying to leave debate and attempts to convince each other behind. These dialogues were not the only ones, but definitely those I will remember for a long time:[1]

———

"What happened on March 1, 1986?"

"Everybody in Ukraine and Belarus went to the Mayday parade. Nobody was notified about the danger coming from the Chernobyl catastrophe."

"It was necessary."

"Why?"

"People would panic. Instead they were enjoying the sunny weather."

———

"Everything went down with the fall of the Iron Curtain."

"Why?"

"Now Russia is full of murders, violence, abuse."

"Do you think this wasn't happening in the USSR?"

"At least we didn't know and hear about it."

———

"What are the numbers 1932–33?"

"1932–1933 was a man-made famine in the Ukrainian Soviet Socialist Republic. According to various different sources, 2.4 to 7.5 million died of hunger."

"That is not true."

"My granny told me quite a few stories about how her family and neighbourhood tried to survive in Ukraine during those times."

"Mine too. Nothing like that happened."

"Where did your granny live in those times?"

"In Russia."

———

"Soviet times were the best, everything was so easy and affordable."

"Yes, but Soviet consumer goods didn't have a big range and diversity."

"That's not true, all my friends had exquisite old furniture."

"Were those pieces produced during Soviet times?"

"No, my friends bought them at the flea markets. Some of these friends were imprisoned afterwards."

———

"What is this: 18.05.44?"

"The forcible deportation of the Crimean Tatars from the Crimea was ordered by Joseph Stalin and carried out on March 18th in 1944. A total of more than 240,000 people were deported in two days."

"It would have been better if Stalin had killed them all back then."

"What have these people done to you that you wish them dead?"

"I had some business in the Crimea in the '90s, I met some very unreliable Tatars."

———

"Why do you come here to tell us how bad the Soviet times were?"

"I don't, I just state the numbers from history."

"Why do you eat our food and stay here if you don't like it so much? The Soviet times were really great. Go back home, nobody asked you to come here!"

"How old are you, if I may ask?"

"22."

———

"Stalin was a great personality. He did his best for the country."

"But… the amount of victims of his regime outnumbers the amount of victims of WWII…"

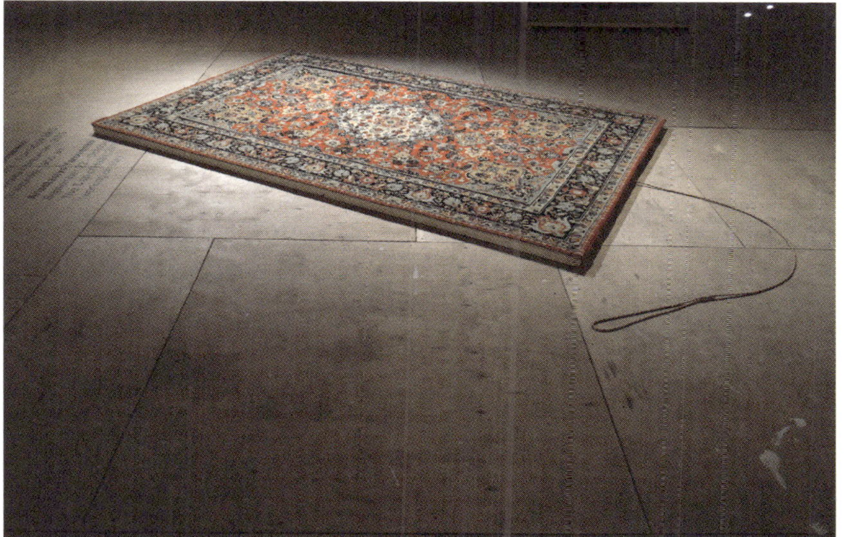

Anastasiya Yarovenko, *The Trap of Habit*, 2015

Otto Snoek, 22 September – 01 October 2015

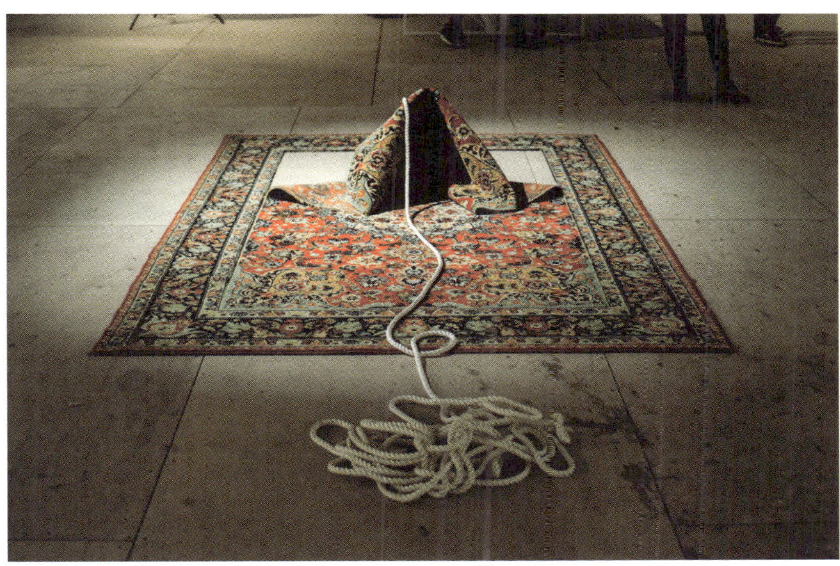

Anastasiya Yarovenko, *The Trap of Habit*, 2015

"He did everything right. I personally support the 'scorched earth' principle. In my opinion, this strategy is efficient in both war and peace time."

———

"What do you think about the current situation in the eastern Ukraine? I find it similar to that of Transnistria."

"What do you think about the Transnistria conflict?"

"I am from there. I would be glad if we could be a part of Russia, and never Moldova."

"Why?"

"Moldova is full of drug addicts."

"Why do you think so?"

"I know it. They have drug rehab clinics, and we don't."

———

(Talking to a participant of Donna Kukama's performance *The Cemetery for Bad Behaviour*[2])

"What did you write in your message that will be buried in the performance?"

"I want to stop the killing of the children of Donbass (the eastern Ukraine region)."

"Only the children?"

"Well, they announced on TV that kids are being murdered there."

1
These dialogues (in a very Buber sense) happened without any attempt to reach conclusions. I see them as "the very pre-requisite of an authentic relationship between man and man". I regard these conversations as a process of thinking together collectively. They allow the examination of preconceptions and prejudices.

2
See page 108.

Birdhead and Daniil Kolchanov — 22 September – 01 October 2015

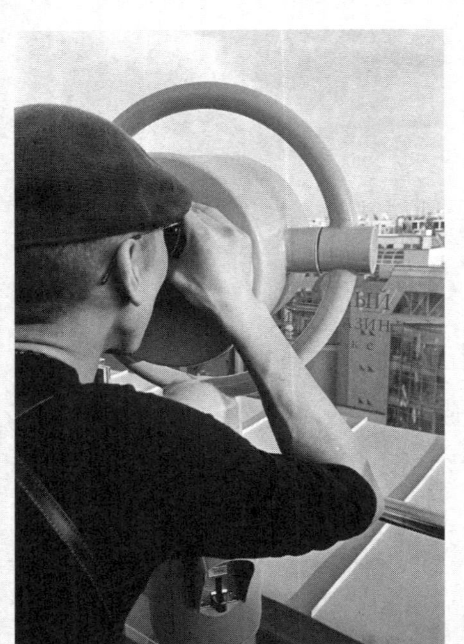

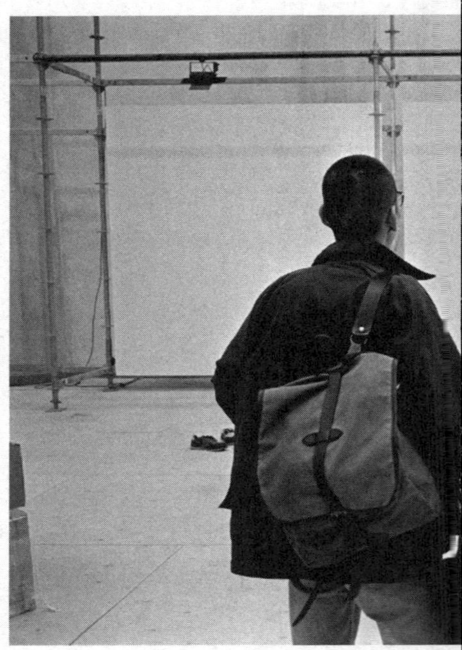

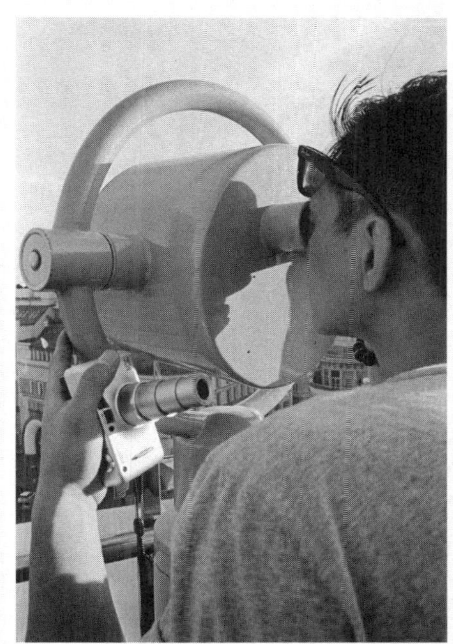

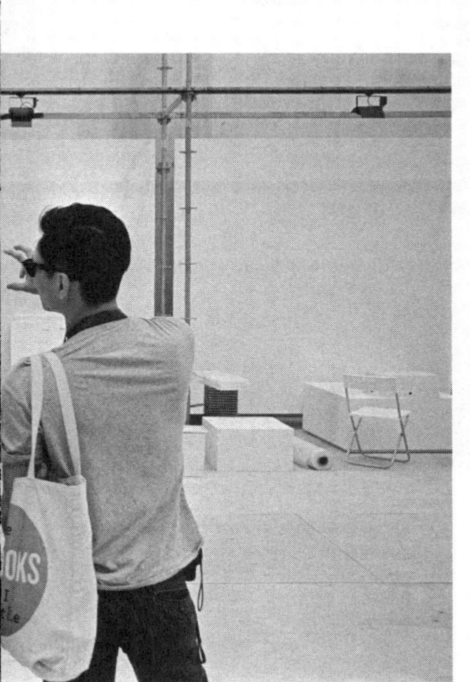

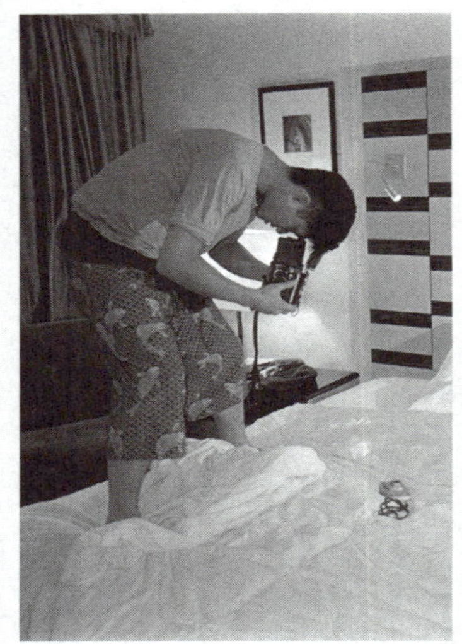

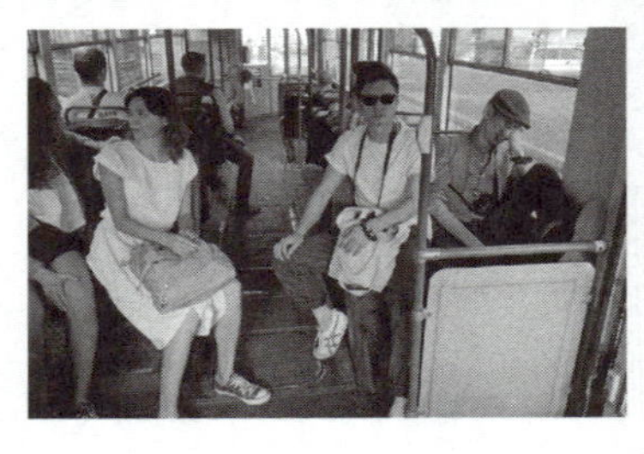

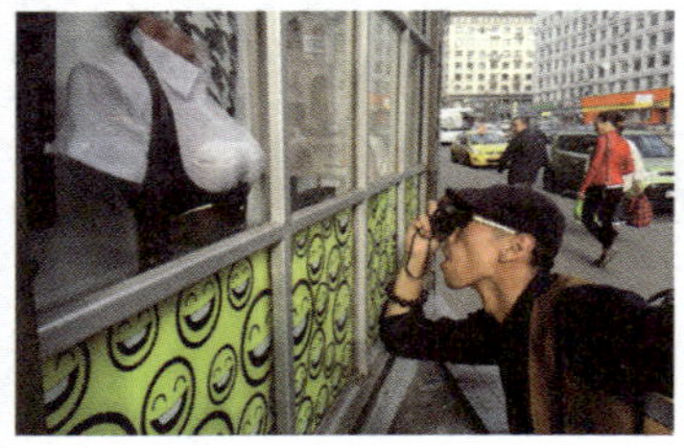

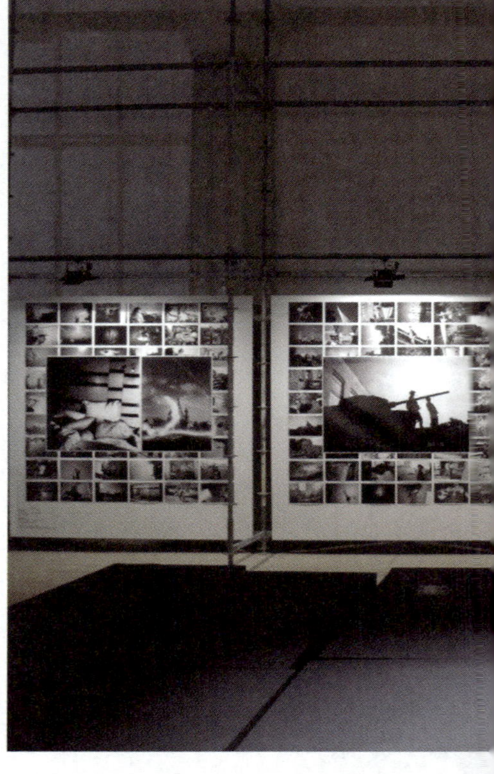

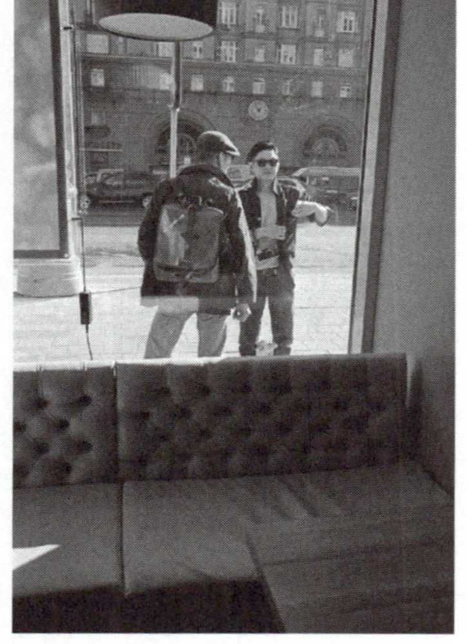

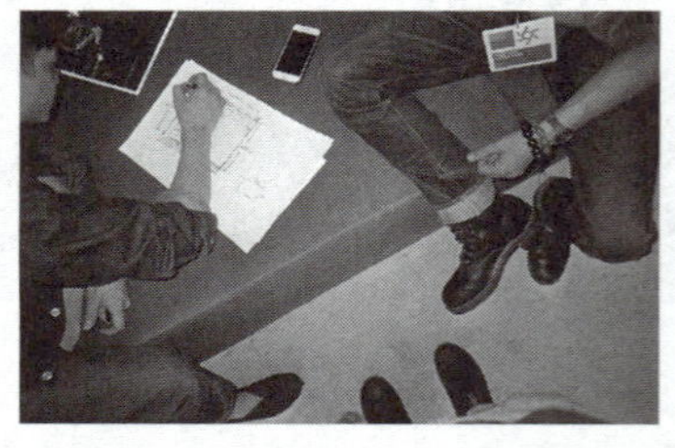

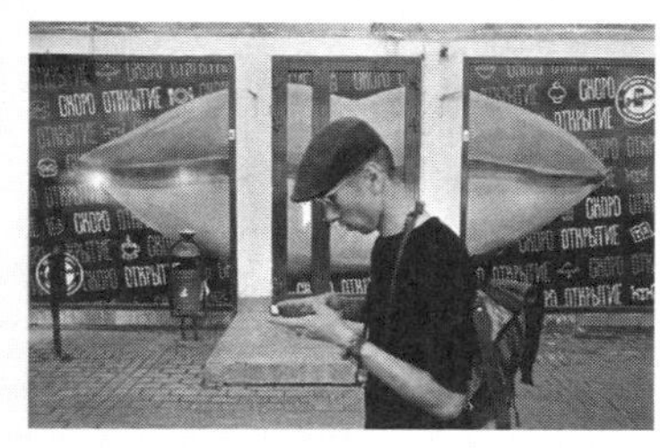
СКОРО ОТКРЫТИЕ

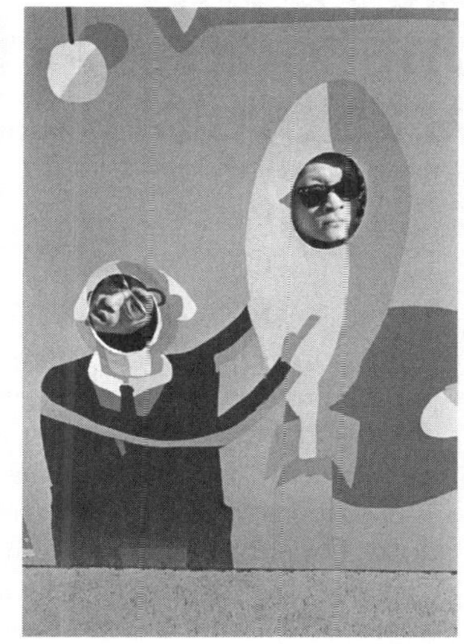

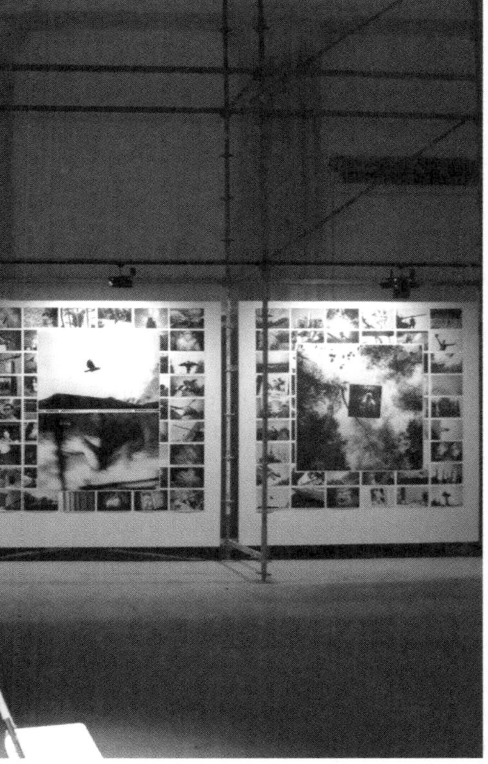

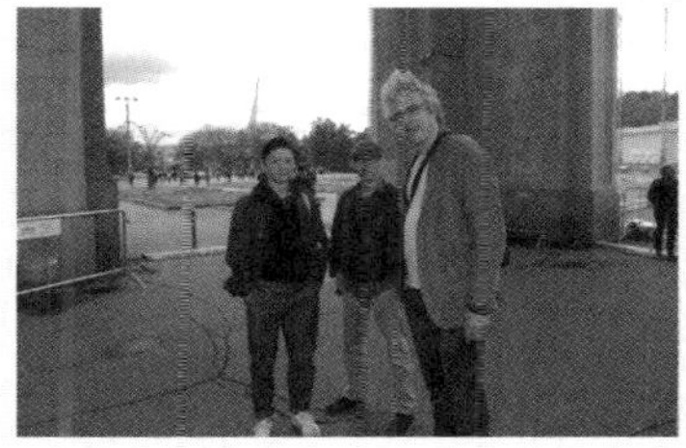

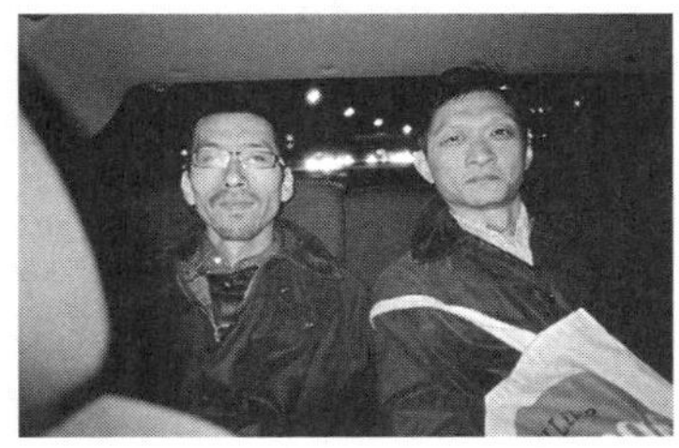

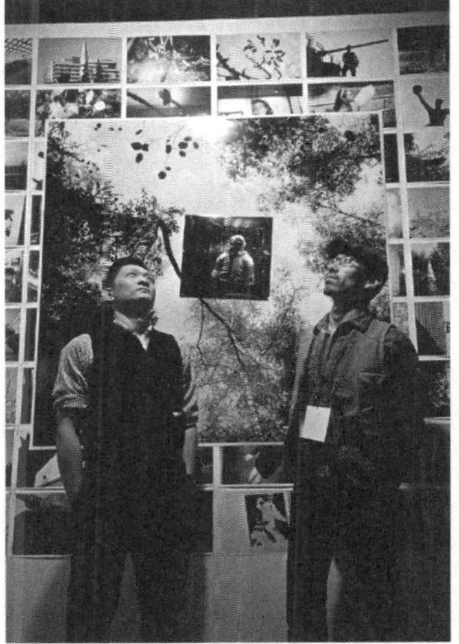

Gleb Berg[1] — Untitled (An Art Story in Three Art Novels) Moscow, October 2016

THE CURATOR

The feverish commotion had abated and I found myself deep in reflection. The impeccably smooth, glinting glass of the windowpane against my furrowed brow had at last warmed up—presumably to around thirty-seven degrees Celsius. I always have a slight temperature when I'm hung over.

Little grey figures pattered along the pavement under my window. Their raincoats were forming a spectrum between the overcast sky and the murky tones of St Isaac's Cathedral. I traced their trajectories and breathed evenly, holding the air in my lungs a bit longer than usual—it's a special exercise for calming the nerves and strengthening the will. With each breath, the windowpane opposite my lips was misting over and then growing clear again.

Where's St Petersburg? Here's St Petersburg! Where's St Petersburg? Here's St Petersburg! I played peek-a-boo with the city.

At that moment I was saying farewell to Russia. Manifesta-100 was now officially history, if still present in the lingering aftertaste of tobacco infused with forest-herb mouth rinse.

The receptionist rang. She was, to judge from the melodious voice, a radiant girl on the edge of womanhood—whipped into line, stultified by strict management, but still possessed of (or not having lost?) an elusive natural coarseness.

"Good morning Mr Curator," she said in a thick Russian accent. "Your taxi is waiting."

"Thank you very much."

"You're welcome."

I descend to the lobby with my suitcase. I check out of the hotel. I give a detailed description of the interior and the people there.

My suitcase is loaded with a thump, followed smartly by the slam of the boot. I wipe the dirt from my fingers and take a seat in the back. The cabbie has the face of a hero from Slavic folklore (I don't know if the Russians have something like the Good Soldier Švejk). Every now and again he casts cunning and moderately curious glances at me in the rear view mirror. Why would that be? He doesn't look like a contemporary art aficionado, so it's unlikely he would recognise me. I begin to wonder whether there's something unusual about me. Only the fact that I'm a foreigner. But you can hardly surprise a taxi-driver in a modern-day metropolis with that. What else? I haven't any scars, no skin irregularities. I'm not wearing a hat. Just an ordinary European in a dark polo neck and sensible jacket.

I fix my gaze on the fir-tree-shaped air-freshener dancing on its string.

The previous evening, the guests of Manifesta's closing party (the art community and its apologists) had descended on the Winter Palace. The very same Winter Palace that had once served as the last bastion of the Provisional Government against the Bolsheviks and revolutionary masses, defended to the last by the women's strike battalion and by the fresh-faced 'yunker' cadets prepared, in all their youthful passion, to see out their oath to the death.

Next, I give a passionate and detailed account of the aforementioned battle, cynically expounding my own attitude to the events of that gloomy October night and their opposing sides, then make a deft transition to a poetic description of St Petersburg's 'white nights', evaluating, as an art critic, the interior and exterior of the palace, putting words to smells, ironically describing the attire of the party guests, and sparing a few words for the lighting.

To resume, I was standing at the bar with an Indian collector and an Italian curator when I caught sight of Maga 'the Stone', a young artist who works with southern Russian, so-called 'Caucasian', identity and issues. I had been aware of Maga's existence for a couple of years (we were vaguely acquainted) and I felt I should probably mark my interest both in this youngster's persona and in his work. But I hadn't quite formulated that interest, whether as a question, a proposal, or a remark. I didn't know what to do with it yet. Now, too, I observed Maga in silence, occasionally picking at a sore hangnail on my index finger. The tiny wound was beginning to swell, but I couldn't stop touching it.

Wearing a black, slim-fit shirt with a high collar and a row of fake (presumably fake) silver *gazirs*[2] across the breast, Maga was dancing the *Lezginka*, a national dance brimming with purposeful gender expression — explicit for men and implicit for women. He was dancing, to the delight of the international art crowd, to a house track. Others, mainly Russians, looked on bemused.

The more vigorous, energetic, and choppy Maga's movements became, the more fluid and graceful seemed those of the lady that joined him in the circle, a young Ossetian artist in a futuristic Japanese outfit.

"ASS-SSA!" Maga shot his arms out one way then the other, landing quick, explosive blows in the air like a master of martial arts, sliding his hands and elbows into place like pistons, as if along a pre-determined trajectory.

His charming and seemingly completely emancipated partner beautifully imitated both the movements themselves and the emotions integral to this traditional spectacle. She danced without raising her eyes, full of gentle humility and, at once, dignity. Then, letting her ancient mask dissolve into lively facial expression, she directed a sheepish, ironic laugh towards Maga and the audience and made way for a young man with a figure like an inverted trapezium. Now it seemed as if he and Maga were tearing up reality with their bare hands, ripping out clumps and throwing them underfoot to trample with their strange, pointed shoes, whose toes strove valiantly for infinity. I caught myself thinking that these shoes, and this dance, and Maga himself would all have been worthy exhibits at Manifesta, either all together or as exhibits in their own right.

By some silly nervous impulse, I bit off my hangnail but it only became worse.

The strobe cut every other second out of the flow of time. I saw how Maga, concluding his dance in a state of frenzy, gave an inarticulate shriek, pulled out a pistol, and started shooting into the ceiling. The shots were drowned out by the loud music and just flashed in the darkness; then splinters of the ceiling fell down, right on Maga's head. Awe at the strength, power, and primitive spirit of this young man turned to palpable fear merged with an inexplicable glee. I knew that if I met this man in a dark alley or open field, he could quite easily kill me if he wanted to. But that power was enticing. The guests scattered; shaven-headed security guards in ill-fitting black suits were already pushing through the crowd, pressing fingers to their earpieces. They started restraining Maga. Evidently realising that he had gone too far, he put away the gun and raised his hands in the air—not so much in an act of surrender, more in the way a footballer who has committed a foul shrugs to the referee and the crowd as if to say "I didn't mean it, honest! It just happened that way."

They began taking Maga away. I squeezed through the crowd and touched him on the shoulder: "Hi! How can I get in touch?"

He looked at me like a baffled child and just said "Hi". I thrust him my business card. "Email me."

Of course, from the point of view of common sense and ethics, I ought to have condemned such a lack of restraint in a young artist; but it shouldn't be forgotten that the boy was from a peripheral, turbulent region, which, although geographically part of Europe, has an entirely different cultural identity.

Here I provide a lengthy description of everything I know about Dagestan and its numerous mountain peoples, then, in detail, the Pulkovo airport (because I'm already getting out of the taxi), all the procedures prior to departure, the Russian customs ladies with their unkempt mousey-brown hair and milk-white skin kissed with a scarlet blush and vanishing under the dull green collars of their uniforms.

I've spent the last few months in England, Belgium, and Holland. I don't intend to waste too many of my allotted words on daily life in western Europe, which everyone knows about, either first hand or thanks to mass culture; nor can I see any narrative justification for dwelling on the ins and outs of my work.

One evening, however, I received an e-mail that made me raise my eyebrows in surprise. I had grabbed a kebab from one-eyed Omar on my way home (he has a small kiosk on the corner), so I got back sated and immediately sat down to a report on… and there in my inbox, nestled among other email correspondence, I noticed a message from Maga the Stone with the subject-line 'please take me'. It was a video. I double-clicked and began to watch.

[Description of song and dance by Maga, who offers the curator his artistic services.]

My housemaid came on Tuesday, like she always does. In November, I had to fly to London on urgent business; economy class was full, so I was forced to slum it up in business. My mother's cat died and my sister gave her a kitten. They decided to call the kitten Sofia II. The chain of events with significance for our narrative took place not long after New Year, in early 2015. A chance encounter at the opening of an important exhibition promised exciting creative developments. There followed a period of waiting, enquiry, and scheming through friends and friends of friends. Eventually a definitive breakfast took place in a restaurant for bobos (all in tasselled or 'bearded' shoes). To cut a long story short: I was invited by a certain art functionary to curate the 6th Moscow Biennale. I thought it over and decided to take a chance.

And here I am on the plane to Russia again, only this time to Moscow. The budget halved in the time it took me to pack my bag, and something tells me that's not the end of it. Naturally, the Russian financial crisis is to blame for everything. Aside from the budget, there's also a complication with the walls: in the designated exhibition area — a majestic pavilion in the imperial style — nothing can be done to stop the centuries-old plasterwork from crumbling. I'm not entirely sure what to expect from the Russians and I'm hoping for the best, but I can still feel the fear deep in my gut.

"Chicken or fish?" asks a Russian stewardess, smiling a stale official smile. Her red uniform is completely absurd, as if the designer had intended to parody the very role of stewardess.

"Chicken," I smile back.

"Ai!" bursts out my athletic young neighbour: having volunteered to pass my tray, he has brushed the hot tin-foil of the container and burnt his hand. He vigorously shakes his wrist, licks the unfortunate finger, and gives me a patronising smile. "Barbarbar!" he babbles in Russian. Unfortunately, I don't know the language, but amicability needs no translation.

The hours in the air — at neither the point of departure nor the point of arrival, at neither midday nor two in the afternoon — this period of timelessness or, rather, of extra-historical time, I usually spend behind a book. While I'm reading, the Dutch landscape, seemingly drawn with a ruler, has been replaced by its chaotic Russian counterpart. As we descend to Moscow the cloud passes by and a great frozen plain rises to meet us, a vast back riddled with the mould of forests, the eczema of fields, and the amorphous birthmarks of human settlements. So much land was available when this enormous nation was forming that there was never any need for rigorous planning. And even Moscow itself, the ancient capital, grew for centuries according to the same principle, its courtyards and palaces seemingly tipped from a sack.

We finally land. Almost all the passengers, including my neighbour, applaud ebulliently. Then, without waiting for the plane to reach a standstill, clamber out from their seats, fetch hand luggage from the overhead lockers, and, ignoring the protests of the stewardesses, form a no-nonsense queue in the aisle.

"Barbarbar!" somebody hails me in the deserted arrivals hall. It's the young lad, my neighbour from the flight, who has doubtless been held up on the way through customs.

"No taxi?" he asks in broken English and winks.

"No," I shrug and sardonically show the screen of my phone.

"One minute!" He raises a significant finger, lifts his phone to his ear, says "Allo!", then laughs, then starts cursing, then laughs again.

His friend appears and they greet ebulliently, hugging and lifting each other into the air. Some people turn and look.

The three of us get into a presentable German SUV with blacked-out windows. Kazbek sits in the front, in the non-driving seat and promptly fastens his seatbelt behind his back.

"Barbarbar," says Nose, who is driving.

"Barbarbar?!" snaps back Kazbek.

"Bar!" Nose promptly pulls a shiny object out of the glove box, leans into the back and plugs it into the seat-belt socket between the back seats. "That's to stop the beeping!" he smiles at me ironically. He's got an identical object in his own socket: an oval metal buckle with rhinestones in the shape of a revolver.

Despite the winter frosts, Kazbek is wearing a tight, brightly coloured short-sleeve shirt with a white collar and elaborate white edging framing the sleeves. He leans on his left elbow, propping it on the wide panel between him and the driver's seat. He has a very muscular arm: the taut white hem looks in danger of snapping from his bulging bicep. He has a long, thoughtful scratch of his thick stubble, then of his broken ear, which looks as if it has been turned inside out, then produces a prison Rosary made of dried bread and starts to finger the beads. A gold ring glints on his middle finger, emblazoned with the logo of a major fashion house; a watch the size of an alarm clock jangles on his wrist. His friend, Nose, sings along quietly to American hip-hop, but garbles nine out of ten of the words. He's dressed in a flashy navy-style jacket, while his face is dominated by a nose of cartoon proportions, crowned by slanting soot-black eyebrows. He seems like a nice fellow. I ask what the guys do for a living. They say they're gangsters—then laugh and admit that they're sociology students at Moscow University. They're only twenty.

"And what about you?" asks Nose, whose English is in another league to that of his friend.

"I work in contemporary art."

"What?"

"Contemporary art."

"What's that?"

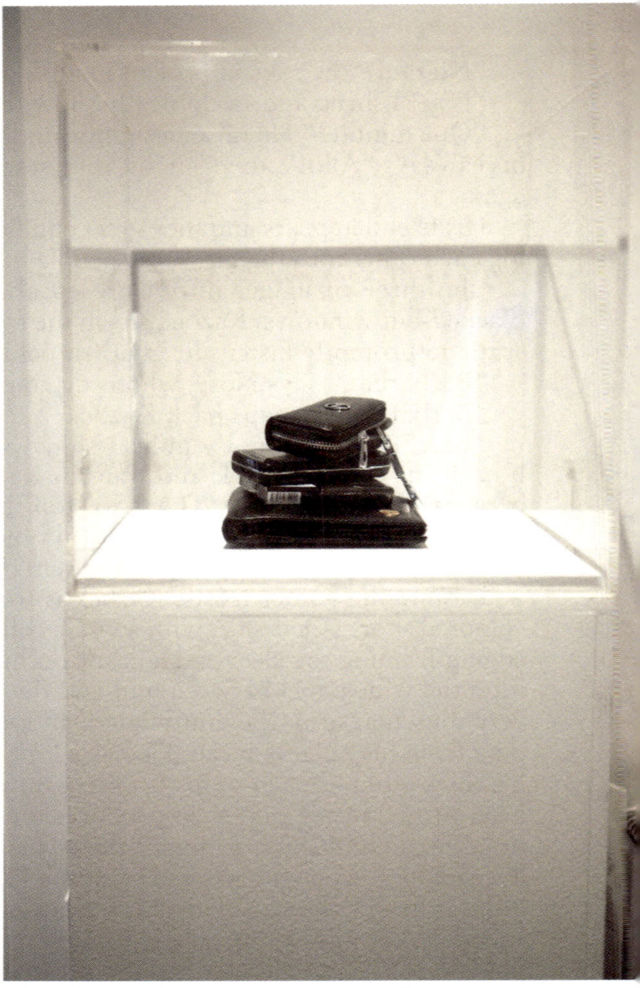

The Unbound, The Greater Caucasian Pavilion, 2015

“I’m here to arrange Moscow’s biggest exhibition this autumn — the Moscow Biennale.”

“Oh! Art! It’s like paintings and stuff, yes?”

Nose translates our conversation for Kazbek, who suddenly becomes animated and dictates the text of a new question. “Do you know artist — Maga the Stone?”

“Yes, we’re acquainted.”

“He is our friend.”

“What a strange coincidence!”

“Yes. Where do you know him from?”

“We bumped into each other in St Petersburg last summer.”

“Ah, we were there too… He’s a whack artist, eh?”

“He’s pretty interesting and original.”

Beyond the foreground of wide, illuminated highway, miles of forest flash by, occasionally making way for the gigantic car parks of gigantic shopping malls. On the other side of the road, shabby districts of tower blocks suddenly rise up out of the impenetrable thicket: the Moscow suburbs. Kazbek lowers the electric window to throw out a chewing gum wrapper and I notice that the car has double windowpanes: the inner panes are tinted, the outer are ordinary transparent ones. Nose explains that it’s illegal to tint your car windows in Russia, so he was forced to exploit this loophole.

“And what’s Maga up to now?” I ask.

“He’s in prison. But he’ll be out soon. His relatives sorted it.” Nose casts me a sly, smiling glance in the rear view mirror.

“It’s a shame he’s in prison, but I’m glad to hear things will be sorted soon.” I answer and decide not to ask how exactly Maga ended up there.

“Hey, you’re lucky you met us at the airport, right? You’d probably still be waiting for your taxi,” grins Nose mischievously.

“Yes, it’s good that I met you. Thanks for offering to drop me off. It’s not a big detour for you, I hope?”

“Well, to tell you the truth we were going in a totally different direction. But we’re happy to help, you’re a good lad.”

‘Lad?’ I think to myself. ‘I’m ten years older than the two of you put together.’

“Listen,” says Nose. “Soon they’ll release Maga and he’s going to need work. Take him for your exhibition. His father will be grateful.”

“I haven’t decided exactly what the exhibition will be about yet,” I answer politely. “But I’m impressed by Maga’s work. I’d be happy to chat to him. I can't promise anything though—think of it as a casting."

The word 'casting' amuses Nose. He translates to Kazbek and the two of them laugh and make obscene gestures. By now we are drawing up to my hotel.

The guys get out of the car to say goodbye and help me with my bag.

"So, what about Maga?" asks Nose again. I give him my business card, which he stows in his pocket without so much as a glance. "Take my number as well," he responds sternly to this gesture. I get out my mobile and start taking down Nose's number, but I fumble with the buttons. He grabs the phone out of my hands and enters the number himself, then produces his own phone. It's made of gold, is studded with precious stones, and has a customised engraving where the logo would otherwise be, evidently his monogram. The display of the golden phone lights up with a call from my number.

"Now I've got you too," clarifies Nose. "So we definitely won't lose touch."

Kazbek, meanwhile, with an incredibly straight back and wide, open shoulders, is busy bumming a cigarette.

THE ARTIST

"Dear diary,

I'm making this entry with a Caucasian accent. Basically, my exhibition went good. Spoke to some people, kicked about, here and there. A gallery from Berlin was right into me. I gave them my number, they gave me theirs. My cousin Abubakar was up from the region. Petersburg is a foreign land to me, but I had to show it my Abubakar somehow. So I took him to the Manifesta after-party.

Europeans, I don't mean no harm, they're dignified men. But the genes of their ancestors—all those Vikings, Goths, and Gauls—you feel it, they're not what they were. That's why they can't take their eyes off our brothers, all bold and strong and sharp as knives, AOOVEOO!"

"You actually write that, 'aoo-veoo'?" laughed Kazbek.

"Yup! I couldn't help it, I let off a banger."

"You're high!"

"He is, bro." Nose graciously cocked his leg and gave several energetic shakes of the hip.

The room was dark, apart from the television. Smoke hung in the flickering white light. Abubakar had passed out on the sofa. I had to stand on top of him to reach the window. "Gai! Gooy!—shouted the contestants of a Japanese game show. I settled back into the armchair and started eating ice-cream with a big spoon, straight from the plastic pot. To be honest my eyelids were already drooping.

"Now he thinks I'm cool"—as I drifted off I remembered the previous night in the Winter Palace and the expression of that curator. Clusters of crystal glinted dimly beneath the ceiling.

I woke in the armchair to morning TV and the fake smiles of plastic presenters. Abubakar and those two animals, Nose and Kazbek, were still asleep. I closed my eyes for a couple more seconds, then opened them very wide, leapt up, and began looking for a cigarette. The contents of the hotel room were strewn everywhere; nothing was where it was meant to be. I had a gurgling pain in my chest and a little higher, in my throat.

There was a rectangle of dry, pale grey asphalt under the awning over the front door. To either side the pavement was black from the drizzle. A five-star sign gleamed samovar gold and a red carpet retracted into the gloom of a hallway like a long tongue.

I felt a shiver run down my arms. I exhaled a puff of slate-grey smoke and it was immediately taken by the wind, straight into the face of the old doorman.

"Eyu! Colonel!" I called out. "Eh! Sir! Let's swap places, you're getting all my smoke. That's no fun for me either."

Yes, it was a nothing summer. I shuffled my bare feet in my flip-flops and huddled with every toke. That whole morning I replayed the shooting at the Winter Palace in my head. Not when the Bolsheviks and yunkers had kicked off… when I had done the shooting, the day before yesterday, at the after-party. I turn into a complete animal when I drink…

I shuddered.

"Now I'm ashamed to ring that curator all sober," I thought, looking dumbly at his matt black business card as I turned it over in my hand. "Only blood can wash away such a disgrace… No, but really, what else?! You *khaivan*![3] To screw up like that in polite society… Now he must think this Maga the Stone is a complete savage, and I'm not. Well, just a little bit savage. There is that…"

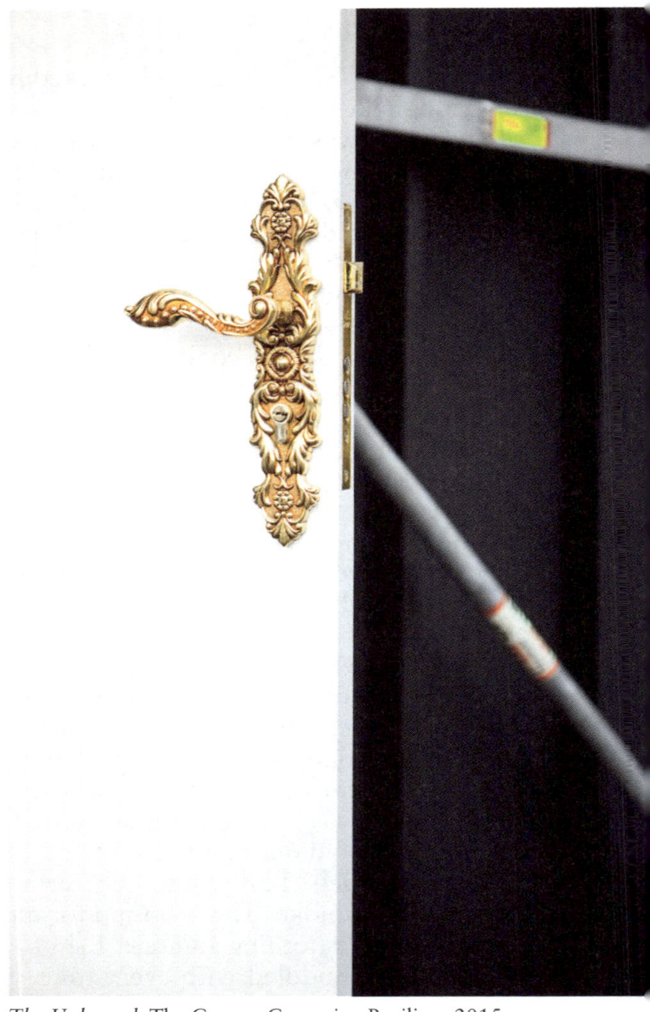

The Unbound, The Greater Caucasian Pavilion, 2015

It was still drizzling. The lads came downstairs — all crumpled, cotton-wool faces, tracksuits and flip-flops with the Russian coat of arms.

"What's all this, eh?" Kazbek poked my goose-pimpled arm.

"This? It's a triceps, bro."

"Nose, hear that?" said Kazbek with a lazy laugh. "What's all this?" I ask him, and he tells me it's a triceps. Got a dangerous one on our hands here."

"Uhuh…" answered Nose and gave a muffled snigger. His eyes were like glass buttons.

And that was the start of it… depression or something… I needed to reflect, to reboot, to somehow fill this nagging emptiness. I suddenly longed for Makhachkala.

And before long I was peering through the plastic oblong of the aircraft window at white peaks fringed with cotton-wool. There it was: my sweet native land, the beloved corner of the world I call home.

Here I give a detailed description of the Uytash Airport, named in honour of the two-time Hero of the USSR Amet-Khan Sultan. I describe the taxi drivers, the friends and relatives saying their hellos and goodbyes, the shawls, the oriental knapsacks, the branded suitcases. I describe the journey to my home and the house itself, a three-storey gothic mansion with turrets and all the rest of it… Makhachkala's full of them now, in every imaginable style: Baroque, Rococo, and so on. In the last twenty years they've built thousands. My parents, family life, the daily to-and-fro — I won't describe that. Suffice it to say that it's a good family, respected people in the Republic. Besides, if you want to know about daily life here you can always read Alisa Ganieva. She says it like it is.

"*Le-e-eh*![4] You're still alive, bro! What brings you here?" laughs Ali, a childhood friend.

"I'm alright — much more surprising that you're still alive! You were born just for a joke and only for five minutes, but look at you now, one serious piece of kit!"

We hug on the corner of a busy street; Alishka feels my bicep and says: "What kind of a beef cake are you? You're a real stone! You're wasted on painting — you should have been a cage-fighter!"

We sashay along the sidewalk — Ali and I. I'm wearing white brogue boots with leather soles, Alishka's wearing red loafers in suede, or 'shaggy leather' as he calls it. For a third time, enormous puddles on the pavement force us onto the carriageway.

"*Leh*! Want to kill me, eh!?" Alishka shouts at a car that blasts past as some lad thrusts himself out of the window in a virtuoso *dzhigitovka*.[5]

"Damn, check the fool out, is he immortal or what? His back's almost touching the ground, huh!" Alishka nods approvingly as a low-rider *Lada Priora* speeds away carrying the daredevil with it.

"Tradition adapted for modern reality... we've resaddled from horses to cars, but it's the same old *dzhigitovka*."

"Do they get up to tricks like that in Moscow?" asks Ali.

"Some lads do. Not often though. The locals never."

We meet up with the lads, a proper gang of us now, and 'patch out at the hump'. That means hang out on a little patch outside a local store. We pass a spliff around and everyone starts to loosen up and enjoy themselves. I decide to record a song for the curator, to make a joke of the whole situation. Maybe then he'll get me in on some project. I warm up my voice and get in the spirit.

Yes, yes, yes, yes, yes, this is Kavkaz!

No, no, no, no, no, this is Kavkaz!

Alishka films it on his phone. At first I'm a bit self-conscious, but then I pull myself together and start to sing one very old, very beautiful song in my own language.

I've hardly got going before the impromptu drummers come in, their hair like Ringo's in the good years.

"Gogydi-gogydi-gogydi-gogydi!" join in the baritones, lifting the tempo in the background. They're all in Gabi hats, those thin wool beanies with no turn-up and a big logo on the forehead that almost all the Caucasian lads in Moscow are wearing, and down here too.

People disperse around midnight. Alishka drives off to some Bombita. It's like the Mexican 'Chiquita', only it's from the word 'bomb'. It's our Caucasian version: all those Rhinestone Uggs, leopard skin, the lips, the eyebrows, you know.

It's already dark, and Gamzatbek and me are meandering back along the dusty roadside. The edge of the asphalt crumbles and drops away like Fjords, and every now and then we pass a street lamp. We can hear music from a roadside bar. We've only just met, because Gamzatbek used to live in a village in the mountains and then I was away for a long time. But he's a fine lad, I liked him straight away.

"Don't you want to move to Moscow then, brother?" I ask him.

"It's not an option now," he says and clicks his tongue forlornly.

"My mother's old. She's not well. My older brother got shot dead, my younger brother's just a lad still. We haven't got anyone else."

I wish his old lady good health from the bottom of my heart, and offer to help if ever he needs anything.

"Thanks brother, appreciate that," replies Gamzatbek. "But we've pretty much got all we need."

The housing blocks end and the fences begin: tacky wooden ones, towering stone ones, all jumbled up together. A police siren silently flashes from around the corner.

"Like I said, I've just arrived only few hours ago. We're walking home now, me and my friend… So what is it we can help you with, commander?"

The patrol squad check our documents. They search us with gusto.

They find a knife on Gamzatbek, which he allegedly used to stab some lad in a fight. They handcuff him and start beating him up there and then. I picture his poor old mother, his younger brother, their grief, their tears—their fate if this man is sent far away for a very long time. And that's if he even makes it there alive… We're all family in the Caucasus: it's the done thing to help each other out, especially your neighbours.

"It's my knife. Let the man go!" I shout to the cops.

My dad will get me off, I hope; but nobody will get Gamzatbek off.

INTERCULTURAL DIALOGUE (FROM THE AUTHOR)

The black bonnets of expensive SUVs shimmer beside a garish oriental façade. Behind it there is a restaurant in a generic Eastern style, more *Aladdin* than *Mulan*. Waiters in gold-embroidered waistcoats scurry between the tables delivering hookahs; in keeping with the theme, they're all called 'Abu'. It's a well-oiled machine: the Abus stoke up the aromatic hookahs on the move, deftly brandish their tongs, blow on the coals, and serve the guests specially cooled pipes. There's every flavour under the sun: double apple, strawberry and melon, coke and lemon, sushi and shrimp…

The curator and artist are sitting in a separate compartment, accompanied by Nose and Kazbek.

"My main idea is that we Caucasians don't integrate with modernity, we adapt its achievements to our own customs and traditions. Take the *dzhigitovka*," says Maga the Stone and recounts his walk with Alishka through Makhachkala.

"That's interesting," nods the curator, who has been listening intently. "Because, the main theme of the Biennale is specifically going to be about intercultural dialogue."

Maga takes a long drag of flavoured shisha and a thick stream of smoke escapes his nose. The food and drinks arrive. Nose asks the waiter to bring a bowl of fruit so the table won't look empty.

"Or shoes," continues Maga. "We always wear flamboyant, elaborate shoes, and I think that comes from our national temperament. Why are you wearing simple, understated shoes, while Kazbek is wearing red loafers with gold buckles? Even two hundred years ago your ancestors were walking around in sturdy leather boots, while Kazbek's were strutting their stuff in three-league boots with looped toes."

"And why is that, in your opinion?"

"Because while your forefathers were cultivating thrift and restraint in the demonstration of wealth and saw that as one of the most important virtues, ours—*dhzigity* and *abreki*—were risking their lives hijacking merchant caravans and plundering neighbouring states, all so they could go back to their auls and show off their beautifully crafted weapons, their golden fabrics, and their priceless jewels..."

"And because they were hot-bloods... the unbounded ones!" adds Nose gravely and brings down the back of his hand on the table.

"And it's not just national colour. It's not just Eastern rugs, Russian birches, German beer... On their own, these things aren't charged at all. They're meaningless."

"Just symbols of themselves..." the curator's eyes have clouded over with a murky haze.

"Yes. But I want to show the authenticity of these things, their essence. I want to use them to expose the ethos behind them. Because they're fragments of real forms of life. They're a part of nature."

The artist and curator are bent over the table now, face to face. It is a very important conversation for both of them. Kazbek leans back on the sofa and speaks to Nose under his breath:

"Maga's a hot shot. But this guy seems to be scared. There's fear in his eyes."

"No, he's just thinking."

“It’s just like they’re playing chess or something.”

Maga goes on.

“Look at our friend Kazbek’s signet ring. Many men in the Caucasus wear one. But why? Very few people have a family coat of arms and you definitely won’t find anyone sealing letters with one. Actually, it’s obvious when you look at the history: the engraving on a real signet ring needs to be mirrored, but on today’s rings it never is.”

“That’s right, to leave the right imprint. But today Europeans consider signet rings an anachronism. That’s why they mostly wear them with the engraving on the inside, facing the palm.”

“But not in the Caucasus. Because, for us, the engraving on a signet ring is just part of the decoration. It doesn’t have any practical meaning. So why does Kazbek wear one?”

Maga poses this question to Kazbek, who diligently chews his kebab and answers in Russian.

“He says it’s to show he’s fashionable and successful,” interprets Nose for the curator.

“Or take another phenomenon;” Maga points to the wallet, smartphone, and car-keys arranged in a pyramid on the table. “The ‘Caucasian sandwich’, as I call it. Young lads, grown men… they all carry this artefact around in their hands, for exactly the same reason Kazbek wears his ring.”

“So ultimately it’s a status symbol, a sort of regalia… like a mitre and sceptre in the hands of a tsar.”

“Exactly.”

Maga picks up the ‘sandwich’ and pronounces a series of stereotypical phrases with colourful gestures to match.

“See? It’s a subtle psychological thing. I’m not empty-handed any more. The ‘sandwich’ is an extra string to my bow… an additional argument.”

And so it is settled; the details are laid out; they shake on it. Maga and his gang, ‘the Unbound’ art collective, will present the ‘Kavkaz’ pavilion at the 6th Moscow Biennale for Contemporary Art. Nose and Kazbek are overjoyed.

“Bang, bang, bang!” Maga the Stone makes a gun with his hand and shoots the air, then gives the curator a good-natured wink.

The shisha coals burn down. Nose asks for the bill. The curator brings his fist to his chin, screws up his eyes, bends back his index finger, and asks Maga about prison.

"It's alright, more or less. Not the worst year of my life," Maga wistfully stirs the green tea in the bottom of his tea-bowl, then looks the curator straight in the eye. "Before, I only knew about prison from what other people told me. Plus I'd read something about it. Now I know how it works from the inside. I met a lot of people and a lot of savages. Something will come of this experience. Very soon.

"And... how do you feel now?"—asks the curator.

"Well, how to say... It's spring." Spreading his arms, Maga turns towards the panoramic window and the street beyond, where the houses are squinting in the bright, slowly brightening sunlight.

1
Gleb Berg contributed this text upon invitation by The Unbound.

2
Gazirs—Caucasian gunpowder cases, typically worn in a cartridge belt across the chest, incorporated into the local folk costume and Cossack dress.

3
Khaivan—Dagestani slang for a fool or idiot (the word originally means 'animal' in the Avar language).

4
Leh!—a Dagestani greeting (generally for men) or an exclamation equivalent to the English 'Eh!' or 'Hey!'

5
Dzhigitovka—various special stunts performed on a galloping horse, originally practiced by Caucasian mountain peoples and Cossacks.

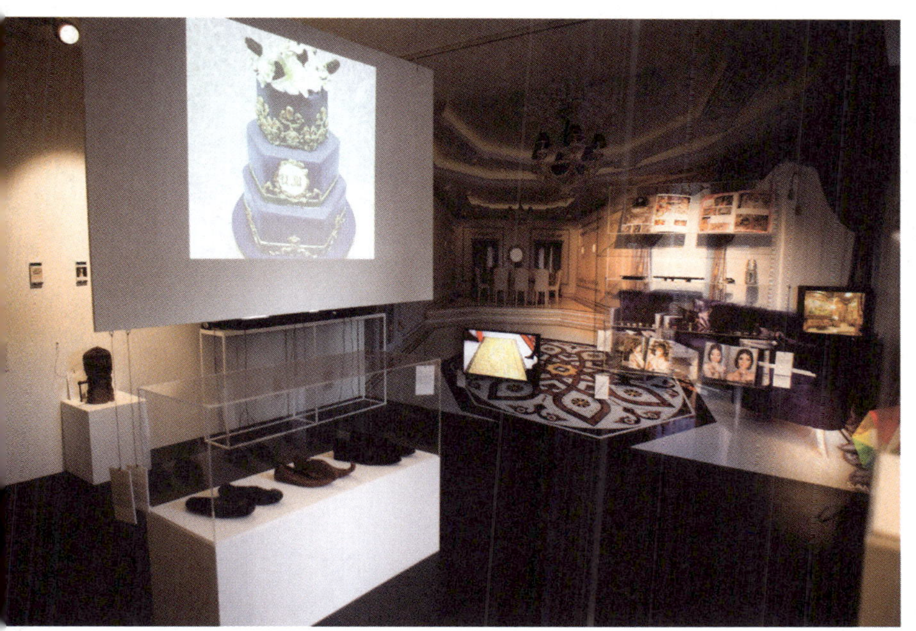

The Unbound, The Greater Caucasian Pavilion, 2015

Konstantin Zvezdochotov — About Ezgin Altinses

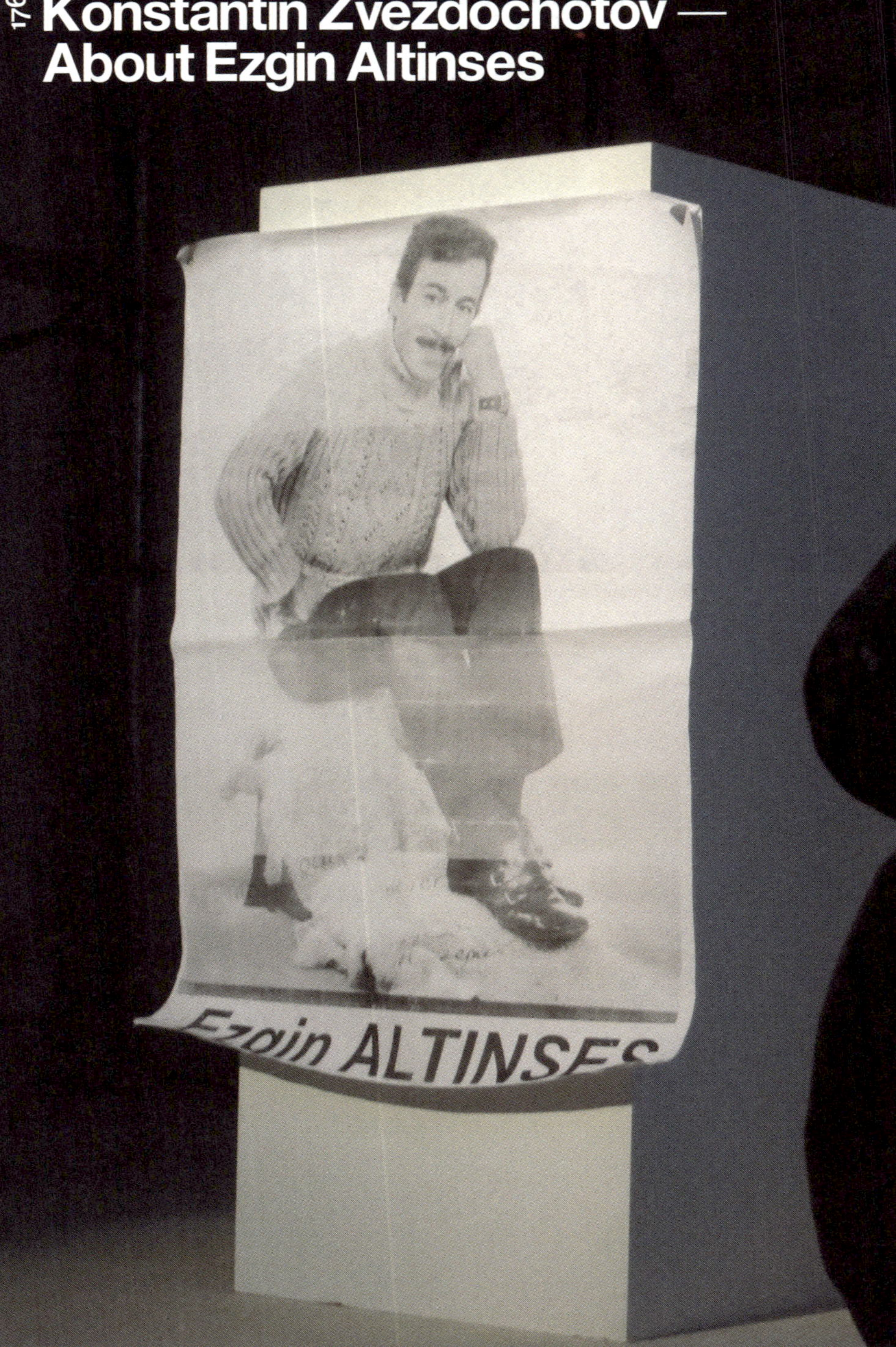

On one cold autumn morning I was hurrying along the boulevard to my new job.

For this season I was working as an artist at the Biennale, and since I was no longer used to working, I was experiencing a degree of discomfort.

Some guttural singing echoed along the whole length of the boulevard, accompanied by some sort of folk instrument.

The boulevard was filled with fog and was relatively free of people, so the singing that filled it sounded clearer and reverberated all the more.

When I came up level with the singer, I found that he was a small, and to put it mildly, very plainly dressed man, with a *saz* in his hands.

I thought to myself that he must be some kind of Caucasian, or an arrival from Central Asia.

Street artists of every possible kind are a common occurrence on our streets, which is why—at first—I didn't stop.

But then, something made me turn around and go back.

I came up to him and attempted to start a conversation, but he only repeated, "Turkish-Turkish." I could not establish contact using either Russian or English, and was about to continue on my way.

But then, a little Kyrgyz woman came out from behind the bushes. She turned out to be the musician's friend and translator. Through her, I could establish that they both came here from Istanbul, where they had met and had become friends. I found out that her name was Aigul, and that her friend was an extremely well respected person in his home country. She told me his name, but I cannot remember it now. What I do remember is his stage name—Ezgin Altınses, evidently because, as far as I understand, *altın ses* in translation means 'golden voice'.

For some reason there was something familiar and homely in these two unknown to me foreigners. I even felt like I had met them before.

Though ordinarily being an indecisive person, I suddenly showed an extreme degree of quickness and brazenly proposed that they come with me at once.

It seemed to me that the appearance of this pair would somewhat enliven the atmosphere of VDNKh, which had, like any other event of the international contemporary art scene, a light touch of routine-ness to it.

Moreover, the appearance of a distinctive Turkish note would give our project greater 'Eurasian-ness', since it is no secret that there are only three countries in the world that are located both in Europe and in Asia at the same time: Russia, Kazakhstan and Turkey.

And besides, Kazakhstan features in the Russian consciousness as a kind of continuation of Russia, while Turkey is its mirror image (that is, everything is the other way round there: the left hand is the right, and the right is the left).

So, it is probably on the basis of this highly profound reasoning that I ventured to invite our strangers to take part in our common cause.

To my surprise they quickly agreed, and together we rushed to face new challenges.

What happened afterwards was very sweet and touching.

The public received the artist with both curiosity and tender emotion. My old acquaintance Babi surrounded him with care and attention. Our curator Defne Ayas, whom I had unthinkingly thought to be German, turned out to be Turkish, and she likewise welcomed our new friend with all tenderness of heart. He was even slightly stunned by this reception. The poor fellow nearly wept.

In all, an unusually warm and intimate atmosphere came into being.

And you know, I dare say that all our exhibitions come and go and are forgotten, and perhaps it was only for the sake of what I described that putting together the whole biennial was worth it.

I have a suspicion that the 'Finger of Fate' exists, after all.

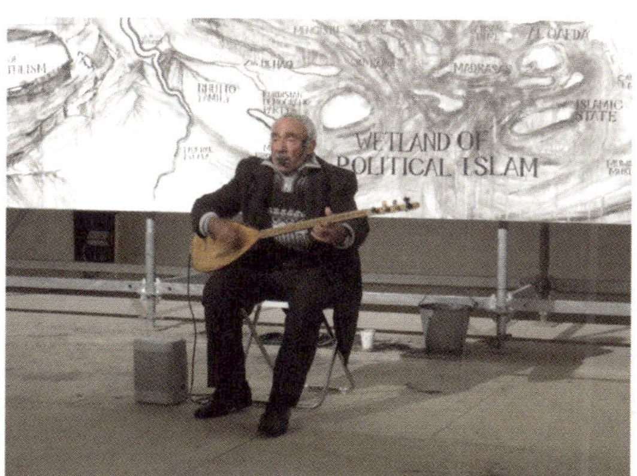

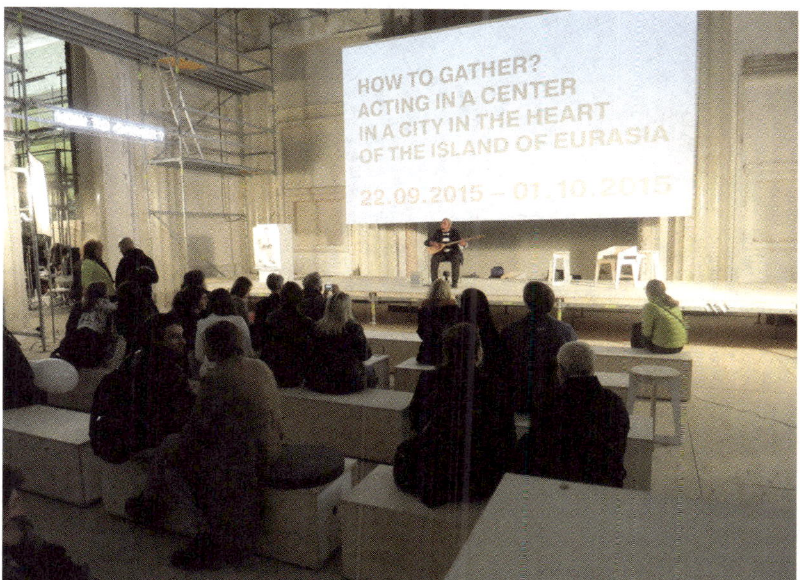

Performance of Ezgin Altinses, Moscow Biennale, 1st and 2nd October 2015

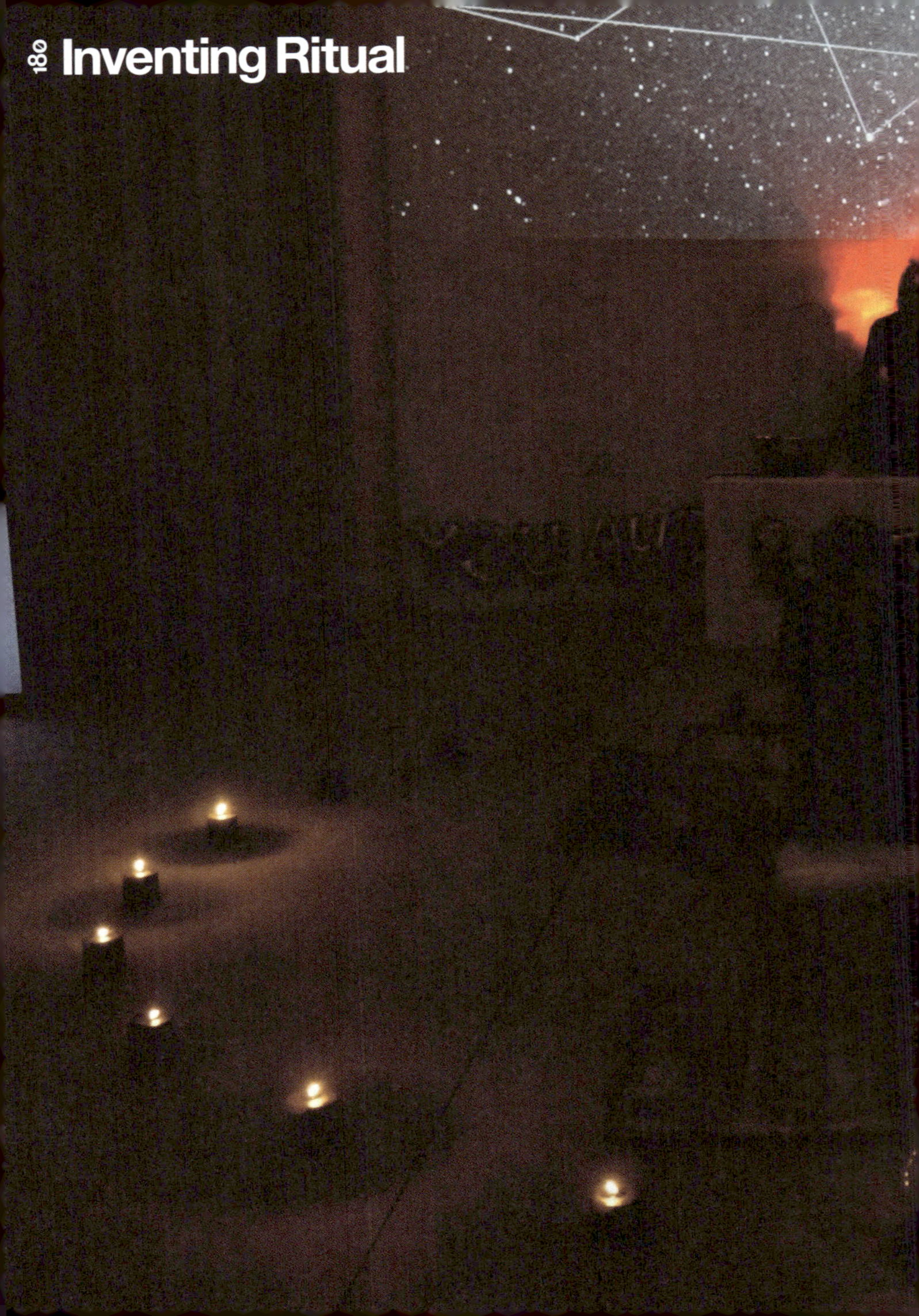

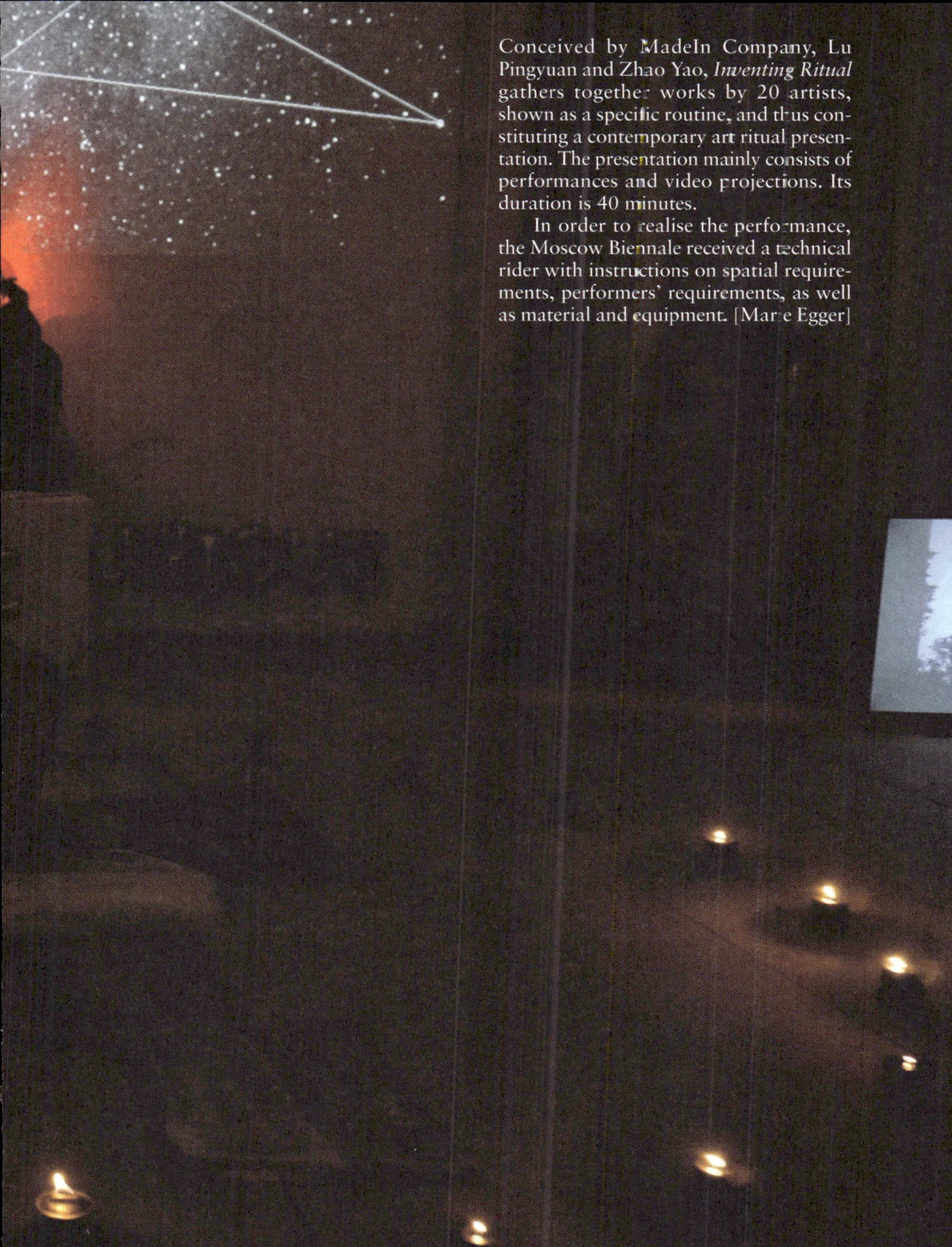

Conceived by MadeIn Company, Lu Pingyuan and Zhao Yao, *Inventing Ritual* gathers together works by 20 artists, shown as a specific routine, and thus constituting a contemporary art ritual presentation. The presentation mainly consists of performances and video projections. Its duration is 40 minutes.

In order to realise the performance, the Moscow Biennale received a technical rider with instructions on spatial requirements, performers' requirements, as well as material and equipment. [Marie Egger]

2. PERFORMERS REQUIREMENTS

- **ONE RITUAL MANAGER**
Man or woman, adult, average height and weight, with sportive background (yoga, dance or other)

- **TWO RITUAL MANAGER ASSISTANTS**
Women, 20-35 years old, pretty and svelte.
(Please send pictures of possible candidates whenever possible)

- **ONE VOLUNTEER**
Man or woman, adult, unrelated to the art field. The identity of the volunteer should be hidden to the performers.

3.1 REQUIRED MATERIALS (to be prepared by the exhibiting venue)

All the equipments with an "A" reference number should be provided by the venue.

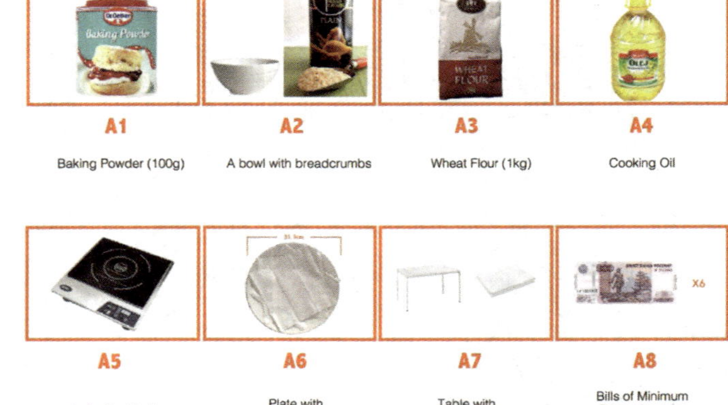

A1 Baking Powder (100g)

A2 A bowl with breadcrumbs

A3 Wheat Flour (1kg)

A4 Cooking Oil

A5 Induction Cooker

A6 Plate with Kitchen Towel

A7 Table with White Tablecloth

A8 Bills of Minimum Denominations from Local ATM

3.2 REQUIRED EQUIPMENTS (to be prepared by the exhibiting venue)

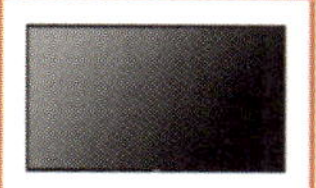

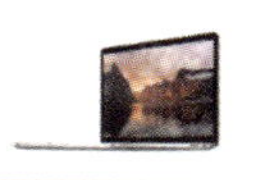

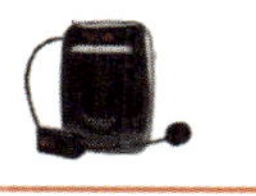

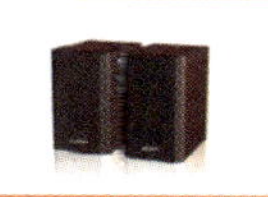

A9	A10	A11	A12	A13
55 inches monitors x 2 (to be fixed on the wall)	Projector with 2 HDMI ports (4000 lumens minimum) and its remote control	Macbook computers x 2	Portable microphones if any	Speakers

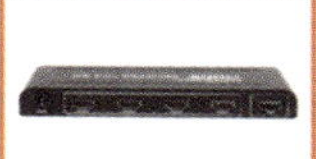

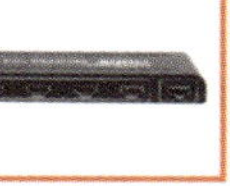

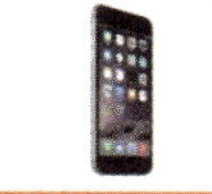

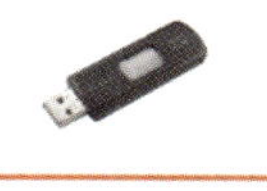

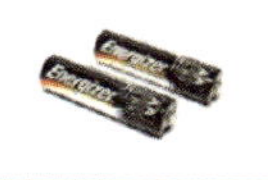

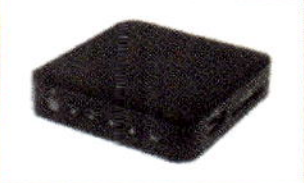

A14	A15	A16	A17	A18
TV Synchronisers	Smartphone x 2	USB×2	AA Battery (Type 316) x 32 for each performance	HD player

3.3 MATERIALS & EQUIPMENTS provided by the curatorial team

All the equipments with a "B" reference number should be provided by the curatorial team.

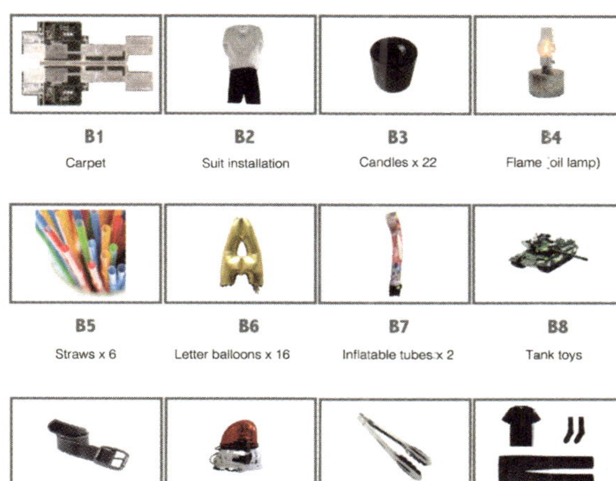

B1	B2	B3	B4
Carpet	Suit installation	Candles x 22	Flame (oil lamp)

B5	B6	B7	B8
Straws x 6	Letter balloons x 16	Inflatable tubes x 2	Tank toys

B9	B10	B11	B12
Belt	Helmet with rotating light ×2	Tongs x 2	Performers outfits x 3

3.3 MATERIALS & EQUIPMENTS provided by the curatorial team

B13

Foam Tape

B14

Masking Tape

B15

White Medical Glove

B16

White Cotton Glove

B17

Strainer

B18

Large bowl x 2

B19

Bubble wrap x 3 rolls

3. Display of the objects on the table (A7)

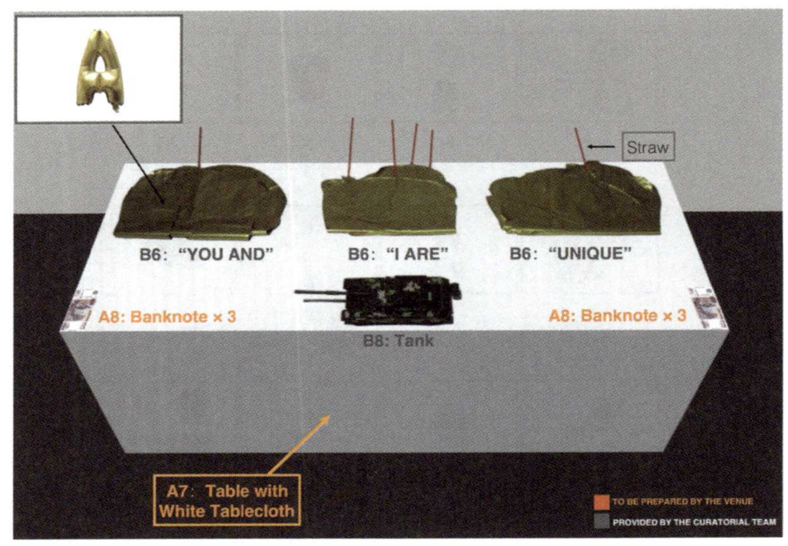

3. Display of the objects on the table (A7)

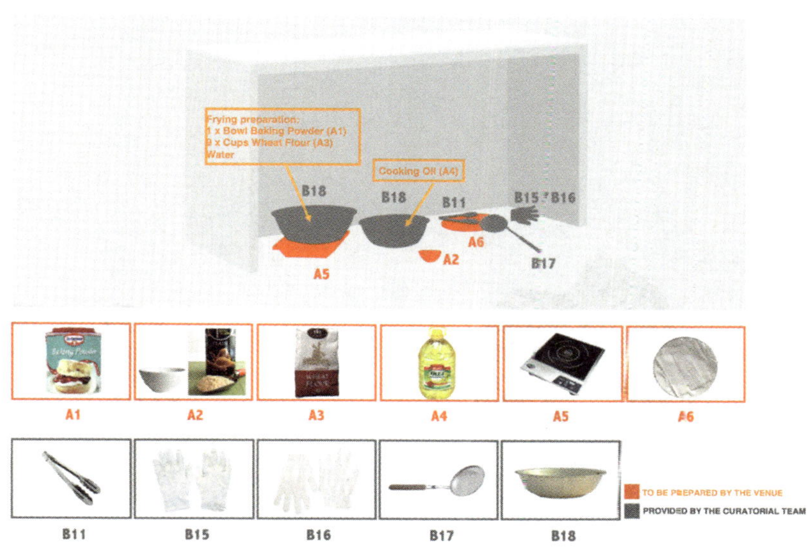

4. Performers' equipments

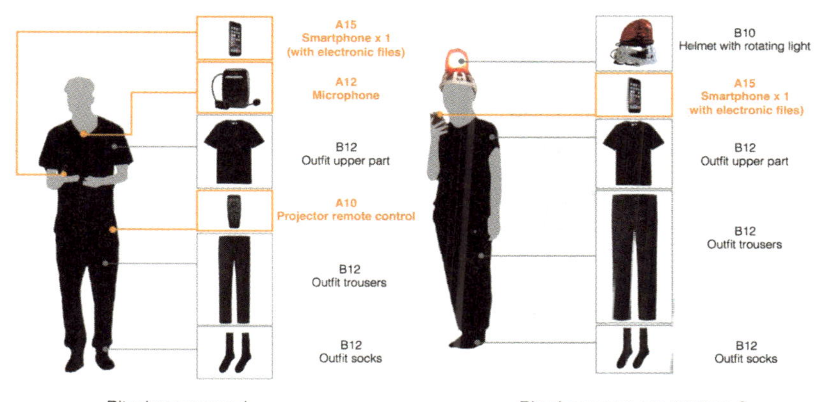

In case size of the outfits aren't appropriate please prepare similar clothing.

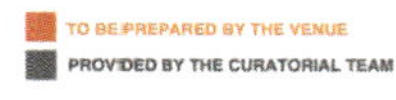

Gabriel Lester — MurMure

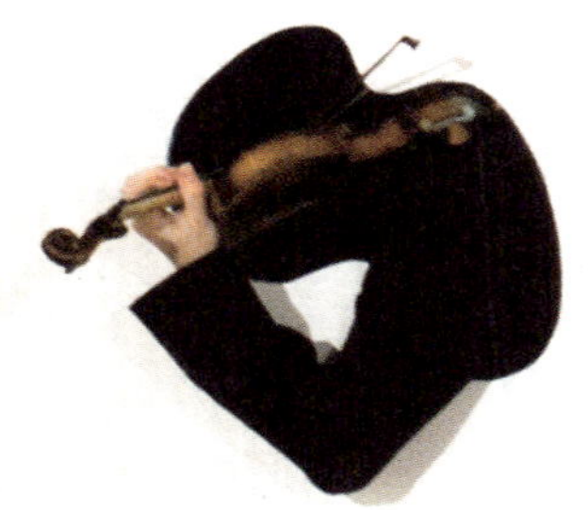

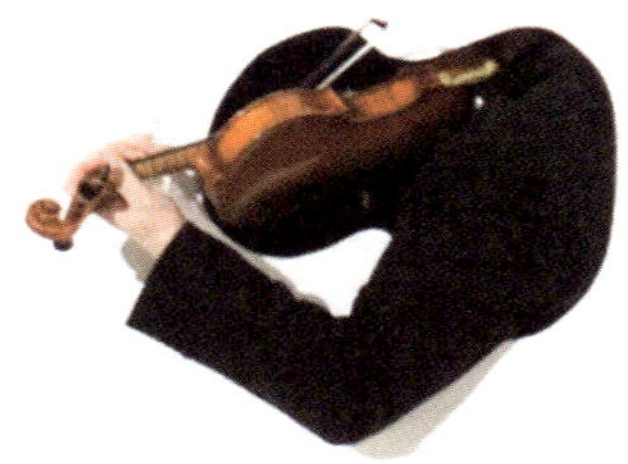

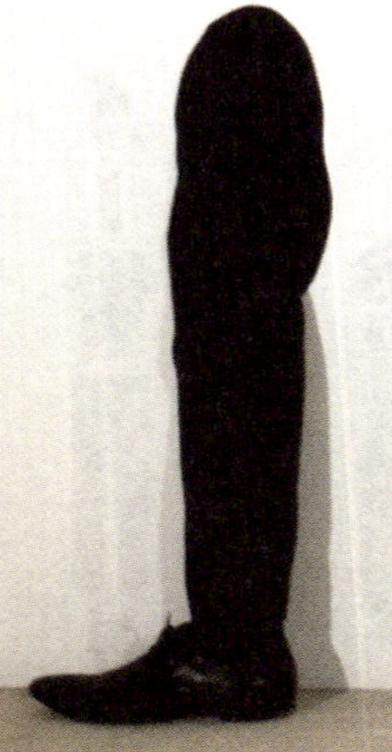

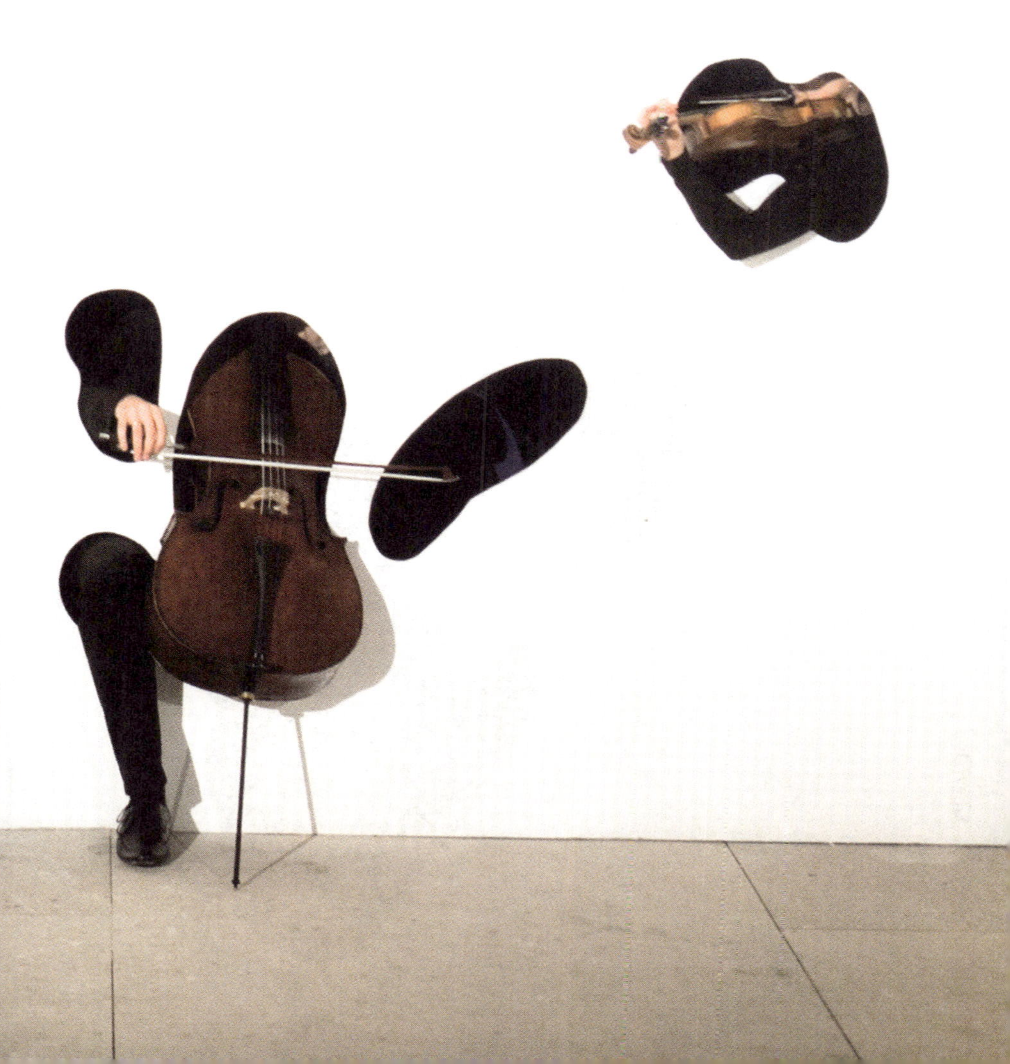

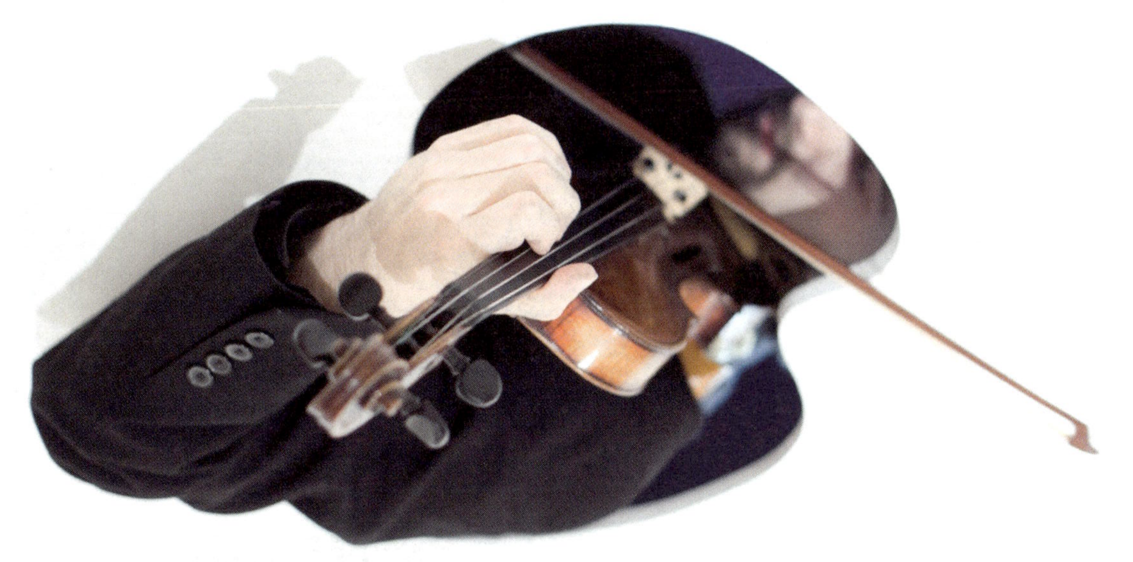

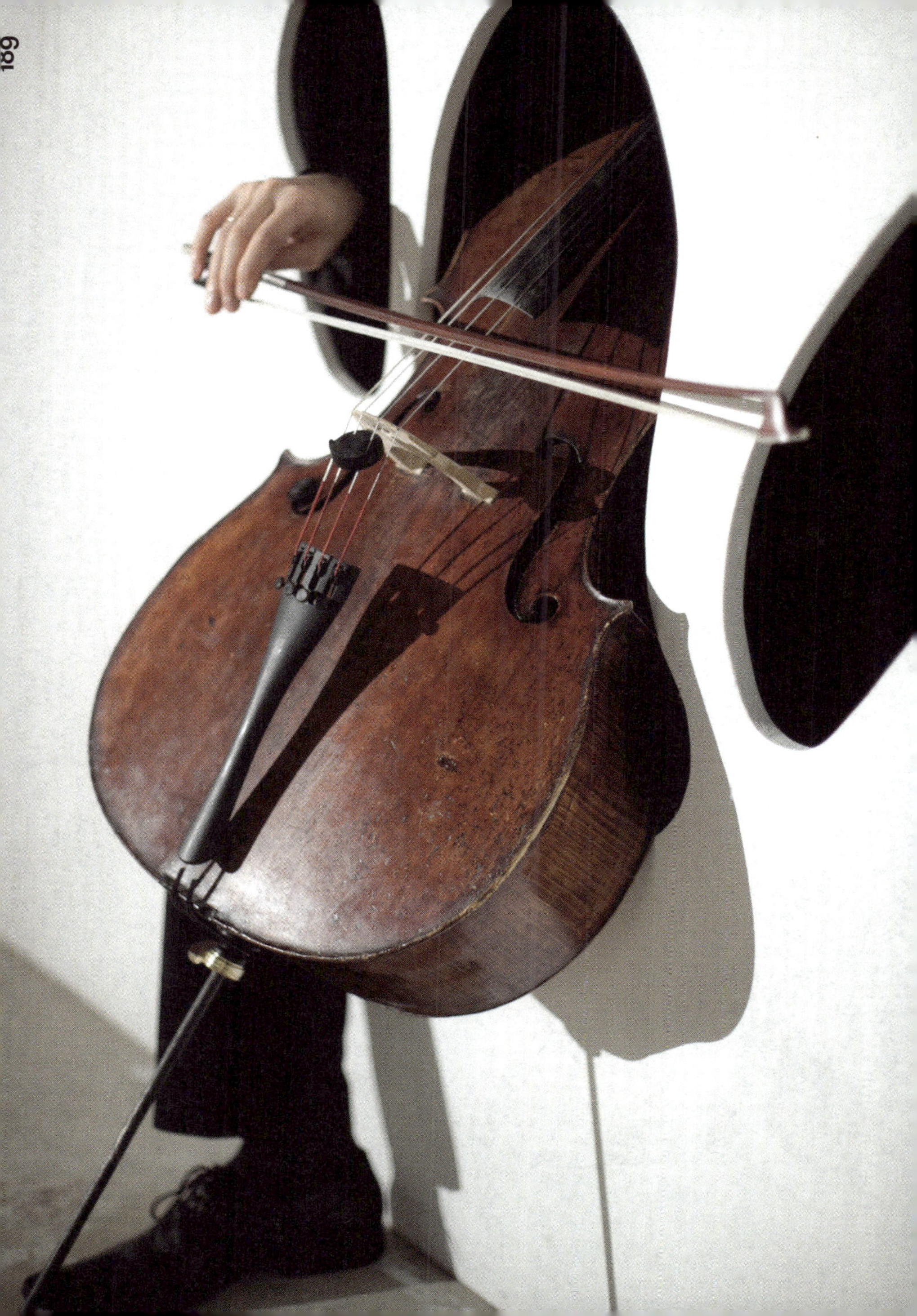

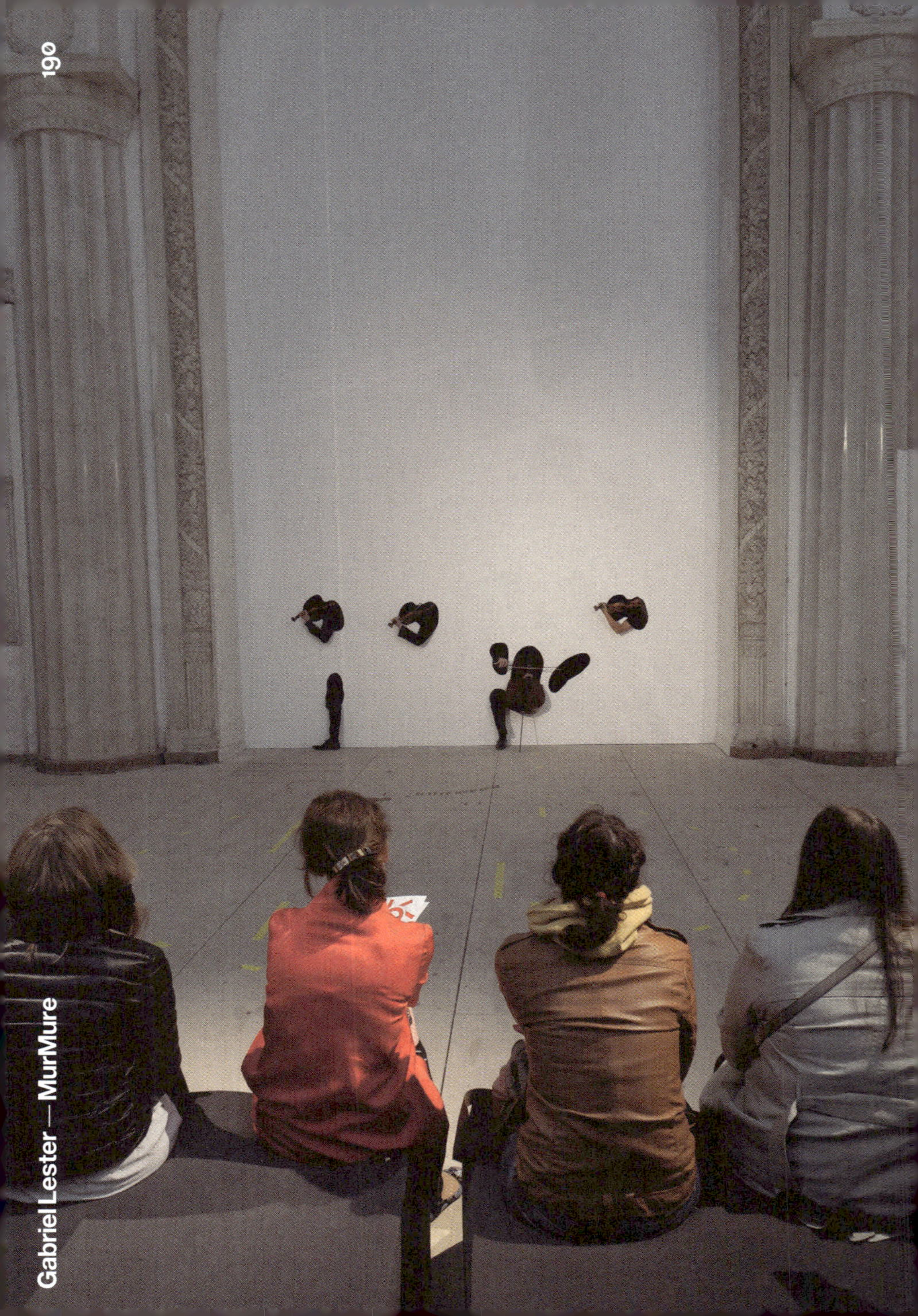

Gabriel Lester — MurMure

Frank Bridge

An Irish Melody

"THE LONDONDERRY AIR"

FOR

STRING QUARTET

PARTS NET 2/6
MINIATURE SCORE NET 1/6

Augener Ltd.
LONDON
18 GREAT MARLBOROUGH STREET, W. 1.
63 CONDUIT STREET (Regent Street Corner) W. 1.
57 HIGH STREET MARYLEBONE, W. 1.

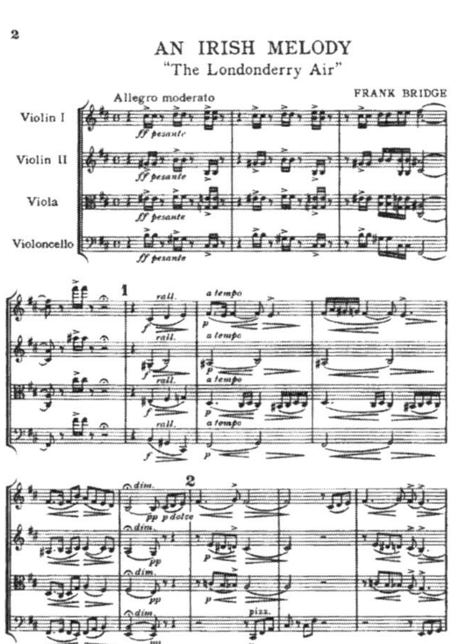

Copyright 1915 by Augener Limited

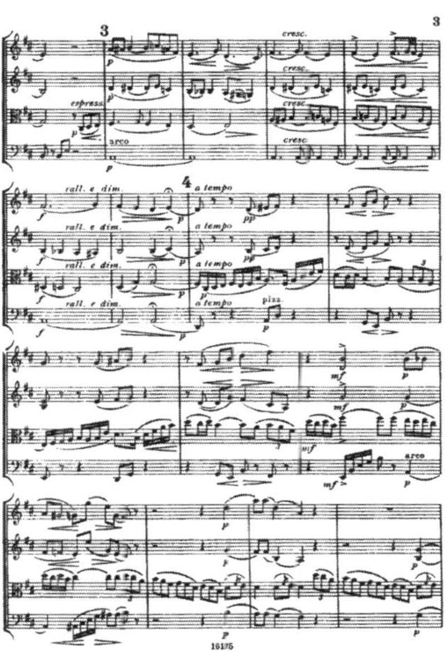

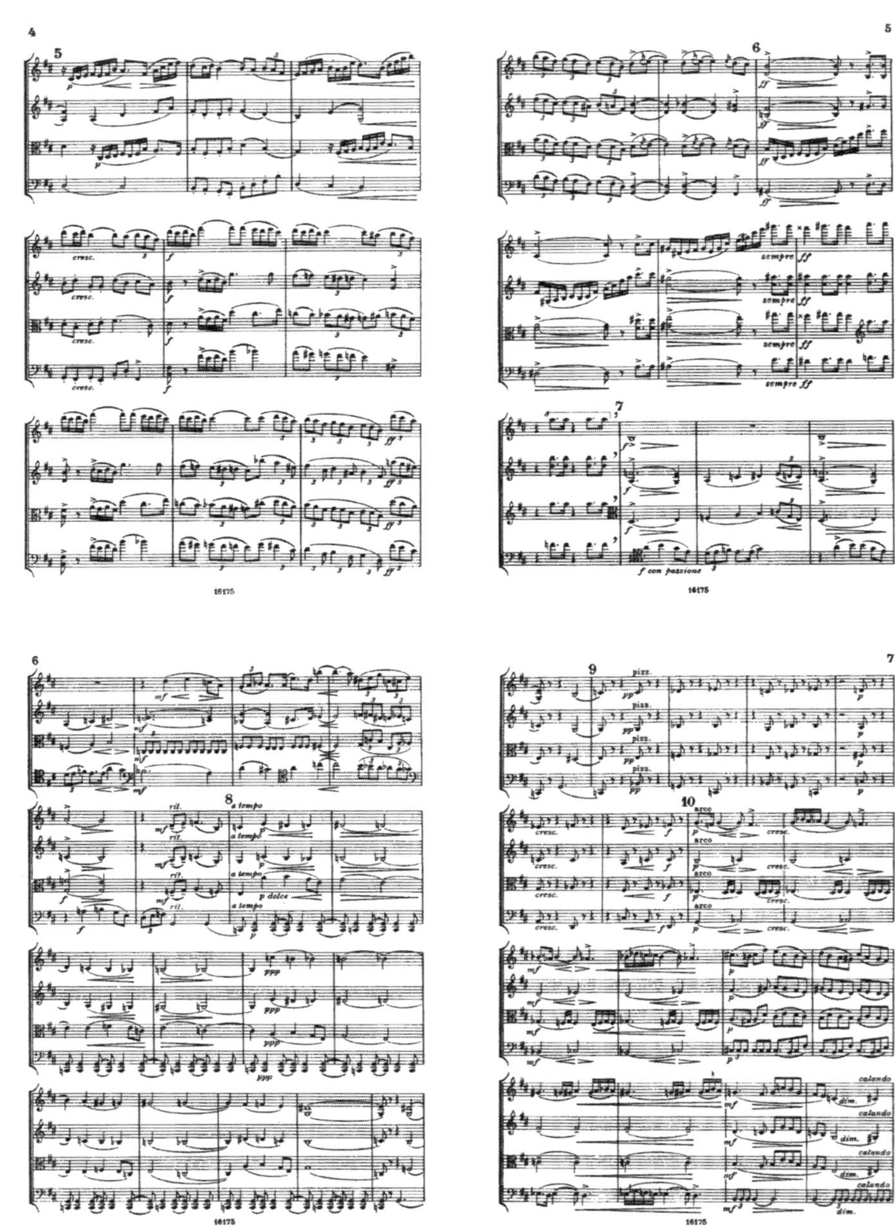
4
5
cresc.
16175
6
sempre ff
7
f con passione
16175
6
rit.
8
a tempo
p dolce
ppp
16175
7
9
pizz.
10
arco
cresc.
calando
dim.
16175

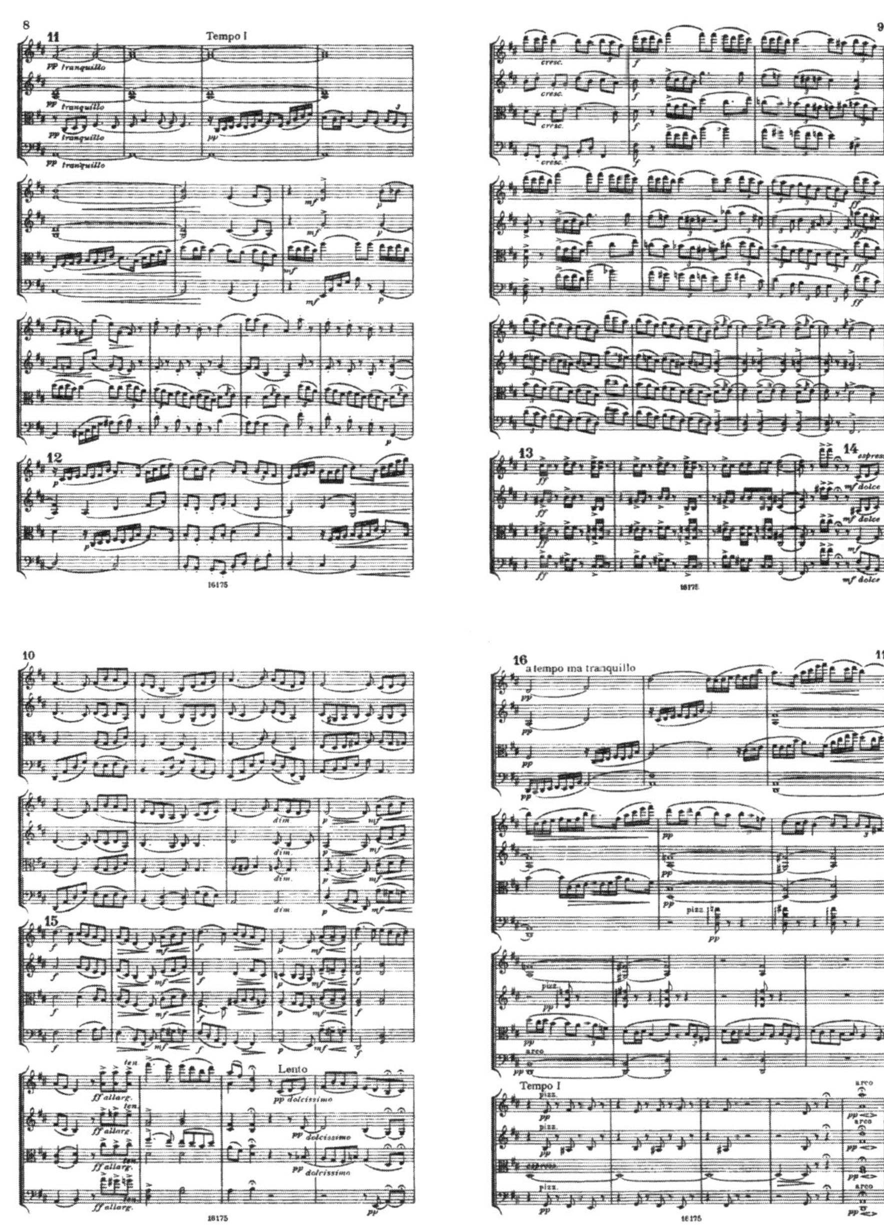

Printed in England by Augener Ltd. Acton Lane, London, W. 4

MurMure/Shopot is a performance in which musicians play from inside a wall. They wear, as it were, a wall. Performed for the Moscow Biennale 2015, the work was born from an interest in thinking about the ubiquitous, almost constant performances of self we maintain and enact in our networked reality. In contrast to this constant management of our profile, the performance attempts to use concealment as a methodology. The performance simultaneously hints at a contradiction between the anonymity of the producers of the objects that we use to perform these public selves, versus the innate desire within the self to be known, to be recognised.

Honoré δ'O — The Ten Commandments

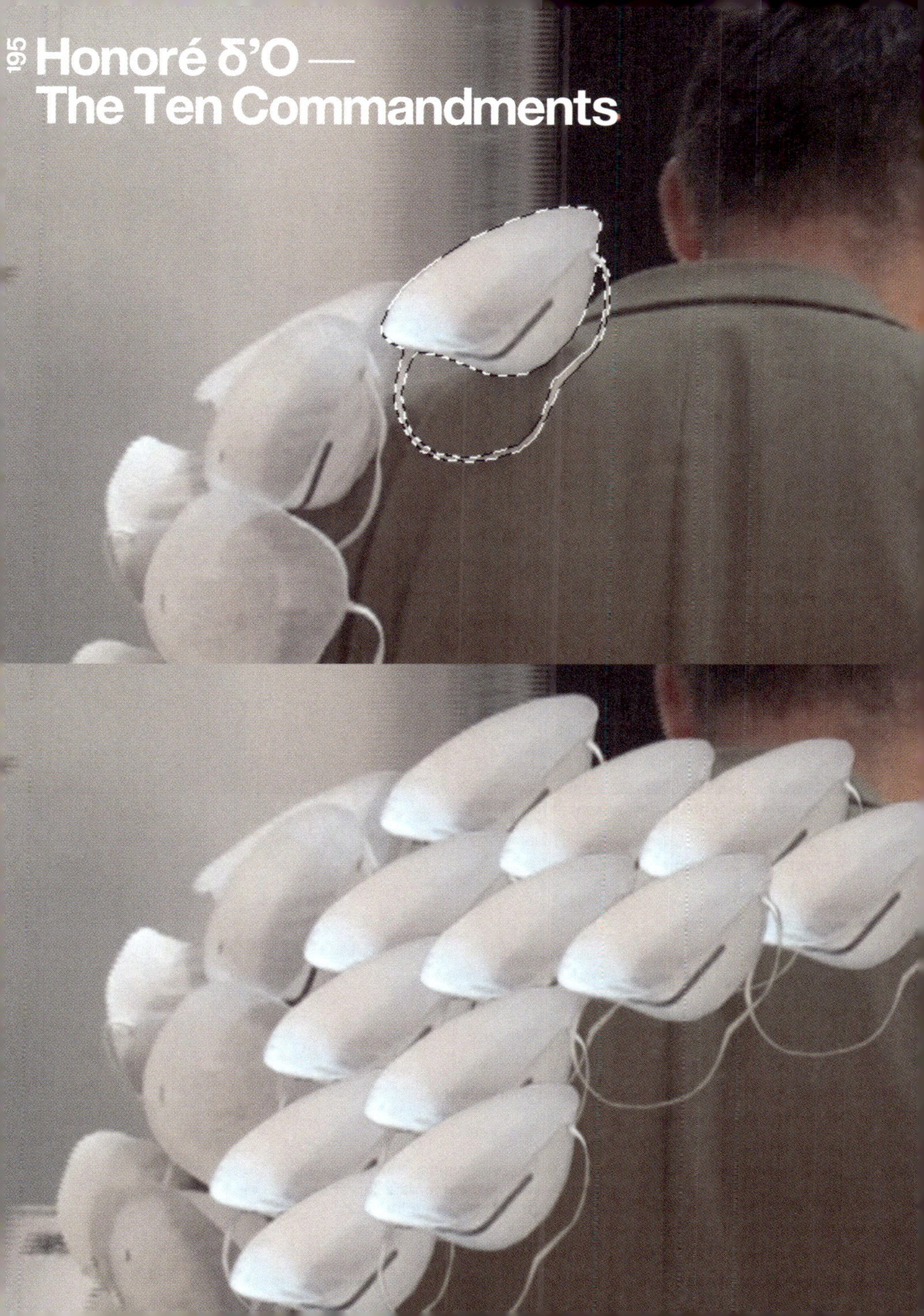

(01) 02 03 04 05 06 07 08 09 10 11 12 13
(01) 02 03 04 05 06 07 08 09 10

14 15 16 17

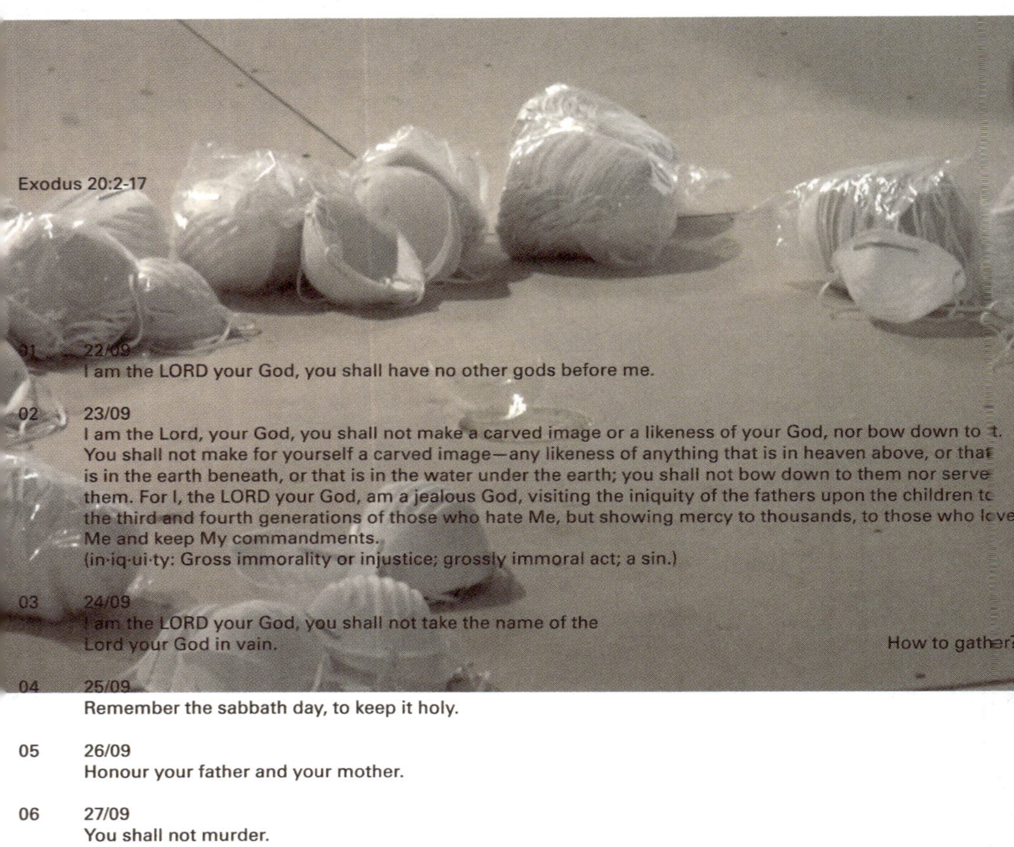

Exodus 20:2-17

01 22/09
I am the LORD your God, you shall have no other gods before me.

02 23/09
I am the Lord, your God, you shall not make a carved image or a likeness of your God, nor bow down to it.
You shall not make for yourself a carved image—any likeness of anything that is in heaven above, or that
is in the earth beneath, or that is in the water under the earth; you shall not bow down to them nor serve
them. For I, the LORD your God, am a jealous God, visiting the iniquity of the fathers upon the children to
the third and fourth generations of those who hate Me, but showing mercy to thousands, to those who love
Me and keep My commandments.
(in·iq·ui·ty: Gross immorality or injustice; grossly immoral act; a sin.)

03 24/09
I am the LORD your God, you shall not take the name of the
Lord your God in vain.

How to gather?

04 25/09
Remember the sabbath day, to keep it holy.

05 26/09
Honour your father and your mother.

06 27/09
You shall not murder.

07 28/09
You shall not commit adultery.

08 29/09
You shall not steal.

09 30/09
You shall not bear false witness against your neighbour.

10 31/09
You shall not covet.
You shall not covet your neighbour's house; you shall not covet
your neighbour's wife, nor his male servant, nor his female servant,
nor his ox, nor his donkey, nor anything that is your neighbour's.

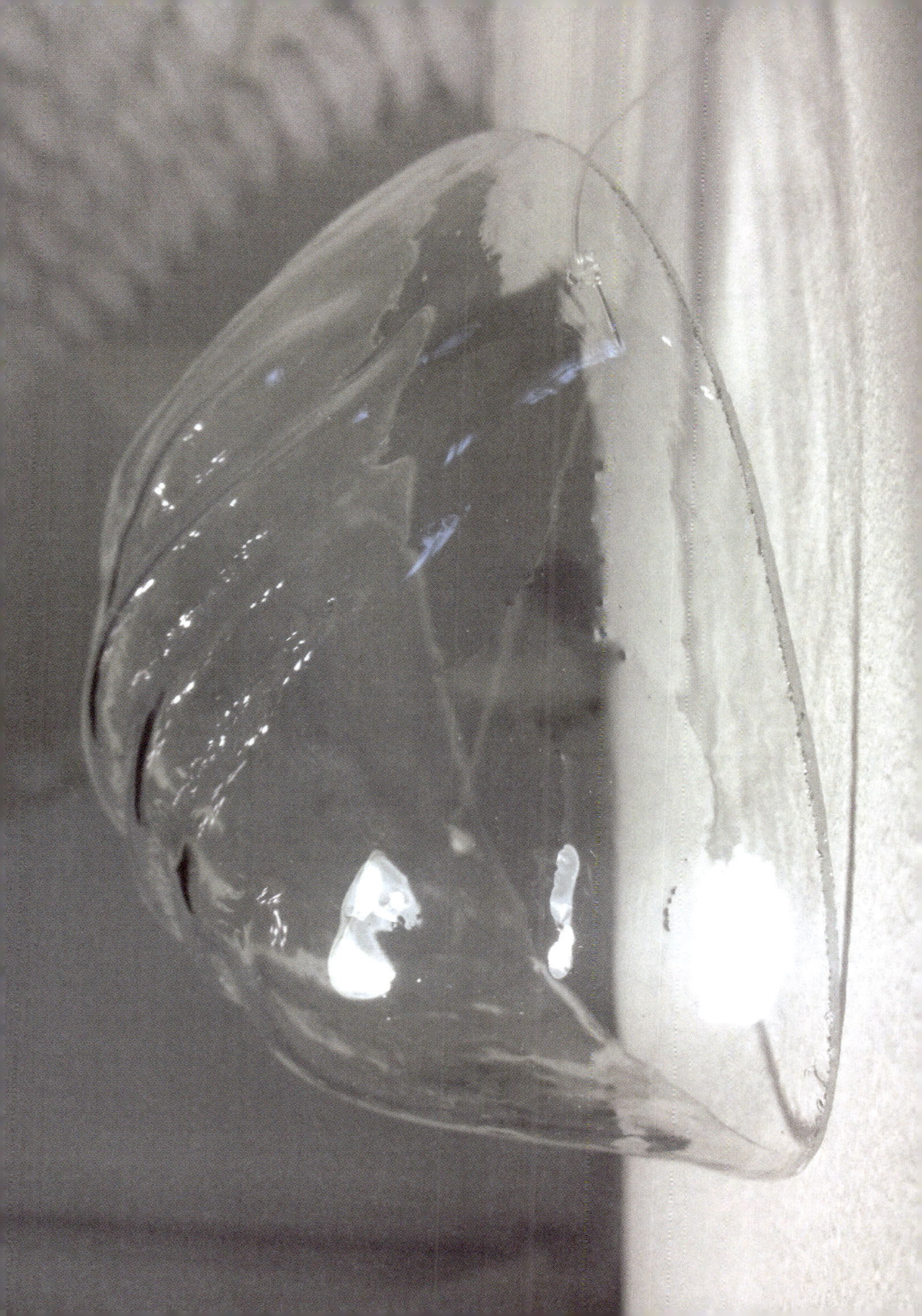

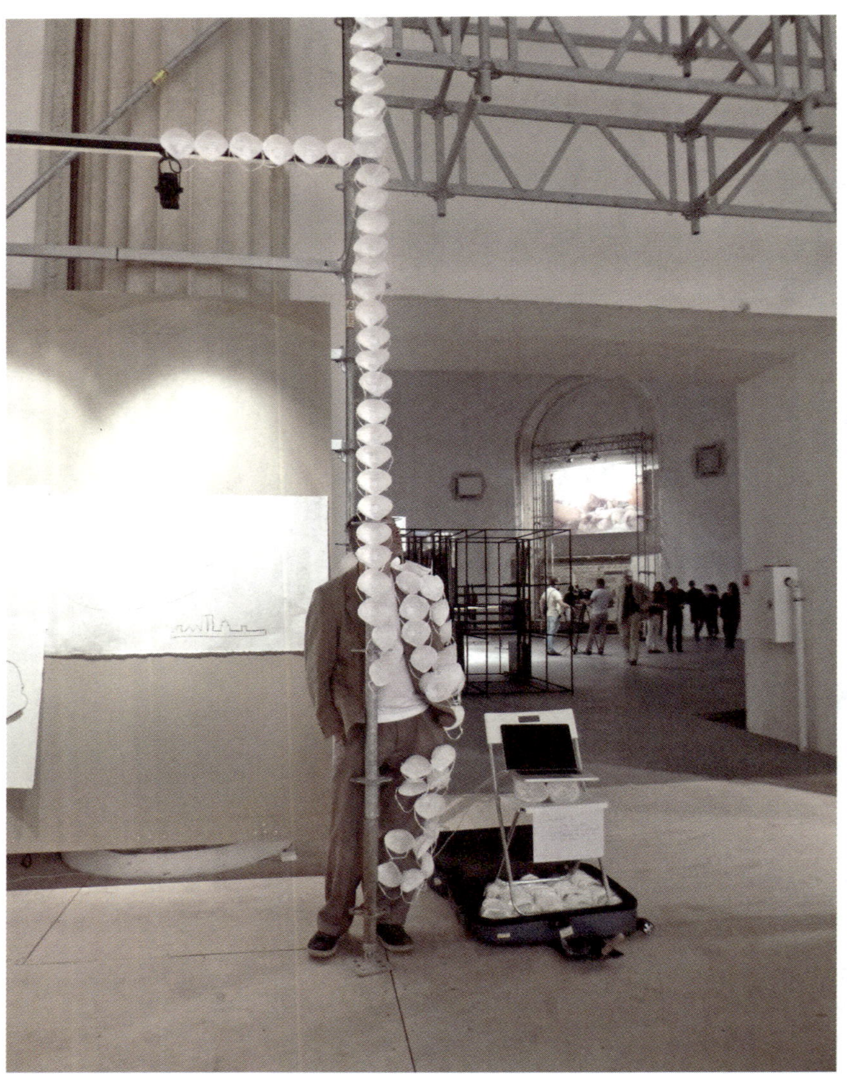

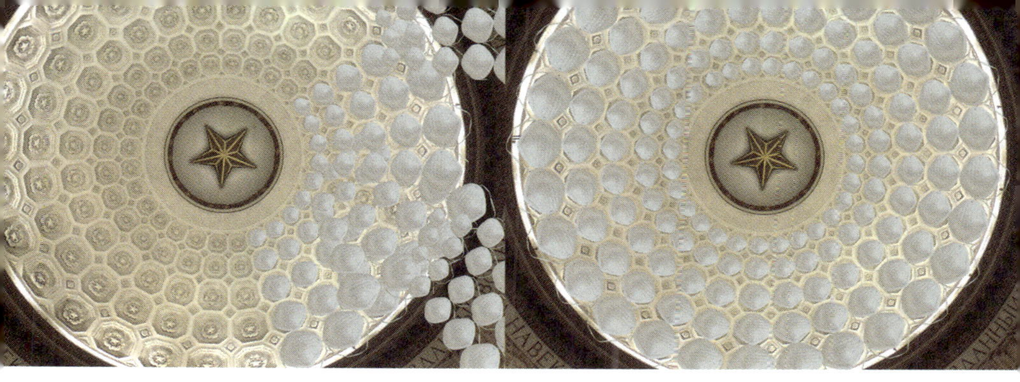

10 days of exhibition > 10 Commandments
1 Commandment / day

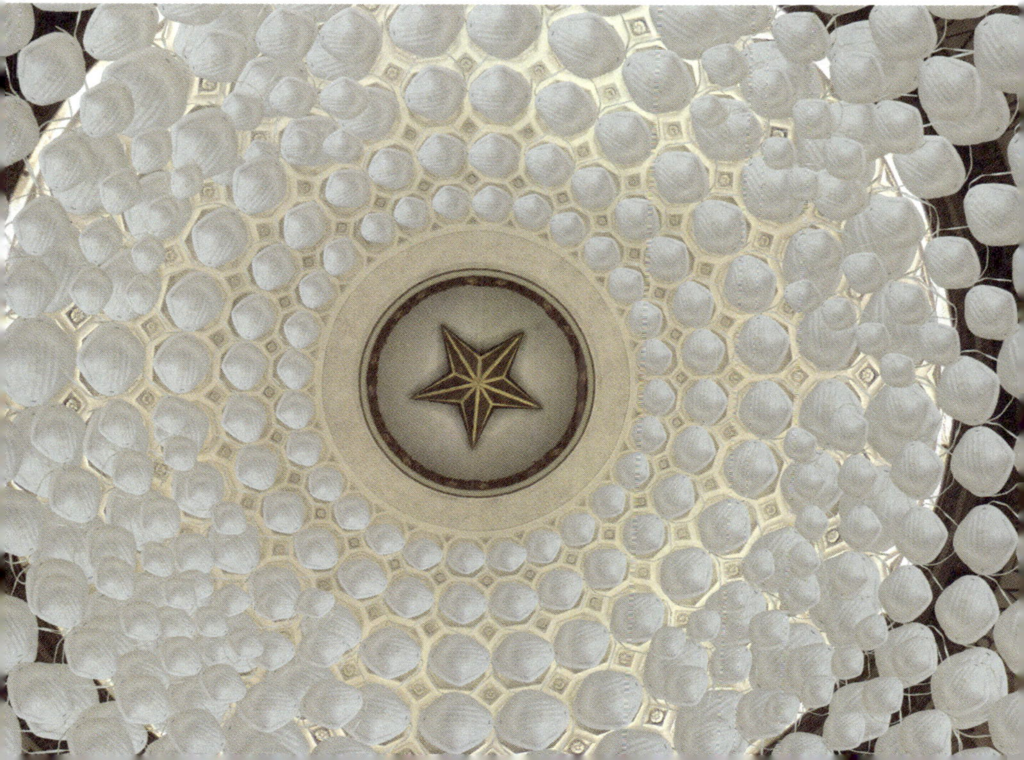

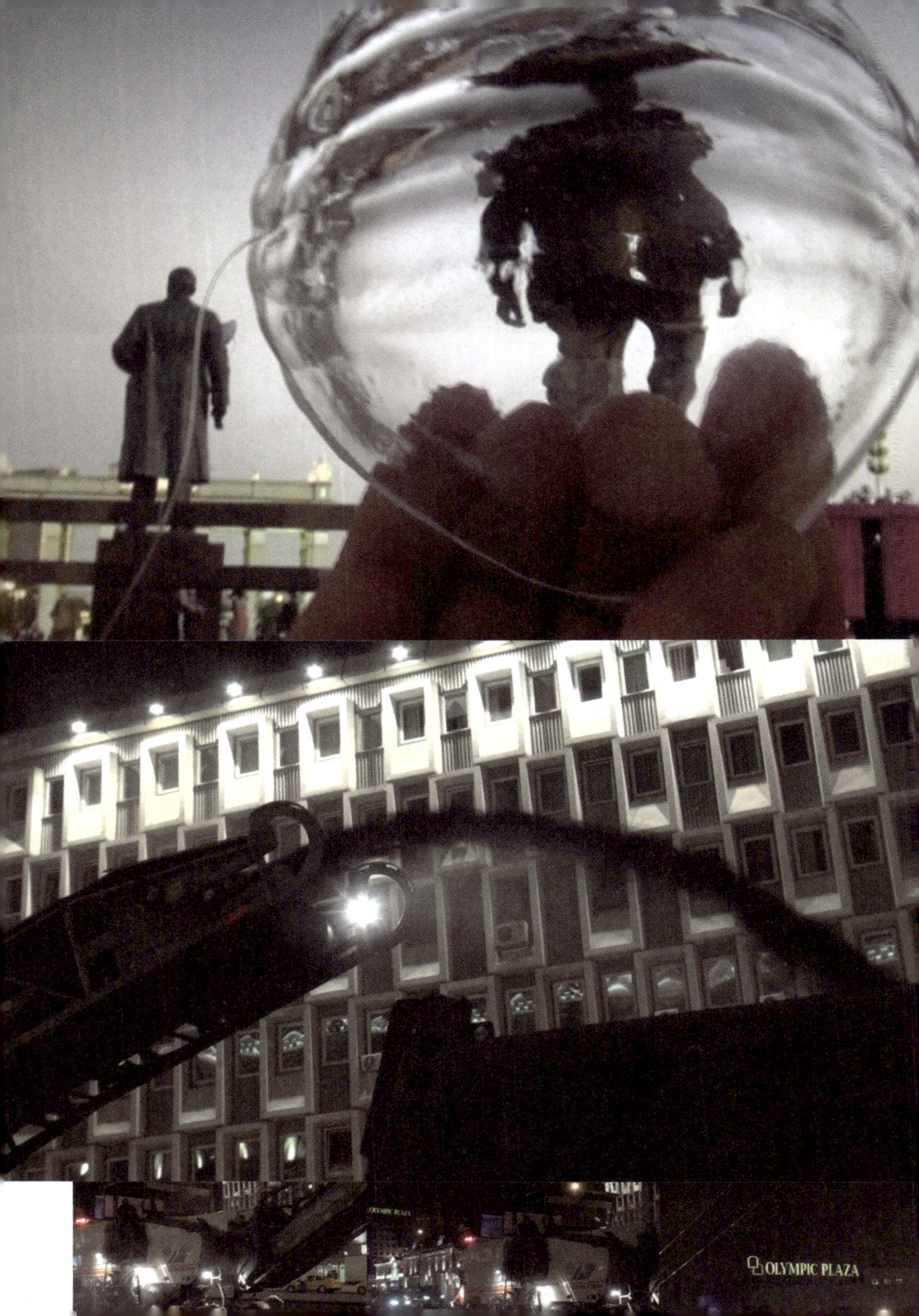
OLYMPIC PLAZA

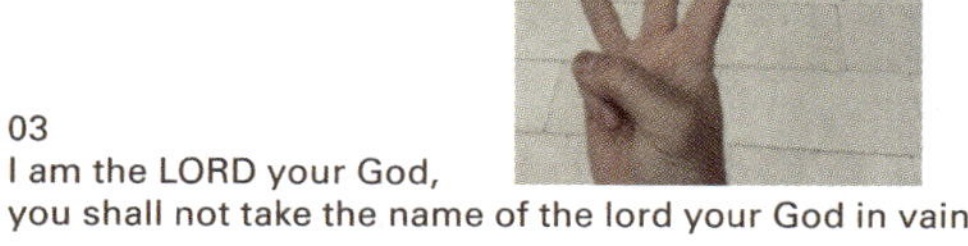

03 24/09

I am the LORD your God,
you shall not take the name of the lord your God in vain.

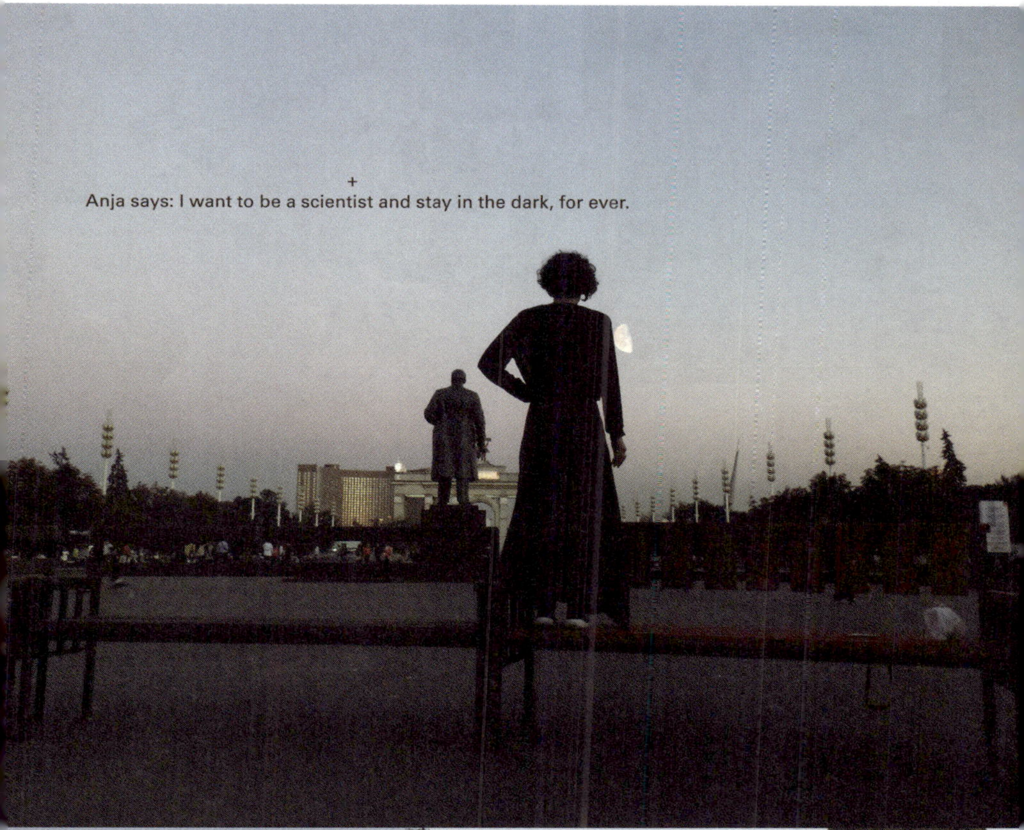

+
Anja says: I want to be a scientist and stay in the dark, for ever.

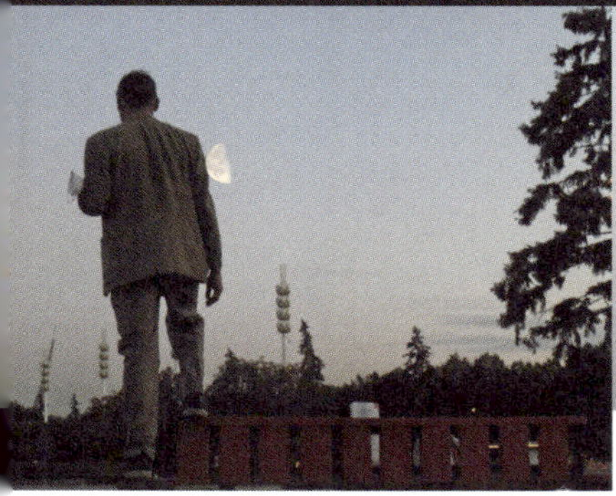

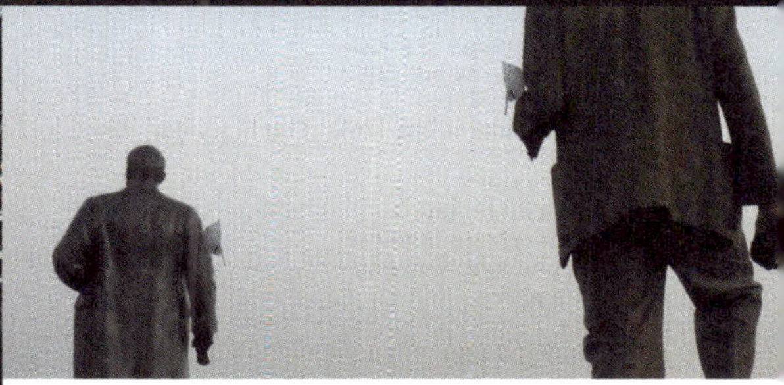

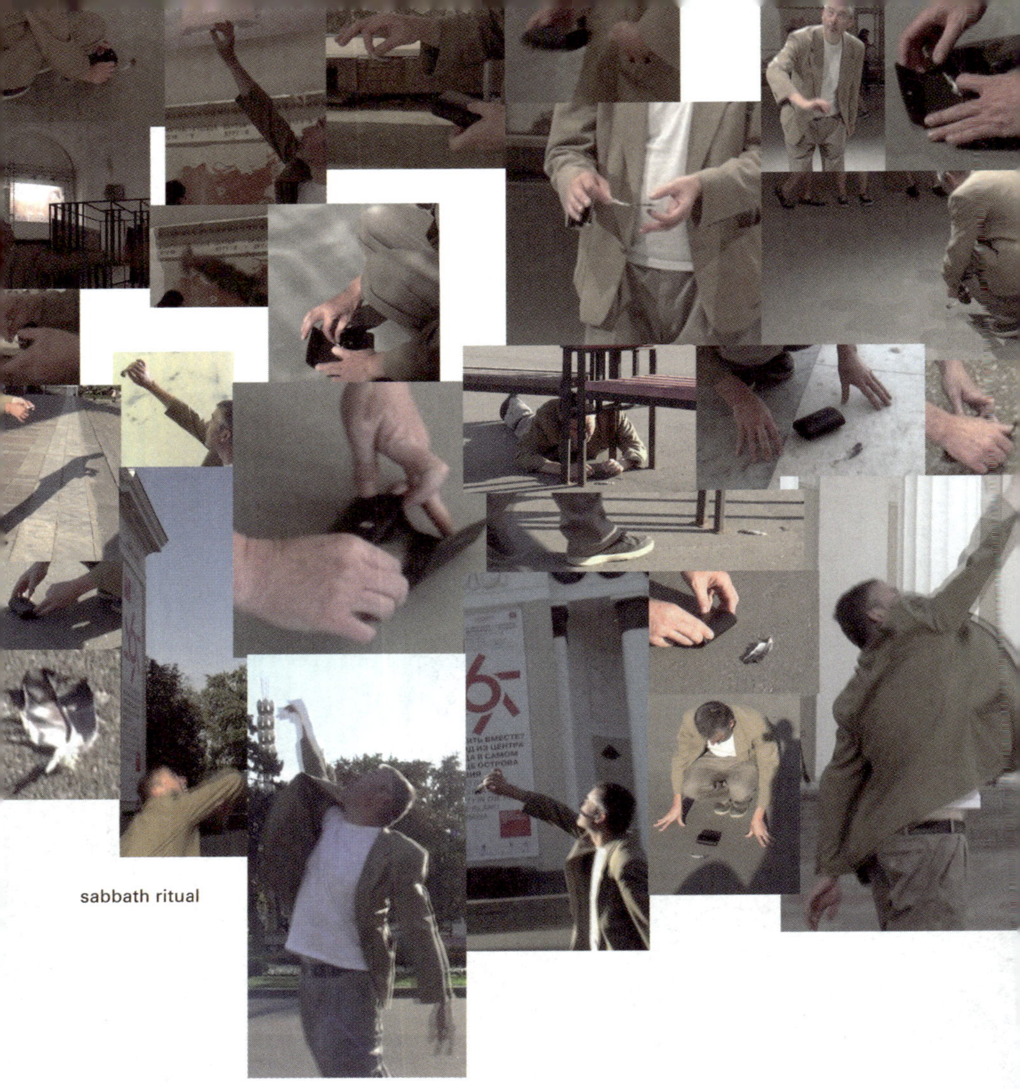

sabbath ritual

Throw the plume to the sky
Let the plume fly and fall
Find the plume
Rescue the plume and cover it up in a safety box
Walk
Come to a halt
Open the safety box
Throw the plume to the sky
Let the plume fly and fall
Find the plume
....
Continue to do so

spasibo

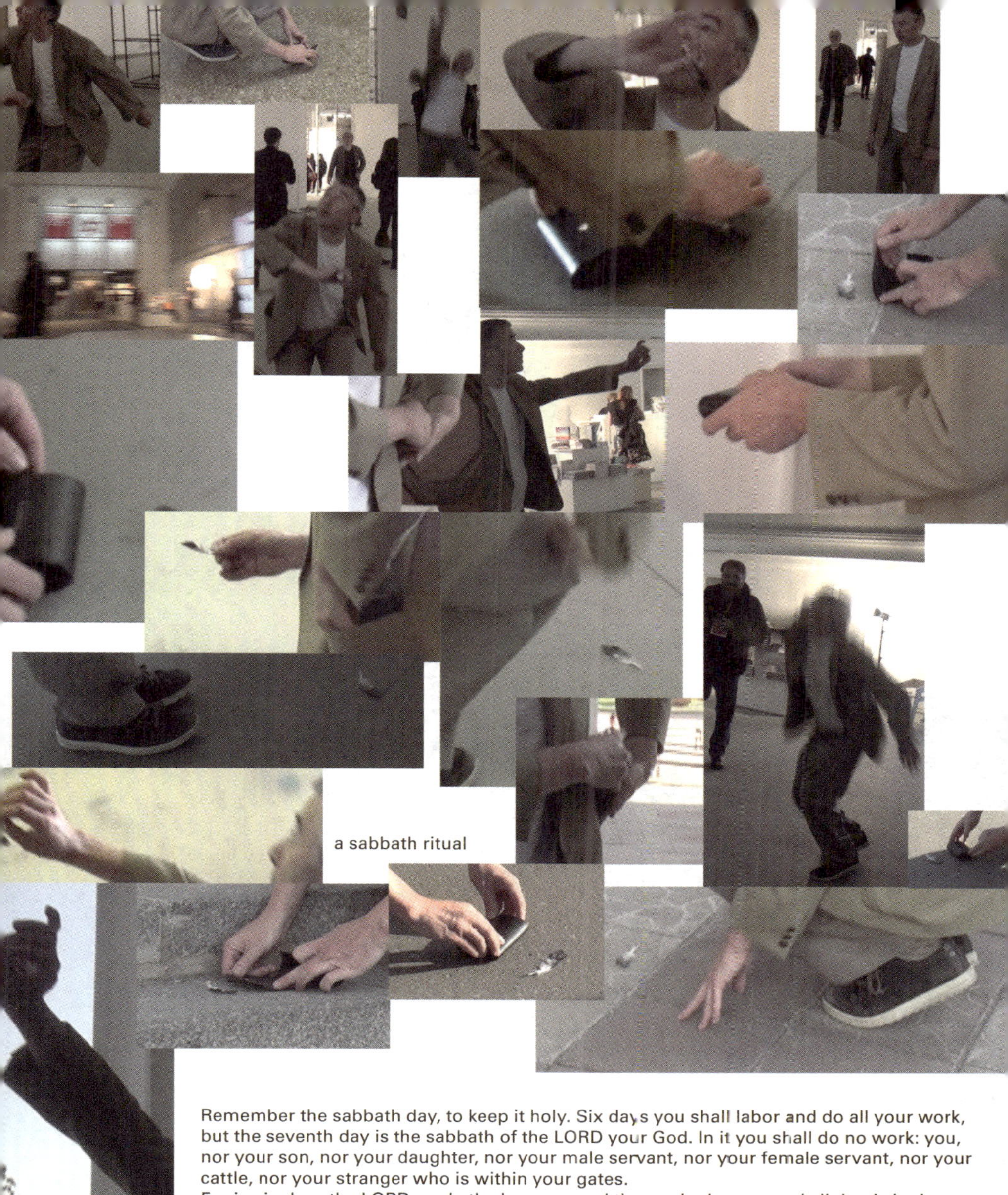

a sabbath ritual

Remember the sabbath day, to keep it holy. Six days you shall labor and do all your work, but the seventh day is the sabbath of the LORD your God. In it you shall do no work: you, nor your son, nor your daughter, nor your male servant, nor your female servant, nor your cattle, nor your stranger who is within your gates.
For in six days the LORD made the heavens and the earth, the sea, and all that is in them, and rested the seventh day. Therefore the LORD blessed the sabbath day and hallowed it. Kak dela? Horosho.

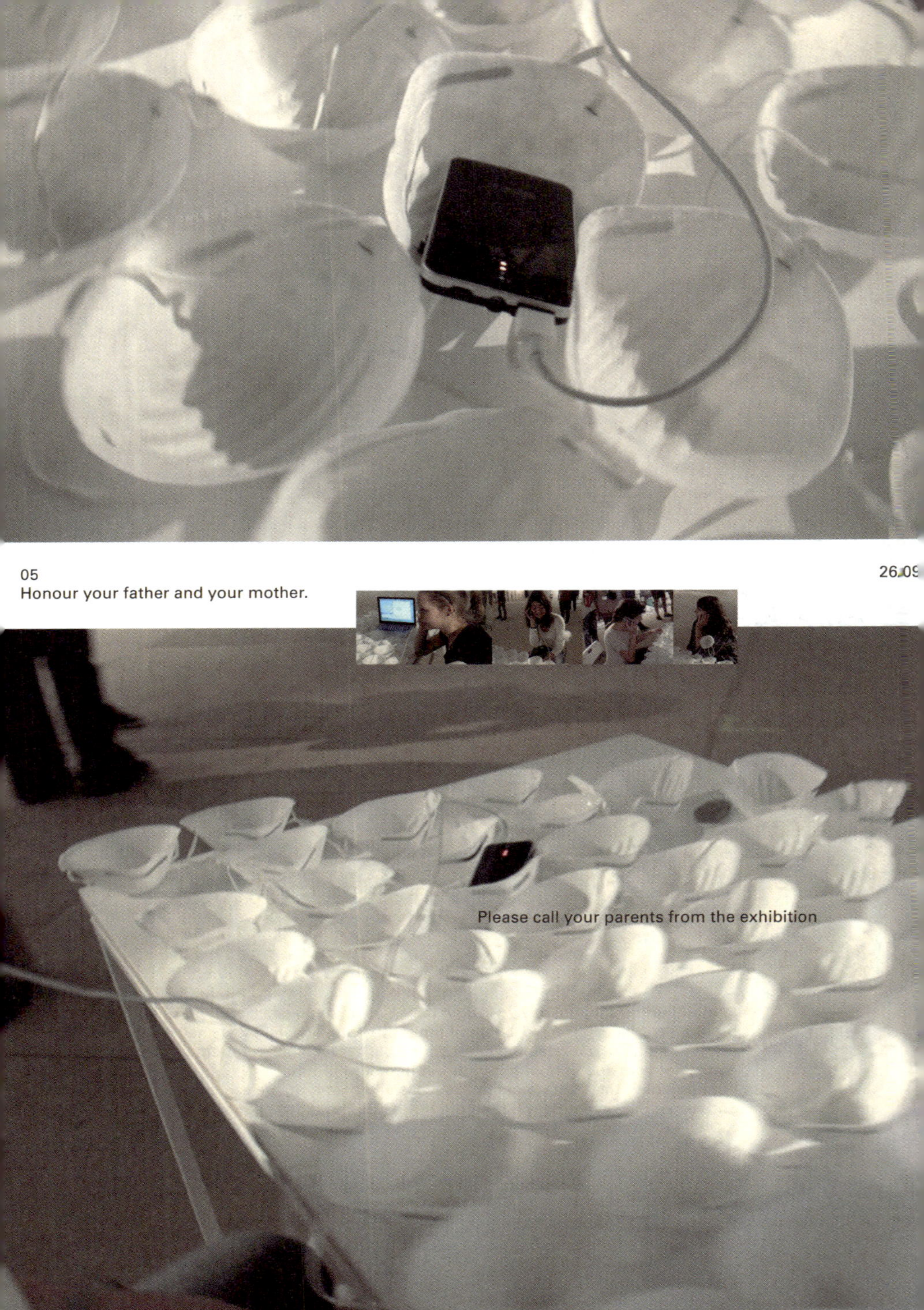
05
Honour your father and your mother.
26.09
Please call your parents from the exhibition

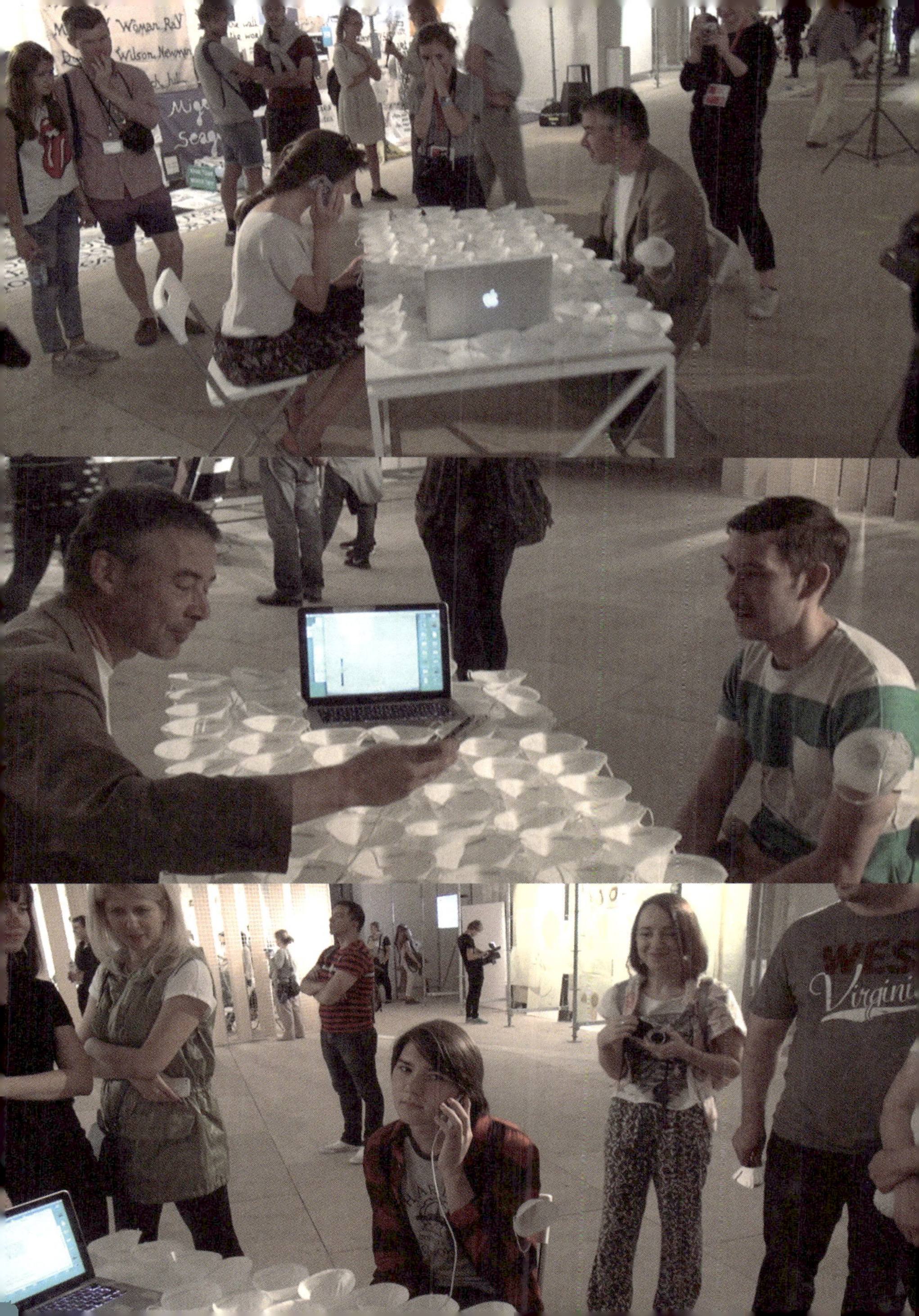
Woman Ray
Wilson Newman

06
You shall not murder.

27/09

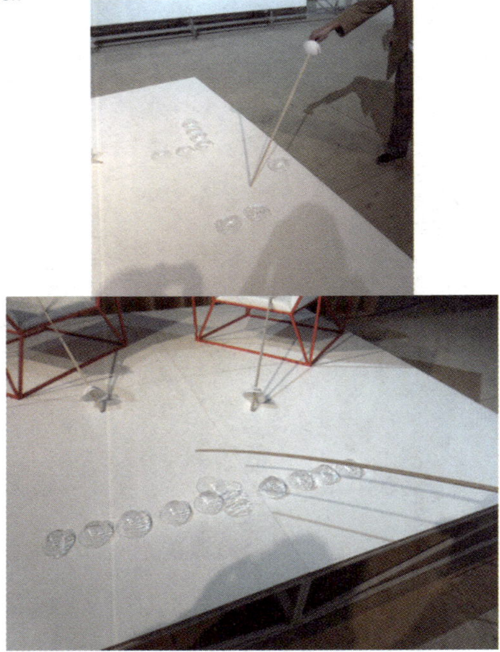

Play 'Murdering' alone
Choose a dress-sword
Turn the ten glass masks one by one
Play the game till one glass breaks
You are the victime

WAIT

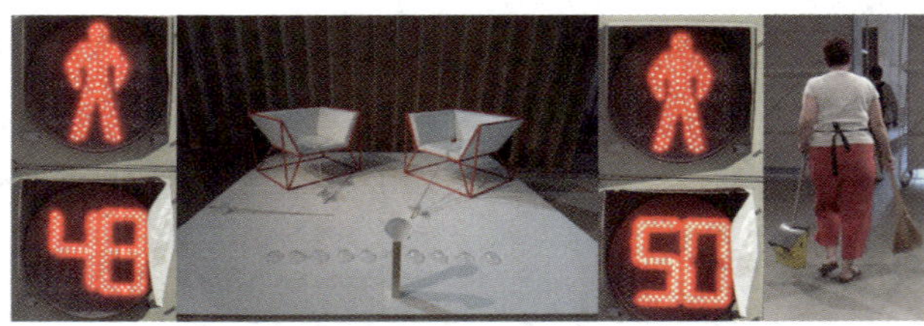

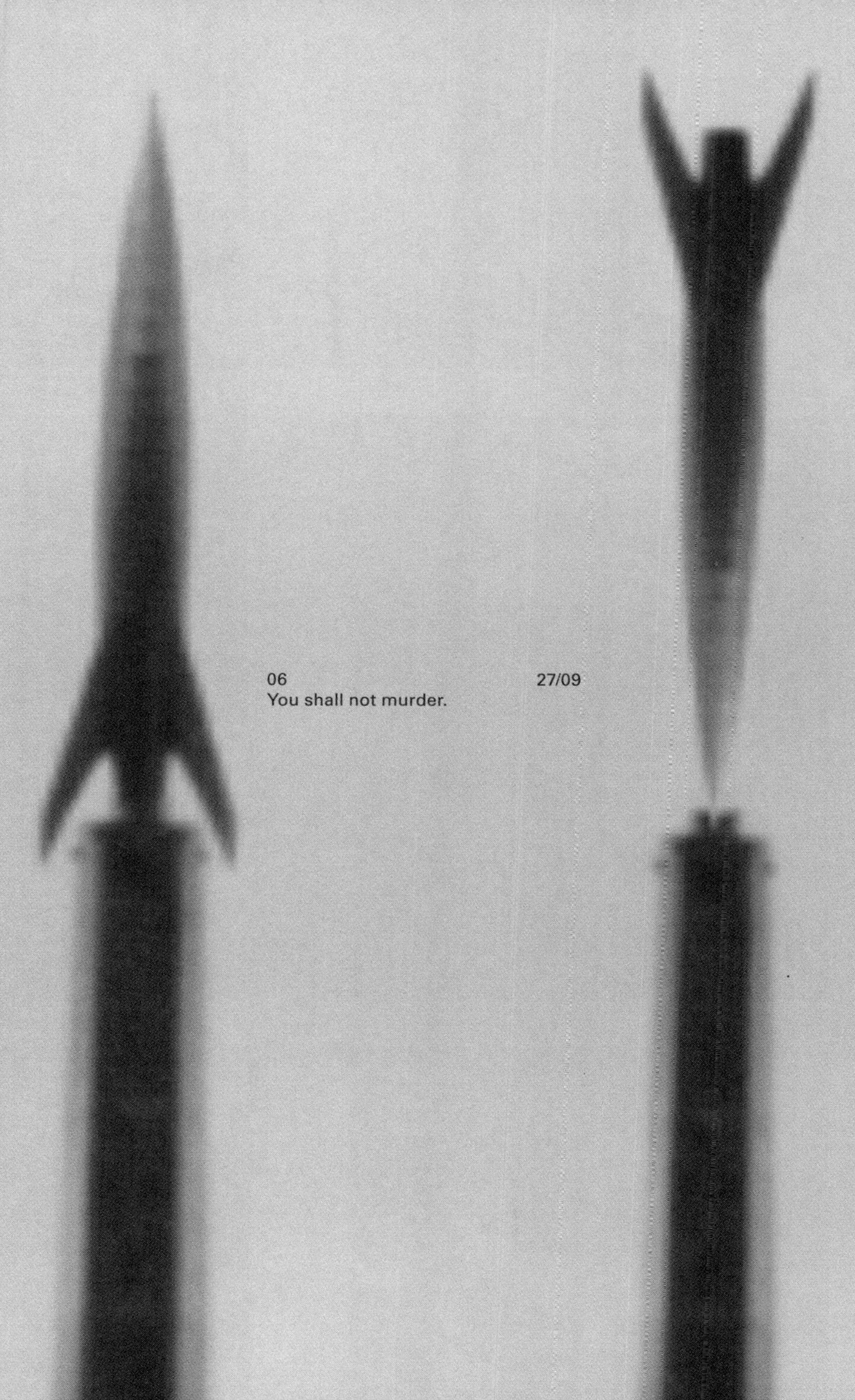

06 27/09

You shall not murder.

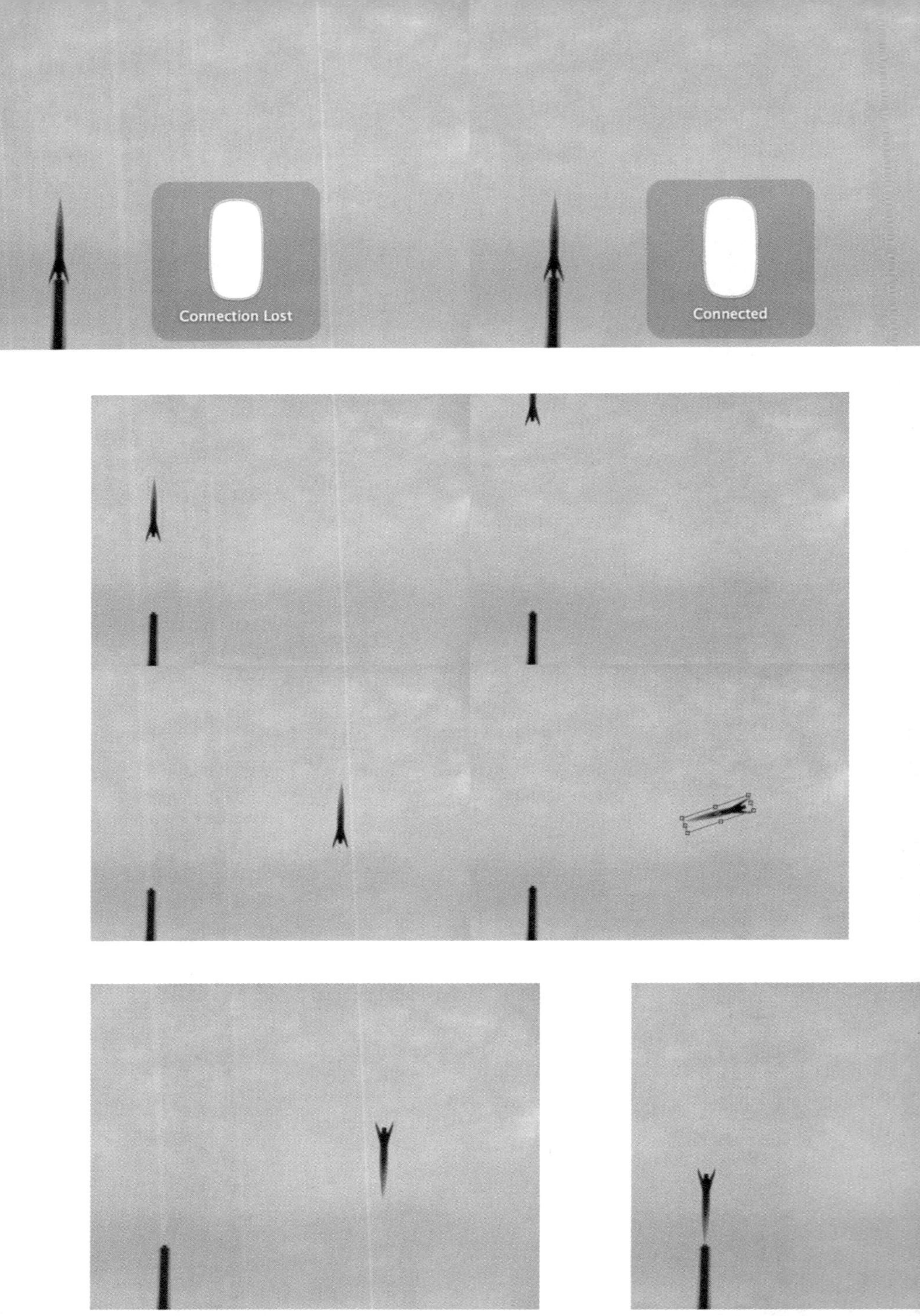
Connection Lost
Connected

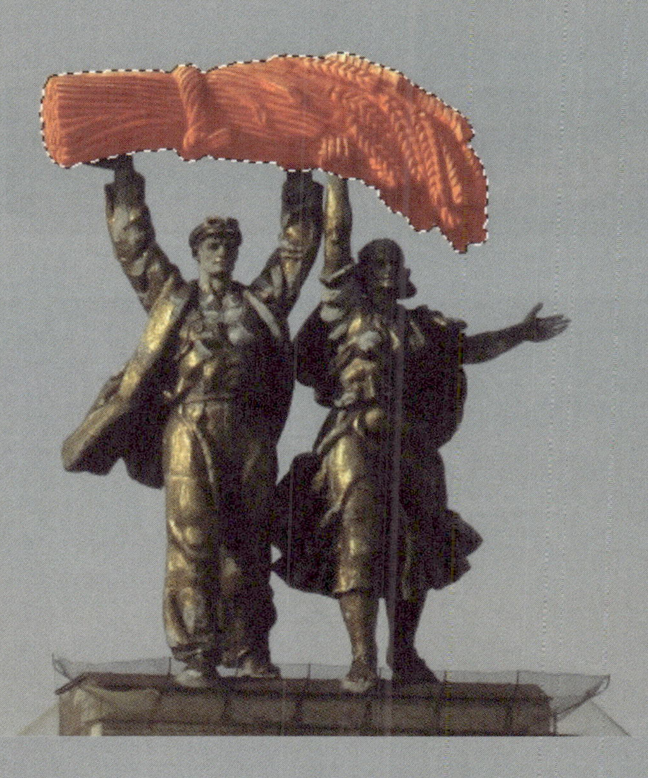

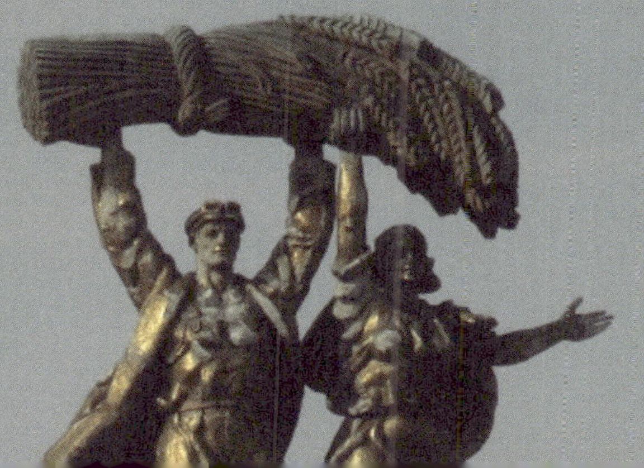

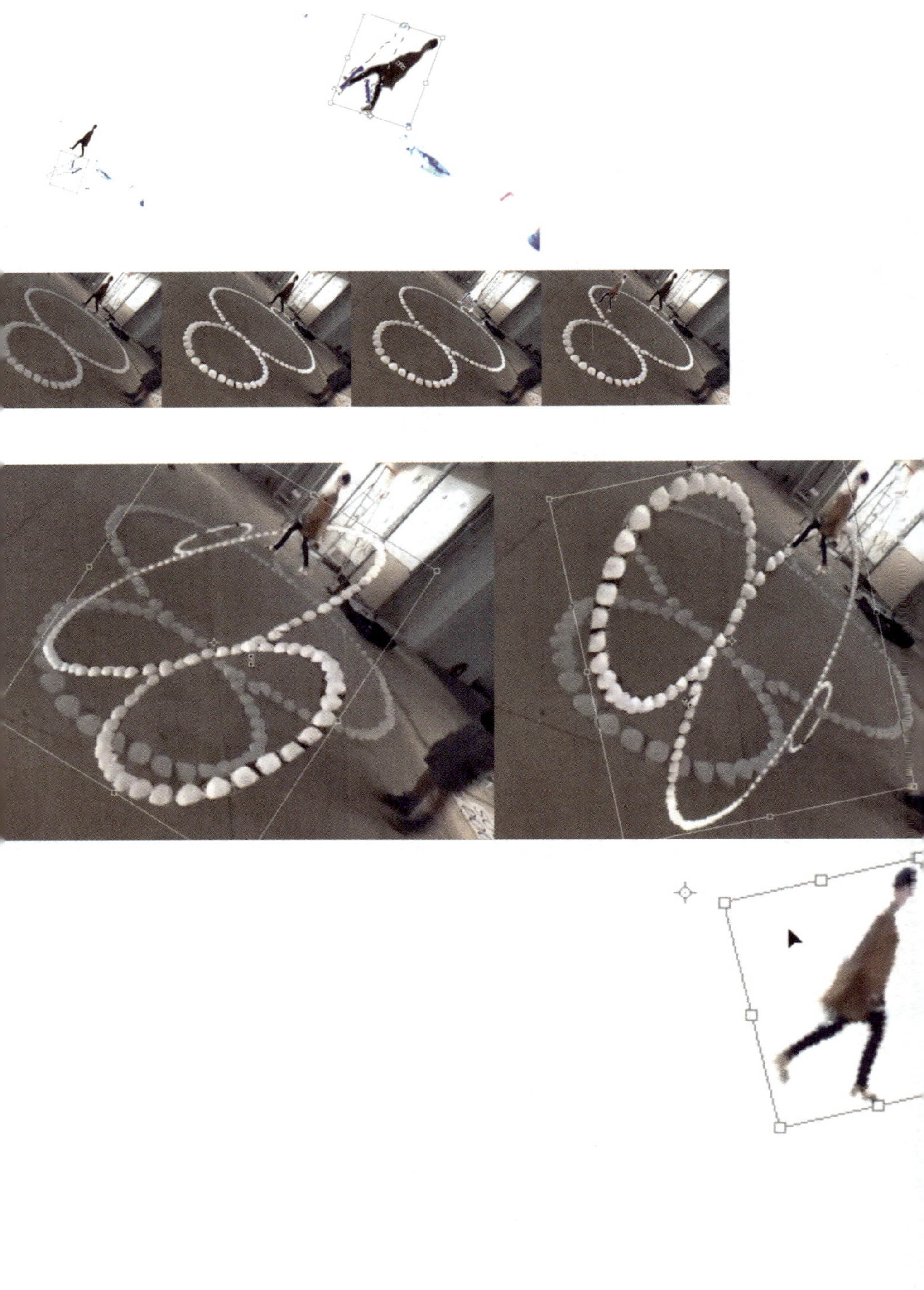

08
You shall not steal.

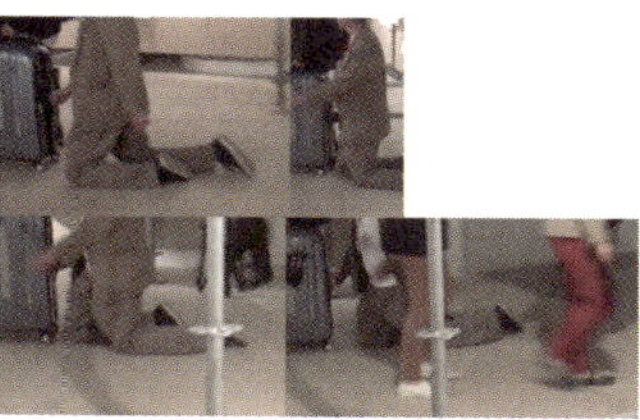

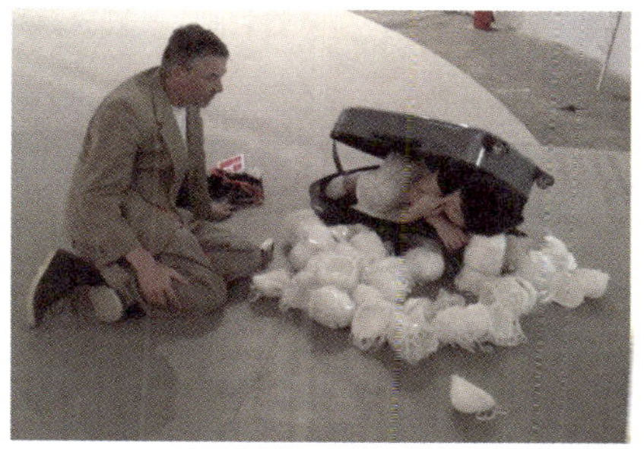

Theft Through, with Anastasiya Yarovenko

Ho-Homage to Michelangelo Pistoletto's *Terzo Paradiso*

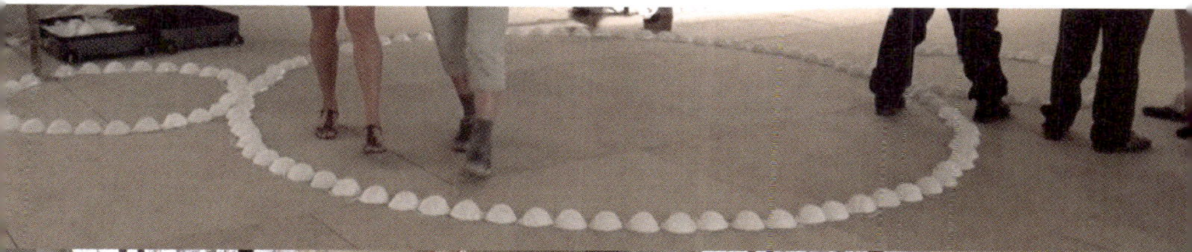

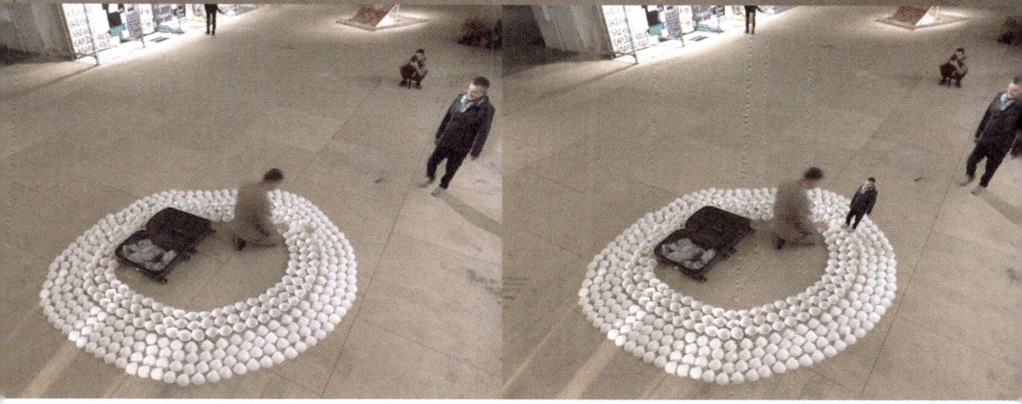

Turning the masks, with Fabrice Hybert

Turning the masks
One by one
From center to periphery and periphery to center
Stay silent
Move slowly
Focus on the spiral
Spiral on the spiral
Ritualise the continuity

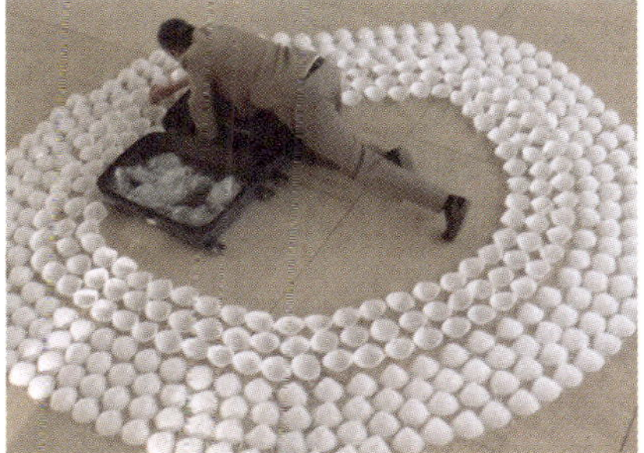

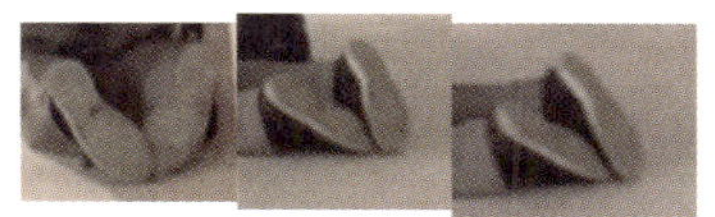

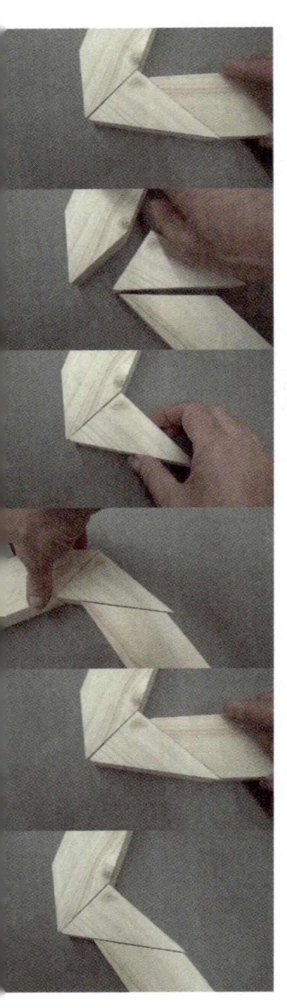
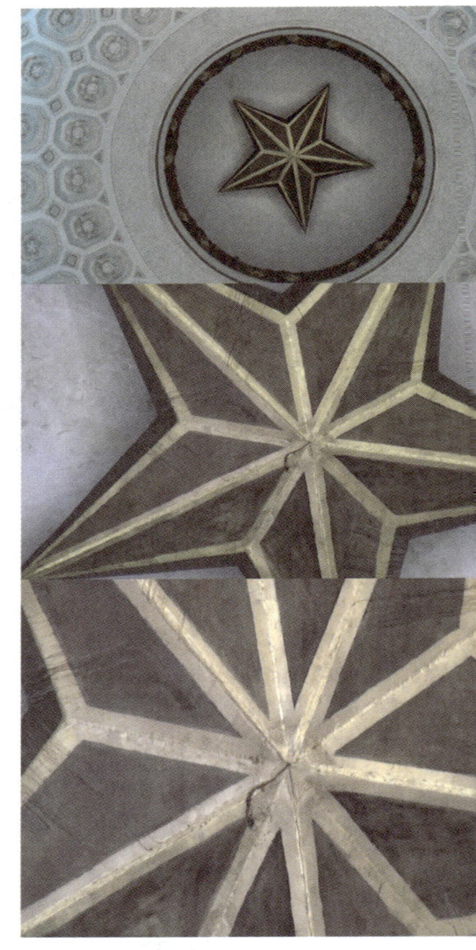
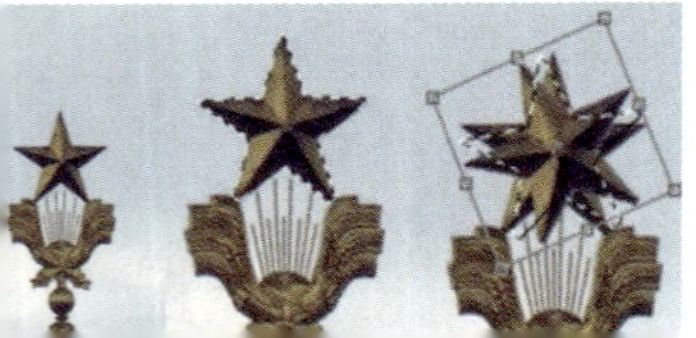

09
You shall not bear false witness against your neighbour.

30/09

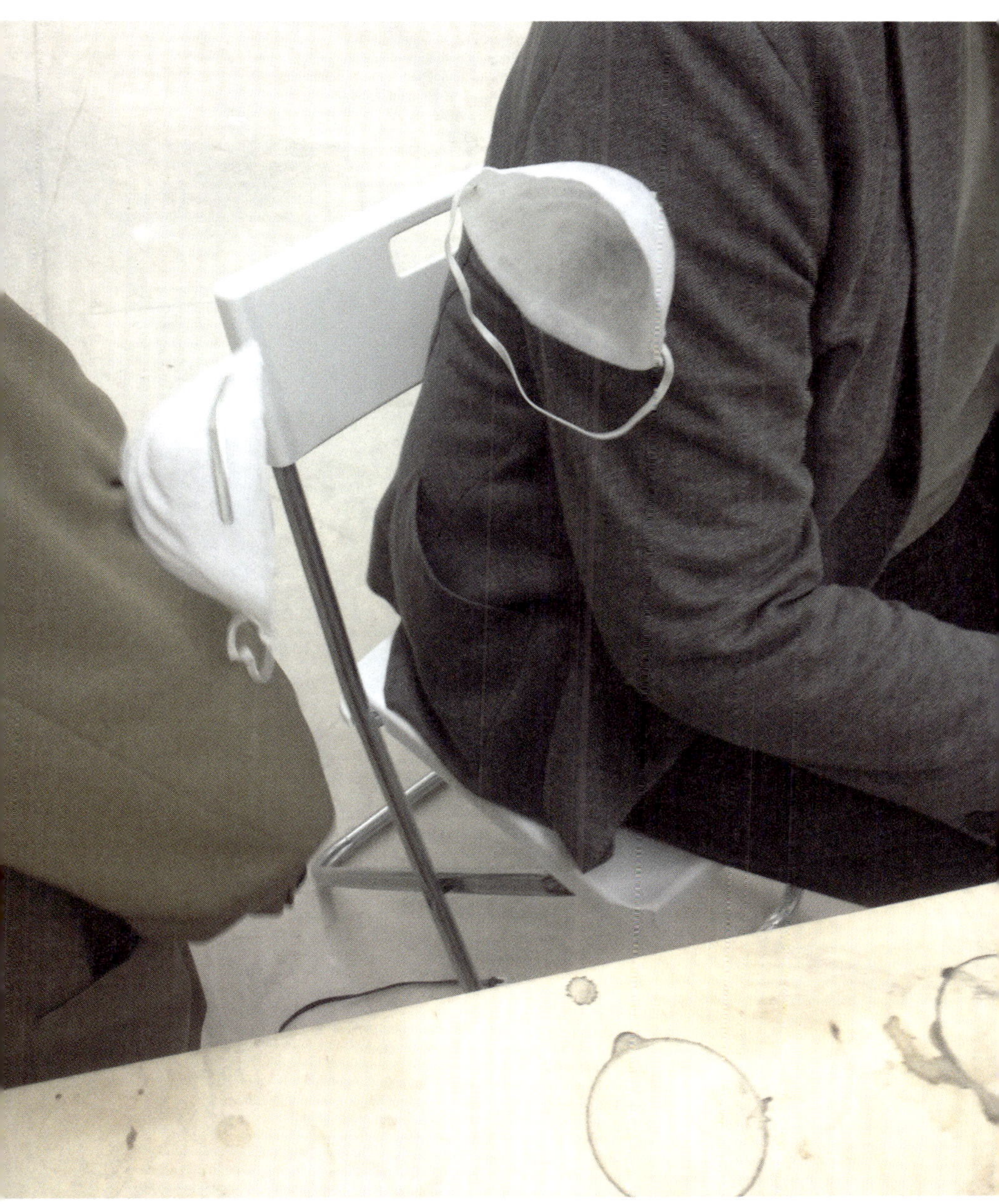

Vaast Colson —
Ten Side Notes as Warm Up

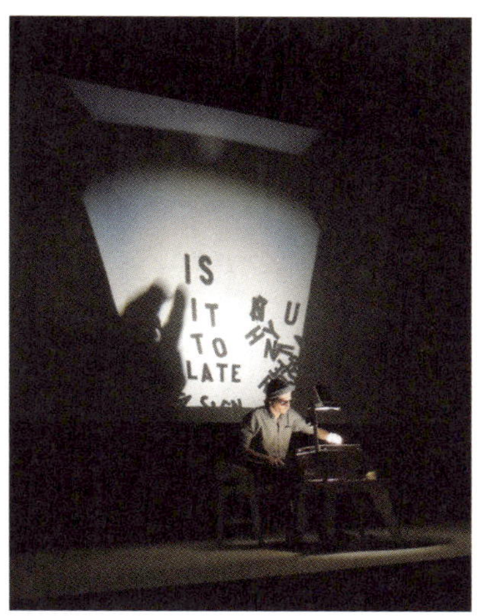

Séance I,
22nd September 2015

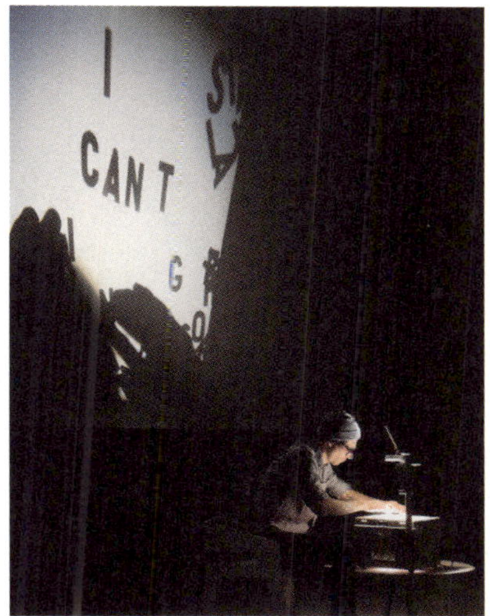

Séance II,
23rd September 2015

Otto Snoek, 22 September – 01 October 2015

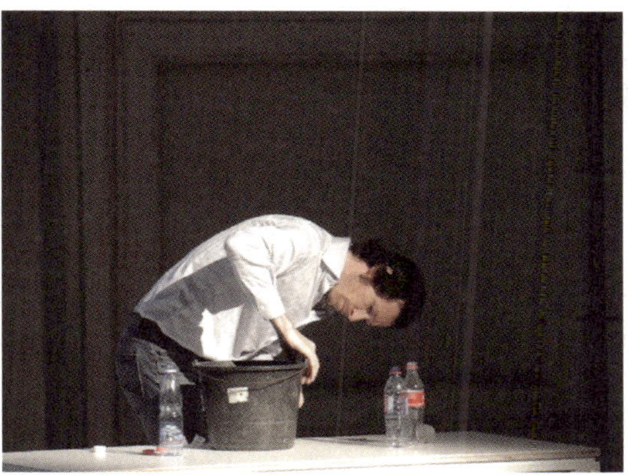

How to Produce a Wishing Well,
24th September 2015

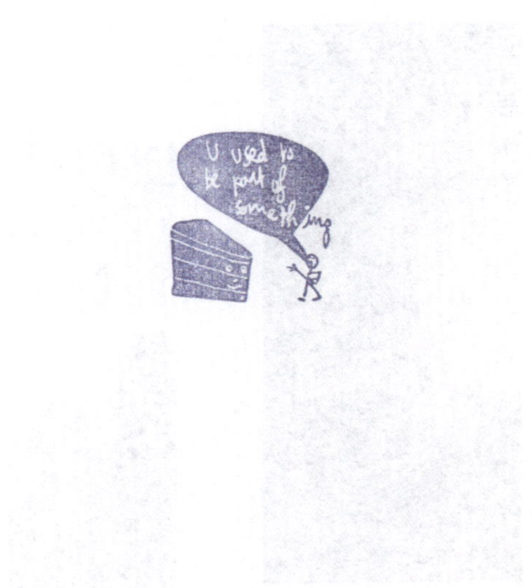

500 times White Space,
25th September 2015

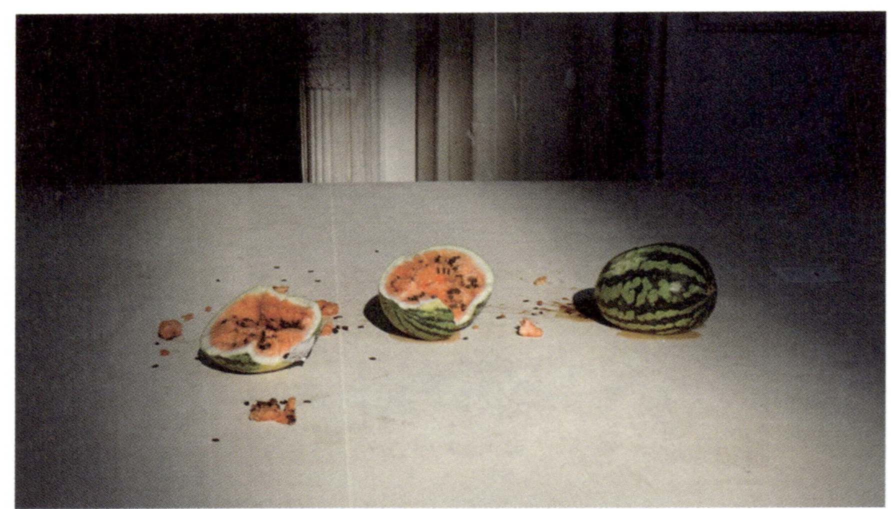

Eventually Melons hit the floor,
26th September 2015

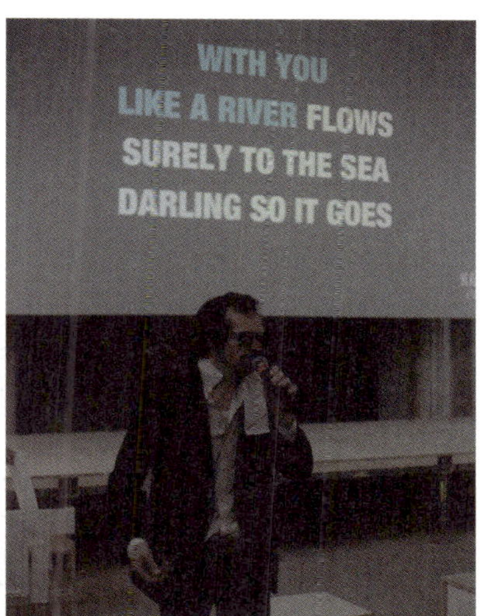

Falling in Love With Elvis,
28th September 2015

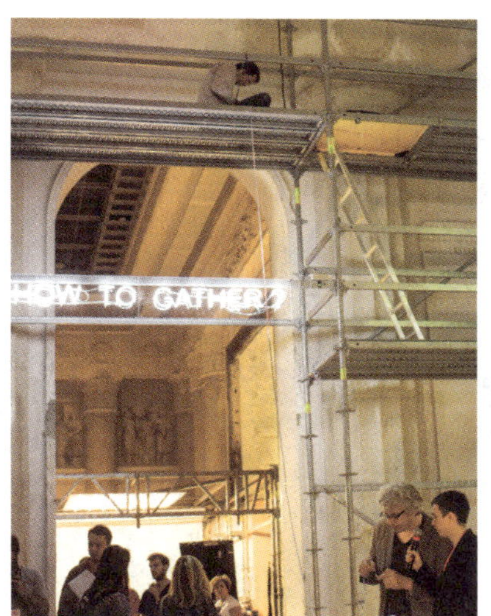

First Orbit,
27th September 2015

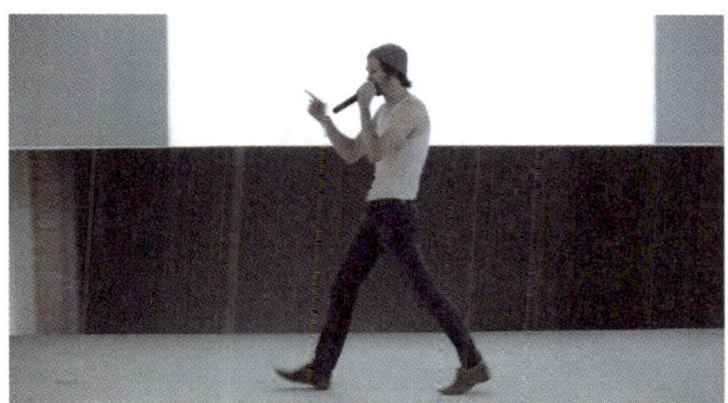

Onstageoffstagededicatingsongsdilemma revisited,
29th September 2015

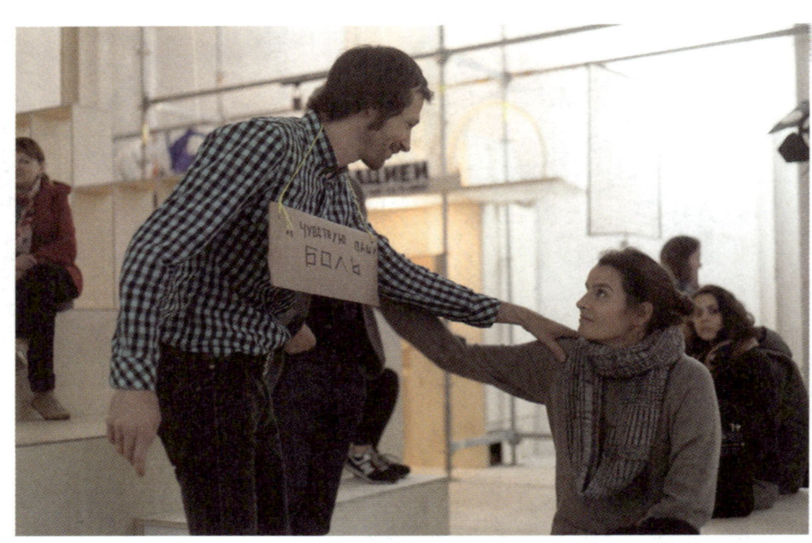

I Feel Your Pain,
30th September 2015

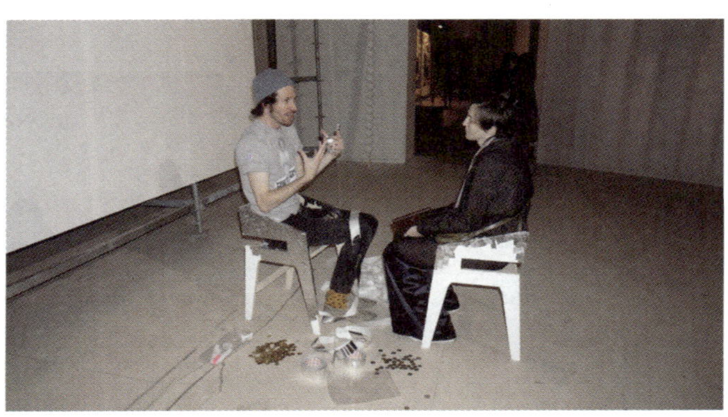

Euro Chair – Ruble Chair,
1st October 2015

Andrey Kuzkin — Balloons and Nails

Every other day, visitors encountered Andrey Kuzkin sitting on a stool in front of Pavilion No. 1 at VDNKh. Two boxes next to him were filled with white balloons and nails. Each visitor got offered one nail and a balloon inflated by the artist. [Marie Egger]

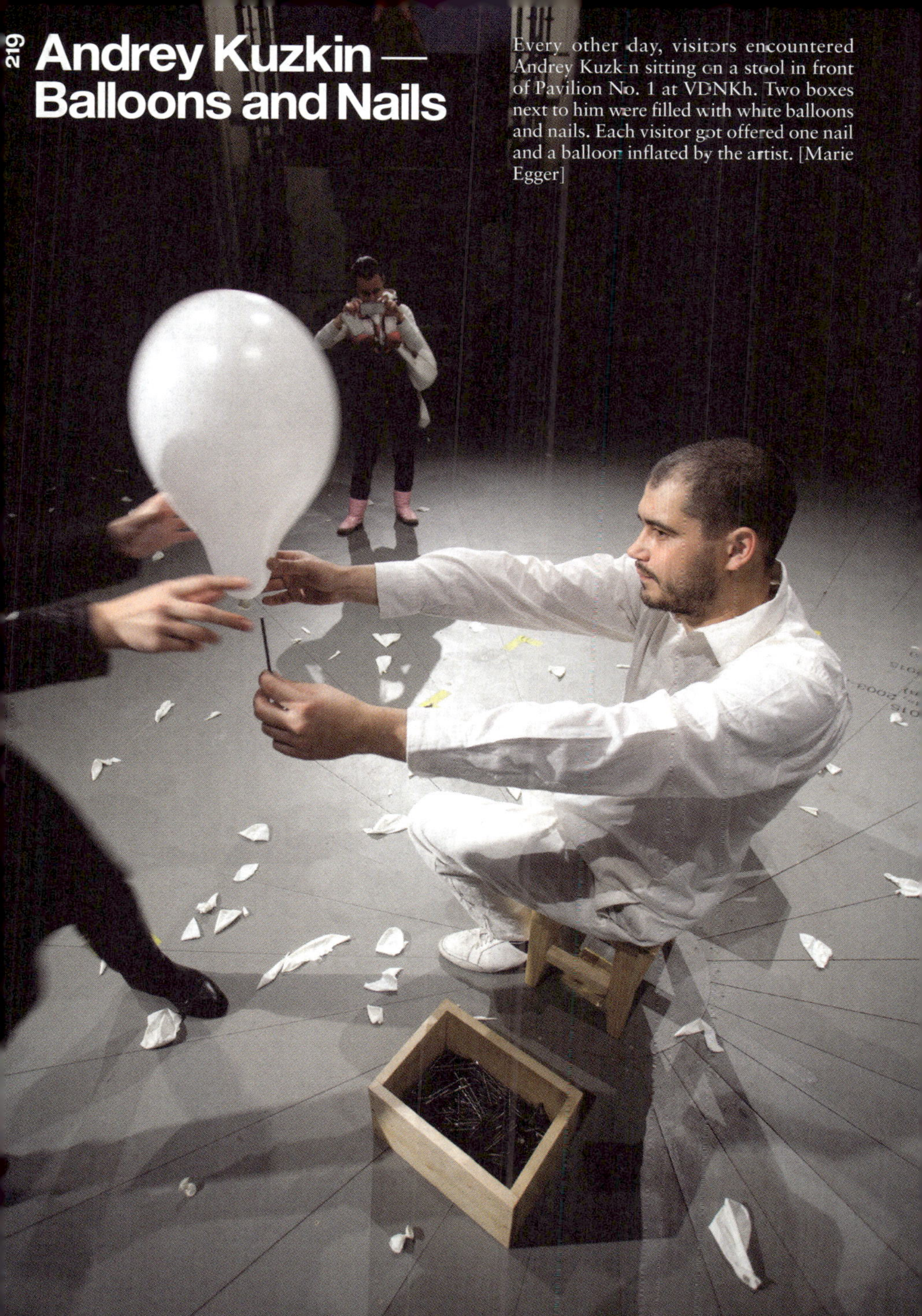

Isa Genzken — Die kleine Bushaltestelle (Gerüstbau)

The Biennale asked four artists for an image, that this might also be a capacity and focus of artists, defined as such, rather than a generic 'artwork'. Isa Genzken was one of the four.

This image was extracted from Isa Genzken's video *Die kleine Bushaltestelle (Gerüstbau)* ['The small bus stop (scaffolding)']. It shows two prostitutes, mimed by Isa Genzken and the artist Kai Althoff. Their conversation about love, acceptance and rejection is one of several episodes in the video, in which the two change characters and appear in various identities and situations.

Isa Genzken glances at us with a whimsical smile. Wearing a see-through bra, a wig and sheer pink stockings she drinks a glass of champagne. With Kai Althoff whining next to her in such an extrovert manner that the scene becomes a parody in itself, Isa Genzken's image may be read as a joyful celebration of the liberty to live out one's creativity, sexuality, friendship and individuality. Placed in the central dome of Pavilion No. 1, the picture appeared somewhat distant and staged, challenging its proximity to local contexts. [Marie Egger]

PAPER GAME NO. 1[1]

The notion of togetherness also has a reverse side. How do you keep your own, individual voice within a community of collaborations? How to keep your own voice and your individual perspective in a world that consists largely of dense networks of social relations and professional and public opinions? Shouldn't our main questions these days be How to be alone with oneself? And what to do in that moment?

One point of view is not enough for two eyes. We need to look with both eyes.

And act together. Overcome our own egocentrism. And observe how ideas are born out of collective discussions. We need to face misunderstanding, rejection, opposing views, and thus affirm and refine our own selves.

To get a buzz from polyphony.

Often, a state of discomfort and frustration is a more fertile ground for expressing something and trying to change something. What, other than discomfort, forces us to fight?

What will be the outcome of that fight? Comfort? The power to causes changes in society needs no motivation—it is pure inspiration.

We only dream of comfort.
We must come to terms with that.

Alexander Zhuravlev
Anna Zhurba
Ivan Isaev
Sona Stepanyan
Maria Stepkina

1
This text is a result of the Young Curators Workshop, conceived by V-A-C Foundation as a discursive platform to reflect on the notion of togetherness. During their meetings, the participants came up with several contributions to this publication. This one evolved from a paper game where everyone wrote a short hand-written liner on a folded piece of paper, to form a consistent text once the paper is unfolded.

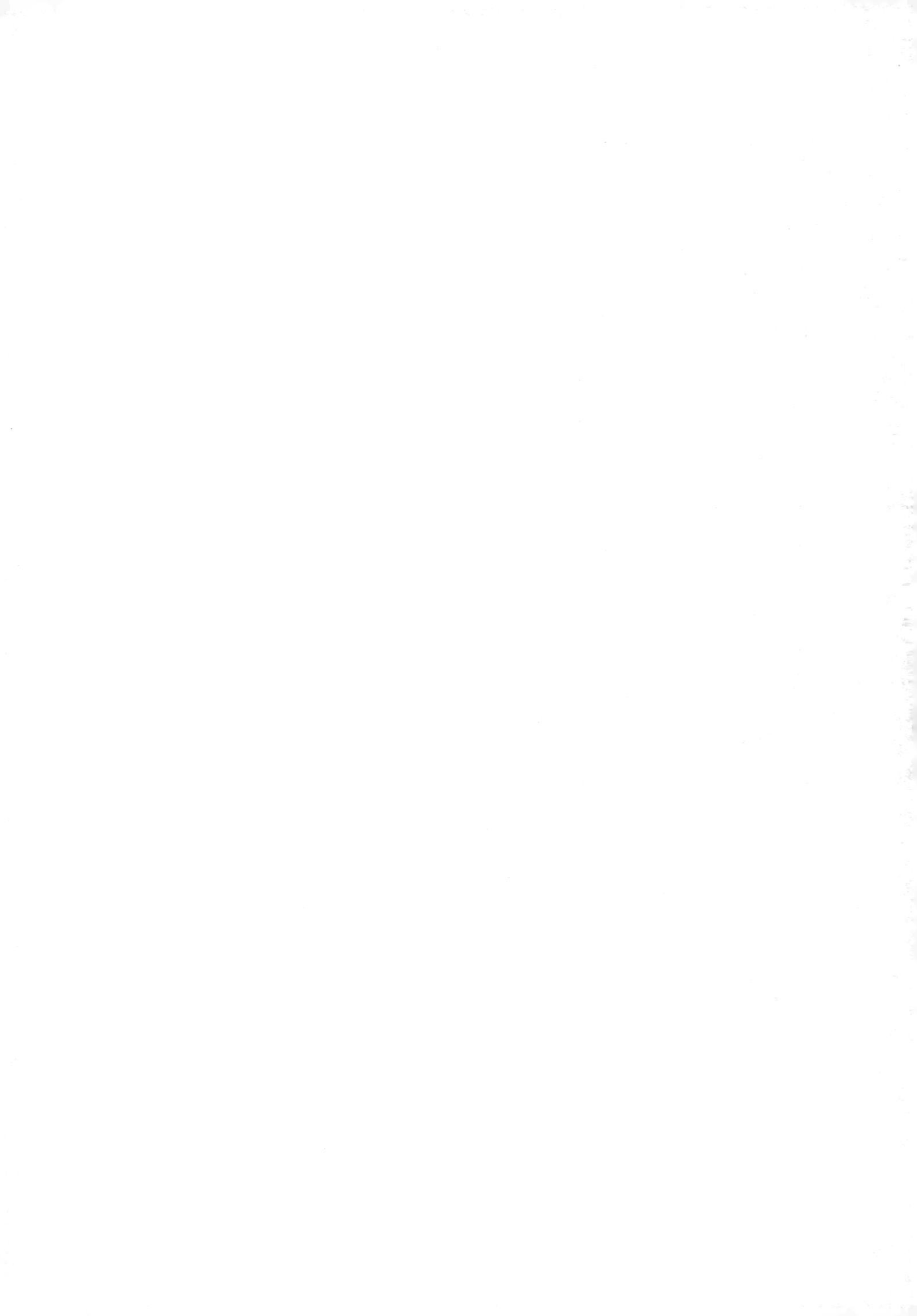

Part

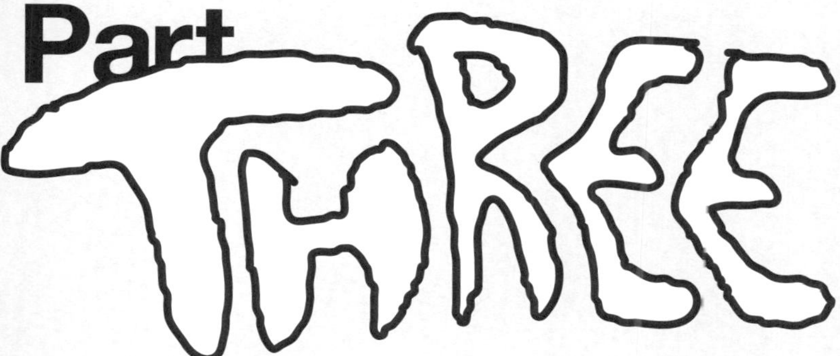

Political Gestures

Anna Jermolaewa and Vanessa Joan Müller — Political Extras

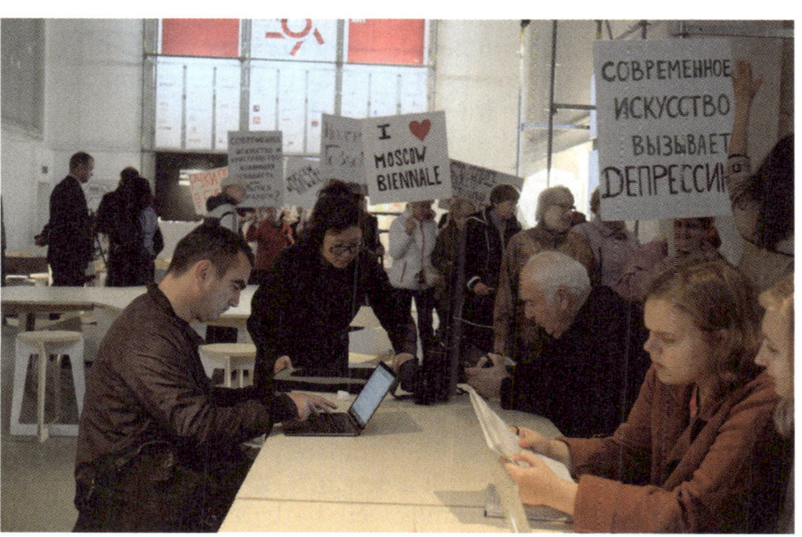

Otto Snoek, 22 *September – 01 October 2015*

Anna Jermolaewa, *Political Extras*, 28th September 2015

Anna Jermolaewa's performance *Political Extras* took place on 28th September 2015 on the occasion of the 6th Moscow Biennale for Contemporary Art. Subsequently, the artist produced a two-part video installation from documentary footage of her performance. The piece was then also presented at the Kunsthalle Wien. In January 2016, Vanessa Joan Müller, dramaturge at the Kunsthalle, spoke with Anna Jermolaewa about the concept of the piece, about its political inclinations and about art and culture as a hitherto underrated populist territory.

VANESSA JOAN MÜLLER: Anna, how did this piece come about? At first, this seems to be a fictitious idea—to stage a demonstration and invite people to protest in exchange for money.

ANNA JERMOLAEWA: I was invited to create an artwork for the Moscow Biennale for Contemporary Art and already had the idea of working with political extras, though I'd had no opportunity to realise it until then. It needed a particular context and institutional backing. And more importantly the idea also demanded a great deal of logistical coordination. *Political Extras* is probably one of the biggest and more important works that I have done so far. It required my undivided attention, especially because I was working with people—and, in a way, exploiting them for the purposes of my project. That is something I thought about a lot.

These kinds of demonstrations first took place in Russia in 2012—the year of political protests. Up until then, critique had been voiced more over social media. Nobody demonstrated. Then the votes were rigged at the election and a number of YouTube videos appeared online showing how the election results had been tampered with.

I think that was the catalyst. Afterwards people took to the streets. It was a very powerful moment and went through Russia like a wave from late 2011 onwards. A huge wave of protest. Unfortunately that chapter is now closed; you might call it a defeat.

At the time, thousands were in the streets demonstrating against Putin and for fair elections. 10,000 people were present at the biggest demonstration in my hometown Saint Petersburg on December 10, 2011. It was an incredible feeling. I flew back to take part in it and I'm so happy to have had that experience. Today, something like this would not be possible. It was a special moment. Something was in the air. You had the feeling that you could change something in this country.

But in order to counter this movement the party in power, Putin's United Russia, developed a new strategy. To offset the media coverage, they organised even bigger pro-Putin demonstrations, on the same day even, that took place at more prominent venues. Thousands of people attended, too. They were more organised. Many students took part, as well as factory workers. I assume there were some voluntary participants, but many of the protesters were told to attend as otherwise they would have been fired or thrown out of university. With that amount of pressure, they were forced to demonstrate. During this time, an online platform was established that made it possible to buy protestors for a cause which is still used to this day. I too made use of it for my piece.

The website *massovki.ru* offers different categories to hire extras for films, for adverts and so on, as well as the category "Political Demonstrations, paid". I advertised there. People who want to organise a demonstration write in and say how much it pays for how many hours. It's almost never mentioned what the demonstration is about. And it doesn't interest anyone either. I organised my demonstration in this way, recruiting participants through that website. All of them were professional demonstrators.

I wanted to develop a project with these bought political bodies for the Moscow Biennale. I let people actually demonstrate—both against and for the Biennale and contemporary art, because the latter is also a huge issue in Russia and is very heavily criticised by the Church for example. The Russian Orthodox Church is one of the main enemies of contemporary art.

I prepared slogans for the participants—readymades taken from media and online blogs. Finding rallying cries against contemporary art in the news was far easier than finding statements in favour of it.

VJM: The protest signs showed real arguments for and against contemporary art, taken from the news?

AJ: Yes. I even found an official text by the regional government explaining why contemporary art should receive less funding. It literally stated that contemporary art leads to alcoholism and drug abuse, that it destroys families and so on. We used that in our slogans. There is also an article in the constitution that can easily be used against contemporary art and, in fact, often is in Russia. By criticising the Church, for example, you run the risk of being convicted under this article.

VJM: I see a fascinating interplay between your video and Goshka Macuga's large-scale work *Notice Board* (2011). In her work, Macuga gathered material on convictions and lawsuits against contemporary artists who are often accused of offending religious sensibilities in her native country of Poland. A very well-known sculpture by Maurizio Cattelan, for instance, shows the then-Polish Pope struck by a meteorite and sinking to the floor. It was ultimately destroyed by two members of a right-wing populist party in the name of the people and in the name of morality. As a Western European I find it paradoxical that the former Eastern Bloc countries that were always incredibly secular would suddenly appeal to religion when it is really a question of censorship.

AJ: I don't know… I have recently had two big solo shows in Poland, both of which received a lot of interest and good feedback. I found the people living there to be very switched on. I think it's different in Russia. The Russian Orthodox Church is very strong at the moment. Cossacks regularly show up to exhibition openings and destroy artworks. This happens every day. People in uniforms simply damage works that, in my opinion, they take a dislike to. Things aren't quite that bad in Poland, but the situation is comparable. I think that Goshka Macuga's large sculpture *Model for a Sculpture (Family)* (2011) would be well received in Russia. It fits the nation's idea of what art should be.

VJM: How was your demonstration received? It seemed very convincing. If you didn't know it was a performance, you would think it was real.

AJ: We didn't say much in advance about what was going to happen. I didn't lie to anybody, but the participants didn't ask what exactly they were supposed to be doing there either. For them it was just another demonstration in a long line of demonstrations. My assistants from the Moscow Biennale helped me a lot throughout the whole process. Accompanied by two of them, we went to pick up the people at the Metro station on the day of the demonstration, as is customary. We had a small sign as agreed upon with my name on it and we also brought a notebook. When we arrived I almost got scared. It was as if there were hundreds of people there instead of the anticipated one hundred. They saw us and started running towards us. We asked them to write their names in the notebook, people started to try and grab it and almost trampled over one of my assistants. It was scary and I began to fear that things were getting out of hand. People started complaining, saying "Normally they put us in rows. And where are the coupons? We normally get coupons."

Suddenly a few people took over, organising the group. They asked for more money for that later. But then everyone had formed rows and we marched to the premises.

I let the participants decide which protest sign they would like to carry. They had the choice demonstrating for or against the Biennale and contemporary art. I had a wonderful encounter with a woman who came up to me with a sign that read, "Art is the driving force of society!" who said, "I love this sign and am very happy to have gotten it."

Another woman grabbed a random sign. My camera crew filmed her saying "Young man, can you look up what this word means on your smartphone?" He looked it up and said "Biennial: A contemporary art exhibition that takes place every two years." She looked at her sign and said "Oh! Looks like I picked the right one then!"

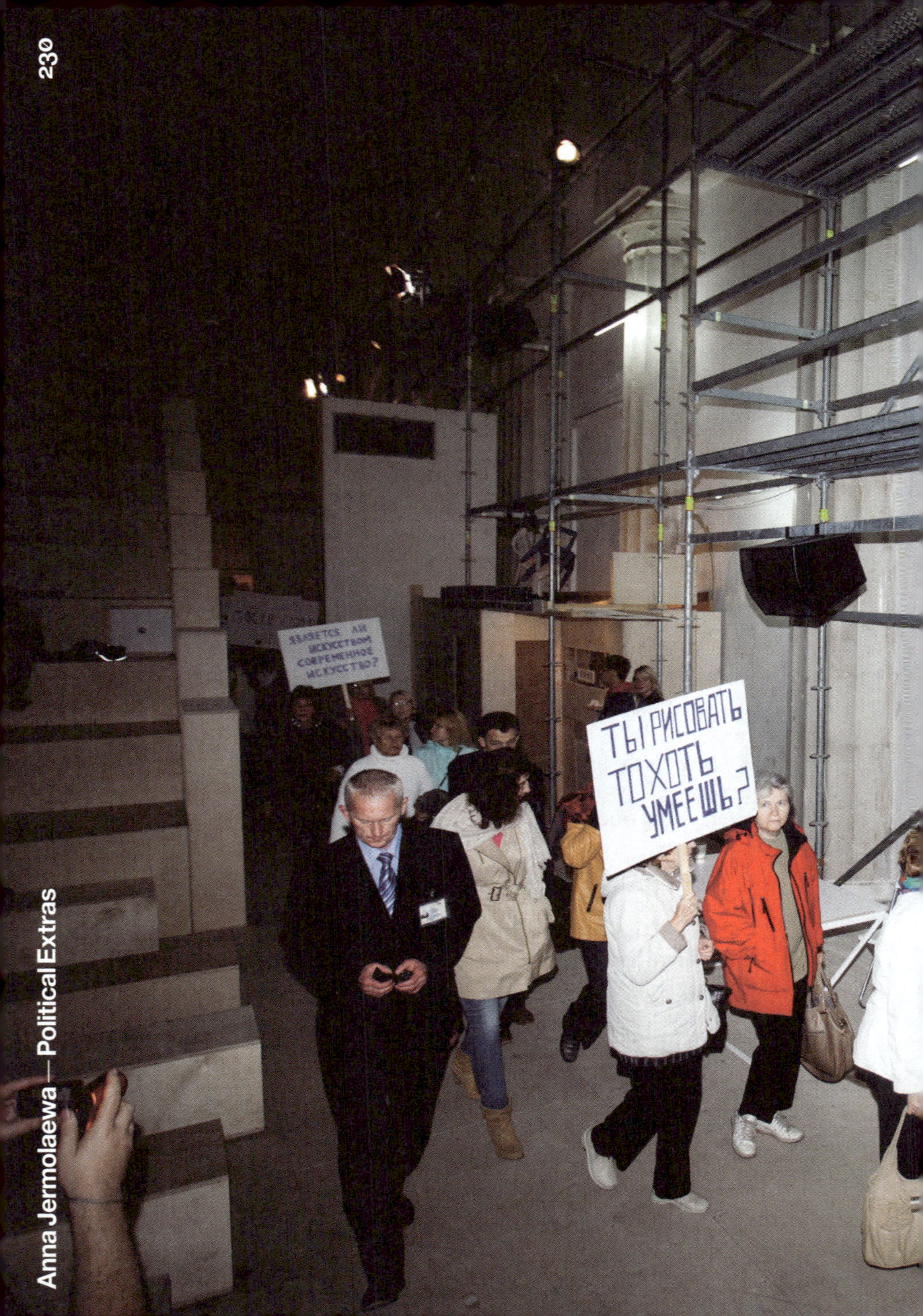
ЯВЛЯЕТСЯ ЛИ
ИСКУССТВОМ
СОВРЕМЕННОЕ
ИСКУССТВО?
ТЫ РИСОВАТЬ
ТО ХОТЬ
УМЕЕШЬ?

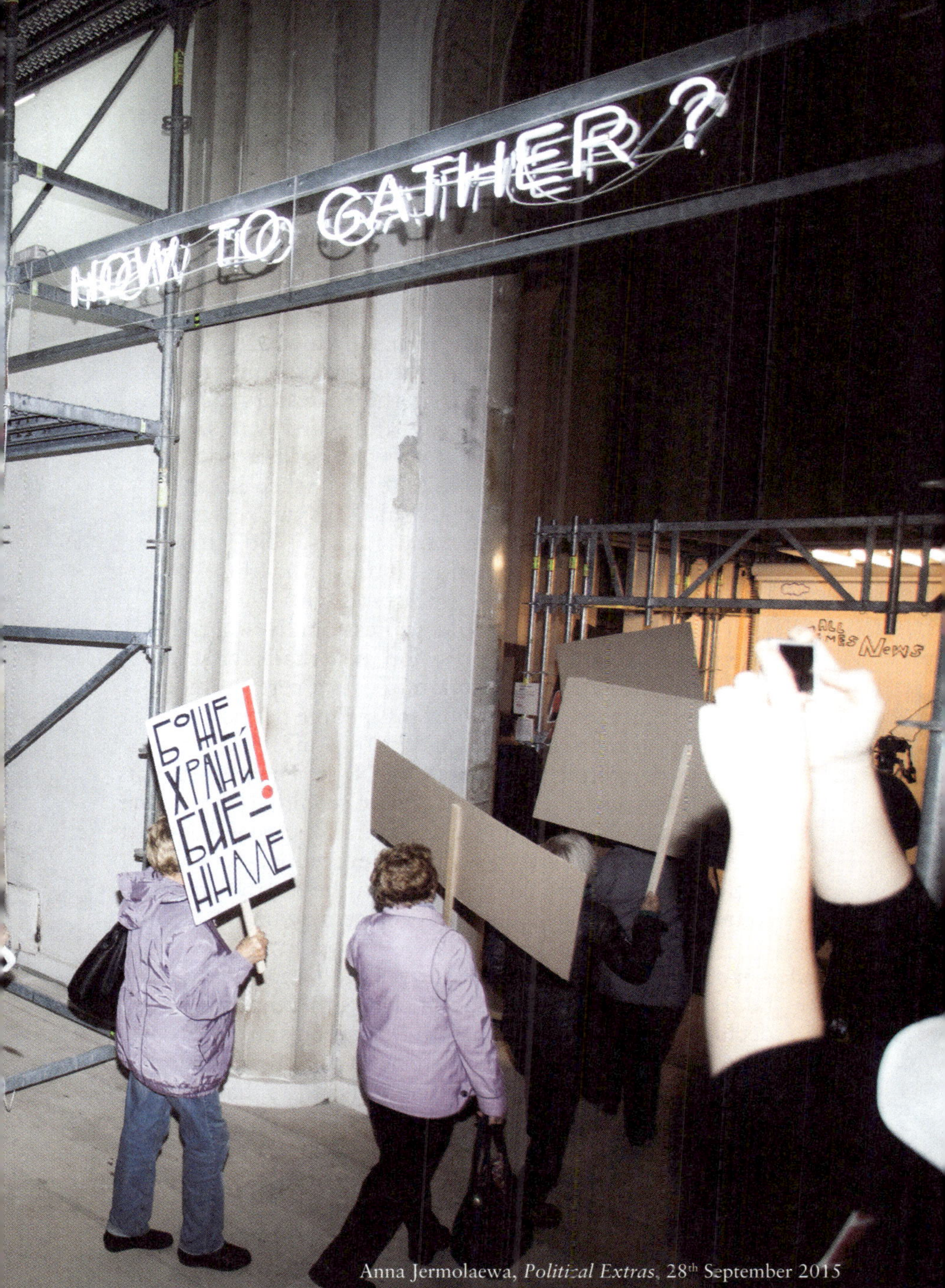

Anna Jermolaewa, *Political Extras*, 28th September 2015

Her sign read "Make Biennial, Not War." We then marched around the Pavilion and outside. For four hours they did what I wanted. It was actually quite unsettling.

VJM: And how did the public react? Was this a location where you would expect demonstrations or did the whole thing have more of a performative character within the context of the Biennale?

AJ: We were outside as well, but primarily interacted with visitors of the Biennale. I refrained from saying much, telling the journalists to address the protestors themselves. A woman came up to me afterwards and said, "A journalist just asked me if we were paid to do the demonstration and I said 'No'. He also asked if we painted the slogans ourselves. I said 'Yes, we're activists. We spent all night painting these slogans.' Did I answer right?" I nodded and she said, "I know how this works! Call me for the next one; I'll help you with everything."

These people really do this professionally and they know how to talk to the press, because that's what it's all about ultimately—to communicate a certain image in the media. Also very important: people get paid in a backyard straight after the demonstration. I had set up a table at the exhibition space in VDNKh. The participants were all concerned that some people would get too much money and the others none, which had happened the last time. They formed rows again and everyone got their 500 rubles. Almost everyone asked when the next protest was to take place and asked me to call them again.

VJM: That all sounds like a pretty surreal and amusing undertaking, all in all—but in fact it shows the absolute decline of democratic values and discredits any form of protest. You start asking yourself if it is the same people telling national as well as foreign journalists that they are activists when they are probably merely briefed on the more politically controversial issues beforehand. Do we forgo the possibility of drawing media attention to important issues by exploiting freedom of speech in public spaces in this way? Do you believe anything anymore after having experienced a project like this and seen how well it actually works? Every demonstration or form of protest—be it for and against a cause—surely seems suspicious after that.

AJ: Yes exactly. It sounds amusing, but I actually experienced a surge of protest within myself and felt slightly ashamed. Something I also wasn't aware of beforehand was the fact that most of the protestors were older retired women who clearly couldn't live off their pensions and relied on these demonstrations as an alternative source of income. I felt bad for them. My task was to expose and draw attention to these mechanisms, and in that way you are completely right.

VJM: You talk about exposing mechanisms. Is this something that everybody knows about in Russia? Or do these things mostly happen in secret, so that it is merely suspected that protestors don't always participate voluntarily?

AJ: I don't know how widely known it is. People really do try to pay the participants in secret so that they're not found out. There have been absurd cases—two years ago some participants were not paid and so went to the police and said "We demonstrated, but were not paid." (laughs)

VJM: I'd be interested to know if you see yourself as a political artist—it sounds like a banal question, but it is actually quite complex.

AJ: I don't think I like this term very much.

VJM: Interesting. Perhaps because it's been, well, not discredited, but when talking about political art we imagine art as a form of activism which aims to have a direct effect on society. Would you describe yourself as a socially engaged artist?

AJ: I prefer the sound of that. I have been working with issues surrounding manipulation for a long time and I am interested in social structures. I explore this in an abstract or a narrative way. If that is political art then so be it. But I think you can also express yourself in very abstract ways.

VJM: Apart from that, could your art be described as a documentary form of art that directly processes political events? Or do you take more of an activist approach, using the art scene as a platform to draw attention to and work through certain issues?

AJ: I want my works to have a direct impact on society. Before becoming an artist I was active in the dissident movement in Russia. Prior to moving to Vienna I knew practically no artists. In the dissident scene we organised demonstrations, published newspapers and founded a party. I was politically active and had certain goals and certain methods. I am still socially engaged, but now I am an artist and have different methods. A statement of Vladimir Tatlin's that I like to use is "Our art pre-empted the Russian Revolution." The avant-garde really believed that their art was the catalyst for the ensuing political events in Russia. And what can be more beautiful than an art that intervenes so directly in society? That is a benchmark for me now.

VJM: Now that's an openly declared belief in socially engaged art! What I find particularly appealing is your belief in the impact of art. Many artists featured in the exhibition *Political Populism* at the Kunsthalle Wien were born and raised in one country, but have lived somewhere else for many years, and yet still continue to engage with the issues, problems and conflicts of their native country in their work. Goshka Macuga, for instance, lives in London, but frequently addresses the current situation in Poland in her art. The same goes for you. In 2013 you produced the work *Untitled (Hermitage Cats)*—portraits of cats working in the Hermitage Museum to rid the storage rooms of the rat plague. They are volunteers in the service of art and the conservation of the Hermitage's treasures. This is also an artwork that takes something commonplace and anecdotal and uses it to paint a complex picture of the situation at hand.

AJ: Yes, I use this sense of superficiality to do this. The forty cat portraits really are bordering on kitsch. But they are aesthetically pleasing and I use this as a point of entry. I draw the viewer in and then tell a gripping story of my hometown Saint Petersburg—cats have been working at the Hermitage for over 250 years. The Empress Elisabeth employed them in the 18th century because she was scared of mice and a plague had just broken out. Since then there have only been two periods in history in which no cats have been present at the Hermitage, the first time being during the Siege of Leningrad in the Second World War. All of the city's cats, including those from the Hermitage, were eaten by the inhabitants. Against this background, what appears to be kitsch feels completely different.

My grandmother lost two babies in the Siege of 1941, they starved to death. The Siege is part of my family history. I read many diaries as part of my research. Many people talk about having had to cook their favourite cat in order to survive the winter.

Here I address the people who share the same opinions as me, because we meet at museums or cultural venues. That was different when I wasn't an artist and I often think about this. I spoke to someone who was first an artist and then a politician. I really admire that. It's such a logical step. He says that it's not that easy. As an artist you have more options. He said that the artist is like the court jester; they can get away with a lot. As a politician you're more restricted. This conversation gave me a lot of hope and the drive to continue doing what I'm doing.

VJ: It wouldn't be a bad idea to have more politicians that formerly were artists. They have internalised different patterns of thinking and have other strategies at their disposal.

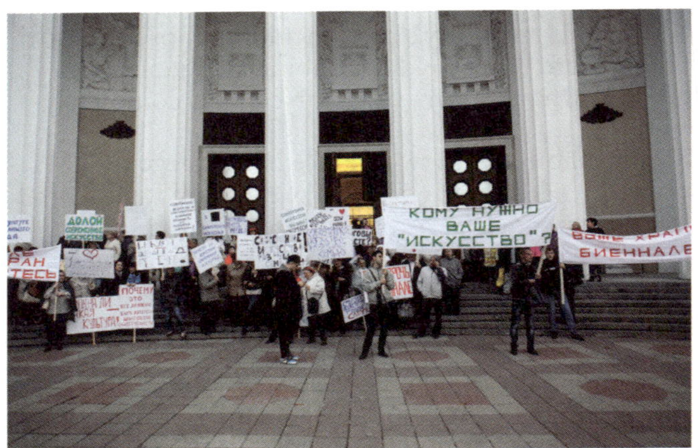

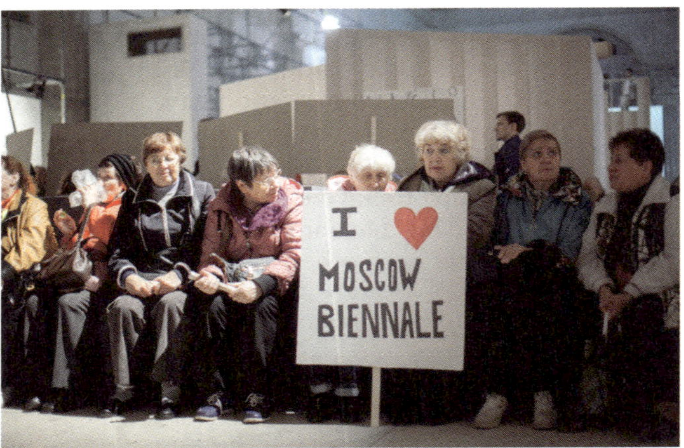

Anna Jermolaewa, *Political Extras*, 28th September 2015

Leon Kahane — Figures of Authority[1] Berlin, Summer 2016

About eight months ago, I took ten days of ballet lessons as my performative contribution to the 6th Moscow Biennale for Contemporary Art. The intention of my piece was to confront Russian high culture with the liberal arts. In totalitarian systems we can witness strong support for high culture and tradition, whereas in more liberal societies the liberal arts are more widely accepted and appreciated. I looked at how Russia's political environment has a direct impact on the way art is dealt with and how it is being received. The liberal arts in Russia are mostly received as an oppositional political expression or statement, regardless of whether the intention of the work is political or not. Thus, high culture, just as it is with religion and politics, becomes untouchable and almost sacred, a narration of ingeniousness, ultimate perfection and prophecy that must reflect on the roots of one's identity.

On the occasion of composer Piotr Tchaikovsky's 175th anniversary, Vladimir Putin was asked about his opinion on Tchaikovsky's homosexuality. His answer was "We love him, but not for this." As implied in Putin's answer, the idea of a minority perspective influencing an artists' oeuvre is incompatible with the concept of homogenous national and racial unity.

For a satellite project of the biennial, I was invited to realise a project in Izhevsk, the capital of the Republic of Udmurtia. Tchaikovsky was born in Udmurtia in the city of Votkinsk and the whole region celebrated his 175th anniversary on April 25, 2015. I proposed that the Udmurt National Orchestra to put on a live arrangement of the Tchaikovsky passages from Walt Disney's film *Fantasia* (1940). Though a Cold Warrior and fierce opponent of communism, Walt Disney was nevertheless a passionate admirer of Russian Romantic music. However, the dialectics of my project weren't clear to the conductor of the orchestra. During negotiations, the young director of the Izhevsk Opera, in favour of the idea, proposed to open up their programme towards Europe and the West. Suddenly, the project was cancelled.

A local politician, who was also supportive of my project and present during the negotiations, gave me a short video documentation of the meeting where I pitched the project to the orchestra and some representatives of the Ministry of Culture. Instead of the initial work, I showed this two-minute-long video.

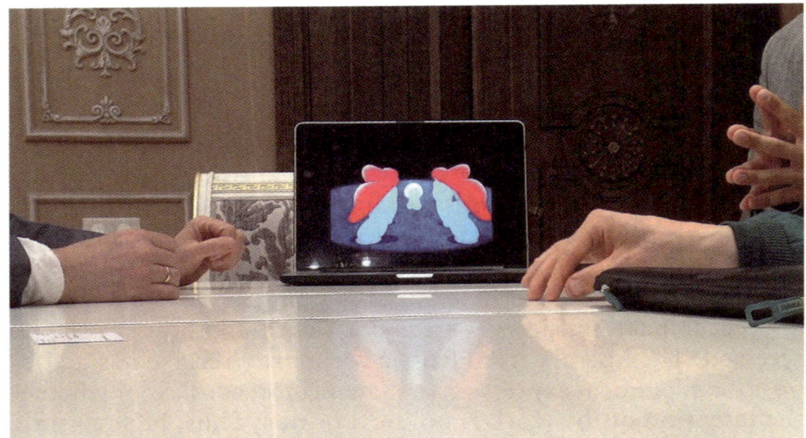

Leon Kahane, *Fantasia*, 2015, single channel video 2 mins., still

I had never been to Russia before I started to work on these projects. When developing my works, I reflected on my experiences growing up in an artistic family in the GDR and its aftermath, on my time in a Jewish school where most of my fellow students were refugees from Russia, as well as on the recent political developments in the European Union; specifically in relation to Putin's Russia, which serves as a projection for all kinds of EU critics.

After Russia annexed Crimea in March 2014, a polarising public debate ensued. The relations between Russia and the European Union became a major aspect of the formation of the PEGIDA movement in Germany. They are also central to the political agenda of AfD (*Alternative für Deutschland*)—a right-wing populist party in Germany. One of the most important connections of the so called *Querfront* movement, or Third Positionism, between the radical left and right, is their policy towards Russia: For the far left, it is the anti-Western rhetoric that makes Putin attractive, for the far right it is the protectionist (conservative) position on culture and tradition. EU-sceptics feel confirmed by Putin in their bigoted, exclusionary and uniform idea of culture. They hail him from left to right and he sends back his congratulations for all their great political victories.

As I write this text, Great Britain is embroiled in the consequences of the Brexit. Nigel Farage has resigned as the leader of UKIP (UK Independence Party) stating: "During the referendum I said I wanted my country back… Now I want my life back," and Boris Johnson has become the new Secretary of Foreign Affairs. There is a consensus within the field of art regarding how fucked up the current situation is. What we somehow do not yet understand is our own role in this situation. We underestimate the importance of art and culture in the entire debate. Art is considered elitist. The Brexit was an anti-elitist movement, but it was also constructed and fuelled by an elite. It is the populist and narcissist drive, the understanding of the power of the 'we' and the 'unity' against an abstract 'them'. An enemy is being created whose antithesis is identity establishment.

Those who foresee the end time for the European Project argue with 'our' tradition and 'our' culture. They profit from the self-scepticism of the Western art world and despise its individualism at the same time. A mindscape like this leaves no room for liberal art. The Nazis' idea of so-called *entartete Kunst* ('degenerate art') can be taken as an example: the counterpart to artists who were depicted as representatives of 'entartete Kunst' were people like Wagner, Furtwängler, Breker and Speer, and perhaps most importantly Goebbels' cinema, which underlay and supported his entire propaganda machinery. The Nazis used some painters to represent their ideology as well, but their potential to serve as multipliers of the idea was too little. We don't want to imagine what would have happened if the Nazis had had social media networks.

The widespread belief in the collective and the movement in the field of art and the rejection of so-called elites conforms with the AfD's and PEGIDA's idea of the people's unity and rejects liberal and cosmopolitan life concepts.

In summer 2016, eight months after my participation in the Moscow Biennale for Contemporary Art, the discussion around the Volksbühne theatre in Berlin, as well as a central contribution to the 9th Berlin Biennial, provide scenes of such bias. The *Verkultung* (mythification) of the Volksbühne as "the last bastion of GDR's socialist culture in Berlin" and Babak Radboy's Verkultung of fascism with his slogan "Why should fascists have all the fun?" plastered around the city, alongside an installation of disinfection dispensers by Puppies Puppies in the staircases of

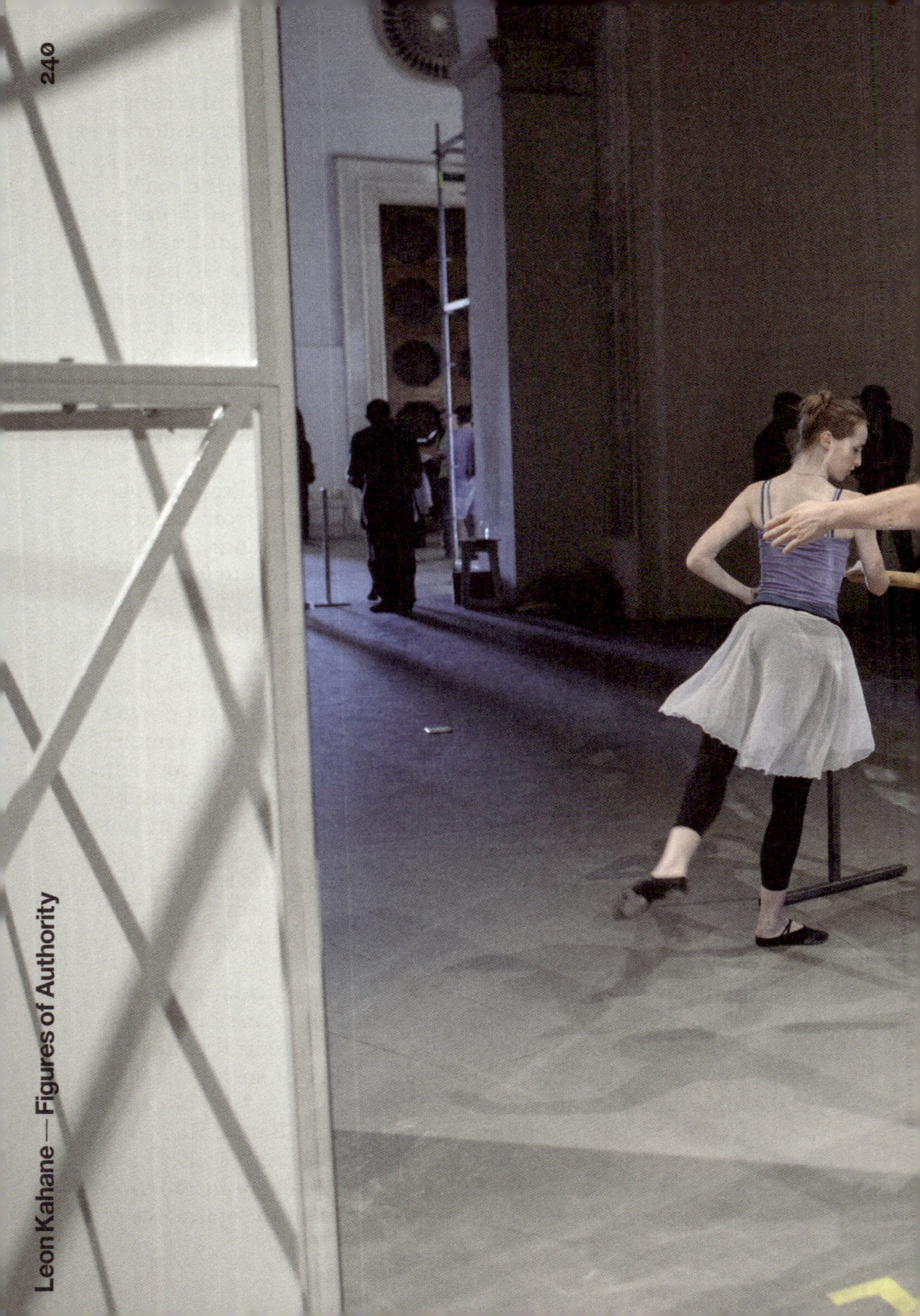

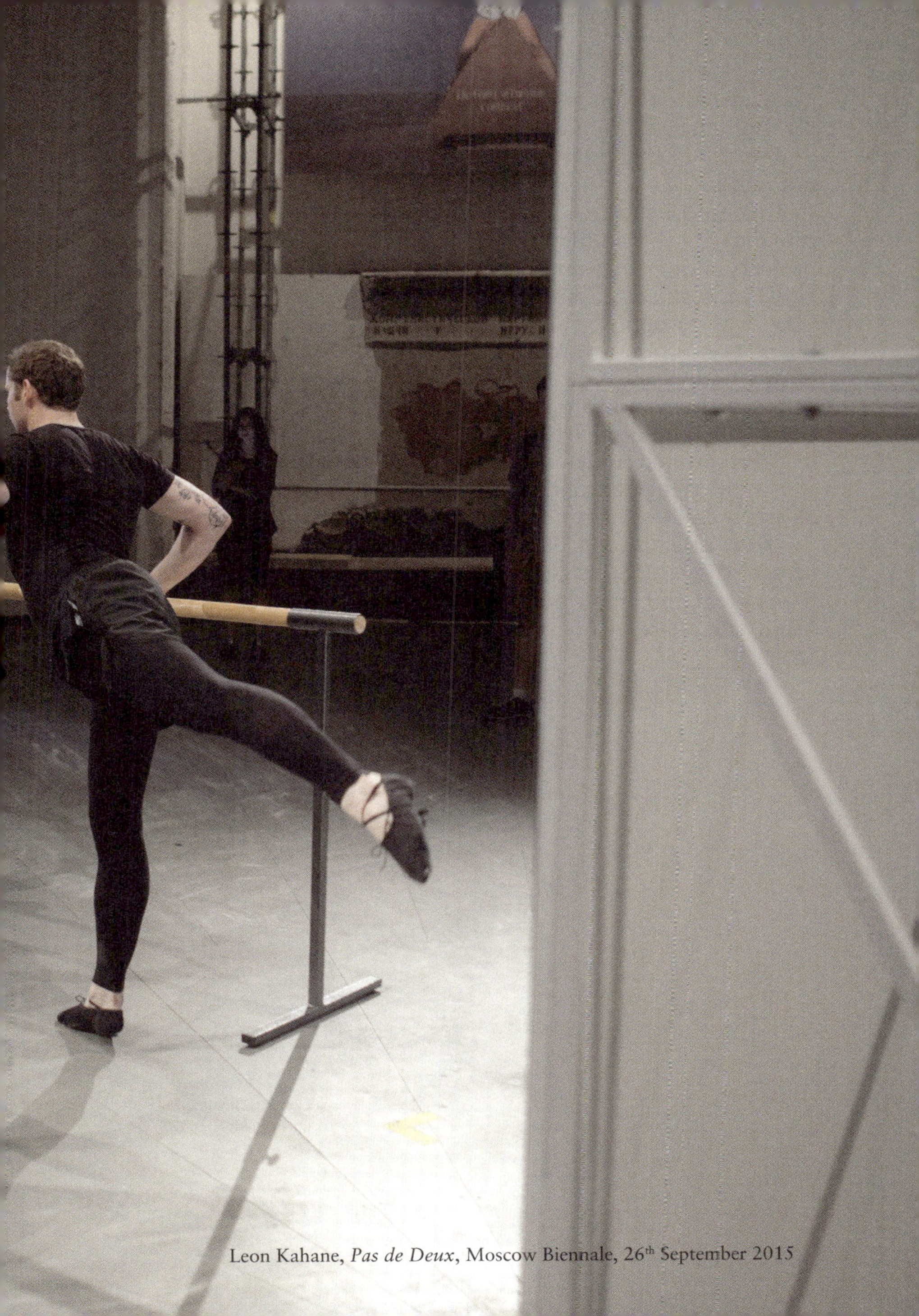

Leon Kahane, *Pas de Deux*, Moscow Biennale, 26th September 2015

the KunstWerke, one of the Biennial's main venues, are exemplary for a privileged thoughtlessness.

But the exclusionary socialism of the GDR and fascism are not punk.

It is no coincidence that the remnants of those extremes have found each other in the Querfront (Third Positionism) through a projection of Putin's authoritarianism.

Fascism still exists and is, in fact, celebrating a new high. There is no way to oppose this rise in fascism if we don't support the liberal oppositions in autocratic systems, but discredit their liberal efforts with a self-centred approach to appeasement.

If anything indicates the democratic condition of a political environment, it is the freedom and diversity of art and culture and its liberty from traditions. The Moscow Biennale was an important step in the right direction. The approach of the three curators was clearly a child of its time.

Now, after Joseph Backstein announced his resignation, the future of the biennial is uncertain. Nevertheless, having met so many great and ambitious artists from inside and outside Russia, I think there are plenty of reasons to remain optimistic.

1
See: Benjamin H. D. Buchloh, *Figures of Authority, Ciphers of Regression: Notes on the Return of Representation in European Painting*, in: *October*, Vol. 16, (Spring, 1981), pp. 39–68.

Nástio Mosquito — SOUTH

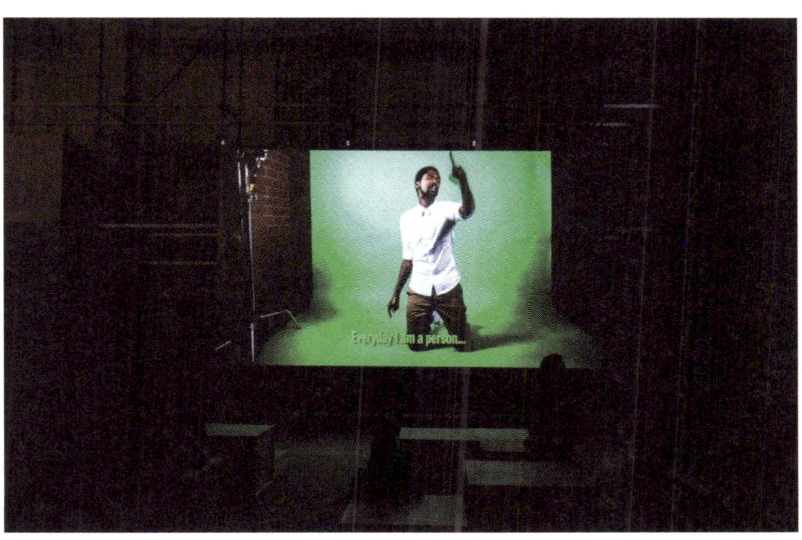

Nástio Mosquito, video screening, Moscow Biennale 2015

There was a time I was targeting coherence... then I found out that it's about integrity. There was a time I said "fuck information, consider only, without denying context, knowledge!"... Then I found out that it's about understanding by revelation; who knows it becomes enlightenment in favour of daily focus.

There was a time I nurtured legitimacy... Yep! I ended up finding that it's about the cultivation of the power that is love, as one's motivation.

There... well, I found 1 Corinthians 13.1-13 and just fucking stopped concluding shit...

(I wonder what afflicted that man... Paul I mean... shit!!!!)

It came out of my mouth, "It's funny to see Europeans in trouble for a change!" Nothing as idiotic had departed from my mouth in a long time... Not because it's not funny, but because even in troubled times there are no guarantees of a learned lesson at the end...

(Only Humans could be so arrogant as to conceptualise such a well-defended trick, even when away from its prodigious manufactured tangibility... THE END.)

"There must be an openness of the West to understand that we, the Third World, have tools of creative survival that can provide a new fresh perspective. With a new point of view of our challenges, there are no limits to the possible outcomes." It was on my brain and it did indeed come out of my mouth... then I recognised that as much skill as one must have when under pressure, perhaps even more skill, and tools, one must apply to a circumstance when lack of time is not the crucial element to consider... just ask Abraham Lincoln; maybe.

We have an opportunity here... not Europeans or Third World, nor Westerners or Southerners but we, we that defecate and fornicate using the word pleasure to express the sensation of executing both adequately. We...

To change is extremely demanding. There's no easy way of doing it... and no easier way than desperation to bring change into the forefront of our circumstances... true but not sustainable.

These are times of change. These are times where our preconcepts are being challenged. This is a time where to survive, whether we are babies or not, we've got to move into solid foods. These are times, for us that believe we possess a vision of what is really happening, to, once and for all, understand that we are not the ones that will achieve change… If we have any chance of really taking this window of opportunity and turning it into a celebration, we must understand that we are the transition team. We will not witness the rise of a new system in the production of art and all its players. We will not witness the contemporary separation of art doers from artists. We will not… well, if there's any chance of us taking a peek at it, we got to serve. Service… what of?

Galleries' commercial relevance is dead.

An artist with no eloquence to his practice functionality is dead.

Art that cares not about communicating to its audience is dead.

Like a cockroach without its head; dead. Moving but dead. Sensing but dead. Heart-pumping but… yes, dead.

The battle is between preservation of identity, credibility of legitimacy and blindness…

That is not new, this in a global context, right?

In all systems, all arenas, in all contexts, in all bodies…

What is art by the way? Functionally speaking? Yes, bloody utility…

So what tha fuck?!?

I would need more time with you, for us…

I do not give a fuck about where you are from.

(Would be quite cool to know where you are going).

I want to know what you believe in and XCVBNM…

I might need you to remind me that I can do what I do, I might need you to tell me that I am 100% of who and what it is that I can, may and will do.

Where did you say you were going again?!?

Saâdane Afif — Play Opposite

playopposite.tumblr.com

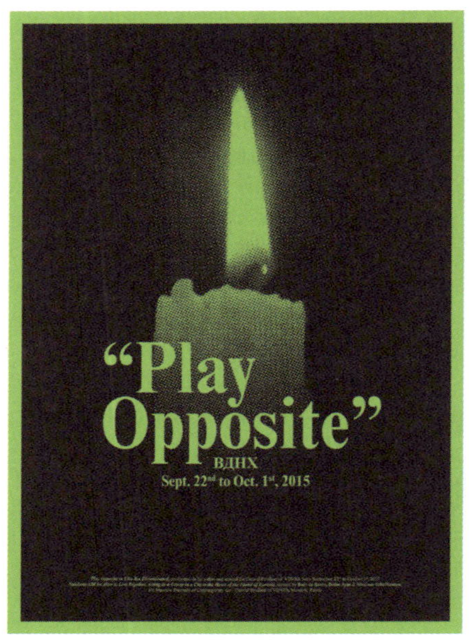

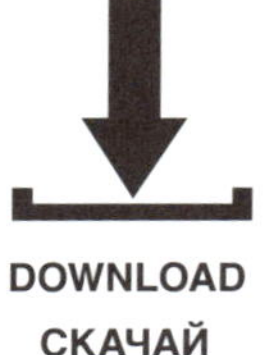

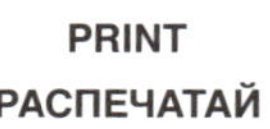

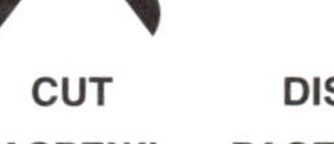
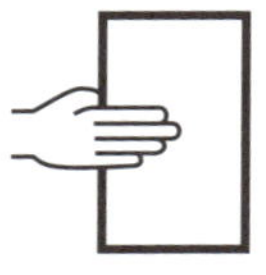

DOWNLOAD	PRINT	CUT	DISTRIBUTE
СКАЧАЙ	РАСПЕЧАТАЙ	РАЗРЕЖЬ	РАСПРОСТРАНИ

Saâdane Afif's response to the 6th Moscow Biennale's question How to Gather? was a performance called *Play Opposite*, set up to last for the whole duration of the exhibition. From the 22nd September to the 1st October, Afif relocated his studio to an office space within the Biennale. Using the Russian translation of the play *Ubu Roi* written by French author Alfred Jarry, the office printed out every single line on unique editions of A5 leaflets every day of the Biennale.

A website now hosts the text, which you can print on flyers to re-enact the performance of Saâdane Afif as it happened during the Moscow Biennale. You can make it happen whenever and wherever. You will just need a printer, a paper cutting machine and some helping hands to distribute the flyers. [Marie Egger]

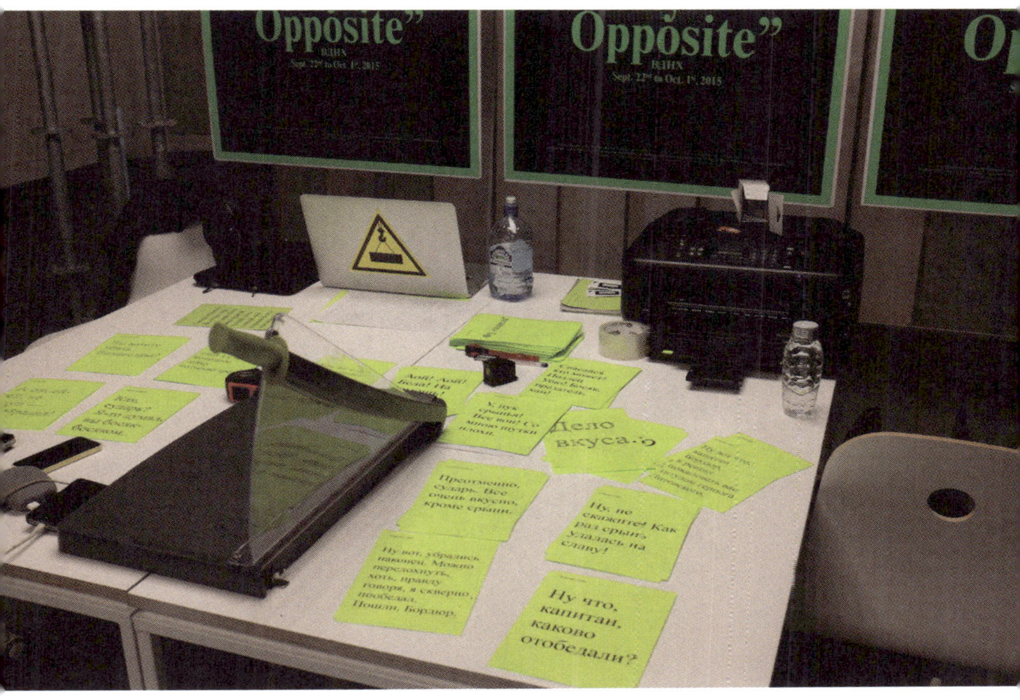

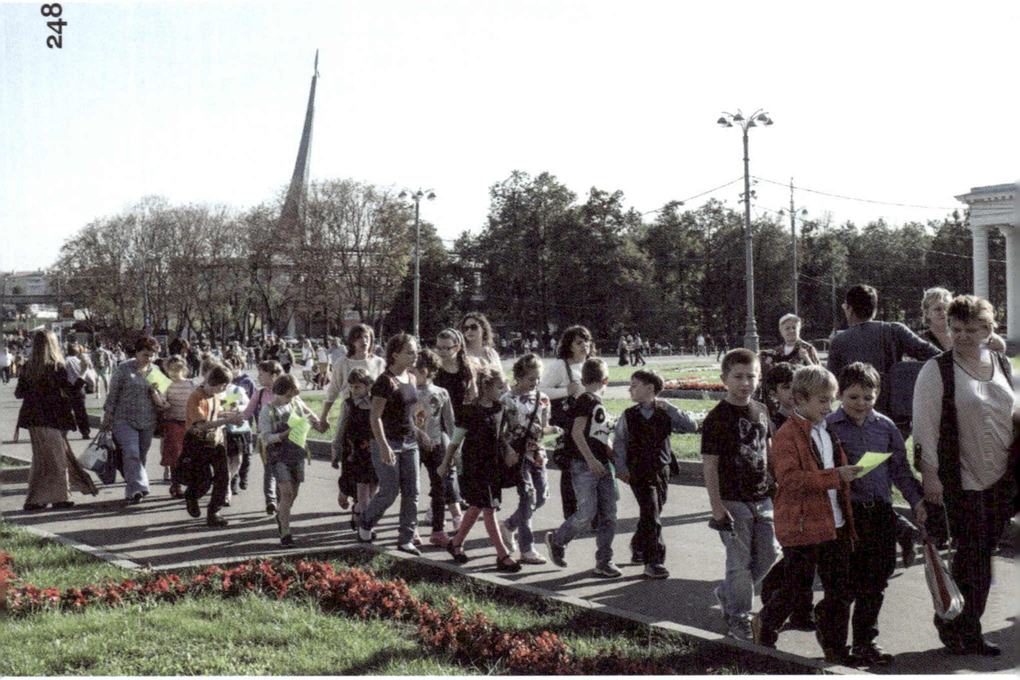

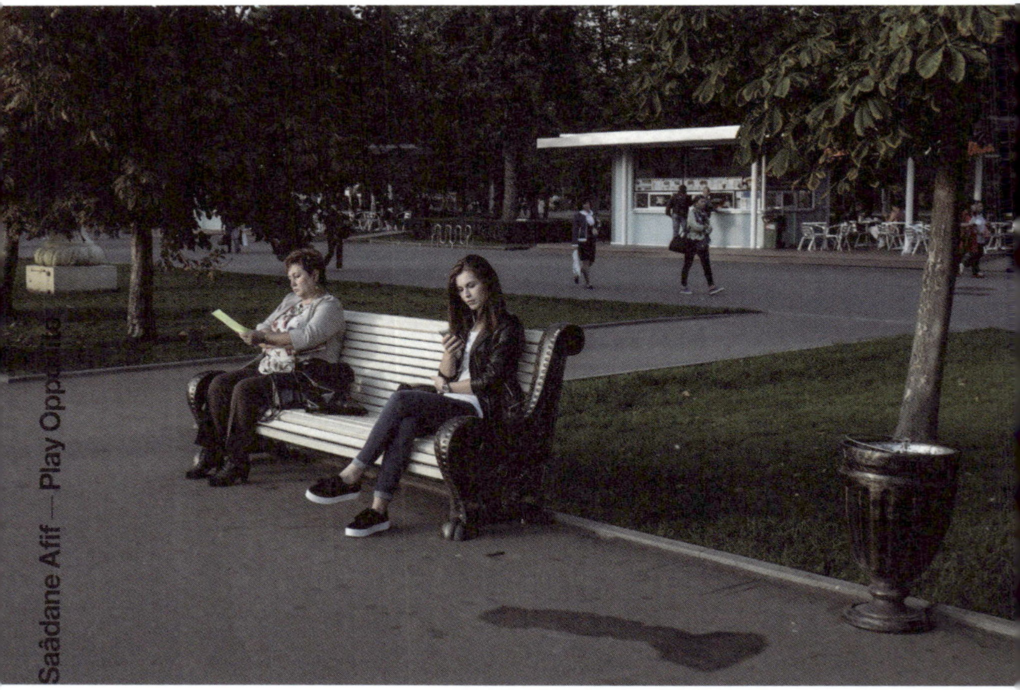

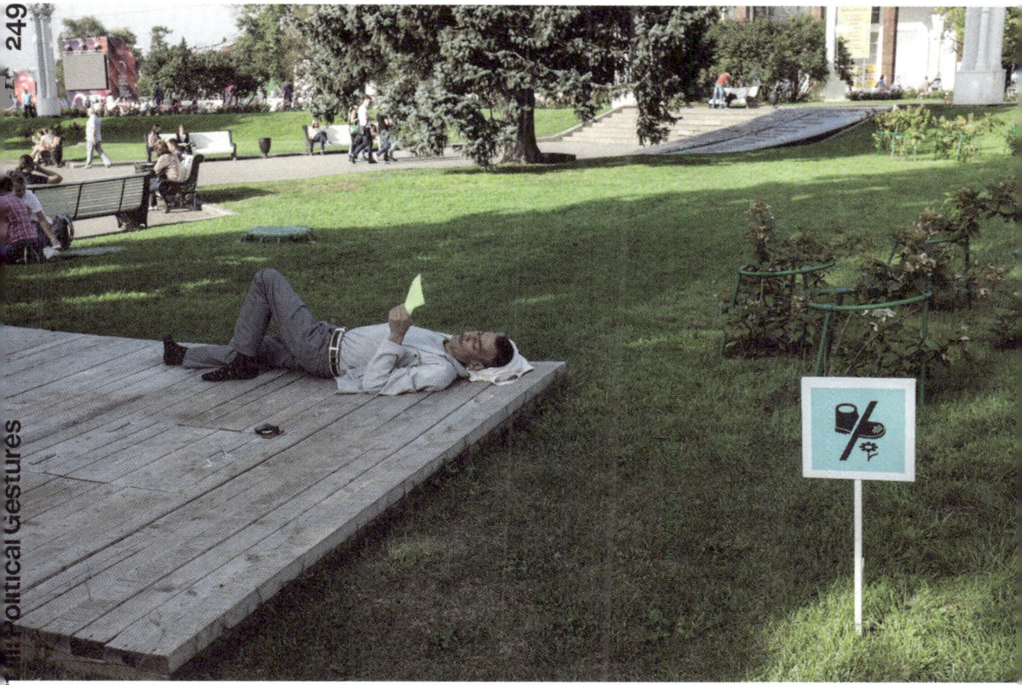

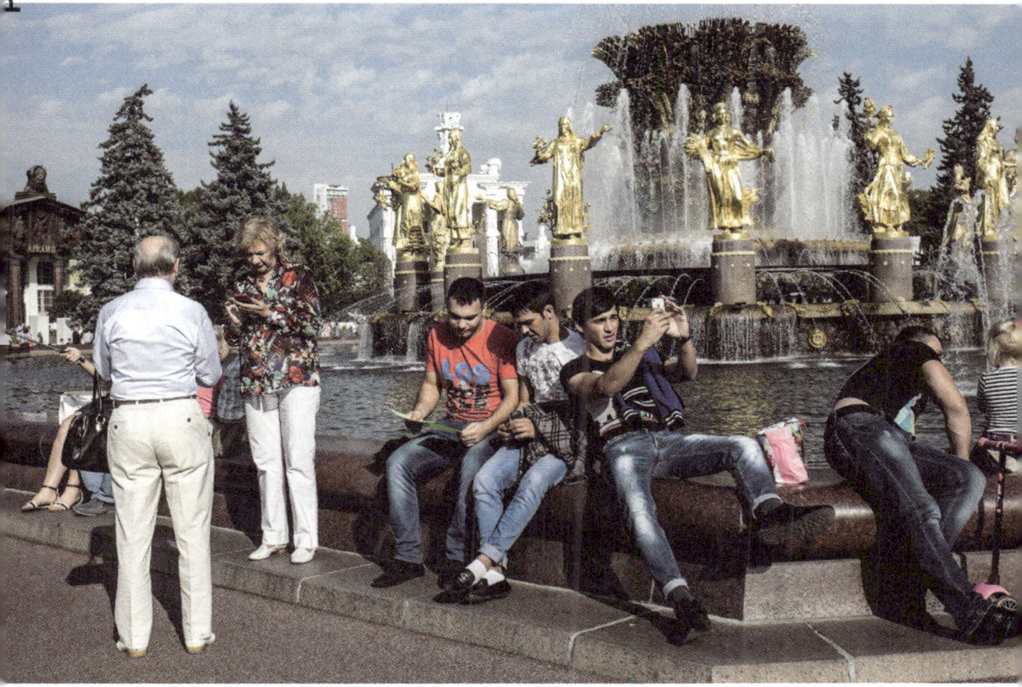

Can You Pull in an Actor With a Fishhook or Tie Down His Tongue With a Rope?

SCRIPT FOR A SOUND PLAY BY RANA HAMADEH

ACT I: [A CRIME SCENE]

FIRST MOVEMENT:
[THE SLAIN AS THE GRAMMAR OF MURDER] – [ORATION]

The orator's voice is heard through a series of horn speakers before his body reaches the central platform. The horn speakers, hanging at ear level, address the audience, adding a metallic texture to the orator's voice. As he clears his throat repeatedly, his oration sounds like a rehearsal.

[ORATOR]

We kill a man__________

The words reverberate throughout the 2000 square meter factory-like space and return to the audience's ears as fragmented phonic avowals.

PAUSE

<u>W</u>e <u>K</u>ill a <u>M</u>an_______________

W K <u>I</u>ll

<u>K</u>

The reading is interrupted by feedback and interference noise from the speakers.

Peeeeeeeeeeeeeeeeeeeeeeeeeeep

A man from the audience uncovers a green-washed irregular hexagonal piece of wood hanging on the wall, with seven white Latin letters painted on it: The letters W, K, M, S, O and I at each angle, and the letter <u>P</u> closer to the center. He points at the letters as the orator speaks. He gesticulates with intended carelessness, as if he has been hired to do this same demonstration on a regular basis for a long time.

[ORATOR]

Here is our <u>M</u>achine.

[AUDIENCE]

Ma.chine!

[ORATOR]

<u>W</u>e call it the blood letting <u>M</u>achine. An <u>I</u>ngenious <u>P</u>iece of engineering this <u>I</u>s. <u>W</u>ith <u>I</u>ncorporated automated <u>O</u>perations that show Sensitivity to the <u>P</u>sychological State of the <u>P</u>atient <u>W</u>ho is being bled. It also encourages patients who cannot cry to give the appearance of crying – It's like an acting course, but with real blood___________ you see?

The man from the audience, carries a wooden board and walks casually leading the group in the way a tour guide would, through one of the machine's vaults: A room furnished to resemble a court-room. The board features a reproduction of Paulus Furst's 1656 copper engraving of Doctor Schnabel of Rome [The Plague Doctor]. He appears wearing a beaked mask, a leather cloak and carrying a cane.

[AUDIENCE]
chant collectively in a uniform male-dominated voice

As long as the doctor is not touched by death, the government says, he will never be infected by it.

[ORATOR]
takes a deep breath and starts singing his lines, adding a gasp to the end of each phrase

Now look at this fortress-like structure for instance eeeeee. This in fact forms the principal motif for our machine eeeee. It comprises a series of ten doors that open each time a specific quantity yyyyy of blood has been gathered in the basin,
eh ehe ehe heh____________________

The ten doors also lead to ten isolated rooms. While the orator continues his deliberations on the machine, the audience wander around the rooms, checking out possible hidden CCTV cameras, hidden microphones, gesticulating in front of windows assuming they must be one-way mirrors, checking out the empty metallic drawers and so forth.

[ORATOR]
resumes singing his script

3

On the first day, I played the murder.
On the second day, I played the murderer.
On the third day, I played the sword.

Reading interrupted by feedback and interference noise from the speakers.

Peeeeeeeeeeeeeeeeeeeeeeeeeeeep

On the fourth day, I played the witness.
On the fifth day, I played the onlooker.
On the sixth day, I played the verb.
On the seventh day, I played the bearer.
On the eighth day, I played the noun.
On the ninth day, I played the slain.
On the tenth day, I played the name.

Then, the audience shall enter the court-room BLINDFOLDED.

In the court-room, long black pieces of cloth hang successively from the ceiling, bearing hand-painted passages from the script at hand. The ceiling fans hit the suspended cloth causing a faint rhythmic noise: shoot shoot shoot shoot shoot shoot

shoot shoot shoot shoot shoot shoot
shoot shoot shoot shoot shoot shoot

[ORATOR]

Let's start again!

E U h h h h ! A h h h A h a h a h a ! ! !
Ehehehehehehe____________________

The first day is the inevitability of murder. How can something without a body be beheaded?
Is it not through slaying that the slain gains access to language? Beheading – the utterance – becoming the body of language? Eh eh eh ehehehehe… Ohohohoh!!!!

Groups of men, women, and children set up small improvised hospital tents in the pathways, propping them against rows of chairs on one side and loud speakers on the other. They recite the part of the script that describes their entrance into the courtroom, until they reach the sound of the fans hitting the suspended cloth.

[AUDIENCE]

Then, the audience shall enter the court-room again BLINDFOLDED.

In the court-room, long black pieces of cloth hang successively from the ceiling, bearing hand-painted passages from the script. The ceiling fans hit the suspended cloth causing a faint rhythmic noise:
shoot shoot shoot shoot shoot shoot
shoot shoot shoot shoot shoot shoot

[ORATOR]
continues reciting his lines in a louder, emotionally charged voice

The second day is the assassin becoming law. The assassin is clean-shaven and the law wears her like a pretty dress.

The third day is a machine.

5

**Hands up in the air! Hands up!
Hands up!
Hands up in the air! Hands up!
Hands up!**

**A bloodletting machine.
An ingenious piece of engineering with two rotating scribes, one for immunity and the other for hygiene. Chant with me! One for immunity and one for hygiene!**

[AUDIENCE]
chants with excitement

**One for immunity and one for hygiene!
One for immunity and one for hygiene!**

[ORATOR]
continues

The fourth day is a testimonial machine, borrowing the eyes of narrative to see – to see the cut that narrative inflicts between the eyes.

The fifth day is an audience of battered legal subjects: the desire to speak with no tongue and to perform stage fright.

[ORATOR]
singing and wailing at once

**The sixth day yyyy ehehehehehehe…
The sixth day is a hand beating itself, claiming the bodies of the oppressor and the oppressed at once.**

Sound of chestbeating *Chak*

The seventh day is an event. A tacit event of bearing masqueraded with a bodily scar.

Sound of chestbeating *Chak*

The eighth day is the invention of the article, 'the'. Concepts become institutions. Dissent becomes the state. Justice becomes the law.

Sound of chestbeating *Chak*

The ninth day is the slain crossing towards theater.

Sound of chestbeating *Chak*

[ORATOR]
in gasping choking voice.

The tenth day is Hussein.

[ORATOR]
wailing

Waaahhhhh Husseinaaahhhhh!!!!

[AUDIENCE]
wails slightly lagging from the orator

Ehehehehehe uhuhuhuhuhuh!

[ORATOR] and [AUDIENCE] exit the courtroom. The temporary hospital tents are dismantled. The script remains suspended from the ceiling

7

[INTERLUDE]

'Off with his head!'
'Off with his head!'

Screaming with passion, the Queen of Hearts orders the beheading of the Cheshire Cat.

↪ The Cheshire cat in Lewis Carroll's Alice in Wonderland is a mysterious cat known for its distinctive and mischievous grin and for its ability to appear and disappear at will.

'Off with his head!'
'Off with his head!'

The Cheshire Cat, foreseeing its fate just before the Queen of Heart's utterance, had settled upon the fact that enough of it had already appeared: Its grin. Off with his head! The Queen of Hearts screams, thereby ordering the beheading of a cat that is not actually a cat, but a 'grin of a cat' – 'a grin of a cat' when cats cannot even grin!

How can something without a body be beheaded? What is more intimate to the possibility of simultaneously wounding and altering the wound than the linguistic expression that holds the two together? Is it not the verb in its infinitive form that constitutes the domain of ethics?

TO SLAY,
TO WOUND,
TO KILL,
TO REVIVE,
TO RESURRECT,
TO RESIST,
TO DEFY,
TO TOUCH,
TO

This script is an extract of *Can You Pull in an Actor With a Fishhook or Tie Down His Tongue With a Rope?*, a cacophonous and delirious sound-play developed under the umbrella of Rana Hamadeh's ongoing project *Alien Encounters*. The work decodes and re-orders the theatrical affects of the Shiite ceremony of *Ashura*, and takes the ceremony's political, military and legal actualisation within the Lebanese/Syrian context as its field for commentary and research. An annual ritual during which mourners re-witness the slaying of Imam Hussein, a highly regarded figure for Shiite Muslims, the Ashuraic oratorical tradition is addressed as a structural dramaturgical framework that underlies the politics of oppression in the region. The script included in this publication was initially designed for the 8th Liverpool Biennial by Julie Peeters. Rana Hamadeh performed the work at the Moscow Biennale for Contemporary Art in 2015. [Defne Ayas]

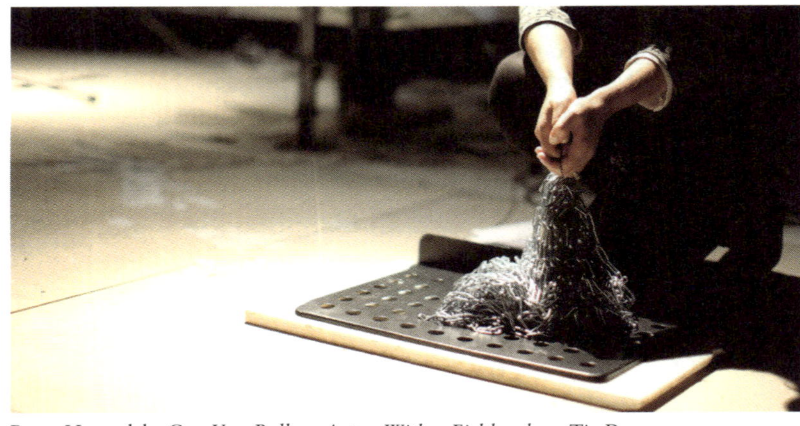

Rana Hamadeh, *Can You Pull an Actor With a Fishhook or Tie Down Its Tongue With a Rope?*, performance, Moscow Biennale 2015

Daily, the central dome of Pavilion No. 1 at VDNKh is temporarily covered with carpets, as mobile racks with socialist paintings by Caucasian artists are put forward and a group of gymnasts performs an acrobatic show to present famous works of 20th century Dagestani art. This show for the mobile museum changes every night. Every evening, artist Taus Makhacheva selects the paintings for the next day from the storage facilities on site.

The performance is a continuation of her last video, *Tightrope* (2015), dealing with her interest in the unstable situation of art in history and exploring local cultural heritage: A tightrope walker moves from one hilltop to another. He carries different paintings and uses them to balance while walking with no safety net.

At The School of Kyiv Biennale in 2015, Taus showed *Tightrope* for the first time. Asked whether it was scary to manage such a shoot, she said that every time the tightrope walker took a piece of art and stepped on the rope over the gap, she would turn away and pray.

At the Caucasus Pavilion close by the Biennale's main venue, an exhibition was set up by the anonymous art collective The Unbound. I only know a few things about the team: This is a friendly informal company of writers, artists, designers, musicians and curators who research the contemporary visual language of the Caucasus and compile its dictionary. In a small, stuffy pavilion, I encounter an anthropological collection that consists of objects found by the curators; of documents, artworks and neo-folk artefacts. It is a condensed collection of typical clichés about the modern-day Caucasus: kitsch, glitter, the *Lezginka*, patriarchy, beards and Ugg Boots with a Chanel logo.

I remember only one artist credited in this exhibition, Farhad Farzaliyev. The other objects and videos got mixed up in my mind and I saw them as one critical work that looks at current cultural codes of the Caucasus and their reproduction by people of non-Caucasian origins.

What fascinated me the most was a YouTube video of kids (two boys and a girl) dancing at a kindergarten celebration. At some point, one of the boys began a fight with the other and then gloriously continues a *Lezginka* dance to the sound of cheers and approving laughter from the mothers and preschool teachers gathered in the hall. Little kids reproducing a model of masculinity and religious education in a ritual dance with the total approval of the community was something scary to see.

I met with Taus Makhacheva to talk about this exhibition and the Moscow Biennale:

MARIA KRAMAR: Taus, how do you think the approach of The Unbound is relevant today? How does it fit with the main programme of the Moscow Biennale for Contemporary Art?

TAUS MAKHACHEVA: Judging from what I saw has been done by The Unbound, this is about building a different world—one that would be the other in relation to the central part of Russia. This is also frightening. I see both an exoticisation and deciphering of that other. In the exhibition, you also find very poetic texts. That is another level of perception.

Generally, the main element of the Moscow Biennale is the time you invest in it. It is an exhibition without an exhibition. It is an exhibition without objects; where everything is in process; where everything is done and everything is changing in real time. The Caucasus Pavilion is a strange anthropological project to show a world excluded from the mainstream. I try to work more delicately, in a poetic way. The Unbound absolutely rock this place out. I wouldn't allow myself to exhibit the set of nipples in sequins. It's clear this is a found object and that such things exist in the Caucasus, but nevertheless this implies a certain message you project to the audience of VDNKh. At the same time, the guards told me that visitors have been asking whether they could buy the Chanel Ugg Boots.

I like that The Unbound worked not only with people from an artistic environment. There is one artist, but the others are people from outside the contemporary art world. Shamil Omarov for example, the owner of a design studio, produced an amazing object: a wardrobe that represents the kitschy interior taste of many people from the Caucasus. And the context of a Caucasus Pavilion at VDNKh, the Exhibition of Achievements of the National Economy, implies that these are the things we have achieved in the last ten years in the Caucasus—a change of ideology, a change of desires. People have a completely new lifestyle and completely new dreams.

MK: Don't you think the curators use established clichés and images of the Caucasus (beard, *Lezginka*, sport) and operate within the same discourse; thus not going beyond its borders?

TM: Of course, you can look at it that way. But again, if you invest some time, the texts will show you that there is something beyond that set of clichés and stereotypes. Like a palace with sparkling gems; If you perceive it as a shop, it remains as a shop. But if you really take the time, the optics can be changed.

MK: Why do you think anonymity and/or fake critical statements are so popular today? Why did the curators not declare themselves?

TM: I don't know, maybe it brings a certain freedom. I often think that for the last two years in Russia I've been living in a movie with a completely mixed reality. You watch the news and don't understand whether it's news or a novel or a fiction film. Artists are especially attuned to this. It is possible that these phantoms inherent to our time are the stuff legends are made of. This is a mirror of our time. It's rather ugly, but, unfortunately, quite objective.

MK: As we speak, almost half of the Biennale is already over. How do you feel?

TM: Generally speaking, the whole concept of biennials is out-dated. I am very happy that this exhibition is radically different from all biennales I've visited before, because you usually see a vicious circle: the same artists send in the same works with incredible insurance, in incredible crates and with lots of instructions. The whole process is very much connected to the art market and supported by galleries. Here, everything is absolutely different. I'm learning a lot, communicating with colleagues and listening to the lectures. The only critical feedback I might have, is that people don't want to invest their time in this, and that's exactly what they need to do. It is very sad that I see so few colleagues here. On the one hand, I don't visit the openings of my colleagues, while on the other hand, I want to listen to the lectures and discussions and watch the performances that are put on here. It's not just about having fun at the opening parties. I want to have real conversations, real dialogues, because there are so many good and experimental works. For example, Fabrice Hyber draws portraits with oil. It is generally outside of his artistic practice, but he really enjoys it.

MK: Is it true that you brought him the oil? Is it Dagestani oil?

TM: Yes, it is Dagestani oil. It was difficult for the Biennale team to find oil in Moscow. In fact, Dagestan has a lot of it. I just made a hole in the pipe and it poured out. I got four bottles and brought it to him. By the way, there are four different bottles and four different coloured oils. I did not know about that. Fabrice told me that from different wells, even if they are as close as a couple of yards from each other, the oil is different in colour.

Maria Kramar
Taus Makhacheva

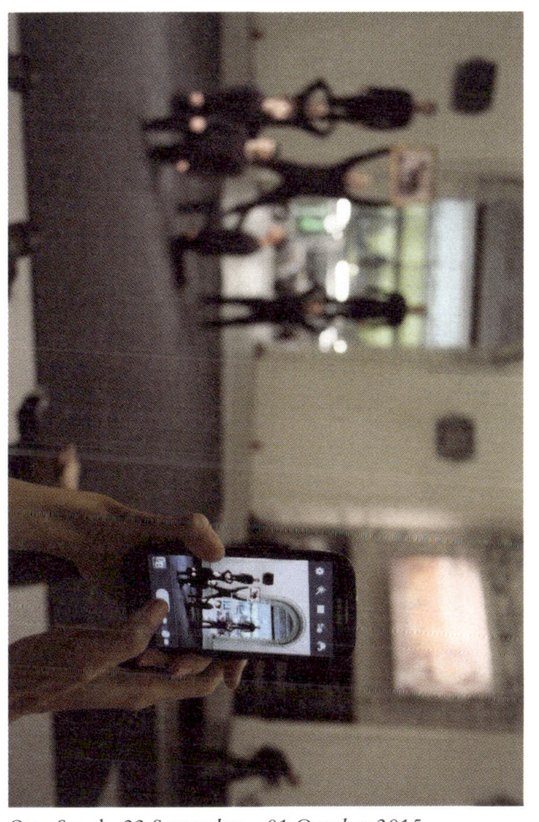

Otto Snoek, *22 September – 01 October 2015*

Taus Makhacheva — Interviews with Acrobats

Moscow, May 2016

My performance *On the Benefits of Pyramids in Cultural Education, Strengthening of National Consciousness, and the Formation of Moral and Ethical Guideposts* emerged from various conversation with the staff at Dagestan Museum of Fine Art named after P.S.Gamzatova. But one story that I have heard struck me in particular:

It was the story of a museum attendants Maria Korkmasova and Khamisat Abdulaeva, who saved the canvas *Abstract Composition* by Alexander Rodchenko, seizing it from a robber's hands in the early 1990s. Khamisat Abdulaeva worked as a museum attendant in room 6, and Maria Korkmasova in room 7 where this work was hanging. Some robber cut out the picture, rolled it up, tucked it in and rushed away. Khamisat noticed an empty frame, told Maria quickly, so Maria ran after him and seized the canvas and thereby prevented the robbery.

The lack of second thoughts and the urge to save a historic work of art made me think about bodies as support structures. I have imagined acrobats as a similar museum network, a network that artworks can lean on. With this work I have also tried to ask a question about daily institutional labour visible and invisible.

Thinking about possible reflections on the biennial, I have decided to speak to each acrobat about their thoughts on the performance, their thoughts on invisible labour in circus art and the notion of the collective body:

———

TAUS MAKHACHEVA: When you saw and understood what was happening, what did you think?

ALEXEI TESLIN (18): I felt comfortable in that building because I was watching something that was new for me and something I did not quite understand. That girl on a swing was something unusual for me—that was the moment I thought art was being created.

TM: To what extent is there an element of fear in circus art to which you are going to devote your life?

AT: There's a fear that the audience might not understand, or might not like you. But in principle, here it's almost the same. You are the organiser, you were probably worried more than we were, because everything was on you: all the good, all the bad, and all complaints would be addressed to you. So, in fact, we were only worried on your behalf. We wanted to help you and do our best.

TM: Is it scary to prepare and perform a circus routine or is it simply a matter of training the body in some way?

AT: Well, preparing isn't scary. You rehearse, and then, when you go on stage you make your debut and you're scared that the audience won't understand and you might fail. But this probably happens only rarely. Even now I'm preparing a new piece, a tragic one for the first time, and I'm afraid that the audience won't like it, even though the teachers say it is very good. You worry anyway, when you go on stage for the first time.

———

TAUS MAKHACHEVA: Why do you think all the pyramids were loaded with pictures?

DMITRY SARAFANOV (22): Perhaps this had a special value or significance within the artwork. All these pyramids were a kind of mound of burdens that we presented to the audience.

TM: In your view, what was your role in the group performance?

DS: It was to support the aforementioned art, as we were holding the pictures up there. That means we were supporting an element of this art.

TM: How did your thoughts change about this project from when you started to when you finished taking part?

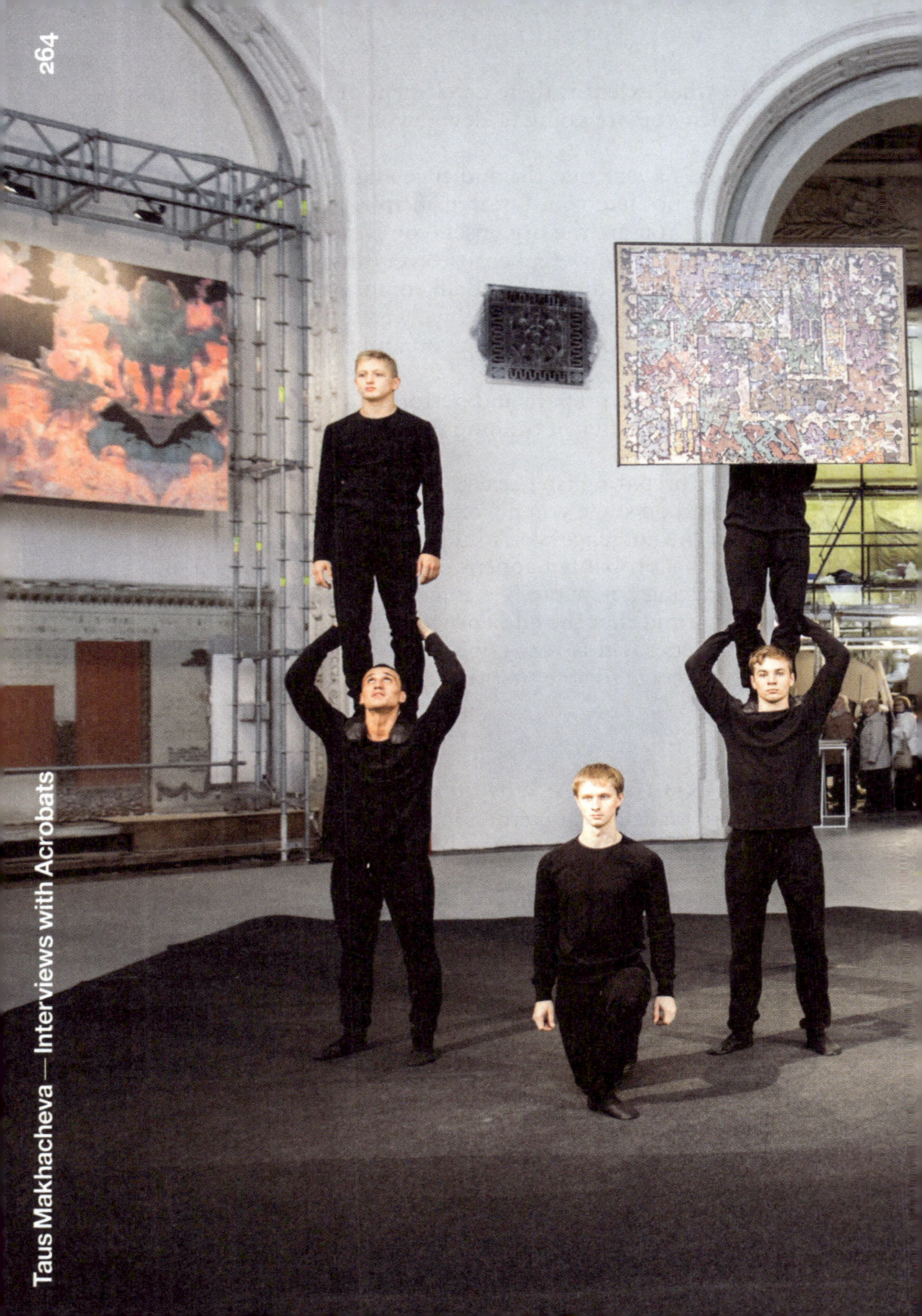

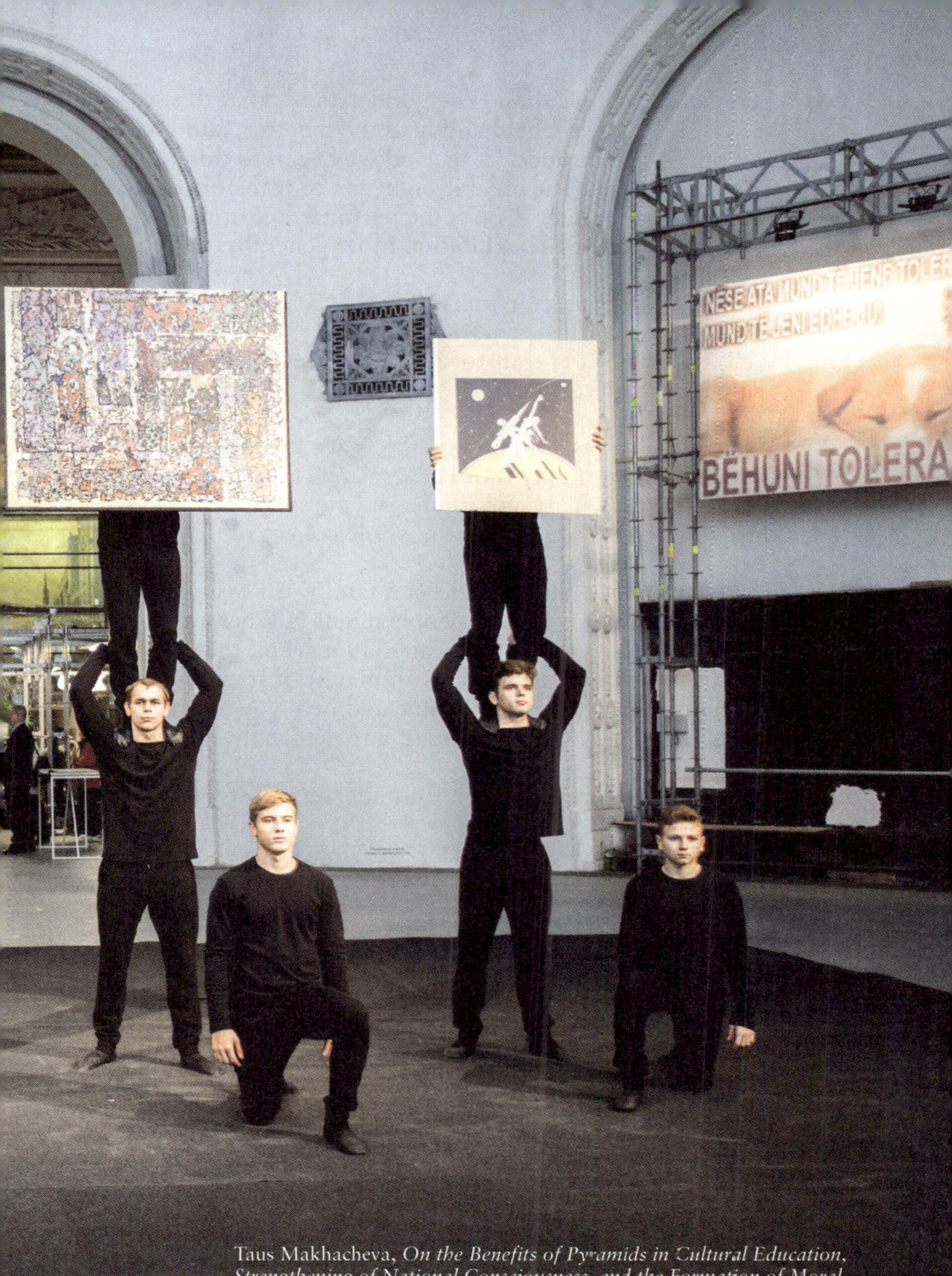

Taus Makhacheva, *On the Benefits of Pyramids in Cultural Education, Strengthening of National Consciousness, and the Formation of Moral and Ethical Guideposts*, performance, 2015

DS: When we started, we didn't even understand what this was at first. In short, we held and held the pictures, and built and built the pyramids. In the end we began to think more carefully… The exhibition began to transform and get its own character—both the performance in which we took part, and the exhibition more generally.

TM: What kind of character was that?

DS: Well, the exhibition transformed from grey into something more festive.

TM: What is the circus community like, if we take your school or a circus community more generally? These communities exist everywhere. What interests me specifically is this: what does it mean to be a whole collective?

DS: The circus community is at least a family. This is why I know for sure that though people might talk behind your back at times—good or bad, no matter what, they can just speak behind your back—ultimately, if something bad happens, everyone will come and help you at once, immediately, without thinking of any personal vendettas.

TM: So there is a support system, if I understand correctly?

DS: Well, yes. There is also a rule in the circus: "In the circus, everything goes around."

TM: What does that mean?

DS: Well, here everyone knows everything about everyone. You can't hide anything here. You say something to someone, he tells someone else, then he… Generally, everything goes around. Even in our school everything is in a circle. All the objects are in a circle.

TM: And what does 'objects in a circle' mean?

DS: If you go to the first floor at the school, where we have the auditorium, we have various props we use for education and training. They are placed around the manège in a circle.

TM: At the Moscow Biennale, what reaction did you expect from the audience, and what did it turn out like in reality?

DS: I didn't even think that the audience would react to it. They would come and see the work, since they must focus on admiring the pictures after all. They probably didn't expect to see the pyramids. That is, the combination of visual art and circus art yielded its own fruit and caused the audience to be surprised. They reacted with… astonishment.

TM: I have a question about 'invisible labour', because this work was also partially about the 'invisible labour' of museum workers, who through their physical efforts symbolically 'hold up' those paintings. I wonder—is there a concept of a circus collective body and an invisible circus labour?

DS: Only if you take a narrow view… We have group numbers: the partner at the bottom throws his partner up, and as a rule, the partner at the top gets all appreciation from the audience. That's because they admire the flight of the partner being thrown and don't usually notice the work of the partner left on the ground. The one at the bottom is left in the shade. Likewise, a teacher's work might also not be appreciated by every audience member. We didn't learn all of those things on our own, we were taught by our teacher. So, his work is also left in the shade.

———

TAUS MAKHACHEVA: Why were these particular moves chosen for the performance?

DENIS GONCHAROV (22): Well, they had to do with a story about a man who carried the pictures from one place to another after a fire. And we tried to capture the essence of how difficult it was for him to do this. Every picture had an individual quality to it. We didn't show just a group of pictures, but tried to show that every picture has its own essence and purpose.

TM: Why do you think there were metal constrictions in place?

DG: They also have their own meaning, because they were some kind of museum artefact too. After the fire he carried them from one museum to another.

TM: Do you have a preference for a particular picture among those being held up?

DG: I only saw the back of the pictures, and during the exhibition I learnt to distinguish them by their backs, and I noticed that the pictures I held were made out of different kinds of wood. There were two kinds of wood. Oak and maple, I think. They smelled nice.

TM: What does the circus community mean to you?

DG: For me it's life. All collectives, all communities have advantages and disadvantages. There's bad and there's good, just like in life in general. Likewise, here there are good collectives and collectives that are made up of people a little bit unsuited to each other. Every community differs. There is a circus community and its 'subclasses'. I have not met a community that is wholly communal. For example, a community of circus performers in which they are all together. No, in any case, separate groups form, and it is only from these groups that a community grows.

TM: What is contemporary art for you?

DG: Everything that is new or the well-forgotten old is contemporary art.

TM: What were you thinking about during the performance?

DG: To do our job to the full in order to allow the audience to understand what we wanted to communicate to them.

TM: And what was that?

DG: That carrying the pictures meant… that we were saving them. We are carrying them, saving them, these works of art.

TM: Did the audience at the exhibition differ from the one for which you usually perform at the circus?

DG: It's pointless to compare them. In principle they are two completely different things, two different genres. Here they came to see art, paintings. Because every person understands pictures in his or her own way. But they come to the circus to relax and wonder. They are like two different planets, different epochs. Each has its own audience.

———

TM: Why were these particular moves chosen for the performance, and what did they mean, according to you?

ARTYOM TKACHENKO (22): They meant bringing art into the public in a literal and figurative sense. Some carried those who carried art, we carried the pictures through time; we were shown a video of how a man carried them across an abyss on a tightrope. And so did we, as it were, carry them through difficult times. Someone carried, someone helped, others carried those who were carrying.

TM: Why do you think there were metal structures there? What did they remind you of?

AT: A cage in some way. A prison maybe. I don't know. At first, I thought it was just a convenient construction to put the pictures on. Then it turned out that they couldn't be put on them. Each picture has its own place.

TM: What turned out to be unexpected?

AT: Unexpected? The people who came to the exhibition, they were completely different. They had a different perception of things. You know, they were calm, peaceful, they wanted something spiritual beyond understanding. That was unexpected. The audience differed, and the things you thought would surprise them turned out to be completely different from those that actually did.

TM: What surprised them, in your opinion?

AT: It's like in the circus, you know, a gymnast flies and performs a difficult element, but it doesn't look so difficult. We are professionals, we know it is difficult, but the audience doesn't understand that. When a gymnast comes down and does just the splits, the audience says "Wow". However, this is simple for him, even without a warm-up. It was the same here. A simple pyramid surprised them more than a complex one.

TM: What is fear in circus art?

AT: Look, I am a support. I don't fly, I throw people in the air, so to say, and the most terrifying thing is not catching your partner, because you are responsible for her life, for her. If you don't catch her, you are the one who is guilty. It doesn't matter if it was her mistake or not. You have to catch her. Another terrifying thing is trusting your partner. When you're not working alone, you have to trust your partner.

TM: What impression did the place where the Biennale took place have on you?

AT: There was such a big hall, high ceilings. The space had amazing acoustics, there was such a silence. But there you could also hear outside sounds, as if you were in a cave.

———

TM: What was your understanding of the performance in which you took part?

DMITRY LAVROV (20): Maybe, as the representatives of a

new generation, we made different forms to show—through a new generation—the classics of typical genres. These pictures were not made all at once, they belong to older times, don't they? Through these difficult tricks I communicated the difficulty of the painting painted then.

TM: Why do you think those certain moves were used? Why the pyramids?

DL: Maybe every picture conveyed its own meaning. Maybe the artist survived something, maybe something happened. With the help of exactly those moves, with the form of the pyramid, the artist showed the tenacity of those artists who survived something and brought art through to our times.

TM: What is a circus community?

DL: As far as I know, in the theatre or in cinema an individual stands up only for him or herself. Only very rarely does someone support another, because they struggle against each other, step on each other's toes, always in competition. Here, we all stick together, everything is friendly. For example, I perform in my genre and I am good at it, but you certainly help others, too. You won't find anybody here who says "These are my tricks and I want to keep them all to myself". You share your experience, help each other, and support each other. I've never seen anything else; here there is always support.

TM: How did the audience react during the performance?

DL: People came there deliberately, they came to see something new. Nobody had come thinking "Oh, let's go there and have a laugh". They looked at the piece with the burden of their own experiences, they looked consciously and understood what they saw. They shared their opinions, and experienced something. To me, they had the look of reasonable grown-up people; there was no childishness, they didn't laugh, even if someone did

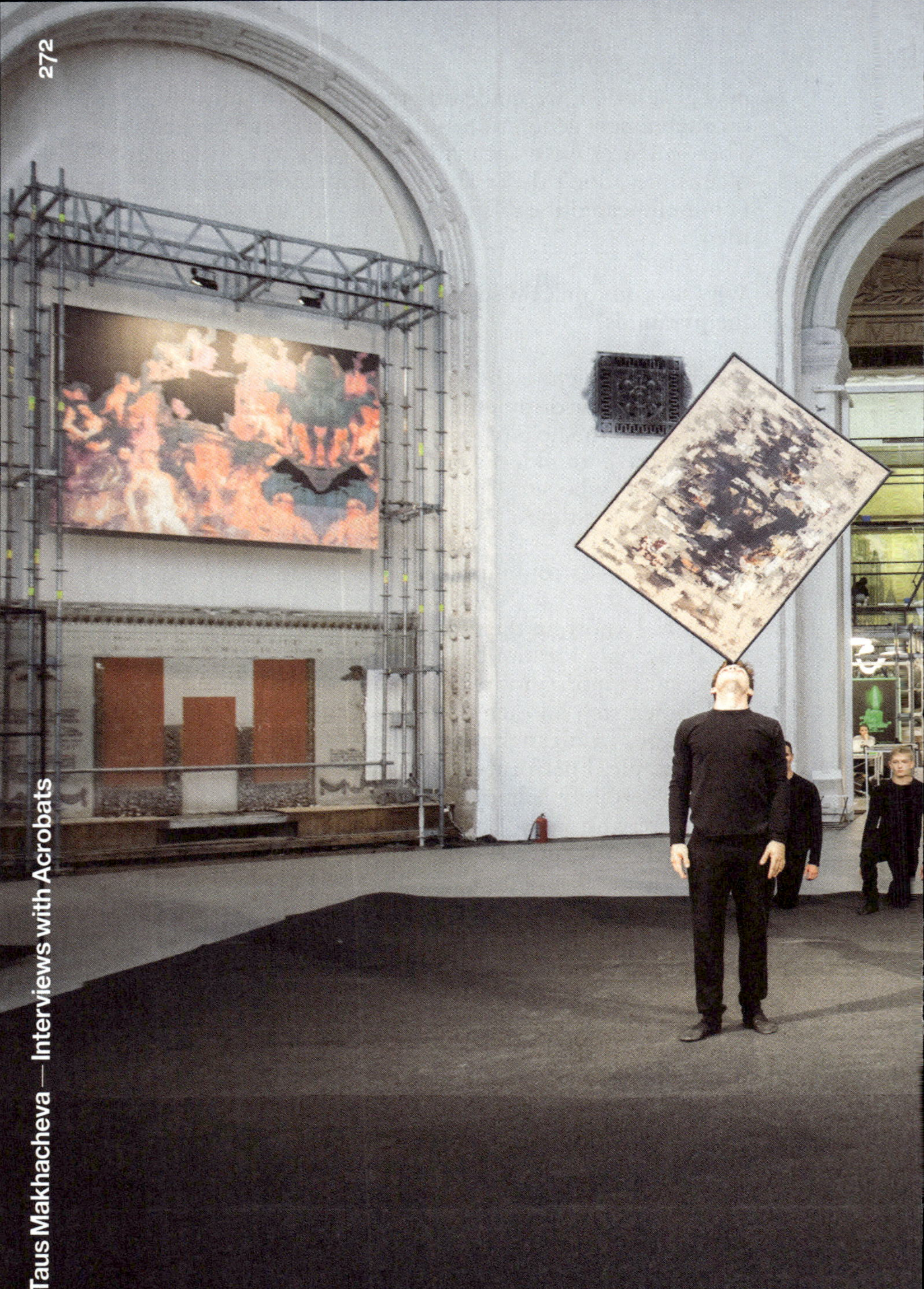

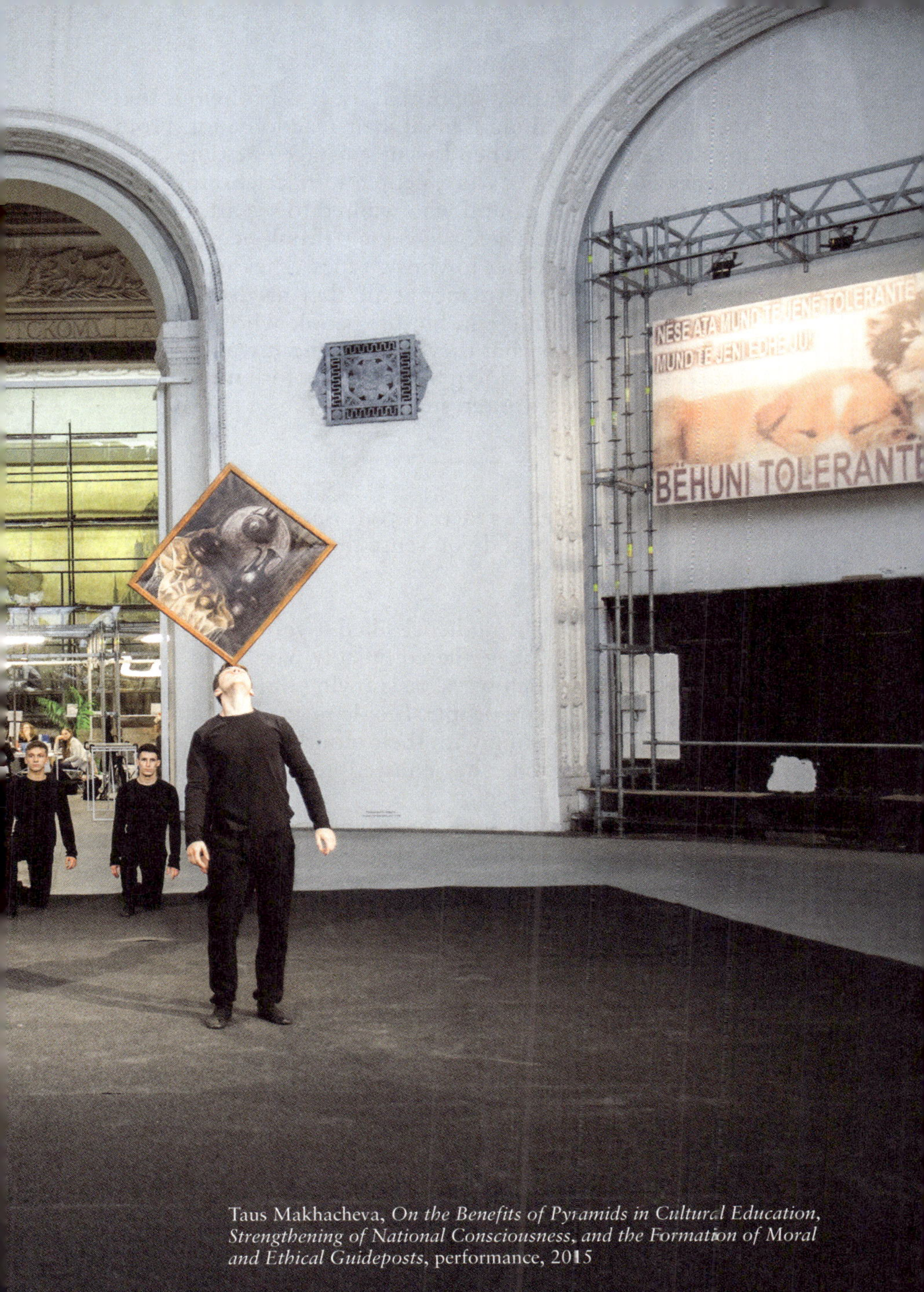

Taus Makhacheva, *On the Benefits of Pyramids in Cultural Education, Strengthening of National Consciousness, and the Formation of Moral and Ethical Guideposts*, performance, 2015

something wrong, they supported us. It was obvious that they noticed everything. I liked their reaction a lot. From my own experience, when I went on stage one time on Victory Day, the 9th of May; people were celebrating and there was nobody around who wanted to see art, or to see something new. There were some drunk people and, forgive me, some rather lowbrow types. They weren't interested in the performance at all, they needed something completely different, but the people who came to the Biennale knew what they wanted and it was great to know who you were doing all this work for and know that they were really interested.

TM: How did the audience react, in your opinion? What feelings or emotions did you sense they felt during the performance?

DENIS TRUNOV (18): The audience liked it very much. It was noticeable that people gathered quickly. Very quickly; towards the end when we were showing our final piece, there were many more people. People reacted with interest. Everybody was looking with their mouth open, so to say. It got them interested. They enjoyed it.

TM: Did your understanding of modern art change after your taking part in the Moscow Biennale?

DT: Of course, I became interested. I began looking carefully at pictures wherever I saw them from then on. I began looking at the world differently. In any case, somehow your imagination, your perception changes… you begin imagining something… creativity develops.

TM: Why do you think the pictures were in the pyramids?

NIKOLAI KOZIN (22): Today of all days, what comes to mind is that it is art. We were the bearers of art, we put on the action, we were those who were art, and art… is the experience of people; art is their feelings, emotions, their souls. We, as ordinary people, moved them and gave it all a certain form. We were the engine, and we took that art into the future—forward. With those pyramids, we somehow varied this movement.

TM: What do you think the metal structures looked like?

NK: The metal structures? The first one reminded me of a mountain, because everything was growing upward, in various different ways. And the second one reminded me of something more manmade, maybe a town, maybe a house. specific places. Out of something unsorted, we were already making a something like a system.

TM: Was there, perhaps, something that surprised you? In a good way or in a bad way?

NK: I liked the exhibition itself; there were many extraordinary, unusual performances. For example, this man with a balloon, who blew up balloons every day and gave them to guests. It's a very good indicator of how people think—outside the box or not. In general, it's an indicator of what's in people's hearts. That girl on a trapeze, who swung back and forth endlessly. I really worried about her. And the part where a man was drawing a picture day after day; it was also interesting to watch the process of what happened, how the work started and what it might turn into during the space of a day.

TM: And what do you think contemporary art is?

NK: Contemporary art? I don't like the term contemporary art. Because art is art. Well… Okay, contemporary art means that people take all the feelings, wishes, and everything they can do—their art, and adjust this to contemporary trends. Because if we use the word 'contemporary' we mean that there are certain interests, demands placed on art and you have to do something to bring your art to the world, to be recognisable, and to do so the artist has to cater to those demands. But art, just as it was in the past, is now, and will be, remains art.

TM: What was the audience's reaction?

NK: I felt responsible and proud that I was representing a certain form of art, someone's experience and worries—and a national art as well—and I helped to display all this. Responsibility mixed up with pride. I was proud of doing it. What did people like? They liked everything—the atmosphere, the art and the means of expression. I saw photos and there must be a video where all of this is well demonstrated. If I were a viewer who'd just come in from the street, I would have liked all this very much.

TM: Can you describe any emotion or feeling that was in the air?

NK: There was tension but not an oppressive one. There's sometimes a feeling when a space begins to weigh down on you. But this was a tension of expectation, the audience was waiting for something. They were watching, watching, watching and probably feeling something. But this tension was present, like a taut string of an instrument, in the air all the time.

TM: Are there examples of collective bodies and supporting structures in the circus?

NK: Speaking of a collective body, I work in a genre at the moment that is quite collective. I work with at least one other person, or, if I'm lucky, with a large number of people at once. And speaking of invisible labour, everybody has it all the time. Yesterday I saw a pastor who said that we should all try to develop and work without being noticeable. Then, after a while, and this only happens after some time, people will see the result, without having seen what you did and how. However, in the end, the result will be visible and you will have finished with dignity.

TM: This is an abstract question, I understand. Not even a question, but a line of thinking.

NK: Since we are all social creatures, to have harmony in everybody's life — no matter what kind of community — people must learn to understand each other, and respond to one another, not only for their own purposes, but so as to not forget that they're not the only ones living in this world. In collective work, the same thing happens. You must understand that your actions affect not only your life and your body, but also the health and fate of those working with you. This is very important to understand from the beginning, because, strange as it may seem, people forget about it all the time. Only when everyone realises this, will they begin understanding each other and then new work will begin, and something completely new will appear in their art and their communication.

———

TM: Why do you think there were pyramids and paintings?

RUSLAN POLYAKOV (22): I think the way we lifted the pictures up on the pyramids with people looking at them from below was something of value. It's unusual; people usually look directly ahead, but here they looked up from below. Every picture can be understood in your own way and from different angles.

TM: What do you think the metal structures looked like?

RP: The metal structures themselves? I understood that they were like a cage in which those pictures were locked. And our task was, in my opinion, to reveal this art to the world, to show that it exists.

TM: What thoughts did you have when you started taking part in this performance, and how did your attitude toward this work change by the last performance?

RP: At the first performance I had a task — to not drop the pictures. In fact, I just wanted to let all this go through me, and when I took hold of every picture, I tried to understand and let the feeling go through me, looking people in the eye. I wanted to let their feelings go through me. I wanted to see how they perceived the pyramids appearing and pictures being. And I lowered the picture a little so they could look and see.

TM: What was the most unexpected thing about the work?

RP: The most unexpected thing was when we were told that half the pictures would not be there. I was surprised why. When they told me the reason, I understood that it was also interesting how people would react to that. On the one hand there is a picture, and on the other hand, there is not. But you must also ask the audience about how they reacted to this.

TM: Why do you think this was interesting?

RP: Well… we can understand it in our own way—an artist in his way and a viewer in theirs. I thought that an artist doesn't always have the whole image; he has an empty spot as well that he wants to fill in with something. This is also very interesting.

TM: I wonder if there are any examples in the circus where your work is invisible but very important? Or, for instance, where there is already a collective circus body instead of separate people?

RP: Of course there is. Even in the olden days when we didn't have these mechanical devices and people with safety wires. The audience doesn't see the team holding a rope and pulling together behind the scenes; this is also invisible collective labour. When all the safety team stand and pull together on the rope of a performer who is flying under the dome, and all his work depends on them—if they don't pull together or keep in time with the music, there will be no performance at all.

———

TM: Why do you think there were pictures and pyramids?

SVYATOSLAV SAVIN (21): Maybe because the pictures mean something big and meaningful and that's why the pyramids were built so high.

TM: What was the idea of this performance?

SS: It might be something connected with a person's inner world, what he feels, and all this is expressed through pictures.

TM: And what was the most unexpected thing?

SS: I don't know, but there was nothing that would have excited people. The unexpected thing was when I had to go up, to stand above the others, because I wasn't familiar with this. During one of the performances, someone forgot to climb up; I was standing there, and boom! I got up, climbed up to the top, and took the picture without understanding what was going on, or how I'd appeared there. That was unexpected.

TM: What is circus society to you?

SS: It's like a big, big family, because everybody sticks together, they help each other. It doesn't matter who works in what genre, because everyone will help each other. Everybody has to be good at everything. If you're a juggler, you have to be able to jump like an acrobat; if you're a gymnast, you also have to be able to juggle; if you're an equilibrist, you also have to be up in the air. Everything has to be interrelated; everyone has to be able to do everything.

TM: Do you think you managed to fill the space where the exhibition took place?

SS: We managed to draw attention to ourselves, so yes, I think we filled the space. People looked at us, not in any other direction.

TM: Is there an invisible support system or invisible labour in

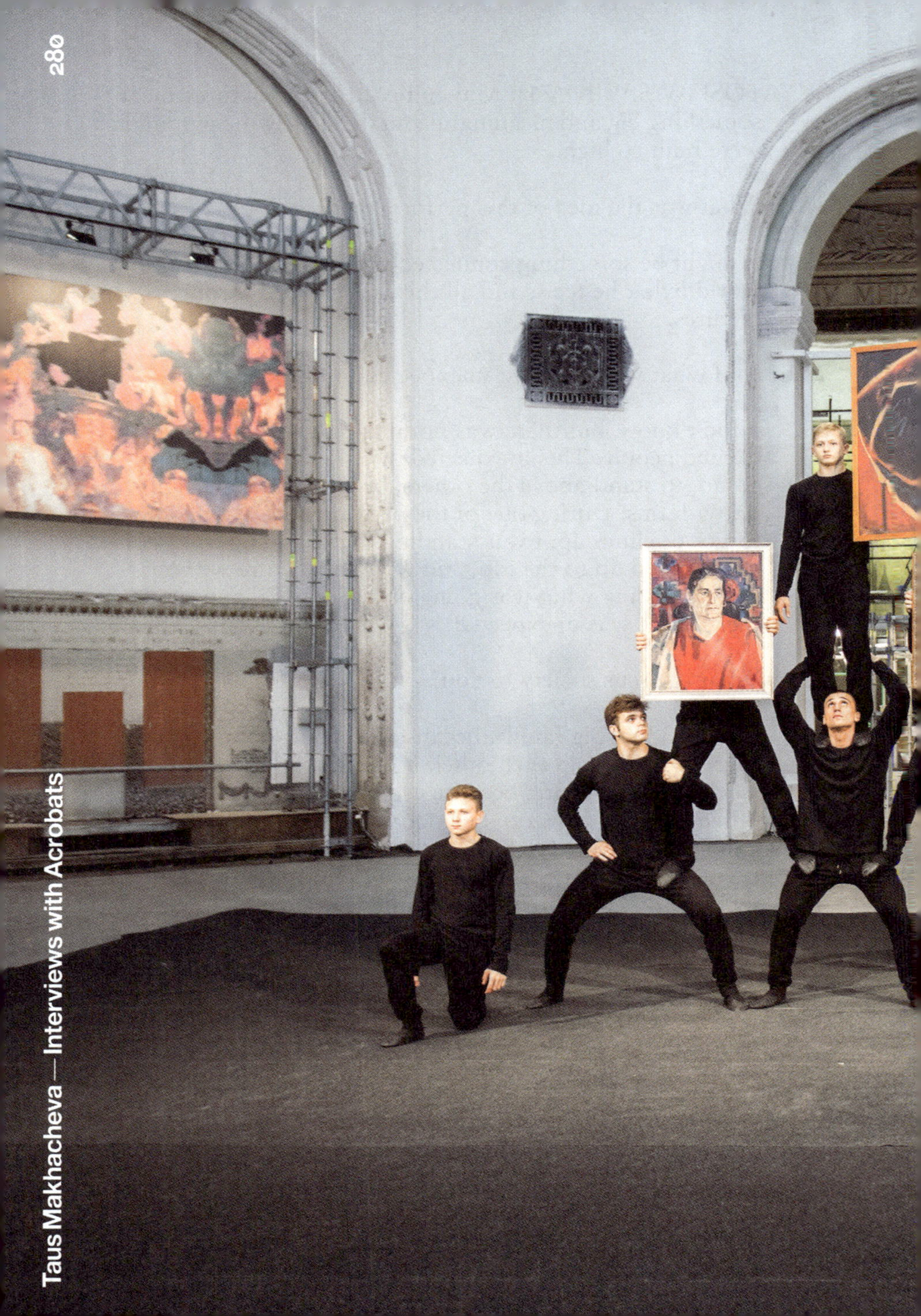

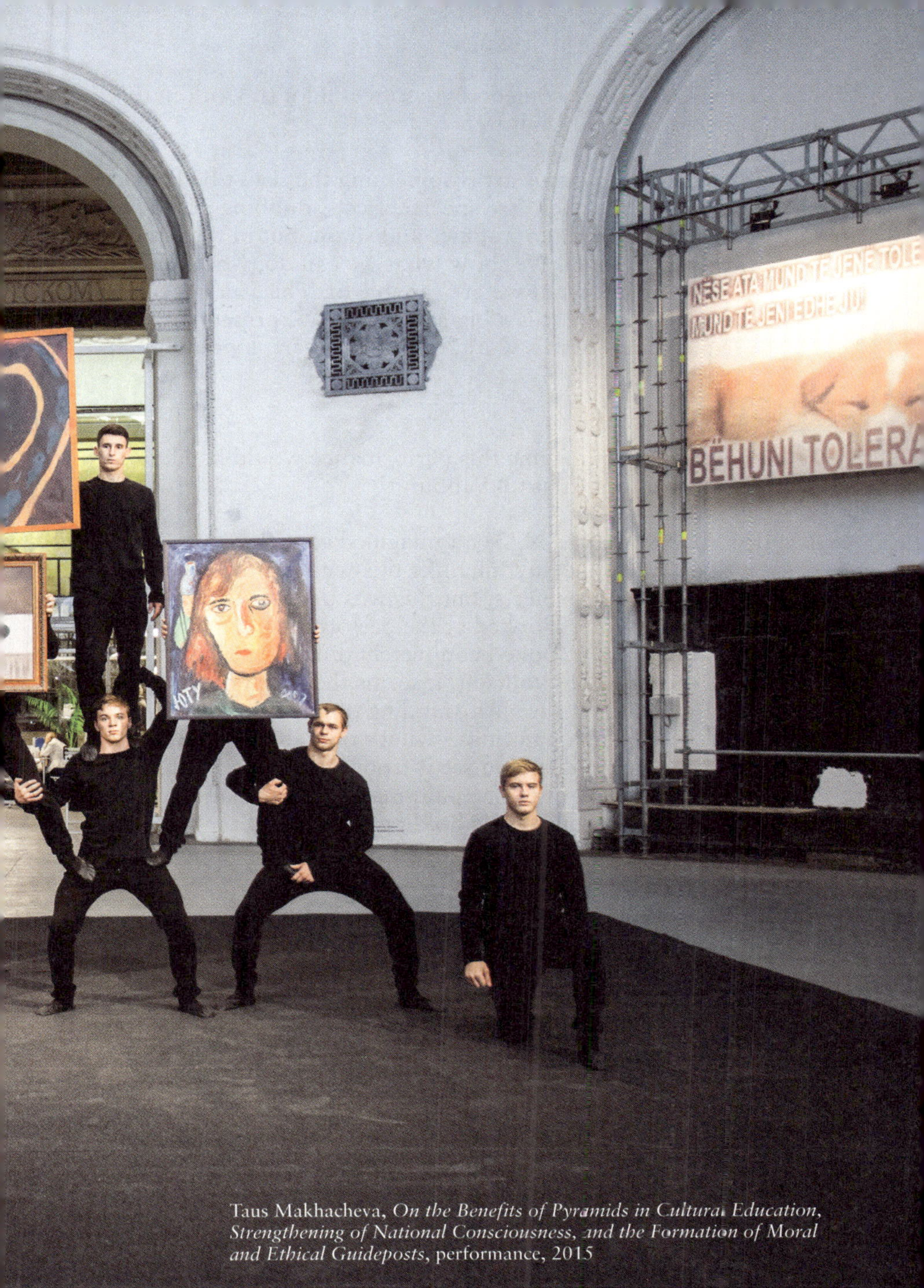

Taus Makhacheva, *On the Benefits of Pyramids in Cultural Education, Strengthening of National Consciousness, and the Formation of Moral and Ethical Guideposts*, performance, 2015

circus art, where somebody sacrifices a lot to work in this sphere to support culture?

SS: In general, the circus art is something that can't be faked. Films are shot, there are special effects, dubbing actors, stuntmen, computer graphics and so on, but in the circus this is impossible. We show what we can do, what our bodies can do, what we are capable of. This is a huge amount of work; it is a big art indeed. We preserve it, we are guardians of this work, of this great art, I would say.

TM: What did you imagine this performance would be like when you were first told about it?

RAFIK KARAKHANYAN (21): I imagined something unusual; we've never done anything like this with pictures. There had been other projects, but this was the first time with paintings. When I looked at the performance from the side, on video, it looked completely different. When you hold the paintings yourself, it seems that nothing unusual is happening, you are just standing on the shoulders of others, holding a painting—what's odd about that? But when seen on video, you see it from a different angle, a more interesting one. The painting is not just hanging on a wall, but someone is holding it, standing on top of another person.

TM: Why were there these metal structures?

RK: To me they seemed like supports for the paintings, nothing strange. The first metal structure we brought out was like a ladder, from the way it built up towards the top, and the second like bookshelves. These were my associations.

TM: How did your perception of the work change from the first performance to the last?

RK: At first, I thought that all I needed to do was to hold the paintings—that's all. By the end, when I watched the video, I knew that I was holding not just paintings, but that they'd been made by someone, and had been passed down through the generations. I no longer had an attitude then of 'I came, I finished my work, I left'.

TM: What was most difficult?

RK: In principle, there was nothing especially difficult. When we first starting making the pyramids, everyone was in a heap, which was slightly tricky. It was also very hard to stay in position and to not start laughing. Actually this was the most difficult part, because when a circus artist performs, he or she smiles and attempts to energise the room, here we did not need those emotions. When people looked at us or did something, we hid behind the paintings and laughed, because when you can see that someone is trying not to laugh, everything becomes even funnier. That was most difficult, and then there were the tricks.

TM: What about the tricks?

RK: The support was three people: two in the middle and one at the top—which was the most difficult position in terms of balance, so as to not drop the painting. We were mostly worried about the paintings, not wanting to damage them.

TM: What was the most unexpected thing within this work?

RK: It's one thing to hold small paintings, and quite another when you're holding large ones… with them in your hands you feel bigger. I hugely enjoyed bringing out the big paintings for 'Atlantis'. It was really cool to be holding such a big painting, a big image and a big meaning, so that when you walked underneath it you were not just a small person.

TM: What do you think about during the performance?

RK: About the audience. You can be in a particular state of mind when you're just going to rehearse; nobody's there, you don't feel excited and it seems like your number is dreadful. But when you work for an audience, when you come out and people applaud, you get excited and you captivate your audience with your energy. The number turns out to be bright and colourful. Contact with the audience is hugely important.

TM: What is contemporary art?

RK: Firstly, I think it's being different from previous generations, it's about being contemporary to our times, and it's perfection within different genres. For example, we've started to combine juggling with acrobatics, gymnastics with balancing acts. That which we perfect over time and that which we do now; that's contemporary art for our times.

TM: So contemporary circus art is a mix of genres?

RK: Before, the juggler only juggled, and the equilibrist only stood. Now, over time, we have begun to mix this. Having performed for a while as a balance master, you come down to jump and dance for a while—we've started to mix all this, where the juggler juggles and then jumps.

TM: Do you think that that's similar to contemporary art, e.g. what you saw at the Moscow Biennale?

RK: Yes, now there are shows like Cirque du Soleil, for example—there's a show on Vernadsky Prospect—*The Messenger*. Everything is without a break, you don't stop, and everything is communicated through these circus numbers.

TM: What reaction did you expect?

RK: The first time, I got lost because there was no music—we came out in silence to the sound of our own footsteps. When we came out, we didn't know what to expect from the audience—would they clap, would they stay or go—but then everything fell into place. It was good to be in silence, like reading in a book in silence, in calm. And it seems to me that it was the same for the audience too; nothing distracted them from the paintings in that calm.

TM: Was there a pyramid that was particularly memorable?

RK: The most difficult one, when we held one big painting, and at the end, when we jumped.

TM: Why did you yourselves decide to jump?

RK: Sometimes magicians do that. The audiences watches, and you do something striking, and the audience instantly wakes up. So we jumped in silence with the painting in the end… and they woke up.

Ilya Budraitskis — Art as a Partisan? Moscow, September 2016

The question of what it means to live together — posed at the 6th Moscow Biennale — is best understood as a question of lost values — ones that art ought to return to society. Tolerance and attention to others, a culture of debate, hospitality, equal opportunities, an inclusive politics rooted in the desire to work together — these are all values that we have long been accustomed to thinking of as necessary but absent. Art, including the kind that is perceived as critical, is supposedly intended to constantly remind us about ethics, which are invariably proclaimed as an ideal, and which are rejected by default. These are the rules one needs to know in order to avoid following them in practice.

In his famous manifesto *Industrial Society and its Future*, Theodore Kaczynski[1] accused the American left of *over-socialisation* — that is, aiming to take the moral codex of society seriously, while society's real life was based on permanently deviating from that codex. We loathe, envy, and get pleasure from a sense of superiority, even though we know that each of these manifestations is against the rules that a person is supposed to follow. The sum of these deviations constitutes the norm, the endurance of which is ensured by an unattainable moral ideal. For the stability of this state it is necessary that somebody constantly remind us of this ideal. According to Ted Kaczynski, the *moral minority* of the left takes on this role. "The goals of today's leftists are NOT in conflict with the accepted morality," Kaczynski writes. "On the contrary, the left takes an accepted moral principle, adopts it as its own, and then accuses mainstream society of violating that principle. Examples: racial equality, equality of the sexes, helping poor people, peace as opposed to war, nonviolence generally, freedom of expression, kindness to animals."[2] The leftist moralists appeal to the conscience of society, to the sense of guilt felt for not being compatible with the moral law that is consistently impossible to fulfil.

One might add that the majority of escapist alternatives — ethical cooperatives, self-managed enterprises, meetings of the Occupy movement (at least, if they are understood as a ghetto, where morally lofty individuals are able to practice 'direct democracy') — may also be related to over-socialised behaviour. This kind of preaching by the left becomes stronger proportionally to the loss of actual political positions and ability to somehow influence the situation.

Pointing to the discord between declaration and action, a focus on the ambiguity and hypocrisy of the existing order of things not only doesn't pose a threat to this order, but in fact gives it strength. Critical art, having long left the traditional place of art in society, has become a key institution of moral criticism. This criticism upholds the consensus and turns moral guilt into a stabilising feeling, which balances out the amoral everyday existence of an individual agent within market relations. Such critical art actually becomes a bastion of socio-democratic and emancipatory values, which no longer have a backing from mass parties or protest movements from below. Art appears as a kind of ghost, a shadow of such movements from the past, borrowing their agenda and turning it into a set of aestheticised views no longer connected to any kind of general political logic.

It's as if, through radical moral statements, the critical artist attempts to piece back together a world that is disintegrating, a world in which the spheres of religion and politics have almost completely lost any connection with the spheres of economics and labour relations. Aggressive conservatism, fundamentalism and xenophobia are today superimposed onto the deregulation of the economy, the destruction of a social sphere and the chaos of individual strategies of survival. Actual oppression again goes into the zone of invisibility, and its victims are deprived of their own voice in politics. Critical art alone continues to remind us of this connection—not in the form of a programme of political action, but as a lofty rhetoric of guilt and responsibility cut off from reality. These days, this art in fact is becoming a new heart of a heartless world.

In his famous 1929 essay *The "Old Mole" and the Prefix Sur in the Words Surhomme and Surrealist*, Georges Bataille declared his break with the Surrealists, having contrasted the Icarian determination to soar toward the sun—a sublime and unreachable horizon—with the strategy of the mole, which, by contrast, sinks deeper and deeper into the black hole of reality.[3] The basis of individual rebellion against reality, according to Bataille, is the desire to give renewed strength to old principles and to enliven illusions and hopes instead of allowing them to rot away completely. The way toward true change will begin only when morality, achievement, and everything that looks like "the liberation of consciousness", evoke no feelings other than disgust and revulsion. Following Marx, Bataille repeats: decay is a laboratory of life, and the more it affects modern society, the closer we come to that, which will come to replace it. Bataille contrasted the crude mass movements, rising up from the thickness of the earth, with the elevated movements of the spirit. The proletariat does not appeal to destroyed morality, and does not attempt to salvage lost values. It does not invoke the moral code when this code is in a state of internal disintegration.

Within the communist movement's break with any kind of consensus, within its escape from the framework of the law, is precisely where the 'conservative revolutionary' Carl Schmitt found his principle of the *partisan* and brought it to a degree of implementation. The main threat to sovereignty of the modern era first appeared at the beginning of the 19th century in the form of a most audacious challenge of the Empire of Napoleon, the most ambitious Universalist project of power and order. The French army, unmatched by organised state armies, received its heaviest blows from peasant partisans in backward countries—first in Italy, then in Russia. The strength of these partisans was in their defiant ignorance, in their natural rebellion against everything orderly and rational. The partisan rejected the laws of war, which had been the highest achievement of modern Europe, already pledged during the Peace of Westphalia in 1648. The partisan was fundamentally not public—he did not wear a uniform (or, rather, constantly changed it). He did not know the borders between battle and rest. He was in his element in nature, among forests and mountains. He appeared suddenly out of the darkness to deliver an instant blow, and just as quickly disappeared. Neither fully a soldier, nor fully a civilian: he could be one or the other depending on the circumstances. According to Schmitt, a partisan is one who is full of absolute hatred and ready to take an absolute risk. Respecting no laws when it comes to his enemy, he equally expects no mercy towards himself.

The first kind of partisan of the modern period was, in the words of Schmitt, a "telluric" warrior, connected to his native land. The archaism, the militant anti-modernity of this figure gave him an incredible strength: it's as if the partisan absorbed all the hidden, pre-state, communitarian and anarchic beginnings of the peasantry, which awaken at the moment of war and strike the modernity that attempts to encroach upon them. The basic novelty of the figure of the partisan that distinguished him from the heroes of antiquity was that his appearance, congruent with the awakening of earth's dark forces, became possible only in response to the high-ranking, to sovereignty and desire for order and transparency. The telluric partisan, a "defensive autochthonous defender of the homeland"[4] for Schmitt, was however only a harbinger of a genuine threat. The essence of the partisan changed when the hidden anarchic forces of the earth connected up with a radical philosophy, the gaze of which was directed not upward, but downward, toward matter, to *Les damnés de la terre*.

In the 20th century, Marxism and its Leninist manifestation created the figure of the global partisan, moved by absolute hatred toward the existing order. Just as the proletariat became economically separated from ownership and from the means of production, the partisan cut himself off politically from his connection to a specific territory, turning the entire world into his sphere of action. The proletarian has nothing that is *his own*, thus his stake in the struggle is not a native piece of land, but all homelands taken as a whole.

The subversive force of the theory of historical materialism, combined with an insurgent who has broken the shackles of hierarchy and law, created, according to Schmitt, the greatest threat to sovereignty. It is the terrifying prospect of the appearance of 'the academic Pugachev', the prospect of which the counterrevolutionary thinker Joseph de Maistre had warned the ruling elite of the Russian Empire about as far back as the beginning of the 19th century.[5]

Now any worker, whom the masters had become accustomed to ignoring, could become a 'speaking instrument' and could turn out to be a secret partisan, adept in revolutionary politics and carrying a feeling of absolute hostility toward capitalism and the state. In this way, the boundary between war and peace disappeared irrevocably. If Clausewitz considered war to be an extension of politics, then, for Lenin, politics was war, devoid of any rules or internal constraints. The global partisan did not seek agreements and the consolidation of the balance of power as a result of military action. He had nothing, and yet his goal was to take the whole world. He would not settle for any less. "Only revolutionary war is true war for Lenin, because it derives from absolute enmity. Everything else is a conventional game," wrote Schmitt.[6]

The strength of the partisan is in his irregularity, in his incredible dynamism and his changing of guises. The reverse side of this impermanent appearance, which confuses the enemy, is a constancy of a strategy that is defined by open battle being impossible. From this angle, Leon Trotsky's famous maxim — "no peace — no war, demobilise the army"—delivered after the failure of the Treaty of Brest-Litovsk in 1918, was the credo of the Schmittean revolutionary partisan. The success of Bolshevism had been not in the military clash with the forces of capitalism, but in the struggle for the souls of people—of citizens, who no longer belonged to their nation states. It is worth waiting for the blow not on the visible front line, but in the rear, where the proletariat could at any moment rise up against their government.

The partisan's main actions take place on the dark side—there, where one expects him the least. He changes not only the meaning of war, but also its spatio-temporal dimension. Schmitt compared the partisan to a submarine, which "in the same way adds an unexpected dimension of depth to the surface of the sea, where old-fashioned naval warfare was once played out."[7]

Thus, we may conclude that the partisan is one who strikes a blow from the underground, from grey, obscure and unexpected places, while forever avoiding open conflict (and therefore its conclusion in the form of a peace agreement). His pantomime with his constant changing of clothes, revealing the absurd conventions of any uniform, is nothing but the seriousness of enmity, revealing the ludic, frivolous and compromising beginning of any 'regular game on the open stage'.[8]

The war of the partisan is not a solders' war inasmuch as his politics is not a *politicians' politics*.

Is it possible to say that, in our days, it is precisely art that can become one of the sources of a new partisanship? That very art that we are used to perceiving as a sign of consensus and compromise? After all, it is this new role of a carrier of social consensus, reconciling society with itself, which has given art the opportunity to go far beyond the bounds of its own traditional territory. The contemporary artist, as if endowed with the extraordinary powers of a peacemaker today, can now act as a scholar, as a political activist and as a courageous explorer of the hidden mechanisms of power. The critical artist has accumulated within himself all aspects of the guerrilla tactics of the past, so as to use them to call for peace and moral renewal. Yet having been given these opportunities, is he able to use them for diametrically opposite aims? The international art actionism of the 2000s, from Yes Man to Pussy Riot and Pyotr Pavlensky, shows how a political activist—in the guise of an artist—finds opportunities for public critique and propaganda that are incomparable with the possibilities of a normal political activist. These new opportunities almost exactly correspond to the main features of the Schmittean partisan — irregularity, increased mobility, and political involvement. Taking on the guise of an artist for the purposes of gaining strength is likewise appropriate for the leftist theorist, the strategist of social movements, and for the fighter against gentrification. This mimicry is gradual, and it is not consciously recognised as a strategy, as an overall unifying line that is able to give the artistic partisan a global character and necessary depth. However, in the context of accelerating social decay, political degradation and militarisation of the world, the role of art as a power of compromise will sooner or later lose all its meaning. Partisanship is not only an opportunity for a new art strategy, which takes advantage of art's situationally consensual character, but also for a new form in which art will — in principle — be able to maintain itself in the future. The way to this realisation for art lies in criticism directed inward toward itself, through a thoughtful undermining of its own accommodating and moralising position, and through its assertion of a deep partisan spirit of hostility. That is the spirit that will be able to unite a community of artists and viewers and give them the real power to "live together".

1
Theodore John Kaczinski (*1942) is an American scientist and anarchist, famous for mailing letter-bombs. He became known as the "Unabomber" (university and airline bomber) through media reports. Between 1978 and 1995 more than twenty scientists and corporate employees became victims of Kaczynski's assaults.

2
Theodore Kaczynski (Unabomber), *Industrial Society and its Future*, in: *The Washington Times*, 22nd September 1995: http://www.washingtonpost.com/wp-srv/national/longterm/unabomber/manifesto.text.htm.

3
See Georges Bataille, *The "Old Mole" and the Prefix Sur in the Words Surhomme and Surrealist*, in: *Georges Bataille, Visions of Excess. Selected Writings 1927-1939* (Minneapolis, University of Minnesota Press, 2008), pp. 33 – 44, p. 38.

4
Carl Schmitt, *The Theory of the Partisan*, Moscow: Praksis, p. 49.

5
Joseph de Maistre TBC.

6
Carl Schmitt, *The Theory of the Partisan*, Moscow: Praksis, 2007, p. 81.

7
Ibid., p. 108.

8
See ibid.

Ines and Eyal Weizman — Between the Dissident and the Activist Moscow, 28th September 2015

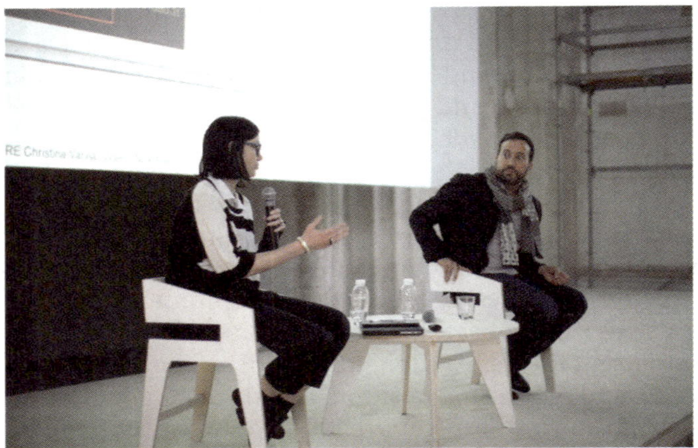

Keynote Ines and Eyal Weizman, 28th September 2015

INES WEIZMAN: VDNKh, the location of this biennial, reminded me that I have in fact already been on site before—about thirty years ago. To verify this I looked through my family album. In 1985 my parents had saved up for a truly unusual journey: a family holiday in Moscow. It was not that easy for an East German to travel to the Soviet Union. Months before we had to apply for travel documents and had to be lucky enough to be selected by a travel agency that would eventually organise the trip. It was also my first flight. We visited all the important monuments and museums of Moscow, but skipped the Mausoleum at the time for a shopping trip. We preferred to buy some classical vinyl records for my parents and a plastic tennis racket for me, which was the latest fashion back then. We also spent a whole day at the Exhibition of Achievements of the National Economy of the Soviet Union [VDNKh]. We wandered from one pavilion to the next, trying to see as many exhibits as possible. We saw the cosmos exhibition—which left no doubt as to why our bloc had won the space race. It was a strange mixture between a museum, a trade show and a propaganda catwalk that was to celebrate the achievements of the national economy.

So I am happy, after thirty years, to be back and I am grateful that you have also invited my husband Eyal; we do enjoy travelling together. Although we do not directly work together, we quite often meet at the same conferences and events. We meet at events about walls. I would speak about the Iron Curtain that ran through Germany and Eyal about a concrete wall that still runs through Israel/Palestine. Ours—I am referring also to the audience here from Moscow—has collapsed while his has actually come up.

For us, one grey November evening in 1989, it was all over. A few sharp wounds of concrete and a space, larger than outer space, opened up. Only when lying there like a corpse, its terrifying life draining out of it, was it possible to get near it, even to touch it. The Wall, on our side, was a perilous territory that was not confined to its actual physical presence. It existed throughout our country, our ideological bloc. For those not living in Berlin, the Wall was nothing but a mental and political condition rendered concrete by a physical artefact. We knew it existed but never saw it. The eyes of its watch-towers were already built into our personalities. Eyal will speak later about the wall in Israel/Palestine. But what distinguished the two walls was that ours, mine and yours, appeared to us invisible, while his was not a wall at all. The two historical conditions gave rise to two different relationships between politics and aesthetic practices. The two walls enclosed communities and ideas in different ways. We could say that the Soviet wall was there to stop people from running out and away while the wall in Israel was built in the West Bank to prevent people from coming in. This logic also gives birth to different types of political and aesthetic practice.

While on our side, say in East Germany, uttering one's opinion and thoughts freely put one at risk (to take away every little freedom you had to pursue one's work, studies, or put you in prison), in Israel/Palestine, the possibility of contestation does exist, at least for Israelis on the Israeli side. Our historical condition enclosed by one type of wall gave rise to the figure of the dissident, while the other gave birth to the activist. The activist and the dissident are very different positions, very different modes of speech and action, and they have very different aesthetic practices.

This spectrum between the dissident and the activist is at the heart of our conversation tonight. They bear on our ability to act as artists in relation to the unfolding of our different political presents. Politics, as according to Chantal Mouffe and Ernesto Laclau, is "a practice of creation, reproduction and transformation of social relations […] and those social relations are articulated in a field crisscrossed with antagonisms."[1] The question of the political cannot be reduced to just institutions of politics, to state and party, but to agents and groups operating independently and agonistically. We can perhaps understand this category when thinking about the creative and precarious, sometimes dangerous practices of dissidents in the Soviet Bloc. As in aesthetic practice it was turned into a somewhat cunning manner of double speech that used art and architecture to deliver and exploit well-coded messages, articulated in music, theatre, installations, performance art and also, indeed quite incredibly so, in architecture.

They wanted to transform, to break away from stained socialism and its empty propaganda and political slogans. Artists wanted to transform, but could not express it in a clear articulation of a claim. The dissident was always an agent without a party—seemingly outside politics, a-political and hyper-political. Or political on the meta-level of framing the possibilities of speech and vision. It is the dissident, as an agent operating outside state institutions, outside party affiliations or any officially sanctioned order, that I try to identify and portray.

What can we learn from the tension between the activist and the dissident? What is the difference between them?

INES WEIZMAN: While Western human rights activists could use the media for "naming and shaming", dissidents in the Soviet Bloc (here and in East Germany) had to work largely underground with *samizdat* publications, declarations, exhibitions, performances, gatherings, open letters and communiqués—always under the omnipresent risk of persecution, intimidation, physical violence, imprisonment, forced exile, social discrimination and even death. One could say that on the one side of the Wall was the Western activist while on the other the Eastern dissident. The former is the prominent model for modes of political engagement in the world, the latter seemingly now extinct, is a mode of retreat from it.

How to write the political history of dissidence?

INES WEIZMAN: It is paradoxical perhaps that the dissident itself is a seismograph of transformation for what happens at the moment when the thing contested, such as the collapse of communism, disappears. 'Dissidentism' could have collapsed with the Soviet Bloc that gave it a target and meaning. But it did not. Mostly, the dissidents of Eastern Europe wanted to change the meaning of socialism or communism. They wanted free elections, more freedom to travel, and, most importantly, freedom of expression—not a reversion to capitalism, and certainly not the predatory crony capitalism that we see in some of its states today.

Dissidents do not share a single ideology. What they do share is an essential engine for politics—discontent—transformed into political action. But dissidence is different from revolutionary politics, a form of political practice that does not seek to overthrow and replace government or to take over the power to govern. Instead, dissidence is determined by radically and fundamentally contesting the way in which subjects are governed. It is a fundamental questioning of professional, cultural and political conventions.

Architecture is perhaps the least likely of practices to articulate a dissident position. Producing buildings requires political powers that control the two main conditions necessary for construction to occur: land and money. These are largely conservative and institutional. But the position of architecture—at the nexus where political, commercial, financial, military, ideological and cultural forces operate—also has the potential to serve as a medium for articulating ideas of resistance, critique, reform or invasion.

Can there be dissident architects?

INES WEIZMAN: My research on architect dissidents began actually with a cultural critique, during the moment of transformation after 1989 in East Germany, after the reunification with West Germany. We actually had a disastrous cultural policy of trying to erase anything looking socialist, a sort of running against these buildings. Out of this sentiment, I found it important to frame the reform movement at that time; it was actually a story that did not fit into this kind of celebratory mode of looking at the successful reunification project. I looked at the dissident reform projects as a sort of spectrum of dissidents, a spectrum of possible practices from the almost unnoticeable or definitely invisible practices, to others which approached more the boundary with activism. Looking at the covert reform practices and daily dissidence in architectural work, I realised that the work of architects had not been appropriately framed and appreciated. Dissident practice, I found, exists as a spectrum of possible interventions. I will present now a work by two architects that seemingly burst the boundary between dissidence and activism:

It is found in the work of the two architects Christian Enzmann and Bernd Ettel, whose imagination and fantasy did not remain in the domain of the private but rather burst through the elastic boundary between private dissidence and its public expression with dramatic effects, having personal consequences for the architects. These two architects, research fellows at the architecture school in Weimar, smuggled competition briefs into the GDR from West Berlin and smuggled out their submissions with the help of a network of Austrian monks. The format of their foldable drawings (letter-sized sheets) was chosen to deal with the constraints of the monks' perilous journey from East to West Berlin—they were able to hide them in their sleeves while crossing the borders to bring these drawings to West Berlin.

The unlucky moment occurred when, in 1983, one of the jury members reviewing Enzmann and Ettel's submissions in West Berlin was most likely a Stasi informer and alerted the East German authorities.

Enzmann and Ettel had decided to participate in a competition in West Berlin that was one of the first in a series of competitions for a building now known as the Topography of Terror. It actually addresses the memory of the Hitler regime in that part of Berlin. Their drawing was headed with four large-typed lines saying: *DIKTATUR*. Rather than making a reference to the dictatorship of the Third Reich, they drew a wall-strip, watchtowers and tree-lined pathways in an apparently idyllic landscape design, making an obvious, but ironic connection to the architecture of surveillance of the GDR regime. They operated by seeking to produce architectural narratives, legible in built form. These architects expressed their dissent in the drawings in full awareness of the consequences. Aiming to push the system to show the limit of its intolerance, perhaps in order to expose these political limits that were still very real during the gradual meltdown of the Eastern Bloc, or else, eager to be deported into the West, they preferred to go to prison as a step on their way out of the country.

Although it was an anonymous competition and the architects were not at first found, eventually the information led back to East Berlin. The two architects were then captured, charged with offending the GDR, and imprisoned for 20 months.

If we think of dissident practices as a rather delicate interplay between the private and the public domain, between subtle gestures of refusal, subversion and outspoken critique, the work of Enzmann and Ettel seems to have pushed this boundary. In its radicalism it marks the limit of the possible range of dissident architecture.

We can see here how dissidence embodies inherent paradoxes and, in an almost Faustian pact, it invites power —its actors and executors (and sometimes executioners)— into a complex dance with uncertain and precarious results. Here, distance from power represents the extreme unknowns and on-going dangers of this practice as it shifts from complicity to complexity, from being instrumentalised, to managing, to achieving real and effective change.

Even if dissidents have not sought power, they have nevertheless been supported and abused by those who did. Dissident practices have therefore faced different orders of traps and contradictions, which makes the diagram of these conflicts more complex than a simple conflict along the vertical dimension between top-down imposition and bottom-up dissent.

The history of the dissident is also the history of complicity. We all know those dissidents that finally fell prey to regressive politics or new regimes—where they became political figures. Today, in the political reality that I inhabit, as a director of the Bauhaus-Institute in Weimar, there is almost an inversion—and dissident practices are no longer a radical replacement of communist ideals with the freedom to consume, but rather to protect and salvage what is still precious in communism and in socialism. To distil and insist. And this has an architectural manifestation. In my research, in film studies and in my work as a teacher, I am trying to combat the destruction and demolition of neighbourhoods and buildings that were once appreciated by their architects and inhabitants under socialism, but that have come under a harsh cultural attack. In a strange change of sides, I am involved in a quest to invert the obvious equation: no longer the demolition of these dysfunctional housing blocks, but rather an understanding that they were dysfunctional because they were never completed, or their very design had been corrupted somewhere in the planning process.

Sometimes history plays bizarre tricks on us, when this position—seeking to complete what socialism had started—was referred to by the new planners of my city as radical and dissident.

EYAL WEIZMAN: I would like to talk about activism within a force field. Within a force field, architecture is no longer static. The building of a wall in the West Bank marks a transition point between what Ines spoke about and my subject: It seems like the most direct, solid embodiment of top-down state power. In fact, the power of the wall in the West Bank lies precisely in it being elastic and dynamic. The wall's wiggly line around settlements and smaller sections shows not its quality of solidity but of elasticity. Therefore, we need to look at categories of viscosity, when the wall stretches in curls like the tongue of a frog to capture small outposts to include them in either the Israeli or Palestinian area. They affect the path of the wall, which is thereby forever elastic and dynamic.

When investigating the force field of viscosity, activism can never remain outside. It is always part of the field, an intervention in it and forever complicit with it. The wall in the West Bank is no continuous line, but fragmented across its entire terrain. Also, there is no direct line to separate the Israeli control area from the Palestinian, but instead there are islands, like splintered worms, where the wall curls around individual settlements. It is not only divided in plan, but also in vertical section. There is a road under Israeli sovereignty, spanning above a valley under Palestinian sovereignty, proceeding into a tunnel to then continue under a Palestinian town. The division between both is completely fragmented in space, which creates an Escher-like effect, in which the walls operate in three dimensions.

The spaces that my research agency Forensic Architecture has mapped are in continuous transformation. We may look at a still-shot of them, but the domain remains viscous. This is what we call a political plastic. For an activist, space is always a political plastic — as much as a force field can be translated into form. We assume form is a way of sensing force. The complexity of a map of the Israeli and Palestinian areas and their division is a consequence of a very complex force field that is continuously changing. To view that map properly, we would need to look at it in animation, to see how it is constantly transforming and thus visualising how force and form are interrelated. Our way of reading it would then imply reading each one of the twists and turns as very complex shapes as well as the force fields that created them.

In order to understand the paradox of activism, I would like to introduce an example from an Israeli court two years ago, in which a group of Israeli activists were trying to petition, together with Palestinians, against the wall. The main evidence to support their claim was architectural. Thus, architecture enters the court as a means of activism: The judges are being told which area is where, where they overlap etc. but cannot fully understand and therefore ask both legal parties to build a model and bring it back to the hearing. That is how the first architectural model of the wall was produced — not by the people who are building the wall, but by those who are trying to resist it. This case shows the problems the wall inherits: The model is one of a settlement. Of a green line to separate the territories and two more: a red line and a blue line.

The red line represents the wall as the state, the Israeli military, wants to build it. The blue one is the one the activists are arguing for. They want to improve the initial proposal to create the best of all possible walls, or the least evil wall. It still runs through occupied territory, but along a slightly better route to leave the Palestinians more land under their control. The architectural evidence (the model) is brought into the court, carried by two porters. An additional table is brought in from the cafeteria to put the model on, so that it may be presented to the judges. However, since the table is too low for the judges to see the model, they have to step down, for the first time ever, from their seats and assemble around the model. Now the model is no longer an object of representation, but it organises the discussion and puts legal protocol out of action. The legal session becomes a material design session where everybody is pushing and pulling between the red and the blue line.

A fantastic thing that happens when you put an architectural model into a room is that everybody is smiling. You cannot not smile when you see an architectural model, because it is a kind of reduced world under control. One of the main judges of Israel inspects the model and measures a particular part of the wall, arguing, pushing and pulling the wall—attempting to 'redesign' it. The proposed new line's distance to the red planned wall is 400 metres, this is the distance between the evil and the less evil wall. But something else happened in that courtroom: The very presence of the wall was justified.

A simple design participation, in which the communities ask to comment upon a design that is being put in their environment, creates a situation where the victims are asked to participate—the force field brings everybody to it. It is all-pervasive; they can act, but by acting they are creating the very reality that they are opposing. And this is different to the reality Ines was speaking about, of a dissident that is outside of politics and the force field.

When Forensic Architecture was asked to look into this case study of the village of Battir in South Jerusalem and help stop the building of the wall, we decided to change the language of contestation. We no longer appealed to human rights. (As a field of activism, human rights have been abused.) We decided to represent the environment. We decided to take as our clients the trees and rocks and terraces. We treated the landscape as if it were a person. My colleague Paolo Tavares called it non-human rights or the rights of the non-human. By thinking like this, we produced a new model that actually won us the case recently. There was no wall built there. And if a wall were to be built there, it could not legally be realised at this little garden, on these terraces, it would forever remain a protected hole.

Let us think of activism between dystopia and utopia. With a group of friends I am working in the West Bank where we have our own office in residency and are projecting images for a reality that is almost impossible to imagine — the de-colonisation of Israel/Palestine and transformation of all architecture of occupation into other things. For example the transformation of a single family house from a residential place into one with public functions. During a Hamas demonstration, an architectural model of a faithful settlement was burnt. I mention this to point out the influence of architecture on the imaginary.

Our most recent project was one for which we were working very much like pathologists. The level of despair about failure and our political reality, something that is so solidified and ossified, led us to develop a practice that would not only open up a discussion with the larger Israeli and Palestinian public, but in fact somehow instrumentalise architectural history and research as evidence in court. Forensic Architecture is the institution we have established for that. It is now a rather large institution providing evidence for international prosecutors in courts such as the United Nations, national courts or other truth commissions worldwide, both political and juridical. The members of Forensic Architecture are not scientists, ballistic experts or doctors; they are artists, architects and curators, or filmmakers too. Their tools are important and effective in opening up a political process.

The term *forensis*, which is also the title of an exhibition we curated together with Anselm Franke in Berlin, is a Latin term. From it derives the word ‘forensics’. It is the art of the forum. In Rome, the forum meant much more than a legal domain. It meant a public space, sort of chaotic, a space of politics, law and the economy. Only in modernity has the notion of forensics somewhat telescoped into the presentation of science in court. With our aim to open up forensics as a public potential practice, we had to rely on this term.

A lot of our work is undertaken through images, through the interpretation of architecture as captured by all sorts of media. For example, we synced up two videos in order to discover the moment of the killing of a Palestinian boy who was shot without any provocation in the West Bank. From another video, we were able to identify the soldier who was shooting exactly at the time you see the kid falling. Through both videos, we could establish an architectural trajectory between the location of the person that was hit and the soldier who was shooting him. It is a rather media-heavy investigation practice that brings together space and images, often through the utilisation of 3D models and subsequent analysis. In this case it led to the indictment and arrest of that person.

Another of our recent investigations was in Gaza. It is an analysis that Forensic Architecture has undertaken for Amnesty International and for the International Criminal Court (ICC) in The Hague. The project was realised through the syncing up of hundreds and hundreds of images. Many of them had smoke plumes in them. What followed was an analysis of the architecture of smoke plumes, to sync up and understand the evolution of a selected one from last summer's Gaza war, by plotting all images available on a timeline. The problem was that all the images we received out of Gaza came without any intact meta-data (info on the location, time etc.). This is why we were looking at the form of the cloud for any time indicators, to read it as a physical clock within the image. Luckily, we got hold of a high resolution satellite image of Rafah from that day on which we could see some of the smoke plumes. And since we knew the time the satellite image was taken, we could locate the original images collected in space. Concluding from the smoke plum visible on the city plan in the satellite picture and from its elevated version in the collected photograph, we started syncing up the timeline; thus undertaking a very careful kind of measuring and study of clouds as architecture and indicators of time. This link between a cloud shape and time would then allow us to look at any other image of the battlefield. Whenever we saw the same cloud shape, we could determine at what time the image had been taken. In a number of images we identified an identical hairline and could then create a timeline of all images from social media from that day. These were actually thousands of images produced by people in Gaza. The entire syncing up of that day's battle was undertaken by turning to an investigation of the form, the morphology of the cloud. Thus, we are talking about dynamic architecture. Considering that the cloud only existed for eight minutes, it was a building in gas form.

From a careful look at the clouds, we started noticing other things we were able to isolate in micro frames from the image: We could see the bomb dropping. The lawyers who were working on the case wanted to know who had manufactured that bomb, which killed 16 people. Because we were able to locate the images in a 3D model, we could measure it (the image itself and the bomb) and in fact determine the exact shape and size—simply by departing from a freeze shot. Finally, it was clear that this was an American-manufactured bomb, which was dropped in the middle of a residential neighbourhood.

These case studies underline how a very complex set of practices defines the edges and contours of possibilities for political action through architecture. On the one hand, providing evidence, and on the other hand, a proposal of a reality that seems impossible to imagine in de-colonising architecture, both complementing the idea of the dissident that was articulated by Ines.

BART DE BAERE: I have a question, to which I do not find a solution. To put it very boldly: When are these actions really successful, what is their aim, maybe to analyse and to see there is one bomb from that mark? That is a moment, but in broader lines dissident and activist activities always face a system which they are discontent with. What could be the dream of a dissident or the dream of an activist? The dream that would help define terms of success of dissidence or success of activism. Because it seems to me that they are always about a direction of failure. Even if they succeed along the way, still they fail, because they end up with another regime. My question derives from this energy of discontent, the different operational modes that enter relations with a force field, what might be the best we might dream of?

INES WEIZMAN: The dissident will not change politics. He or she is essentially against any kind of politics. They are producing a space in which you can think. In that sense it does not have the proper results, because the action cannot directly be implemented. While activism, as Eyal has shown, has consequences. It takes larger risks and is no longer about creating the space in which you can think and trying to create an outside, to describe new questions in a situation that seems hopeless—when you do not even see your enemy clearly. Dissidence is trying to describe that space, and for that you also need aesthetic practices, a form of creativity to find what you are looking for. I find it fascinating that dissidence has to shift to activism at some point. A dream may empower dissident practices to maybe build together a quantity so that activism can happen. Then there is a community, an Eastern European university, subversive or underground universities, that would form an idea and at some point be able to translate it into activism. I guess the kind of activism Eyal was presenting here has direct legal consequences; it is not remaining just an idea or ideal.

EYAL WEIZMAN: I want to reinforce what Ines was saying. We try to simplify only as much as we draw to limit consent. When complicit with it, you are engaging with a tool, a grammar of power, to find out which bomb it is, who manufactured it etc. Political practice today needs to exist in-between and needs to rethink its position on that spectrum: entering a negotiation in a force field (when assembling around a model in court with the danger of reaffirming some realities that we do not agree with) and always considering that absolute withdrawal and refusal exist.

The question is not only which bomb fell that day, but what is the world that allows for that bomb to fall into that place? Then we are talking about a chain of manufactures, of trades, of legal reality, political, geopolitical and economic reality. Around every moment there exists a whole world. We never allow ourselves to sink into the hole of detail without seeing through a glass ball in order to unpack a larger political force field. Similar to the work of a historian — and as such we write the history of a day in Gaza, with the tools of contemporary history: media, media analyses, architectural analyses, cloud analyses, shadow analyses, etc.

The evidence we seek to investigate always depends on the form it is presented in. It is weak evidence if it does not have a political implication to it and is carried by a certain form of political gathering. There are always moments where one needs to withdraw. By thinking in terms of a perhaps old-fashioned Maoist auto-critique, this should exist inside the organisation. Inside Forensic Architecture we have a critical unit that would seek to understand the wider politics of that court, of the force field and whether to enter it or not. The possibility of withdrawal should always exist.

For me, presenting in an Israeli court is something we do not do anymore. We will not submit our evidence to them because we think that it is their instrument of power. We prefer to intervene by releasing the information into the public domain so it can embarrass them, exactly at that moment when they arrive at the proceedings for a particular situation.

1
Ernesto Laclau and Chantal Mouffe, *Hegemony and Socialist Strategy: Towards a Radical Democratic Politics*, Verso, 1985, p. 153.

Alevtina Kakhidze — All Times News

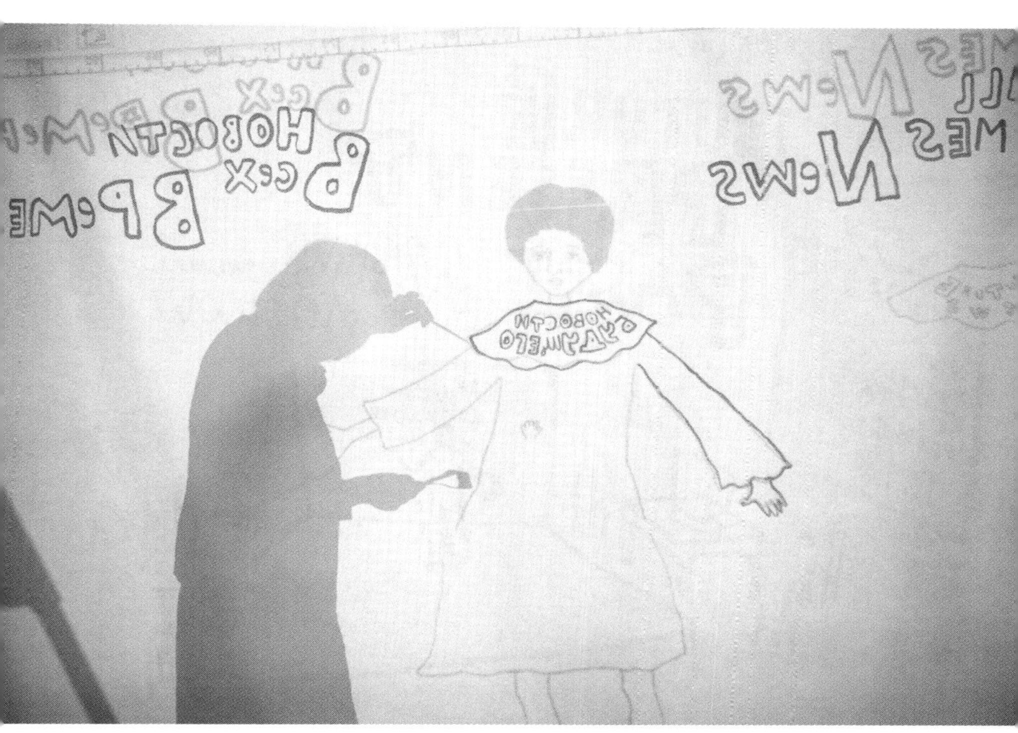

Alevtina Kakhidze, *All Times News*, Moscow Biennale 2015

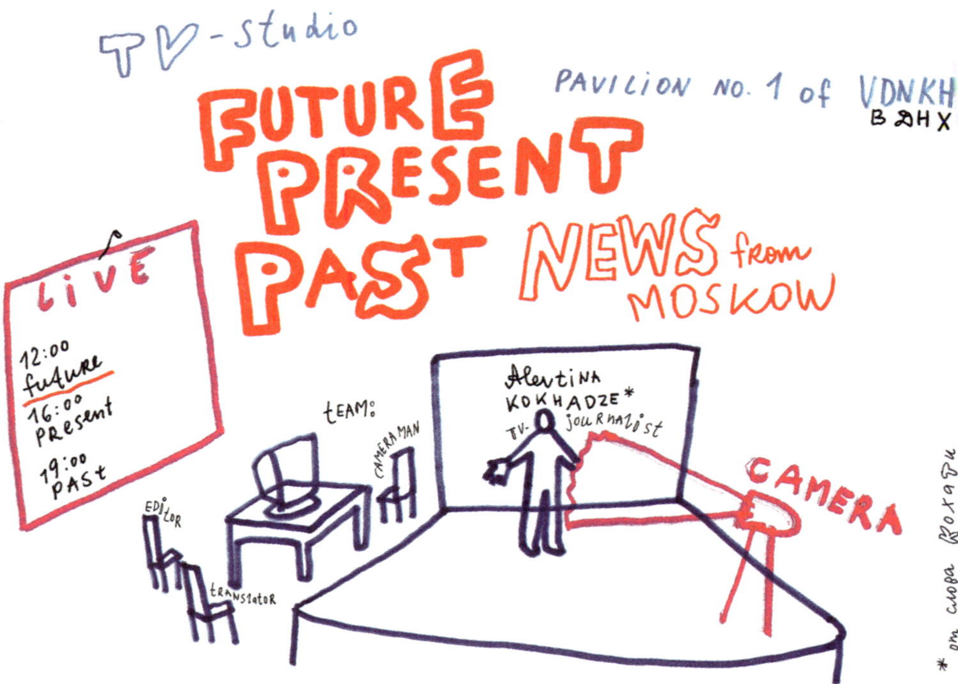

TV-studio
PAVILION NO. 1 of VDNKH
ВДНХ
FUTURE
PRESENT
PAST
NEWS from MOSKOW
LIVE
12:00 future
16:00 Present
19:00 PAST
TEAM:
CAMERAMAN
EDITOR
TRANSLATOR
Alevtina KOKHADZE*
TV-journalist
CAMERA
* от слова Кохати

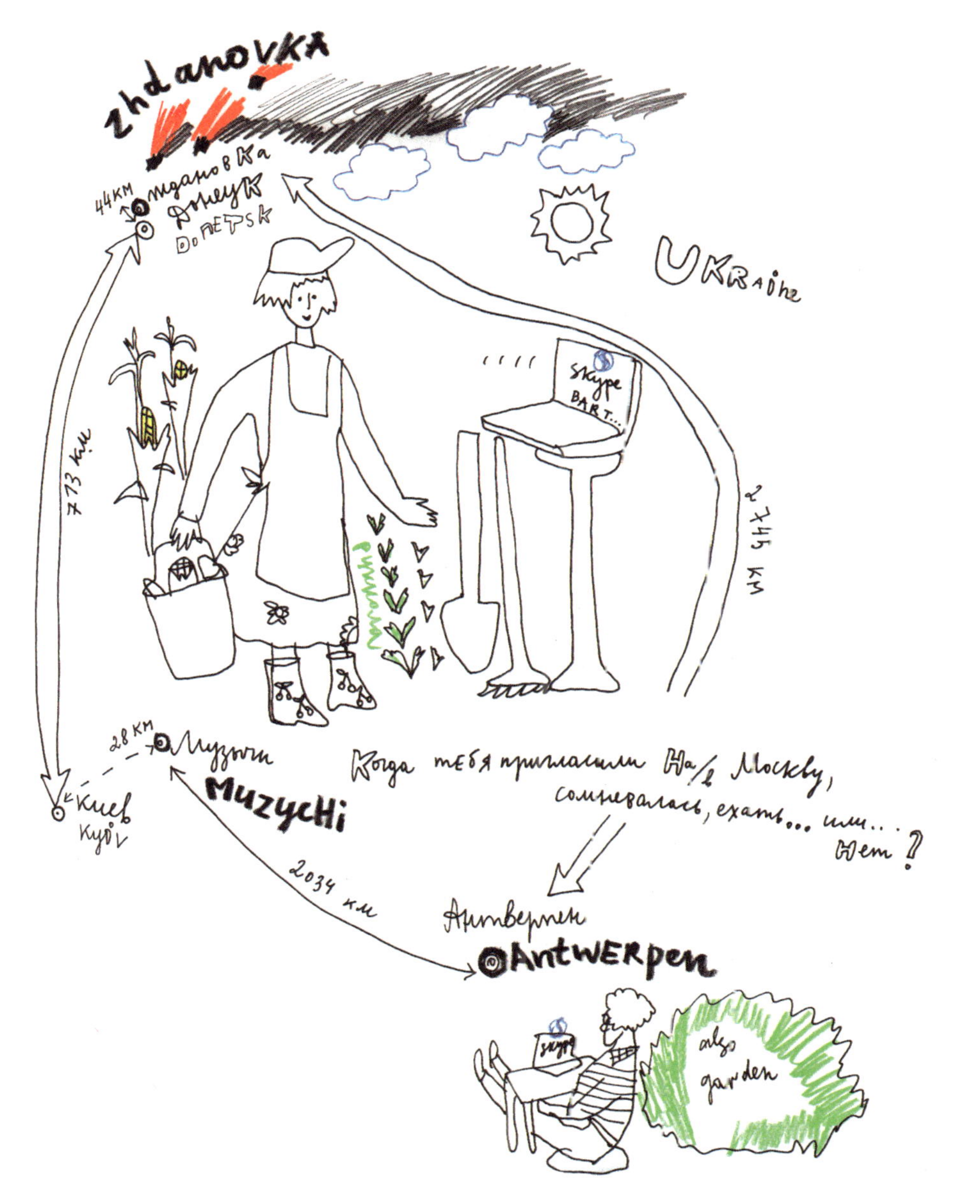
zhdanovka
44 км
Жданов Ка
Донецк
Donetsk
Ukraine
Skype
BART...
773 км
2 745 км
28 км
Музычи
Киев
Київ
Muzychi
Когда тебя пригласили на/в Москву,
сомневалась, ехать... или...
нет?
2034 км
Антверпен
Antwerpen
skype
algo garden

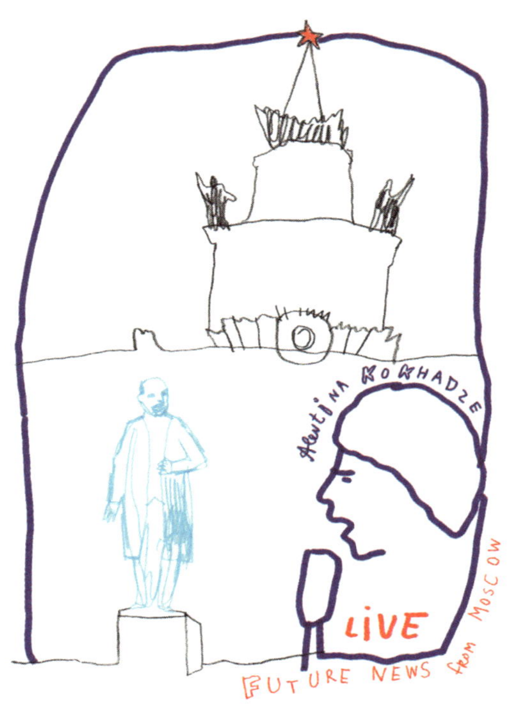
LIVE
FUTURE NEWS from MOSCOW

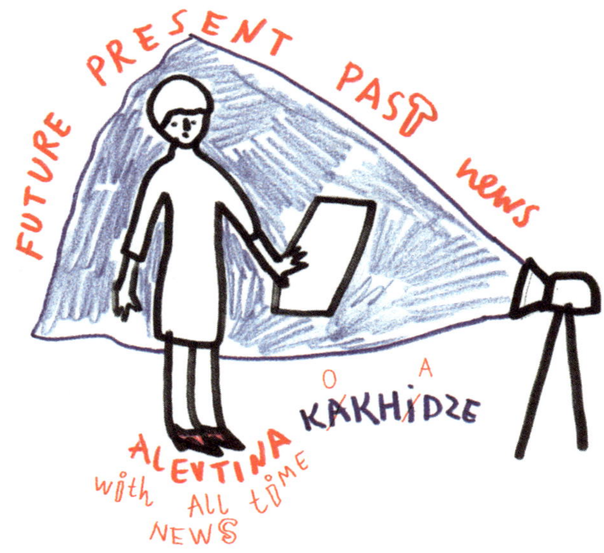
FUTURE PRESENT PAST news
KAKHIDZE
ALEVTINA
with ALL time NEWS

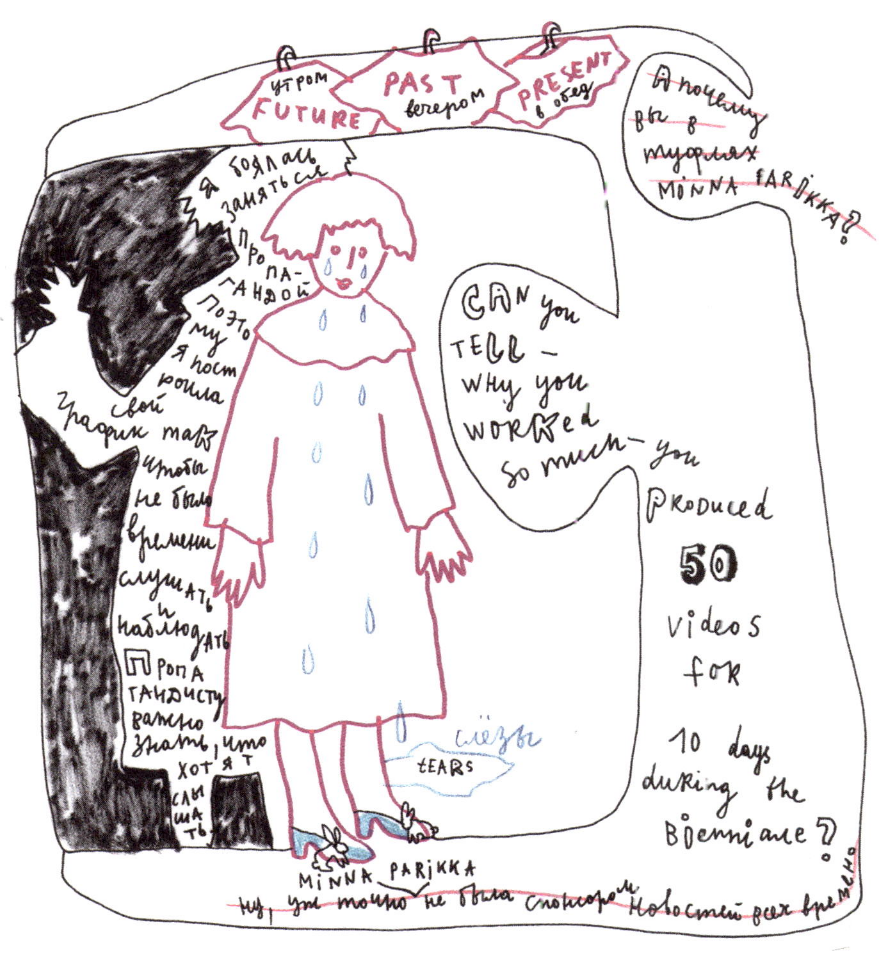
утром
FUTURE
PAST
вечером
PRESENT
в обед
А почему вы в туфлях MINNA PARIKKA?
Я боялась заняться пропагандой поэтому я построила свой график так чтобы не было времени слушать и наблюдать. Пропагандисту важно знать, что хотят слышать.
CAN you TELL – why you WORKed so much – you PRODUCEd 50 videos FOR 10 days during the Biennale?
слёзы
TEARS
MINNA PARIKKA
ну, уж точно не была спикером новостей всех времен

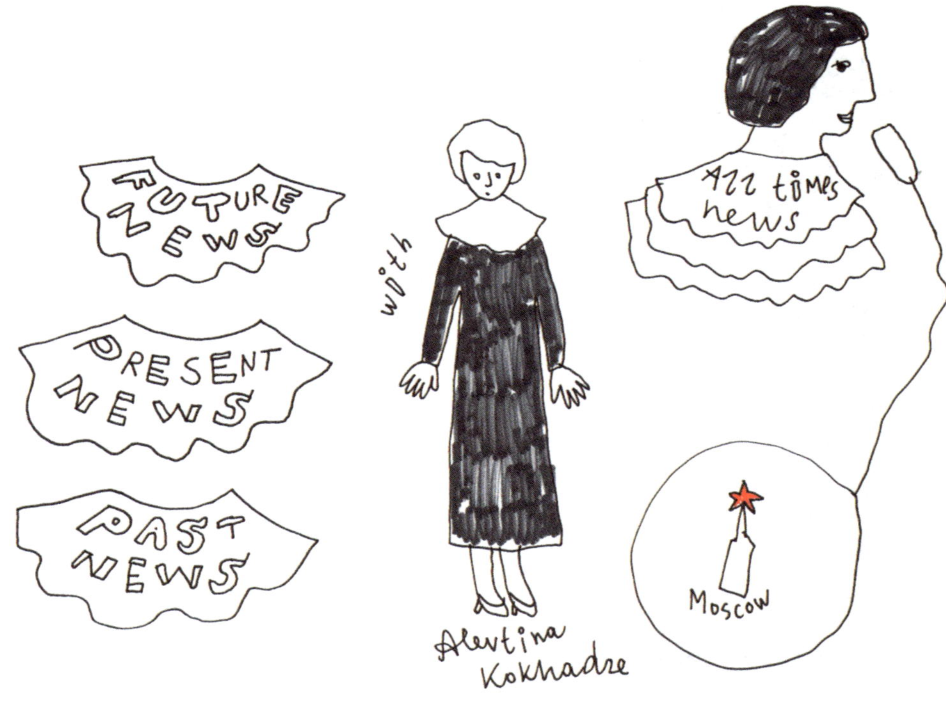
FUTURE NEWS
PRESENT NEWS
PAST NEWS
with
Alevtina Kokhadze
All times news
Moscow

HOW TO GATHER?

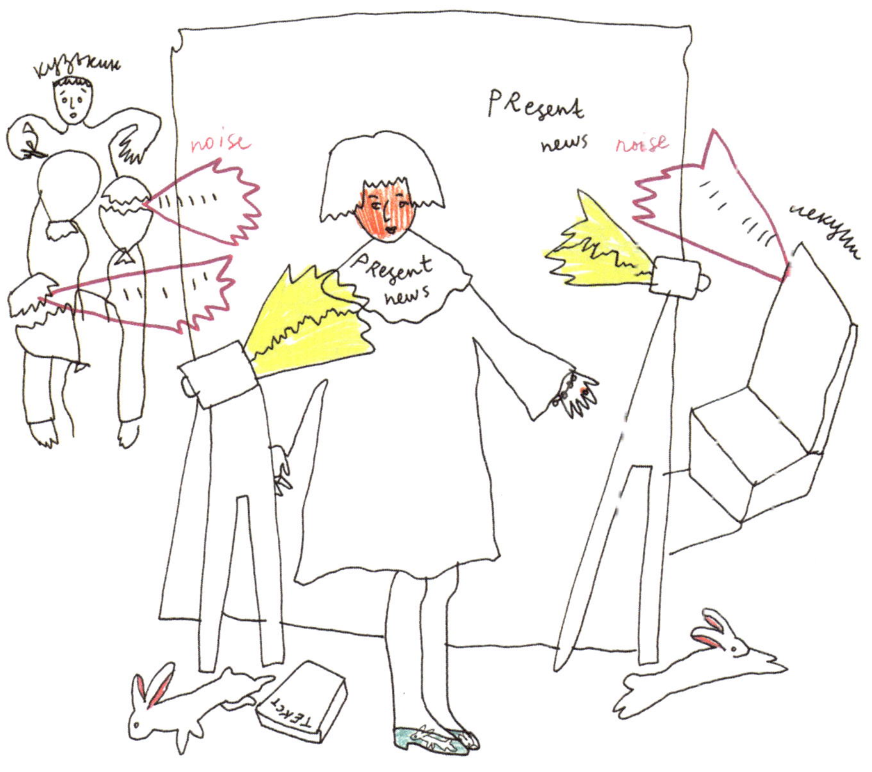

MOSKOW

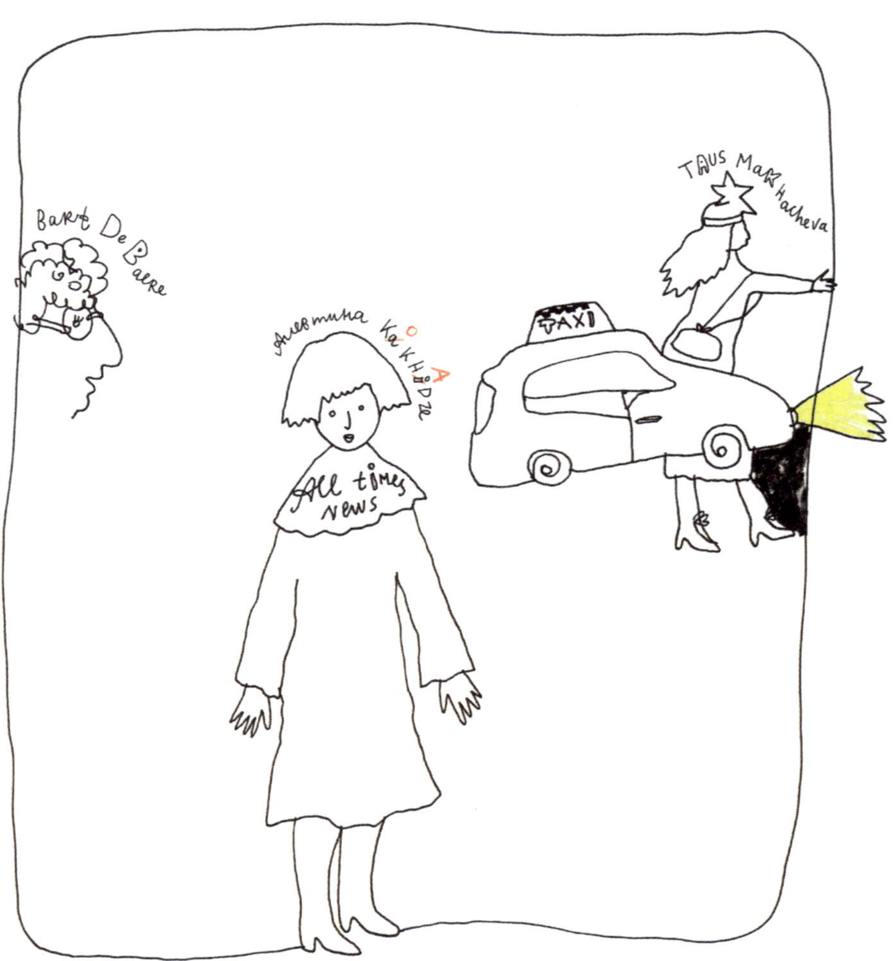

Bart De Baere
Алевтина Kakhidze
All times news
TAXI
Taus Makhacheva

Part

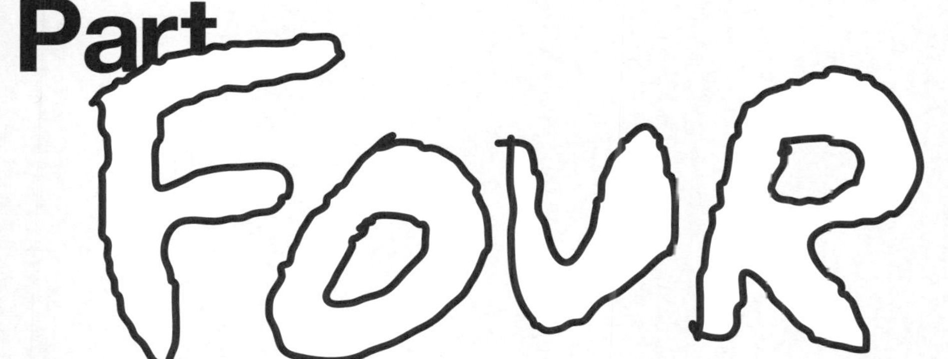

Systemic Shapes

Ackbar Abbas — Living Together in Volatile Spaces Moscow, 26th September 2015

I.

To say the world is an enigma is commonplace. But to say that the world is an enigma composed of its various solutions requires the intellectual subtlety of a Nietzsche. Following Nietzsche, we might say that the question of how to live together is also an enigma composed of its various solutions. If this is the case, then instead of trying to come up with quick solutions, which would only make living together even more enigmatic, we might begin by trying to understand the various dimensions of the enigma: the enigma, of how to live together in spaces that are increasingly volatile.

Volatility is arguably what is most characteristic of our times, the one aspect that politics, economics, and art have in common. What then is volatility? What makes spaces volatile?

A space that can be conceived of in terms of a single frame of reference is never volatile. Action and movement in such a space may be perplexingly complex, but complexity is not volatility. There is volatility only when you find multiple frameworks that overlap, and each framework pulls in a different direction. Hence, in a volatile space, movement loses clear directionality and takes on the randomness of Brownian movement, while time loses its chronological sequentiality, and various kinds of anachronisms take over. One good example of a volatile space is China today and its 'socialist market economy', as if only a catachresis were accurate enough to describe it. What is the socialist market economy? Are we dealing with another phase of socialism? Or is it the case, as it is often said in the West, that China today is capitalist in everything else but name alone? Or, even more paradoxically, are we dealing with neither the life nor death of socialism, but with its afterlife, with what I might call a 'posthumous socialism' rather than a post-socialism? Socialism in posthumous form can have a vitality stronger and more volatile than ever before. It is not a case of socialism being more alive than dead in China today, but a case of socialism being more alive when dead.

Spatially and temporally then, posthumous socialism is more volatile than post-socialism. Whereas in post-socialism, one set of conditions is seen to succeed and replace another, in posthumous socialism we are forced to inhabit overlapping time frames. A socialist past is not just succeeded and replaced by a capitalist present, but co-exists with it; and a single party system, where the state is the final arbiter in all important matters, co-exists with the rise of a consumer society, where individual choice and preferences are given priority. In posthumous socialism with its overlapping timeframes, anachronisms of a new and peculiar kind are everywhere. Anachronism here does not mean being behind the times; rather, it is a sign of the times, a product of the speed of historical change. For example, in a China that seems to the outsider to be obsessed by famous brand names and consumerism, we still find as a common occurrence the anachronistic singing of revolutionary songs. What we will see then in the coming period is not just a change from socialism to consumerism. In fact, it is not change in any familiar sense that we need to understand. Rather, what we must grasp is how change itself has changed.

It is perhaps not coincidental that volatility as a consequence of overlapping frameworks resonates so strongly with the theme that this Moscow Biennial has formulated: *Acting in a Centre, in a City, in the Heart of the Island of Eurasia.*

The notion of Eurasia points to overlapping frameworks, namely the overlap of Europe and Asia; so structurally speaking, the notion has something in common with the socialist market economy and other volatile spaces. Furthermore, to describe the largest land mass on earth as an island suggests that under volatile conditions (what Paul Virilio would call conditions of speed) space loses its measure and even our perception of dimensions, of large and small, can come unfixed. Finally the Chinese box effect of a centre, in a city, in a heart, and so on, suggests that centre, city, and heart are not single focused entities, but each a multiplicity made up of overlapping frames, and each a site of volatility.

II.

We cannot think of volatility then as simply speed of movement or quickness of change or the absence of rules. Volatility can no longer be captured by Futurist images of bullet trains devouring space, or even by the influential image of globalisation as time-space compression, which still has something directional about it. A more accurate image might be time-space distortion, which follows a less predictable trajectory than the image of compression, which still suggests movement in one direction. Volatility has many paradoxical features (like the blurring of fast and slow, or of large and small) and some of them can be discerned if we take even a brief look at contemporary theories of finance, of cinema, and of reading and interpretation.

Take finance: in options trading, volatility refers not to the actual price movement of a stock and its expected returns, but to a statistical history of how the stock tends to deviate from its own mean; in other words, to what is called the 'spread'. The spread then is a measure of deviation from a statistical norm, and not a measure of actual movement; that is to say, what the spread measures is the movement of movement. The greater the spread, the higher the volatility, but a small difference in the spread can produce a huge difference with regard to volatility. Note too that the spread as a measure of volatility has a slow temporality. It operates not in actual chronological time where frantic price movements take place, but in the time of meta-movements and statistical deviations that cover longer time periods and move more slowly — the time of duration.

There are clear parallels to finance theory in contemporary cinema. In *Cinema II*, Gilles Deleuze, the French philosopher, argues that contemporary cinema begins with the crisis of movement and chronological time: "Thus movement can tend to zero… (or it) may also be exaggerated, be incessant, become a world movement, a Brownian movement, a multiplicity of movement on different scales." Such devious movement then, from zero to exaggerated, is Deleuze's cinematic version of the spread. Deleuze continues: "We no longer have a chronological time which can be overturned by movements which are contingently abnormal; we have a chronic, non-chronological time which produces movement 'necessarily' abnormal, essentially false…"[1] What marks contemporary cinema then is how movement loses clear directionality and takes on some of the randomness of Brownian motion, or what Deleuze calls 'false movement'; while time loses its chronological sequentiality and various kinds of anachronisms take hold.

As for reading and interpretation, it can be shown that the challenge of what is still perhaps the most influential model of reading — the deconstructive or allegorical readings of Paul de Man — comes from its relation to volatility. His seminal text entitled

Allegories of Reading can be understood also as 'Volatilities of Reading'. Such readings do more than break down binary oppositions, or explicate a text. As de Man describes it, a literary text has a structure very much like the structure of overlapping frameworks found in volatile spaces: "Things do not happen as if a literary text moves from a certain period of time away from its centre, then turns around, folding back upon itself at one specific moment, to travel back to its genuine point of origin. These imaginary motions between fictional points cannot be located, dated and represented as if they were places in a geography, or events in a genetic history… the three moments of flight, return, and the turning point at which flight changes into return or vice versa, exist simultaneously on levels of meaning that are so intimately intertwined that they cannot be separated… Our entire argument lies compressed in such formulations."[2]

One conclusion that de Man does not shy away from is that the volatility of the literary text makes it impossible to read. Hence, reading is never correct; it is always accompanied by error. The more rigorous the reading, the more aware it is of the volatility of the text, and of the unreliability of reading: this is the challenge of de Manian poetics. Reading, de Man argues, is not "an emotive reaction to what language does, but… an emotive reaction to the impossibility of knowing what it might be up to. Literature as well as criticism—the difference between them being delusive—is condemned (or privileged) to be forever the most rigorous and consequently the most unreliable language in terms of which man names and transforms himself."[3] In de Man, as I think these quotations show, reading is not a method of interpreting or domesticating volatility, whether with a hermeneutics of belief or a hermeneutics of suspicion. Rather, reading itself is a volatile act, where rigor and unreliability go together.

III.

With some of these paradoxical features of volatility in mind, let me now turn to one specific case of art in volatile spaces. The case of Ai Weiwei is as good as any. Among Chinese artists, as I think all of us know, he is the one most outspokenly critical of the state and its abuse or neglect of human rights. He has also been called an entrepreneur and self-promoter, and is certainly one of the richest artists in China. The official reason for his recent house arrest is tax evasion. His position is a curious and contradictory one. He is by turns beaten up or arrested by the authorities, and tolerated or even deferred to; when the police arrest him, they apologise. At times, his work is banned in China; at other times he is the country's unofficial artistic emissary on the international stage. The state plays a game with Ai Weiwei, and he plays a game with the state: a dangerous *pas de deux*. However, the ambiguous position of Ai Weiwei is itself produced by China's volatile space. The present regime in fact encourages creativity in the arts, just as it encourages private enterprise. We see the proliferation of art districts, state sponsored art biennials and so on. But on the other hand we also see the palpable presence of censorship, which can be both crude and irrational. What is disturbing and confusing in China today is not so much a lack of freedom; there is in fact ostensibly much more freedom now than during the pre-Tiananmen era. What is disturbing is this constant oscillation, this constant switching back and forth, between permissiveness and prohibition, free agency and control, at all levels of social and cultural life.

It seems to me that no formal art historical analysis of Ai Weiwei's artworks would take us very far. It is only when we situate aesthetic form within the volatile space of the socialist market economy that we catch a glimpse of what is at stake. Now the obvious way of reading Ai Weiwei's artworks and performances, which the artist himself might endorse, is to read them as emancipatory gestures, designed to subvert state repression and to see the artist as a fighter for human rights. However, a more volatile alternative is to read him as someone who has learned how to live under extreme conditions, like those organisms that microbiologists have recently discovered that can thrive on toxic waste. What defines his art is the game that Ai Weiwei plays with the state, sometimes with serious consequences. The game is to turn censorship itself, toxic for art production, into something enabling; to thrive on and not simply survive these conditions; to swim and not just float in the destructive element. This means nothing less than enlisting the repressive state as a collaborator, and to make repression itself a source and resource of emancipatory art. This is a dangerous and paradoxical game, which is why some of Ai Weiwei's admirers, especially those in the West who know nothing about what is at stake, think he should leave the country—except that this might be the worst thing for him as an artist. Take away

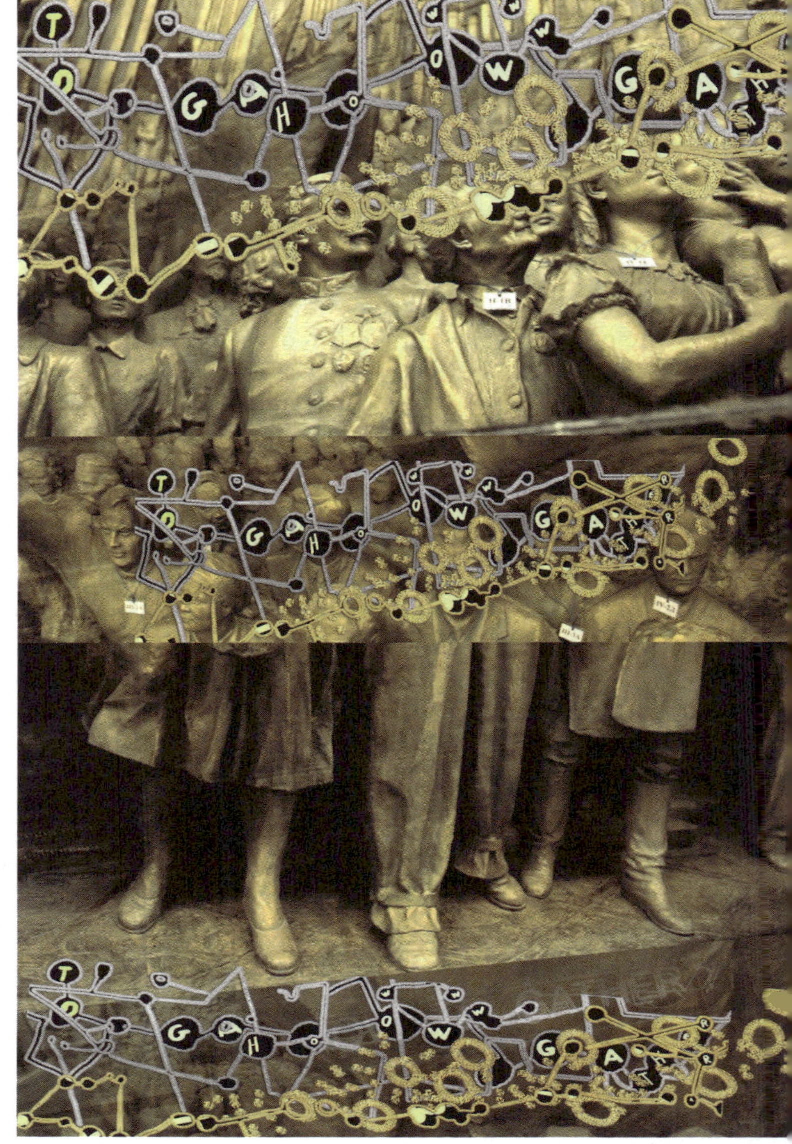

Almagul Menlibayeva

the destructive element and Ai Weiwei will be like a fish out of water. Adulation in his case could be less productive than repression itself.

IV.

For an artist, living under conditions of censorship that have become unpredictable is of course not a happy situation. Yet, as we see in Ai Weiwei's example, creative work can still be done within this context. In fact, it could be argued that toxic conditions can sometimes function as necessary stimuli. This raises the question of what kinds of relationship should exist between 'living together' and 'happiness'.

What does it mean to be happy together? This is the subject of Hong Kong director Wong Kar-wai's 1997 film *Happy Together*. The film is about a gay couple running away from a sexually conservative Hong Kong to Buenos Aires in search of happiness. But after a very graphic homosexual scene (for Hong Kong cinema) at the beginning of the film, the couple starts bickering for the rest of the film. It is as if they could be happy and not together, or together and not happy, but never again happy and together at the same time. Nevertheless, what both Ai Weiwei and Wong Kar-wai are suggesting in their different ways is that while living together may not result in immediate happiness, what it offers is even more important: the promise of happiness.

Immediate happiness in the form of success and recognition is possible if we are willing to conform to the values of our times. This is why the existentialists used to say that happiness is nothing but a bourgeois fantasy: witness the fact that for some Chinese youth today, happiness means living in a consumers' paradise. In contrast, the promise of happiness is a much more volatile notion. It forces us to imagine a much more subtle and complex form of happiness that does not just passively reflect a society's predispositions but works to transform it. Let me briefly trace the genealogy of this phrase, *la promesse du bonheur*, first in Stendhal, who introduced it, and then in Theodor Adorno, who understood it in a completely different way in order to apply it to art and politics. What Stendhal originally wrote was "love is never more than a promise of happiness." The model is that of flirtation that promises everything and delivers nothing, an erotics of deferral and duplicity. In Adorno, the phrase becomes "art is the promise of happiness", a notion that figures prominently in two of his most important works, *Minima Moralia* and *Aesthetic Theory*. The question Adorno asked in these and other works was the following: can art transform society and not just collude with it or withdraw from it? In other words, he was asking the question of how to live together.

The negative part of Adorno's answer is that the condition of capitalism has irreparably damaged our ability to live together and has reduced art's transformative potential. *Minima Moralia* is subtitled *Reflections on damaged life*, because for Adorno, a life under capitalism is already damaged. A key aphorism from *Minima Moralia* reads "Wrong life cannot be lived rightly." In such a desperate situation, the only ethical option open to art, its minima moralia, is to fail. But in a crucial twist, it is in the principled and creative way in which art fails that we find the promise of happiness. Failure here is not the opposite of success. It calls success into question, through a complex relationship to happiness, as we see in another aphorism from *Aesthetic Theory*, where Adorno writes, "For the sake of happiness, happiness is renounced", and it is only through this renunciation that the promise can be kept. Failure as minima moralia also announces the emergence of a new kind of artist. For Adorno it was someone like Samuel Beckett, whose comments on art as failure written some time ago we are only just beginning to understand. Beckett writes:

"…to be an artist is to fail, as no other dare fail, that failure is his world and the shrink from it desertion, art and craft, good housekeeping, living…" Beckett goes on to outline 'an art of failure': "…I know that all that is required now is to make of this fidelity to failure a new occasion, a new term of relation and of the act which, unable to act, obliged to act, he makes, an expressive act, even if only of itself, of its impossibility, of its obligation."[4]

An art of failure, it should be clear, is not the same as failed art. In Adorno and Beckett, failure is both an ethics (wrong life cannot be lived rightly) and an aesthetics that makes of failure an expressive art; that makes of the impossibility of art the starting point for a different kind of art; just as De Man's insistence on the impossibility of reading results in an exemplary kind of reading. Understood in these ways, failure is related to a main concern of this Moscow biennial: how to act, particularly in spaces that we do not accept, or do not feel we can live with.

V.

This issue of how to act also lies behind an event that challenges us to think through the problem of living together in volatile spaces. I am thinking of the Hong Kong Occupy or Umbrella Movement that took place over several months at the end of 2014. I want to conclude with a brief discussion of how in this event, the ethics, aesthetics, and politics of living together overlap in important ways. The movement was a genuine event and not just an occurrence. There is an important distinction between an event and an occurrence. An event is not just something that happened, but something that happened that had never happened before, which is what distinguishes an event from an occurrence. An event always catches us by surprise. It is beyond the reach of facts, against the run of history as pattern, with an outcome that cannot be determined in advance. Hence it is always volatile spaces that produce events. To discuss the Umbrella Movement, we have to distinguish between what happened, which was almost predictable, and why it was an event whose implications we are still trying to grasp.

Briefly, what happened was as follows: The immediate issue was the method of electing a new chief executive. One of the things agreed upon when Hong Kong was returned to China in 1997 was that, by 2017, elections would take the form of one-person one-vote. Beijing followed the agreement in principle, but added further stipulations, like limiting the number of candidates and so practically pre-selecting them. We find here the control mentality of the old socialism together with the neo-liberal strategy of seeming to allow freedom of choice while re-containing it at the same time; or in the famous words of Henry Ford about his 'Model T' motorcar: "You can have any colour you like, as long as it's black."

Led by the charismatic eighteen-year-old Joshua Wong, the student leaders understandably refused this deception. Their tactic was simple: to disrupt the system by disrupting traffic in strategic areas of the city with barricades or their own bodies. There was initial public support for the young students, but as days turned into months, sentiment turned against them from taxi drivers, from small retailers relying on street businesses, and from old people who could not get to hospital. The government was remarkably restrained about using force. It played a waiting game of attrition, believing, rightly as it turned out, that time was on its side. In a last ditch effort, Joshua Wong went on a hunger strike, but by then the movement was almost over. That was what happened more or less. But what were the implications and what can we say about the Umbrella Movement as an event? Let me make three sets of comments.

Firstly, as the leaders are young high school students, some critics have been tempted to see the Occupy Movement in terms of a generation gap, and its participants as passionate, idealistic, but basically naïve and immature. The movement has been called many things, from an impractical form of populist democracy to a phony disobedience movement. But it could as accurately be said that what we saw really was an imagination gap. One important aspect of the Umbrella Movement was that it provided an outlet for the city's creative energies, which had so far been too narrowly channelled and directed towards instrumental goals. Those who took part in the movement were able to see their city in a different way. They became aware that spatial configurations other than the established ones were possible. Interestingly enough, the protest sites were also the chosen venues for weddings and even births to take place. They were also the places where we saw art works being produced. These artworks were on the whole ephemeral products of the moment, sometimes crude and hardly masterpieces. However, they took their energy from what was happening on the streets, and this gave them an edginess that separated them from kitsch. Just as the Umbrella Movement changed our perception of the city and the streets, so its art changed our perception of art: art not as someone else's work that we stand back from and admire when we have the time, but as something that we ourselves can do.

Another unpredictable aspect of the Umbrella Movement, which marked it as an event, was its relative longevity and the reasons for it. When participants were asked about why they stayed even against the advice of their parents and teachers and the personal risk to themselves, many of them said it was because the intense friendships they experienced in the movement was something that they had never experienced before. Friendship in this context clearly has a political meaning. A politics of friendship means organising a movement or a society not from 'top-down' or even 'bottom-up', but laterally; where we find not the paternalistic relations of parents to children but relations between brothers and sisters or better still, between friends. The movement was not an abstract lesson in democracy. It was a practical lesson that we are still trying to understand on how to live together. And one part of the lesson, it is important to admit, is that 'the politics of friendship' did not work. The idea took hold for a while, but turned out to be too unstructured as an organisational model.

And this leads me now to a final comment, which concerns whether the movement has failed. The protest sites have been cleared and it would seem that Hong Kong is back to business as usual. These outcomes were of course entirely predictable right from the beginning, given the tremendous odds against the students ever succeeding in getting their demands met. However, one outcome was not predictable. Even as it became clear that resistance was futile, it continued. We find here not a failure of resistance, but rather failure as resistance; a politics of failure that is not the same as a failed politics, and that has a kind of heroism to it, quite different from the heroism of other times. For example, the motto of Kant and the Enlightenment was 'dare to know'; in other words, have the moral courage to combat prejudice and superstition. But in the volatile spaces of today, where knowledge itself is linked to power and control, our model may have to be 'dare to fail'. Failure, we might say, is the moral heroism of our time, in social life as well as in art. This is what allows us to act and create under conditions of impossibility; to act not because we have hope, but because we refuse to give in to despair.

1
Gilles Deleuze, *Cinema II*, translated by Hugh Tomlinson and Barbara Habberjam (Minneapolis: University of Minnesota press, 1996), p. 128.

2
Paul de Man, *Blindness and Insight* (New York: OUP, 1971), p. 163.

3
Paul de Man, *Allegories of Reading* (New Haven: Yale University press, 1979), p. 19.

4
Samuel Beckett, Grove Centenary Edition, Vol. 4 (New York: Grove Press, 2006), p. 563.

Simon Denny — The Innovator's Dilemma

Moscow, 27th September 2015

ALL YOU NEED IS DATA — THE DLD 2012 CONFERENCE REDUX (2013)

I'm going to go through a few projects that I've made over the last 5 years. The first project that I want to talk about is a show that I made in Munich. It was about a tech conference that happens in Munich every year, put on by German publisher Hubert Burda since 2005. It's called *DLD* (Digital-Life-Design Conference). I wanted to do a snapshot of the tech-industry at that point through a documentary exhibition that framed a bunch of key players in that scene at that time—investigating what they were interested in, what they were looking at…

Generally, these conferences are a big part of tech culture, and there are many of them across the world and in Europe. DLD is one of the more prominent ones in Europe. In 2012, they had invited people like Sheryl Sandberg from Facebook, Jack Dorsey from Twitter, Jimmy Wales from Wikipedia—some really big,

1

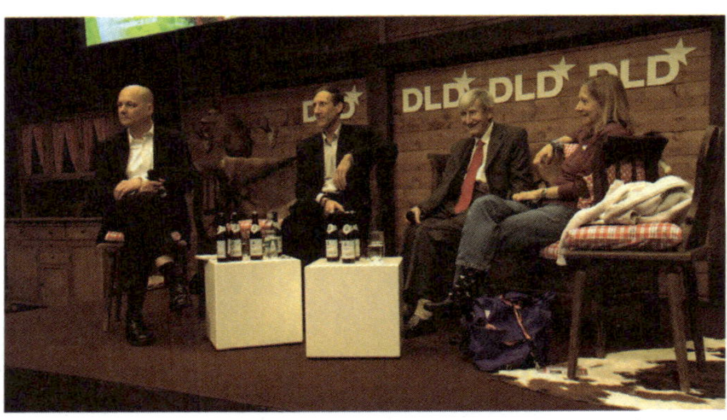

DLD (digital life design) used two elaborate stage sets as backdrops for their conference talks. Pictured here is a set that suggests an Alpine lodge, the other stage depicted a futuristic Alpine scene with pastel gradients. I interpreted these designs in my skeumorphic canvas summaries of each talk.

important thinkers and cultural icons of that context. But they also realised a huge build-up, an amazing stage set. My aim was to reflect on this community and repackage them through looking at this one moment, this one snapshot.[1]

Brian Chesky, one of the leaders of the 'sharing economy' and co-founder of Airbnb, showed a slide that aesthetically made a nice relationship to what was discussed in the talks. It led me to the graphic register I finally appropriated for my documentary exhibition: *Skeumorphism*. This means using images of objects to stand in for functions. It has been used in computer interface design at least since the 1970s, most popularly by Apple. At the DLD 2012 conference everybody was using Apple. It was a high point of the iPhone revolution. iOS 5 was the dominant platform at that moment and it really didn't get much more skeumorphic than this. Meaning, you had an image of a full old bookshelf for your iBooks, a writing pad for your notes... et cetera. To me, this was the perfect language to use to describe that community. So I made canvases with quotes and images from each talk. And added quotes from each speaker that I considered interesting or representative.

I took the stage background, made a graphic version of that and laid over each a relevant text in a handwriting font which is often used, for example in the note taking app in iOS 5. The layout also included Polaroids of the main speakers. A great quote is this one from the talk by Andrew Mason (co-founder of Groupon, one of the unicorns of that time with a growth rate of 500%): "Let's start having fun. Let's get funky. Let's announce everything. Let's be wildly positive in our forecasts. Let's take this thing to the extreme. If we get whacked on the ride down who gives a shit? The time to get radical is now. We have nothing to lose." This gives you a sense of the amazing momentum happening in the tech industry in 2012.

Another side of the tech industry was highlighted with Jimmy Wales speaking to Russian entrepreneur Pavel Durov, who was at that time the head of VKontakte, the Russian version of Facebook. (Durov later on had to sell that company to the state and flee Russia.) Back then he was riding high and donated one million dollars to Wikipedia while on stage at DLD, which was an amazing moment in the event. These are the kinds of things that were going on there and which I included in the documentary exhibition.[2]

I grouped the talks and made one panel for each. With ninety presentations over three days, I made ninety canvasses that were

2

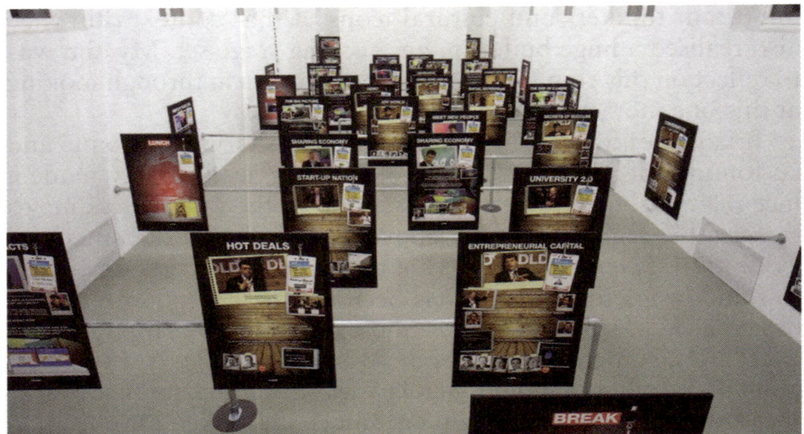

One panel represented one 'panel' talk in the three day conference's program. A total of ninety canvasses were then presented in a maze-like walk-through timeline, mounted on poles, in a dead end formation similar to stanchions one passes through when lining up at a bank or airport.

then presented in a maze-like walk-through timeline, similar to the set-up one has to pass through when lining up at a bank or airport. As you go from panel to panel there is an overwhelming amount of information. It's quite an interesting scale because each canvas had an A0 format so that the portraits were almost human-sized. You would look these people in the eye and maybe get a sense of what it feels like being at a big conference. The canvases were all facing forward and thus only visible in terms of their content from the front. So, if you made your way through the timeline, when you looked back there was just no content in view. The content was only visible looking forward. And a timeline was one of the most important organising tools of the dominant platforms at that moment such as Facebook and Twitter. I felt that making a sculpture like this was a good way of reflecting the values of that community.

All You Need is Data combined tech conferences and participants with documentary exhibition making and mobile interface design. All of this came together as a snapshot of the tech industry in 2012.

DISRUPTIVE BERLIN (2014)

I realised this project in Berlin at Galerie Buchholz in 2014, which was an interesting moment for a more localised subgroup of this same tech community. Berlin is and was coming to reimagine itself as a tech hub — like many cities that want to reimagine themselves as the next Silicon Valley, Berlin was trying to become that for Germany. *Factory* in Berlin is a location there that was built a couple of years ago and is now a prominent incubator where young companies start out. During construction works, Mozilla placed an advertisement on the scaffolding saying “Doing good is part of our code”, so “don’t be evil” is the message there — like Google’s famous early maxim.

hy! was another highly-produced conference that happened in Berlin, which was backed by Axel Springer, another publishing company from Germany. And another was more of a grassroots style event, called Tech Open Air (TOA) — showing that conferences of different sizes and flavours are very important in the calendar of the tech scene in Berlin. That year, *TechCrunch Disrupt* also came to Berlin. TechCrunch is the most internationally known blog in tech. A lot of the dominant conversations pass through that blog at some point in Silicon Valley. They organise a regular event called *Disrupt*, which is, again, a conference. Berlin was important enough for them at that point to decide it was worth holding the conference there.[3] (Now they’ve actually moved it to London.)

3

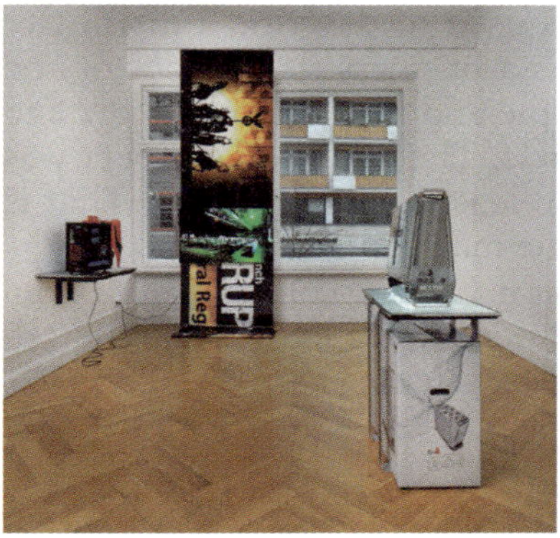

In “Disruptive Berlin” I included a banner from the conference TechCrunch Disrupt to show how the city was used as a backdrop in their graphic identity. The design focuses on an explosion behind the Brandenburger Tor with “Disrupt” passing through it.

My intention was again to make a sculptural picture of that community and of a city reimagining itself. At that time, I was looking into competitive computer gaming culture and really loved what they call case mods. If you are a competitive gamer, maybe some of you are, some people in that community like to make badass looking cases with all the best hardware and express themselves through how their computer looks. I decided to make a case mod for each of the top ten start-ups in Berlin.[4] Each of the mods was conceived on the one hand as a monument to each of these top ten start-ups as they were emerging, but also as a little miniature possible headquarters space. I wanted to create a sort of cityscape in the gallery. The material I used was off-the-shelf material that you can get if you are in the case-modding context —and I basically branded each case. Another company was Sociomantic, where the mod included the letters ROI for "return on investment" which was important for them. Clue, the only female-founded tech company in the top ten that year was also included in the selection. Gender balance is not something which is well represented in tech culture in Berlin or anywhere else. Soundcloud is probably the most well-known Berlin-based company that I created a mod for. The case mods were shown together with the Mozilla banner I mentioned before. Its dimensions gave a sense of scale to the exhibition space with a kind of miniature cityscape under a real, full-scale outdoor banner.

I also blew up book covers and key diagrams from tech literature and installed them on construction fences that were popping up around Berlin. Books such as Clayton Christensen's *The Innovator's Dilemma* informed the way that these companies bring themselves together and imagine themselves. In *The Innovator's Dilemma* the word 'disrupt' was used to describe a disruptive business for the first time. That is a business that comes in and completely changes a market. Apple and the iPhone are key and clear examples of what disruption is. The cell phone market was completely irrelevant after they released their product. That is how they 'disrupted' the cell phone market.

For the exhibition Disruptive Berlin, young companies in Berlin meet the idea of "disruptive innovation" and a Berlin city rebranding exercise to form a disruptive ecosystem.

4

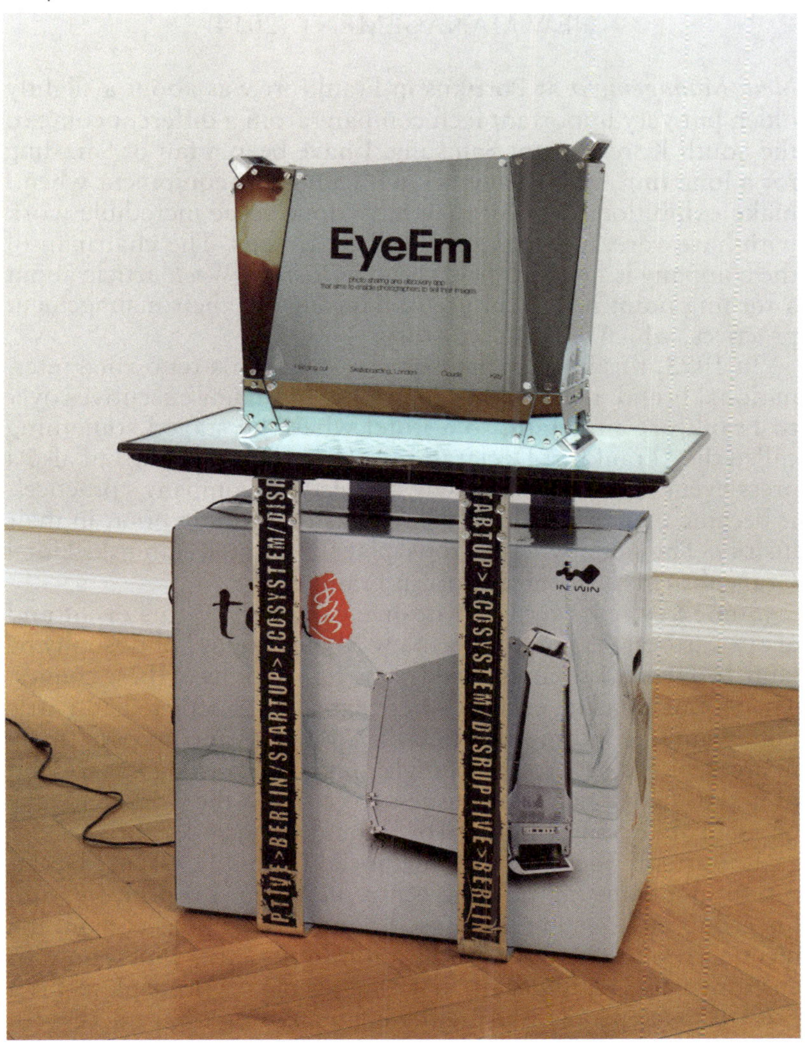

This is a case mod (customized gamer computer cases) representing EyeEm, a prominent Berlin based image-sharing startup. Initially a kind of German Instagram, the company soon pivoted towards being a user-generated stock-image sales platform. This was adapted from an off-the-shelf, fully mirror-glass computer case, at once recalling miniature a corporate tower and the photographic process

NEW MANAGEMENT (2014)

New Management at Portikus in Frankfurt was about a slightly older, but very important tech company from a different context: the South Korean giant Samsung. I have been a fan of Samsung for a long time and often work with Samsung equipment when I make exhibitions. I think they have done some incredible work with hardware, e.g. making excellent screens. The chairman of the company is Lee Kun-hee. I read a *BusinessWeek* article about a turning point in the culture of Samsung, in their management practices, which was a great story:

In 1993, this is when Samsung wasn't such a renowned international brand, Lee Kun-hee flew all of his major executives over to Frankfurt am Main, to a hotel where he staged something called the "Frankfurt Declaration". This was a meeting but also a press-event where he completely changed the company's practices. It became memorialised by the firm as the turning point in their history. The hotel where it took place was the Kempinski Hotel Gravenbruch, near the airport in Frankfurt.

Some key texts by Lee Kun-hee came out of this event and also a cartoon version of the "New Management" philosophy he launched there. I commissioned some translations of these comics. There is an amazing excerpt where Samsung is depicted as a little bunny and the international markets that it wants to participate in are depicted as ferocious jungle animals. Samsung has to kind of find its own inner ferociousness to go out in the world and take on giants like Sony, Honda, Toyota and General Motors.

Reportedly there exists a memorial to this Frankfurt Declaration in a Samsung training centre in Yogin. Lee Kun-hee and his group at Samsung purchased a number of objects from the meeting room where the Declaration took place, which now sit enshrined as a reminder of New Management's principles. It is a private space people outside the company don't have access to. This inaccessibility inspired me to make a public version of this important corporate cultural monument to a key moment in global consumer electronics.[5]

My version of the memorial included a re-painted faux Canaletto painting in front of a desk chair supporting a print of Lee Kun-hee during the Declaration. I put a double-sided mirror opposite the table, chair and painting to complete a circle of New Management speculation. I also installed Plexiglas walls sandwich-

5

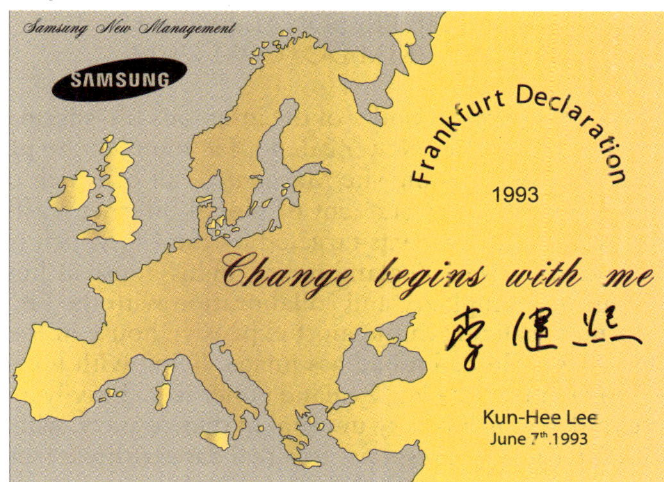

Here is a Samsung plaque design produced during the period of the Frankfurt Declaration. It features the catch phrase "Change begins with me", a key quote from chairman Lee Kun-hee superimposed over Europe; the Korean giant claims territory.

ing the monument, including modified Samsung air-conditioning units with quotes from New Management printed on them—like "When a group is changed, a society can be changed." During the exhibition, these were live and circulated air through the quotes around the exhibition.

On the walls, I installed a reproduction of Samsung's corporate history timeline from their History Hall in the Frankfurt headquarters; a collection of items from the Samsung-owned Shilla hotel in Seoul; a model of the Burj Khalifa in Dubai, which Samsung's construction group built; and finally a kind of timeline of cell phones that describe the path to Samsung's breakthrough Galaxy smartphone—an industry leader.

The *New Management* exhibition took Samsung and Lee Kunhee's management principle, mixed it with the Kempinski Hotel Gravenbruch in Frankfurt and a dream of international expansion and global markets, and condensed them all into a copy of their New Management monument.

THE PERSONAL EFFECTS OF KIM DOTCOM (2013)

Kim Dotcom, the founder of the infamous file-sharing site *Megaupload*, is based in New Zealand. He founded the platform and Internet video-hosting site *Megavideo*, all of which occupied, at one point, about 4 per cent of global internet traffic. It was a massive thing. Kim was targeted by the US, which resulted in a huge raid by New Zealand police on his house in January 2012, in unusual complicity and collaboration with the FBI.

Kim was living in the most expensive house in the country at that point. He had a bad-ass image, living with lots of cars and trophy items. The New Zealand police were heavily armed during the raid—which is very unusual in that country, which felt more like theatre than a response to a real danger/threat from Kim. The indictment that followed this raid included a list of things that were confiscated from Kim in the seizure. There were 110 items on this extraordinary list. When I first saw it published I was convinced this could be an interesting proposition for a group of things to stand in for the conversation around Kim, a kind of subset of his collection.

I wanted to make an exhibition around issues that I felt that the Kim Dotcom phenomenon somehow stood for: Who has sovereignty? What is the role of the US in international justice? What is privacy today? What does copyright mean in a Google/YouTube world? Where are these rules enforced and where are they ignored?... So many issues, which swelled so poignantly around Kim's raid, felt somehow carefully framed by the US authorities. Kim Dotcom had around 64 bank accounts on the list seized and a number of objects; tech hardware, TVs and servers, and vehicles as well as artworks. The indictment list could be framed as a collaboration between Kim and the US courts—in a certain sense as a curatorial project that highlighted part of his collection.

There were amazing press images of police contractors removing objects from his home—among them amazing sculptures from Colin Christian, a giant TV screen and a *Predator* statue... Kim Dotcom appeared in major New Zealand papers almost daily for about a year and continued as an important public figure for much longer. I contrasted those mainstream media depictions of him with Kim's own tweeting practice, which started a few months after the raid.[6]

6

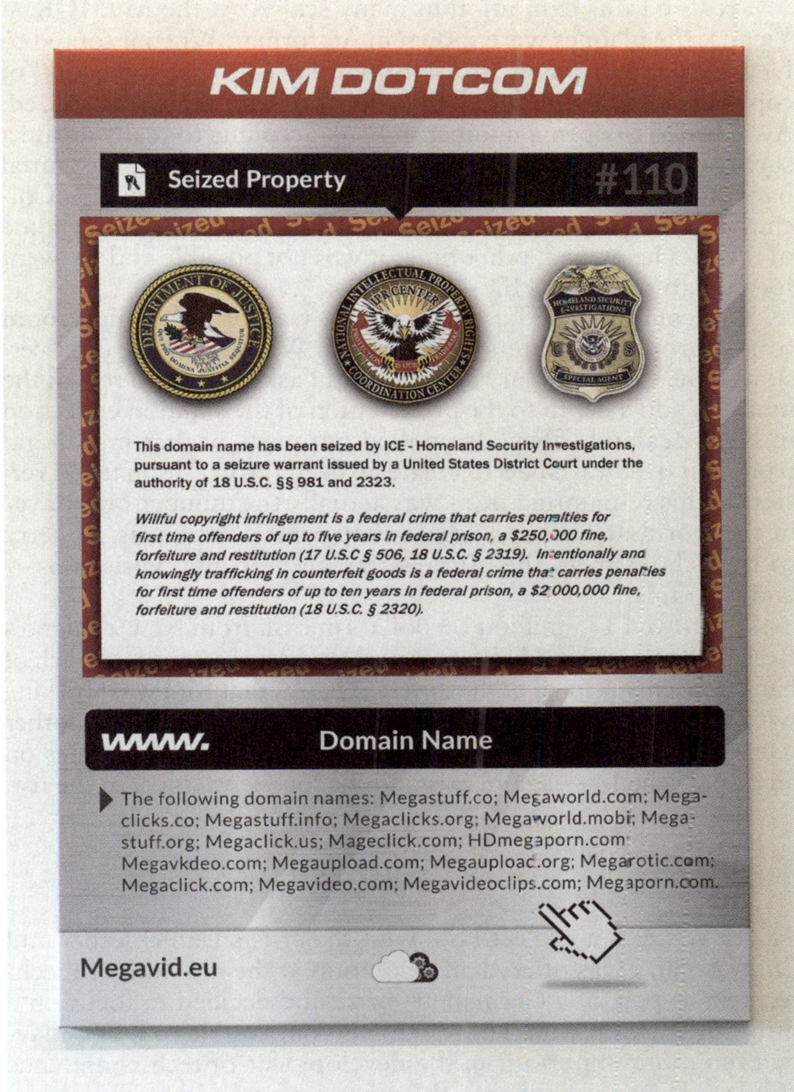

For each item on the indictment list issued by the US courts to Kim Dotcom, I designed a plaque like this one to make the list more tangible in exhibition form. Objects represented many of the items as well; hinting at the many versions online content takes in copied form, often in vastly differing levels of quality.

I realised this exhibition in many scales. At the MuMOK in Vienna, the plaques were shown in A6 format. When it toured to New Zealand they had an A0 format. I tried to get some kind of copy/version/stand-in for all the objects of Kim's that were seized. Also, I tried to open a number of bank accounts to really create a surrogate group of things from the list to stand in for substantial bank accounts. At one of the versions of the exhibition in Colchester, England, we were able to get full-scale versions of some of the cars he owned, other times it was not possible and we went for miniature—less 'HD'—stand-ins.

Kim commissioned a mural on the wall of his gaming room from a group of painters in Auckland. When working on a version of the exhibition in New Zealand I asked them to repeat the mural to add a depth to the presentation of the stand-in collection in New Zealand. They also pulled out parts of that mural and painted it over my labels to create an even further dramatised version of this re-painting. Kim was actually the number one player in the world at *Call of Duty* at that point. There was a poetry to the echoes from the mural—imagery of men with guns—and the raid.

I borrowed 175 million US dollars in cash from New Zealand's Reserve Bank in shredded currency. Also, I tried to open a bunch of bank accounts—in all of the different banks that Kim was working with. The result was a long paper trail with no success. Another part of the exhibition was reproductions of the license plates on all of the vehicles—again, as stand-ins for the vastness of the list.

TEDX VADUZ (2013)

TEDx Vaduz is a project I did with the artists Daniel Keller and Emily Segal. I was offered an exhibition at the museum of Liechtenstein as part of a German art prize and decided to focus on a direct interaction with TEDx. TED is comparable to DLD, maybe even more important in the development of tech conference culture. They are probably the most recognised brand in tech-conferences; a premium brand active since the 1980s. Since 2009 they have licensed out their brand to external people in different countries to do more self-organised versions of conferences.

Since there had never been a TEDx in Liechtenstein, we thought it would be great to do one in Vaduz. Liechtenstein was a very interesting context to interface with at that point because many of the voices I was following in Silicon Valley were speaking about moving outside of general society and creating separate societies —a kind of tech secessionism. This included ideas of the outside, offshore, sea-steading culture, of going to live on a boat in international waters or creating a whole new country that would not participate in existing sovereign systems. Regulation from existing nation states was being framed as having the potential to get in the way of radical innovation in tech.

Larry Page spoke about this very visibly at the Google I/O. Peter Thiel, another prominent founder and venture capitalist from Silicon Valley, was involved in and speaking about sea-steading. Liechtenstein has been described as an offshore tax haven. That is why we found it an interesting idea to overlay the exit impulses of people from Silicon Valley (or the ideals of Silicon Valley as represented by TED) onto a country or principality, which is known for a kind of outside. Daniel Keller and I applied for and received the license from TED to do TEDxVaduz.

There are many guidelines you have to follow when you do a licensed TEDx. But actually, stage design is an area that has some but not so many rules, so we took that as a space where we could add our voice or take. We created a word-cloud backdrop of all the most used words ever in TED talks. Think, thank and thing come out on top. Our stage design had Liechtenstein rendered as a tropical island to visualise it as an offshore location.[7]

7

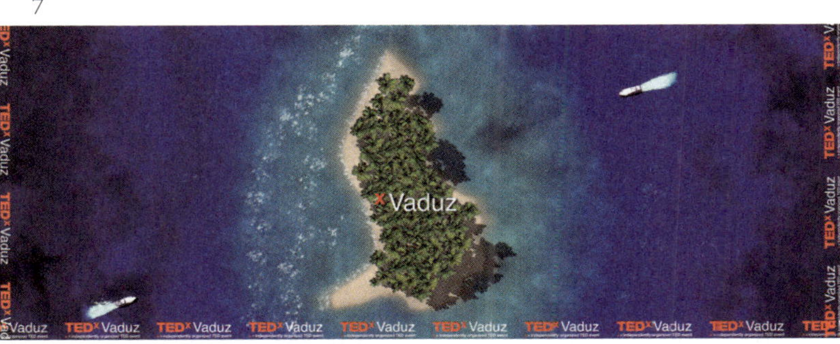

This stage design for the TEDxVaduz talks depicted quadruple land-locked Liechtenstein as a tropical island, underlining the 'offshore', tax-haven reputation of the principality.

Emily Segal gave a talk called "The changing face of luxury". Femke Herregraven spoke about her research into offshore networks that take money around the world. She invented an amazing game where you get the best outcome for your money at each country. Peter Fend designed different taxation systems based on better land use in Vaduz. Katja Novitskova spoke about ecology online and the appeal of cuteness as a kind of technology.

I then made an exhibition to mark the TEDx, including artworks by these artists. The show also included atmospheric, memorial Plexiglas vitrines with a commemorative cake at their centre. Iced onto the cake was the successful TED application that granted us the license for the event. The vitrines also featured a key quote from each of the talks in the exhibition.

SECRET POWER (2015)

Like everybody in June 2013 I was completely floored by the experience of looking through the relics of organisational culture and communication within the USA's intelligence agency NSA, as the *Guardian* and Edward Snowden released classified internal documents. New Zealand, where I grew up, was shown to be part of the USA/NSA-led Five Eyes intelligence community. I was captivated by the amazing journalistic and artistic work done around this incident.

I was particularly interested in how these programmes were imaged. The kinds of logos and visual language that were used surprised me. The cartoony, jovial style felt at odds with the activities the intelligence organisations that developed them seemed to be doing. One of the highlights from the many logos was the imagery used to describe Mystic, a phone tapping program that had a kind of wizard carrying a sceptre with a flip phone roughly collaged onto it as its logo. Another stand-out icon inside the documents was the SSO (Special Source Operations) logo, which is a giant eagle carrying the earth in its talons. Monumentalising this material through reinterpreting them either in higher resolution re-renders or as objects, grouping them into sub-sections of similar imagery, seemed to be one way to try and locate where clues to the value systems of the intelligence agencies might sit.

This project was partly realised in the *Biblioteca Marciana* in the middle of Venice, which we used as the New Zealand pavilion for that year, along with the Marco Polo Airport. The Marciana Library is a well-known building and one of the most important in Piazza San Marco. Designed by Jacopo Sansovino, its interior is decorated with dense imagery, beautiful paintings from Titian, Veronese and other Renaissance masters. The whole building was conceived as an architectural allegory for the value of acquiring and keeping knowledge. Each of the paintings in its interior reflects this theme. The library also contains a number of maps and beautiful globes from the Renaissance period. To create a dialogue between the ways in which intelligence imagery and geographic, geopolitical imagery is produced and used by a state today and the way state-commissioned images behaved in sometimes similar ways in the past, the building played a key role in framing the material.

Looking at the Snowden-leaked logos and illustrations, I wondered about the people who had made them. What were the artists' tasks in an organisation like the NSA, and what is the role of these designers? Why do they choose this kind of imagery? As I was doing that research I came across David Darchicourt's LinkedIn profile. Darchicourt was a Creative Director of Defense Intelligence at NSA for ten years from 2002 to 2012. This was a key period—post 9/11, when many of the most controversial programs the NSA uses were developed or accelerated. His profile stated: "My work was instrumental in communicating the NSA mission, vision and projects through brochures, flyers, posters, maps, ads, exhibit displays, newsletters, banners, signs, presentations, and promotional pieces." He was also responsible for "complex senior level visual communication initiatives throughout the Agency and the intel community." It was clear from his CV and examples of his work that he was likely involved in designing the leaked NSA slides.

In my exhibition in the Marciana Library, half of the room was dedicated to spotlighting the excerpts from the Snowden slides which I thought were particularly poignant. The other half of the room was dedicated to proposing an artist figure as a possible author of the Snowden material. I foregrounded a self-portrait that Darchicourt had made of himself, which me and my team had redrawn and blown up in scale.[8]

I included interpretations of excerpts from artworks found on his online profiles; for example, I had some miniatures made from images of exhibition designs he had done for the NSA's own public

8

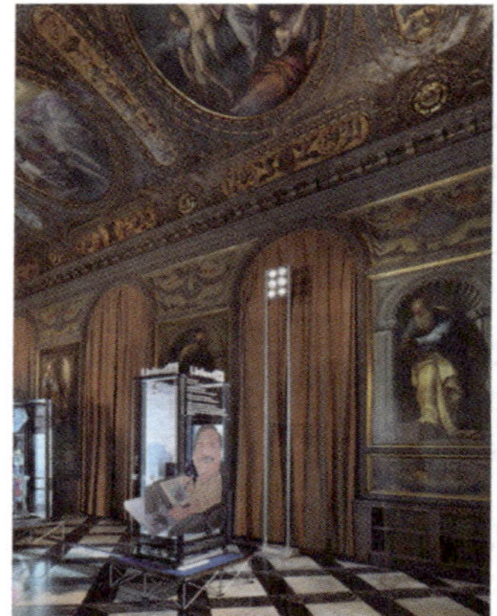

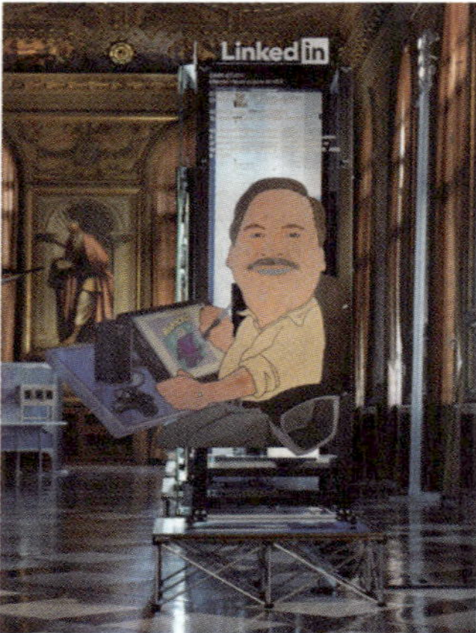

A sculptural monument, adapting a computer data server rack as vitrine, featuring former NSA illustrator David Darchicourt. Darchicourt produced some of the graphics used in NSA documents that were leaked by Edward Snowden. This exhibition contrasted his work as a visualizer of contemporary data collection with masterpieces in the Marciana Library, Venice, which was designed as an allegory for the value of acquiring and keeping knowledge in the Renaissance.

9

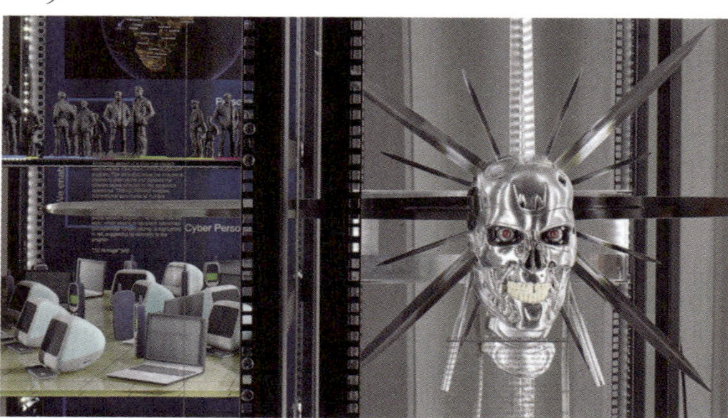

Detail of a sculptural monument exploring the Snowden-leaked graphics describing the NSA's Google-map like geo-location program "TREASUREMAP". Ironically, the program was represented using imagery from the *Terminator* films, a film warning of the dangers of military A.I.

museum, the National Cryptographic Museum. I also spotlighted his cartoon work for the museum's education department called CryptoKids—a group of cartoons which introduced children to the way the NSA did their work. These cartoons were redrawn and printed on the brushed aluminium panels which surrounded the exhibition miniatures.

I also engaged a commission with Darchicourt. The designer I was working with on my pavilion, David Bennewith, commissioned two drawings directly from him through his profile. One of them was a New Zealand version of CryptoKids. I wanted him to follow the style of all the amazing images he had created for the NSA, but apply the style to a Tuatara, a New Zealand native lizard. For the exhibition, we combined those with what he had done for the NSA (like mouse pads, intelligence awareness posters, security posters…) and monumentalised them in sculptural vitrines made by altering computer server racks with custom display elements and lighting. The images from the Snowden-leaked slides on the other side of the room were treated in the same way.

He designed *Dive into Social Networking*, a shark-themed card game for kids to educate them on the dangers of sharing personal information on social networks. He also created a board game called *Positive Press*, which is designed to keep people optimistic. Across both the Snowden-leaked and the Darchicourt-authored material, gaming cards and images derived from magic and fantasy gaming kept reoccurring. Management charts representing pyramidal forms were also common. But common to both the contemporary images I chose to exhibit and the Marciana Library's interior paintings were mythic wizards, different kinds of white bearded wise men holding receptacles of knowledge—books and globes in the paintings, and computers and tech devices in the contemporary JPEGs.

Another really interesting group of slides was made for a program called *Treasure Map*. This program is kind of the NSA version of *Google Earth*. They used a *Terminator T-800* skull with sword-like compass points erupting from it as a seal for that program, which I thought was incredible! Here is an artist, somebody like Darchicourt if not Darchicourt himself, choosing to use an image which is associated in popular culture with the Terminator and the dangers of using AI as a military tool, as the logo for a program which potentially does exactly that. A very interesting choice.[9]

Darchicourt's involvement as an author of at least some of the Snowden-leaked images was confirmed when *Guardian* journalist Charlotte Higgins contacted him as a part of writing an article on my Secret Power exhibition. "He had, for example, designed the logo used internally at the NSA for the program Poison Nut—which was designed to break through security measures taken by potential targets of surveillance," read her article published on the opening day of the Venice Biennale, also confirming to me that aesthetic research can lead to amazing outcomes. Attribution of any of the material up until then in the Snowden-leaked slides had not been possible—some governmental voices in New Zealand were still claiming at that point that all the slides were fictitious.

Mariana Mazzucato — The Innovative State[1]

Moscow, 25th September 2015

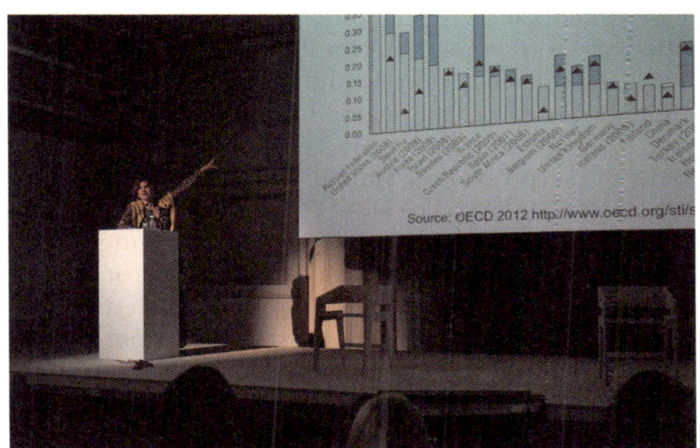

Otto Snoek, 22 September – 01 October 2015

GOVERNMENTS SHOULD MAKE MARKETS, NOT JUST FIX THEM

The conventional view of what the state should do to foster innovation is simple: it just needs to get out of the way. At best, governments merely facilitate the economic dynamism of the private sector; at worst, their lumbering, heavy-handed, and bureaucratic institutions actively inhibit it. The fast-moving, risk-loving, and pioneering private sector, by contrast, is what really drives the type of innovation that creates economic growth. According to this view, the secret behind Silicon Valley lies in its entrepreneurs and venture capitalists. The state can intervene in the economy—but only to fix market failures or level the playing field. It can regulate the private sector in order to account for the external costs companies may impose on the public, such as pollution, and it can invest in public goods, such as basic scientific research or the development of drugs with little market potential. It should not, however, directly attempt to create and shape markets. A 2012 *Economist* article on the future of manufacturing encapsulated this common conception: "Governments have always been lousy at picking winners, and they are likely to become more so, as legions of entrepreneurs and tinkerers swap designs online, turn them into products at home and market them globally from a garage," the article stated. "As the revolution rages, governments should stick to the basics: better schools for a skilled workforce, clear rules and a level playing field for enterprises of all kinds. Leave the rest to the revolutionaries."

That view is as wrong as it is widespread. In fact, in countries that owe their growth to innovation, the state has historically served not as a meddler in the private sector but as a key partner of it—and often a more daring one, willing to take the risks that businesses won't. Across the entire innovation chain, from basic research to commercialisation, governments have stepped up with needed investment that the private sector has been too scared to provide. This spending has proved transformative, creating entirely new markets and sectors, including the Internet, nanotechnology, biotechnology, and clean energy.

Today, however, it has become harder and harder for governments to think big. Increasingly, their role has been limited to simply facilitating the private sector and, perhaps, nudging it in the right direction. When governments step beyond that role, they immediately get accused of crowding out private investment and ineptly trying to pick winners. The notion of the state as a mere facilitator, administrator, and regulator started gaining wide currency in the 1970s, but it has taken on new-found popularity in the wake of the global financial crisis. Across the globe, policymakers have targeted public debt (never mind that it was private debt that led to the meltdown), arguing that cutting government spending will spur private investment. As a result, the very state agencies that have been responsible for the technological revolutions of the past have seen their budgets shrink. In the United States, the budget "sequestration" process has resulted in $95 billion worth of cuts to federal R&D spending from 2013 to 2021. In Europe, the EU's "fiscal compact," which requires states to drop their fiscal deficits down to three per cent of GDP, is squeezing educational and R&D spending.

What's more, thanks in part to the conventional wisdom about its dynamism and the state's sluggishness, the private sector has been able to successfully lobby governments to weaken regulations and cut capital gains taxes. From 1976 to 1981 alone, after heavy lobbying from the National Venture Capital Association, the capital gains tax rate in the United States fell from 40 per cent to 20 per cent. And in the name of bringing Silicon Valley's dynamism to the United Kingdom, in 2002, the government of British Prime Minister Tony Blair reduced the time that private equity funds have to be invested to be eligible for tax reductions from ten years to two years. These policies increase inequality, not investment, and by rewarding short-term investments at the expense of long-term ones, they hurt innovation.

Getting governments to think big about innovation is not just about throwing more taxpayer money at more activities. It requires fundamentally reconsidering the traditional role of the state in the economy. Specifically, that means empowering governments to envision a direction for technological change and invest in that direction. It means abandoning the short-sighted way public spending is usually evaluated. It means ending the practice of insulating the private sector from the public sector. And it means figuring out ways for governments and taxpayers to reap some of the rewards of public investment, instead of just the risks. Only once policymakers move past the myths about the state's role in innovation will they stop being, as John Maynard Keynes put it in another era, "the slaves of some defunct economist."

THE FAILURE OF MARKET FAILURE

According to the neoclassical economic theory that is taught in most economics departments, the goal of government policy is simply to correct market failures. In this view, once the sources of failure have been addressed—a monopoly reined in, a public good subsidised, or a negative externality taxed—market forces will efficiently allocate resources, enabling the economy to follow a new path to growth. But that view forgets that markets are blind, so to speak. They may neglect societal or environmental concerns. And they often head in suboptimal, path-dependent directions. Energy companies, for example, would rather invest in extracting oil from the deepest confines of the earth than in clean energy.

In addressing societal challenges such as climate change, youth unemployment, obesity, aging, and inequality, states must lead —not by simply fixing market failures but by actively creating markets. They must direct the economy toward new "techno-economic paradigms", in the words of the technology and innovation scholar Carlota Perez. These directions are not generated spontaneously from market forces; they are largely the result of deliberate state decisions. In the mass-production revolution, for example, the state invested in both the underlying technologies and their diffusion across the economy. On the supply side, the US military-industrial complex, beginning in World War II, invested in improvements in aerospace, electronics, and materials. On the demand side, the US government's post-war subsidisation of suburban living—building roads, backing mortgages, and guaranteeing incomes through the welfare state—enabled workers to own homes, buy cars, and consume other mass-produced goods.

As Michael Shellenberger and his colleagues at the progressive think tank the Breakthrough Institute have documented, despite the mythmaking about how the shale gas boom is being driven by wildcatting entrepreneurs operating independently from the state, the US federal government invested heavily in the technologies that unleashed it. In 1976, the Morgantown Energy Research Center and the Bureau of Mines launched the Eastern Gas Shales Project, which demonstrated how natural gas could be recovered from shale formations. That same year, the federal government opened the Gas Research Institute, which was funded through a tax on natural gas production and spent billions of dollars on research into shale gas. And the Sandia National Laboratories, part of the US Department of Energy, developed the 3D geologic mapping technology used for fracking operations.

Likewise, as the physician Marcia Angell has shown, many of the most promising new drugs trace their origins to research done by the taxpayer-funded National Institutes of Health, which has an annual budget of some $30 billion. Private pharmaceutical companies, meanwhile, tend to focus more on the D than the R part of R&D, plus slight variations of existing drugs and marketing.

Silicon Valley's techno-libertarians might be surprised to find out that Uncle Sam funded many of the innovations behind the information technology revolution, too. Consider the iPhone. It is often heralded as the quintessential example of what happens when a hands-off government allows genius entrepreneurs to flourish, and yet the development of the features that make the iPhone a smartphone rather than a stupid phone was publicly funded. The progenitor of the Internet was ARPANET, a program funded by the Defense Advanced Research Projects Agency (DARPA), which is part of the Defense Department, in the 1960s. GPS began as a 1970s US military program called Navstar. The iPhone's touchscreen technology was created by the company FingerWorks, which was founded by a professor at the publicly funded University of Delaware and one of his doctoral candidates, who received grants from the National Science Foundation and the CIA. Even Siri, the iPhone's cheery, voice-recognising personal assistant, can trace its lineage to the US government: it is a spinoff of a DARPA artificial-intelligence project. None of this is to suggest that Steve Jobs and his team at Apple were not brilliant in how they put together existing technologies. The problem, however, is that failing to admit the public side of the story puts future government-funded research at risk.

For policymakers, then, the question should not be whether to pick particular directions when it comes to innovation, since some governments are already doing that, and with good results. Rather, the question should be how to do so in a way that is democratically accountable and that solves the most pressing social and technological challenges.

A SMARTER STATE

State spending on innovation tends to be assessed in exactly the wrong way. Under the prevailing economic framework, market failures are identified and particular government investments are proposed. Their value is then appraised through a narrow calculation that involves heavy guesswork: Will the benefits of a particular intervention exceed the costs associated with both the offending market failure and the implementation of the fix? Such a method is far too static to evaluate something as dynamic as innovation. By failing to account for the possibility that the state can create economic landscapes that never existed before, it gives short shrift to governments' efforts in this area. No wonder economists often characterise the public sector as nothing more than an inefficient version of the private sector.

This incomplete way of measuring public investment leads to accusations that, by entering certain sectors, governments are crowding out private investment. That charge is often false, because government investment often has the effect of 'crowding in,' meaning that it stimulates private investment and expands the overall pie of national output, which benefits both private and public investors. But more important, public investments should aim not only to kick-start the economy but also, as Keynes wrote, "to do those things which at present are not done at all." No private companies were trying to put a man on the moon when NASA undertook the Apollo project.

Without the right tools for evaluating investments, governments have a hard time knowing when they are merely operating in existing spaces and when they are making things happen that would not have happened otherwise. The result: investments that are too narrow, constrained by the prevailing techno-economic paradigm. A better way of evaluating a given investment would be to consider whether it taught workers new skills and whether it led to the creation of new technologies, sectors, or markets. When it comes to government spending on pharmaceutical research, for example, it might make sense to move past the private sector's fixation on drugs and fund more work on diagnostics, surgical treatments, and lifestyle changes.

Governments suffer from another, related problem when it comes to contemplating investments: as a result of the dominant view that they should stick to fixing market failures, they are often ill equipped to do much more than that. To avoid such problems as a regulatory agency getting captured by business, the thinking goes, the state must insulate itself from the private sector. That's why governments have increasingly outsourced key jobs to the private sector. But that trend often rids them of the knowledge necessary for devising a smart strategy for investing in innovation and makes it harder to attract top talent. It creates a self-fulfilling prophecy: the less big thinking a government does, the less expertise it is able to attract, the worse it performs, and the less big thinking it is allowed to do. Had there been more information technology capacity within the US government, the Obama administration would probably not have had such difficulty rolling out HealthCare.gov, and that failure will likely lead to only more outsourcing.

In order to create and shape technologies, sectors, and markets, the state must be armed with the intelligence necessary to envision and enact bold policies. This does not mean that the state will always succeed; indeed, the uncertainty inherent in the innovation process means that it will often fail. But it needs to learn from failed investments and continuously improve its structures and practices. As the economist Albert Hirschman emphasised, the policymaking process is by its nature messy, so it is important for public institutions to welcome the process of trial and error. Governments should pay as much attention to the business school topics of strategic management and organisational behaviour as private companies do. The status quo approach, however, is to focus not on making the government more competent but on downsizing it.

PROFIT AND LOSS

Since governments often undertake courageous spending during the riskiest parts of the innovation process, it is key that they figure out how they can socialise not just the risks of their investments but also the rewards. The US government's Small Business Innovation Research programme, for example, offers high-risk financing to companies at much earlier stages than most private venture capital firms do; it funded Compaq and Intel when they were start-ups. Similarly, the Small Business Investment Company programme, an initiative under the auspices of the US Small Business Administration, has provided crucial loans and grants to early stage companies, including Apple in 1978. In fact, the need for such long-term investments has only increased over time as venture capital firms have become more short term in their outlook, emphasising finding an 'exit' for each of their investments (usually through a public offering or a sale to another company) within three years. Real innovation can take decades.

As is the nature of early stage investing in technologies with uncertain prospects, some investments are winners, but many are losers. For every Internet (a success story of US government financing), there are many *Concordes* (a white elephant funded by the British and French governments). Consider the twin tales of Solyndra and Tesla Motors. In 2009, Solyndra, a solar-power-panel start-up, received a $535 million guaranteed loan from the US Department of Energy; that same year, Tesla, the electric-car manufacturer, got approval for a similar loan, for $465 million. In the years afterward, Tesla was wildly successful, and the firm repaid its loan in 2013. Solyndra, by contrast, led for bankruptcy in 2011 and, among fiscal conservatives, became a byword for the government's sorry track record when it comes to picking winners. Of course, if the government is to act like a venture capitalist, it will necessarily encounter many failures. The problem, however, is that governments, unlike venture capital firms, are often saddled with the costs of the failures while earning next to nothing from the successes. Taxpayers footed the bill for Solyndra's losses yet got hardly any of Tesla's profits.

Economists may argue that the state already receives a return on its investments by taxing the resulting profits. The truth is more complicated. For one thing, large corporations are masters of tax evasion. Google—whose game-changing search algorithm, it should be noted, was developed with funding from the National Science Foundation—has lowered its US tax bill by funnelling some of its profits through Ireland. Apple does the same by taking advantage of a race to the bottom among US states: in 2006, the company, which is based in Cupertino, California, set up an investment subsidiary in Reno, Nevada, to save money.

Fixing the problem is not just a matter of plugging the loopholes. Tax rates in the United States and other Western countries have been falling over the past several decades precisely due to a false narrative about how the private sector serves as the sole wealth creator. Government revenues have also shrunk due to tax incentives aimed at promoting innovation, few of which have been shown to produce any R&D that would not have happened otherwise. What's more, given how mobile capital is these days, a particular government that has funded a given company might not be able to tax it since it may have moved abroad. And although taxes are effective at paying for the basics, such as education, health care, and research, they don't begin to cover the cost of making direct investments in companies or specific technologies. If the state is being asked to make such investments—as will increasingly be the case as financial markets become even more focused on the short term—then it will have to recover the inevitable losses that arise from this process.

There are various ways to do so. One is to attach strings to the loans and guarantees that governments hand out to businesses. For example, just as graduates who receive income-contingent student loans get their repayments adjusted based on their salaries, the recipients of state investments could have their repayments adjusted based on their profits.

Another way for states to reap greater returns involves reforming the way they partner with businesses. Public-private partnerships should be symbiotic, rather than parasitic, relationships. In 1925, the US government allowed AT&T to retain its monopoly over the phone system but required the company to reinvest its profits in research, a deal that led to the formation of Bell Labs. Today, however, instead of reinvesting their profits, large companies hoard them or spend them on share buybacks, stock options, and executive pay. Research by the economist William Lazonick has borne this out: "The 449 companies in the S&P 500 index that were publicly listed from 2003 through 2012… used 54% of their earnings—a total of $2.4 trillion—to buy back their own stock."

An even bolder plan would allow the state to retain equity in the companies it supports, just as private venture capital firms do. Indeed, some countries adopted this model long ago. Israel's Yozma Group, which manages public venture capital funds, has backed—and retained equity in—early stage companies since 1993. The Finnish Innovation Fund, or Sitra, which is operated under the Finnish parliament, has done the same since 1967, and it was an early investor in Nokia's transformation from a rubber company into a cell-phone giant. Had the US government had a stake in Tesla, it would have been able to more than cover its losses from Solyndra. The year Tesla received its government loan, the company went public at an opening price of $17 a share; that figure had risen to $93 by the time the loan was repaid. Today, shares in Tesla trade above $200.

The prospect of the state owning a stake in a private corporation may be anathema to many parts of the capitalist world, but given that governments are already investing in the private sector, they may as well earn a return on those investments (something even fiscal conservatives might find attractive). The state need not hold a controlling stake, but it could hold equity in the form of preferred stocks that get priority in receiving dividends. The returns could be used to fund future innovation. Politicians and the media have been too quick to criticise public investments when things go wrong and too slow to reward them when things go right.

THE NEXT REVOLUTION

Past technological revolutions — from railroads to the automobile to the space programme to information technology — did not come about as the result of minor tinkering with the economic system. They occurred because states undertook bold missions that focused not on minimising government failure but on maximising innovation. Once one accepts this more proactive state purpose, the key questions of economic policy get reframed. Questions about crowding out private investment and unwisely picking winners fall by the wayside as more dynamic questions — about creating the types of public-private interactions that can produce new industrial landscapes — rise to the top.

Today, many countries, from China to Denmark to Germany, have settled on their next mission: green energy. Given the potential benefits and the amount of money at play, it is crucial that governments back this mission the right way. For starters, they must not only pick various technologies or sectors to invest in but also ask what they want from those sectors. For example, if what governments want from the energy sector is a stable energy supply, then shale gas will do, but if the mission is to mitigate climate change, then it won't. In fact, mission-oriented policies need to foster interactions among multiple fields. NASA's mission to the moon required the interaction of many different sectors, from rocketry to telecommunications to textiles. Likewise, the green energy revolution will require investment not just in wind energy, solar power, and biofuels but also in new engines, new ways of more efficiently maintaining infrastructure, and new ways of making products last longer. Accordingly, the state should take its cue from the venture capital world and diversify its portfolio, spreading capital across many different technologies and enterprises.

In making green investments, governments should fund those technologies that the private sector has ignored and provide a strong, clear direction for change, letting various entrepreneurs experiment with the specifics. Governments should provide ambitious targets, not in the old command-and-control style but through a combination of carrots and sticks. The German government has followed this approach in its energy-transition initiative, or *Energiewende*, which is designed to phase out nuclear energy and substitute it with renewables; it is doing this by setting lofty goals for carbon emissions reductions and subsidising technological development of wind and solar power.

More broadly, governments should strike agreements that allow them to share in the profits from their successful investments. And most of all, they should build the public agencies of the future, turning them into hotbeds of creativity, adaptation, and exploration. That will require abandoning the current obsession with limiting the state's intervention to fixing problems after they have happened—and smashing the popular myth that the state cannot innovate.

1
This text appeared in *Foreign Affairs*, Volume 94, January/February 2015, pp. 61–68.

Chapter I
The Urals, Russia

— copper deposit in Rezh
— gold mine in Berezovsky
— metallurgical factories in Nizhniy Tagil
— asbestos mine in Asbest

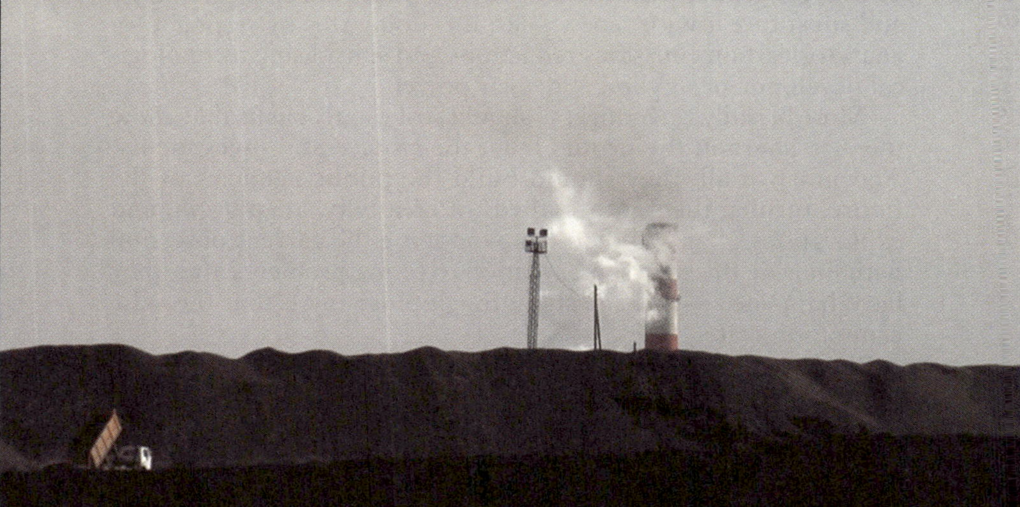

Chapter II
Deutsche Börse in Frankfurt am Main, Germany

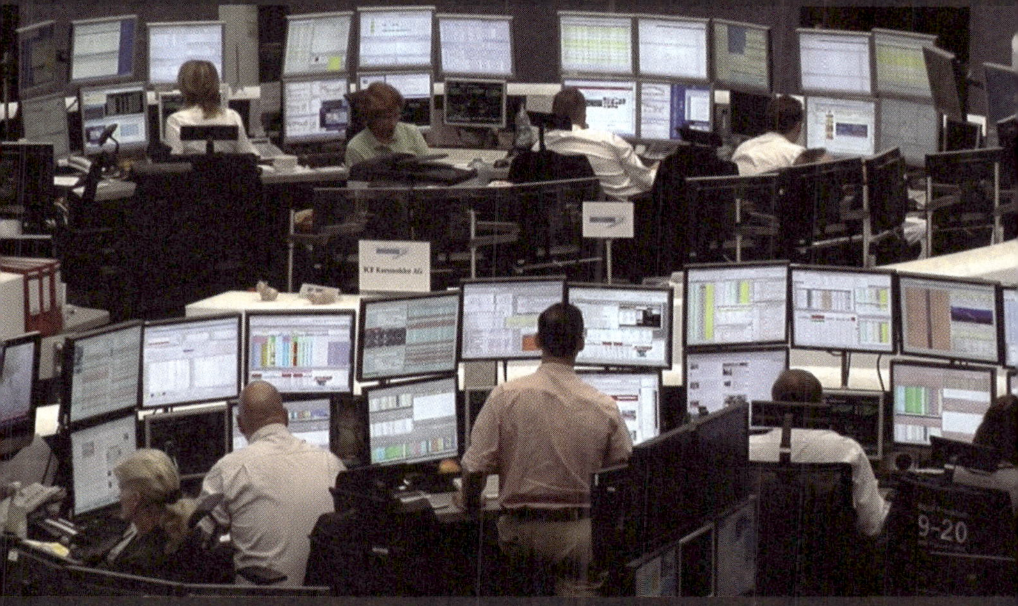

Chapter III

— EVN collection 95–05, book
— "Art at Work", Deutsche Bank, Frankfurt am Main, Germany
— entry hall of Commerzbank, Frankfurt am Main, Germany

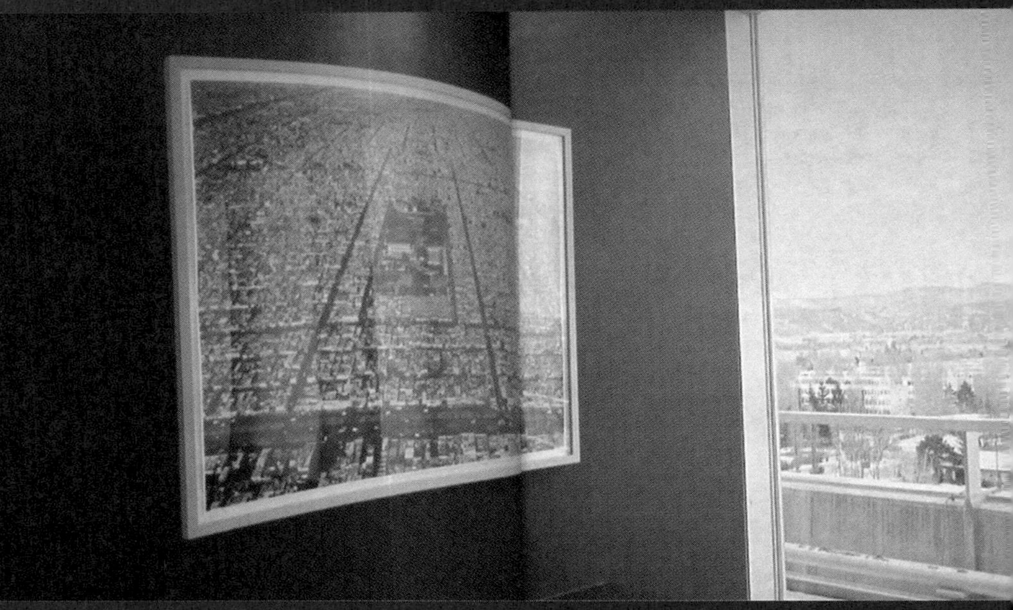

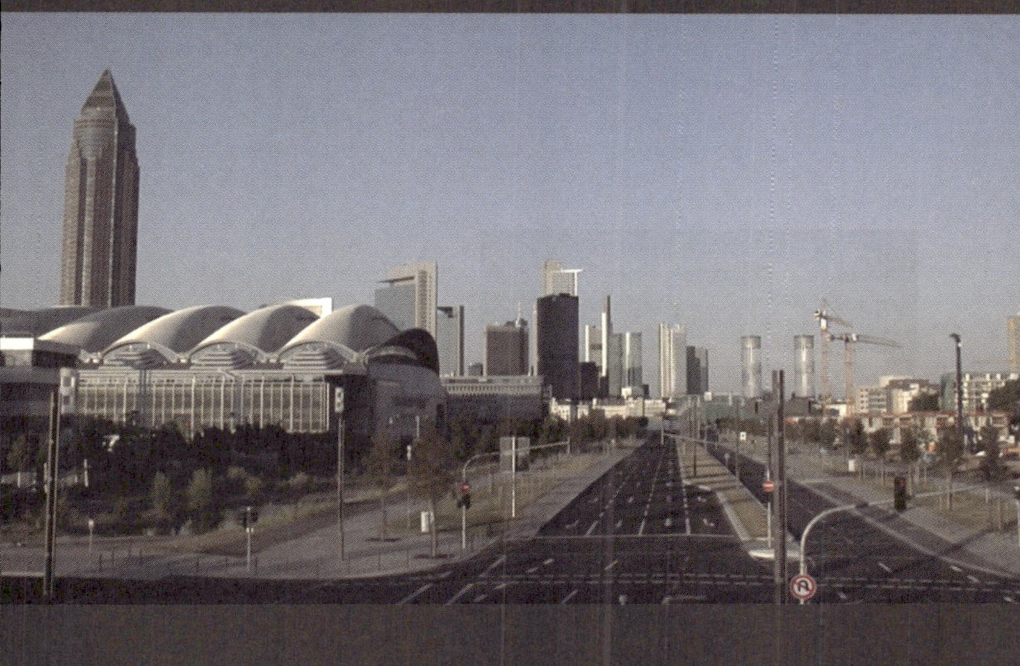

Estate is a sequence of shots from post-industrial locations in Russia and Germany, to unfold a narration on global economy and comment on corporate collections of contemporary art. [Marie Egger]

Yanis Varoufakis — What am I doing here?

Moscow, 1st October 2015

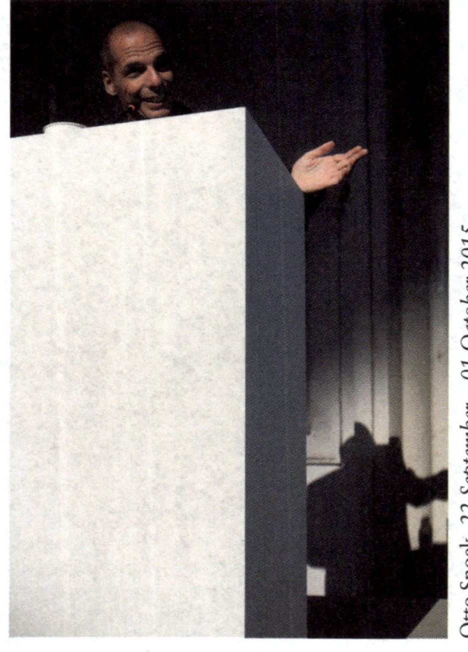

Otto Snoek, 22 September – 01 October 2015

What am I doing here? A political economist and politician. It is not immediately obvious why I am speaking at the Moscow Biennale for Contemporary Art 2015. Let me be more specific and self-critical about this: Economics is a very stale, uncultured discipline; students of economics are taught to think as if economic life can be fully described and understood independently from culture, art or music—somewhat like a military academy. As part of their officer training one of the things they learn is savoir-vivre, good manners. They come in handy if you are a general of the Russian, the French or the American army and your president invites you to dinner. You need to be able to know the right spoon, the right fork. But it is completely irrelevant for you doing your job properly on the battlefield. Manners are something good to have. They are additional to what is necessary in order to perform mass murder, which is what you do as a general. Similar to this, in the world of economics, culture is a good thing to have but it is completely inessential to understand how the economy works.

Politicians look at culture as a veneer, as a source of legitimacy. Culture serves a politician to become a minister of culture at one point in their career. It is not an essential ministry and very low down in the pecking order of government. So if you have been a minister of finance or foreign affairs and afterwards you become the minister of culture it is considered a demotion. At times, it may be good to have this title, it gives you an aura. Cultural professionals, for example artists and curators, lend a degree of social, narrative power to politicians. Somehow like having a bishop next to you, eulogising you. But it is not seen as essential in the running of a country. The minister of culture has a minor position in government. He does not have very important things to say when the big issues are discussed in the cabinet.

I am a politician. I am a political economist. I am an economist. All this endeavour is only tangentially and, if you want, imperialistically linked to art. In a sense, the curators of Moscow Biennale for Contemporary Art 2015 were mistaken to invite me, because if I really believed in the practices of the economists and the politicians, I should not have been invited as, in the end, deep down I would be contemptuous of the world of art. I would see it at best as something good to have on top of important things but not as something crucial in our lives, as something essential.

The attempt to isolate the quest for what matters for a good society from the aesthetic, and from the musical, has always been alien to me. I recall various political and social conflicts that I tried to understand when I was a young man, before I became an economist and politician. And I remember that to make sense of what was at stake, the aesthetic and the musical were always very important: In the 1980s' Nicaraguan Revolution, the conflict between the Sandinistas and the Contras was also polarising the West: Who is right and who is not? Who were the good and who were the bad guys? Listening to the music the Sandinistas played or sang and to the music that the Contras played gave me information that no article, no book, no degree of politicisation could show. And further back in the 1930s, when comparing Picasso's *Guernica* with Franco's art: one quick look already tells you a great deal about the essence of the Spanish Civil War. Listen to Beethoven's Ninth Symphony and compare it to the Prussian anthems of the time. Or even compare it to the music Napoleon was listening to, to whom Beethoven dedicated the Third Symphony. Then listen to the music Napoleon was listening to after Beethoven tore up the dedication to Napoleon, due to Napoleon's abandonment of the ideals of the French revolution. Compare the aesthetic of Leni Riefenstahl to the aesthetic of Sergei Eisenstein—through the eye of the artist and by looking at the aesthetic, we can always recognise the political and economic differences.

If you had studied politics or economics you would not have this cultural input, you would have missed out on a great thing of essence. When I met my wife Danae, I had the opportunity to experience what I had always been convinced about, but in practice; due to the fact that she actually grabbed me away from my office and my armchair and made me travel with her around the world to experience up close and personal all those concepts which I had found intriguing from a philosophical or an academic point of view: globalisation, harsh divisions. We travelled around all the continents, tracing dividing lines, the United States and Mexican border, the separation wall in Palestine, Belfast, Ethiopia, Kashmir, etc. It was interesting for me to see how much more I understood about concepts which I thought I had grasped while looking at these experiences through her lens—the lens of an artist. Also, to see that there was a direct correspondence between the method of an artist and the method of a mathematician. I remember, when I was a student, my struggle to solve an equation and the click when you suddenly knew how to do it. It is very similar to the way an artist struggles with a concept and at some point 'it' clicks and the work is complete, conceptually, in the head. These are the experiences which—thanks to her—confirmed what I had already known theoretically: Art is not a luxury—it is an essential part of making sense of the world we live in.

Some of you may have heard that I had something to do with the Eurozone Crisis, I am not going to bother you with an explanation of what is wrong with the euro. However, the euro, Europe's common currency, is terribly constructed. The reason why Greece is in the news, is because we are the flimsiest part of a monetary union that simply was not designed for the world we live in. As it is fragmenting under pressure from global capitalism, the flimsiest part of that union is traumatised and continuously pushed down a black hole. I was the minister of a bankrupt country that was at the forefront of this. But if you really want to take a glimpse of what is the matter with the euro, you should take out a euro note and look at it—aesthetically. What do you see? A very boring design. No matter whether it is a 5 euro note or a 10 euro note, a 20, a 50, a 100, or, if you are rich enough, a 500 euro note. Its two sides depict either a bridge or an archway. That is the main design of the euro notes. But these arches and bridges do not exist. They are figments of some second grade artist's imagination. They are not pictures of real archways or existing bridges. Europe, despite its extremely rich cultural and artistic heritage, has not depicted any of these treasures on its notes! Do you know why? Because they could not agree which ones to select. The idea of the Colosseum or the Parthenon on the 50 euro note was a no-no in Frankfurt in the Bundesbank. Why? Not because they have a problem with the Parthenon or the Colosseum, but they thought: The association is going to lead from the Parthenon to Greece to the Euro to that of a 'soft' currency. So they decided against the Parthenon on the Euro notes. Without the Parthenon or the Colosseum or a precious Michelangelo image, they could not then include the Cologne Cathedral either, so they could not select any existing work of art. A decision was then made to commission third grade artists to produce fourth grade designs of non-existing arches. You do not need to understand economics or politics in order to understand that the Euro was going to be in trouble—just look at it aesthetically.

The theme of previous keynotes of the Moscow Biennale was about doing things together, about collective action. In Europe, ever since the Euro Crisis began, we have a delicious irony: a continent that was uniting, that was doing things together, under many different cultures and languages for decades after the Second World War, was divided by a common currency. Oscar Wilde once said that Britain and America are divided by a common language—we went one step further and are now divided by a common currency.

Let me take you to the period of time when that common currency was being designed: The euro came to us at the time when the Berlin Wall was coming down. Indeed, German reunification and Europe's common currency are historically intertwined. One of the conditions for the German reunification was the monetary union. The French and the Germans (President François Mitterrand of France and Chancellor Helmut Kohl of Germany) came to the agreement that a reunified Germany should be embedded in a European monetary union by sharing a currency as a first step towards a federation of a united states of Europe. Around that time, when these debates where happening, with the Iron Curtain (not just the Berlin Wall) being removed, beginning in Berlin but also in Moscow, what was the cultural milieu at the time?

I believe that if we look back at 1991, that essential year, we will recall that there was an urge from among Europeans, among Russians, and from among all of us, to come closer together, to overcome the divisions the Cold War had erected. As the Iron Curtain was coming down, there was one particular movie, which touched me very personally: *The Double Life of Véronique* by Krzysztof Kieślowski captured this spirit elegantly and reflected upon the emotional impact of the ending of Europe's post-war division, but also conveyed a certain brooding, a certain angst amongst those of us who were dreaming of a borderless Europe. The device in the movie that Kieślowski came up with were the bonds between two identical looking strangers: Veronica in Poland was one woman and Véronique in France was another. They were both played by the same actress, Irène Jacob. The paths of the two women only cross once in the movie, as Europe is about to be reunited. There is a scene where jubilant crowds in Cracow in Poland are interspersed with one girl, Veronica, who has been invited for an audition for a singing part. After that she rushes through a demonstration (in favour of the reunification of Europe) in Cracow's main square. A protester accidentally knocks her, the sheets music falls to the ground, she reaches down to pick up her music folder, and as she is coming up she sees Véronique—her double—getting on a tourist bus. This is the only time the two women see each other. They only meet for that fraction of a second. After the successful audition, Veronica lands the solo part. And while on stage, singing her heart out in the performance, she collapses and dies. And at that very moment, Véronique in Paris experiences an overwhelming deep sorrow, which is completely inexplicable to her. That emotional musical bond between Véronique and Veronica — the radical absence that Véronique in Paris felt when Veronica died in Cracow, symbolised, from my perspective, a solidarity and a cultural spiritual connection between Western Europeans and those who were left behind the Iron Curtain. Even solidarity with Southerners in Greece who had been left out because of the dictatorship we had in the sixties and the seventies.

Another movie, I would bundle together with *The Double Life of Véronique*, is Costa-Gavras' *Z* (1969), which had become a symbol in the West of the bifurcation, of the division between Northern Europe and Southern Europe, and the manner in which a film, an artwork, can heal such divisions. These movies epitomised European unity. Europe as a unit that not only survived but actually grew in the shadow of the harsh divisions of the Cold War. Could a beautiful movie like that, emerge from today's Europe? Could Kieślowski have filmed *The Double Life of Véronique* today?

The irony of our present moment is that the eradication of borders, at least within the European Union, and the triumph of the single market which was heralded as the cement that brings us together and solidifies the unity of Europeans — that these symbols of homogenisation, of globalisation have devalued and fragmented Europe's cultural goods. Nowadays, the Polish Veronica might get a recording contract in Paris or in London, but her music would be homogenised within a global market place for music and for the arts, a market place that knows no boundaries and lacks a heartland, an anchor. Music, art, even theatre, have come under the aegis, under the dominance of market forces. They are guided by bureaucrats in Brussels, by funding institutions which are increasingly in the pockets of commercial power. They are showcased in blockbuster exhibitions in large museums or heavily marketed at concert series, at forums in which the stars are the postmodernist curators, inviting economists like me to give a lecture to artists. Economists who are extending the imperium of finance and the logic of the market to the artistic market place. And of course they are influenced by celebrity contractors and corporate sponsors who determine everything. Instead of being bonded by music like Veronica and Véronique were (because they listened to the same music), instead of being bonded by motion, by guilt, by culture; today Véronique and Veronica would probably be bound by a contract drawn up by a global legal company from New York, or Paris, or most likely London, and the French Véronique would probably be worried that the Polish Veronica would move to Paris and steal her job.

Now let me take you to another movie. Recall the scene in the Orson Welles movie *The Third Man* (1949), when looking down from the heights of the famous Ferris Wheel at Prater in Vienna, when Harry Lime, played by Orson Welles, uttered an impertinent theory of culture: "In Italy for 30 years under the Borgias they had warfare, terror, murder, and bloodshed, but they produced Michelangelo, Leonardo da Vinci, and the Renaissance. In Switzerland they had brotherly love—they had 500 years of democracy and peace, and what did that produce? The cuckoo clock."

This is very impertinent and unfair to Switzerland, because the history of Switzerland is a lot more nuanced and richer than that. But yet, he is right in that scene when he says that the beautiful culture, art and music of Europe was drenched in blood and underpinned by conflicts. Art and music are far from benign features that sit decoratively on top of civilisation. Picasso once said (and I love this quotation) that a painting is not meant to decorate, a painting is meant to work as a weapon against the enemy. Beethoven, as I mentioned before, dedicated his Third Symphony to Napoleon and then tore up the dedication in anger. D.H. Lawrence supported a raging contempt for democracy; he was a thoroughly nasty character and a great poet with a sprinkling of virile anti-Semitism thrown in for 'good' measure. Ezra Pound is a poet who celebrated his immense love for European culture while at the same time being a great supporter of Benito Mussolini.

When talking about culture and doing things together, we must constantly remember that, however much we despise anti-Semitism,—and I do despise anti-Semitism more than I despise anything else—however much we despise conflict, however much we despise treating others as enemies, Picasso's point about using painting against the enemy has to been taken very seriously. The enemy not being other people, but the enemy as in destitution, the enemy as in racism, the enemy as in all those forces (economic primarily) that are pushing people and societies apart, therewith setting one proud culture against another. Art must not be anodyne, culture cannot be decorative. Herman Göring once quipped that: "When I hear the word culture I reach for my Browning!" (referring to his gun). He was right to think that culture is indeed a dangerous weapon. You folks in here, you artists and curators, should be feared by the powerful in our societies. If you are not considered dangerous by the powers-that-be, you are not doing your job properly. As long as culture resists commodification, it is going to be a great threat for those who use commodification in order to extend their own realm as far and further afield as possible. Now, of course, culture is becoming commodified. This is being accomplished by expert gallerists, postmodernised by cunning curators, sanitised through the meat grinder of the European commission's funding formulae for the arts. Göring never understood that he had no need for his revolver. The market did the job of turning culture into an anodyne accomplice of the powerful, better than the gulag, better than threatening artists with imprisonment. Culture could and is being diffused simply by making it go through the revolving doors between the Single Market and the Brussels bureaucracy. Indeed, why send the stormtroopers into the theatres and into the artist's studios when the bureaucrats, the auctioneers, and the curators can eliminate the potential of culture for political subversion, turning it into another realm where playfulness and where subversion are traded in the stock exchange of art, of culture alongside jewellery, cars, gadgets and toxic financial derivatives of the kind that Wall Street knows how to produce in droves?

For several decades, three decades at least, exchange value has been wiping the floor clean with any other form of value, including cultural values. In about the 1970s, the bankers were kept very tightly in a box, and banking was very boring until the 1970s under the system that the New Dealers in the United States designed, also known as the Bretton Woods System. The collapse of the first phase of post-war capitalism begat financialisation in the seventies, when finance and banking was unleashed. Its collapse was to herald a number of developments such as financialisation, the complete emancipation of the banker to do as he pleases, and the sequels of events that eventually brought down the Soviet Union… But that is a long story not to be told now. All we need here is to recall how, since the 1970s, finance has been subordinating industry, and neoliberalism (which is the ideology of emancipated finance) has been subordinating liberalism's respect for industry, labour and parliaments. It is the ideology of the bankers whose penchant for greater liberty for themselves ushered in the new creed according to which markets are an end in themselves—that they are only answerable to… markets. Liberals in previous eras believed in markets as instruments, not as objectives, not as something to be fetishised. After the early 1970s, however, this is what neoliberalism did. Being neither particularly new nor liberal, this neoliberalism was all about the fetishisation of the market: the market as an objective, not as an instrument with which to achieve other objectives.

This process led us to a radical failure, a radical inability to think thoughts that a more confident past used to allow: The thought, for instance, that a song or a poem can be valuable independent of its market value. The thought that value is irreducible to price, and that not everything is a matter of demand and supply. That the economist is not somebody who can know everything about humanity, including all thoughts that are potentially useful to an audience like this one. That the inability to privatise the smell of the meadow in springtime is not a problem to be fixed by a technical trick by which to market the smell of meadows.

While commodification is a global phenomenon, it took a particularly virulent form in the European Union around the time of Véronique's release in 1991. That is not because Europe became too pacified without any more wars. I am not suggesting that we should go back to the battlefield so that culture can be revivified. It is not at all that we became too re-unified for culture to flourish. The problem was the constant retreat of the public sphere. There is nothing wrong with the idea of a single market from the Atlantic to the Urals, or indeed, since the topic is Eurasia, to Vladivostok and China and Japan, and beyond that to Australia. There is nothing wrong with that. Borders are awful scars on the planet and the sooner we dispose of them the better.

The problem is that market economies require a powerful *demos*, a people, the word from which the term democracy derives. A market without a powerful *demos* to counterbalance, to stabilise, to civilise it, is a market that fails even by market-criteria. To keep Europe civilised, to keep Russia civilised, to keep Europe and Russia capable of producing culture that is dangerous to the powerful, a single market, a market economy requires a democratic state. A state that is controlled not by those who gain the greatest power from the commodification process, but which is controlled on the basis of one-person-one-vote. When you and I go to a shop, we vote with our rubles, our euros, our dollars. Every time you buy an iPad, it is a vote for Apple. And the higher the demand for iPads, the more expensive they are and the more votes we give to Apple. So in a sense, the market and politics involve voting systems, except that in the market place it is not-one-person-one-vote, you have as many votes as you have rubles, yen, euros, or dollars. The beauty of democracy is that you have one vote, and that you have the same number of votes (one) whether you are rich, poor, well-educated, stupid, Russian, Greek, or whatever. And unless you have the political process to stabilise the market process, the one-person-one-vote against as-many-votes-as-you-have-dollars system, you are not living in a potentially stable market society.

In the same way that art and culture are not useful add-ons to embellish politics and economics, democracy is not a luxury for those in credit; as opposed to in debt. Democracy is a political process which is necessary in order to stabilise the market itself. And those who prioritise the market and turn it into an end in itself, they are not even good at being liberals, because they are promoting a kind of market that will fall on its face. Capitalism produces crises in the same manner in which it produces iPods: naturally—it is in its nature. To keep our social economy civilised, we have to remain exceptionally sceptical of the market place as a realm that can substitute for culture, for politics, for democracy. If we do not follow this instinct towards stabilising the economy by putting it under the control of democracy and under the critical scrutiny that only artists, musicians and cultured people can conjure up and supply our societies with, if we fail in doing that, we will end up with gigantic markets and colossal bureaucracies that are incapable of stabilising those gigantic markets. This will lead, as it always does, to an unholy alliance between exchange value (that is, price) and bureaucratic authoritarianism, all at the expense of cultural and political values that we Europeans, Russians, Greeks and Germans so painfully produced over the last few centuries.

Let me take you to an interesting moment, in 1978: It was autumn, it was September. Two suited men entered Aachen's cathedral where the remains lay of Charlemagne, the great Christian king who unified Europe into the Holy Roman Empire. The two suited men were President Giscard d'Estaing of France and Chancellor Helmut Schmidt of Germany. The reason they went, according to what they told us later, is that they had just signed a treaty. It was called The European Monetary System Treaty. It was the beginning of Europe's common currency, when they decided to create a monetary union between France and Germany that, in the end, brought as the euro. So why did they go to the cathedral, to the tomb of Charlemagne? Their own explanation is that they felt trepidation, anxiety and they needed Charlemagne's blessing. This is a cultural reference. It is a bit of Eurokitsch and reminds one of the Eurovision Song Contest's aesthetic. But let me also draw another two historical parallels. In 1993, when the European Central Bank was created, the president of that bank (called The European Monetary Institute at that time), felt that he was doing his duty according to… Charlemagne! Let me give you now a third dimension, which is pretty nasty. It is December 1944. The last fresh unit of the SS is formed in Berlin. It comprises 11,000 Frenchmen who were collaborators of the Nazi regime. They were the ones who fought tooth and nail to defend Hitler to the last moment. Of those 11,000 only 13 survived as they fought to the bitter end. What was the regiment called? *Charlemagne*.

What I am saying is this: Europe has a brilliant and a disgusting history all wrapped up. Our attempts to get together are essential. Doing things together is important because if we work against each other we shall fail. The idea of re-nationalising ambition, of going back to our national currencies, of doing things separately, of hiding behind the cocoon of the nation state — those are steps in the wrong direction. We have to do things together in Europe. But just because we are integrating and creating a common currency, just because we have a vision of pulling French, Germans and Greeks together, this is not necessarily going to augur well for Europe. The idea of a common currency was first discussed in a conference in Berlin in 1942, under the Nazis. Charlemagne can be the symbol of Giscard d'Estaing, who was a great democrat and Europeanist, but also of Frenchmen willing to die in defence of Hitler. As Spanish anarchists (whose flag featured red and black colours) said during the Spanish Civil War, beautifully reproduced in Ken Loach's *Cry Freedom*: We have to keep hope alive with the colour red, but also have the colour black to remind us of the dark side of our soul.

In Europe, over the last few years, we have seen how Helmut Schmidt's and Giscard d'Estaing's Eurokitsch pilgrimage to Aachen, and their excellent ambition to bring Europe together under the common currency, have backfired. Today, the Germans hate the Greeks, the Greeks hate the Germans, the French and the Italians loathe the Germans who look at them with contempt, the Greeks have begun to turn against the Greeks and, very soon, the Germans will turn against the Germans… Europe's peoples are, in short, being torn apart by their common currency. It has not worked well. Because we have not done it properly. And we have not done it properly because we separated the economic from the political; the socio-economic from the artistic. We have separated the notion of getting together in a Single Market from the public space. We have diminished the public space, thinking that the private sector must dominate. It cannot, without shooting itself in the foot. These divisions, these separations are lethal, they are toxic, they undermine the best intentions, they turn Europeans against themselves, they turn Russians against themselves. It is about time we transcended them.

I shall finish on a comment about Europe. People say to me: You are very critical on the European Union, although everyone wants to be part of it. The Baltic states wanted to join it, the states of former Yugoslavia, Croatia, Slovenia, Serbia… At that point I remind them that the Roman Empire imploded when its inner core became too brittle while its borders were expanding eastwards. Why? Because its inner core was imploding both economically and politically. This created a cultural vacuum also known as the Middle Ages. Today, the European Union is also seeing its core disintegrate at the time of eastward expansion. One proud nation after another is being subjected to the kind of treatment our government was subjected to in July 2015 — what I call fiscal waterboarding, a form of financial torture. One people is turned against another, with no serious discussion of how to create a rational economic architecture for Europe; with some Europeans increasingly convinced that they are more deserving then other Europeans.

There is a tendency among the elites towards expansionism, towards reconstructing Charlemagne's empire in Western Europe, the old Soviet Union here in Russia, a 'Great America' on the other side of the Atlantic. But at the same time, Western Europe's, Russia's and America's inner cores are fragmenting. Promoting expansionism at the expense of a moral, ethical, economic, political, cultural core is a major threat for civilisation. Before the fall of the Iron Curtain, a film like *The Double Life of Véronique* resonated perfectly like this in Moscow, in Cracow, in Stuttgart, in London, in Athens, and in San Francisco. Today that movie would have been a flop. Véronique and Veronica would share no bond, no mystical connection, except the bonds that lawyers and multinational corporations would have. They would have been pitted against each other in the context of a ruthless, single, unstable, dystopian globalising market.

Almagul Menlibayeva — Center of Eurasia

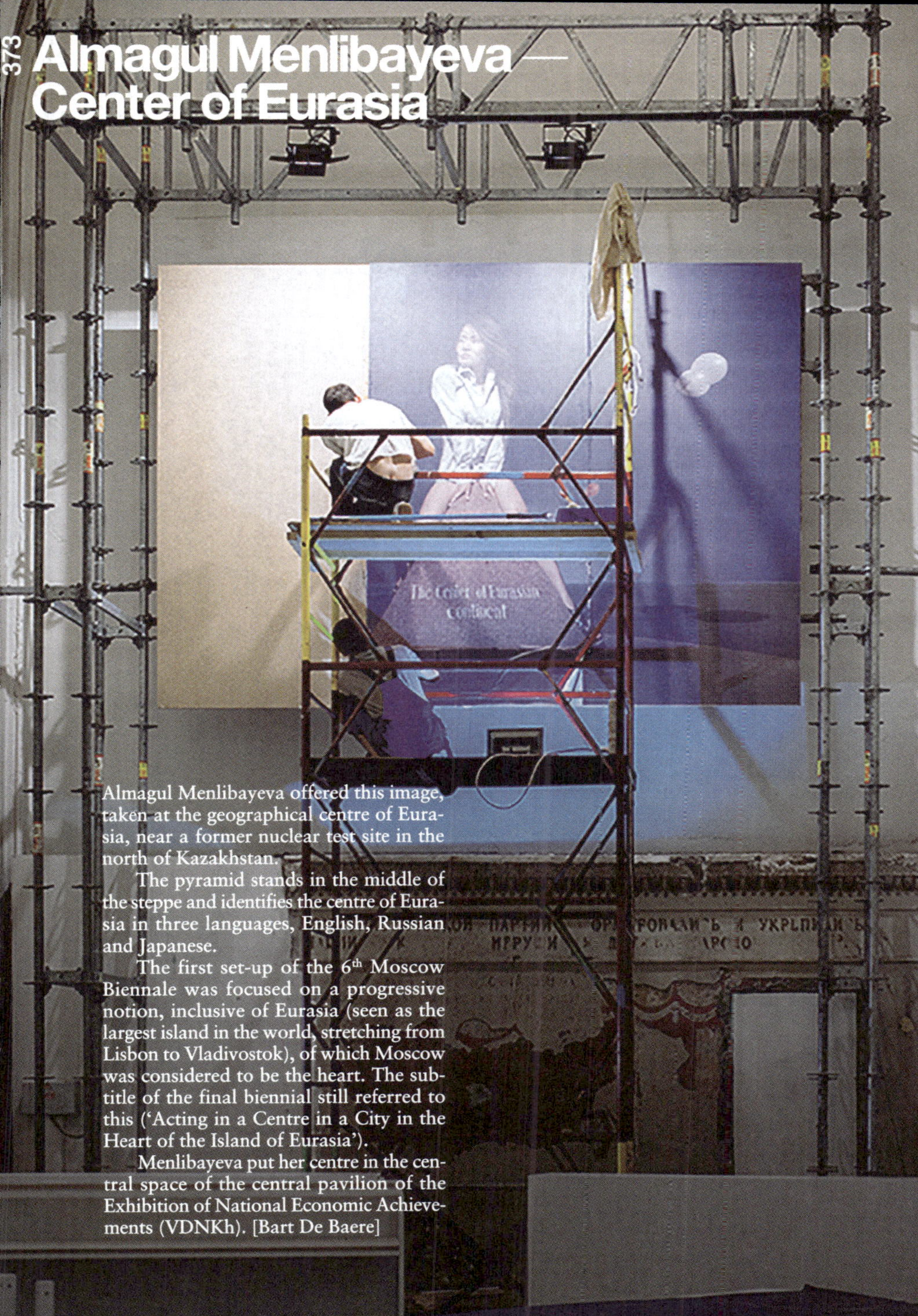

Almagul Menlibayeva offered this image, taken at the geographical centre of Eurasia, near a former nuclear test site in the north of Kazakhstan.

The pyramid stands in the middle of the steppe and identifies the centre of Eurasia in three languages, English, Russian and Japanese.

The first set-up of the 6th Moscow Biennale was focused on a progressive notion, inclusive of Eurasia (seen as the largest island in the world, stretching from Lisbon to Vladivostok), of which Moscow was considered to be the heart. The subtitle of the final biennial still referred to this ('Acting in a Centre in a City in the Heart of the Island of Eurasia').

Menlibayeva put her centre in the central space of the central pavilion of the Exhibition of National Economic Achievements (VDNKh). [Bart De Baere]

Park Chan-kyong — Anyang, Paradise City

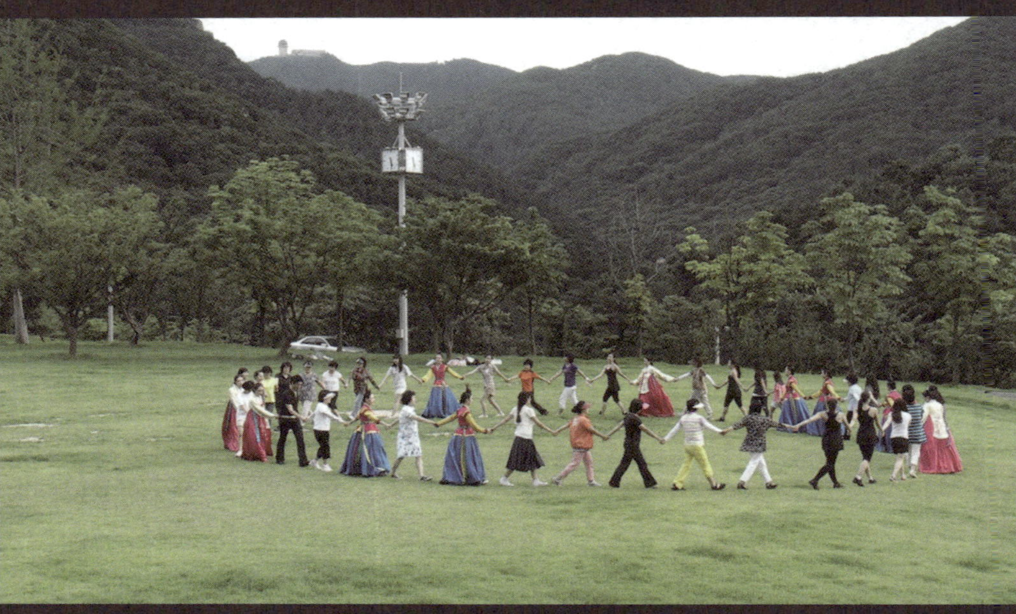

Park Chan-kyong, *Anyang, Paradise City*, HD Film, 101 mins., 2010, video still

Anyang, Paradise City is a feature length film by Park Chan-kyong. One of its first scenes shows a group of women dancing the Korean folk dance *Ganggangssullae*. It is one of the oldest Korean rites and is traditionally performed on a summer night at full moon to guarantee a rich harvest later in the year. The dance was included in the programme of the opening ceremony at the 1988 Olympic Games in Seoul. A symbolic ritual for Korean national identity, the dance was announced as an intangible cultural heritage. It is usually performed exclusively by women.

Park's film tells a semi fictitious story of a group of filmmakers who research the case of a fire in a factory that happened in Anyang, on the outskirts of Seoul, in 1988—shortly before the Olympic Games. During the fire, 20 young women died because they were locked in the factory that also served as their dormitory. The young protagonists of Park's film follow the traces of this incident to the present, where it is set.

With an eye on Korean heritage and its current situation, on the role of female workers within this history (as well as in a global context), and on the exploitation of traditions and neglect of valuable heritage, Park encounters the dualisms in Korean culture. His observations may sensitise us to the other, to the dual, and encourage ways to try and review our situation together. [Marie Egger]

Ulrike Guérot and Robert Menasse — Europe: the Reconstruction of the Free World [1]

National borders are a reality—and for most people, they are something that is taken for granted and indeed necessary. But are they really the normal state of affairs? A critical and historical approach suggests this is in fact a very recent development. By recognising this, we can start to open our minds to imagine new ways of including 'Others' within our own borders. A radical futuristic plan for a borderless Europe.

In political psychology, even schizophrenia is normal. When citizens of any state are at home, they want to know that their state borders are defended and policed as rigorously as possible. But when they travel abroad, they want borders to be as porous as possible, and ideally invisible. They don't want to be held up at borders, but they want others entering their country to be stopped at the border and prevented from entering. At their destination, they want to experience the 'Other' as 'an interesting different culture', but at home they perceive the 'Other' as a threat to 'our culture'. The sudden disappearance of borders can spark euphoria, as we saw with the fall of the Berlin Wall, and indeed of the rest of the Iron Curtain, but citizens want the borders back again when it appears that the people from 'over there' want to come over here looking for work. They drive 'over there' themselves if it's cheaper to buy stuff there, but they don't understand it when people want to come 'over here' to earn more. When they want to claim their human rights, concerned citizens can quote chapter and verse to prove these are 'universal'; but in the face of claims by others they want to fence them off as a part only of their own national law. This is what passes for 'normality' nowadays.

Historically, however, political borders are anything but normal. On the contrary, the system of political borders, which today are generally regarded as normal and which are once more being constructed and defended, is the historical exception, and in the foreseeable future it will be regarded again as a short and untypical historical interlude.

THE BORDERS THAT BIND

The so-called four freedoms (the freedom of movement of people, goods, services and capital) are the greatest post-war achievement of the European integration project. However, they are not a new phenomenon in European history, but only a step towards the restitution of historical normality: An absence of borders was the natural state of affairs in Europe from the Middle Ages until well into the 19th century.

In the Middle Ages, the German Reichstag, or Diet of the Imperial Estates of the Holy Roman Empire, was a peripatetic—a sort of mobile—assembly with no fixed location of the German Prince-Electors in different European cities from Luxembourg to Prague, not all of which still lie within the borders of today's Federal Republic. Mediaeval students followed their teachers from Rotterdam as far as Bologna. Cultural, culinary, linguistic, religious and geographical borders, certainly, but not national ones, were important and palpable in Europe, but these cultural borders did not divide: on the contrary, they bound Europe together. Even topographical borders such as rivers or mountains were not able to divide homogenous cultural regions: the Basque people live south and north of the Pyrenees, the Tyroleans south and north of the Brenner. The Rhine, on the other hand, never became the national border of France. And it was possible to travel from the heartlands of the Habsburgs through Bohemia and Moravia to Galicia on tracks which, for hundreds of kilometres, crossed no borders. Before 1914, you didn't need a visa to travel by cab from Paris to Moscow, changing horses in Berlin, as Stefan Zweig described. Nor was it necessary to change money then, neither guilders nor thalers, and nor did one have to leave Europe if one took the coach from Vienna to Lvov and stopped over in Budapest. "Before 1914," wrote Heinrich Mann, "'abroad' was just a figure of speech."

Moreover, what we understand today of the term 'passport' has only existed since 21st October 1920. That was when the League of Nations defined what should be in a passport and how it should look in order for it to be recognised by the world's states as a document enabling travel and the crossing of borders. The preamble to the League's definition of an internationally-recognised passport is interesting (but sadly forgotten): namely that the introduction of the passport had only provisional validity until the "complete return to pre-war conditions which the conference hopes to see gradually re-established in the near future".

To think of today's borderless 'Schengen Area' as a unique historical phenomenon, an absolutely revolutionary achievement of the recent European history of integration, is therefore misleading. On the contrary, it is important to remind people that a borderless Europe was, for hundreds of years, accepted as the normal state of affairs, simply so that we can talk about what this European area should be today—namely, what it always was: a palimpsest of borders, which aren't actually borders at all, but which instead merely defined the cultural regions that have always created out of the cultural diversity of Europe the single European space.

To remind ourselves of this is also important so that we can discuss how the European region can and should manage the refugee crisis.

EUROPEAN HISTORY—AND TODAY'S EUROPEAN REALITY

If Europeans understood European history, rather than simply believing that what they now know as normality, then it goes without saying that they would wish to re-establish the historically normal state of borderlessness in Europe that endured for hundreds of years and which was only brutally and bloodily destroyed in the 20th century by the two world wars—by Europe's 'second Thirty Years War'. But the EU today is distancing itself at great speed from precisely that option, and not just since the so-called refugee crisis, which is being exploited as an opportunity to link back to the darkest chapter of modern European history, with border controls and border fortifications, with even the construction of fences and walls within Europe. In fact, in the European discourse, to see the EU as a project whose founding purpose was to Europeanise Europe again and to overcome the nation-states, is an ambition that was already abandoned some time ago. There are many reasons for this: the contemporary political elites are too young to have understood at the time the founding purpose of the European project, but they are too old to be able to imagine anything other than what they are used to—the national system in which they have made their careers. And what they know for certain is that they are only elected in national elections, which is why they must maintain the fiction of national interests in order to rally the support of their electorates for their offices, though not for the European project.

The refugees are now intensifying this regression at the European and the national level. If a European solution to the refugee issue is not in sight—neither with regard to the repartition of refugees within Europe, nor, as a minimum, to common defence of the external borders, as is now often being called for—and if in addition a common and coherent European foreign policy has yet to be realised, then all that remains is the flight to national withdrawal; which, however, is available in practice only to those European states without an external EU border, for example Germany or Denmark. But Greece or Italy, or the countries on the Balkan route—whether EU members or not—have no choice: they will be overrun by refugees whatever they do to prevent it. Because as long as the EU doesn't decide to lay barbed wire across Mediterranean beaches, or to turn back refugee boats with armed force, the sea border of the EU to the south cannot be 'defended': the EU cannot cut itself off from the Mediterranean—which, it is worth remembering, is in cultural historical terms, as *Mare Nostrum*, the quintessential European sea—and from whose trade routes the EU most certainly does not want to cut itself off.

The question today is therefore how it will be possible in future on an organisational level to deal with the fact that Europe wants and needs open borders for trade, but not for people. The fact that the border closures that have already taken place and those that are to be expected within the EU may affect (and threaten) lorry traffic—and thus business, production, trade and consumption, and ultimately our living standards—and that closed borders mean quantifiable bottom-line costs; that just-in-time management and efficient customer inventory management are only possible if lorries are not wasting time held up at borders; all of this is now beginning to dawn on the economic ministers of the member states. But a border that is open to lorries and at the same time closed to refugees is not possible. The only realistic option that remains for the EU is to open up—it will have to share its space and its place with the 'others': with the people who want to come to Europe.

MERGING ASYLUM RIGHTS AND CIVIL RIGHTS

There are, at this moment, 60 million people fleeing war, hunger and destitution around the world. The USA, Australia and Canada, each of which only grants asylum to around 10,000 refugees each year, have effectively withdrawn from the 1951 Geneva Refugee Convention, which stipulates that the community of nations has a shared responsibility towards refugees, and that every refugee is entitled to asylum. Social welfare entitlements for state citizens arise out of civil rights; basic human rights to shelter and to welfare provision arise out of the right to asylum, independent of citizenship, and both are increasingly merging into one. Everyone has a right to a homeland and to security. In times when many are forced to become nomads in search of a new home, the decisive question becomes: How can this process be organised without conflict and in a way that is humane for all?

The Belgian author and psychoanalyst Luce Irigaray coined the expression "sharing the world" as a modern extension of Kant's "right to universal hospitality", which assumes that all people are born equal and therefore have an equal right in principle to live anywhere in the world. Given this human right, states cannot define a territorial right of abode for people. In the future, the challenge must therefore be to organise extra-territorial democracy and to realise the promise contained in the Universal Declaration of Human Rights: that the recognition of human rights should be independent of any specific 'state citizenship'.

The coming climate catastrophe, with all the consequences of the global reduction in fertile soils it will bring about, will put nation-states under even greater pressure: they will be unable to maintain their insistence on territorially-based statehood as a privilege which enables them to reserve land within their state borders for their own citizens (and for millionaires who buy their way in). This applies to the European area as well. So it's about the global right to a homeland; about universal access to the global commons beyond the nation state; about providing a homeland for all in times of permanent migration.

In the future, everyone must have the right to cross national borders and to settle where they want, especially since, for everything else except people, the globalised world is already one single system of networks, of permeability and of borderlessness: from pipelines to broadband to the high speed trading of the financial

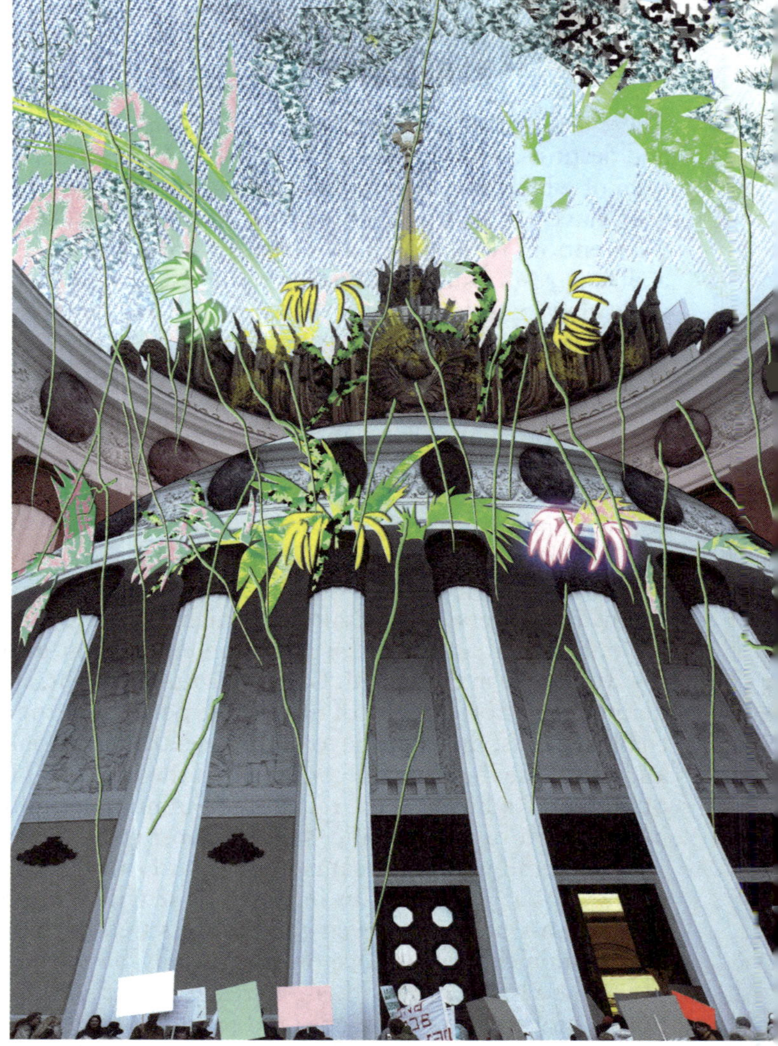

Almagul Menlibayeva

markets and product supply chains, everything has already in practice functioned for a long time unhindered by national borders. The challenge now is to reflect this fact in a new political institutional system. What is needed is to develop a political form of the diverse and many-layered global network, instead of delimiting national enclaves which cannot be justified in Kantian terms. What is needed is for homelands to be bound together: this must include bonds in both the legal and normative senses. The legal bonds tie everyone to one constitution; the normative bonds enable the participation of all in whatever affects all. Everyone has a stake in the system, and everyone contributes to it. What is needed is the free organisation of 'Otherness' in a legal system of obligations, in the words of Luce Irigaray; that is, a novel form of direct connection between the local/regional and the global beyond the state, and thus a merging of asylum rights and human rights. This leads to the creation of an unlimited transit area. In future, it would no longer be the salvation of ethno-cultural homogeneity by homogenous populations which would count as 'European', but the dissolution of borders as limits to homogeneity. This creates a gigantic space of potential for real-life plans and modes of living existing alongside each other. Sociology teaches us that segregation is also a form of tolerance. Against this background, the question arises of whether the current EU refugee policy is the correct one, focused as it is on integration, which carries within it the risk of large-scale social unrest.

GIVING SPACE TO THE 'OTHERS': CITIES FOR MIGRANTS?

Let us look back into recent history to seek inspiration from solutions that have already proved to be sustainable: What did the European migrants do who emigrated to the New World in their masses during the famines and political crises of the 18th and 19th centuries—the Irish, the Italians, the Balts, the Germans…? They built their cities there again.

Across America we find cities with names such as New Hannover, New Hampshire, New Hamburg, and so on. In Little Italy in New York, the Italians occupied an entire district. It didn't occur to anyone then to divide families, or to place them in separate accommodation, or to haggle over family reunification. Nobody was given asylum-seeker status, or received state money, or had to commit to language courses or even to a *Leitkultur*, a dominant national culture. The European refugees simply arrived in a new homeland and reconstructed their old homeland there. We can learn from that.

What if refugees in Europe were to be allocated building land neighbouring the European cities, but at a sufficient distance to maintain 'otherness'? That would create a space of potential for real-life plans and modes of living existing alongside one another. In this way, New Damascus and New Aleppo, New Madaya and so on could arise in the middle of Europe. Or New Diyarbakir or New Erbil and New Dohuk for the Kurdish refugees. Perhaps also New Kandahar or New Kunduz for the Afghan refugees, or New Enugu or New Ondo for the Nigerian refugees. Europe is large (and will soon be empty) enough to build a dozen or more cities for new arrivals. Then we don't need to stress over integration. We don't need to cram the refugees into our—sometimes dilapidated—suburbs or into the—sometimes sprawling and desolate—no man's landscapes in the countryside between them. We don't have to concentrate them in refugee homes to be burnt down to warm the hearts of patriotic nationalists. We don't have to play off their rights to housing and work in their new homeland against housing and jobs for the lowest quartile of our own society. We don't need to rub up against each other and rub each other up the wrong way. In short: we don't need integration. We respect 'otherness'—and we let the new arrivals be in their 'otherness'.

The new arrivals then look after themselves, in accordance with their culture, cuisine, music and social structures. They recreate their cities in Europe, their squares, their schools, their theatres, their hospitals, their radio stations and their newspapers. And EU law applies to everyone. And that is important: *Aequum ius*, equality before the law—for old EU citizens as well as for the new arrivals. Instead of 'Leitkultur', civic rights for all.

Europe gives building land as support to get started—improved land, that is, land already connected up to infrastructural services such as energy, ICT and transport, but otherwise free for development by the new arrivals. All the money that we now give out for integration and language courses, for fences and border protection, for security and policing, can be given by Europe to the refugees to help them make a start. As urban construction is not a quick process, Europe, with the support of the UNHCR, can help to begin with by providing temporary dwellings—that is, exactly the kind of container dwelling that is provided now. Town planners who are involved with refugee camps and who have researched them report that refugee camps soon turn into towns, as long as the refugees are left in peace. Building towns seems to be human nature. In Lebanon, the carefully positioned and rigidly aligned UNHCR containers were moved around and re-positioned after only a few weeks. Big thoroughfares and small side streets emerged — for example, the main street in one Lebanese refugee camp was christened the Champs-Élysées. Out of nothing, trade began to take place, and little boutiques sprang up; street-smart handymen and amateur mechanics built mopeds out of scrap; suddenly there were little theatres and dance festivals. Experts say that in less than six months a refugee camp turns into a town.

IMAGINING NEW WORLDS

In short: what is needed is a multi-coloured Europe, proximity with respect, an alliance of alterity under the same European law, a creative network of diversity.

Over time, the residents of the different towns would mix together quite naturally. The new arrivals would make their way to the nearby 'European' towns to work. Or they would open their boutiques there, sell what they produce there. Nobody would need asylum-seeker's support. The residents of the older indigenous towns become curious. The new arrivals have different and interesting food, and an unknown spice or two. Artists come to look, to paint and to write poetry. Hipster cafés spring up. Students seeking cheap accommodation rent flats to share in New Damascus. Then come the first love stories, and then the first children. Then the first visits from parents. Three generations later — that's how long it usually takes — the children of the children of the first generation of new arrivals have learned the language of the new homeland — simply because it's more practical. Another hundred years later, it will probably only be the town's name — like New Hannover, or Paris, Texas, or Vienna, Virginia in the USA today — that reminds people that its founders came from a different world.

1
This text appeared first in the German issue of *Le Monde Diplomatique* on 11th February 2016. An English translation was released in the *Green European Journal* on 1st March 2016.

Saskia Sassen — Who are we, the citizens?

Moscow, 22nd September 2015

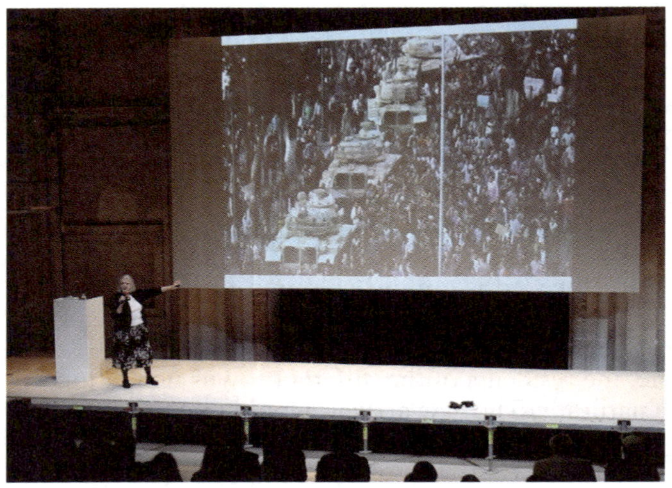

Keynote Saskia Sassen, Moscow Biennale, 22nd September 2015

A majority of us exists in ways, in domains, in spaces; and we are managing rather well. If you look at our big, rich cities, they are mostly becoming bigger and richer, building beautiful stuff. I want to take you across a set of systemic edges. These are not the borders of countries; they are systemic edges constituted inside national territories, inside cities. They are in the interiority. The systemic edge is a moment in a process where the familiar becomes so extreme that we lose it. It is so extreme that our conceptual categories, our language, cannot capture it. Thus, their very material conditions have a capacity to become invisible. Partly because we are almost by definition theoretical in how we see; seeing with another eye. If we could see everything, if we took in everything, we would go crazy. When we walk into a room, we select. We are actually capable of rendering invisible that what is standing right in front of us… that which is highly material.[1]

The clearest example for me is the amount of dead land and dead water we have in the world today. And I use the terms 'dead land' and 'dead water' rather than climate change. Climate change sounds too beautiful, too pretty. I want the brutality of the word 'death'.

The city and its citizens are the target of this talk. The citizen is a construction we have made and which has come to us through multiple epochs. It seems to me, that we, the citizens, are losing rights in our liberal democracies. And when I speak about the citizen, I am really thinking about the citizen as a subject made under certain particular conditions in the West. Under the conditions of liberal democracy or, in other words, capitalism. From the beginning, the 'sub-' in 'subjects' was constituted when liberal democracies first took off; fundamentally unequal. Within this system we can never overcome that foundational inequality. It is built into liberal democracies.

Thinking about the current time, we are dealing now with a very negative moment. This is one of the worst periods in liberal democracy. No matter that our cities look more beautiful, richer, with better buildings… That is just one little piece of a big pie. Today, we are makers. We make. This is a kind of accomplishment (Fig. 1). We made this. In 20 years, we managed to reduce this vast sea to a sliver. We made that. And I mean a very collective we. We have the equivalent all over the world. It is a capability. I cannot just stand back and say: "Oh my God, how terrible!" I also stand back and say in full horror: "Amazing, we pulled that off."

Fig. 1
A comparison of the Aral Sea in 1989 (left) and 2014 (right)

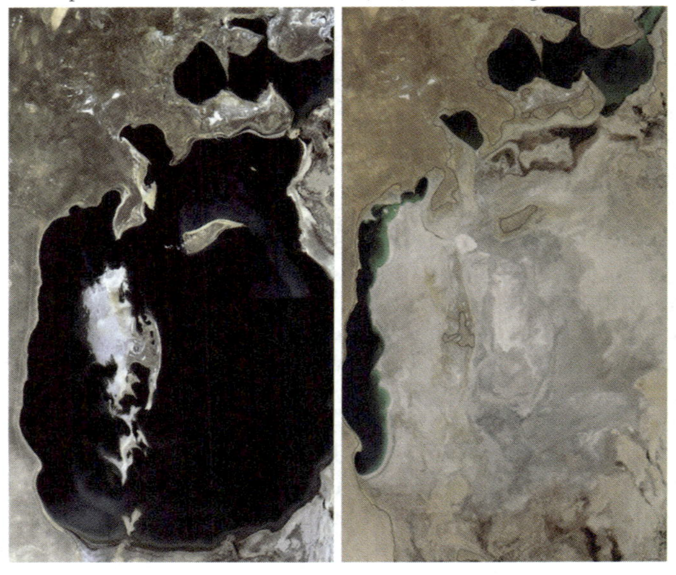

Source: NASA, Accessed June 2, 2017. https://commons.wikimedia.org/wiki/File:AralSea1989_2014.jpg

Fig.2
Extent of Surface Melt over Greenland's Ice Sheet

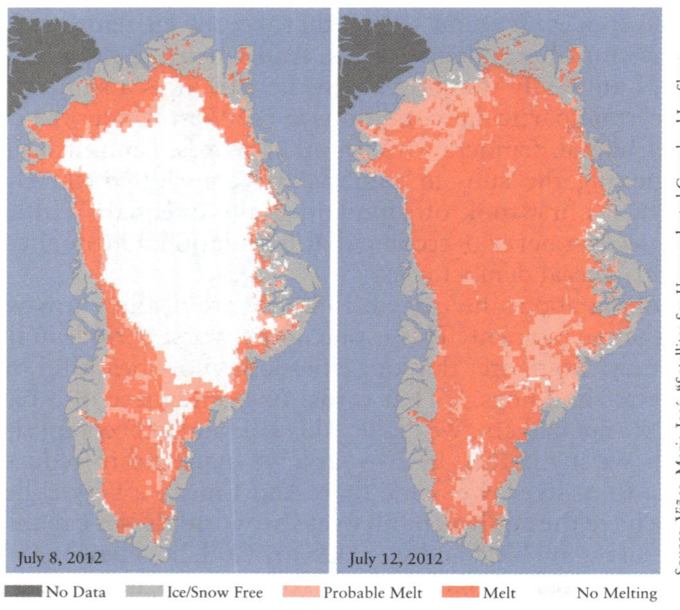

Source: Viñas, Maria-José. "Satellites See Unprecedented Greenland Ice Sheet Surface Melt." NASA. Accessed July 30, 2012. http://www.nasa.gov/topics/earth/features/greenland-melt.html.

We also made this (Fig. 2). In a very short period of time we eliminated something that had existed for billions of years. We have come to the melting of the permafrost. Methane gas will emerge from this. The whole world, we did that.

These are very problematic ways of making but I want to emphasise the fact of our nature as makers. This is just one part of us. But it is this particular line that I want to take because I cannot cover everything in a short period of time.

Now, one place that we have made is a people's place in principal, it is the city. I think of the city as a complex but incomplete system. In that mixture of complexity and incompleteness lies the capacity of cities to outlive powerful actors like kings, governments of all sorts, multinational corporations, et cetera. Cities survive through different epochs, they incorporate the past. It is that mixture of complexity and incompleteness which makes this possible. (An office park, for example, is not a city. It is a closed system and is very soon to be obsolete. Then it will be finished. And you will have to rebuild something else in its place.)

I like to think of citizenship as an incomplete contract with the state. I am using state here in a very generic sense. And citizenship too, because it is complex and incomplete, has outlived many epochs. It is not going away. Neither the city, nor the citizen are. And this means the citizen in a broad sense: a resident, someone who lives in, who occupies the place… But both the city and the citizen today are in crisis.

WHO OWNS THE CITY?

There is a new development taking off after the financial crisis of 2008, when suddenly big corporates have decided that buying property is a very good investment.[2] Actually, Moscow is also on my list of a hundred cities that are the main recipients of corporate investment, both national and foreign. Whether this is national or foreign is completely secondary. What matters is that it is corporate. And it is very large. The minimum investment, in New York for example, is $5 million. We are not talking cute little houses. We are talking big corporate investments and often they buy multiple units. The numbers refer to just one year. This is a development that took off a few years after the financial crisis (Fig. 3). From mid-2013 to mid-2014, US$ 600 billion were invested in buying

Fig. 3
Total Investment Volumes In Top 50 Recipient Cities (Q3 2014- Q2 2015)

Metro	Volumes (US$)	Growth*
1. New York	74,799,870,615	36.3%
2. London	55,206,679,357	13.4%
3. Tokyo	37,971,179,153	0.7%
4. Los Angeles	37,457,376,509	14.4%
5. San Francisco	32,355,485,613	35.9%
6. Paris	22,955,312,136	-0.2%
7. Chicago	20,036,200,994	39.4%
8. Washington	18,515,548,212	29.5%
9. Dallas	16,296,780,618	13.4%
10. Atlanta	16,022,394,226	60.7%
11. Miami	15,949,703,541	74.5%
12. Boston	15,365,776,426	43.2%
13. Hong Kong	14,447,415,389	4.9%
14. Sydney	14,075,615,656	7.9%
15. Houston	12,365,902,892	-6.2%
16. Berlin	11,814,090,834	-6.2%
17. Seattle	11,609,540,148	31.9%
18. Melbourne	11,078,147,297	33.1%
19. Frankfurt	9,845,334,528	14.4%
20. Phoenix	9,312,751,061	53.5%
21. Denver	9,029,533,977	19.6%
22. Austin	8,046,028,787	45.3%
23. Shanghai	7,978,366,830	-19.6%
24. Amsterdam	7,942,738,059	13.3%
25. Munich	7,271,540,067	9.9%
26. San Diego	7,251,264,452	-0.3%
27. Madrid	7,097,274,018	164.3%
28. Orlando	6,981,214,900	55.1%
29. Stockholm	6,338,824,520	-20.7%
30. Hawaii	6,048,702,620	48.5%
31. Osaka	5,839,892,968	26.1%
32. Hamburg	5,794,518,685	23.7%
33. Toronto	5,780,113,060	-23.9%
34. Singapore	5,575,750,013	-24.4%
35. Beijing	5,408,756,455	-25.9%
36. Brisbane	5,368,732,014	39.2%
37. Philadelphia	5,333,247,720	-22.0%
38. Seoul	5,264,240,793	-16.0%
39. Nanjing	5,190,516,937	142.6%
40. Minneapolis	5,098,620,802	64.1%
41. Raleigh/Durham	4,867,567,697	86.1%
42. Charlotte	4,763,778,197	46.2%
43. Tampa	4,763,108,826	55.5%
44. Portland	4,459,699,959	91.5%
45. Milan	4,258,359,663	142.1%
46. Dublin	4,257,624,236	-3.7%
47. Oslo	4,250,853,127	92.7%
48. Manchester	4,224,580,070	25.2%
49. San Antonio	3,727,740,580	58.7%
50. Birmingham (UK)	3,708,838,018	27.4%

* Compared to the previous 12 months. Source: Cushman and Wakefield, Real Capital Analytics.

Source: Cushman & Wakefield, also based on information from Real Capital Analytics, Oxford Economics, Guardian News and Media Ltd., The World Economic Forum, Urban Land Institute.

existing property—this excludes new development and construction... if this were added, the figure doubles. And from mid-2014 to mid-2015, it went up to over a trillion US dollars. These are significant amounts.

Many people say that this is gentrification. I do not think it is. For instance, the Qatari royals now own more of central London than the Queen of England. Frankly, who owns more is not the point. The point is that this is not gentrification—these are two very rich royal families. It is something else. This is something deeper, that we have not quite thoroughly understood. I explore this in depth in my contribution to *The Quito Papers* we presented at the 2016 Habitat meeting in Quito.[3]

If I may digress, I make the parallel argument about the migrations that are currently happening. That is not migration, nor is it just about refugees. There is a deeper history in the making for which we lack a language. Ultimately, this is about a massive loss of habitat; habitat in the full, complex sense of the word—a place where you can live. This loss of habitat is partly made in cities. The loss of habitat is partly made through dead land and the death brought by environmental destruction. It is made in mining; it is made in many different ways.[4]

And cities capture this in a very acute way insofar as so many of the migrants and refugees wind up in cities, including most of all in the cities of the Global South—Europe keeps thinking it is being invaded, but the largest refugee camps are in the Global South! This is a moment for which we do not have adequate language to capture the severity. There is a rupture and there are systemic edges beyond which, once crossed, it all becomes invisible; where we lose track of it all because our categories for analysis fail us.

Back to the main subject of this lecture!

There is an invented market, which sets minimum prices for super prime housing in international cities. It also lists the main nationalities who are buying in those cities (Fig. 4). This privately made market deals with buying up pieces of the city. Everyone wants to come to Shanghai, for example, and buy. It is similar in New York and Paris. In Hong Kong, prices are much higher, but the majority of buyers are Chinese—that is also very interesting. This is not gentrification either. It is something else. These big acquisitions account for a considerable amount of urban space, reducing the habitat for many modest-income households—there

Fig. 4
Foreign Buyers in the Superprime Housing Market 2007–2012

City	Country of origin of foreign buyers	Minimum price to qualify as superprime (in millions of $)	% foreign (of all buyers) 2007	2012
Monaco	Russia, CIS[a], United Kingdom, Italy, Switzerland	18.9	100	100
Paris	Russia, CIS[a], Italy, France, Germany, United Kingdom, United States	8.8	90	95
London	Russia, France, South Africa, Italy, India, United Arab Emirates, Greece, Australia, United States, Canada	15.9	75	85
Dubai	Kenya, Somalia, Tanzania, Saudi Arabia, Russia, India, Iran	8.0	45	60
New York	United Kingdom, France, Italy, Spain, China, Singapore, Australia, Brazil, Argentina, Canada	10.0	50	50
Shanghai	Hong Kong, Taiwan, United States, Canada, Japan, Malaysia, Germany, France	6.4	34	10
Singapore	Indonesia, China, Malaysia, India, Australia, United Kingdom	8.3	24	31
Hong Kong	China	15.4	12	35
Moscow	CIS[a]	7.8	10	10

Source: Powley and Warwick-Ching 2012

Note: a) CIS refers to the Commonwealth of Independent States, which includes the following countries: Armenia, Azerbaijan, Belarus, Kazakhstan, Kyrgyzstan, Moldova, Russia, Tajikistan, and Uzbekistan.

are now housing crises in more and more of these cities for the more modest middle and working classes. This adds significance to the question: Who owns it? Why do cities matter? As I understand the city, it is a complex but incomplete system. But it is also a space where those without power get to make history.

200 years ago, for the West, the frontier was at the edges of empire. I define frontier as a space where there is an encounter between two actors who belong to different worlds, for whom there are no established rules of engagement. Where is the frontier today? It is not at those edges. It is right in our big cities. There are many encounters: you may have the same nationality or the same religion but you may belong to different worlds: poor, rich, et cetera… There are many mixed cities; many different nationalities and religions coexist in our big cities. The frontier is inside, and it is a combat zone. But one where those without power can stand up and say: "We are present, we are here." They do not become empowered by this, but their powerlessness becomes complex and that is what cities can do. They do not necessarily make you powerful, but they can enable you to have complexity in your powerlessness. In Latin America we have a beautiful phrase which is *Estamos presentes*. It means 'We are present.' We, the poor, the discriminated, without power, without money…; we are not asking you for something, we just want you to take note we exist. A city makes that possible.

An office complex, a mega project, however, even if huge and dense, is not a city, and it is not necessarily marked by urbanity in its full sense—it is a private space where those without power cannot come in and stand and say *estamos presentes*—not in an office complex, not in a privatised mega complex. This is why these massive investments in cities are so disturbing: They take a whole part of a city, of the urban tissue, and transform it into a privatised mega project. It may be far denser then what was there before but it is far less urban, it is not a city. There is no frontier zone. So in that sense, one of the things we have made collectively, across time and across space, is cities. And they matter enormously. The more privatised they become, the more we are losing something very important.

Now, at the other side of all those investors is something else: A story about the capability of finance. Finance is a capability. It is the sector that has dominated the last 20 to 30 years. And it is not about money—it is a capability. Finance sells what it does not have. It has to invent extraordinary instruments and invade sectors and extract what it needs. It does that by very fancy means, and with such highly complex instruments it can also extract from very low incomes. To this extent, finance is a negative capability like the ones I mentioned at the beginning.

According to the US Central Bank, millions of households (of one to two, three, or many more persons) are evicted every year. Over 15 million households have been thrown out of their homes. You see vast stretches of empty housing in certain parts of US cities. 15 million households means at least 30 million people. Both the empty houses and those 30 million people are basically invisible in all their materiality. Why would anybody go to areas where there are all these empty houses? You just don't go there. It is not because you do not want to; you do not think about going there. We have a lot of empty urban land and when you look at the corporate investments you can see what one possibility is at least.

What I am really asking is: Who are we? The citizens today. How many more rights are we going to lose?

It is a hobby of mine to look at the rights that we are losing —no simple task in a liberal democratic system. We do not exist as a Christmas tree where the rights are decorations; where if one is missing you say: "Oh, my God, we've lost a right!" No, we do not exist as the citizen in Western law. We exist across a distributed set of specialised laws. That is where you have to go digging: to see if you have lost a right here, and here and there, and so forth. It is not easy to find out if we are losing rights. But I have a network around the world, that is, in the mostly Western democracies, where we are trying to track this. And I could talk quite a bit about the rights that we are losing: some are big, some are small. But they matter. What is important is this: We are a certain kind of subject right now.

NEW SYSTEMICS

The city has been a critical space for us to construct our citizenship, to actually develop it. A question that I ask myself when I juxtapose these different worlds, is: Are we really dealing in today's world with a new systemics?

Corporate profits grew and grew and shot up until the financial crisis (Fig. 5). After that short critical moment, corporate profits kept growing even further while most households are still in crisis. A lot of citizens' money is put into the sector to generate an actually higher rate. At the same time, think of all those displaced people: 50% of the people who live in New York City are below the poverty line! Yet we have a growing concentration of wealth. Corporate assets keep going further. The disturbing thing is that there is a divergence: some gain and some lose. And that is partly the story we are seeing.

I want to clarify how finance has to be seen as a capability that can enter all kinds of domains, even modest little houses. Before I describe this, let me tell you that these brilliant physicists have developed sixteen enormously complex steps to make use of a modest asset but not to allow its modest value to be present in the financial instrument. So, the backrooms of the big financial firms, where the secretaries used to sit, are now full of physicists developing these kinds of instruments. One of my arguments is that today we have incredibly complex forms of knowledge that we really admire, such as physics. And I always think that the forms of knowledge of this period have to be able to manage complexity and openness. And there are two: physics and continental philosophy. But many of the physicists have been recruited by the

Fig. 5
Corporate Profits after Tax in the United States, 1940s–2010s (in billions)

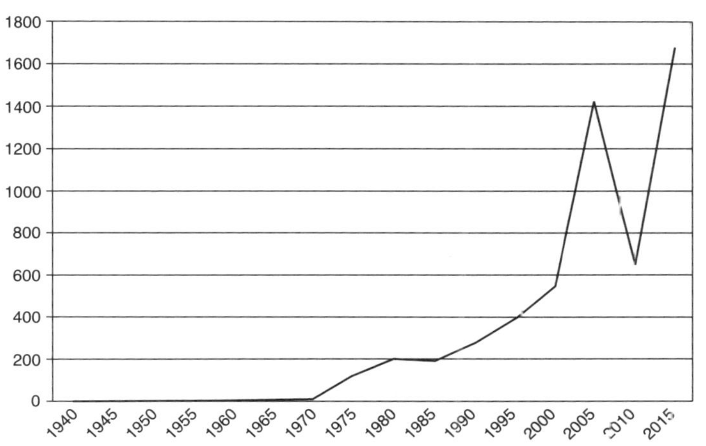

Source: Federal Reserve Bank of St. Louis 2013a, in Saskia Sassen, *Expulsions: Brutality and Complexity in the Global Economy*, Harvard University Press 2014, p.19

financial sector to develop these enormously complex instruments that are then used by the financial system to extract value from more and more sectors.

Now, back to finance as a capability. Fig. 6 is an example of the capacity of finance to jump orders of magnitude: For instance, the value of credit default swaps rose between 2001 and 2007 from under US$1 trillion to US$62 trillion; it took just a few years. Hardly anything has that rate of growth. In 2007, that value of $62 trillion represented just 10% of the global value of finance as measured by outstanding derivatives—the basic measure used for finance. And the US$600 trillion value of finance is several times that of the value of global GDP—the GDP of all the countries in the world.

I work with pretty standard data from the US Central Bank, from the IMF, but I keep interrogating these data, rather than just accepting these numbers as normal. For instance, I ask, when I look at the currency you and I deal with, what the value is of all the currencies issued by the central banks of all the countries in the world. It tends to be higher than the GDP, but is much less than the total value of finance. At that point in 2007, it was perhaps almost a third. Today the value of finance stands at over a

Fig. 6
Rising Value of Credit Default Swaps, 2001–2008 (in trillions of $)

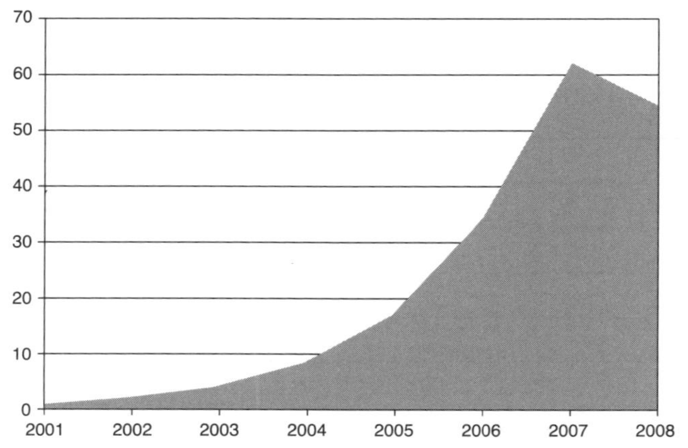

Source: Varchaver and Benner 2008, based on data from ISDA in Saskia Sassen, *Expulsions: Brutality and Complexity in the Global Economy*, Harvard University Press 2014, p.142

quadrillion dollars—three zeros more than a trillion! While the global GDP of all the countries in the world stands at 270 trillion dollars. And this tells you something about finance, namely that it is not about money, or currency, it is something else. And the best way to understand it and its powers is that it is a capability. Can we put it to good use? Can we bring it down to ground level and materialise it into transport systems, social housing, or the clean-up of toxic dumps? That is a very difficult task. But there is also brilliant knowledge to be found here. Too often these brilliant intelligences and their knowledge are put to the service of truly problematic and not at all impressive purposes and, at the elementary limit, very simple forms of brutality. So I think of finance as an extractive sector. It is unlike traditional banking which sells money at a price-interest. We all need loans. Rather, it is commerce. Finance sells something it does not have, and thus it needs to develop complex instruments to invade other economic sectors. Yes, it is extractive… and yes, this is not the usual way in which finance is understood. Financial instruments are one part of the story that produced almost 15 million households being thrown out of their homes in a short brutal history of ten years. This is not innocent brilliant knowledge.

IN THE SHADOWS OF URBANISATION

You know the famous phrase: Most people now live in cities. The question for me is: what don't I see? When I just say: "Oh my God, most people live in cities." One element we do not see when we focus on cities alone are the land grabs, especially, but not exclusively, in the Global South.

By the way, JP Morgan once tried to buy land in Russia. A very complicated procedure: They had to create a fictive entity that they listed on the stock market, it was not easy to buy at all. And Goldman Sachs bought land in Ukraine. Anyhow, the main destination is still Africa. This also takes off after the crisis—the buying of land, rural land. Africa is the main market, but it is also happening in Europe. For instance, when the crisis hit, a lot of young French people who had had French-style farming in their family wanted to go back to farming. They tried to buy land in certain areas, in the good rural areas of France. They couldn't. It had all been bought up by corporates. The Mormons of Utah have bought a vast stretch of land around Cambridge, England, around the university…

When you begin to look, when you put on the lens of "Who owns this land?", you will find that other story that I have come up against: Who owns national territory?

This may be seen as imperialism, but it is an imperialism of a very different kind. When these buyers come and get all that agricultural land… 1) They want to make plantations, to set up mines and basically evict fauna and flora so the land and earth die more quickly. They evict small farmers, they evict rural manufacturing, and so forth. Where did all of that go? It goes to the slums of the big cities and goes to cities. Which is why all that growth in urban populations, especially in certain parts of the world, was partly caused through these investments. 2) This is a very different type of imperialism, because it has nothing to do with the old-style imperialism. They get whatever piece of land and will use it until it is dead and they move on. They do not care at all about getting the whole country involved. The image that I have is of these geographies of dead land and dead water that are left behind, but also of geographies of privilege. We now have geographies of privilege and that are centred in cities; that cut across north, south, east and west. There are parts of the Chinese financial system that are totally embedded in Western finance. And others that are not. These are very particular geographies and all that matters is that particular set. The latest addition to one of these geographies is Luanda, the capital of Angola. A predatory elite in Angola is building up Luanda as a platform to access natural wealth. The international corporate world is doing that. Right now, Luanda is the most expensive city for high-level professionals to go to because there is almost nothing there. Luanda has been fully re-invented as a platform for accessing natural wealth. And when they are done with that, they are out of there. It is not about developing anything in the rest of Angola. This is very problematic.

WHO ARE WE, THE CITIZENS?

There are 10,000 plus buildings that are gathering data about all of us, full-time. If you have been in the USA for 2 days, you are in that data-set. It is huge. It includes a million people with top secret clearance and is very international. If your best algorithm builder is an Indian mathematician, she is in the data-set. She does not have to be an American. The system keeps gathering information about all of us. So, again: Who are we, the citizens? The UK, France, Germany—all countries in the West have these systems. Their logic is a very peculiar one: For security, we, the citizens, are all being surveilled. It is really data gathering more than surveillance, but it is used for surveillance. So, for our security, we, the citizens, first, are positioned as suspect for our security. Problematic.[5]

Coming back to cities and to the citizen, I think that spaces of indeterminacy are becoming critical today. They are frontier spaces. But not only that. Think of the street as not just a *rue*, but as an undetermined space that can be used in many ways. I'm not talking about a highway that might be running through a city. A lot of the stuff that I have described to you is doing away with streets. The street is a sort of space where, at least for a moment, we are all urban subjects. We are not religious, we are not ethnic, we are urban. During rush hour in Manhattan, the rich, the poor, immigrants, probably murderers too, we are all running to catch the train. We are all urban subjects. I like that image, not necessarily the murderer, but you know what I mean. The street is one space besides other urban spaces that can be thought of as enabling urban capabilities, in this sense a positive thing.

I have written a piece about this, asking "Does the city have speech?"[6] On speech as a category distinct from the law, as a very significant category of its own. We, the citizens, have political speech because we can vote. It is not chatting, it is talking. I argue in that article that: Yes, we have speech and the city has speech, but we do not know how to see it anymore. This rush hour run that I just mentioned is the way in which the city has speech, it makes us into urban subjects.

Another very simple example that I often use is this: Imagine a beautiful, wonderful car made for any terrain, any road, something amazing. It arrives at a crowded downtown and, puff!, all those capabilities are neutralised. They are gone. The city has spoken. It says: all of that, not here. Here, you go just like a little worm, no faster than a person walking.

What are all the different forms of speech of the city today? Coming back to the street, there is an image that I want to share. It is a familiar image and has all ended in great tragedy, but it captures something about the capacity of the city to neutralise what is not meant to be there (in this case the military) and to urbanise. What I like is the masses of people who neutralise the tanks. This is, of course, in Tahrir Square. That is a very powerful image. The bigger story has ended in tragedy, but not that moment of it.

In that sense, by this notion of the city having speech, we, the citizens, gain access into today's world where we are losing our rights. We need to begin to understand this speech of the city. And artists are often actually very good at it; unlike social scientists.

1
For a full development of the issues raised in this short article, see Saskia Sassen, *Expulsions: Brutality and Complexity in the Global Economy,* Harvard University Press 2014, (now translated into 15 languages).

2
For an analysis as to how the global city debate fits in here, see: http://www.saskiasassen.com/pdfs/publications/the-global-city-brown.pdf.
See: http://www.newyorker.com/business/currency/top-down-bottom-up-urban-design?intcid=mod-latest4
See: http://socdev.ucpress.edu/content/2/2/204.

5
See: http://www.saskiasassen.com/pdfs/publications/the-global-city-brown.pdf.

6
See: http://www.saskiasassen.com/PDFs/publications/does-the-city-have-speech.pdf.

In Saskia Sassen's keynote, she spoke of "a new systemics" that has come to dominate finance—the rise of complex instruments such as credit default swaps that allow firms to in essence sell what they do not actually own. This is what she calls finance as capability (from Latin *capere*, 'to take'), rather than money. But what is perhaps most interesting is her characterising of these financial instruments as forms of knowledge that require skills far outside what we normally associate with the world of banking. As she elaborates in her recent book *Expulsions*:

> At the heart of finance is the work of inventing and developing complex instruments. It is the mathematics of physics and its models that are in play here, not the mathematics of microeconomic models. Exemplifying it all, Goldman Sachs's backroom is well stocked with physicists. The mathematics of the backroom is mostly well beyond the understanding of the highly paid executives of the boardroom.[1]

Indeed, even a quick glimpse at the job postings for Goldman Sachs reveals the firm's on-going thirst for individuals with the aptitudes needed to develop—as the website explains—"quantitative and technological techniques to solve complex business problems," i.e. to utilise their "mathematical and scientific training to create financial products, measure risk, and identify market opportunities." The advertisement for positions in "strats," as the field is known in financial circles, possesses its own curious poetry of capital: "cutting-edge derivative pricing models," "automated trading algorithms," "analyse exposures, structure transactions," "risk management alternatives"... Concretely, the mathematical skills required include partial differential equations, stochastic calculus, time series analysis, and statistics and numerical techniques.

Considering finance as a form of knowledge brings to mind the concept of "general intellect" first developed by Marx but more recently redeployed in a range of post-operaist critical theories. Briefly, general intellect insists on the public-ness of thought, which is no longer to be understood as secluded and solitary reflection but rather as "something exterior and collective, [...] a public good." Intellectual activity, once it finds its place within the means of production, becomes necessarily "exterior, collective, social."[2] But the mobilisation of pure mathematical knowledge, acquired over centuries of painstaking inquiry in the realm of financial engineering, turns this public good toward ends of private gain. This can even be understood quite literally, with the draining of physicists from publicly funded scientific projects into private financial firms. From Switzerland's CERN particle accelerator—one of the most prestigious research centres in the field—scientists have left to work in credit and mortgage structuring at Goldman Sachs, to strats and modelling at Morgan Stanley, to quantitative research at JP Morgan... the list could be prolonged. If, in the 19th century, the general intellect was something fixed in the great machines that powered industry, today it is fixed in the bodies, and minds, of such individuals. And finance is where surplus value is being most effectively extracted from that intellect.[3]

What has this to do with contemporary art? We might begin by insisting that financial engineering isn't entirely foreign to this realm, and not only in the form of the increasingly sophisticated algorithms used to model the behaviours of the art market. It has also long been present as a site that might be occupied by artists. Wasn't this the gesture of Marcel Duchamp's *Monte Carlo Bond* (1924–1938)?[4] As with Sassen's definition of finance—the selling of something that doesn't belong to you—Duchamp hoped to use the sales of these bonds to underwrite his interest in gambling, promising investors a return of 20%, to be funded from his roulette winnings. Despite the ultimate failure of the plan—only a handful of the bonds were ever sold—it was a prescient gesture. Robert Morris would update the strategy four decades later in

Money (1969-1973), a work produced for the Whitney's "Anti-Illusion" exhibition, in which he invested $50,000 of a trustee's funds in the stock market.

How should we consider such occupations of the space of finance and speculation? Perhaps we can find an analogy in art history. In a famous text of the early 1970s, Michael Baxandall analysed the "period eye" of the early Italian Renaissance, exploring the specific perceptual/mental horizons that framed invention of the techniques of perspective. He considered the Florentine merchants who constituted the primary patrons and audience of the paintings and frescoes utilising this new means of representing the world, and suggested that the mathematical tools of calculation—of weight, of distance—that they had to make use of in their everyday commercial dealings were being redeployed by artists, so that one might exercise those same skills in the space of aesthetic observation.[5] For Baxandall, this was a matter of a homology between ways of seeing in the concrete social world and ways of seeing in the visual arts, but might we not see it from a slightly different angle? Rather than insisting on a simple continuity from commercial to aesthetic realms, perhaps this was a matter of artists taking "forms of knowledge" that had been subjected to the means-end rationality of the marketplace and shifting them into a space of perception free of the profit motive. When we make use of our calculative skills to observe a painting, we restore them to their origins in the common, we return them to the general intellect. In a very different economic structure, perhaps Duchamp and Morris perform an analogous operation, diverting finance's forms of knowledge into the "autonomous" realm of art, working on the borders of private and collective property.

But before concluding, we should consider a last, parenthetical comment from Sassen's lecture. After her discussion of financial engineering, she mentioned that there were actually two fields in which truly innovative, creative uses of knowledge were occurring at present: physics, as we have seen, and Continental philosophy. Here too, it is a matter of the general intellect, and of what Alain Badiou calls "the adventure of French philosophy." He names five characteristic aims of this experimental mode of thought: to refuse to divorce itself from existence; to inscribe itself within everyday life; to insist on the unity of theory and praxis; to see itself as an intervention into the political arena; to question the basis of subjectivity; and, finally, to develop a new style of exposition—"to turn philosophy into an active form of writing that would be the medium for the new subject."[6] Perhaps these have their own parallels in contemporary artistic practices—at least those that resist simply submitting wholly to the exchange relation. What else could we ask of art as one component of the general intellect, but to be an active form of creation, a medium for a new subject?

Tom McDonough

1
Saskia Sassen, *Expulsions: Brutality and Complexity in the Global Economy*, Belknap Press, 2014, p. 119.

2
Paolo Virno, *A Grammar of the Multitude: For an Analysis of Contemporary Forms of Life*, MIT Press, 2004, pp. 37–38.

3
See Christian Marazzi, *Capital and Language: From the New Economy to the War Economy*, MIT Press, 2008, p. 44.

4

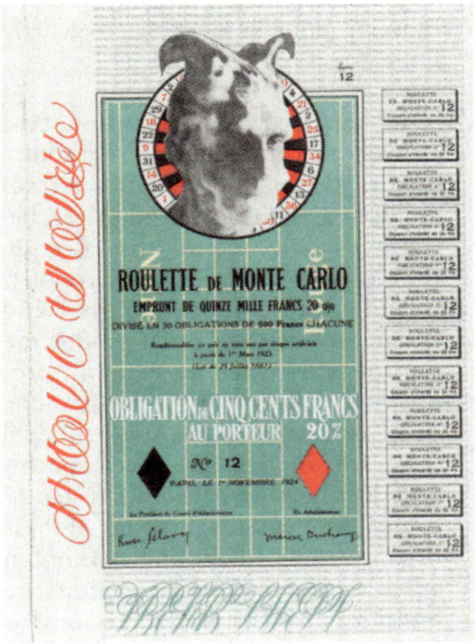

5
See Michael Baxandall, *Painting and Experience in Fifteenth-Century Italy: A Primer in the Social History of Pictorial Style*, Oxford University Press, 1988, c1972.

6
Alain Badiou, *The Adventure of French Philosophy*, Verso, 2012.

On inefficiency[1]

ALEXANDER ZHURAVLEV: The 6th edition of the Moscow Biennale for Contemporary Art was criticised for a lack of ambition. I want to go with that critique but defend it. To me, that lack of ambition is a fairly progressive technique of resistance. Normally, everyone expects a curator of a global, international exhibition to be ambitious, to say something new, to be positive, benevolent and bright. It's the sort of thing that you can really easily hide behind. But perhaps it is time to reconsider: ambitious projects are projects that need more than just money. Maybe the time has come for silent projects, which get on with their business without excessive and loosely defined budgets, quietly but efficiently. Just as efficiently as the 2015 edition of the biennial.

IVAN ISAEV: I want to add to that my partial support for Sasha. You may consider a biennial a mechanism of resistance. At the same time, they are often rightfully criticised for being part of the tourism economy and for contributing to the concepts of neoliberal consumerism. Art always tries to offer an opposition to this regime. From that point of view, anti-productivity, anti-production and dematerialisation of objects are part of a strategy that we may use. We should be inefficient, and as a result also become the opposition. You've already mentioned that the 6th Moscow Biennale was unattended and short, but pleasant enough for those who were included in it. All the same, it does appear to be an instrument of resistance.

ANNA ZHURBA: Are you saying inefficiency is a form of protest?

IVAN: Yes, as in a lack of production and productivity.

ANNA: But you understood that, in the specific context in which this biennial took place, inefficiency is exactly what we need to protest?

IVAN: What do you mean?

ANNA: Social protest in Russia is wholly inefficient in all its forms, from economic to managerial, etc.

IVAN: Economic efficiency always depends on whose interests you have in mind. If you look at the people that our economic system was built for — it was built very efficiently. The system allows people to benefit relatively easy, without risks. That is what certain indicators, such as GDP, rely on. But the well-being of an average person is not a parameter to determine the efficiency of that economy. It is built to serve the needs of a narrow group of people.

ANNA: Still, it seems to me that if we stop thinking only of Russia and start thinking globally, we return to general indicators…

IVAN: In that case, we ought to protest the efficiency of the economy, without a doubt. We should welcome the crisis and welcome the lower oil prices, because it will have a positive effect on the ecological situation in the country. It will make certain marginal and dangerous methods of oil production unprofitable (such as shale oil production). Imagine if the programme of oil production in the Arctic suffered some sort of setback, which specifically led the price of oil to fall significantly. Given all the attempts of these organisations to achieve maximum efficiency, maximising the quantitative indicators for the global economy is at the core of neoliberalism. I believe that we should protest against efficiency in the economy.

MARIA MKRTYCHEVA: It seems to me that Anna wanted to say something against inefficiency.

EKATERINA SAVCHENKO: It depends on how we define efficiency. We may define it in terms of quantitative indicators, for example the pursuit of the largest quantity of oil, of the largest number of visitors, of artists… But can we also define it in terms of quality?

ALEXANDER: Maybe this is naïve, but I think that all modern art carries, to some extent, socialist ideals. Of course, the improvement of the economy for a certain clique of oligarchs is not the generally accepted meaning of efficiency. It seems to me that any project like the Biennale sees society in the broadest sense of the word. I don't know to what extent the curators were able to comprehend our socio-political and economic context, but evidently our country is champion in the field of inefficiency, including communication. Therefore, it is precisely the Biennale… I just oppose Ivan's idea that inefficiency is a form of protest. In our context efficiency would be a form of protest. The idea of groups, gathered together to do something, that's what I call a protest.

IVAN: Well, a gathering in itself is a protest, since as we all know it is forbidden for more than two people to congregate in a public place.

ALEXANDER: I want to speak about what has happened here to the West, to Western realities, and why that is important. In fact, this talk of Russia being seen in the West as a champion of inefficiency is indisputably a plus. Here, we are the champions in the fight against neoliberal economics, and we have won. In that sense, for the West, we are a treasure trove of knowledge about how to destroy any system: the communist one, the neoliberal economy, or anything else.

MARIA M.: And all while achieving our individual goals. In the West it is more complicated to achieve your individual goals, because their system works more smoothly than ours.

ALEXANDER: Yes, I do see that as a downside, because it is very easy once you've destroyed a system to get certain personal gains. But nevertheless, what I was saying is that talking about the efficiency of this Biennale will seem a little strange to the Russian observer.

MARIA STEPKINA: Because they experience inefficiency first-hand…

ALEXANDER: Well, yes, in a way. And to talk in the West about the inefficiency of this Biennale is difficult.

IVAN: There's an example of the 6th Caribbean Biennale, where the whole budget was blown by the curator on collecting a group of artists and theorists, his friends, and taking them all to a Caribbean island to relax. The whole biennial was promoted and financed using all information channels but, in fact, it consisted of people coming together and relaxing at the Biennale's expense. In principle, the observer got nothing out of this Biennale. That's an example of inefficiency, of luxury given by the biennial to the artists taking part and the people who visited. It became a very radical, historic gesture.

ALEXANDER: If we address what the biennial did for the Russian public, it's hard to hide the fact that no one came to this biennial, and that it wasn't understood by anyone. But for the unprepared Russian observer it was just another incomprehensible project in a serious of incomprehensible projects of modern art. To the Western observer it is something avant-garde. The worst thing that could happen to the curators when travelling to Russia is that they become Russian, like the Russians there. They'd get a bit of experience of fighting the system, like we have, of breaking the system down from within…

MARIA S.: When they came to the destroyed central pavilion, they probably understood straight away…

ALEXANDER: Yes indeed, it's all about the destruction of the system. And maybe the biennial, just like Napoleon came here to lose, and Hitler came here to suffer defeat, — maybe the Biennale also has to accept the inevitable…?

IVAN: Do you mean that the collapse of the institution of the Biennale will start with the sixth in Moscow?

ALEXANDER: Well, why not?… Maybe it's perfectly possible; the collapse of big projects like that.

Alexander Zhuravlev
Anna Zhurba
Ivan Isaev
Maria Mkrtycheva
Ekaterina Savchenko
Sona Stepanyan
Maria Stepkina

1
This text is a result of the Young Curators Workshop, conceived by V-A-C Foundation as a discursive platform to reflect on the notion of togetherness. During their meetings, the participants came up with several contributions to this publication. This one is a transcript of a conversation during the several workshop meetings that re-evaluated the biennial with a focus on its impact in Moscow, Russia and beyond.

Pascal Gielen — The Global Civil Parade. Constitutions of Transnational Citizenship Antwerp, October 2016

CREEPING RAGE

The terrorist attacks and pervasive threats that hang over us today distract us from another kind of violence I want to discuss here. That violence includes a form of aggression that rather insidiously oozes throughout the world. Over the past decade we have been startled at intervals by sudden but intense outbursts of rage. The explanation for the kind of violence addressed here is not directly traceable to God or any particular country. That is why it emits as much incomprehension as does terrorism. Although sometimes its immediate cause can be identified, eruptions arise, especially those of unusually large destructive proportions that are beyond any comprehension.

Whether it be riots in the *banlieues* of Paris, in the suburbs of London, in Brussels' Molenbeek district, the cat-and-mouse game around Antwerp's Turnhoutsebaan or the street violence in the Schilderswijk of The Hague;—its cause is often ascribed to controversial arrests, or even deaths caused by police violence. However, the reason the reactions are so severe and why they also, quite massively, trigger a civic roar, remains unclear. Besides, it can be particularly difficult to imagine whether the dam is going to burst or whether there will be no eruption at all. In other words, while the symptom is clear, the underlying disease remains elusive.

Surprised by a sudden eruption, the mainstream media and politicians have already proven to fall short on interpretive frameworks. At the time, Nicolas Sarkozy coined the phrase '*les crapules du banlieues*' [the villains of the suburbs] while Dutch prime minister Mark Rutten talked about '*achterlijke gladiolen*' [dim-witted dung-heads]. When it happened in David Cameron's backyard, the former British prime minister put his moral finger in the air saying, "Young people and immigrants must urgently be re-taught the norms and values of their country." In response to the riots on Turnhoutsebaan, the then mayor of Antwerp abolished the city slogan 'The City is of Everyone'. From then on, the city was no longer for everyone anymore.

Repressive measures such as zero tolerance and more police on the streets are accompanied by a strikingly moralising rhetoric. Citizens must be retaught norms and values, and those who do not want to change must relocate. The city and the country may indeed not simply be for just anyone anymore. Some people are just not worthy of being American, Belgian, British, German, Dutch, Russian or European. Their right to citizenship is, at the very least, doubtful.

The responses to these violent eruptions remind us that citizenship has always existed to create a regulatory mechanism of inclusion and exclusion. However, over the past decade we have been confronted with a notable shift in meaning—from a formal to a moral interpretation of the word: Where the formal concept of citizenship concerns the legal status of a citizen, moral citizenship includes the extra-legal normative interpretation of what a good citizen is, or should be and should do. As the Dutch sociologist Willem Schinkel put it: "Citizenship is a concept that will be stretched more and more in today's policy. The moral side of citizenship becomes the centre by emphasising the formal aspects of citizenship. When 'integration' is then seen as 'citizenship', this will lead to a quasi-elimination of citizenship for many citizens in the formal sense. The state is trying to effect this by adapting the concept of citizenship to promote a discourse that makes clear who is and who is not part of the dream society."[1]

ACTIVE CITIZENSHIP

As soon as feelings have cooled down and insults in the streets and media have calmed, the horizon is clear and open for more rational solutions. The motley crew and their senseless violence must be addressed proactively and more thoughtfully. In recent years, relief has also been sought in improved integration and participation policies. Thereby, ever so often, the notions of 'active citizenship' and the 'participatory society' came to the fore. The 'Big Society' and active citizenship seemed to be David Cameron's ultimate medicine for social diseases such as violent outbursts.

But we also see these concepts emerge on a European level. European citizenship was first officially mentioned in the Treaty of Maastricht in 1992. The notion of active citizenship emerged again eight years later at the Lisbon Council of Europe. There, citizenship was understood as a means of making Europe the most competitive and dynamic knowledge economy of the world.[2]

Over the past three decades, the mission of civic education has transformed the political landscape from one with a humanistic perspective (of learning how to be human) to one of learning how to be productive. That way, education is supposed to help people settle within the labour market. Thus, citizenship includes first and foremost a desire to integrate and participate in the economy. According to the Dutch pedagogue Gert Biesta, these terms of education lead to an interesting re-definition of civic rights and duties: "Whereas in the past lifelong learning was an individual's right, which corresponded to the state's duty to provide resources and opportunities for lifelong learning, it seems that lifelong learning has increasingly become a duty for which individuals need to take responsibility, while it has become the right of the state to demand of all its citizens that they continuously engage in learning so as to keep up with the demands of the global economy."[3]

THE PARTICIPATORY SOCIETY

A similar shift can be observed in the definition of participation. The emphasis here draws equally from influencing policies on political participation to self-reliant participation.[4] The swing from the political to the moral dimension of citizenship implies both a politicisation as well as an individualisation. Thus, again we observe a return of the debate to the balance of rights and duties: the participation right of a citizen is renamed a moral obligation. At the same time, the legal-technical semantics around citizenship are sliding towards a rather affect-laden discourse. Herein, citizens are called upon to care for each other and be less dependent on the government.

The new politicised morality of affective citizenship focuses on the intimate local and affective relationships among citizens themselves, as opposed to the aloof national level and faceless bureaucracy of the welfare state. Moral and emotional ties thus receive more appreciation than legal-technical or political relationships. We see these personal and small dependencies in the return of terms such as 'personal strength', 'civil power', 'personal responsibility' or simply 'taking part'. With the emergence of affective citizenship, focus shifts onto one's own responsibility and active solidarity, clearly reflecting the trend towards individualisation. Solidarity is simply a personal mission and responsibility, and it becomes less and less the duty of the government to organise this solidarity structurally (between generations, between the healthy and the sick, between the employed and unemployed, between rich and poor, etc.).

With the term individual responsibility rulers are already searching for a new balance between government and the citizen. From a political point of view, the notion of regularity is presented as a solution to both the crisis of the welfare state and the blurring of norms and values.[5] Active citizenship with a focus on private (individual) responsibility often implies less responsibility for the government. It requires little argumentation to demonstrate that this signification fits well with a neo-liberal conception of society that represents a receding, minimal state.

FUNCTIONAL CITIZENSHIP

The ever-louder call for personal responsibility saw a shift from a humanistic vision of citizenship toward a functionalist perspective. It is not the whole person which is taken as the subject of civil rights, but the person who can do something, and particularly one who has to do something. Only when a person can prove that he or she fulfils certain functions, or at least intends to fulfil these functions, he or she is entitled to citizenship. The appeal to active citizenship is therefore often accompanied by an appeal to duties. Someone wishing to be a citizen must therefore show that they want to integrate, to participate, to learn the language, but also that they are available (and flexible) for work. Within the new rhetoric, a citizen can only claim civil rights when she or he performs a function for society, the economy and the GNP. If she or he cannot find work, the citizen must volunteer to make his or her services available to society.

In line with this shift from a humanistic perspective to a functional setback, attitudes about government responsibilities have changed as well. At least the government obligations are attached to the notice of civic duties. For example, in Belgium in the autumn of 2015, a political debate erupted on whether to unconditionally grant child benefits without the need for this to be linked to school attendance. Can we coerce parents to teach their children in exchange for child benefits?

The Belgian dispute is an example that shows how welfare benefits such as social security, pension schemes, (free) education, etc. are increasingly questioned. What was guaranteed in the Rhineland model as obvious public services for all citizens is not only being reduced. The remaining public services are simultaneously linked to the increasing obligations of citizens. These citizens do not only take individual responsibility, but they also carry their own risks. The recent transition from scholarships to student loans in the Netherlands, for instance, reduces education as a civil right and collective public duty to a personal choice on one's own account. The same can be said about encouraging private pension savings and private health insurance. The dismantling of the welfare state also generates a 'shrinking' of citizenship, or better-said of civil rights. Or, as one phrase has it, which is popularly doing the rounds: The citizen is stripped.

Nearly everywhere, formal or legal citizenship has been reduced to some version of a minimum package. This 'minimum citizen' will be presented on the other hand with a wide range of tasks. She or he must develop their own talents, they must be dynamic, they must integrate socially or they should simply provide good deeds. On the other hand, we find calls to be courageous, to propose political questions or to adopt a democratic role to be much less reflected in the discourse on citizenship. Thus, structural and macro-political problems are kept out of sight.

The active citizen, according to Biesta, is therefore primarily "the citizen who will contribute to the reproduction of the existing political order."[6] Integration and citizenship are cultivated, in his terms, mainly as a matter of socialisation. That is to say that civic and integration strategies are designed to introduce individuals to an existing social order and culture without empowering competencies that allow them to put this order into question.

Criticism and political action, on the other hand, assume processes of subjectification when individuals are confronted and learn to argument with others and others' opinions. Furthermore, they learn to unravel deeper social, political and economic relations. Active citizenship seems to displace the possibility of critical citizenship. Already, social criticism oftentimes derives

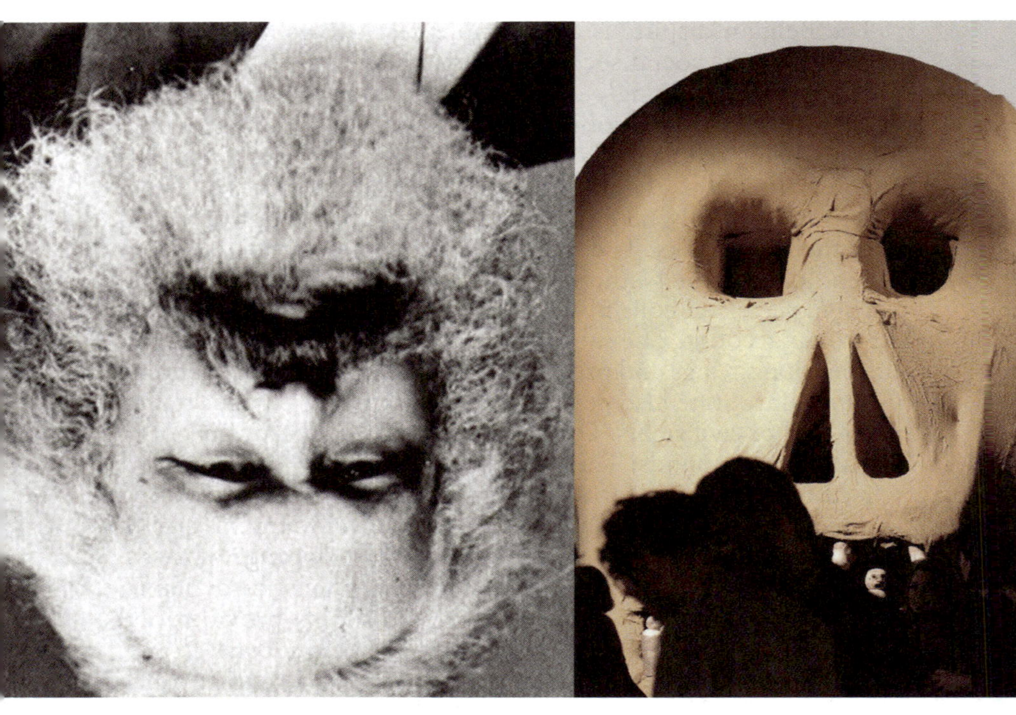

Almagul Menlibayeva

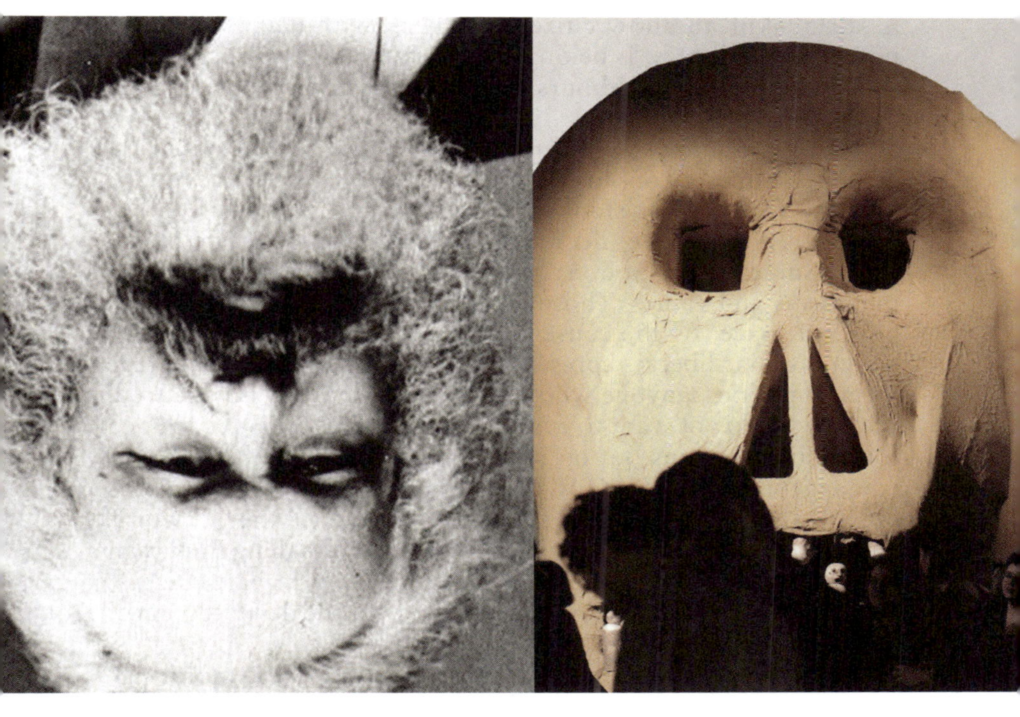

from self-criticism. What goes wrong in the world has to do primarily with one's own limited activity and responsibility. The active citizen is thus encouraged to contribute, but hardly to emancipate. Empowerment nowadays is referred to as primarily a 'social skill' to allow citizens to speak with neighbours and potential employers. It belongs less to the register of active citizenship to incite neighbours or colleagues to activism or civil disobedience.

New conceptions of citizenship fit a democracy of consensus. Which assumes a consensus about the existing political model, but also that the decisions based within and the beliefs about (liberal representative) democracy are in consensus. The model thus assumes also that every potential citizen endorses the existing norms and values. Those who don't, simply fall outside the political space. As the consensus model claims to be correct in assuming that liberal representative democracy is the only true form of politics, anyone who does not endorse this is outlawed. Those who do not want to embrace these values are not excluded for political reasons but on moral grounds. Remember the war language used by George W. Bush when talking about the 'Axis of Evil' after the September 11 attacks, remember abusive words such as '*crapules*' or '*achterlijke gladiolen*' that leading European politicians liked to use after violent outbursts of private citizens. Apparently, the retarded or those who are 'of the devil' can never deserve political rights.

The previously identified transition from formal to moral citizenship is thus in line with the shift from a democratic to a moral discourse in the political arena. The fact that democracy, and especially its shape, must constantly be a topic of discussion, as well as the need for dissent among citizens seems to be replaced by the rhetoric of active citizenship and participatory society. But agony and dissent are the core of (deliberative) democracy. Dissensus does not just mean discussion, argument or disagreement between different opinions. Its main concern is to make visible what is not yet visible, to speak in the words of the French philosopher Jacques Rancière.[7] Dissensus means for example to point out civil rights to those who cannot see them under the prevailing policy (or those who don't want to see them) or to those who the government would not consider entitled to these rights. Dissensus can also mean that the inhabitants of a city may claim certain ecological, social, political or economic rights; rights which no one—apart from themselves—would assume to be allowed to claim. Dissensus questions and breaks the consensus over and over again to always indicate different possibilities.

THE CITIZENS' PARADE

The remarkably positive effect of the outlined evolution is that dissent is mentioned more often. Between governments and markets, between unions and employers, further civil space is opening worldwide. Perhaps the *Indignados* and Occupy brought the global vigour of this civil movement most prominently to light. Today, however, processions of activists and citizens' initiatives are holding a parade across the globe. In many cases, they operate locally, but their activities apparently are so infectious that they mirror all over the world. Virtual networks and social media not only disseminate their messages instantly, also their tactics and organisational forms obtain a direct global resonance.

Anyone browsing the web understands quickly that the Internet today is an instructive manual for citizens' initiatives. Be it a subversive or a revolutionary practice, for fun or reformist activities—new means of communication provide these initiatives an immediate global forum. From the Zapatistas in Latin America to Pussy Riot in Russia, from *Recetas Urbanas* and Sanidad Universal in Spain to the occupation of the Maagdenhuis in Amsterdam, from Anonymous in Canada to Culture 2 Commons and Independent Culture in Croatia, from *Teatro Villa Occupato* in Italy to *Hart boven Hard* in Belgium—however diverse the background of all these initiatives may be, they are all kneaded into a new civil society. It has to be said that their actions often disappear as fast as they pop up. But perhaps it is the continuous sequence of activities that counts. Moreover, their growing global interconnection makes it so that they learn from and strengthen one another.

In his book *Networks of Outrage and Hope: Social Movements in the Internet Age*, the Spanish sociologist Manuel Castells explains in depth how, for example, the Egyptian Revolution connects with the Kitchenware Revolt in Iceland. The flow seems to be unstoppable. However heterogeneous these actions and initiatives may appear, the components for a new civil society are being placed all over the world. Virtual connections and global networks make it so that national governments have less and less control over this phenomenon.

The new civil space that stands in scaffolding has a global scope, and the new civilian will be a global citizen. This may all sound somewhat premature, and optimistic—but while the national governments of Europe think that they can restrain their subjects by means of liberal representative democracy, it is hard to deny that a new democracy is in the making in their own backyard. After all, democracy, as is demonstrated in quite a few nations, in fact appears to fulfil a neoliberal agenda. A balanced budget serves as an excuse to further reduce welfare and solidarity structures. If there is anything positive about the on-going crisis, it's that it is becoming increasingly difficult to hide the true face of the current politics.

MEANING

Liberal representative democracy serves not so much civil rights as private property and capital. Our voting policy hides a political-economic ideology. Emerging global social movements and citizen actions are bringing precisely this into the light. No matter how varied and volatile the activities of these civic parades may be, the subsequent actions breach the democracy of consensus and models of 'natural' competition every time. Harsh repressive politics of liberal economic measures, cuts and restructuring operations, along with technocratic audits, accreditations and monitoring administration seems almost heartless. Authorities, administrators or politicians in general are therefore losing their public support, as management policy deprives citizens of all meaning.

A technocratic policy that only navigates according to economic parameters, hinders the granting of meaning. An accumulating bureaucracy crushes any meaning or professional satisfaction that might have been found in education, justice and health, as much as the economisation of (active) citizenship causes a questioning of the very meaning of it all. "Why am I still doing this?" the teacher asks himself in the evening when he is going through forms on competences and contact hours. "What is the meaning of all this?" wonders the surgeon when he checks off his operations rate. "Where is the pleasure in my profession?" muses the judge who now finds himself in a competitive atmosphere with his colleagues. "And why do they even involve us when we hardly enjoy our civil rights?" the mob thinks when they smash shop windows and street furniture to smithereens.

Both professionalism and citizenship have a great deal to do with meaning. They make it possible to give meaning to our own being, our place and identity in a society. The continuing repressive liberal policy that focuses on quantity now blocks precisely this process of signification. We might put it this way: While workers' revolts and industrial actions were the symptoms of an underlying disease (namely the exploitation of the proletariat in early capitalist times), it is now rather the deprivation of meaning that leads the so-called precariat to despair in the late capitalist era.

For now, the doctor, teacher or judge live their life, not yet in poverty; but newcomers may often be given a very modest income. Besides money, there is something else that makes a civilian life. People are finding it increasingly difficult to give meaning to their work inside the society in which they dwell. As is well known, this results in stress, burnouts and sometimes depression. And while refugees and other newcomers find it increasingly difficult to assign themselves meaning in their country of destination, native citizens too are increasingly losing a sense of their national culture and political identity.

When the state is phasing out structural solidarity, hampering free education and health care, the citizen indeed wonders why she or he still pays taxes. Anyone who is quantified is going to start calculating more themselves. In short, the quantified citizen sees herself or himself more and more in a contractual relationship with society. This rationalised relationship between citizen and state, but also between employee and employer seems simple and functional. What it cannot provide is a 'soul'. Thus the citizen is increasingly deprived of the possibility of a meaningful existence. It is therefore not surprising that the growing group in question comes more and more to rely on violence when faced with the ever-expanding mesh of the dwindling welfare state.

This so-called 'senseless' violence is indeed meaningless in the sense that it is the last straw for many who still demand any sense. When every access to meaning is denied, the fist feels like the last resort to those wishing to be noted, wishing to provide them with significance. And indeed, when the riots do break out, politicians and media suddenly turn their attention to those who have been ignored for decades, who they have neglected in every (electoral) meaning, from whom they have taken away any sense. In short, violence is the final resort of expression for those who are denied any means of expression. Aggression on the street, but also towards oneself (as in suicide) is found, in other words, on the edge of culture. When a culture can no longer provide sufficient signs or sense with which to signify a person and his environment, when a man has been cut off from culture, sometimes violence seems the only way to reclaim meaning, to write oneself into a culture.[8] That is the paradoxical sense of the 'meaningless' frenzy of the '*krapuul*' and '*gladiolen*'.

THE CULTURAL COMMONS

Athwart the senseless violence, however, a vitalistic flood of initiatives emerges to return meaning to work, citizenship or simply to life itself. When the mainstream media finds it ever more difficult to give a hearing to all voices, when even public broadcasters fail to present a picture of the full cultural richness and diversity in their own lives; and when liberal representative democracy finds it increasingly difficult to suffer its citizens, a colourful parade of immigrants, artists, scientists, homosexuals, environmentalists, feminists and trade union activists emerges. What is striking here is that this motley crew is constantly mixing with each other. New social movements are fighting not only for labour rights in their own lives, as the trade unions of yesteryear once did. Anyone who looks at the bullet points of *Indignados* or *Hart boven Hard* will encounter a whole jumble of demands and concerns.

While quite a few mainstream media and politicians easily dismiss them as people who do not know what they want, this is, however, precisely the crux of the matter. The citizens' parade represents a total change that can only lay out heterogeneous demands. The point is that ecologists and trade unionists, migrants' and women's rights organisations, artists and doctors, architects and educators are increasingly finding it easier to join in a common struggle. But what is the shared point?

Presumably this is the already identified matter of meaning. The citizens' parade wants to regain meaning for their existence, their profession, their own being in society. Therefore, the heterogeneous struggle is not exclusively economic, environmental or political but cultural. The actions of Anonymous, Pussy Riot or *Recetas Urbanas* undeniably have aims that are social, political, economic or concern gender equality. But their primary intention is that economics, politics and society are shaped in a new, different way to permit them to give meaning to themselves and society.

The construction of meaning is the central concern of all these movements. Hence culture as a reservoir of meaning and purpose plays a crucial role in their actions. The subversive performances of Pussy Riot, the guerrilla architecture of *Recetas Urbanas*, and the giants of the *Hart boven Hard* parade all have in common that they offer an imaginary space in which to conceptualise the world differently. However fictional or utopian they may appear, they do however generate each of these possibilities and, above all, they hold together a motley crowd with the most heterogeneous demands. Precisely this makes artistic expression possible. They generate an imaginary space in which the most diverse wishes and desires can be projected.

The growing citizens' actions are no longer limited to such unequivocal concerns as a fair income, global warming or discrimination against women, but turning more and more to the very arrangement of our life in its totality, for which all these things form the constituent components. The purpose of the community of this murmuring crowd is, as stated, to give meaning. And the social place they are trying to generate is called the commons.

Between market and government, private and public property, the civilian parade with its public actions, shared city gardens, semi-legal constructions, Wikipedia, open source and creative commons, is restoring a common autonomous place in the city or on the web. When job satisfaction is managed away, professional enjoyment and pride are downsized, and civil rights are calculated away in a civil budget, the commons provide one of the few sanctuaries remaining for meaning.

We should not delude ourselves: The common is not a harmonious community. There is no hippie romanticism here, but a lot of squabbling and bickering set the scene of the commons. Naturally, conflicting demands and desires collide in the battle for meaning and purpose. But it is precisely this dissensus that keeps a true democratic culture alive. And we should be quite optimistic about this. The more rulers hide behind budget deficits, the higher management stacks bureaucracy, and the more civil rights we lose, the bigger the hunger for meaning and culture will become and the harder the commons will act. Sometimes it happens through violent outbursts, but more and more colourful and meaningful parades are being held too. The citizens' parade is spreading worldwide to help bury neoliberalism once and for all, to give life meaning again.

1
Schinkel, W. (2010). *The Virtualization of Citizenship. Critical Sociology*, 36(2), pp. 265–283, p. 48.

2
Biesta, G. (2011). *Learning democracy in school and society*. Rotterdam: Sense Publishers, p. 34.

3
Ibid. p. 66f.

4
Van Hees, S., Horstman, K., Jansen, M. en Ruwaard, D. (2015). *Betekenissen van burgerschap van ouderen in de participatiesamenleving*. Tijdschrift Gezondheidswet, 93(5), pp. 191–196, p. 192.

5
Vrooman, C., Noije, L. van, Jonker, J. J., Veldheer, V. (2012). *Responsabele burgers, regisserende overheid*. In: Veldheer, V., J.-J. Jonker, L. van Noije & C. Vrooman (red.), *Een beroep op de burger, Minder verzorgingsstaat, meer eigen verantwoordelijkheid, Sociaal en Cultureel Rapport 2012*. Den Haag: Sociaal en Cultureel Planbureau, p. 11.

6
Biesta, G. (2011). *Learning democracy in school and society*. Rotterdam: Sense Publishers, p. 43.

7
See Rancière, J. (2015) *Dissensus. On Politics and Aesthetics*. Bloomsbury: New York.

8
See Gielen, P. and Lijster, T. (2015), 'Culture: The substructure for a European common'. In P. Gielen (Ed.), *No Culture, No Europe: On the Foundation of Politics*. Valiz: Amsterdam, pp. 19–66.

Ilya Budraitskis, Boris Dolgin, Evgeny Gontmakher, Dmitry Venkov, Vasily Zharkov — The Invention of Eurasia

Moscow, 30th September 2015

On the occasion of the Moscow Biennale *How to Gather? Acting in a Centre in a City in the Heart of the Island of Eurasia*, historian Ilya Budraitskis, political scientist Boris Dolgin, economist Evgeny Gontmakher, artist Dmitry Venkov and political scientist Vasily Zharkov discussed the notion of Eurasia from an economic and political point of view.

The concept of Eurasia has been a controversial topic of debate in Russia for almost a century. The two main directions of the discourse split into an interpretation of Eurasia as 1) a space without borders, without colonialism, without racial inequality or without exclusion logics and 2) a political project to insist on values and interests that differ fundamentally from the conceptions of Europe and Asia.

ILYA BUDRAITSKIS: Let's talk about the strange and problematic concept of Eurasia. It is located centrally between various ideological, political and cultural speculations. Today, the idea of Eurasia is much more present in the vocabulary of political elites than in cultural and social contexts.

Eurasia needs to be discussed and demystified. What is really behind it? How was Eurasia invented as a project to reflect on a special Russian historical path? How is it rooted in opposition to that of Europe? Can Eurasia be understood not as a state project but as an alternative to the established order of things?

EVGENY GONTMAKHER: I'm not a historian. I'm more interested in geography. From a geographical point of view, Syria is also Eurasia. But the concept of Eurasia has somehow been reduced to one of Russia, Ukraine, Kazakhstan and the Eurasian Economic Union.

The Soviet Union, for example, was created without regard for geography. Its creators probably thought it would later be joined by Germany, the UK and other countries. The same counts for Eurasia. But let's be careful when making use of the word 'geography' for political purposes…

How can we talk of any 'special path' in today's world? We share the same institutions. I'm not talking about democracy or economics, but about the position of the individual in society, in relation to the state. Some love to talk about a specific situation, about traditional values. But, frankly, not a single person in our country has formulated what this means exactly. Is it Orthodoxy? Is it family values?

I think globalisation should not unify, but preserve diversity—linguistic, ethnic and sexual diversity. As long as it doesn't cause ruptures in society, we may refer to it as globalisation. Society can survive when each person is unique and can discover her or his abilities. Thus, variety and self-reflection may become the bases of everything. Eurasia doesn't have anything to do with it.

VASILY ZHARKOV: The title of our discussion *The Invention of Eurasia* refers to the historical theory of constructivism, which explored how the notion of Eurasia was defined as something natural, as if it had always existed. Actually, it appeared in the era of modernity as a result of intellectual efforts and collective expectations, and the transformations then being experienced.

Geographically speaking, Eurasia stretches from Lisbon to Indonesia. But political geography is unnatural; it creates borders. It is a fruit of the human mind. The concept of Eurasianism achieved considerable popularity in the 1920s and 1930s. During the formation of the young Soviet State, Eurasia bore the potential to explain why it was that the Soviet Union was no longer a part of Europe, of the bourgeois world. Here, geography became a tool that allowed parts of the Russian intelligentsia to side with the Soviet power and create for it a framework in which they could legitimise this power.

ILYA BUDRAITSKIS: In his book *Inventing Eastern Europe*, Larry Wolff describes the construction of Eastern Europe as an invention not by its inhabitants, but by Western education, which included Eastern Europe in its universalist paradigms through a process of orientalisation. Eurasianism however, emerged in exactly the opposite way: It was an attempt to understand this space from within. It implied connections with a specific, unique geography (also of political formats) in relation to its culture and traditions, which cannot be exported and universalised. So, Eurasia seems to be a very special political project that cannot be fully entered into from a perspective dominated by Western and American views.

BORIS DOLGIN: It's hardly an attempt to self-orientalise. After the Revolution, a number of new trends emerged in the émigré community: There was a need for new explanatory schemes. Practically, the older systems had failed. There was a demand for new ideas to try and explain what was happening. The concept of Eurasianism evolved in emigration, not in Russia, from a social demand for the establishment of new ideas. One of the movement's inherent features is that it was an attempt to cope with reality and the fact that older concepts, inherited from our forefathers, had failed.

I'm a strong supporter of nominalism. When we have several objectives, separating them becomes a problem. We may classify them however we please. But the question is, what is the purpose of such classification? Some find the concept of the Mediterranean relevant, others the concept of the Arab World... Is there, in fact, a political project of Eurasia? I would say no. And I don't see the need to bring its corpse back to life.

Could I say there was a 'special path'? No. There are special ways. Each country is special and unique in its own way, which is also how all countries differ from one another. There are no similar countries. However, for some purposes, we may combine our goals and find patterns in them.

In 2007, a Russian-Mongolian anthropological expedition spent a summer in Mongolia to collect material. In one of the settlements they visited, they asked a local inhabitant about his beliefs: “How should humans behave?” He answered that the future depends on how a person behaves. If they behave badly, after death (I hardly think it necessary to remind you, but the main religion in Mongolia is Buddhism), they will turn into a demonic creature, like a devil. And if they behave well, they will be reborn in the Kingdom of Shambhala — in America. The researcher asked, “What do you mean ‘in America’?” and the response was “In the United States.” This does not mean that Mongolia has forgotten about the existence of Tibet — no, all is sacred, all is well. But in the everyday mythology, Shambhala is in America.

EVGENY GONTMAKHER: Vasily rightly mentioned that Eurasianism is an evaluation of what we deny. We push off against something, but do not know where we are going. The peculiarity of European thinking — in the broadest sense — is to put everything into question. But that gives rise to chimeras, such as fascism, Eurasianism and others. Europeanness is not something manmade, but a diversity and clashing of opinions that introduces a degree of doubt into everything. Dissidence is the mission of few, but a typically European mission. In this scenario, when people come along who aim to construct everything around themselves and know how to do it, it can be very dangerous. I take the current political manifestation of Eurasianism as a form of violence. Russia, unfortunately, is suffering from the affliction of Eurasianism, special paths, and the construction of a new man. But in an economic sense, too, Eurasianism has no future.

VASILY ZHARKOV: The English language makes America a neighbour of other countries. Thus, geographical identity becomes secondary, making Eurasianism clearly a concept of the past. Now, you can be anywhere — thanks to technical gadgets and the Internet. Today, no matter where you live, your identity is connected with that of others.

ILYA BUDRAITSKIS: The binary opposition of large, overwhelming and gloomy meta-ideas — chimeras such as

Bolshevism, Fascism or Eurasianism — and blooming, pluralistic concepts prone to constant questioning and reflection; these oppositions are also something it is possible to play with. As does the Russian President, speaking of America as a carrier of an expansionist, universalist project of exclusivity, while he, together with his friends like Iran and China, favours exuberant diversity, the ability to cooperate and coexist with different political formats, and a situation that would lead the world into a dance of the distinct paths, followed by separate entities minding their own business. This spirit of doubt is not Eurasian a feature, but a European one, and it must not be forsaken by us under any circumstances.

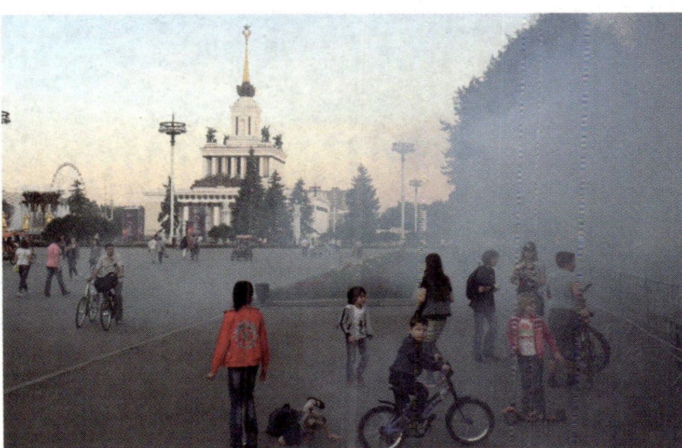

Otto Snoek, 22 September – 01 October 2015

Almagul Menlibayeva — Green, yellow, red and green again

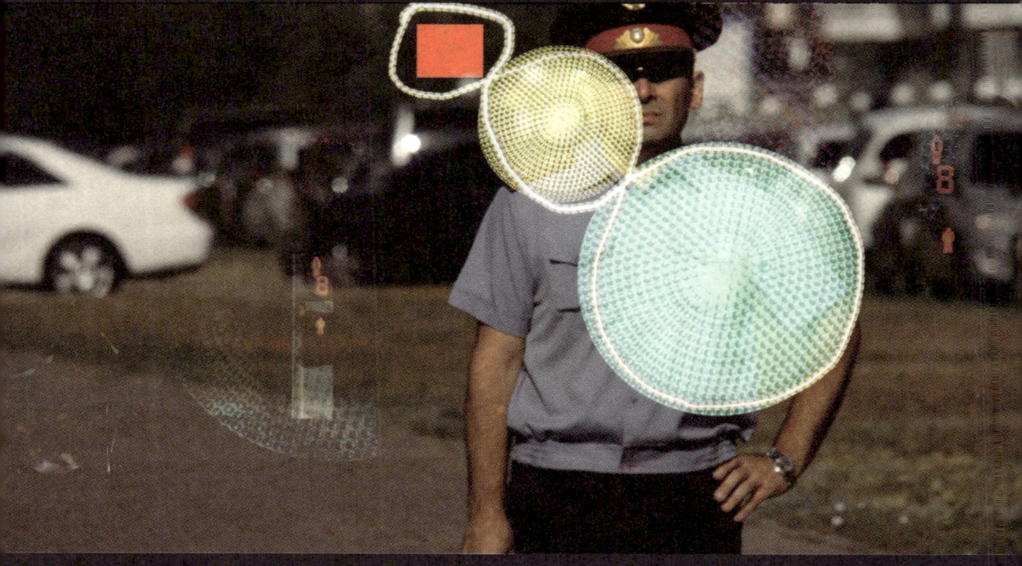

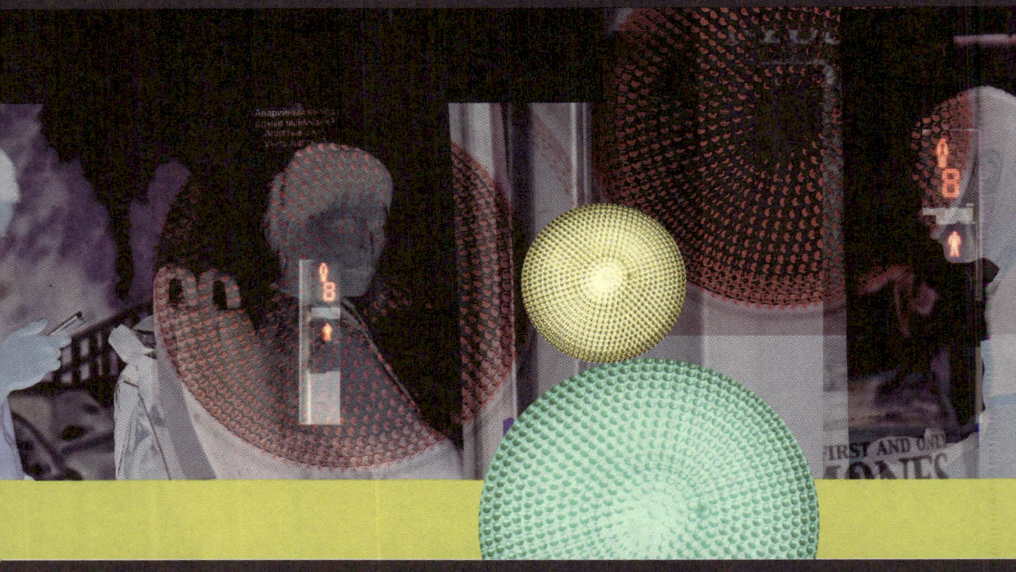

The title of this video refers to a film by the South Korean film director Kim Ki-duk, *Spring, Summer, Autumn, Winter and Spring Again*.

In the video there are groups of people in different cities and countries standing at a crossroads to cross the roads. Watching and waiting for the traffic light. Their combination brings together all the traffic lights in all the cities all over Eurasia in a rhythm with one single language; green, yellow, red.
A group of people from Almaty are looking at the traffic light / edit jump in / at a pedestrian crossing in Brussels or Berlin. It is red. The Almaty people are waiting, looking at / edit jump in / the Brussels or Berlin traffic light. It turns green / edit jump in / for the people on the crossroads in Almaty or Astana.

Or, on the contrary, people at a crossroads in Brussels or Berlin are looking at the traffic light / edit jump in / for the traffic in Almaty or Astana. The traffic light turns green / edit jump in / we see the face of a man from Brussels or Berlin, who understands that he has to cross the road. The video was filmed in different cities, which I visited to meet friends. How to live together? The viewer is as familiar as any observer. [Bart De Baere]

←←
←
Almagul Menlibayeva, *Green, Yellow, Red and Green Again*, video stills, 2015

Jimmie Durham[1] — Bekkah and Son, and Elpidio

I knew Son and Bekkah in San Francisco.

He had a place called 'Sonny's Pima Pizza and Poetry'. It was mostly a permanent stage where he could recite his poetry and sometimes his rap monologs which were only sometimes poems. Every few months he would have an evening of reading from his favorite poets, T. S. Elliot, Walt Whitman, E. E. Cummings; writers I have always intensely disliked. He did not invite anyone else to read, though, and had a mile-a-minute overly-energetic way of talking that allowed no interruption nor discussion.

The restaurant was not exactly in the Mission District, but close by. He said that he called it 'Sonny's' because the name Son had no poetry. Son's mother was Pima, from the Mexican side of that strange border originally, but came to the U.S. as a child. Son was her first born and hence given the name. She had no other children but perhaps intended to have.

Son did not know his father although he always said he was Apache. No, not always, now that I remember. Sometimes he said his father was Yaqui.

Bekkah was a wolf. A mountain lion. What we call a Beloved Woman, if only we had our sense back. She was Cherokee from Oklahoma, except that she was Black. From that community that are descendants of Africans who were slaves 'belonging to' some Cherokee families.

Oklahoma is really racist and Oklahoma Cherokees can be mortifyingly stupid.

Bekkah was a warrior. A Spirit. She had those incredible green-violet eyes you often see in Black Cherokees from the Carolinas. Take your breath away.

Probably not yet twenty when she came out to San Francisco. A lot of people were suspicious of her, even if no one would say what exactly they were suspicious of. Many Oklahoma Cherokees went out to California over the years, though, and a blond-haired Cherokee woman at the Community House introduced Bekkah to Son to see if she could get a job. It's Bekkah who told me this.

She was a good waiter and popular with everyone, helping Son's business more than he knew.

Son often hung out with movie star-types, or maybe they just sort of tolerated him. At least that's the way I always saw it.

Kind of like a pet Indian but movie stars don't really seem to be so loyal to pets.

But there was a guy from Mexico, more an actor than a movie star, and he started hanging out at the restaurant.

One time this guy brought another Mexican; guy named Elpidio.

You know what happened next. He and Bekkah started hanging out together. Easy to see why—Elpidio was good-looking in a way that was really rough, but children cottoned to him right away, and different kinds of older working women who can often act dangerous and bad. I never could figure out how he charmed them without even trying. And he was a good guy. Not funny, but he loved other people's humor.

So you can also see what happened next. Son got jealous. He didn't make a show-down or nothing. Started being bad to Bekkah.

Once they had a fight. He said, 'You even speak Cherokee?'

Bekkah is a warrior. She went cold, as they say. 'You speak Pima?' 'You need my license?' 'My certificate?' 'I told you about us.' 'I do not speak trash like you do.'

It gets worse. Ugly. Son had to go to Los Angeles for a couple of weeks.

Bekkah and a couple of others were taking care of the Pima Pizza parlor. Elpidio was there. About ten thirty on that Friday night in late September two government agents came in and arrested him.

No one ever saw him again.

From what Bekkah could find out Elpidio was not legally in the U.S. She told me later in Boston that Elpidio is Purépecha. 'Legal in any part of the Americas', she said.

When I saw her in Boston those years later we spent a week or so together, or maybe a decade, it was so strong.

She told me she did everything she could but could not find Elpidio. Stayed completely cold to Son. Finally just left. Went east. She'd been reading Louise Erdrich and went east.

I heard from a Penobscot guy that she lived with Darrel Cannuk in Canada for awhile.

She learned French, moved to Paris.

I guess Son is still in California, haven't heard anything.

1
2014, Napoli — This is a piece of fiction, written for the occasion of an art show by Lawrence Paul Yuxweluptun at the Museum of Anthropology in Vancouver. Special note to Canadians: although the word 'Canuck' is used pejoratively against Canadians of French descent it is still a fairly common surname among First Nations people in Quebec and Ontario. j d

Jimmie Durham — Bekkah in Europe

CHAPTER TWO

So Bekkah landed up in Paris.

She knew it was not going to work out with Daryl Cannuk in Montreal; she said he was always acting about himself.

But she didn't just wash up in Paris like James Baldwin had done so many years earlier. She knew Hombart Lyle back in Tulsa and he is the brother of Maryanne Wolf who had been in Paris for more than thirty years. Maryanne had been famous earlier, and she was not only a folk singer but she also sang opera and she used to brag that she never sang *Carmen*. So Hombart gave her Maryanne's address and told Maryanne that she was coming.

Back in San Francisco Bekkah was really a knock-out but now she was beautiful in ways that are not describable. It was like her beauty had found her and she wasn't even expecting anything. She had let her hair grow to shoulder length. It was afro hair but at the same time it was Cherokee afro hair. So much of her hair had turned deep, deep red, blackish red and was more than curly but still not typically African hair. Sometimes her skin seemed to be even darker than it had been and sometimes her eyes seemed to be even more violet than they had been. Ok, sorry, it's just that I was quite often in Paris in those days from being in Strasbourg so much.

Maryanne Wolf you might say had become French. I think she forgot everything about Oklahoma and the life there and I think she was really gracefully proud of the forgetting. She had lived with a composer-guy for a long, long time but then married another guy also French but I don't know what he did in the music business. She had one son who in turn had two sons and a daughter. These three young French people were very proud to be Creek even though none of them had ever been to the U.S. much less Oklahoma. But here now: one of the boys, Pascal, fell more or less in love with Bekkah. I mean, pretty much as soon as she got to Paris she fell in with a crazy bunch and was in a strange way part of a very strange part of Paris life. The artistic music life. She was always happy to be with Pascal but she said later that their cheerful apolitical attitudes began to drive her nuts. At the same time she began to meet other, more interesting guys. So that for the next year she was in what we might call a constant whirlwind of love affairs, political actions and even tried some singing herself.

She had a lot of fights and she was able to; not just because of Maryanne's introduction, but because everyone could see how she was. And over that first year her Canadian French got better and better real French. She got a reputation very quickly for not taking any nonsense. People would say, "How is that you are Black?" And with a fierceness that was almost physical, she would say, "How is it that you are Pink?" People would say, "Do you speak Cherokee?" And she would rattle off some insulting phrase in a way that they had to know that they were being put down.

But there was this one time, there was a bunch of us at Maryanne's house, including a couple of Indian artists from the West Coast. Some woman who was kind of French but maybe Algerian, said to Bekkah, "But do you mean that you and your family are not recognized as Cherokees because you are Black? I have been to Oklahoma several times and I have seen that most Cherokees around Tahlequah look English or Irish! Just because your family were slaves, you are not Cherokee? That's like American Blacks not being American because their ancestors were slaves!" Bekkah looked at her but she didn't say anything and stayed pretty much quiet the rest of that evening.

Not so many people know that the truth about Paris is its suburbs. It is a city of giant and invisible unacknowledged suburbs. Bekkah met a guy and lived out there somewhere. He was kind of like one of those guys who could do anything. He had no money. He had no nothing but he was always up. He was from the Gha tribe in Ghana and once when I was visiting he explained to a bunch of us that although the Gha were not the most populous of the various tribes in Ghana or the most powerful, they were the people who could get things done between all of the other people. He said he was a born diplomat. He was trying to be an artist in a system where there are few artists and a bunch of pretenders. This is the kind of art he was making. He had a big handled ax and a short hatchet. He could take abandoned cars apart with these tools and he tried to make, or maybe I should say, unmake, things with the parts of cars that he could not resell as regular car parts. Now, as strong as this guy was, maybe still is for all I know, he had a mother, Georgina. His mother was even stronger and took to Bekkah naturally right away. Bekkah did not treat her like a mother but like a close friend which she was.

I don't know how to say about what they did but here is what they did: they started an organization and they got many other women involved. First from that neighborhood and then from other neighborhoods. It was as though people were ready for some sort of planned action; kind of spread like wild fire, you might say. Nothing to do with the guy but with just Bekkah and her friend: they went to Ghana. They went to Senegal. They came back and spent a lot of time in Geneva and in Strasbourg. They spent a lot of time in Brussels. Bekkah told me that she saw more racism in Brussels than she had ever seen in eastern Oklahoma. Their organization grew and it never stopped working. Never stopped being right-on. And of course, maybe that was the problem. Another woman in the organization, she wasn't even from Ghana, accused Georgina of trying to have sex with her. Georgina did not deny or affirm it. She just tried to ignore it but then it wasn't more than a couple of weeks later that some woman in the French government said that they might have been embezzling money. Bekkah started spending more time in Geneva and Brussels. Georgina went back to Ghana and before the year was out she was dead.

More than a month past before I saw Bekkah again. She came to Strasbourg where I was staying practically dead herself. It was as though she was dead. I don't know how long she stayed but just a day or two. After that she disappeared. I don't know why but I never ask around for her. I guess I was afraid to. I was in Paris quite often and I would go around to where she often used be but I never asked anybody anything. Two years later I moved back to the U.S. and lived in New York City and never saw anybody who knew her and I still never asked anybody about her.

It was more than twenty years later maybe almost twenty-five, I was in Mexico City and I saw someone from San Francisco from the old days. She was in the city for a conference, she came running up to me. "Did you see Bekkah?", she said? "What do you mean?" I said, "Where?" "Here, she's been here for at least a week." "Where? Do you know where she is staying?" I called the hotel but she had checked out that morning. Then I looked up the woman who had told me about her to see what all she knew. Bekkah had been living in Venezuela. She didn't know how long but a long time.

Bekkah was part of an animal rights group who were doing things with wild animals in north-western Venezuela.

I guess I never stopped being in love with her but I never said that to her and I was never very forceful one way or another. I thought about going to Venezuela but I never did. Then even more years passed by and I heard from somebody that Bekkah was back in Brussels. I was almost never in Europe anymore and pretty much was never in the U.S. either by that time.

Fedor Dubinnikov and Igor Doshlygin — Exhibition Architecture

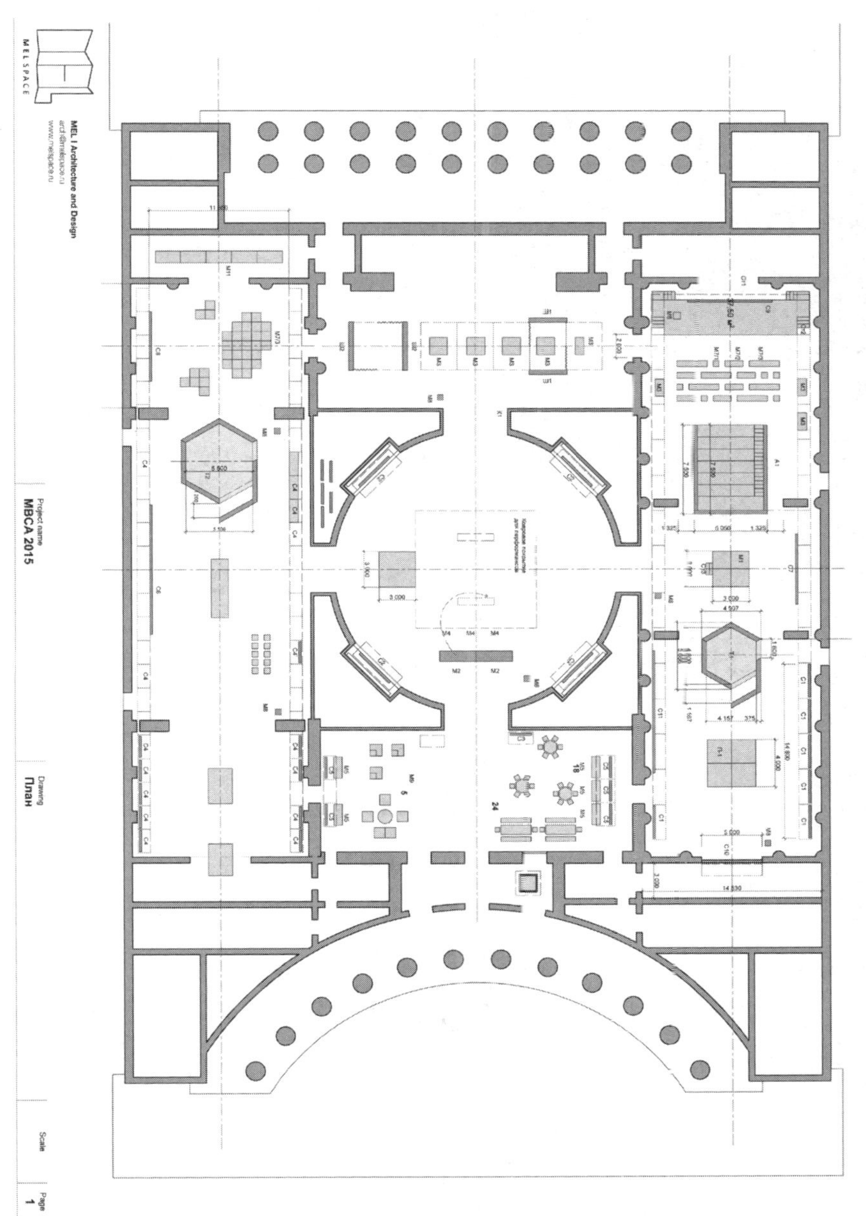

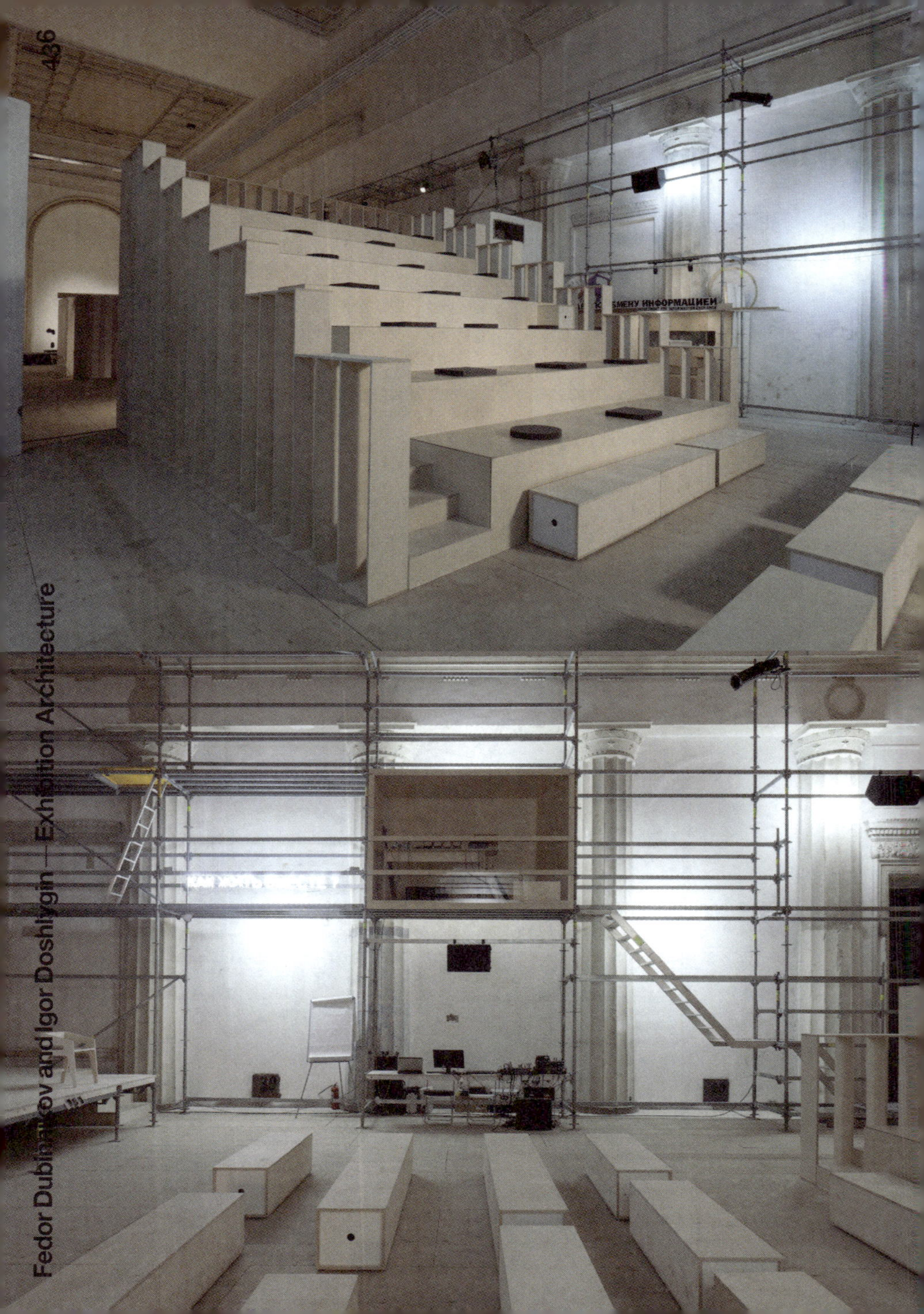

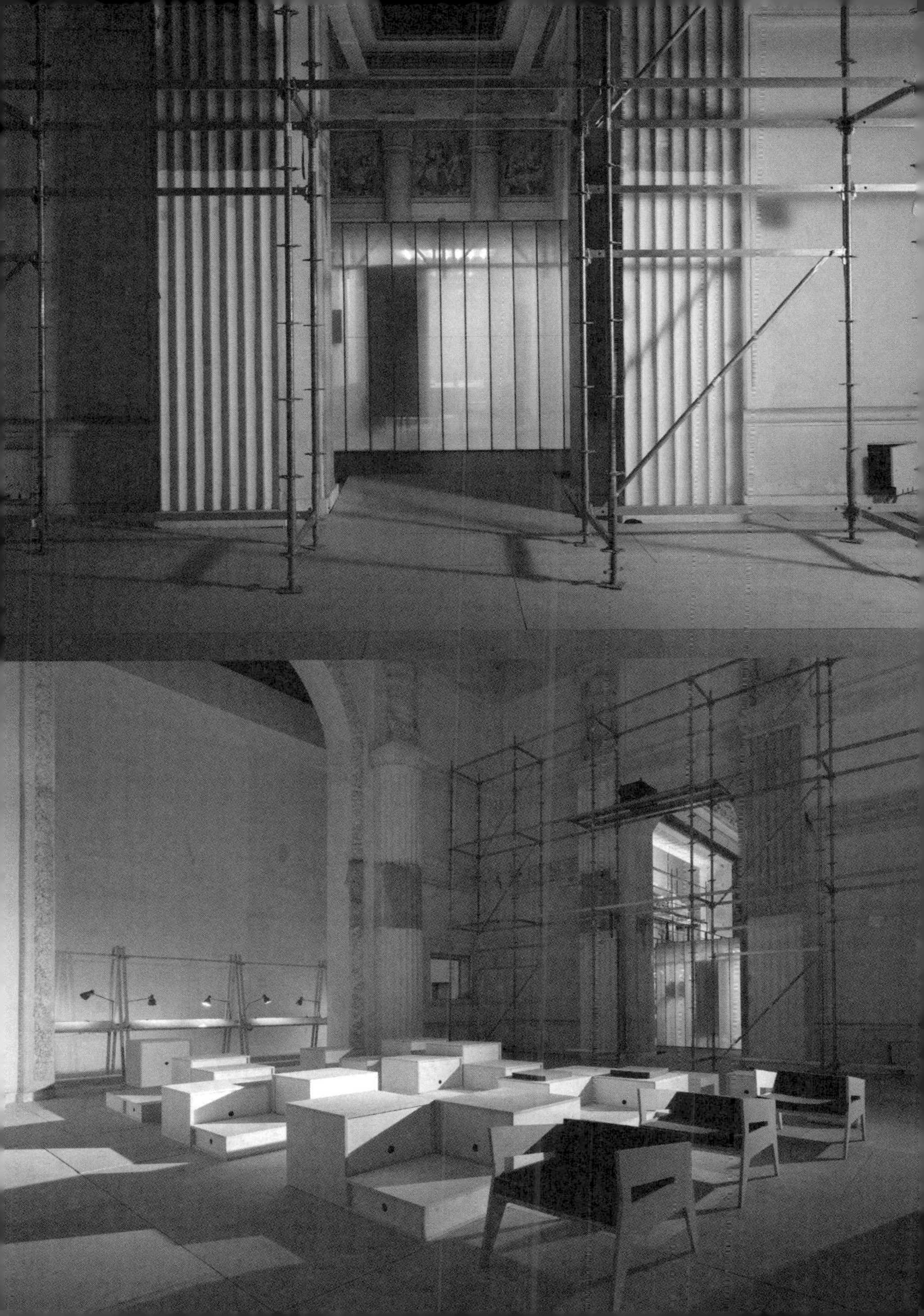

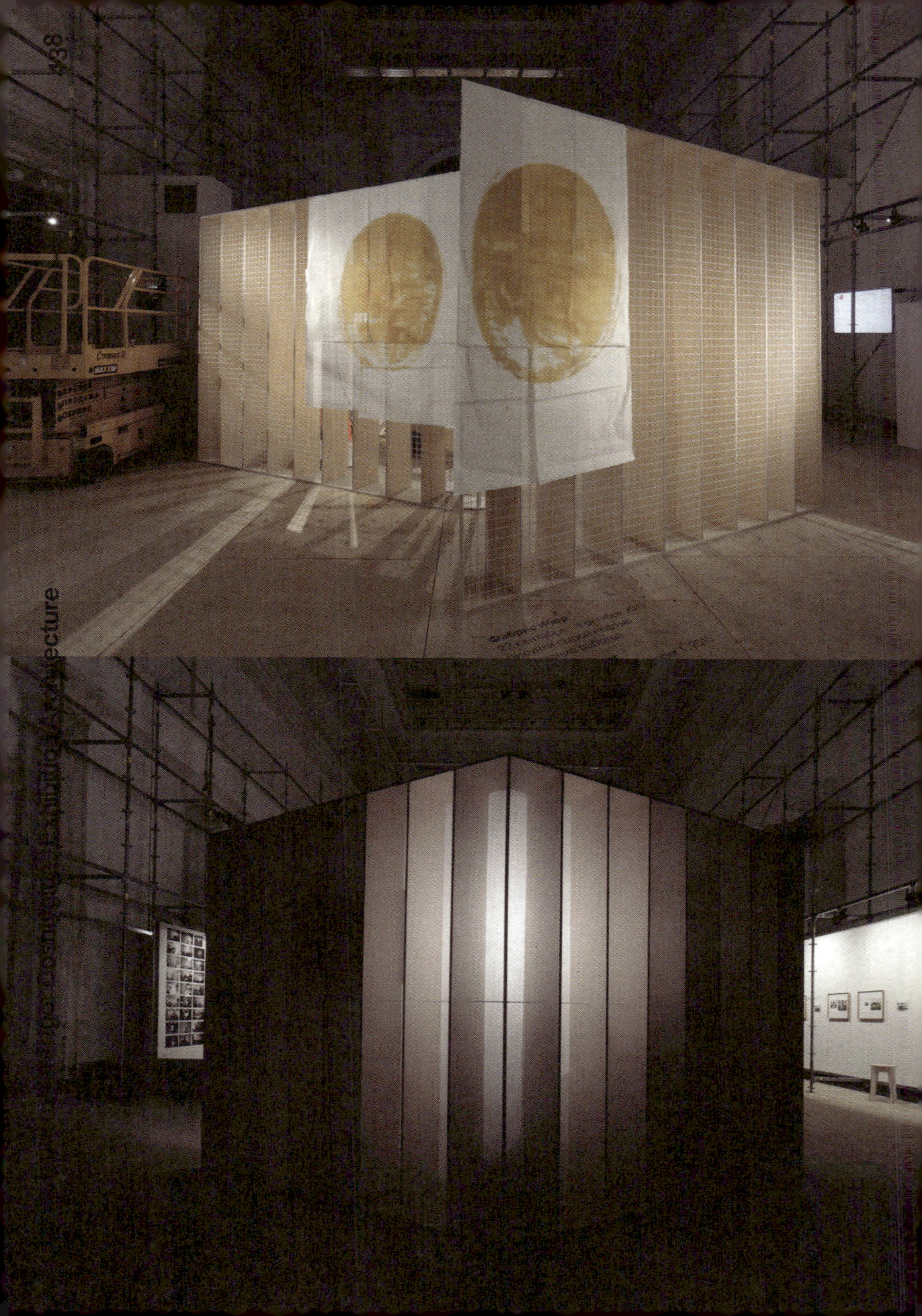

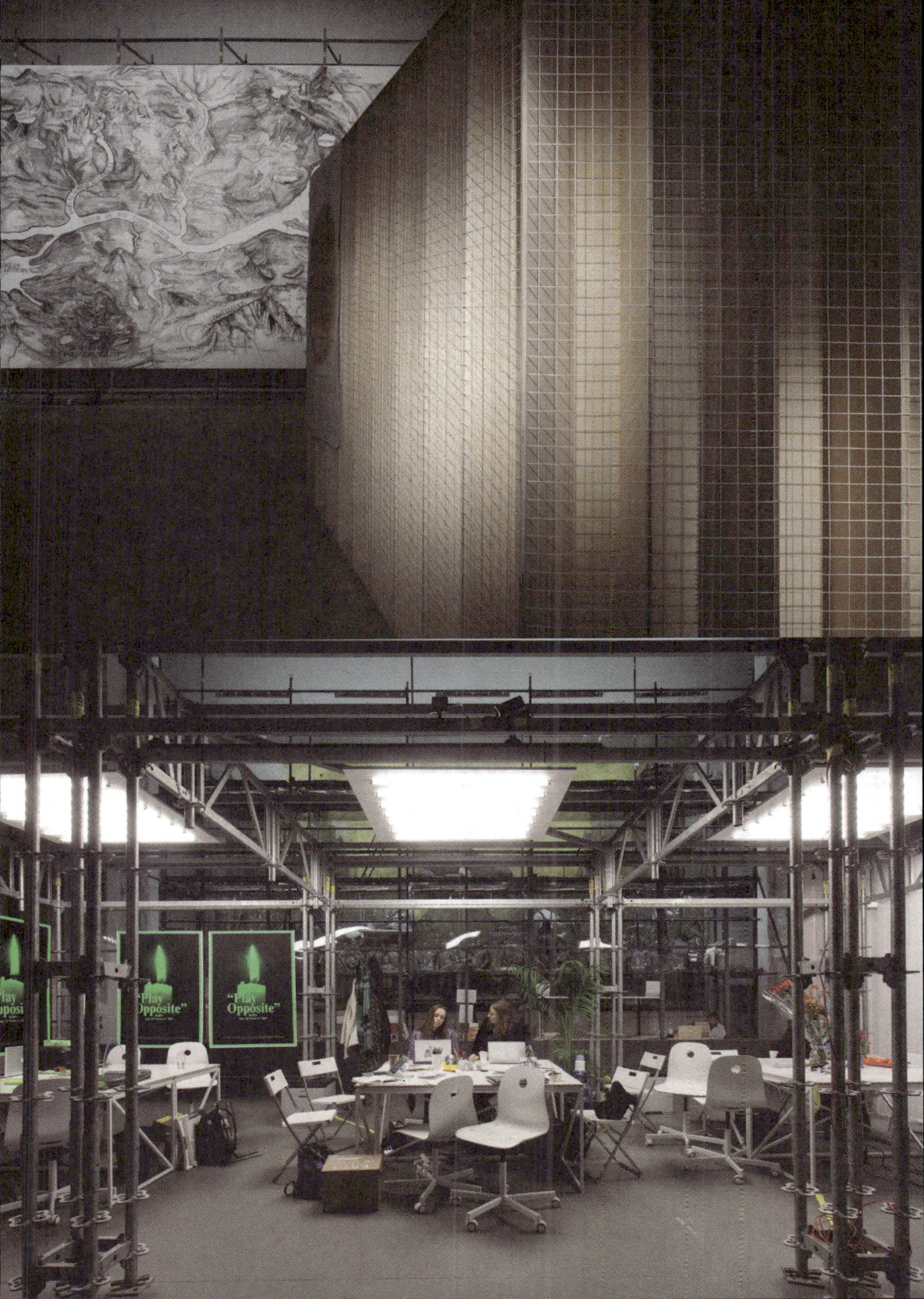
"Play Opposite"
"Play Opposite"

The architecture for VDNKh's Pavilion No. 1, where the 6th Moscow Biennale took place over ten days, was designed by Fedor Dubinnikov and Igor Doshlygin from Studio MEL. Studio MEL specialises in exhibition design and conceived the pavilion as a '*parcours*': They installed pavilions for intimate encounters or working together in groups, scaffoldings for flexible use of wall space, reading areas, mobile podiums, a main stage with the possibility to discuss in a plenum and a media machine for the extended Biennale team to work on site with the artists. The architectural concept took into account the landmark status of the pavilion and the structural needs of the ten-day think-tank where artists, visitors and organisers would meet. [Marie Egger]

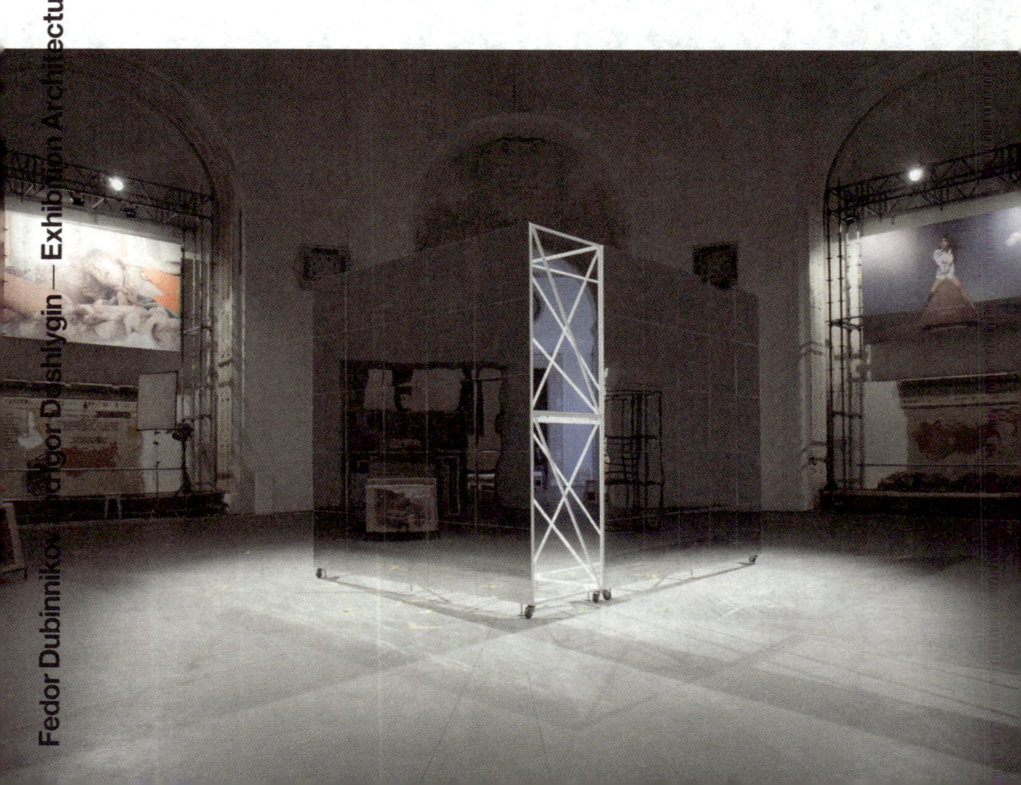

Part 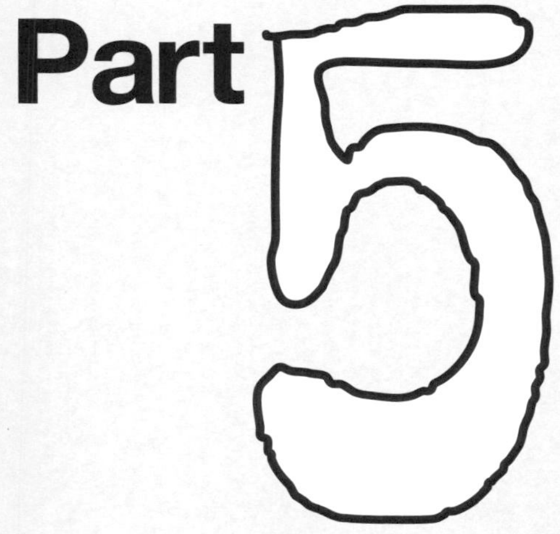

Appearances of Multitude

Flaka Haliti — Bëhuni Tolerante!

The biennial asked four artists for an image, that might also be a capacity and focus of artists, defined as such, rather than a generic 'artwork'. Flaka Haliti was one of the four.

Bëhuni Tolerante!—'If they can be tolerant, so can you!' says the billboard Flaka Haliti sent as her image contribution. A cat and a dog snuggling on a couch advocate for the creation of a peaceful environment and promote tolerance in Kosovo in 2010 — two years after the country's declaration of independence. The picture was part of an image campaign organised by KFOR (Kosovo Force), NATO's peacekeeping force whose task is to help create a secure and democratic environment in the Republic of Kosovo, the artist's home country.

Flaka Haliti transferred the original image, as displayed in the campaign in Kosovo, to the Moscow Biennale for Contemporary Art. Installed as a billboard in the Central Dome of Pavilion No. 1 at VDNKh, the image was kept as it was, gathered from the Internet, without any intervention by the artist, despite the decision to transfer it to a different context. It is exactly this gesture with which Flaka Haliti answers the question "How to gather?" An image that was supposed to impose tolerance between Albanians and Serbs and root Western democratic values in Kosovo, is read as an offensive, top-down act. Not only in the comparison of Serbs and Albanians to cats and dogs, but also in the somewhat offensive tone of the slogan and a perpetuation of Western as opposed to Eastern values.

Without the possibility of obtaining a legitimate state visa, Flaka Haliti could not attend the biennial personally and travel to Moscow. To this degree, her decision to send this image to the Moscow Biennale for Contemporary Art rightfully read the event as one to re-place the image into a new context and quasi-invert the logic that formerly applied to the picture. It became an opaque, neutralised version of itself, including a gaze from West to East and back again, detached from historical circumstances and bearing the potential to be re-observed again — potentially also under future conditions. [Marie Egger]

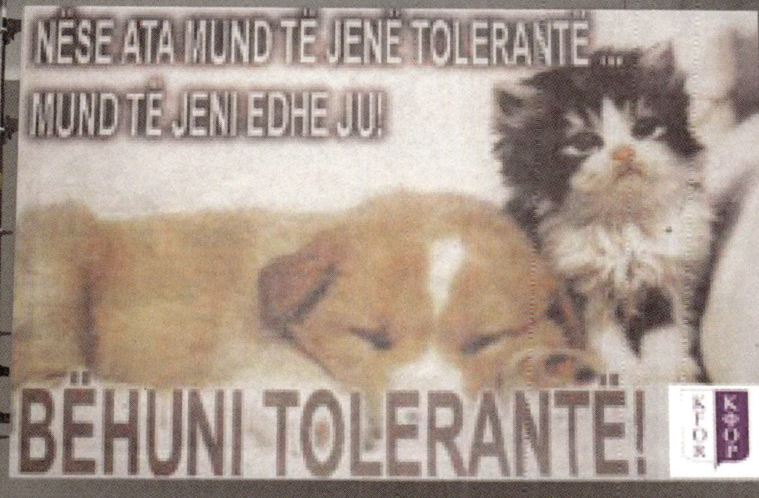

Babi Badalov — ME-GRANT. SHE-GRANT. A STORY OF AN UZBEK MIGRANT

Moscow, 24th September 2015

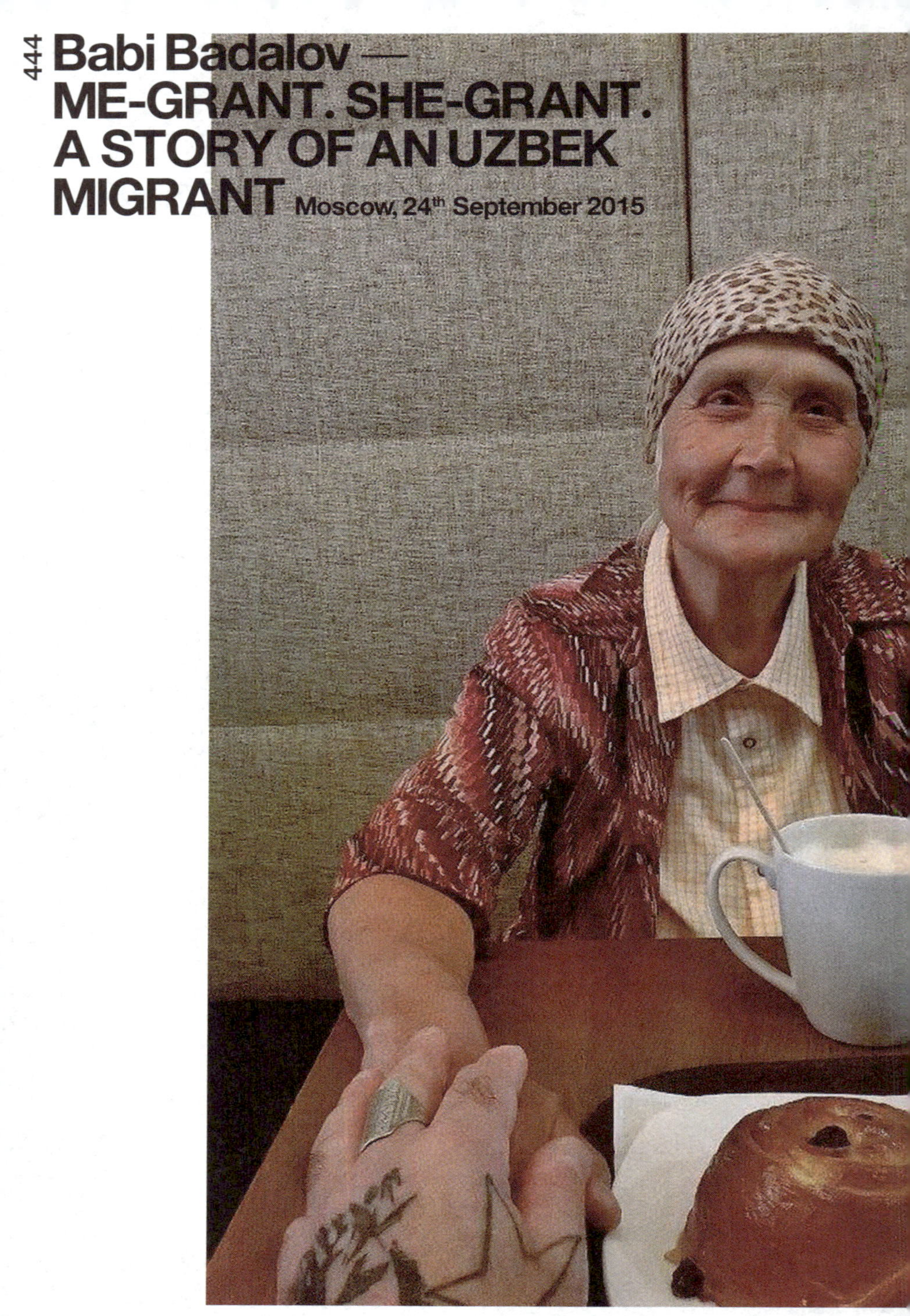

On my second day in Moscow I went to have a coffee. There I met a poor and sad looking old woman with torn plastic bags:

"Where are you going?"

"Uzbekistan?"

"Are you from Uzbekistan?"

"Yes."

"Where are you going?"

"I am going to McDonald's to have some *chai* and cake and use the bathroom."

I suggested that I come with her and treat her to this coffee. So we had breakfast together. She wanted a coffee with milk, a cappuccino. I went and got it for her as well as the cake with raisins and a sandwich to take away.

She couldn't, didn't want to believe it. We sat and she was so impressed and kept saying that Allah had sent me. She slowly ate and drank the cappuccino. Because she didn't finish the cake, she took the rest of it with her. I told her I that I am here for work — she insisted on going to the Metro and showing it to me.

"I will go to the mosque and pray for you."

The woman was 76 years old. Her name was Mahira. She was born in a small village near Tashkent, the capital of Uzbekistan. She has two sons. Talking to her was slightly difficult because she didn't speak good Russian. We were talking in a mixture of Azeri, Turkish, Uzbek and Russian. She was unbelievably happy. I hugged her a lot and told her how beautiful she is. It was very touching.

By the way I met her today as well when I came to McDonald's to buy some water.

←
Babi Badalov with Uzbek woman, Moscow, 2015

TEXT FROM PAPER GAME NO. 2[1]

No to dogma.
No to demagoguery.
No to hierarchy.
No to normativity.
No to the norm.
Yes to freedom, to mutual assistance, to friendship, and to creativity!

Yes to the view from outside.

It is important to feel oneness with the Other. We don't need a universal language. The beauty of civilisation is that which stops us from singing in unison.

Flaws create the most beautiful things.

Without a doubt, preserving individuality, or a flaw, is important. But haven't we seen the prerequisites for World War III in the excessive segregation and upholding of The Other as more important than the rest?

Has the opposition between I and Other not become obsolete? How significantly are we different from one another and from the masses? To what extent are differences important for maintaining peace? Perhaps, after all, No Man Is an Island?

In order to save the world, it is important to not think in categories of different masses. The word mass is associated with something formless and homogenous, like Plasticine, from which one can mould something. In the end, it's not so important how big our differences are if we are willing to recognise and respect their existence.

It seems that what follows from this is that the masses are utopia. Perhaps individuality is the last thing that remains that resembles reality.

Perhaps the only thing that is left to try is to live together individually.

Alexander Zhuravlev
Anna Zhurba
Ivan Isaev
Sona Stepanyan
Maria Stepkina

1
This text is a result of the Young Curators Workshop, conceived by V-A-C Foundation as a discursive platform to reflect on the notion of togetherness. During their meetings, the participants came up with several contributions to this publication. This one evolved from a paper game where everyone wrote a short hand-written liner on a folded piece of paper, to form a consistent text once the paper is unfolded.

Maria Theresa Alves — Tchám Krai Kytõm Pandã Grét (Male Display among European Populations)

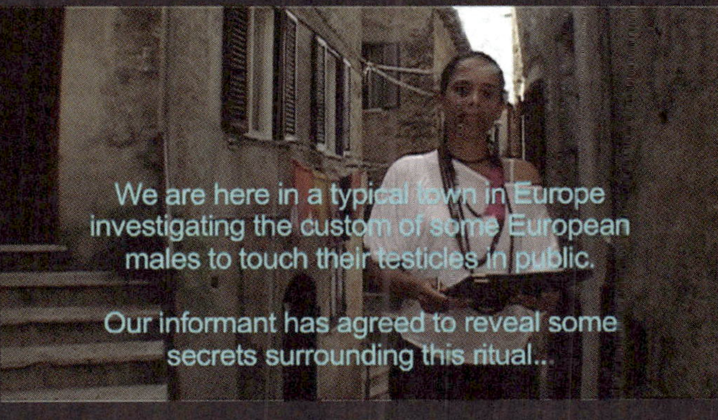

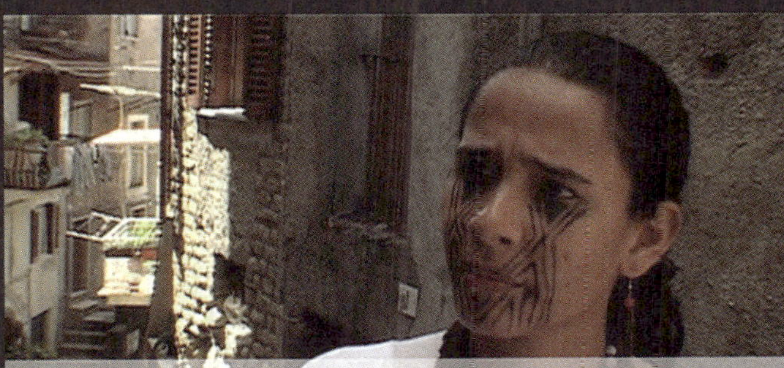

ANTHROPOLOGIST: We are here in a typical town in Europe investigating the custom of some European males to touch their w in public.
Our informer has agreed to reveal some of the secrets surrounding this ritual…
When is it important to touch your testicles and why?

EUROPEAN MAN: A man must touch his testicles if someone says that another man is lazy.
Or if someone says that another man has died.

ANTHROPOLOGIST: And why do you do this?

EUROPEAN MAN: To protect oneself from a similar fate.
Or in case of an empty hearse passing with no coffin, then from a future fate.

ANTHROPOLOGIST: Can you demonstrate?

EUROPEAN MAN: If a black cat crosses the road while I am driving, then I stop the car.
I let the cat pass.
Or if a priest passes.
Or if a nun passes.
Or is a friend is having bad luck, let's say his wife is ill and his mother has died then…

ANTHROPOLOGIST: Any other situations you can think of?

EUROPEAN MAN: For good luck.
If I am going to get married.
If I am going to get a job.

ANTHROPOLOGIST: Any other instances?

EUROPEAN MAN: Crossing under a ladder.
Or when I spill salt.
Or if a mirror breaks.

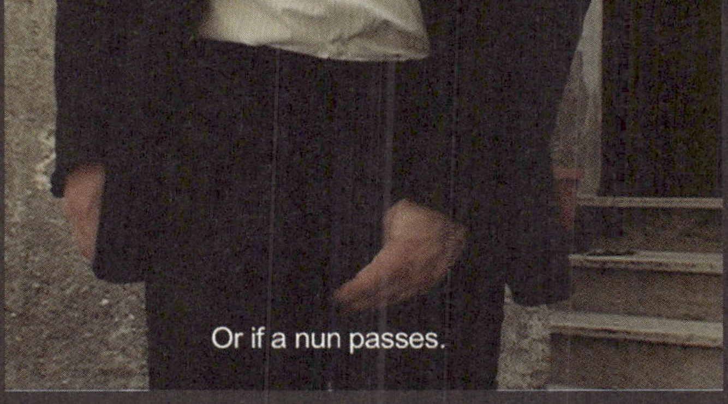
Or if a nun passes.

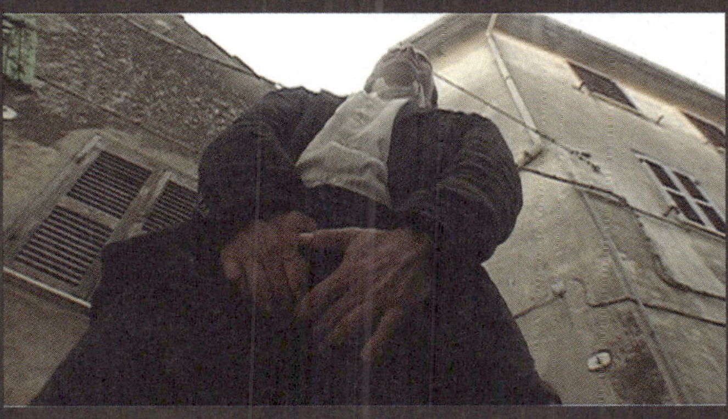

45º Fabrice Hyber — Montmartre Spirit

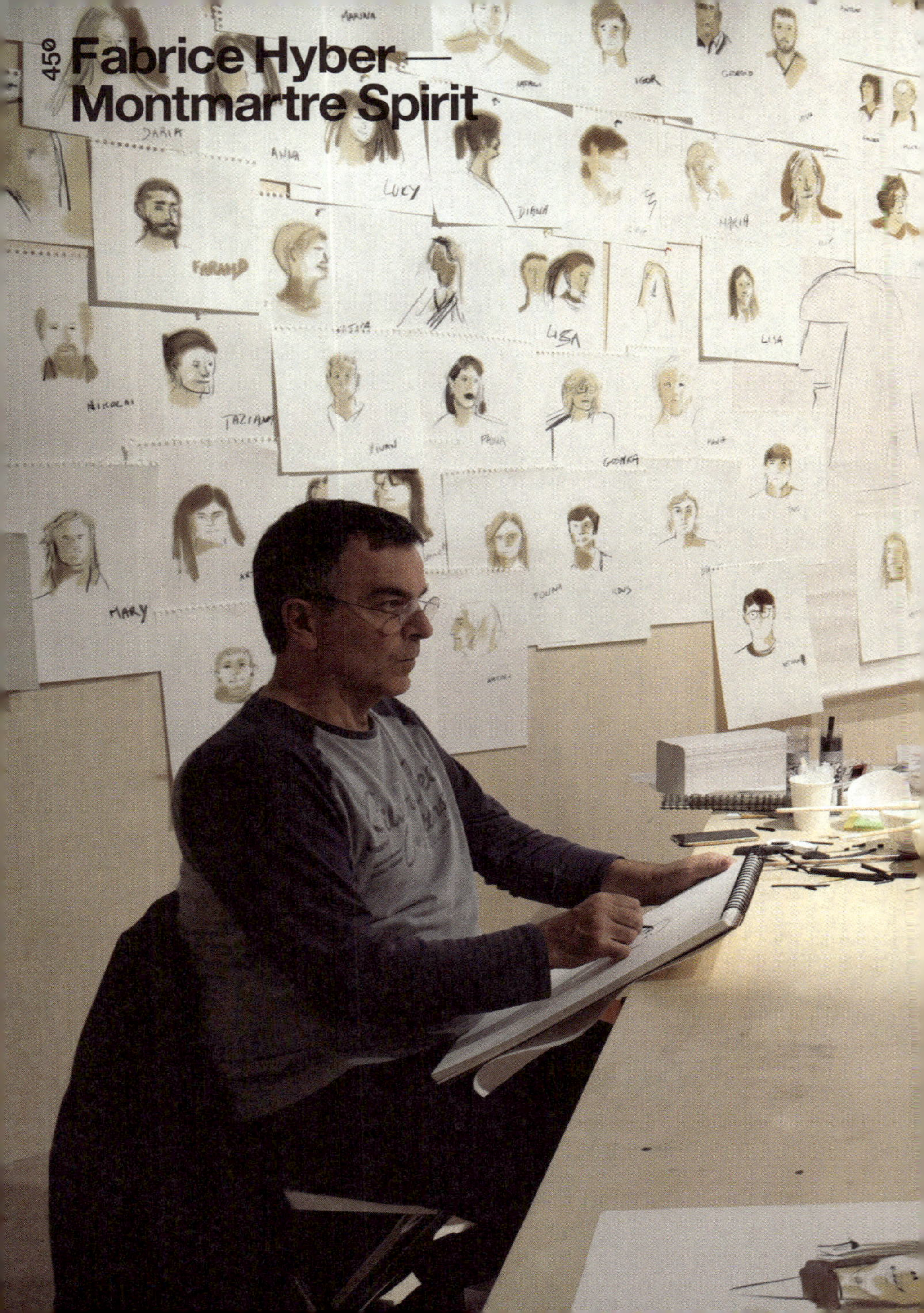

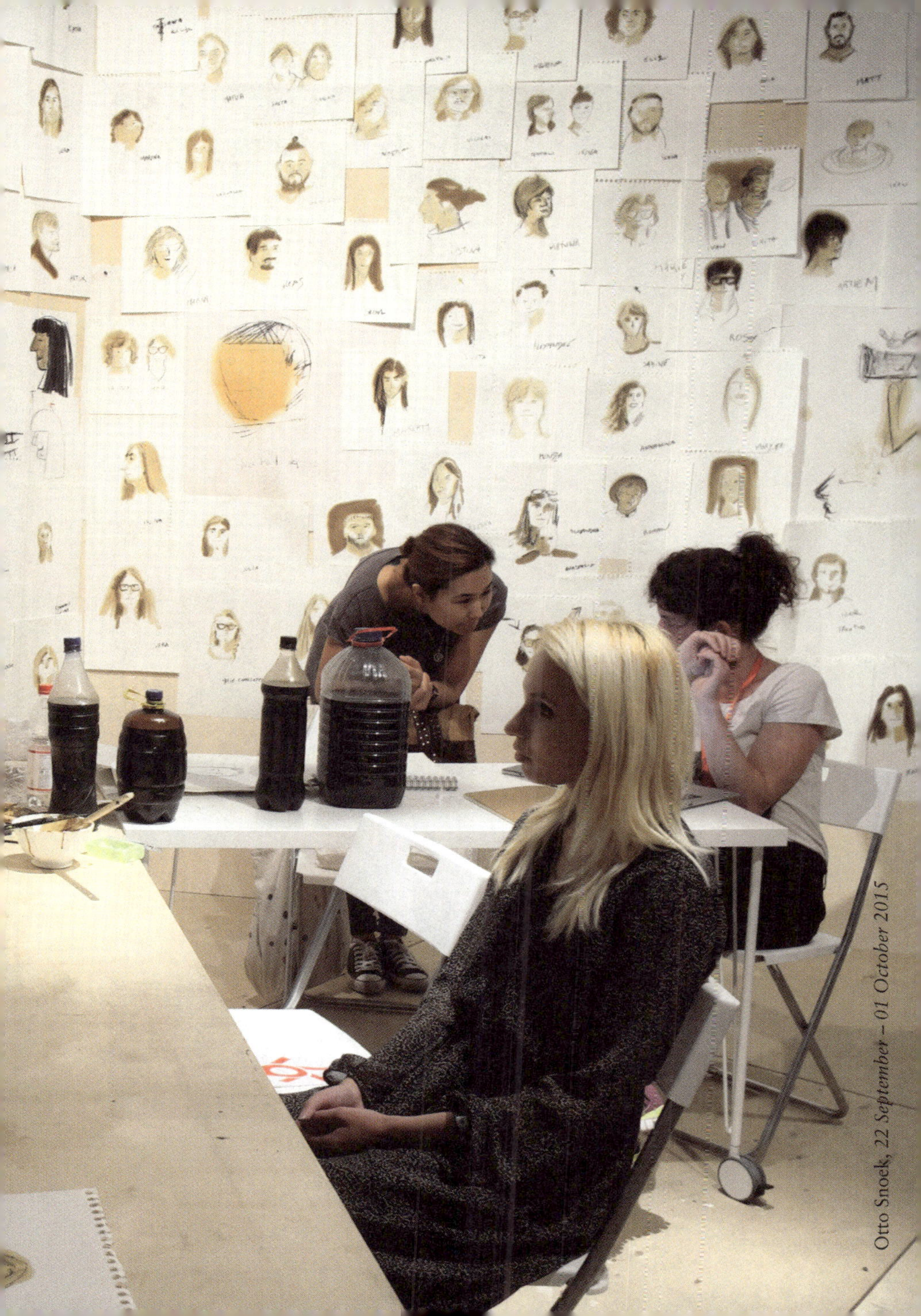

Otto Snoek, *22 September – 01 October 2015*

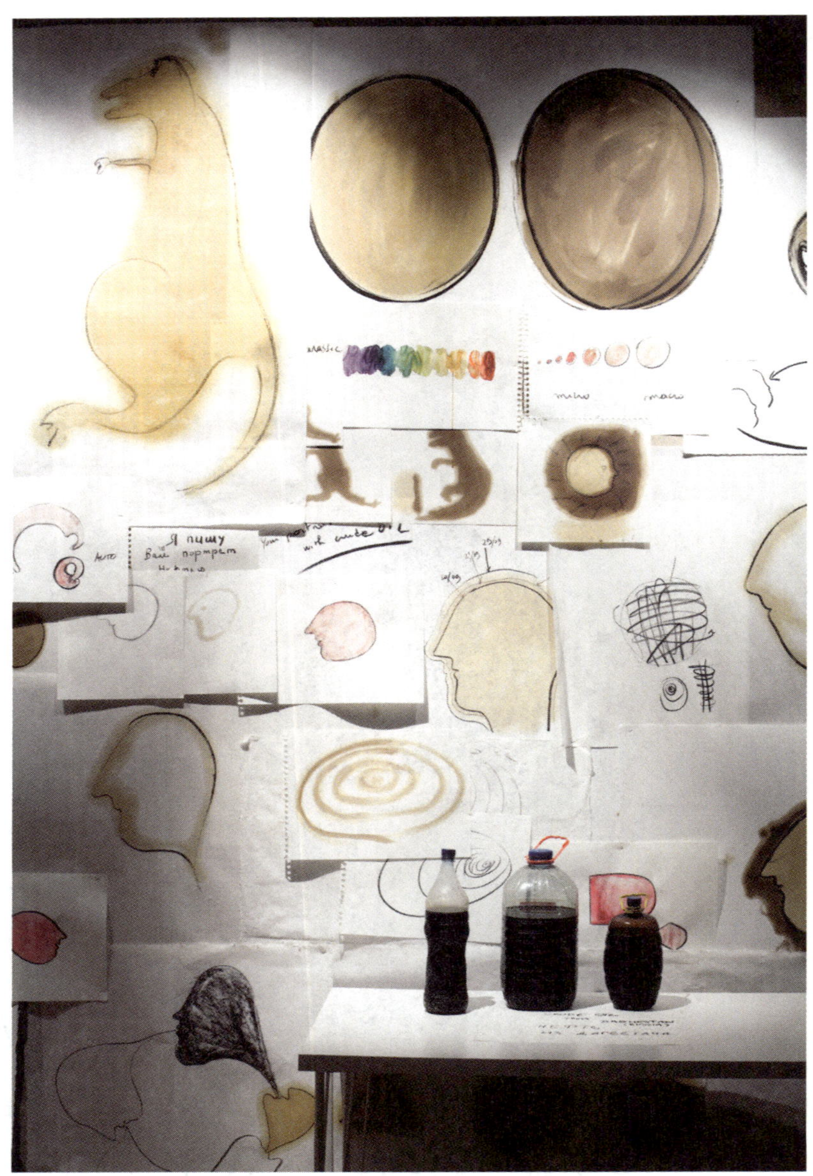

←↑
Fabrice Hyber, *Montmartre Spirit* at the Moscow Biennale, 2015

For this exceptional Moscow Biennale, *Montmartre Spirit* opened a forum of exchange for everyone visiting the Moscow Exhibition Centre's central pavilion, creating an infinite possibility of encounters. French artist Fabrice Hyber, born in 1961, constantly invents, using the rhizome, proliferation and transformation to draw emerging new thoughts and test new behaviours. To capture the movements of the world, imagine shifting points of view, and to create.

In Moscow, he asked each person to sit down and have their portrait drawn just as is done on the Place du Tertre in Montmartre: *Montmartre Spirit*. The hundreds of portraits, made in a few days, became the pretext for a discussion with artists, visitors, housekeepers, curators, children, grandmothers, assistants, journalists, directors, performers and gymnasts from Dagestan. An exchange of words and thoughts between Fabrice Hyber who draws and the subject of the portrait.

Everyone is invited to enter, sit in the chairs, and wander around. There is a large wooden table with all the paper necessary and two chairs on either side. Each person takes their place in front of Fabrice Hyber: just enough time for him to look at their face, to start a discussion, and to draw some lines that allow us to recognise the subject.

To draw the faces of all those who enter this open space inside the central pavilion of VDNKh, Fabrice Hyber uses charcoal from carbonised wood produced in the Vendée and crude oil from Dagestan — fossilised wood that has lain in the Russian soil since the beginning of time. These two raw materials extracted from nature have the same origin but are separated by thousands of years. Here, they become the common denominator of every portrait and therefore of every person. In the utopian space of the Moscow Biennale, creating a representative sample of the world in an instant, the act of drawing the portraits of every person who visits takes on a special meaning. Crude oil spreads out slowly, extending beyond the charcoal which traces the lines of the face: the individual's portrait cannot be perfectly confined to the borders of the outline. Just like the shared thoughts that permeate those who speak, the primitive material diffuses its effects and upsets the line that draws the skin, the boundary between inside and outside.

Little by little, the walls of the *Hexagone* — the caricatured map of France, which hosts *Montmartre Spirit* — are covered with portraits and build a territory which one is perfectly free to enter and exit, to run into one another for the duration of the Biennale. A place for the exchange of words which draws a utopian territory (and a pleasant place) is therefore created. At the end of the Biennale, everyone can leave with their portrait; the memory and the seed of an experience disperse. Discussions and encounters permeate *Montmartre Spirit*, echoing the current concerns over borders. Very real and closed—with the catastrophic consequences that we are familiar with—they are however in no way accessible to numerous flows. Perhaps these borders have already disappeared? Can we conceive the organic movement of populations in a globalised world? How long has the passport existed? And what if we did away with all passports?

If *Montmartre Spirit* evokes a popular custom, the work offers new behaviours, one of the themes that run through all of Fabrice Hyber's work: from the *POFs* (Prototypes of Functioning Objects) to *réalisateurs*, a school in Normandy that gives young artists the opportunity to invent new ways of producing works with businesses. During the Moscow Biennale, it is the act of drawing that offers new ways of thinking and behaving that are sent off with the portraits that each person takes away with them.

Montmartre Spirit, with all the portraits created, is one of the witnesses, one of the traces of what the Moscow Biennale was, which provides a response to the questions asked—How can we live together? How can we gather?—with all the urgency of the present moment, in a centre, in a city, in the heart of the island of Eurasia. [Juliette Malot]

David Polzin — Department for Information Exchange

The *Department for Information Exchange* opened for ten days during the Moscow Biennale 2015. The artist David Polzin returned to the site daily to put in a full day's work at the Department. Visitors could ask to make a deposit at the bank — in the form of information. This information could be true or false. There was no way of knowing whether the Department would check the data delivered to verify if it was correct or not. There was, however, an infrastructure in place that assigned a specific value to the information and would determine whether it was worthy of receiving another intelligence in return or not.

The *Department of Information Exchange* was an organisation, realised, led and run by David Polzin. When the biennial's architecture was nearly fully installed, he arrived on site and built a small, closed-off location; a wooden shed that snuggled itself into the scaffolding of the exhibition architecture. The materials for this office were gathered from the pavilion's basement. Whilst the building took on the new function of housing the biennial, the emergence of this agency during the installation came as a natural part of that transformation. The *Department of Information Exchange* fitted the context organically, while at the same time being as discomforting as any intelligence agency is in a democratic environment.

Inspired by bureaucratic architecture such as fences, barriers, gates, guideposts, interphones, glass walls, cash desks, etc., the Department closed itself off from visitors as a wooden box. Clients would have to ring a bell until a member off staff would come to greet them from behind a glass wall through a counter intercom. With no distinctions made as to who approached the bank or what information they would provide (lies were also accepted as valuable intelligence) the valuation and interpretation of the collected info remained cryptic and opaque. Sometimes, a submission would qualify a visitor to enter the bank and see behind the counter, other times, the information was graded as valueless and simply remained in the bank, without a counter offer being made.

David Polzin was initially invited by Suchan Kinoshita. His presence on site during the full duration of the biennial made him a crucial contributor to witness the happening from beginning to end. To this extent, the *Department of Information Exchange* was realised in accord with the biennial set-up as a whole. Facilities like news services or intelligence agencies gather their data in a grey zone of both public and non-public sources, to ensure the security of the system that installed them. However, they act from an extremely powerful position when gathering knowledge and determining by themselves how transparently they should deal with this. Set up, for example, as a bureaucratic structure subordinate to a democratic body, the collection and interpretation of data and their flow of information is controlled by the agency—with or without the constitutional right to act on the results of its work. [Marie Egger]

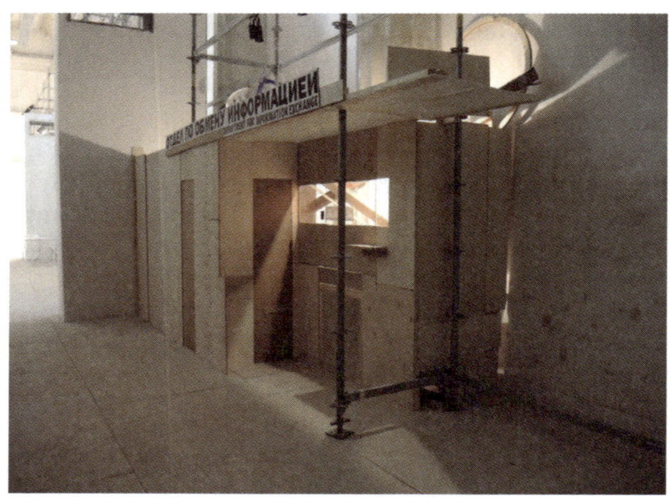

↑→
David Polzin, *Department for Information Exchange*, 2015

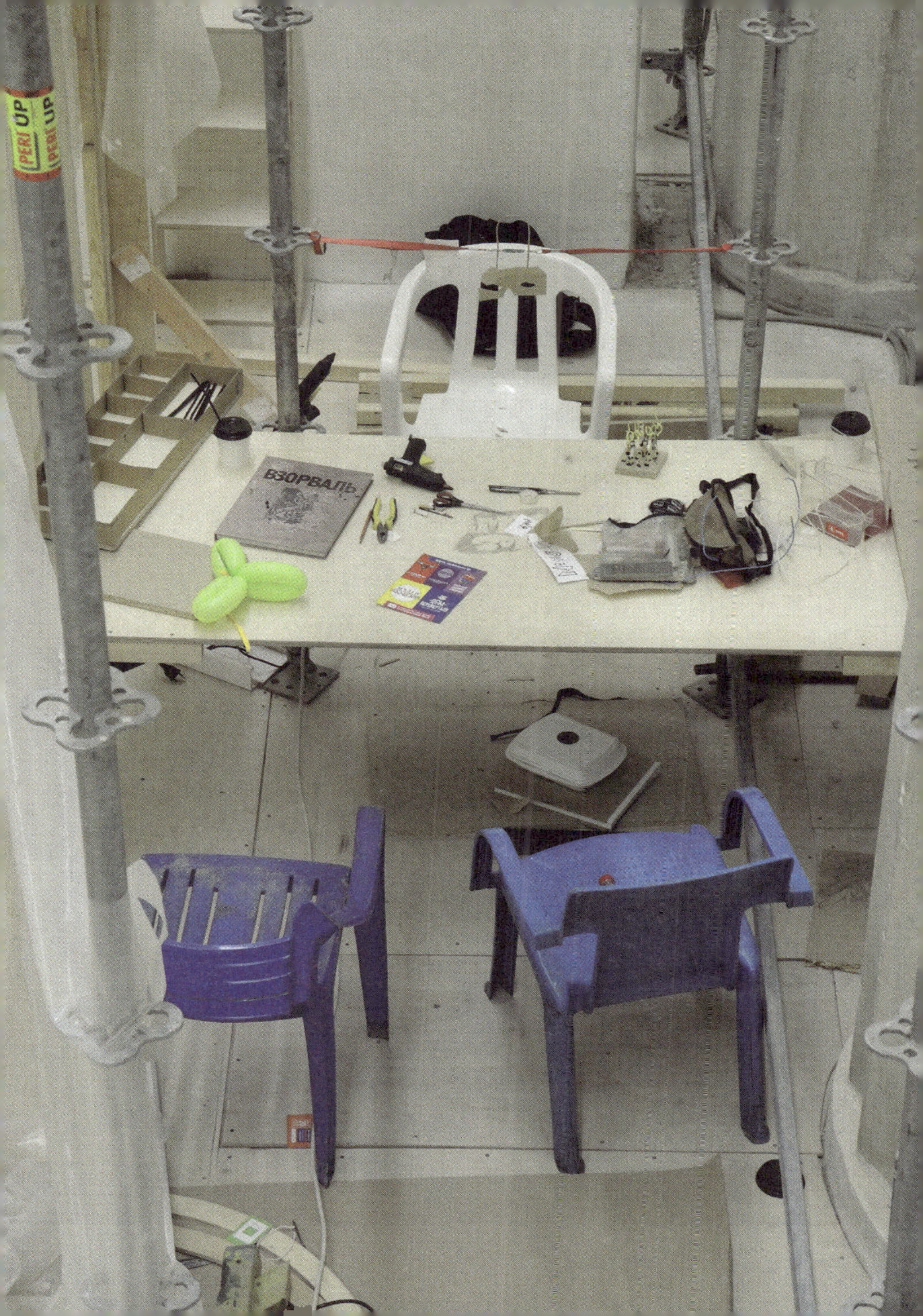
PERI UP
ВЗОРВАЛЬ

Evgeny Granilshchikov — Unfinished Film (Script)

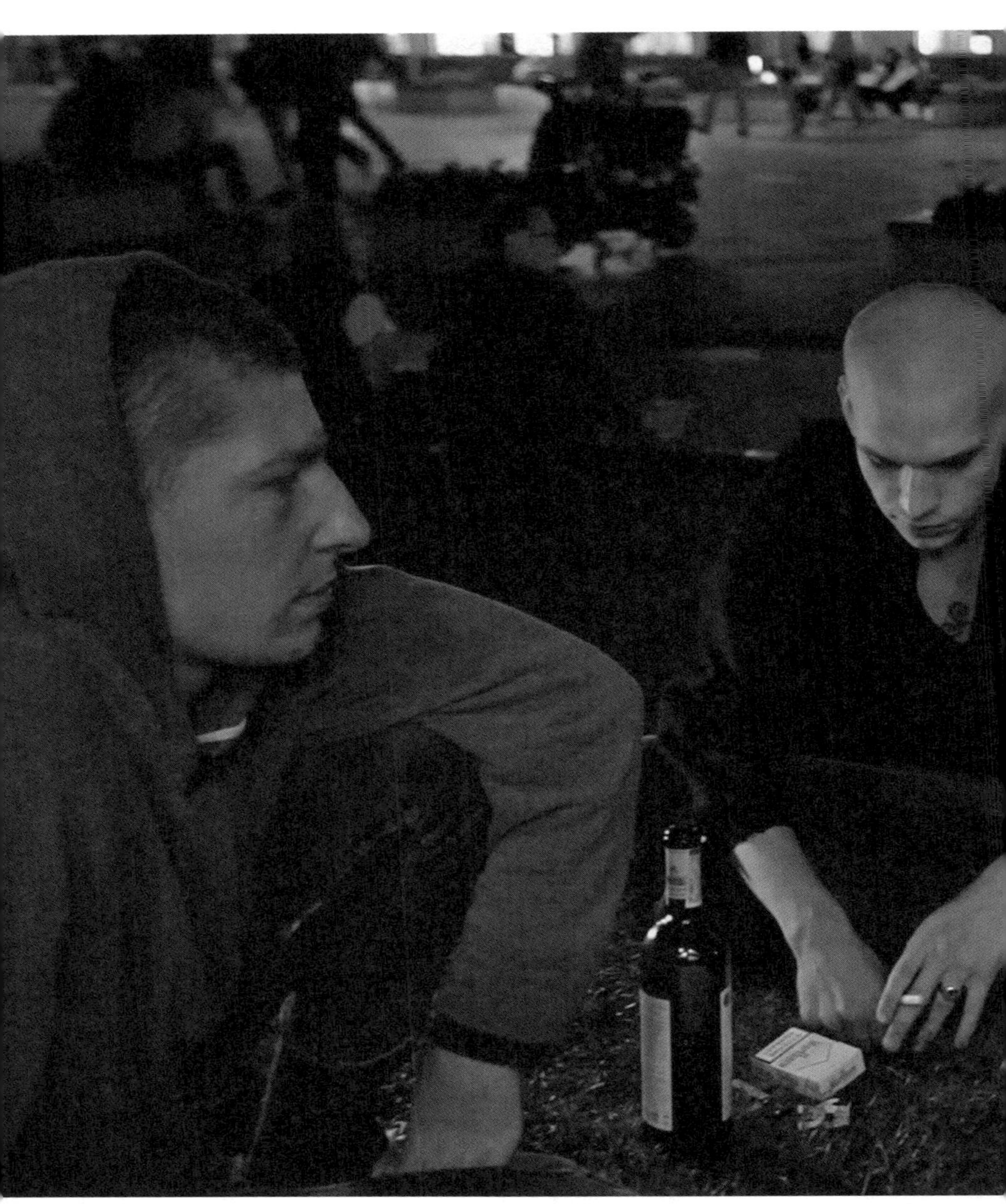

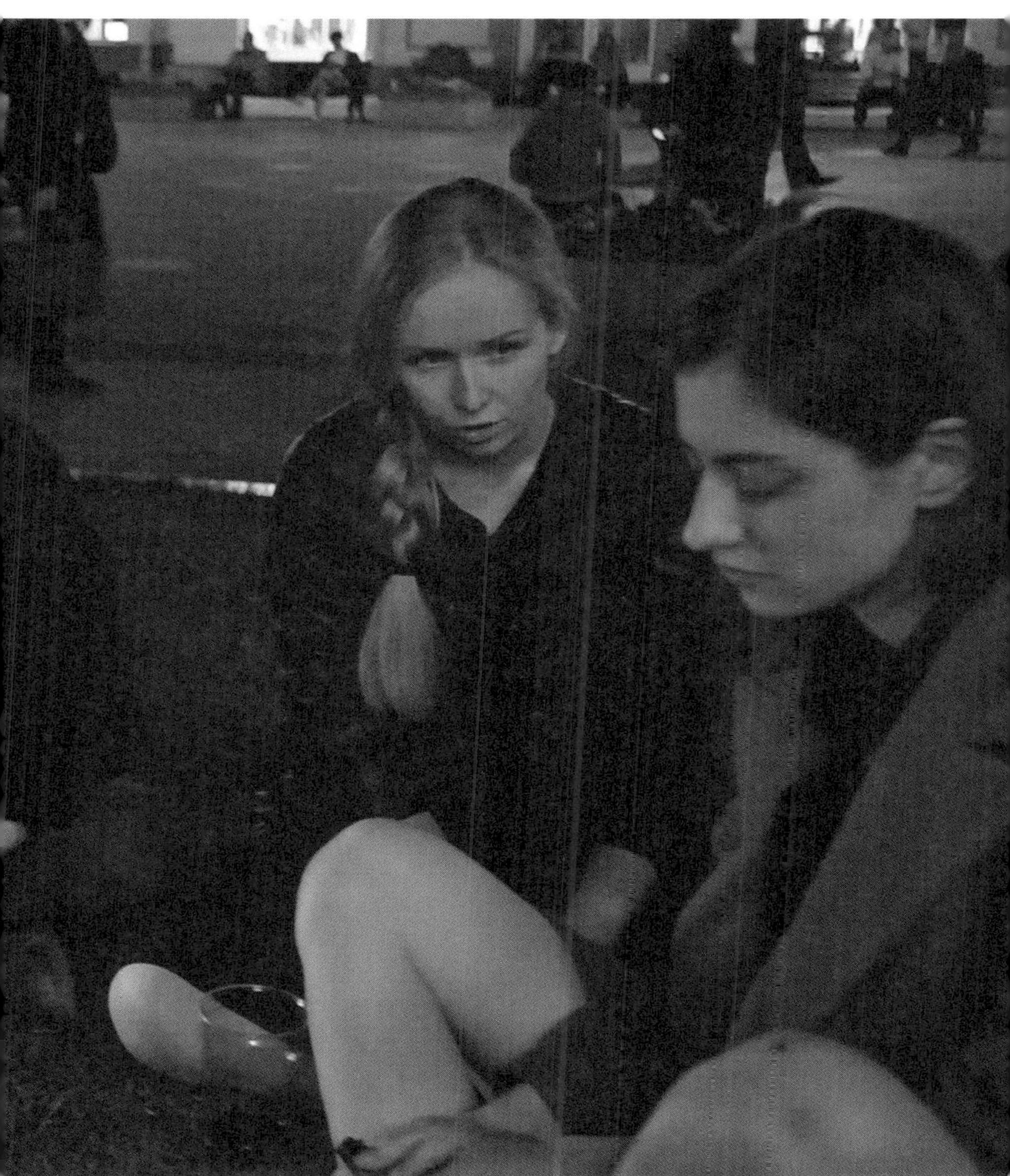

HyperComments will receive the following information:
open profile, list of friends, email address,
and personal description.

Dear Users, access to this resource has been denied.
Please accept our apologies.

Walking…
Downtown. Going back home…
There's nobody here… like early in the morning. Empty streets,
not a single person.
Like a curfew.
But I'm used to it.
Let's try by Friday.
Okay.
Bye.

There're two shops… one in Gazetny…
The other is opposite the Mayakovsky Theatre.
You can't turn into Gazetny here, ahead only, you see?
Maybe on the corner…?
Oh, it's closed.
And that one?
Can't see the widows from here, by the way.
How did these people drive from the other side? Don't understand.
Everything is blocked there.
I think it's totally blocked there.
They're from here… ooh… they're breaking the regulations…
Or maybe they drove from the office?
I do not understand.
Will they fine us for turning here?
Let me turn!
What's wrong with this shop?
I still can't see the windows…
It was hereabout.
Cool…

And this… this loss of some any kind of orientation… well…
Which was after the '90s… the common state of that progressive public
that they're against any ideology…

I often dream that I am in a city. Paris or Berlin, for example. In my dreams these places are much more beautiful than in real life. This makes me deliriously happy. Though sometimes I worry that I won't have time to visit all the sights before I need to leave again. Yeah, I often dream of travelling.

I had a flight at 4 am. I was so scared of being late that I arrived at the airport three hours in advance. I found my gate but didn't want to sit down in case I fell asleep, so I just walked and walked. Somehow I lost track of time. No idea how it happened, but by the time I looked at my watch the boarding gate was closed.

I ran and through the glass doors I could see that the plane was still on the tarmac, but they wouldn't let me board. I didn't hear them call my name because everything is really quiet there. So I went to the check-in desk and explained that I was late and told them to let me on the plane. The officer asked me a million questions about how I happened to be late, where I was, and what was I thinking. And I kept saying: "Can I just quickly board, since the plane is still here?" He started calling someone and it took like 15 minutes.

I went to the smoking lounge and almost suffocated. It was a tiny space filled with smokers. You could barely see through the smoke. I remember sitting down on the floor and thinking: I will probably suffocate in this smoking lounge and no one will ever know.

I'm on Tverskaya.
Say it again.
Can't hear you, bad connection.
In what square?
Wait, I'll go into a side street, it's more quiet there. It's heavy traffic, I don't hear you.
I say, it's heavy traffic.
At an intersection of Tverskaya and Kamergersky.
Say it again.
Bad connection, hey, I say bad connection.

And begin to understand that there's some kind of narrative, but we can't figure it out.
You know, we always create a narrative.
Of course we do, and here too. But we understand that it's inconceivable for us. It's the supreme narrative.
That's the point. Our guess gives a rise to the feeling that it is...
Of course.

Because there is a dialogue between the girl and the old man in the café...
Haven't you watched it yet?
Which was described... or wasn't described... by Sartre... never mind.
Yes, I watched it, yes, started watching but not... not... not until the end.

"—basically, I would like to radically express my views here, but I believe that today that's forbidden by the legislation of the Russian Federation."

Well, it's naturalism and total artificiality at the same time.
I wonder at what moment you suddenly find out that you don't understand if it's a play or an improvisation. Is it a character's own speech or is it a script?

And I want a little more connectedness. Like in a text, you know? There should be connectedness even if it's a stream of consciousness...

Courbet's using of the unusual verb *déboulonner*, that isn't registered in French dictionaries, has lately helped to defend him against accusations on the destruction of the column. André Gill suggested that the unusualness of the word itself pointed at the painter's indifference to the matter.

But for all that—it's written below—in the letter to his father by February 23, 1871, the painter says in a few words, "I wanted to tear the Vendôme Column down but couldn't get the consent

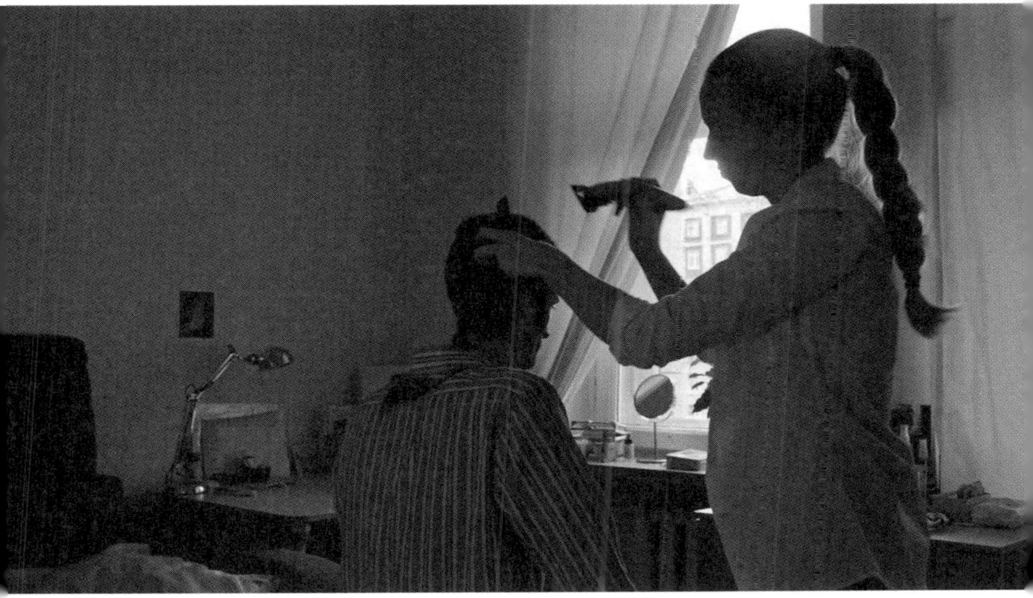

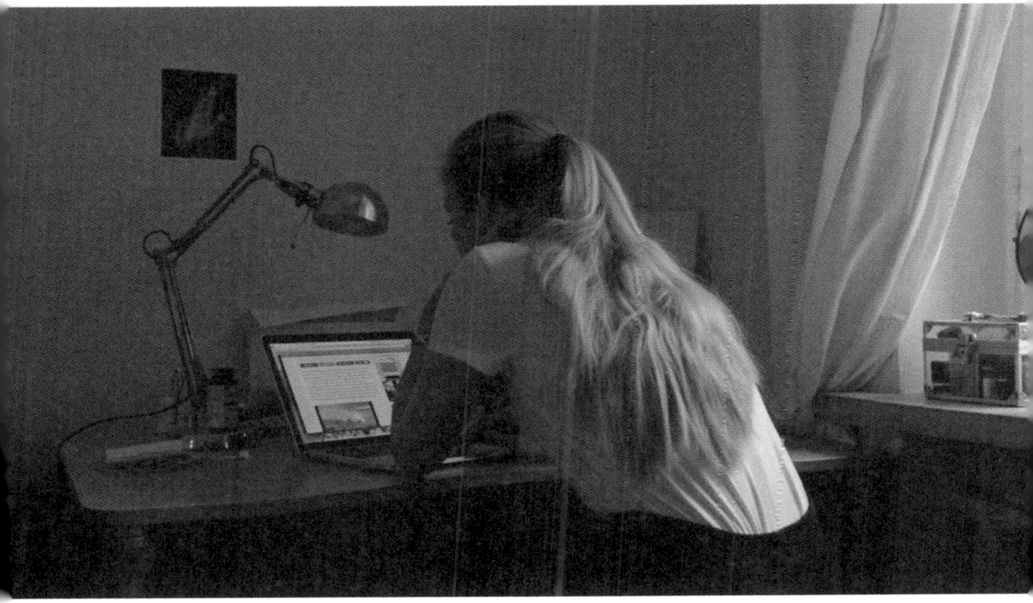

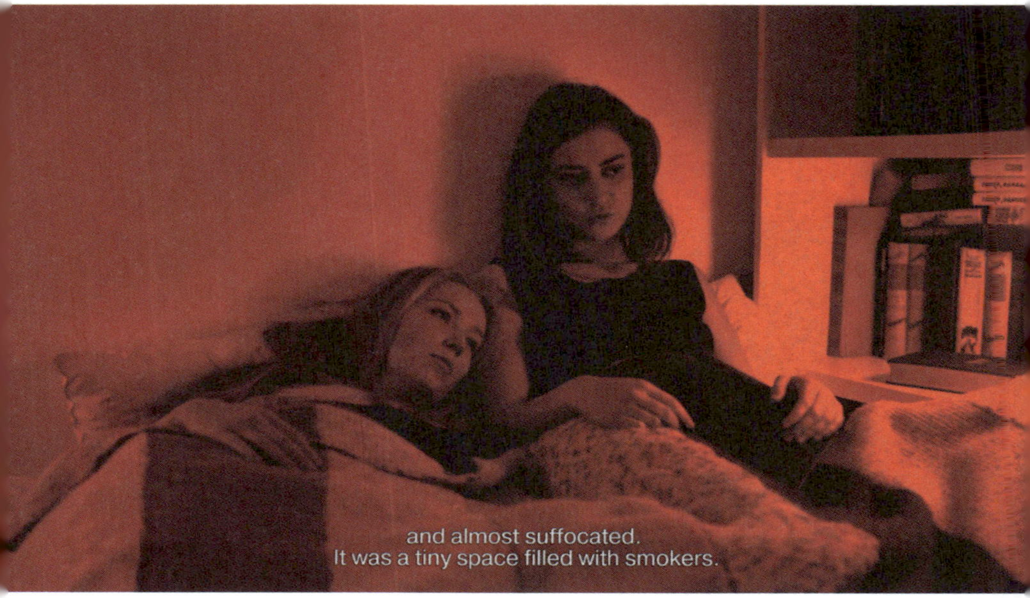

and almost suffocated.
It was a tiny space filled with smokers.

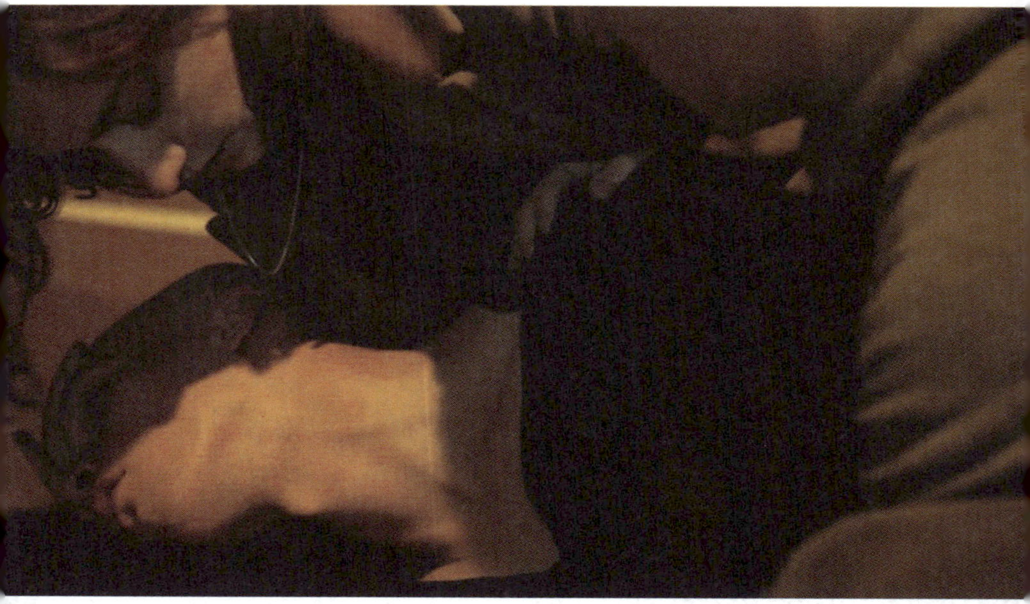

of the Government." The Vendôme Column was the main but not the only target of general indignation with the House of Bonaparte. Soon after the downfall of the Empire, the Government of National Defence took steps to prevent the crowd's destruction of other Empire relicts. About 5:30 p.m. several military bands of the National Guard, which were standing in the corners of the square from the side of Saint-Honoré, struck up *La Marseillaise*. Everything was ready for the wench to start and the rope pulling. It was in tension for several minute, then the column rocked. It leaned and suddenly broke to pieces that fell to the ground with a terrible noise, raising a dense cloud of dust. The viewers rushed to the giant fragments, climbing on them and looking at the lumps of stone. Several members of the Commune delivered short speeches, then they brought red banners from the staff and raised them on the column pedestal.

It's like three hours of infernal anguish, psychological American movie, Stanislavski's system and it's very boring… but I was watching. I don't understand why…

You have one new message.
Sunday. 9:58 am.
— Hi! I wanted to tell you something… Was going to send you an e-mail but…
Better do it by phone.
Just like face to face. But a little more one-way.
To be honest I was hoping that you wouldn't be at home. I thought it would be simpler.
But anyhow it's very awkward.
Oh, well, never mind. Sorry…

If now I hold some political views, it has all formed
because of the painful situation that had taken place in my family.

It would be very difficult for me to leave this country. And if I have to leave, I'll feel… don't know…

And all these taboo themes that are impossible to speak of.

About ten years have passed, but we still can't grasp the Chechen War, for example... Or all these May 6 events... They took place two years ago. And so what? How much did they get? Two or three years because they threw a plastic bottle at a policeman?!

So, nothing has come to an end. And all these actions, all this talking—it's our history. That's what I think. I don't play now. What's the reason of making a film if you don't touch these themes? Yes, it's direct, it absolutely stands out. But there's no any other opportunity. It's impossible not to speak about the plastic bottles. I don't play. This conversation is beyond the bounds of the film. It's not cinematic. Of course, you could have written about it in your script... That's what I want to say. What's the difference between speaking about May 6 prisoners in the words from your script or in my own words? Well, keep this scene for your film.

Jon Rafman — Erysichthon

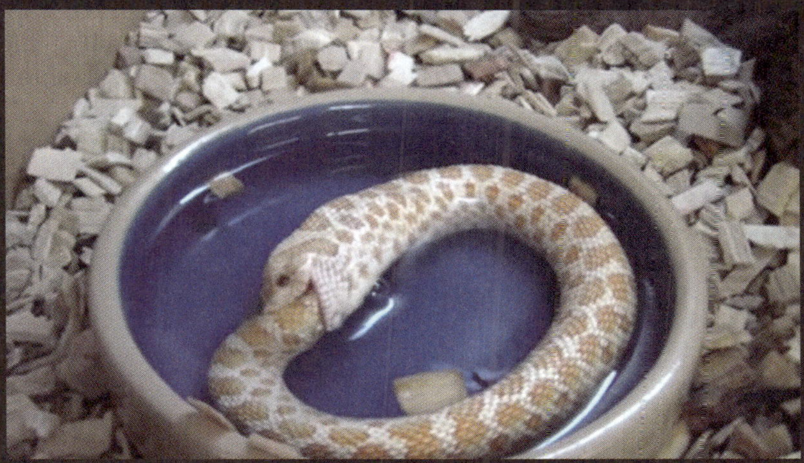

Jon Rafman, *Erysichthon*, 2008, HD video, 8 mins., still

Erysichthon, in Ovid's *Metamorphoses*, is a monarch who one day decides to fell a tree that is sacred to the goddess Demeter. When it won't fall, Erysichthon himself grabs an axe, knocks the head off his incapable servant and brings the tree down. Demeter revenges the act by sentencing Erysichthon to eternal hunger and insatiability. His never-ending hunger would get worse the more he ate. He finally lost all his property and even sold his daughter Mestra, until he finally ate himself.

Jon Rafman's video *Erysichthon* (2008) is composed of footage found online, taken from what you might call the dark net, deep net, hidden corners of the internet, an online landmass or simply a virtual world. The video begins with a shot of ferromagnetic putty swallowing a magnetic cube. Then, the camera wanders along circular server racks. Masks and motifs of self-cannibalism follow, until we see a child on a 360° swing circling around. The unnerving footage, such as that of a snake eating itself, speaks of self-destruction and circular rhythms as well as an endlessness of things. Possibly a reference to the constant consumption of media, news, images, knowledge and information, the video actually never leads to expulsion. It causes a gruelling physical reaction that may lead to one's incapability to watch the video in loop.

Curiously, one still feels drawn into the work. There is no dramatic peak or ending to the video, nor are the clippings decrypted. The *Ouroboros*, a circular icon of a snake eating itself, repeatedly pops up in the video: symbolising an ultimate form of living being, it has no beginning or end. It eats, digests and re-consumes itself, to exist as an auto-entity independent of any surrounding. The Ouroboros symbolises unity, autonomy and infinity through a circular repetition of life's phases. [Marie Egger]

Michelangelo Pistoletto — Third Paradise Moscow, 23rd September 2015

This is the symbol of rebirth, of the *third paradise*. It means there have been two earlier paradises. One circle symbolises the first paradise, where human beings lived totally in accord with nature. The second symbolises the paradise that has been produced up until today by a humanity which has escaped nature. It is distant from the first paradise.

The third paradise is the one we need to build today in order to overcome the distance between the first paradise and the second; in order to mix the natural and the artificial into a third situation that did not exist before.

We need to be able to create a new world departing from the two different situations humanity has previously arrived at. We are thus now entering a third stage of humanity. That new stage needs to be organised to enable the creation of new situations that have never existed before.

The symbol for the third paradise comprises three circles and is based on the symbol of infinity, which as you know consists of two circles. Infinity as a concept is familiar to all of us, but it is volatile; it escapes and you cannot grasp it. Similar to freedom; in theory it sounds fantastic, but you cannot touch it.

In order to make both ends meet, you need to add something to the centre. And that is finity. I felt that the infinity symbol needed some help in between its two circles — a third one — that would represent our life in the world.

Why?

Because we have a constant necessity to put together two different situations, two different conditions, two different elements — that may even be opposite. All those oppositions create conflicts and war. So, to develop a concept of peace, for instance, you have to find a way of combining differences and opposites in a new way.

That is why I use the symbol in relation to a project I call *The Trinamic Concept,* which simply refers to the dynamics of the number three. These dynamics are a creation project. Bearing the potential to overcome the duality of two elements, a central third element is created, which did not previously exist. In chemistry, hydrogen and oxygen are two separate gases but together they create water. United, the two colours blue and yellow create green.

Two voices together create a third voice, a harmony. Masculine and feminine are representative of the two opposites, but if you put them together, you have a child, a third person that did not exist before. Socio-political situations may be described the same way: When two oppositions clash or are in contrast, it may result in war. But we need to find ways of producing and creating something that is the result of an aesthetic and moral solution. That is why this sign, for me, symbolises creation. And I am convinced you can apply this principle to everything. There is always a potential for something new.

The concept may be applied to politics, economy, in education… It enables you to think between systems and try to make connections with them. Between spirituality and politics, for example, or economics and education. It is an attempt to find a way to combine opposites. When teaching in school I usually propose that when you have something in mind, you stop for a moment and look for the opposite of what you were thinking of doing. Then try to make a productive combination of the two.

This project, the symbol I have created, is not something I sell. I prefer to think of it as a certain way of thinking or something that may be used by anyone. I activate the symbol with people. We have also created extensions through other people.

On December 21, 2012, the day that was spoken of as the end of the world according to the Maya calendar—the world was definitely not going to end. Nevertheless, it was an occasion to reflect on our current situation and there is no doubt that we are in a bad condition. With so many crises in the world and a certain way of using our capacities of creating and producing (in science, technology and economics) we are destroying our planet. We are working against nature, one of the two principles. So, in a condition where the artificial is going against the natural we are obliged to find a way to balance the two extremes. We may call this the last day of the world or the first day of the world. A spring, a renaissance. That is why we started to work with the concept and these conditions in many different places. What came out of it was the *Embassy of Rebirth*.

In fact, the idea of rebirth is integrated in the symbol. Thinking that we may have had two births, a natural one and a cultural one, the third time—the third paradise or the third circle, if you will—would result from a combination of the two opposites, creating a third future life. And the moment for that is now.

On the day of the 21st December, many people held big parties. When you celebrate, you do something that is connecting and creating a meaning for something. People were participating everywhere and we hoped that this might help to develop an idea of the capacity for understanding each other in that project of change, of evolution, and of the third condition that has to start from now on, for the future. The sign is thus giving a prospective, saying "We have to go, we have a goal and we have an expectation. And we have to work for that."

Thus, today, we have a job for everybody. A big job for everybody in the world to do something to change the world itself. And that is not something any artist or anyone else could do alone. We have to start from pairs of two. There is always someone in front of us, somebody else who we can arrange to have a creation with, and between. That is what we have to find.

I think the direction this Biennale is taking is going exactly along that way. With the aim of a condition to work together, to meet one another and start to talk and ask: "I'm doing this, what are you doing?" So, what is important is acting. To feel we are finally acting and will find a territory that did not exist before. It will enable this to go on. And that is the moment of creation.

This creation is what the formula of the third paradise aims for. And it is not at all exclusive but may be used by anybody, as well as artists. In the twentieth century, we arrived at individual freedom. Everybody can do something. Artists make fantastic solutions, big surprises and so forth. But I think that this freedom has not changed the world. It was a big revolution in individuality and authority, really. Nevertheless, it was an important revolution because, finally, the artist has the possibility of not being a slave to any religious or political concept of society. The revolution of the individual was an incredible success because it gave artists autonomy and freedom. But now we have to go back to society and make use of the autonomy and freedom in our hands and recognise them for the responsibility they are.

Without responsibility, freedom will not grasp anything in society. We have to offer opportunities to participate in the job of creation to everyone. Starting from schools and childhood. Personally, I may help in thinking about changing the world, but it is the youth, the children of today, who will work over the next 20 years and create something. If we're not giving them the capacity to be able to create, nothing will change. They will keep on fighting as before.

It is the transformation of fights and conflicts into production, into ideas in practical life that I have always been interested in. Through artistic projects in all the different fields of social life. But now we really have to do it, not just consider it in theory.

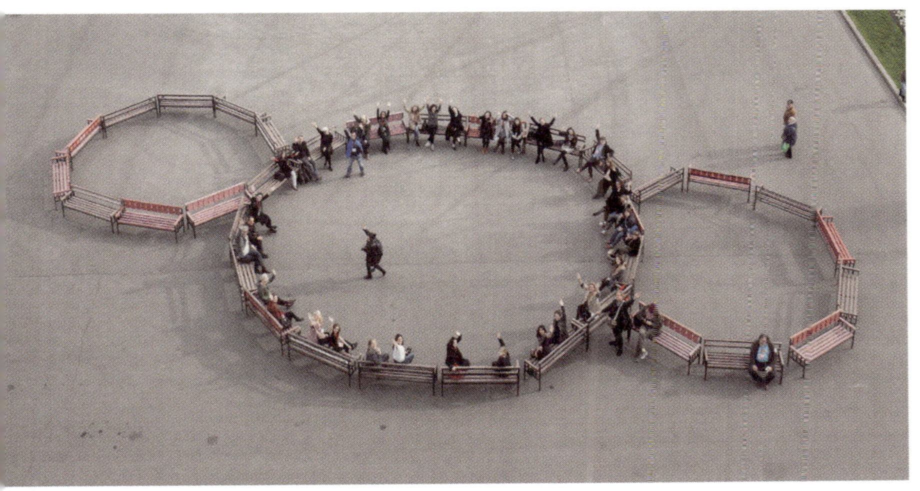

The team of Moscow Biennale 2015 gathered in Michelangelo Pistoletto's installation *Third Paradise*, 2015

Konstantin Zvezdochotov — The Unbearable Luxury of Communal Living

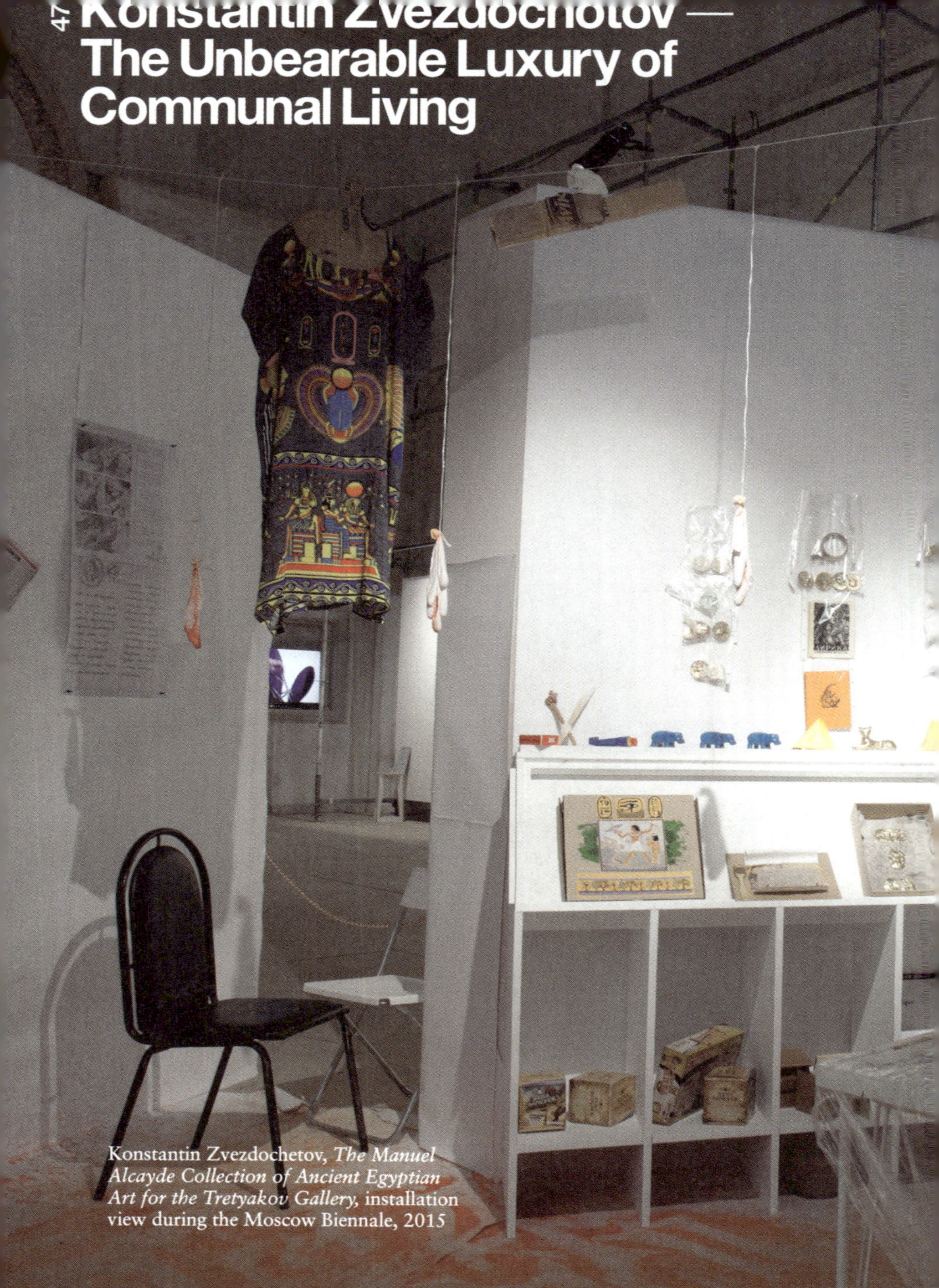

Konstantin Zvezdochetov, *The Manuel Alcayde Collection of Ancient Egyptian Art for the Tretyakov Gallery*, installation view during the Moscow Biennale, 2015

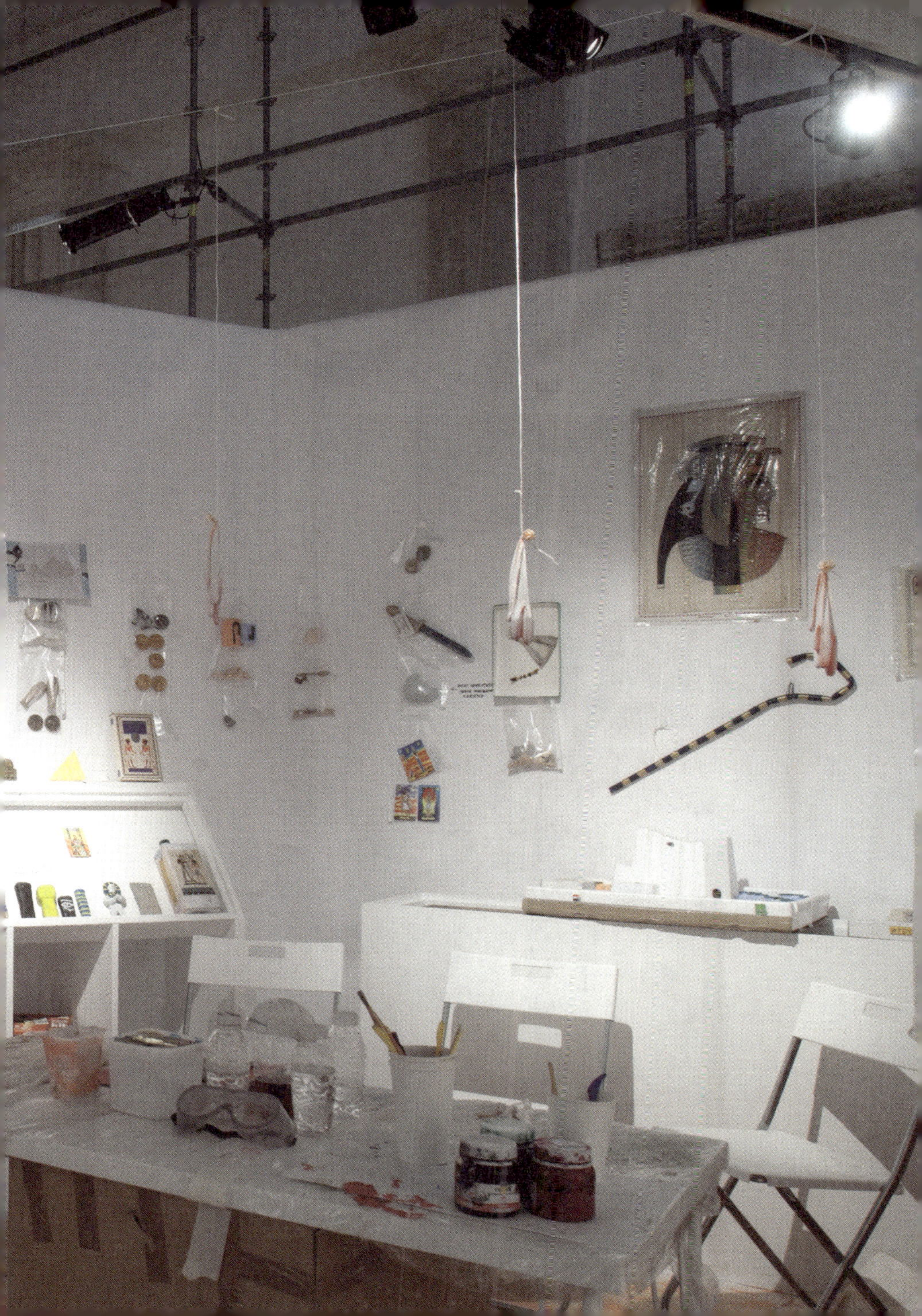

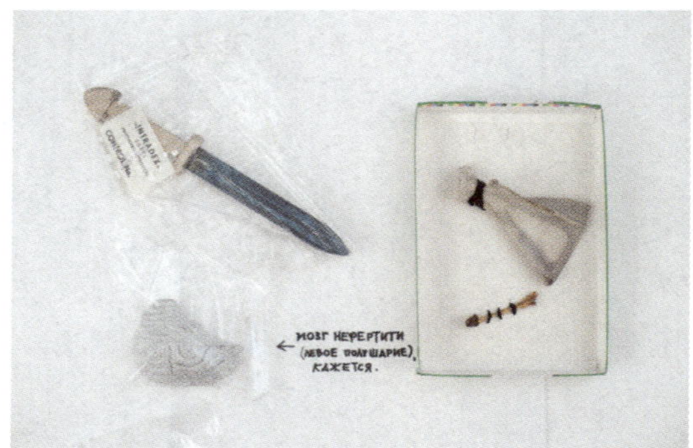

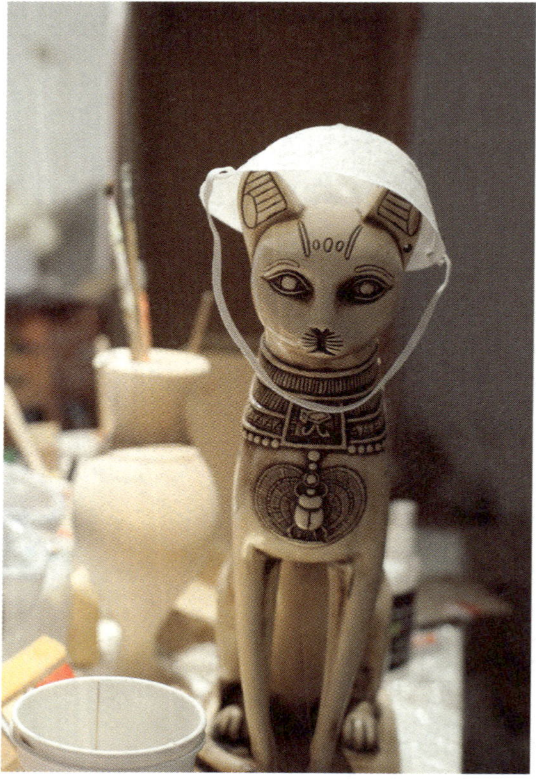

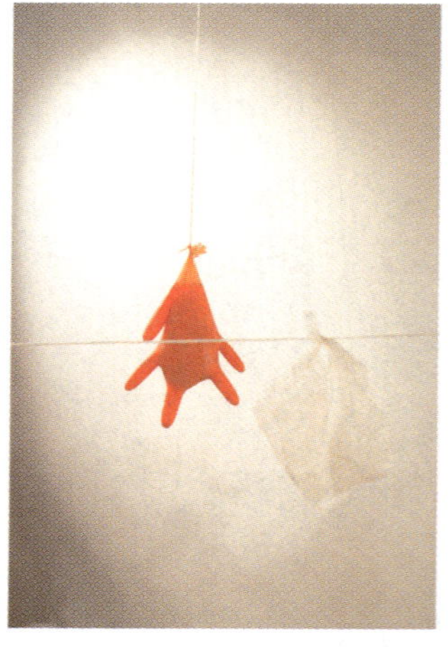

↑→
Konstantin Zvezdochetov, *The Manuel Alcayde Collection of Ancient Egyptian Art for the Tretyakov Gallery*, 2015

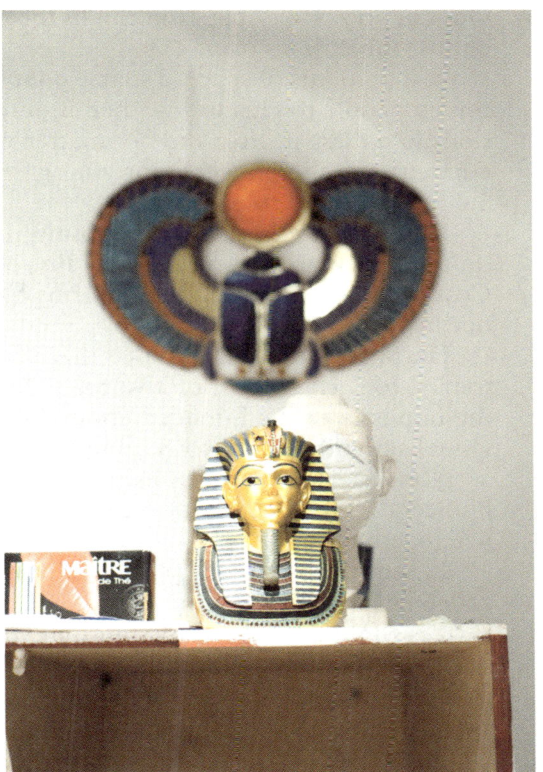
MaîtRE
de Thé

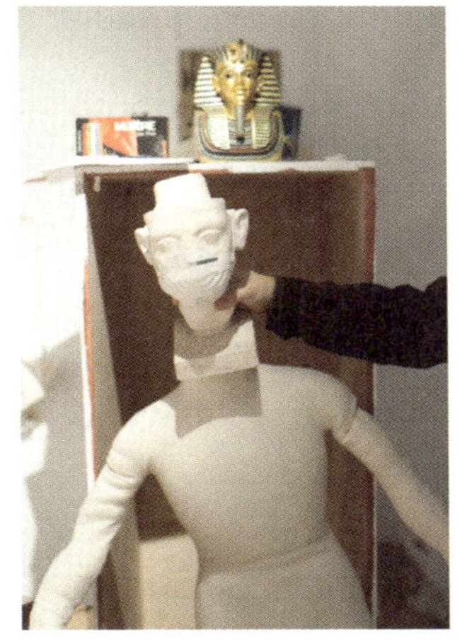

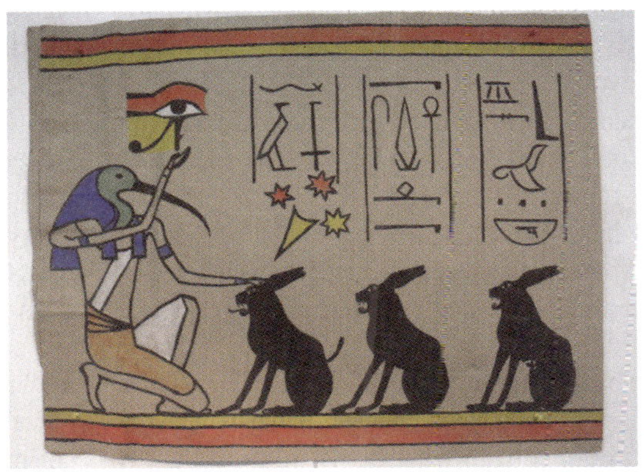

Our country is very big. You can fit the rest of Europe into Russia almost three times over.

Vast amounts of space, a sparse population and a harsh climate forced people to cluster together, if only to keep warm. In situations like these it often did not matter who you were, what your ethnicity or religion were, nor your gastronomic preferences. We ate what we had to eat.

Therefore the peasant community in Russia was something quite particular, and more generally, all kinds of gangs, artels, Cossack troops and collective farms have figured constantly in our history.

The Soviet state exacerbated this aspect of our way of life and took it to such a point of absurdity that it has sometimes led to the opposite of the intended effect, expressed in hysterical individualism and misanthropy.

Nonetheless, dormitories, communal apartments and both Pioneers' and concentration camps strengthened the instinct to live together.

At the risk of coming across as categorical, I would say that collectivism and pluralism are in our blood.

It is therefore not surprising that the collaboration between our group and our Cuban friends began precisely in one such dormitory, which was home to students from all over the world studying at theatrical and art institutions.

Our mutual curiosity and interest in the arts led to us moving on from discussion to action.

Among the Cubans, one particularly active individual in this regard was Manuel Alcayde. At first, he took part in the events and exhibitions of the Mukhomor group, then in the activities of AptArt, and, finally, began to emerge as an independent artist in his own right.

Aside from that, there were so many activities (*The White Snow of Russia*, *Moscow—a Port to Five Seas*, etc.) that he and I organised together.

Largely, however, we spent our time on sheer invention and harangues. Since we were lazy and did not have the technical ability to realise our conceptions, a large part of these projects remained ideas.

Among them was a project called *Collections of Ancient Egyptian Art*. We planned that the exhibition would consist of all kinds of kitsch objects which had been inspired by this theme. It would also include souvenirs brought back from Egypt, boxes, wrappers and crafts made by various unknown oddballs.

Naturally, like any other self-respecting conceptualists (which we considered ourselves to be at that time), we grounded everything in theoretical foundations.

It was like that this time too. Since 1980 we have existed in a kind of informational vacuum, we've had to resort to home grown theorising, perhaps thereby reinventing the wheel. Nonetheless, it was with the greatest degree of importance that we came up with the following pearls of wisdom:

1. Text, which has lost its original meaning and context, passes into the aesthetic plane.
   Example: Ornament and Egyptian hieroglyphics, having ceased to be sacred texts in the mass consciousness, have become a kind of decorative embellishment.
2. Contemporary culture is the culture of reproduction.
   Example: The inhabitants of Siberia do not necessarily need to go to Paris so as to have some idea of *La Gioconda*.
3. Time is illusory, but at the same time people fetishise it, for completely understandable reasons.
   Example: On the one hand, the Parthenon and the Pantheon are — for the majority — almost the same age, while on the other hand, an antique lamp costs more than a lamp from the supermarket.

The fourth postulate was wholly leftist: The majority of the greatest creations have had anonymous makers and are works of collective creation. The establishment of the idea of authorship is a product of capitalism, individualism and commerce.

Based on this profoundly abstruse reasoning, we began to collect. Because of our lack of discipline, the collection turned out to be unsystematic and disjointed. Often our relatives would throw away these artefacts as rubbish. Objects simply got lost among the clutter of everyday life. Then I was drafted into the army, and Manuel left for Cuba. We lost contact and it all came to an end.

35 years later, when Bart invited me to take part in the Biennale, I suddenly remembered our 'Egyptian project' and decided, finally, to realise it. In my mind it was very well suited, both in subject and in its embodied form, to what was going to happen in the main pavilion at VDNKh. What impressed me about

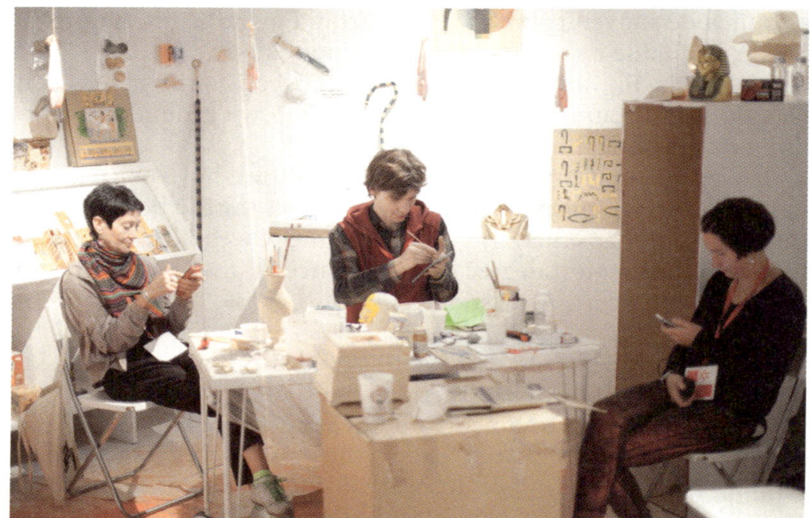

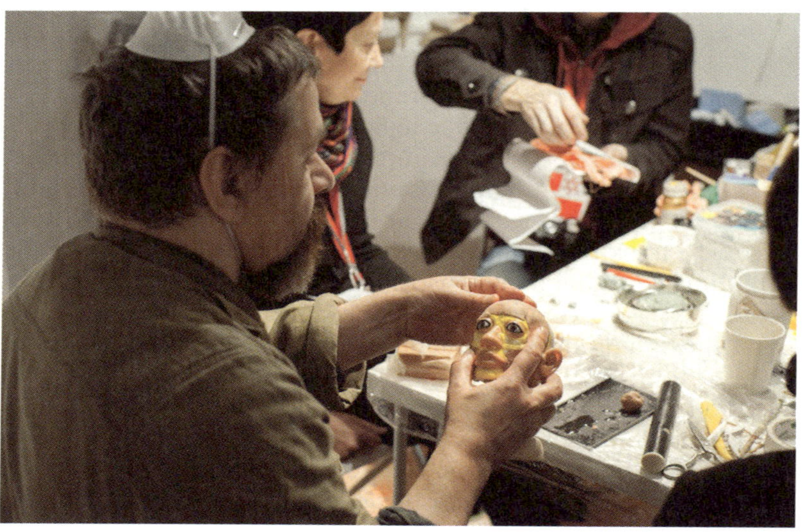

Konstantin Zvezdochetov, *The Manuel Alcayde Collection of Ancient Egyptian Art for the Tretyakov Gallery*, 2015

the project was that the problems of authorship, nationality and artistic value were carried through to the point of idiocy. See for yourselves. This was a Russo-Cubano-Egyptian contrivance, put together either from things made in a 'Skilful Hands' children's club, or from all sorts of junky souvenirs brought from home.

The absurdity of it all was compounded by the fact that all of this rubbish was then passed on to the Tretyakov Gallery as a 'Collection of Ancient Egyptian art' — a place that, as is well known, is a collection made up exclusively of all manner of Russian and Soviet exhibits. I was happy about the thought of such a collection appearing in our national art museum, since this is something that is clearly lacking there, and which makes it inferior to the Louvre and to the British Museum. We accordingly formed a wonderful team that coped extremely well with the task at hand.

As the years pass, I more and more rarely feel a sense of euphoria from my own work. At the Biennale, however, I was accompanied for months by a sense of gladness while co-creating and informally communicating with audiences. This time was filled with genuine drive, enthusiasm, warmth and solidarity, for which I thank everyone.[1]

The Manuel Alcayde Collection of Ancient Egyptian Art for the Tretyakov Gallery

Arina Balantseva
Evgenia Veselova
Denis Sychov
Konstantin Zvezdochotov
Pavel Kuznetsov
Alexander Petrelli
Sasha Sam
Dmitry Shagin
Tatyana Shagina
Alexander Postikov
Leyla Sultan
Ekaterina Bermont
Anna Nepsha
Masha Ivanova

1
PS. Manuel Alcayde now lives in Mozambique. I think that he too would be very pleased with this.

Burak Arikan — The Graph Commons Journal

This is a three-part guide on mapping, understanding, and analysing networks. We will focus on the design and understanding of complex networks through mapping and visual analysis in order to expand your thinking about the network as a creative and critical medium.

PART ONE
CREATIVE AND CRITICAL USE OF COMPLEX NETWORKS

1. Understanding complex systems

Complexity is characterised as something with many autonomous parts interacting with each other in multiple ways. The signalling of neurons in our body, the messaging of devices in the telecommunication infrastructure, transactions between agents in markets, and social formations among people are some generic examples of complex systems.

If we want to understand a complex system, we first need a map of its relationship diagram that is composed of the nodes and links which make a network form. By nature, that form is the fabric of most complex systems:

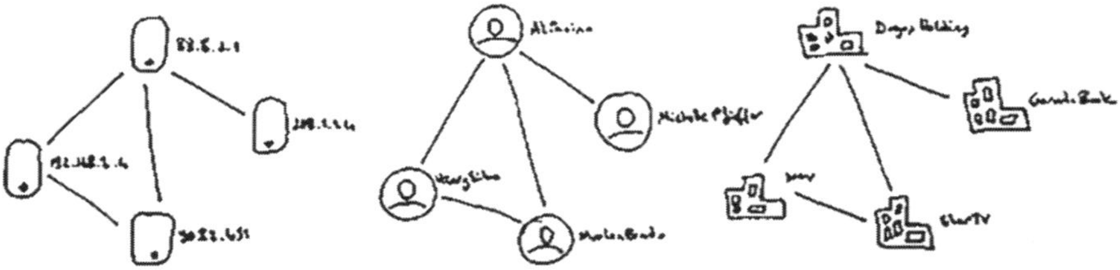

A network diagram like these offers a common language that is both visual and mathematical. This way, from a network map, we can obtain qualitative information by reading its actors and relations, as well as carry out quantitative analysis by computing its connection structure. In fact, we can use this common language to study systems that may differ widely in their nature, appearance, or scope. For example, three rather different systems—1) devices sending messages to each other, 2) film actors connected by appearance in the same movies, and 3) organisations connected through partnerships—may have exactly the same network structure. While the nature of the nodes and the links differs widely, each network has the same graphic representation, consisting of 4 nodes and 4 links. We can use this simple method to begin studying a variety of complex systems.

2. Why is network logic significant today?

Why do networks specifically matter today, after having existed in every society in history? It is known that 3,000 years ago the ancient Phoenician and Greek colonies formed their trade routes and built a network of harbours in the Mediterranean Sea. Today, in the same geography, submarine cables carry messages and enable a global communication system.

What we have today is not just networks as analogue or bare life happenings, but networks that are digitised, in the same way that many aspects of life are now digitised. Thus, networks matter today because electronic and software-based communication systems have made networks measurable. Only in this day and age are networks able to reach a global scale and infiltrate every part of our life. With today's advanced information technologies, the metrics of network effect have become trackable and measurable even in one's daily life, while at the same time structuring the social world as such.

3. Use of complex networks

In fact, we all experience the network effect: from email to e-commerce, from social networking to banking, from telecommunication to transportation. We all acknowledged the fact that the world is more complex than ever. It feels both flat (we can reach anyone any time) and chaotic (our inbox is inundated with information from all directions.) Sometimes we are opportunistic about the Internet, talking about it as a global good,—and other

2

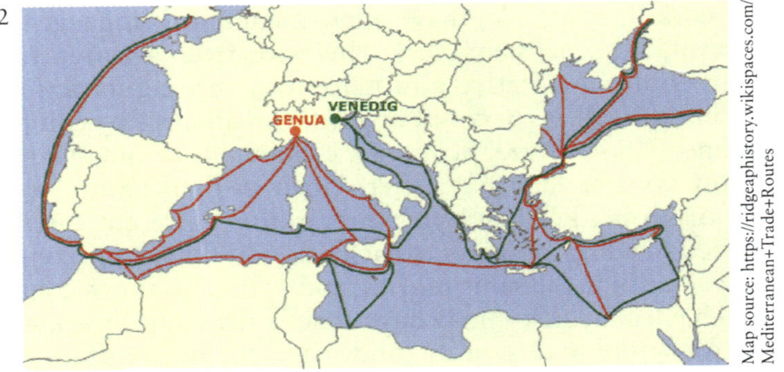

Map source: https://ridgeaphistory.wikispaces.com/Mediterranean+Trade+Routes

From the Phoenicians and Ancient Greeks to the merchants of the Italian city states, mariners formed trade routes crisscrossing the Mediterranean.

3

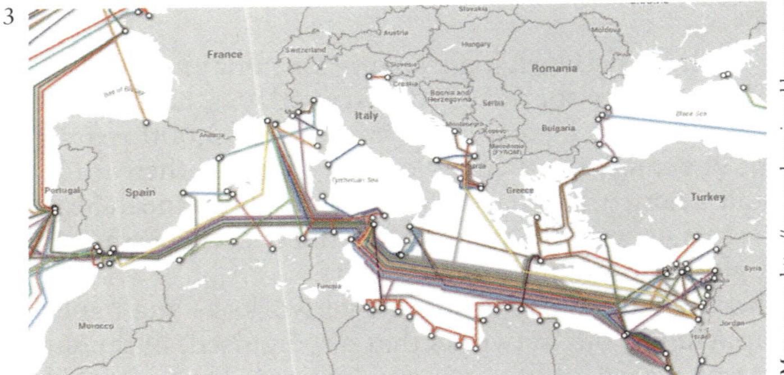

Map source: http://www.submarinecablemap.com

Today, in the same geography, submarine cables are enabling a global communication system.

4

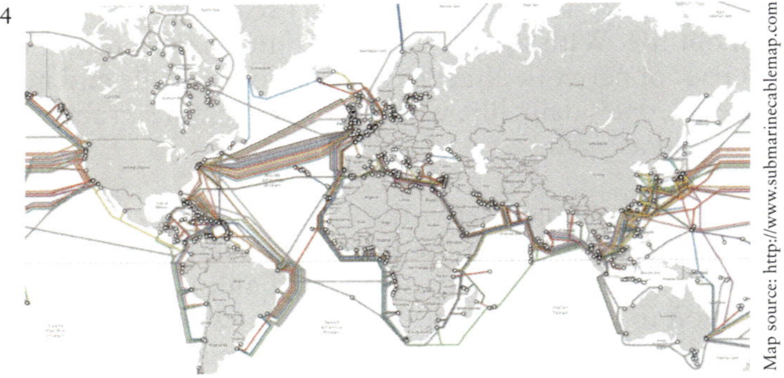

Map source: http://www.submarinecablemap.com

Only in this day and age are networks able to reach a global scale and infiltrate every part of our life.

times we are pessimistic, knowing that we are all under surveillance all the time. In such an antagonistic world that is at once flat and chaotic, the question arises again: Where does power reside and circulate?

Additionally, the state's tactics of monitoring its own citizens in partnership with certain corporations through what has been called 'big data', the NSA leaks, etc., have also attracted our attention towards an inaccessible but quite magical tool of knowing and predicting what people want. This indeed was possible through understanding the interrelated or linkable structure of the information generated by many, but only open to the reach of a handful of institutions. In other words, network logics have been mystified in the eyes of the public. Only experts in certain fields have aggregated a large amount of data and used scientific tools for visualising and analysing it on a relational basis. Neither the relational data nor the tools for visualisation or analysis are accessible to common people.

However, it is a myth that common people have no access to data. Yet, we are the data for the governments and corporations who continuously sense our activity. In fact, interconnecting individual data points around us (the collective mapping of relationships that we can observe) would indeed render complex structures visible and thus discussible. Together we can map relationships and unfold the issues that impact us and our communities. Graph Commons is a step towards allowing you to do so.[5]

5 At Graph Commons, you can collectively compile data about the topics you are interested in; define and categorise relations, and map the issues that impact you and your community on a user-friendly interface. Graph Commons members have been using the platform for investigative journalism, data research, civic activism, strategising, organisational analysis, curating content, etc.

PART TWO
MAPPING NETWORKS

1. Understanding the field—
Who are the dominant actors in the field?

The first question should be what actors there are in the field that you are interested in researching. The actors can vary from real persons to concepts, and from institutions to inanimate objects. Let's say that a researcher is interested in fish farms, the market relations between the farms and the vendors, and how this ecosystem of fishing operates in its processual cycle. The reproduction of fish would then not only rely upon the human subjects in the field, but would also rely on companies that produce fish meal or the fish themselves. In other words, you first have to investigate and list the actants within your field.

2. Detecting the actors and relationships—
What are the critical relationships that can scale?

The second step is to come up with relations that make interaction possible between the actors. These could be interactions like sending emails, collaborating, and influencing, or affiliations such as being a member, belonging to a category, and similarity. For instance, if one is interested in understanding the lobbying activities of a certain pressure group, one would expect to find official as well as organic links that make up the bigger social network. Another relation one would expect to detect would be bribery, which is neither organic nor official in nature. It is therefore a good idea to start with an educated guess as to what kind of relations one might encounter. However, it is also vital not to assume the categories beforehand and overlook the ones that we are deliberately not pursuing. Also, remember that the number of actors can also be limited by your definition of your field and research topic.

There are roughly four general categories for thinking about relationships:

	Transmission Networks: Something actually flows. Water flows, electricity flows, money flows, news flows… Usually physical, and the flow could be broken like a pipe.
	Interaction Networks: Connection is an event, with a specific time. I email you, I buy something, we do an exhibition together… Something passed on during a contact. Explicit.
	Attribution Networks: Connection is an expression of a relationship. You are my friend, I love you, you trust him, she recognises you… Visible only if you state it.
	Affiliation Networks: Connection is a belonging to a group or category. We are in the same school, things are in the same category, organisations are connected by board members… Linked by correlation, similarity, or membership. Implicit.

The relationships you choose will more or less fall into one of these categories. Needless to say, these categories are here to give you guidance to start thinking about relationships, and you can get creative and introduce other relationships outside these categories.

3. Compiling data & making the map

Start gathering data after you have listed the actor and relation types. The best way to organise your data is to put it into a spreadsheet. Use the Graph Commons 'Data Table' feature, which turns your data into a self-organising diagram as you edit. In fact, you can visually add nodes and relations just by clicking on the map canvas.

Alternatively, you can use the Graph Commons spreadsheet template (https://docs.google.com/spreadsheets/d/13sV8DAROJKfGmkb4olOea4-vPVnBMGv8CrtbR1L8RJw/edit#gid=0) to organise your edges and nodes by importance. If you prefer the external spreadsheet option, you will find two separate sheets in the template, one sheet for nodes, and a second sheet for relationships, which will have a column structure as below.

Nodes Table

Simply a list of nodes by rows and their properties by columns.

#	Type	Name	Description	Website	Location	Age
1	Person	Sarah Wilson	Artist	sarah.com	New York	27
2	Person	Ahmad Suphi	Lawyer	asuphi.com	Beirut	41
3	Person	John Travolta	Actor	john.com	London	52

Edges Table

A list of relations—in each row, on the left, from node types and names, on the right to node type and names, and at the centre a single column Edge Type to represent the relationship in between. You can also add weight if you need to.

#	Node Type	Node Name	Edge Type	Node Type	Node Name	Edge Weight
1	Person	Sarah Wilson	Collaborates	Person	Ahmad Suphi	1
2	Person	Ahmad Suphi	Collaborates	Person	John Travolta	1
3	Person	John Travolta	Likes	Person	John Travolta	2

Hand drawing the network that you can now see before your eyes, after your attempts at taxonomisation of the field, helps a lot. Start by drawing circles, writing names and connecting them with lines, from which you can generate a sketch for your network map. This way the nodes and edges will appear to you as they have been slowly emerging while you were listing the actors and relationships.

Your hand-made diagram will get messy pretty quickly. You need to transfer your work to a computer simulation, where things can get organised. The network map on Graph Commons is a self-organising physics simulation program, where the layout is organised based on the connections, showing both similarities and differences between nodes, highlighting central as well as peripheral actors, and revealing organic clusters that you would normally not be able to see.

4. Collaborating on Graph Commons

We get the most out of mapping when we interconnect our partial knowledge about a given issue and build a bigger picture together. Invite collaborators to your graphs, get notified when your collective work is updated, and reuse existing data by cloning nodes from others' graphs.

Graph Commons supports asynchronous collaboration, which means you can clone an existing node to your own graph and incrementally expand from there. This way, you can make mashups of existing and new data points. You will be notified when someone clones your nodes, so that you can track its journey and possibly merge back new data points into your graphs and hopefully start new collaborations.[6]

6 The Graph Commons Interface: See the video tutorials here (https://vimeo.com/graphcommons/videos).

PART THREE
READING AND ANALYSING NETWORK MAPS

We can start analysing a network map by examining its centrality and clustering metrics. Here are some of the concepts for reading and analysing networks in a single image:

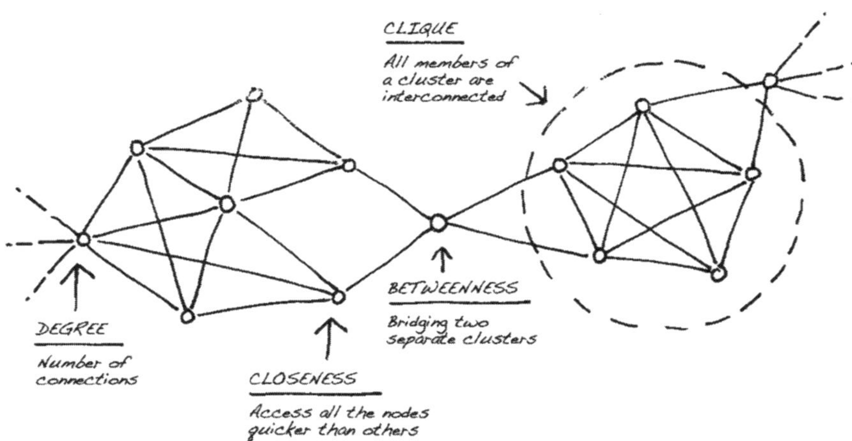

Centrality:
Who are the most important actors and what are their locations in the network? Centrality measure is not just the number of connections an actor has. The question is rather how much of a bridge role a node has between clusters, and how close it is to other members of the network. Who are the connectors and leaders, who bridges, who isolates? What is the position of actors within clusters? Who are in the core of the network, and who are on the periphery?

Clusters :
What organic groups or clusters exist in a network? Discovering clusters of nodes which have more connections to one another than they do to outsiders. You can name the clusters by looking at who are in them. The structural holes between the clusters as well as the bridges between them are as important as the clusters themselves.

Equivalency :
Which actors are alike? Determining actors who play a similar role and have similar positions. These show us alternative paths, as well as redundancy in the network. Refers to the extent to which actors have a common set of linkages to other actors in the system.

Shortest Paths:
What is the distance between two actors? What indirect relationships exist? Revealing normally invisible connections and the degrees of separation between actors.

Graph Density:
How well is a network connected, compared to other networks? Comparing density of networks, as well as connectivity of different regions within a single network.

Graph Diameter:
What is the longest path in the network? Finding the reach, that is, how long it will take at most to reach any node in the network.

u/n multitude — Political Score "Palace of Culture"

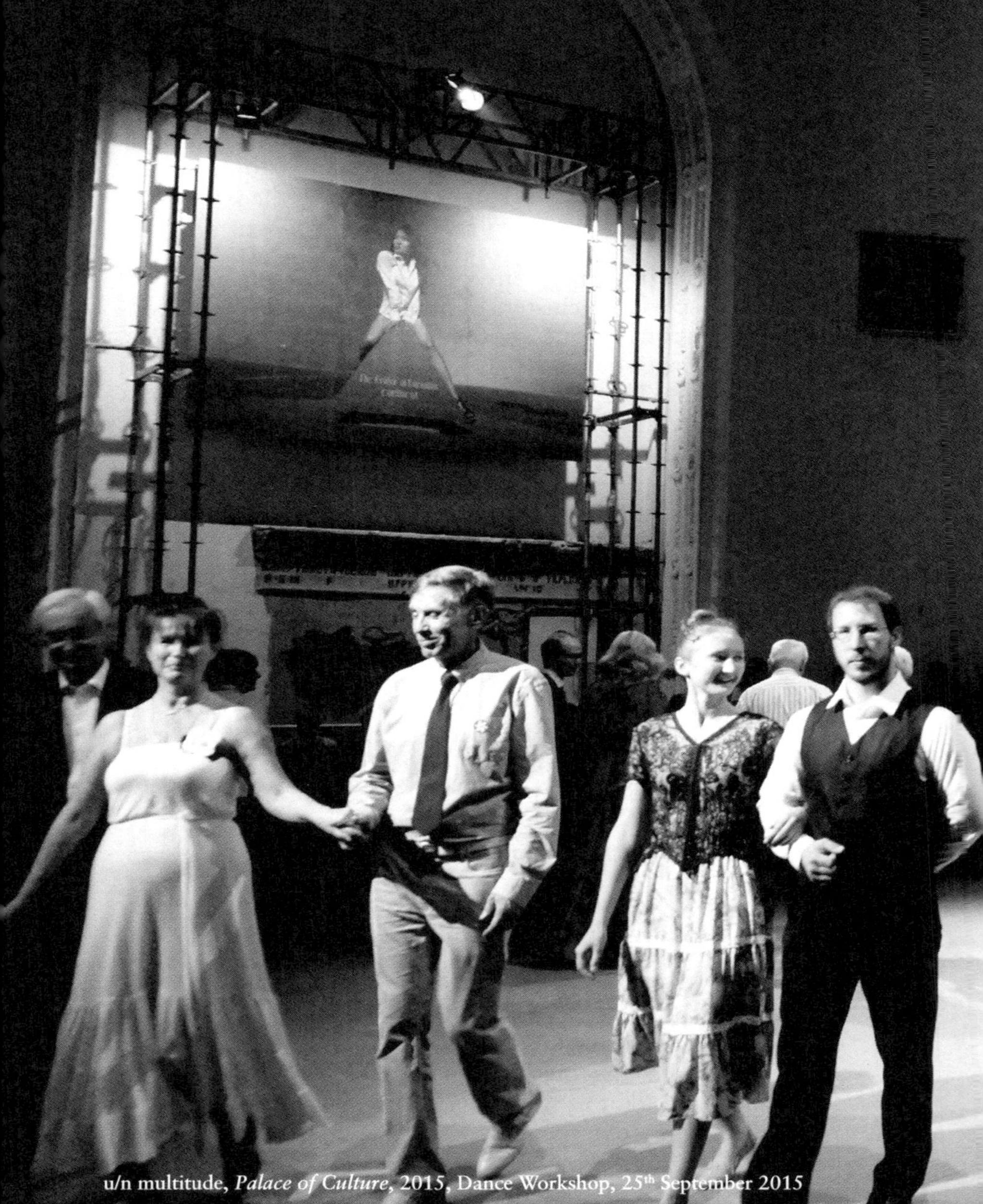

u/n multitude, *Palace of Culture*, 2015, Dance Workshop, 25th September 2015

In Soviet times, a Palace of Culture was a place where cultural and recreational activities for the community were organised and took place. The Palace of Culture was both a means of education, propaganda and collective gathering in leisure time. For the biennial, the art collective u/n multitude organised four public activities to put the notion of the cultural palace to test from a historical point of view—and aim for an actualisation of it, led by the question of how to gather today.

u/n multitude appeals to the institution as the one responsible for mass outreach activities in the Soviet era. For this, they worked with the local communities of VDNKh, such as amateur clubs for dance and drama or vocal-instrumental ensembles. u/n multitude immersed into each of the specific contexts of amateur culture at VDNKh.

Stemming from their interest in the potential of music to spark a confrontation with political and social contexts, all four events were inspired by the notion of scores: As a means of musical notation, scores can organise a whole orchestra, leave room for inspiration for the individual player, or become a tool of exchange and communication through the act of playing and listening. [Marie Egger]

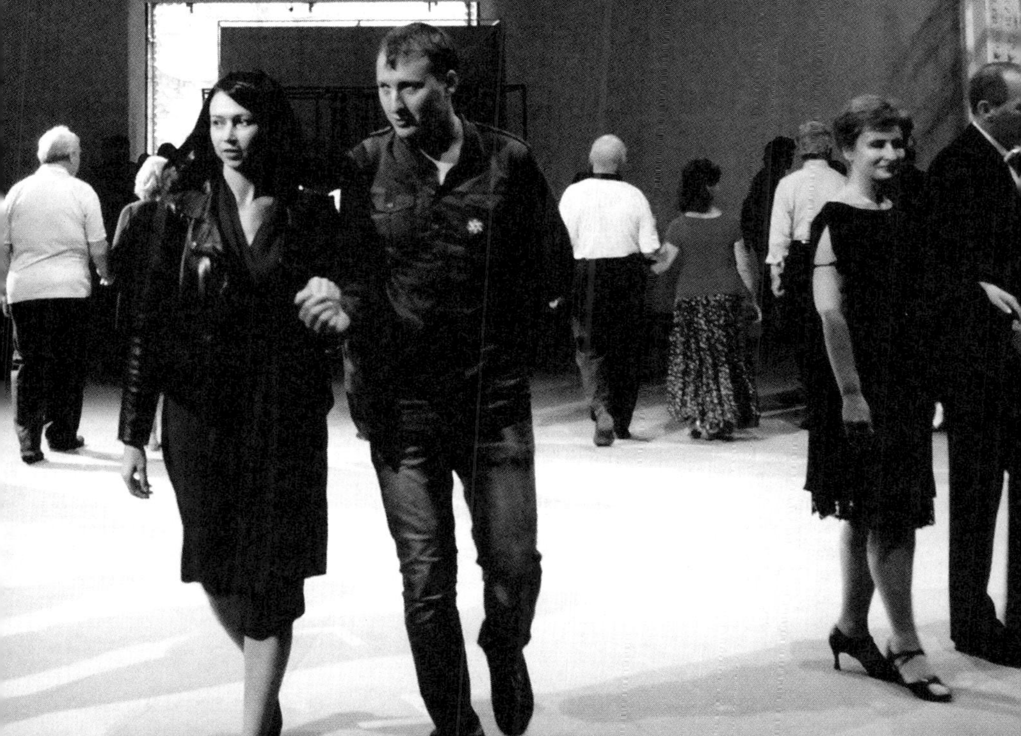

25th September 2015
Dance Workshop

Dance evening and workshop by Anatoly Mikhailovich Mazalov, the head of the historical ballroom dancing studio *Polites*, in the Central Dome of VDNKh.

Participants:

Mikhail Radchenko, Alexei Nikonov, Alexander Pravdyuk, Dmitry Pashkov, Nastya Galitsyna, Igor Trushkin, Olga Chernyshova, Sergei Lebedev, Anastasia Pavlova, Mikhail Pushkin, Maxim Gabrukovich, Vladimir Pleshakov, Irina Myrsina, Galina Demidova, Boris Barabanov, O.M. Odinets, Maria Yakovleva, Natalia Nikitina, Mikhail Ustalov, O. A. Ushakova, V.N. Khakhareva, Yevgeny Zhikharev, Dmitry Tarasov, Tamara Mets, Zhanna Morozova, Viktor Igishev, Irina Ziuzeva, Anatoly Mazalov, Olga Lakireva, Natasha Kulikova, Maria Lyamina, Daria Zakharova, Dmitry Simonov, Yuri Kuznetsov, Yekaterina Nikolayeva, Valeria Solovyova, Vyacheslav Sergeyev, Nadezhda Titova, Tatyana Bodnar, Dmitry Arkhangelsky, Alexander Izmailov, Lyudmila Moskat, Boris Petrov, Svetlana Vasiliyeva, Alex Bender, Zhanna Yanukovich, Yuri Pakhomov, Alexander Antonenko, Vladimir Lenin, Olga Nechayeva, Vladimir Zharkov, Yelena Petrova, Larisa Kudryashova, Igor Silukob, Alexandra Silukob, Maria Varygina, Lyudmila Popova, Artyom Volkhonsky, Marina Vishnyakova, Alexander Yurev, Yuri Shteynikov, Natalia Kaznacheyeva, Igor Kozlovsky, Sergei Prigozhin, Alexandra Krivosheyeva, Lyudmila Batakova, Alexander Semyonov, Margarita Fyodorova, Sergei Ivanchuk, Marina Mironova, Yulia Anokhina, Natalia Bulycheva, Alexandra Vasilyeva, Tatyana Mikhailova, Tatyana Aliyeva, Vladislav Odintsov, Lyubov Muraveva, Inna Pichugina, Vladimir Loginov, Tatyana Barinova, Anatoly Agapchev, Alexander Shchedrov, Oxana Parmanova, Alyona Plokhotnaya, Igor Belov, Tatyana Bodnar, Dmitry Tarasov, Tatyana Osipova, Maxim Dubinsky, Lev Khokholikov, Valery Aronenko, V.V. Prokofiev, Ye.R. Slyunyayeva, Yuri Markeyev, Mila Simakova, Yevgenia Minayeva, Larisa Komarova, Viktor Sokolov, Elvira Vinokurova, Anatoly Usovich, Olga Vdovina, Alexander Yuriev, Tamara Gorbunova, Yevgeny Zineyev, Alexander Yevdokimov.

Programme:

Polonaise
Pas de Grâce
Pas de Patineur
Pas de Zephyre
Moscow Quadrille
Hungarian ballroom dance
Mazurka
Boston Waltz
Figured Waltz
Viennese Waltz
Grand Waltz
Waltz-Gavotte
Waltz-Mazurka
Rhythm Waltz
Spanish Waltz
Svetsky Rucheyok
Berlin Polka
Minuet
Russian Lyrical Dance
Sudarushka
Tango
Slow Foxtrot
Anastasia Waltz

27th September 2015
A Lecture on the Self-Organised Community at VDNKh

At the heart of this lecture lies the counterpoint of two situations: a gatherings of bards — in a circle of friends. During the preparations for the performance, u/n multitude attended the *Republic of Songs* Pavilion each week, observing over an extended period how people well-known to each other gather and a pass a guitar round the circle. These meetings were accompanied by an unpretentious tea party where everyone brought snacks.

During this performance in the Pavilion No. 1 of VDNKh, u/n multitude tried to remain faithful to the nature of the gatherings and the atmosphere of the *Republic of Songs*, opening the invitation to participation of their friends.

As a result, fragments of the lecture and the singing of songs to guitar created the structure of a refrain and episodes, which compared the (extroverted) solo public lecture to the (introverted) chamber group meeting of the bards.

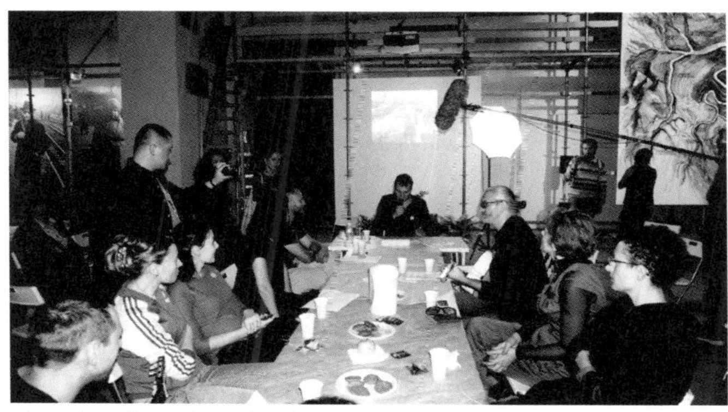

u/n multitude, *Palace of Culture*, 2015, A Lecture on the Self-Organised Community in VDNKh, 27th September 2015

29th September 2015
The March of Enthusiasts

Dedicated to the enthusiasts of two eras: 1) those who erected and built VDNKh and 2) the employees who maintained the complex in the 1990s. On the stage, Chinese artist Li Mu laid out aluminium buoys which u/n multitude had borrowed from the Fishing Pavilion. Simultaneously, musicians reproduced the construction of the Exhibition Centre, climbing up the scaffolding while a voice recited the enthusiasts' names of the two eras in free order. The performance was attended by contemporary enthusiasts—the restorers of the Belarus Pavilion.

March of the Enthusiasts

In the everyday work of great building,
In the merry rumble, the flames and the peals,
Hello, you country of heroes,
A country of dreamers, a country of thinkers.

Across the steppe, across the forests,
From the tropics all the way to the pole,
You spread out, my boundless homeland,
My indestructible land of birth.

On sea or land, we know no obstacles,
We fear no ice bergs, not the clouds.
The flame of our heart, the flag of our country
We carry across worlds and ages!

Is it for us to stand in place?
We are always right in our daring,
Our work is matter of honour,
A matter of valour and glorious exploit.
Whether you're leaning over a workbench,
Or cutting out stone from a wall,
A dream of wonderment, still unclear to you,
Is calling you ever ahead.

Our world was created wonderfully.
The work of centuries has been done in years,
We grasp our happiness by rights,
We love with gusto, and sing like children.
And our stars of scarlet
Glitter, like never before,
Above all other countries and oceans
Like a dream if our heart, the flag if our country
We carry across other worlds and ages!

Anatoly D'Aktil

1st October 2015
Rock Concert

On the closing day of the Biennale, the rock band *Drugie Lyudi* played a concert on the main stage at the Central Pavilion. Usually, this street band performs cover versions of well-known pop-songs at the entrance of VDNKh. The band switched locations with u/n multitude, who were simultaneously performing at their customary spot on the street.

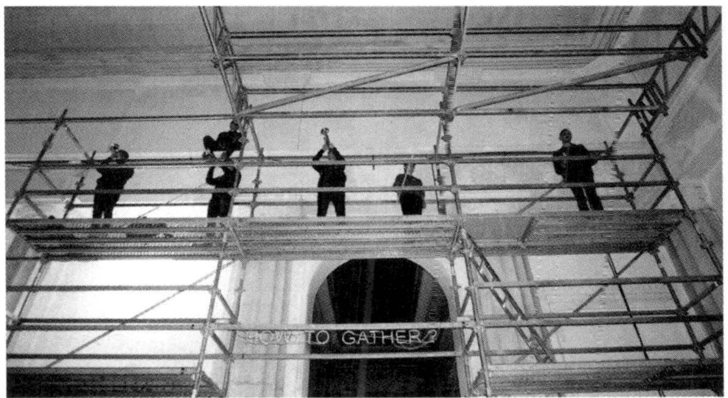

u/n multitude, *Palace of Culture*, 2015, The March of Enthusiasts, 29th September 2015

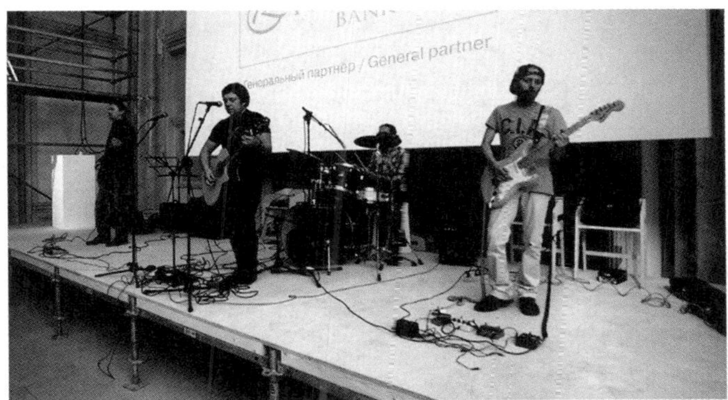

u/n multitude, *Palace of Culture*, 2015, Rock Concert, 1st October 2015

Studio For New Music Ensemble — 6th Moscow Biennale Programme

23rd September 2015	composer Nikolai Popov with string quartet "Studio for New Music" (two violins, alto and cello)
24th September 2015	composer Nikolai Popov with ensemble of 4 musicians — flute, clarinet, violin, cello and electronics
25th September 2015	composer Nikolai Popov with percussionist and real time artist David Ru who is going to paint in real time with simultaneous video screening and sound, depending on the painting
26th September 2015	composer Alexei Nadzharov with electro violin player
27th September 2015	composer Alexei Nadzharov with string quartet and electronics
28th September 2015	composer Alexander Khubeev with ensemble of flute, oboe, clarinet, trumpet and trombone, using both instruments and specially constructed objects
29th September 2015	composer Alexander Khubeev with ensemble of 2 violins, viola, cello and double bass, using both instruments and specially constructed objects
30th September 2015	composer Alexei Nadjarov with ensemble of flute, clarinet, accordion and double bass, with interactive live electronics
1st October 2015	composer Alexander Khubeev with large ensemble of flute, oboe, clarinet, trumpet and trombone, synthesiser, percussion, 2 violins, viola, cello and double bass Premiere of new piece by composer Vladimir Tarnopolsky. Performed by the ensemble and soprano (Ekaterina Kychygina). Conducted by Igor Dronov. With a livestream Skype commentary from Venice by Vladimir Tarnopolsky.

Otto Snoek, 22 September – 01 October 2015

Maarten Vanden Abeele — 22 September – 01 October 2015

Maarten Vanden Abeele was invited to the biennial as one of four photographic eyes. During his presence in Moscow for ten days, he captured what was going on around the biennial, in VDNKh (the exhibition park around the site) and, above all, in Moscow city. His photographs were installed on walls inside Pavilion No. 1 where the biennial took place. The following pages resemble this hanging.

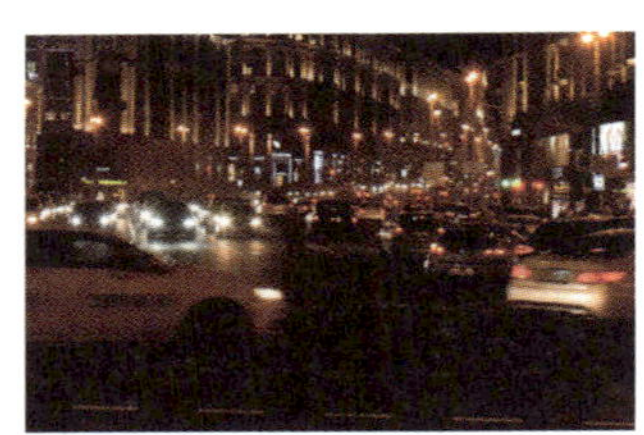

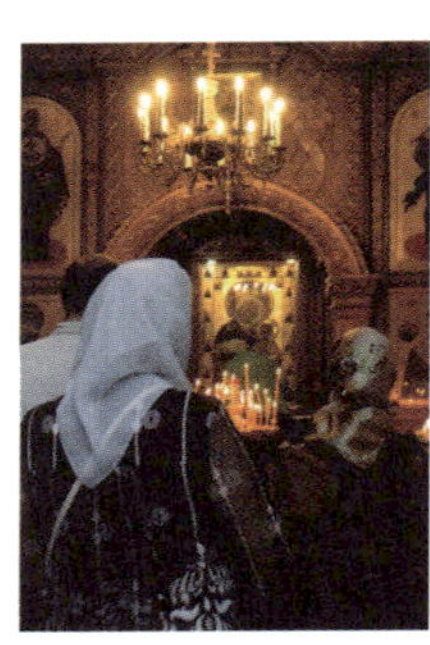

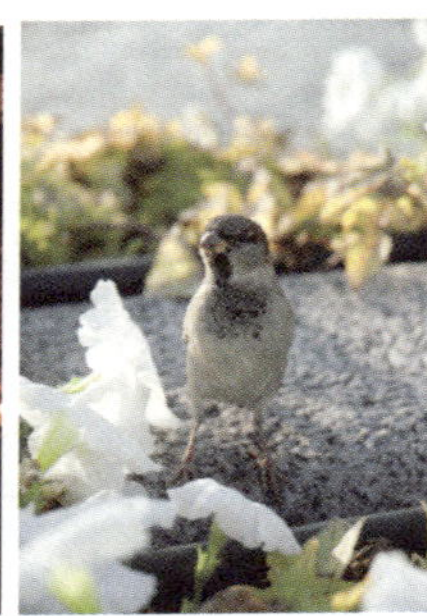

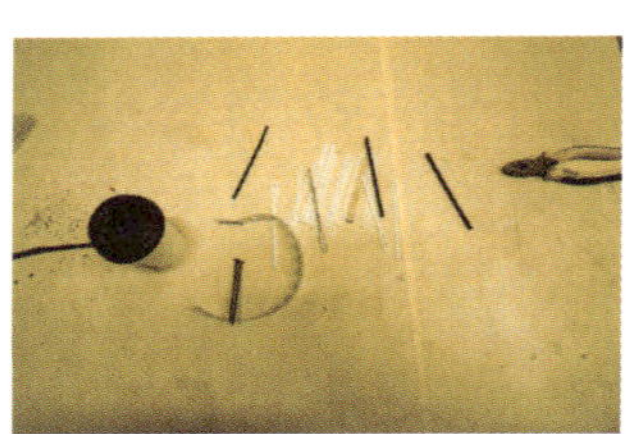

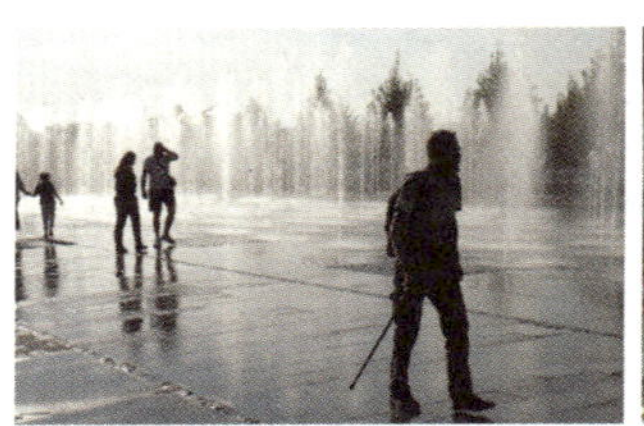

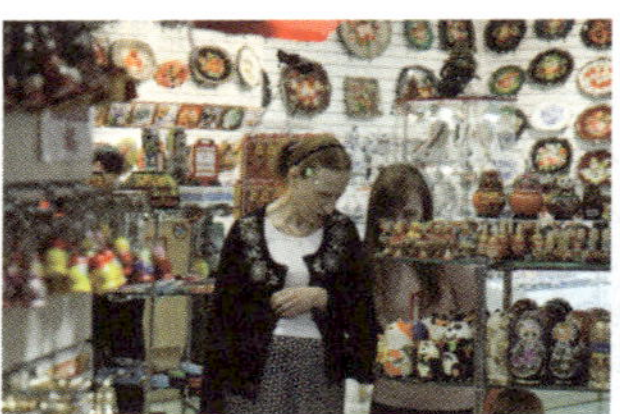

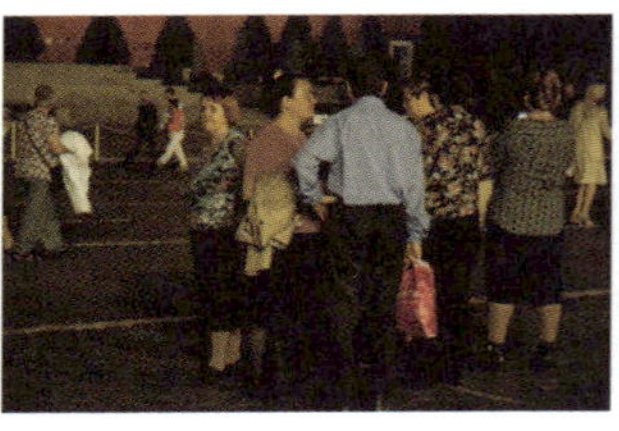

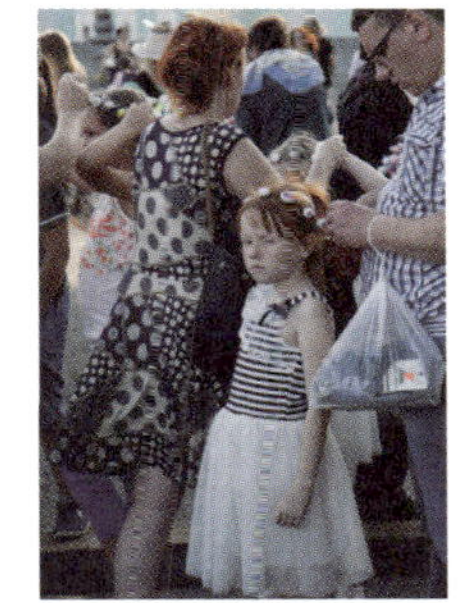
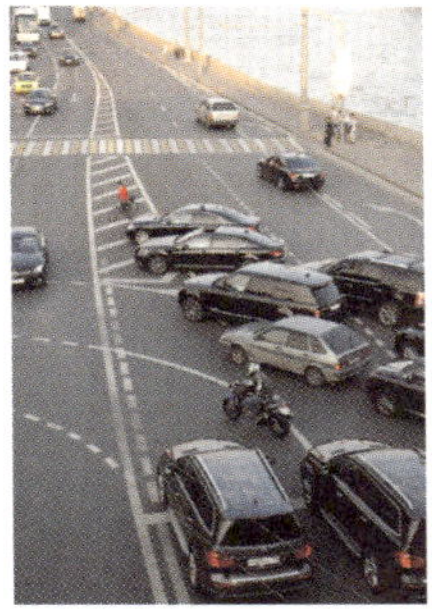
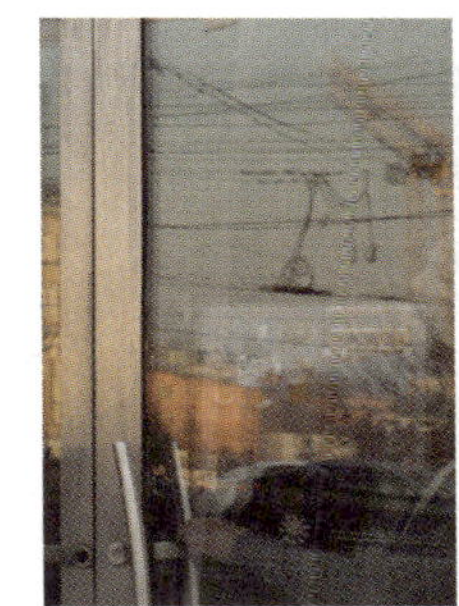
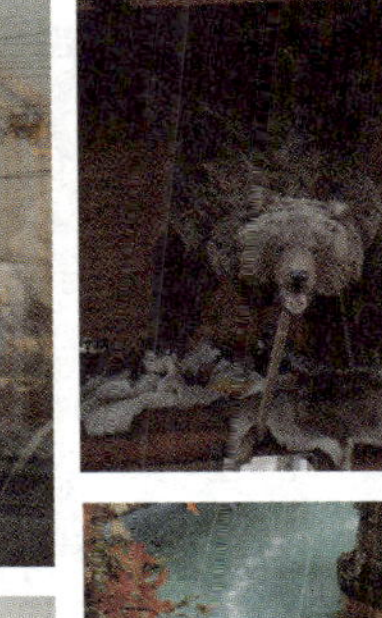
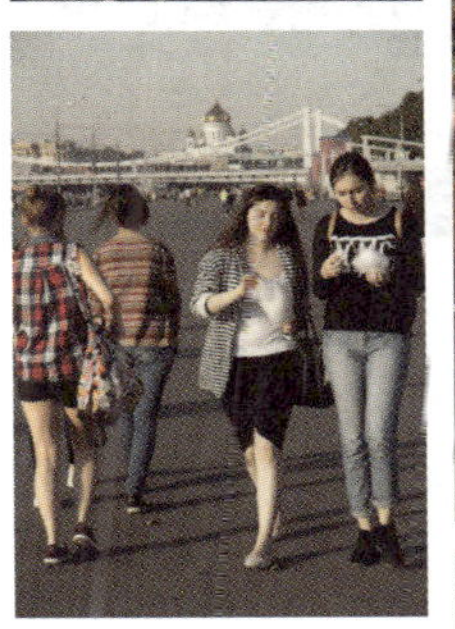
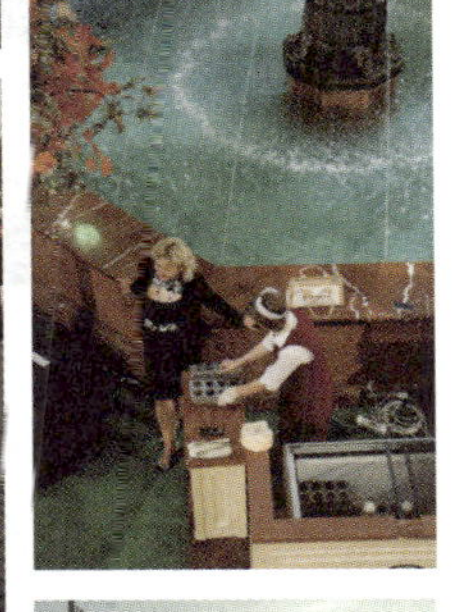
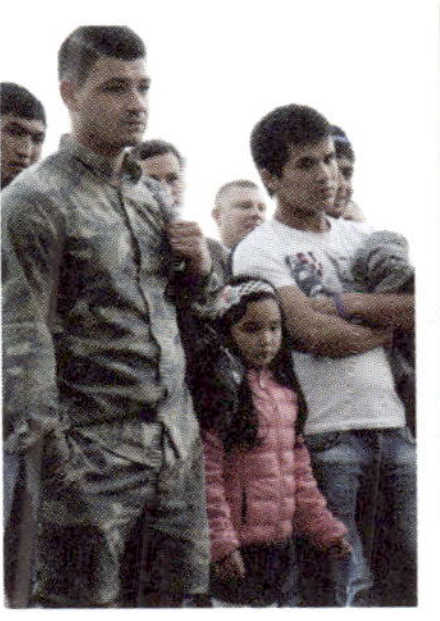
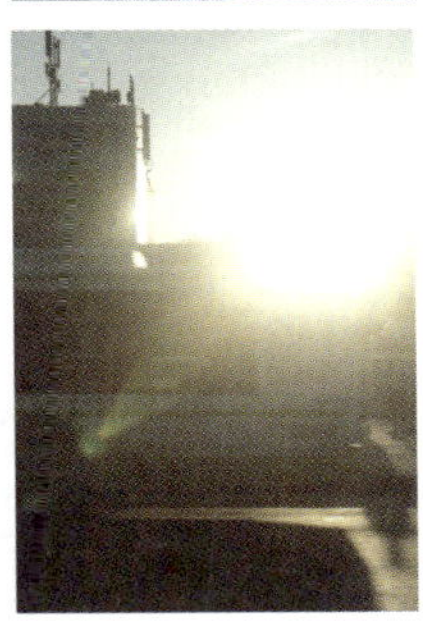

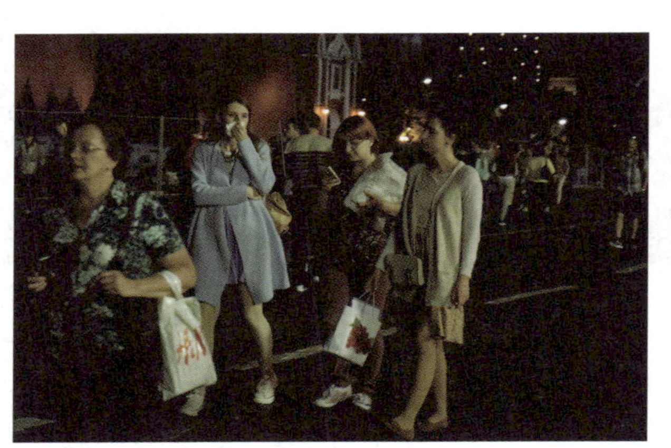

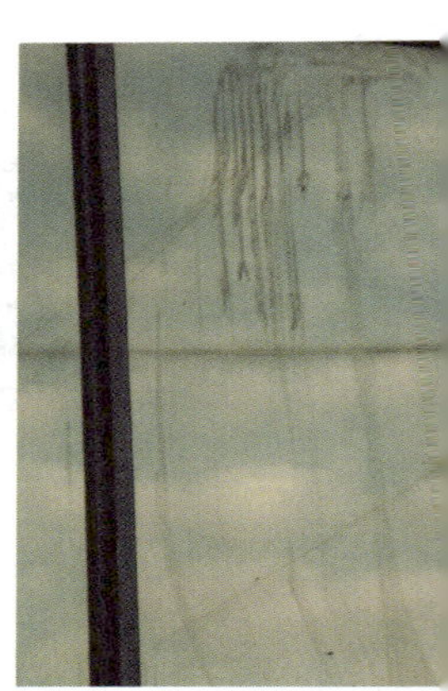

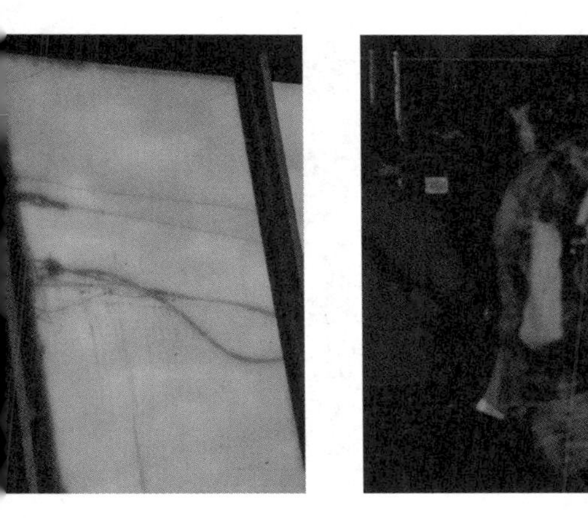

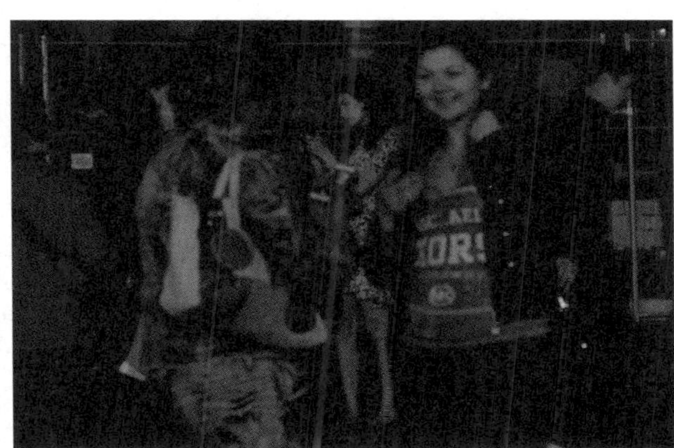

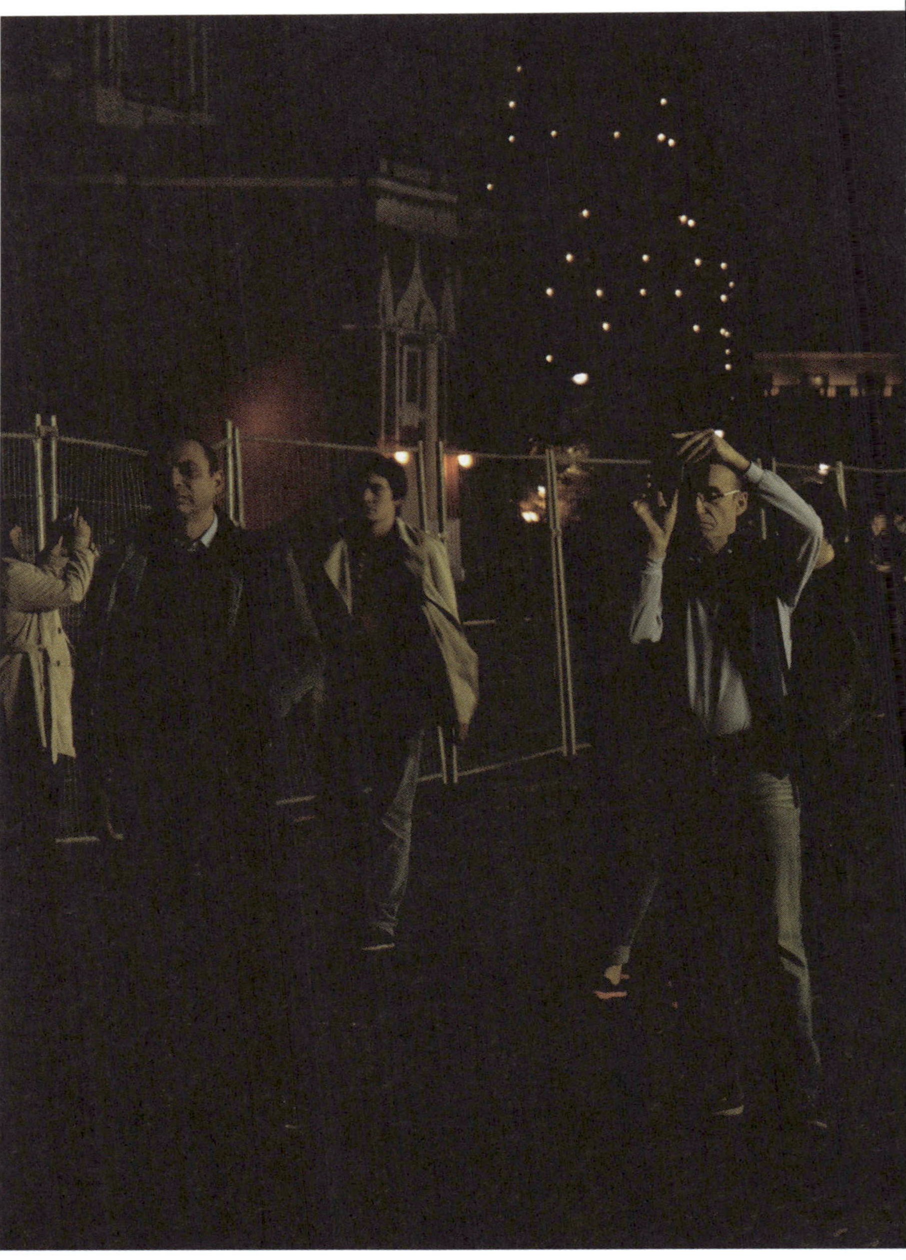

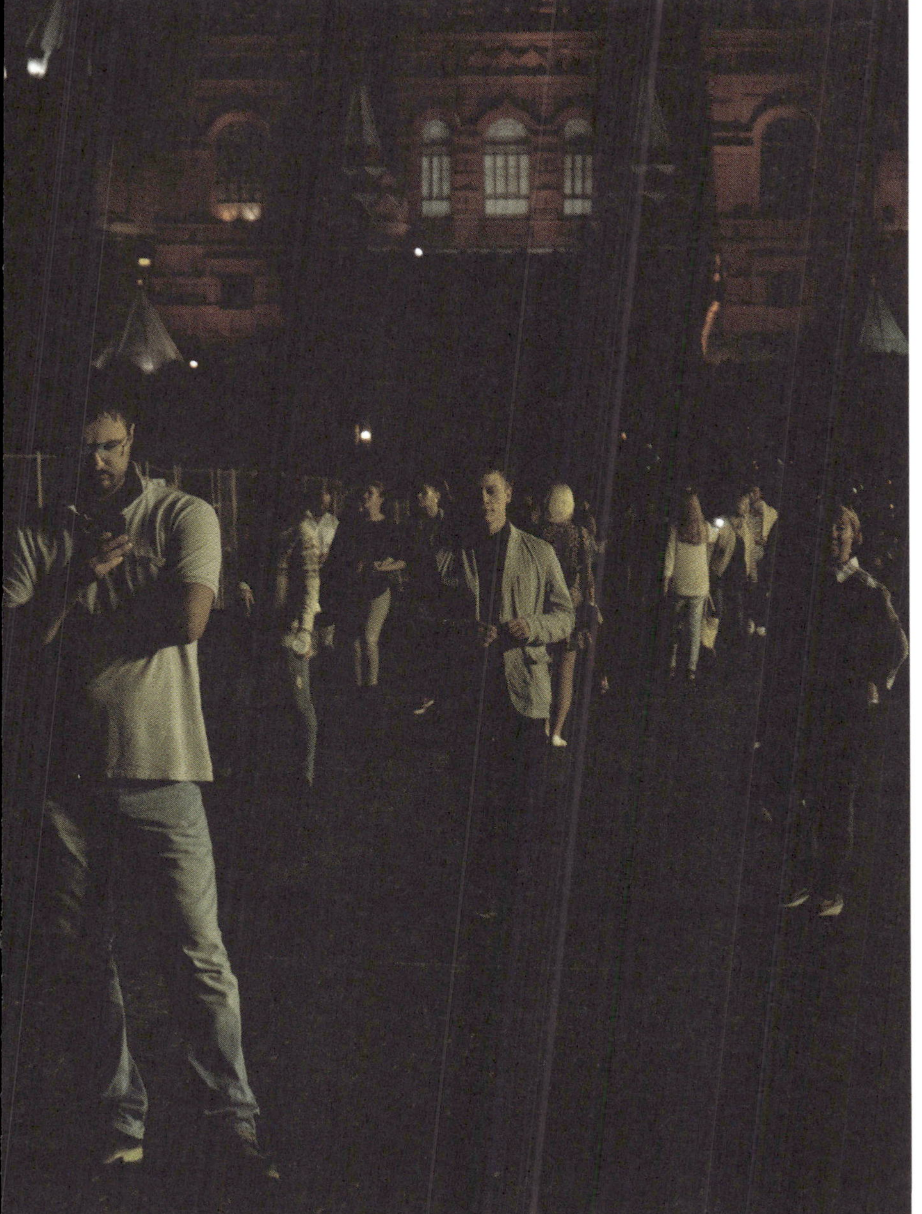

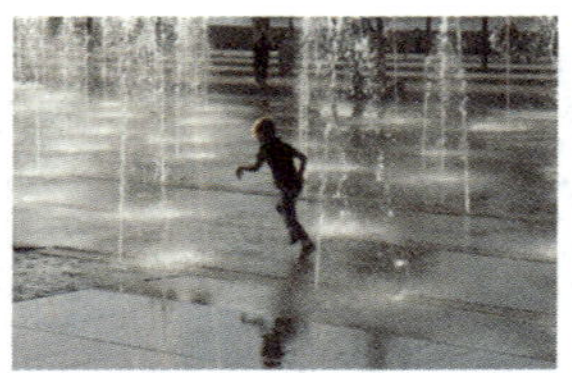

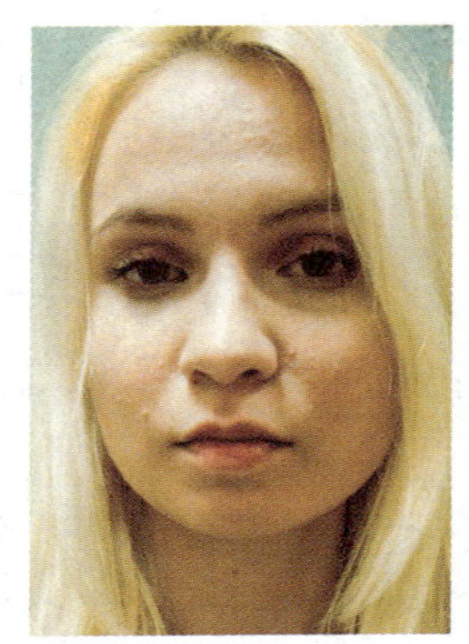

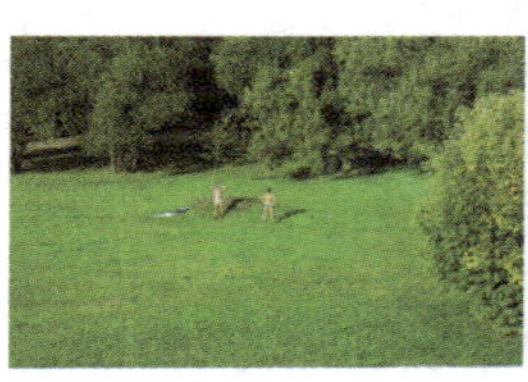

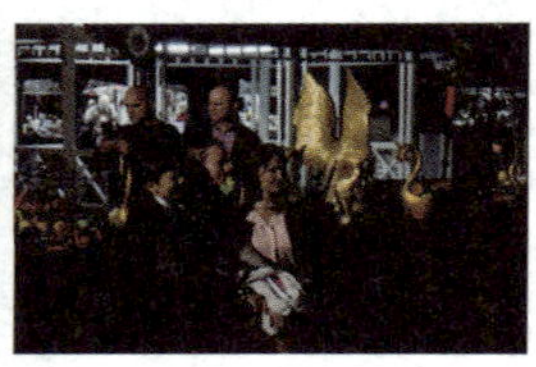

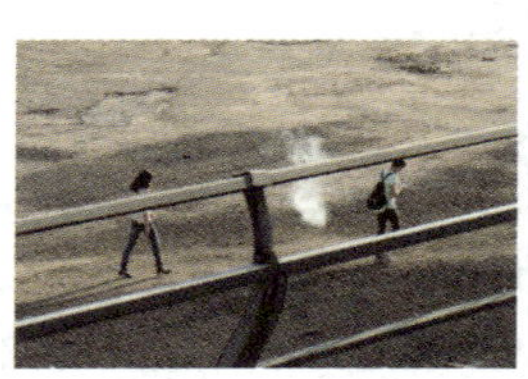

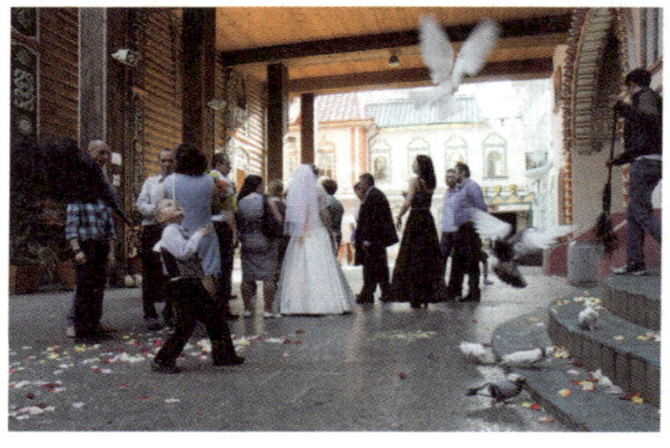

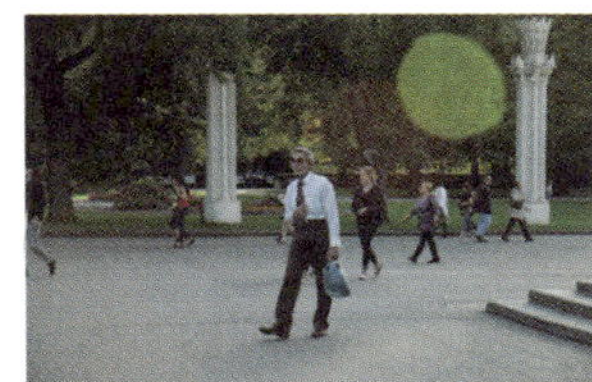

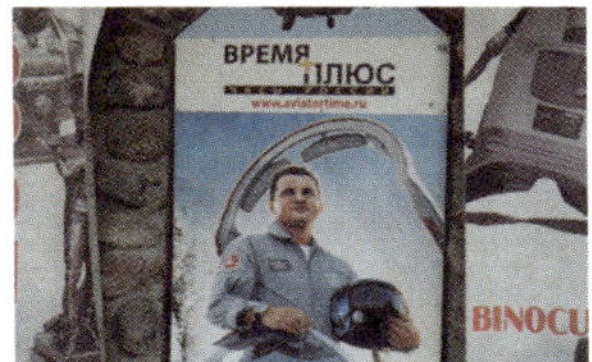
ВРЕМЯ
ПЛЮС
BINOCU

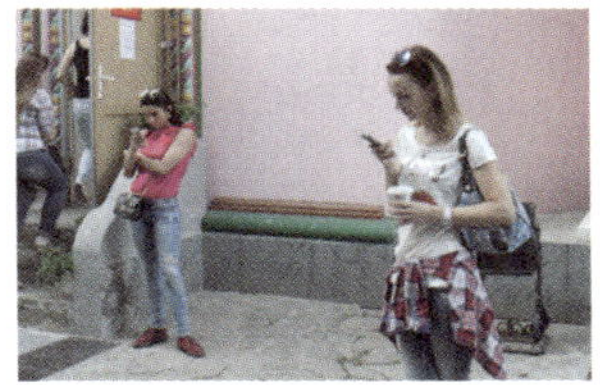

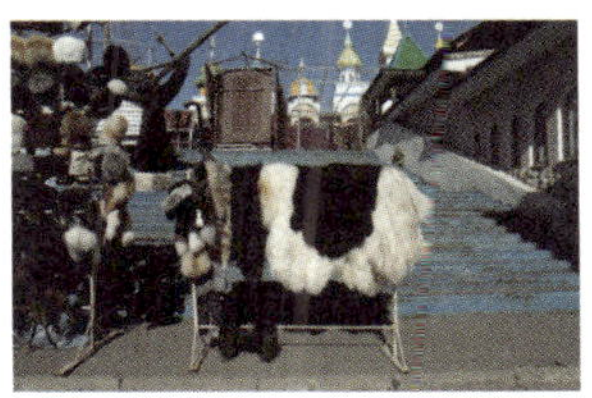

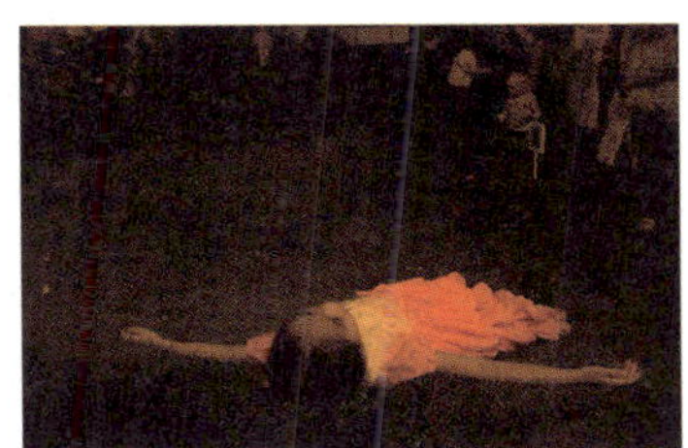

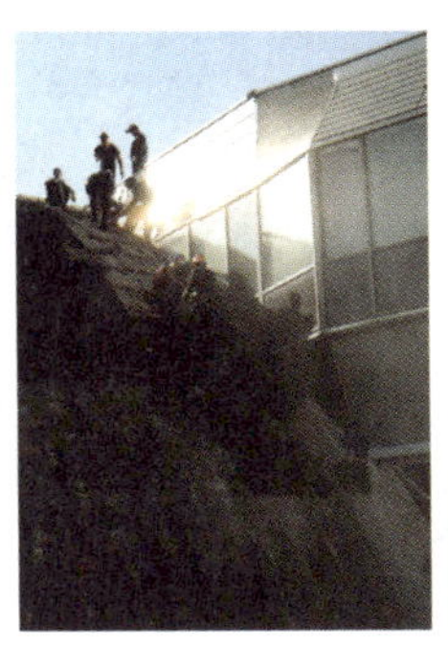

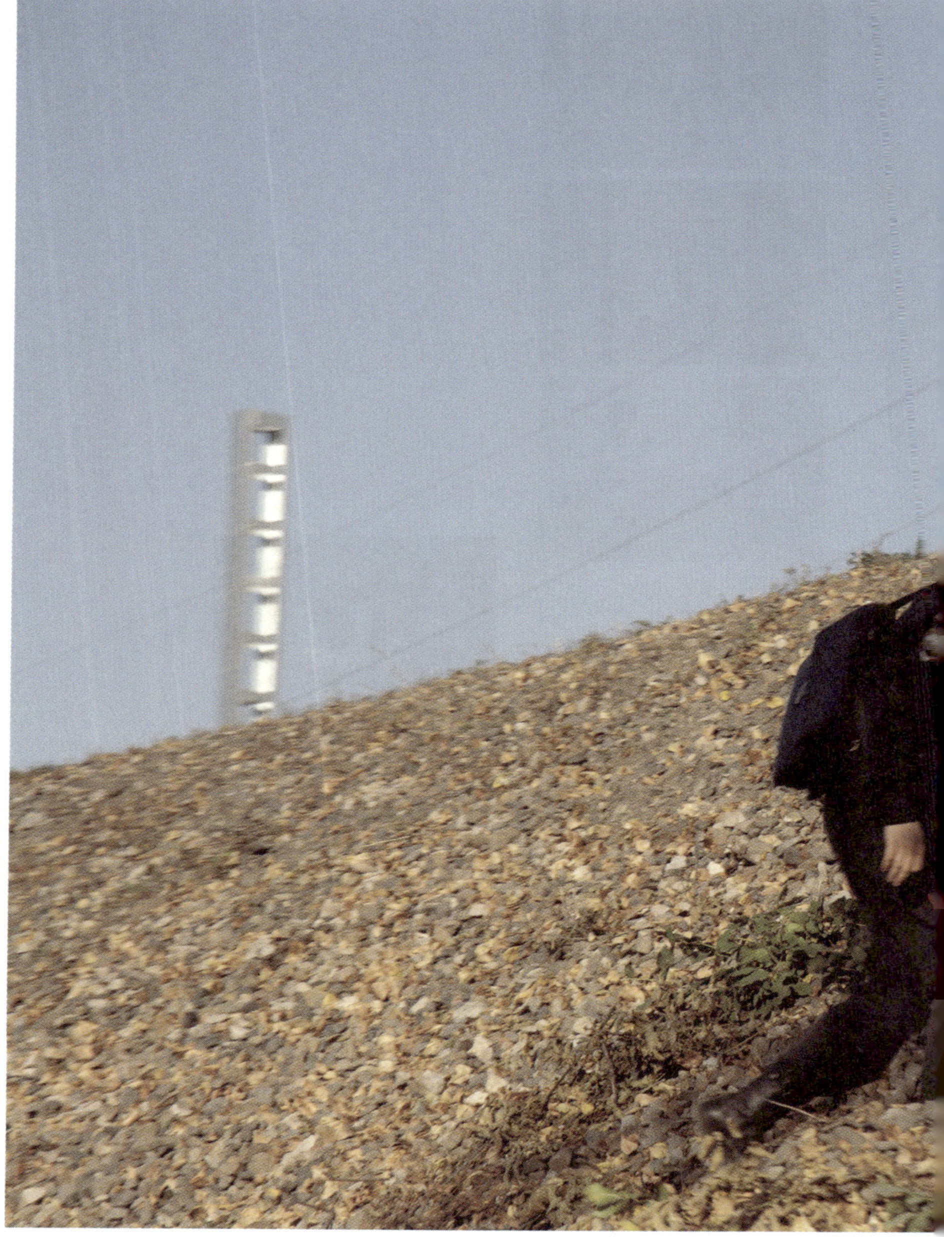

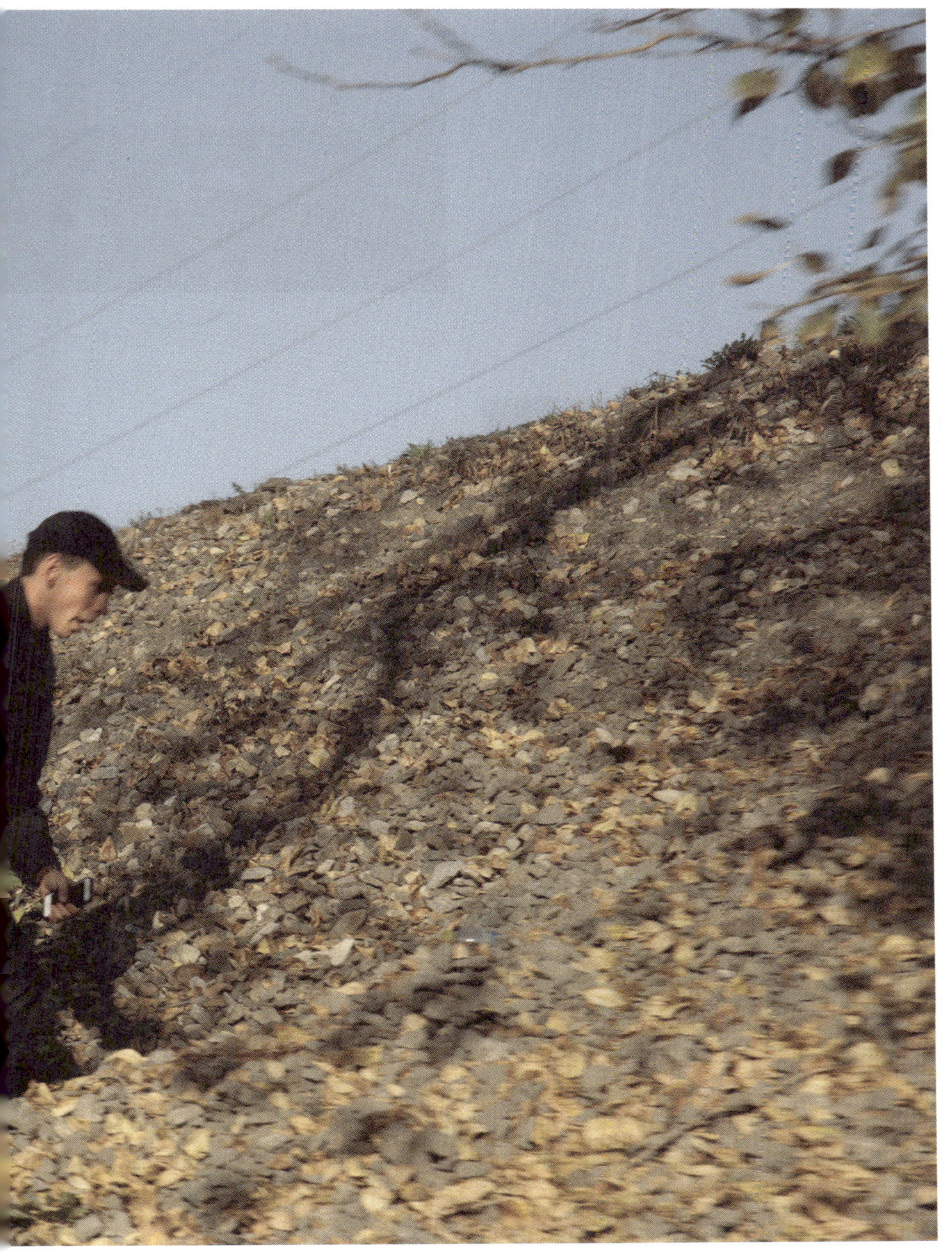

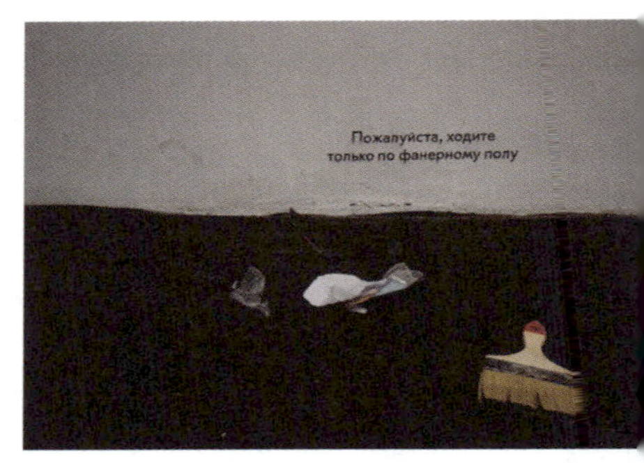
Пожалуйста, ходите
только по фанерному полу

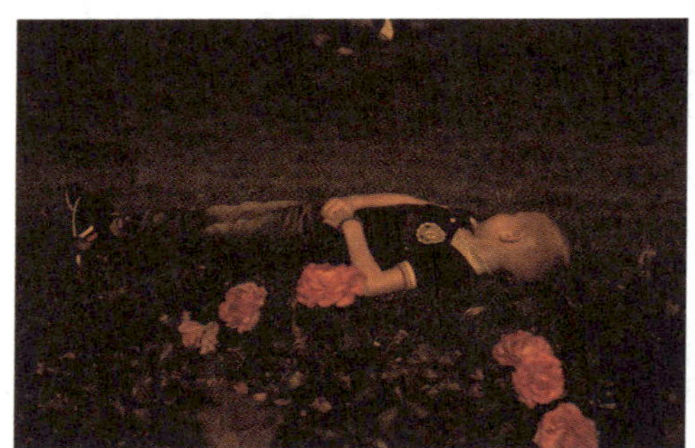

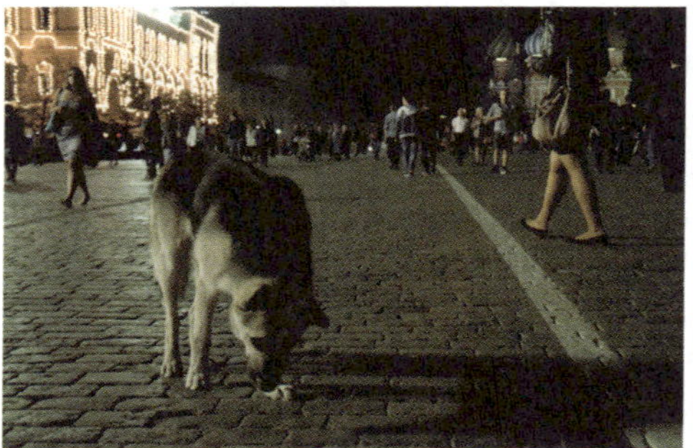

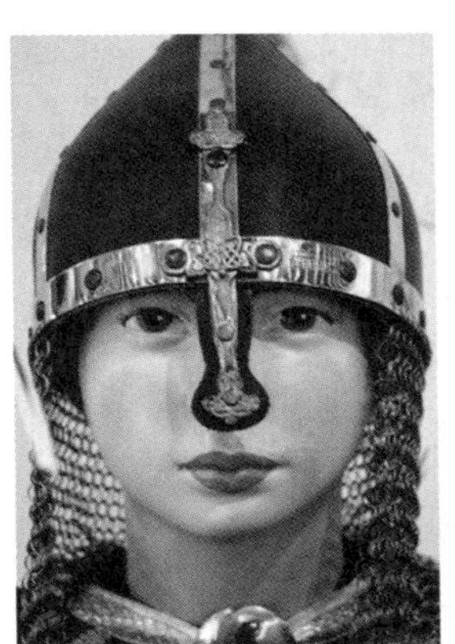

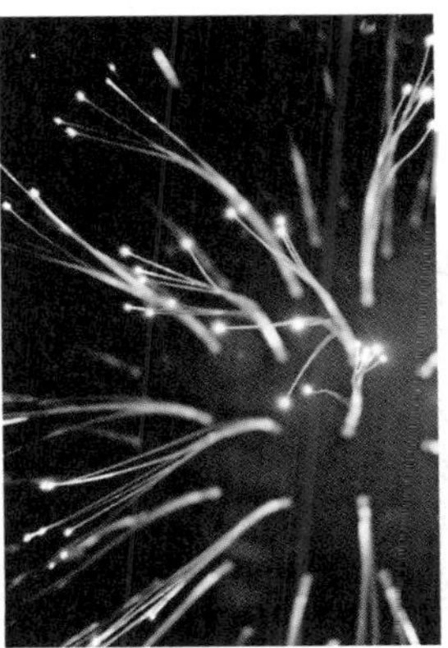

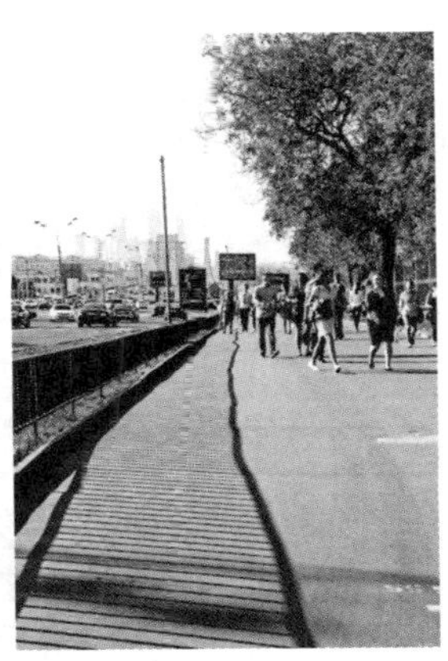

Otto Snoek — 22 September – 01 October 2015

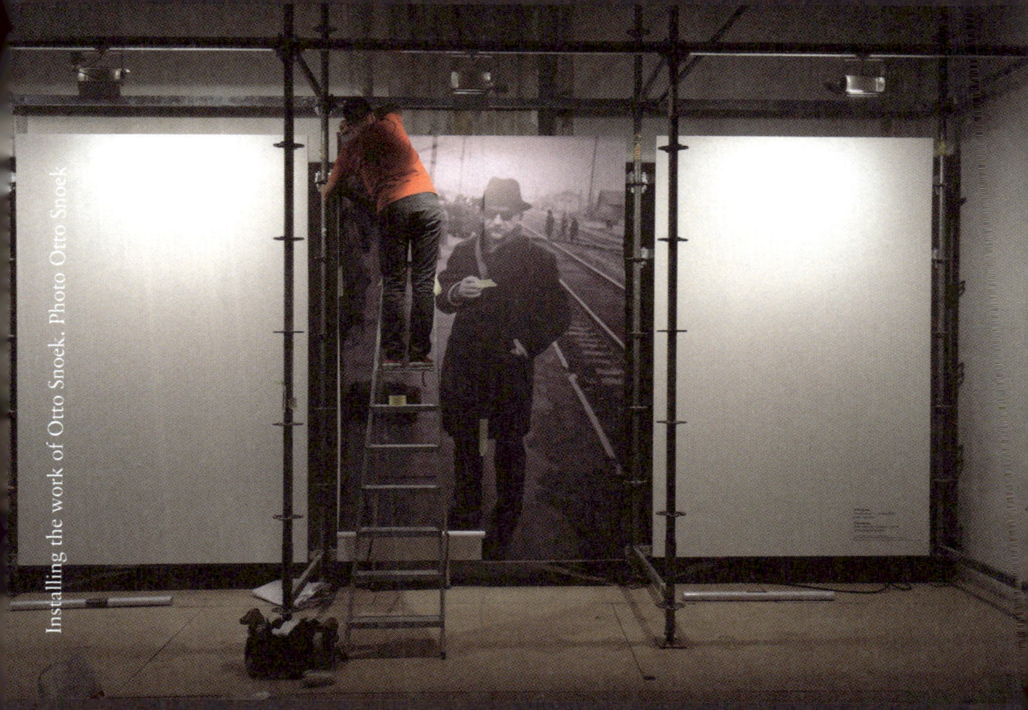

Installing the work of Otto Snoek. Photo Otto Snoek

Otto Snoek was among the four photographers who witnessed the biennial on site. They were encouraged to direct their antennae to what happened outside the Central Pavilion as well as within. Otto's observations from that widened horizon are what he presented at VDNKh after the ten days of the biennial. For this publication, he contributed a number of images he took during the programme — as an always sensitive, sometimes silent observer of the happening on-the-go. His photographs are spread throughout the book in order to mirror the highly subjective but also documentary approach to Otto's practice. See pages 9, 62, 119, 137, 151, 215, 225, 345, 360, 423, 450, 496, 510, 522 and 552. [Marie Egger]

Anatoly Osmolovsky — The End of Modernism in Russia

During the ten days of the Moscow Biennale for Contemporary Art 2015, the artists Anatoly Osmolovsky and Alexander Kutovoy (together with Irina Petrakova, Alexander Plusnin and Vitaly Barabanov, students of the BAZA art school) made a sculpture of the dead poet Vladimir Mayakovsky on the stairs of VDNKh's Pavilion No. 1: *The End of Modernism in Russia*. The sculpture was based on a photographic portrait taken immediately after Mayakovsky's death in 1930. The clay sculpture gradually dried out and fell apart after the biennial. [Marie Egger]

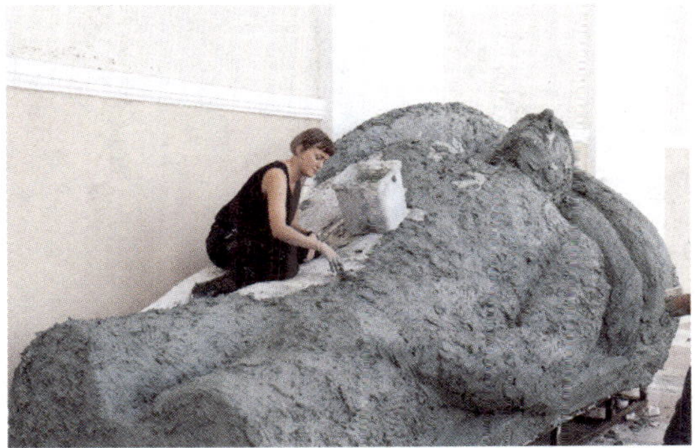

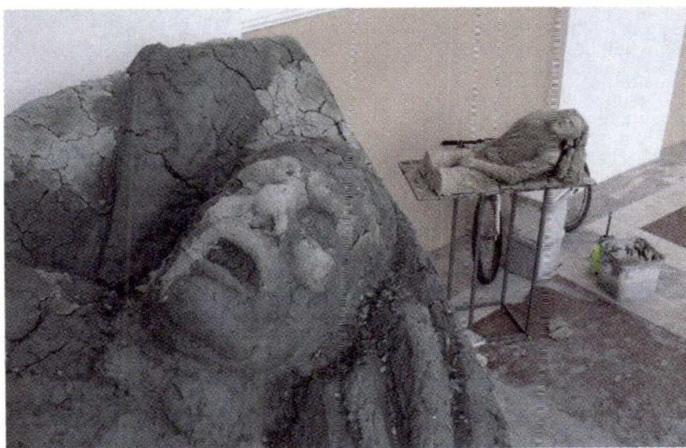

Anatoly Osmolovsky, *The End of Modernism in Russia* (detail), 2015

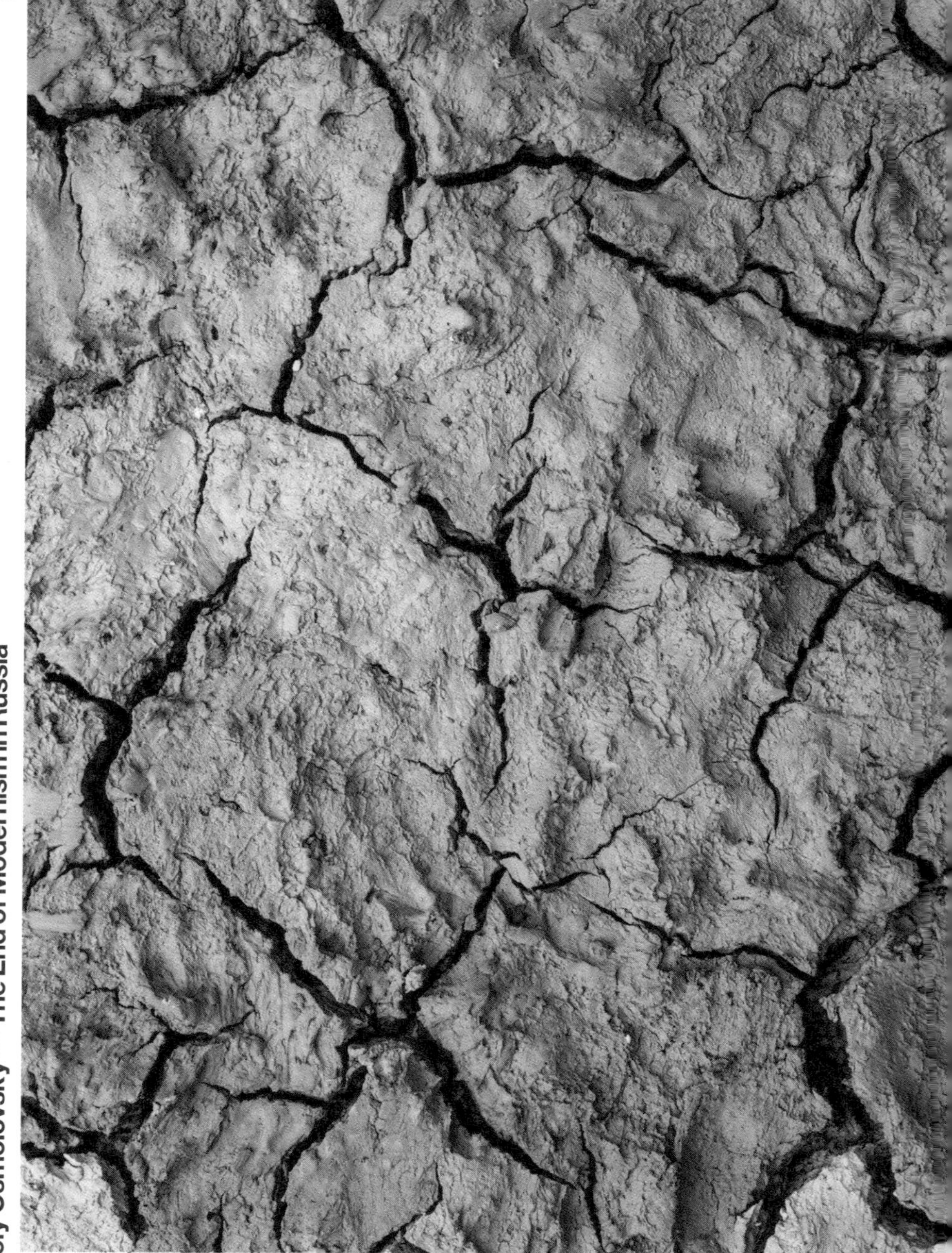

Anatoly Osmolovsky, *The End of Modernism in Russia* (detail), 2015

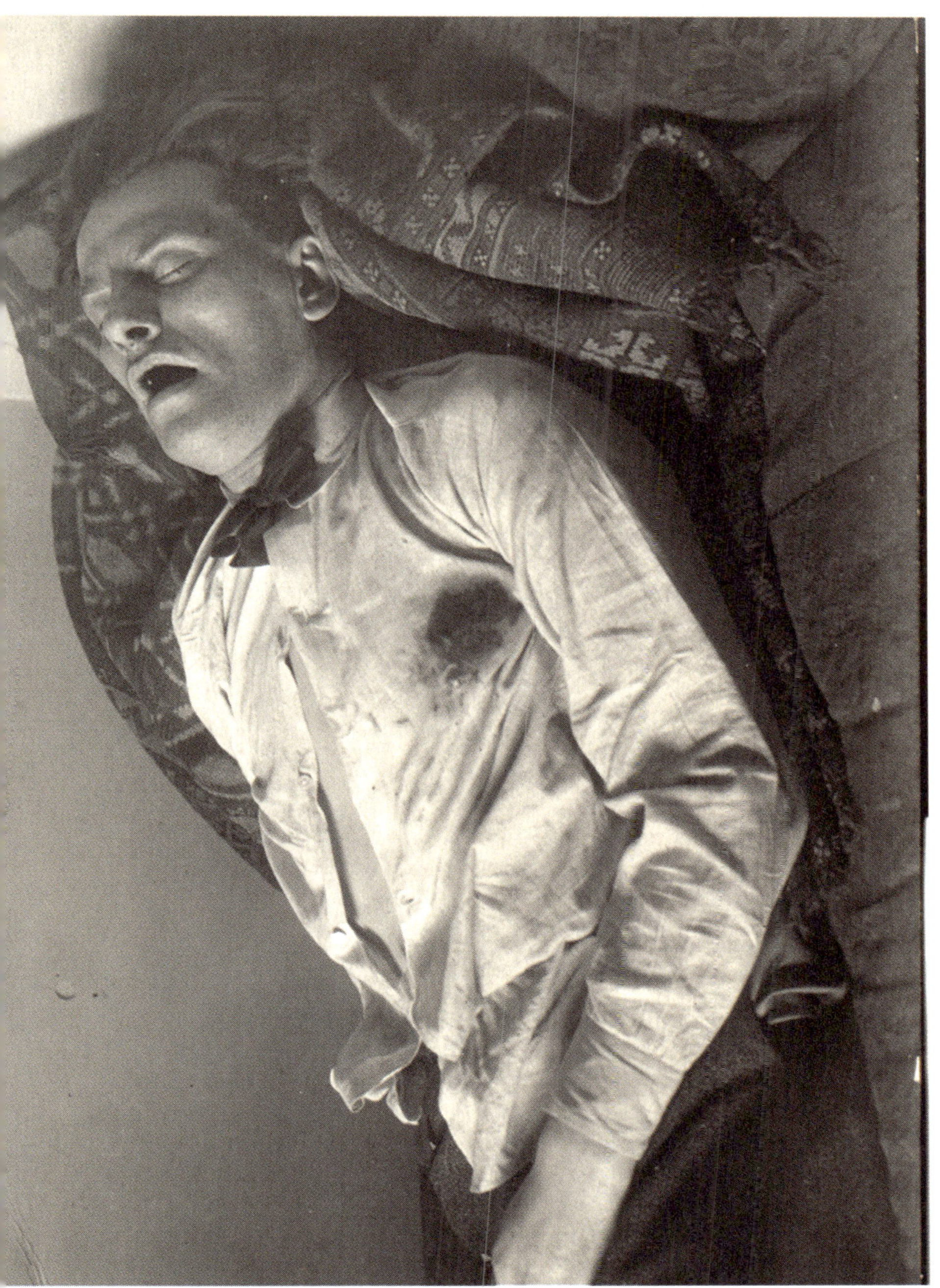

Vladimir Mayakovsky after the fatal gunshot, 14th April 1930

Els Dietvorst — We Are All Driftwood

1. EVERYBODY BECOMES PART OF THE GAME — BUT WHAT MIGHT THE NAME OF THIS GAME BE?

You have those moments where everything seems to fall in place, where the artwork, the artist and the public fall together. A magic spark comes through. They don't happen often.

In July 2001, I participated in a multimedia project called *The Return of the Swallows*. Together with the Firefly, I re-created a mini-society in Brussels. With 30 swallows, immigrants and Belgians, we realised performances and films led by our dreams and desires. In order to become a swallow, one had to become oneself in becoming another — and thus live intensively.

The Moscow Biennale for Contemporary Art also created this kind of magic for me. An open space that, once you were in, you could freely wonder through.

Day 1
It is afternoon.
The heat burns me.
I was not prepared for this.
I thought Moscow was cold.
Like the bears, so cold.
Actually, I had no idea about Moscow. I did not have time to think.
My brother is deadly sick.[1]

There was also a feeling of not belonging. Both Brussels and Moscow were places I did not understand the rules, the people or the language.

Also both projects had a healthy sort of a constant chaos. Presentations and work processes overlapped. Things were going on everywhere. And sometimes, by accident, you walked into beauty. There was a mélange of artists, non-artists, volunteers, labourers, academics, public and crew.

The emphasis was on the process, on the moment where art meets life, where people and things gathered. From morning workouts to shared lunches and drinks. You could freely step in and out. That was articulated by letting the public in to become part of the process and part of the game.

Maybe the only difference was that, in Moscow, my goal was to finish an artwork in 10 days. In Brussels I had had no deadline and we continued until we all, participants and artists, decided it was finished. This would have been an interesting thought for a biennial.

Both projects deal with ephemeral processes and outcomes. Some of the *Swallows'* happenings were not recorded. In Moscow you knew that all the work made would disappear after 10 days. It gave the projects the character of an extended happening.

I think we must try to build these situations more often. That is to say, collective ambiences, ensembles of impressions determining the quality of a moment. According to Guy Debord, these moments are passageways, without a future—indeed, discontinuous moments or events that try to tap real life. Eternity is the grossest idea a person can conceive of in connection with his acts.[2]

It also leads you, as an artist, to other forms of creating, thinking about an artwork differently. Without the constant pressure of production which is a result of a capitalist system and liberal government.

2.
A DÉRIVE

But the essential thing is surely the connection to the people. *The Return of the Swallows* brought together 35 people from different nationalities and very different backgrounds.

In Moscow I was working on *Skull 3*[3] with a group of people of different ages, backgrounds and cultures: migrant carpenters from countries such as Tajikistan, Uzbekistan and Kyrgyzstan. Sukhrob was their leader. Together with Daria, an artist and volunteer from Moscow and Mu, an artist from China, we worked closely together as a team. We had not known each other before and did not have much time meet up besides work. I think we were all open to be dérives.[4]

> Day 3.
> A man stands in front of me, motionless, he does not smile, he blinks his eyes. What's your name, I ask?

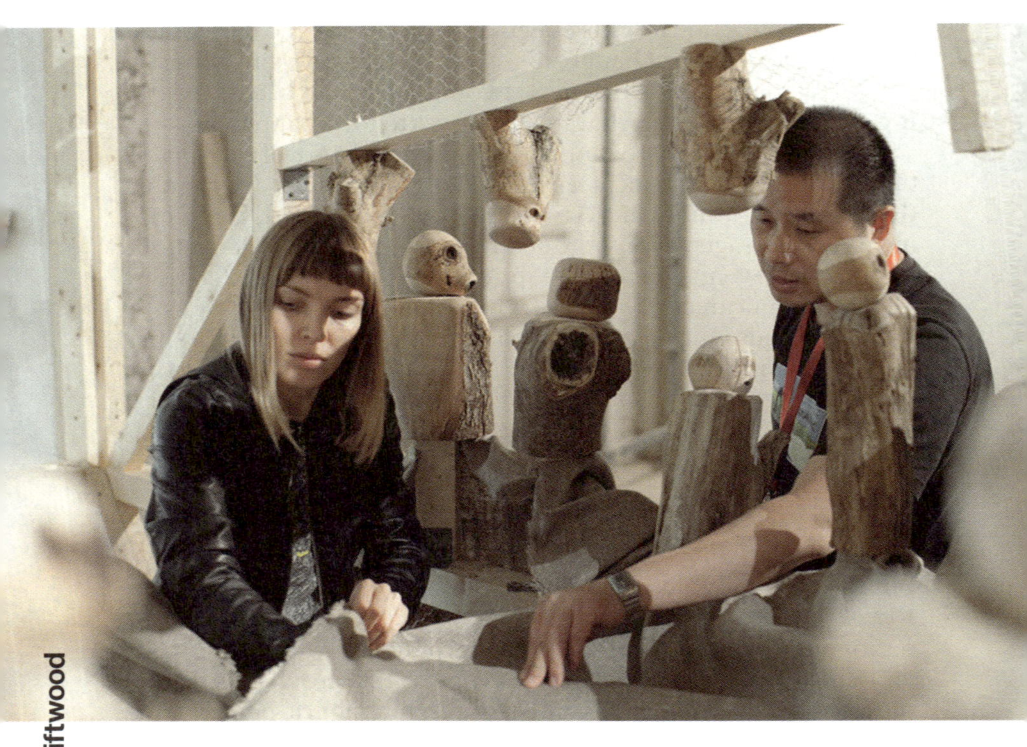

Darya Likhovitskaya and Li Mu installing *Skull*

"The Laborer," he says.
He stretches his arms in front of him… shows his hands, turns them slowly… "I am designated to help you," he says.
I tell him we're going to swear and honour. I give him my grandmother's needle.
I give all of us a needle, we know the stitch, we know the smell, we recognise the tissue of the Skull.
In a backspace we eat together… we eat with our hands… we drink tea.
I think of my brother, he can't eat, he can't drink.
I asked him what would be his first desire. He says… a glass of water I'd kill for.

Day 4.
I give my words, my wallet, my jewellery to Dasha.
I'm not a mother, a daughter, a sister, a wife anymore. I know how you sleep, she says and adds …it is only with the heart that one can see rightly, what is essential is invisible to the eye. "How come you are so clever?" I ask.
"Because I am old," she says.

It was in the process of the making of the skull when we discovered each others' strengths. As an artist, I pulled myself back to float on the energy of this temporary collective. Another artist said, "You have courage. How do you let other people work on you artwork?" But it is in this energetic and open space where a social sculpture is created.

The making of the *Skull* reunited memories and dreams. Sukhrob had never made a sculpture and was very impressed by the process.[5] He took selfies of every step and was very proud to make it into the local newspaper *Metro*. The work reminded Daria of her childhood. Mu said he got power from it.

Day 6.
It's Sunday morning. There is nobody. Just Sukhrob and me. He wants to ask me things, I want to tell him things, we do not understand each other's words. He looks for translations on his phone.
He says "…the nails have elves' heads, the skull con-

fides secrets to us, the shelter is where it all comes together… the hidden tissue. I say I do not understand you, but it sounds nice. We smile, drink tea and look proudly at the *Skull.*

The main structure of the *Skull* was already constructed when I arrived. The process of putting on chicken wire, tissue and loam was followed correctly. In every step Mu, Daria and Sukhrob taught me something new, even though I had been making these kinds of sculptures for over 10 years.

Every day we stepped back and looked at the skull to see if all of us could find ourselves in it. Which is why in the end I agreed with Mu to change the name on the label to mention all of us.[6]

Day 8.
I lit candles for my brother in the Church of Our Lady.
I call my brother, excited, I tell him about the language as sweet as honey, I tell him about the scents and colours, the faces that are like the faces of my sons. I realise that he will never be able to join me. I tell him collaboration exists in the possibility to dream.

3. WHAT IS THE LIGHT?[7]

Because the work process was so intense I was not able to get out of the room I was working in, which created a relation with the in-situ artists in the same space. On the last two days interesting connections were made, the space became ours. Honoré brought parts of his performance to the *Skull*. Fabrice mirrored the *Skull* on his wall and Babi used part of the tissue to make his last artwork. This all started on the last day and it would have been interesting to see how it might have evolved. The energy and social warmth made us believe we could lift the *Skull*, which in my view we did. Because as Bart said, we are all driftwood.

Day 10.
Loftiness is a habit we, mankind made ourselves guilty of too often.

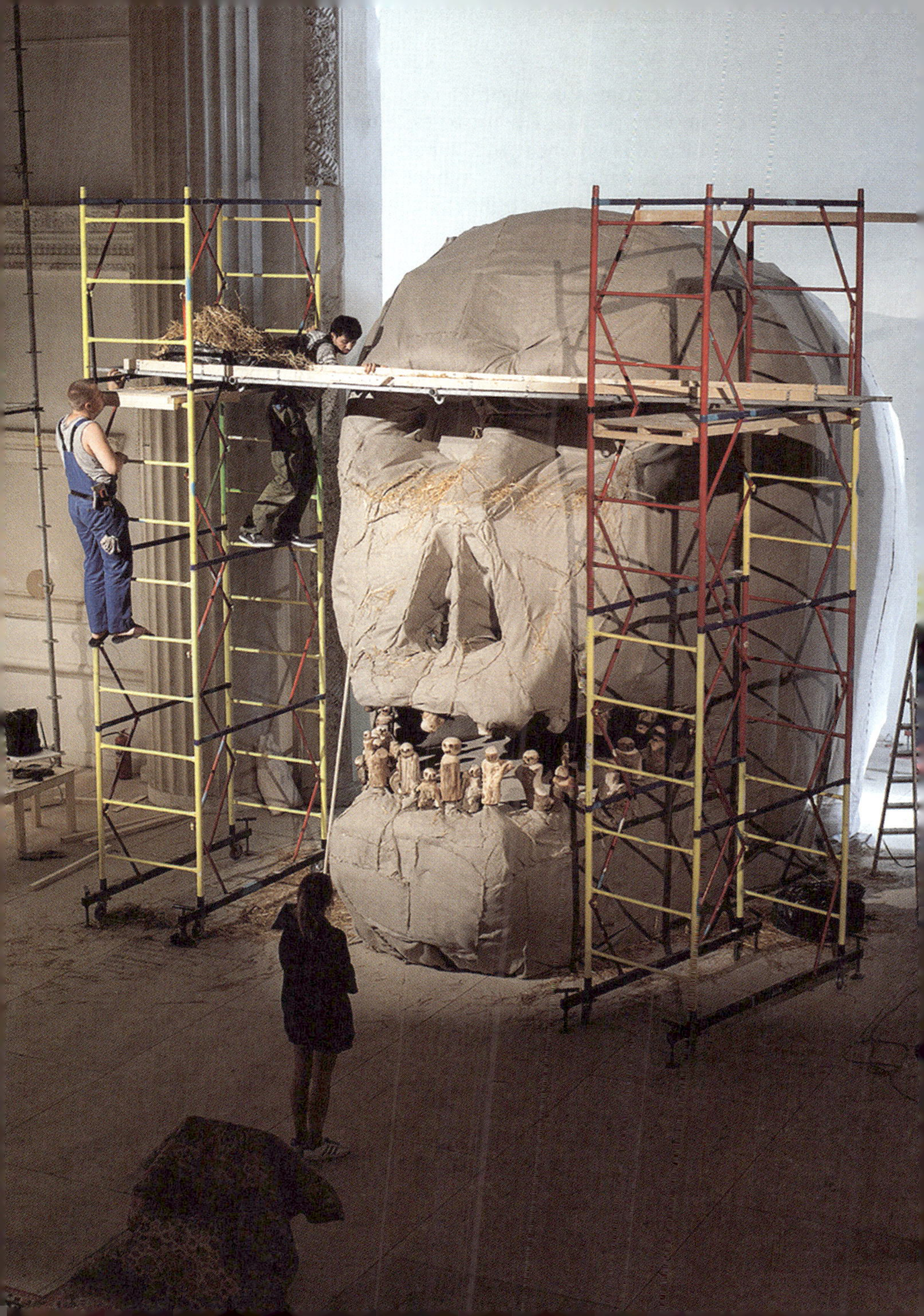

A visitor comes in, another one, can you move out of the way please, I want to take a picture.
And there is where it is… where I no longer exist… where the image blurs… where the Skull lifts itself.
What remains is the light it triggered.

1
All diary entries are from *Driftwood*, a surreal fairy tale based on my experience of the biennial and the loss of my brother.

2
See Guy Debord, *Report on the Construction of Situations*, 1957.

3
Skull series (1999–2016) 1999, I built the first skull in reaction to the Yugoslav War, from an urge to make a strong image to counterbalance all the violence. That skull was suspended from the truss of my studio and made of wood and loam. In 2002, reacting to George Bush's declaration of war after the terrorist attacks in New York on September 11, 2001, I built another skull on the roof of MuHKA in Antwerp. 2015 was the year I created a third skull at the Moscow Biennale for Contemporary Art. That one was inspired by my thinking about migration and became a symbol of transience, vulnerability and solidarity. In 2016, when Gilles Laurent, sound engineer of my films, becomes a victim of an attack in the Brussels Metro station Maalbeek, I make the fourth skull.

4
See Guy Debord, *Theory of the Dérive* (1956). In a *dérive*, for a certain period of time, one or more persons drop their relations, work and leisure activities, as well as other motives for movement and action; and let themselves be drawn by the attractions of the terrain and the encounters they find there.

5

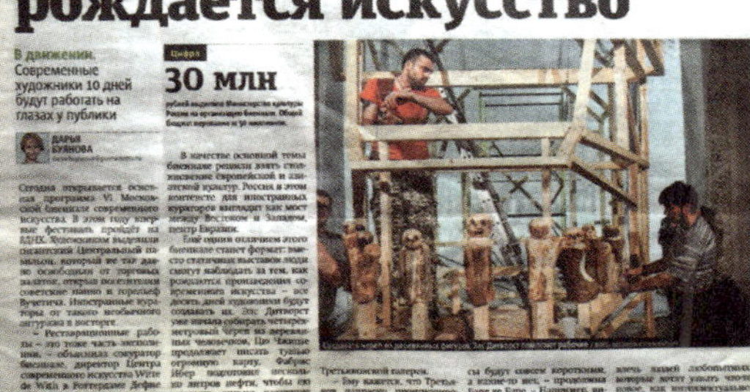

Москвичам покажут, как рождается искусство

В движении. Современные художники 10 дней будут работать на глазах у публики

Дарья Буянова

Цифра

30 млн

(Sukhrob Ganiev: We met with Els at the Moscow Biennale where she created her work *Skull*. In the beginning, the idea of our role and input was not quite clear to me. But when she gave a detailed vision of the project, the picture crystallised. Her interpreter and assistant Daria helped us a lot in terms of communication.

It was the first time in my practice that I had to create a sculpture of such an impressive scale. I believe this was true for each member of our team. Initially, the wooden frame was quite far from a skull shape. For 10 days we struggled to achieve the right form. But Els convinced us that a perfect shape was not the heart (major concept) of her work. The essential details of the skull she brought with her: small, assorted, human-shaped wooden bars. They served as teeth of the skull and looked like carved chunks with polished heads and pyrographed eyes and noses.

Another challenge of our work was to lift the whole construction 20-30 cm above the floor After lots of effort we had to face the bitter truth — it was technically impossible. Finally, we agreed with Els that we would lift it just 10 cm high.

We covered the wooden frame with metal gauze and fabrics on top. We had to make several incisions, stuffing these with hay where necessary to get the right shape of a skull. When we finished this shaping, we covered the whole sculpture with clay to give a flair of time and decay.

We had two major goals in our work: the first was to make Els happy with what we do and the second was to amaze the audience. Hopefully we met Els's expectations. As for the second task, it's difficult for me to judge.

The language barrier was also quite an issue in our cooperation with Els. But it did not discourage her. She did her best and used gestures and Daria's help. We were really happy to work with Els and hopefully it was mutual.)

6

Li Mu's diary (see page 43).

7

Song by The Flaming Lips, 1999. (On an untested hypothesis suggesting the chemical in our brains which enables us to experience the sensation of being in love is the same one that caused the Big Bang which was the birth of the accelerating universe)

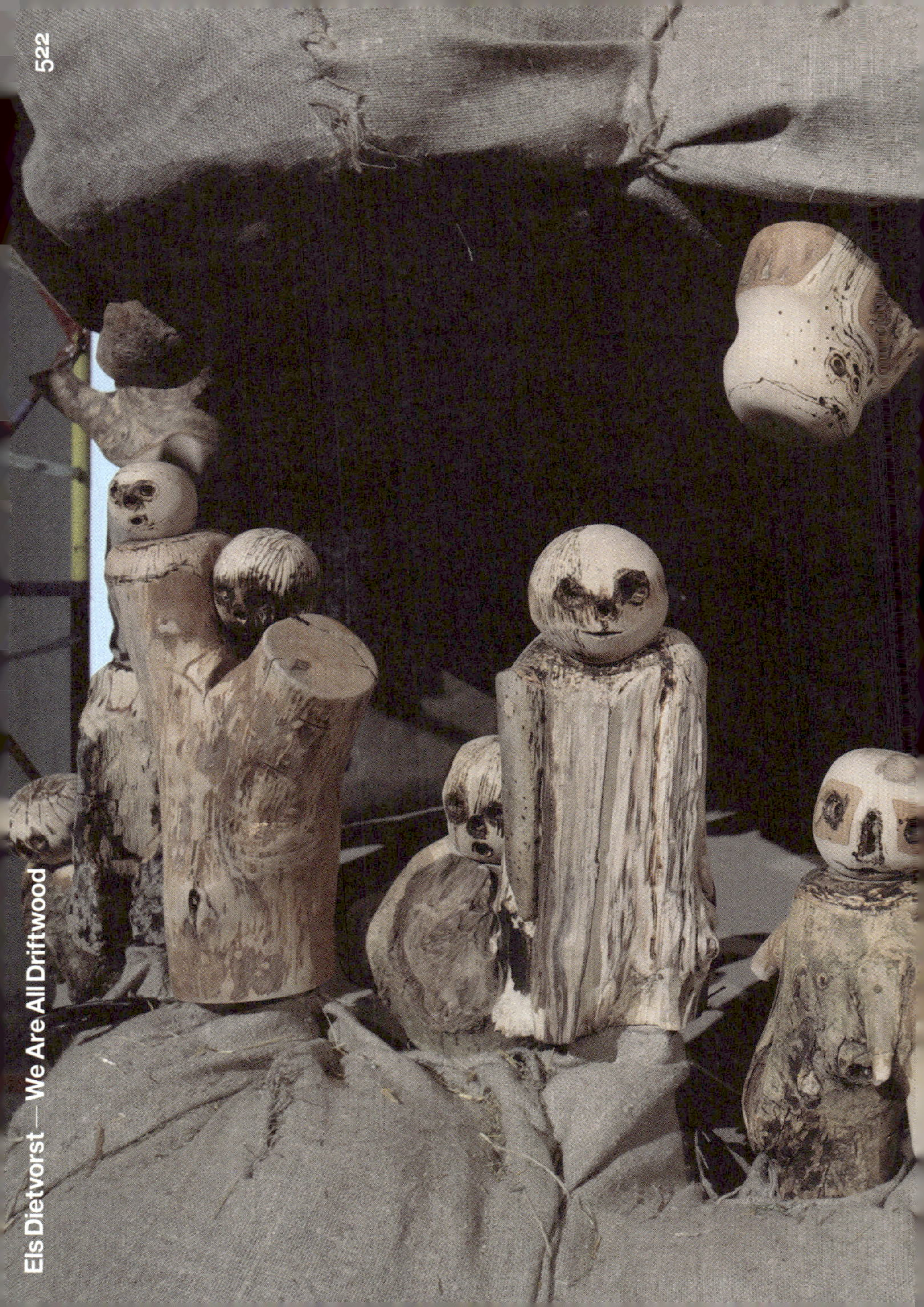

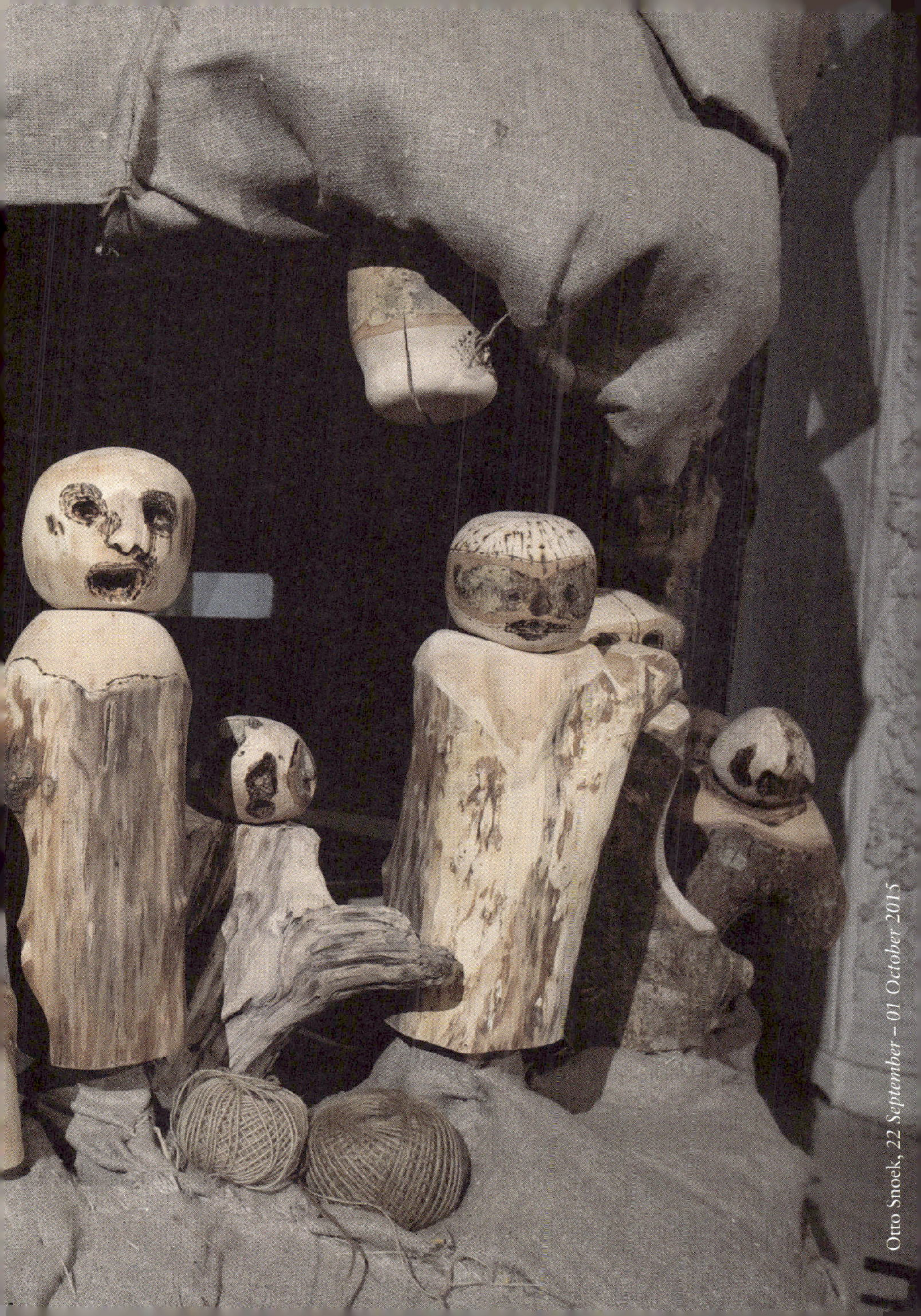

Otto Snoek, *22 September – 01 October 2015*

Part 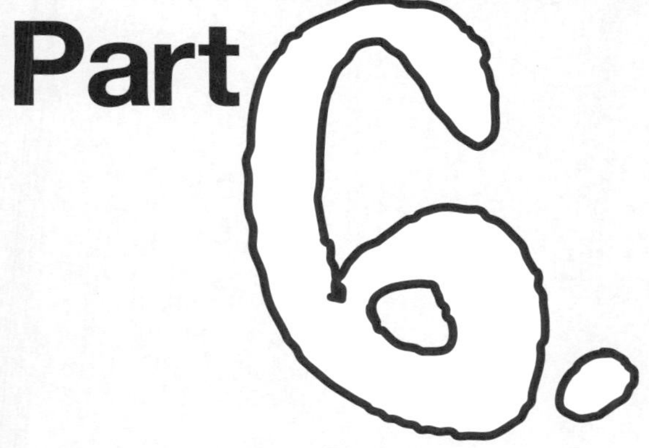

Cartographies of Time

Sergey Bratkov — Eclipse

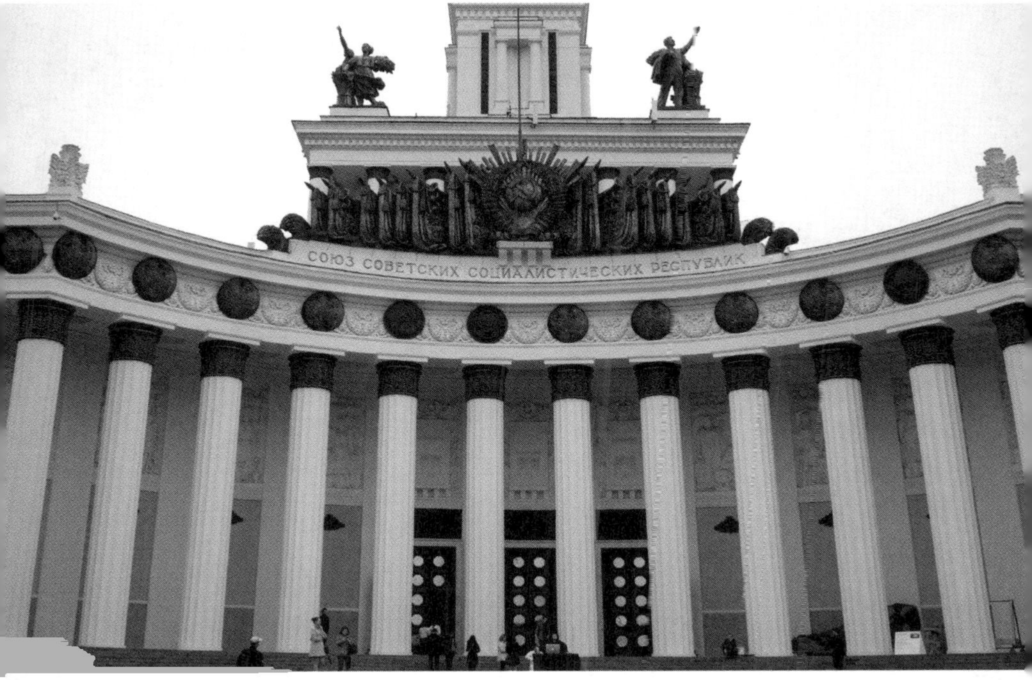

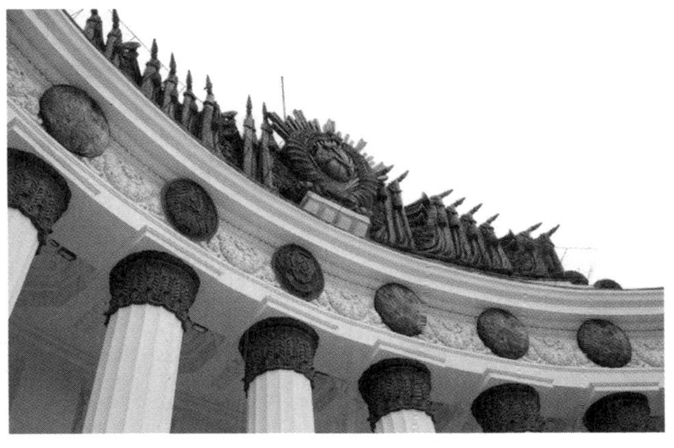

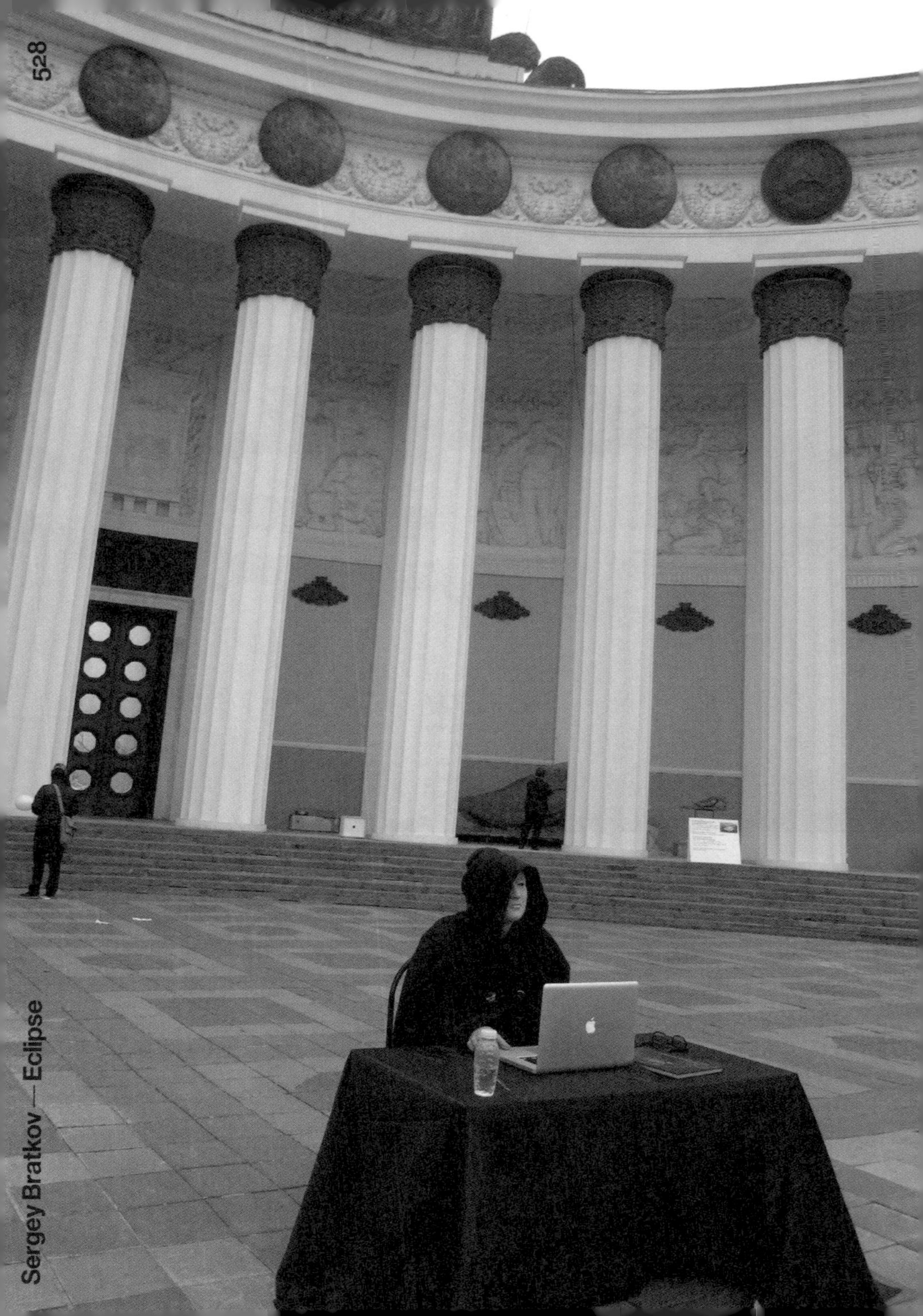

The main *Friendship of the Peoples* Pavilion at VDNKh is one of the sacred places of the Soviet ideological system. There are 16 coats of arms of the former Soviet republics on the pavilion's gable, arranged in a kind of a parade of planets around the sun — the emblem of the USSR. It has been suggested that Vyacheslav Oltarzhevsky, creator of the architectural ensemble of the exhibition park, had wanted to create "not culture, but the occult centre of the USSR". One of his ideas was the resurrection of Lenin, which is why the monumental Lenin before the pavilion building is captured in motion — he has already begun walking.

In my project, 13 coats of arms are under covers emblazoned with the image of the far side of the moon, with only three left uncovered: Russia, Belarus and Kazakhstan — the members of the Customs Union, a prototype of the Soviet Union. The image of the unseen side of the Moon clears the ideological horizon of the Biennale exhibition, disrupting the imbedded idea of its esoteric outcome. The reverse side of the moon works as a reverse side to the Resurrection built into this symbol, though the political vector of today's Russia points in another direction. This can be seen in the reconstruction of VDNKh as a monument to Soviet ideology.

Clairvoyant séances constituted the performative part of the work. The visitors who had their fortunes told also received images in which each of them was placed on the far side of the moon.

←←
Sergey Bratkov, *Eclipse*, Moscow Biennale 2015
←
Sergey Bratkov, *Eclipse*, Moscow Biennale 2015, performance on 30th September 2015

Maya van Leemput — Having Looked for Moon-Time

PARALLEL TIME

At the 6th Moscow Biennale I was cast as a witness. Part of my testimony remains hidden on a canvas graciously donated by Fabrice Hyber for the visualisation of my observations. I drew a mental model on the framed stretch of white plastic, and on the backside I jotted down: "Asked to do the impossible, I came up with this." It may have been an apology for the tangled mesh that was the presentation of my findings with 'moon time' in the centre. To decipher more than that central concept, each line would have to have been traced individually and the overall picture taken in as well. The model, true to the reality it represented, was hard to read but the legend on the back was a confirmation that this was indeed the outcome of a distinctive mission.

For months before I arrived in Moscow, the various elements that made up my interpretation of that mission had been shifting and moving, like the murmuration of a flock of birds. At the outset, only a few winged ideas were clearly discernible. I was to conduct participatory observation and provide a Futurist's reading of the Biennale. I would be on the lookout for qualities of 'gathering'. Later it transpired that we could build a database with tags or labels for the different pieces and performances of the biennial.[1] With such a systematic approach we might help ourselves understand what we were doing, or so it seemed.

Then it appeared that we were to gather for a higher purpose and even aim for the moon. The here and now would serve as a launch pad. The specificity of place and time was obvious "in a Centre in a City in the Heart of the Island of Eurasia" as per the Biennale's full title. Despite the historic weight of the location and the push of current geo-political developments, we had the idea that we might create 'parallel time' and be somewhere or somewhen different all together. We called it 'moon time'. We thought through the potential of such a yet-to-be defined concept and placed bets on it ahead of arriving in Moscow.[2]

Eleven days in a row, I made my way to the VDNKh exhibition park on the north of Moscow. I didn't skip a day and every day was different in the bubble created by the mixed rhythms of activities at the central pavilion. Processes announced themselves, with tentative identities and alliances unfolding into action and repetition, into patterns as well as simple disorder and ordinary everyday life. I liked being there. Our parallel time was plentiful. Participatory observation is a tricky method like that. I was just as much part of the gathering as any of the other participants, many of whom have their own explicit research practices and are into quality conversation and out-of-this-world ideas. This was beyond going native, more like being native. I lived our parallel time — together with the artists, curators, speakers and guests. We were a mixed bunch. I was impressed and enchanted.

A POST-NORMAL GATHERING

The 6th Moscow Biennale was always going to be different to familiar biennial standards; and not just on the surface. Its duration, intensity and content were not merely unusual or innovative. Produced in conditions of high organisational, (geo-)political and cultural uncertainty, complexity, chaos and contradiction, the Biennale in many ways became a post-normal event.

When we were conceiving moon time, our leading question (from the Biennale's title: '*How to Gather?*') was already recognised as a fiendish problem: one that would not sit still and let itself be defined and isolated just like that, or solved by using established physical and intellectual resources. We realised the proven theories and customary practices of our disciplines would not guide us towards a viable answer, as Ziauddin Sardar describes in *Welcome to postnormal times*.[3] We knew we were going to have to try something else. This is the first pointer towards understanding the Biennale as a post-normal event.

In 1999, Jerome Ravetz and Silvio Funtowicz wrote: "We discover that facts are uncertain, complexity is the norm, values are in dispute, stakes are high, decisions are urgent and there is a real danger of man-made risks running out of control." [4] This is a painfully good fit for the political and everyday circumstances of Moscow in 2015. As I put forward in my reflection ahead of the Biennale,[5] the US national intelligence council's *Global Trends 2030* discusses Russia under the mega-trend 'diffusion of power' and the slow relative declines of the economies of Europe, Japan, and Russia. The report cites the increasingly multi-polar nature of

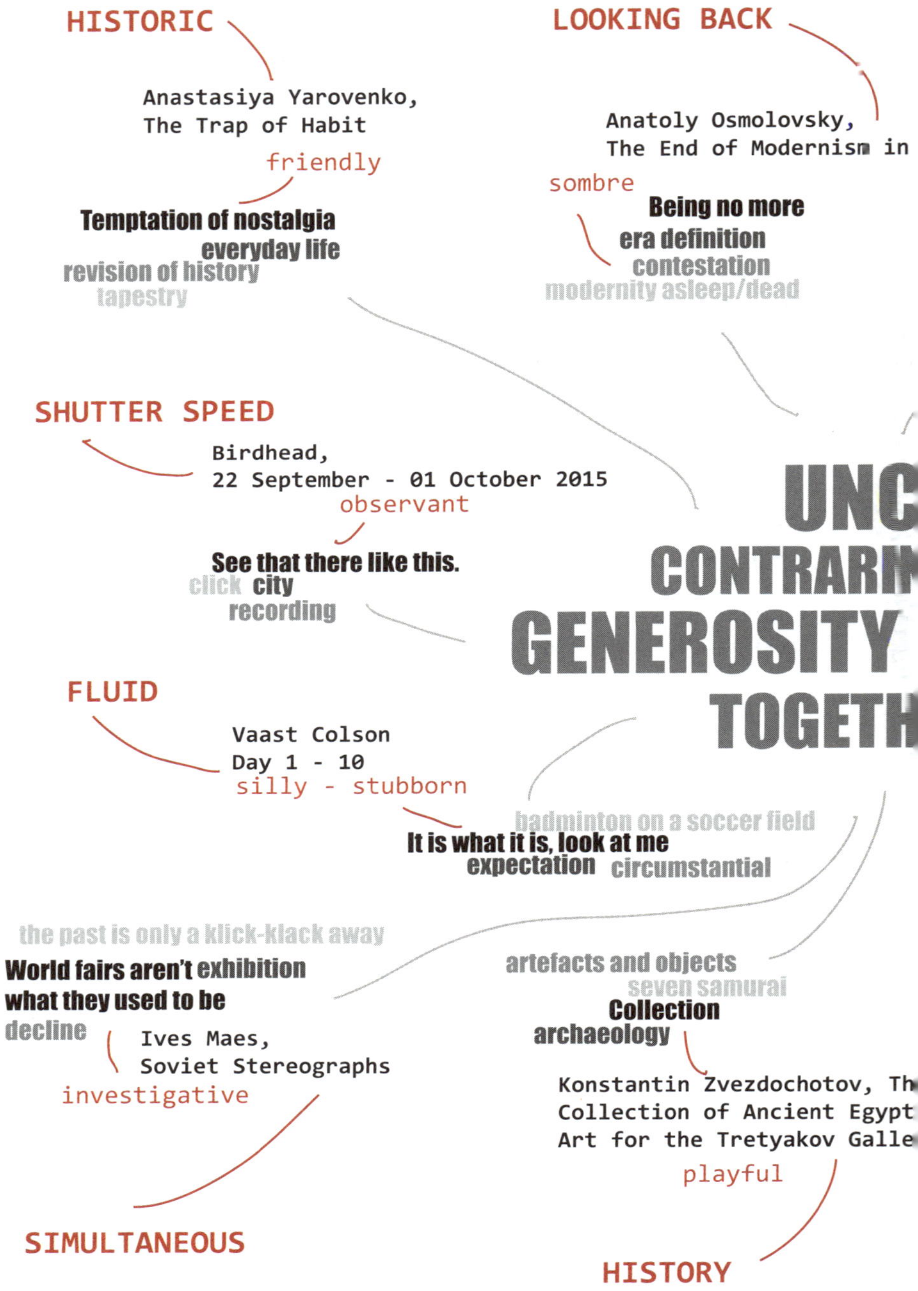

HISTORIC

Anastasiya Yarovenko,
The Trap of Habit

friendly

Temptation of nostalgia
everyday life
revision of history
tapestry

LOOKING BACK

Anatoly Osmolovsky,
The End of Modernism in

sombre

Being no more
era definition
contestation
modernity asleep/dead

SHUTTER SPEED

Birdhead,
22 September - 01 October 2015

observant

See that there like this.
click city
recording

UNC
CONTRARI
GENEROSITY
TOGETH

FLUID

Vaast Colson
Day 1 - 10

silly - stubborn

badminton on a soccer field
It is what it is, look at me
expectation circumstantial

the past is only a klick-klack away
World fairs aren't exhibition
what they used to be
decline

Ives Maes,
Soviet Stereographs

investigative

SIMULTANEOUS

artefacts and objects
seven samurai
Collection
archaeology

Konstantin Zvezdochotov, Th
Collection of Ancient Egypt
Art for the Tretyakov Galle

playful

HISTORY

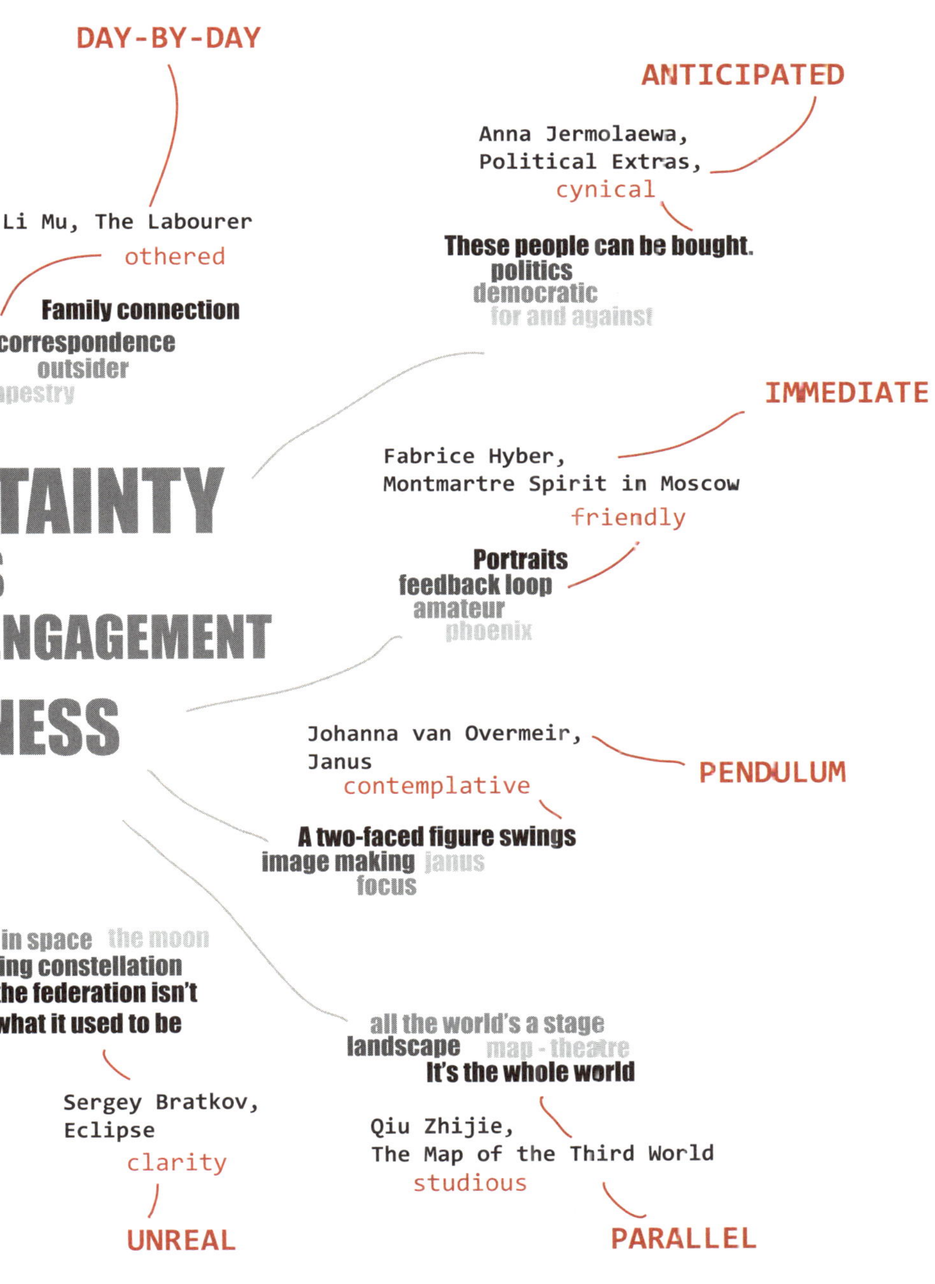
DAY-BY-DAY
a
Li Mu, The Labourer
othered
Family connection
correspondence
outsider
tapestry
ANTICIPATED
Anna Jermolaewa,
Political Extras,
cynical
These people can be bought.
politics
democratic
for and against
IMMEDIATE
Fabrice Hyber,
Montmartre Spirit in Moscow
friendly
Portraits
feedback loop
amateur
phoenix
RTAINTY
S
ENGAGEMENT
NESS
Johanna van Overmeir,
Janus
contemplative
PENDULUM
A two-faced figure swings
image making janus
focus
er in space the moon
nking constellation
the federation isn't
what it used to be
Sergey Bratkov,
Eclipse
clarity
UNREAL
all the world's a stage
landscape map - theatre
It's the whole world
Qiu Zhijie,
The Map of the Third World
studious
PARALLEL

the geo-political sphere with cheerful sounding game-changers for regional instability and the potential for increased conflict added to the disturbing picture. Three sets of risks are listed that "could conspire to increase the chances of an outbreak of interstate conflict: (1) changing calculations of key players— particularly China, India, and Russia; (2) increasing contention over resource issues; and (3) a wider spectrum of more accessible instruments of war." At the time of the Biennale, Russia's role in crises in Ukraine, the Crimea and Syria had caused heightened tensions with Europe. Russia had also just started boycotting Belgian fruit. Madonna refused to play the Russian capital, taking a stand on gay rights. What is more, the choice of theme and wording of the Biennale title placed questions of political geography at the centre of attention of the event.

Not only the conditions of the broader (geo-political and regional) contexts but also the modes of production of this biennial were post-normal. In their concept letter, under the heading "How we gathered, around a sense of urgency,"[6] the Moscow Biennale's curators describe how the 'pragmatic circumstances' of a budget that had plummeted together with the ruble, and the nature of the premises allocated to the event, shaped what the curators put together. Clearly, there were no options for business as usual.[7]

THE ART OF CONVERSATION

Sardar argues that in post-normal times "even a very basic understanding of a problem requires a dialogue on its various dimensions, involving a whole range of perspectives and interests including those of experts, lay, adults as well as children, people of different social and cultural backgrounds, different ethical notions."[8] In Moscow, we were able to try this out in practice. The programme of keynotes, performances, talks and workshops was a multi-disciplinary mix, sourced well beyond the confines of the art world. The involvement of a range of unconventional contributors, myself included, was a further indication of the post-normal attitude of the gathering. The already relatively broad peer community of actors in the field of the arts was extended to include politicians and policy makers, social and political scientists, economists, philosophers, journalists, a futures researcher, historians, local musicians and gymnasts…

Healy explains: "Extended peer communities [...] extend the traditional quality assurance role of conventional peer communities to all legitimate stakeholders and enable their participation in related policy debates."[8] Moreover, extended peer communities enable the use of "extended facts". A clear recognition of uncertainty, ignorance and indeterminacy had the organisers of the Biennale seeking to enrol a widely diverse group of participants in an attempt to generate extended facts, even if the three curators did not use this particular wording from post-normal theory.

Since few of the participants and organisers of the Biennale were experts on the regional and international issues that provided the setting and focus to the event, we sought help from a string of guests for orientation and additional perspective in a special project outside of the regular programme. For this project, seven international press correspondents, well at home in the messiness of Moscow, joined the artists in a series of unconventional lunchtime conversations. Every day a different character was hosted at the table. We sat on simple benches and ate fine food. When there were many of us, we squeezed up to make space for an extra person, holding our elbows near our bodies and tuning our ears to each other's exotic accents. The journalists from Russia, India, Austria, the Netherlands and the United States who accepted our invitation were always pleasantly surprised by the set-up, even if they were not entirely physically or socially comfortable with it.

After the meal and introductions, we would have coffee in the hall where the movement of visitors and the wondering eyes of the security guards posted at the entrance were only minor distractions. Each correspondent was paired with an artist with whom they would compare notes on gathering, on Moscow, on Eurasia, and on art, and attempt to look forward together at what might be possible in the future and what might not be.

The first such meeting brought together the prominent Russian journalist and defence analyst Pavel Felgenhauer with the Indian independent correspondent and businessman Dattan Nair. The latter was deeply impressed by his personal meeting with the former. It was an awkward exchange, saved by the grace of artist Augustas Serapinas. The two older men based in Moscow were obviously minding their words with great awareness, neither of them able to draw a picture of positive political, economic or military developments. The young artist listened attentively to the points they made but didn't let them get away with the sweeping pessimism they had brought to the table. Emphasising the importance of the new, Serapinas pointed out the paradox that when humanity learns something, it always forgets something as well. The ability to understand others, the ability to communicate, however, should never be lost, he argued. In the uneasy conversation between the well-known imposing Russian and the careful and honour-stricken Indian, the mere fact of connecting, the search for a common ground where the exchange might be fruitful, was by itself a kind of victory.

Probably the warmest of the lunchtime meetings was between Belgian artist Els Dietvorst and Austrian journalist Carola Schneider. They talked about motherhood. They talked about Ukraine and about migration. Keywords were fear and trust, justice, patriotism, migration and hate. The duo concluded that gathering by itself is a hollow word because gathering needs to be for something and with someone. In this conversation too, the idea that communication should never break down and that real effort should be put into learning trust and overcoming fear, was central. The focus on trust in this and other conversations at Pavilion No. 1 is not surprising in the context of a post-normal gathering. As Healy explains, "trust underwrites both the dialogue central to extended peer communities and the functional utility of the knowledge so created."[9] Moreover, just as trust in 'normal' science has been lost, trust in the mechanisms of international politics is now absent and this necessitates 'the cultivation of trust by other means'. The conversation between Els and Carola was a good example of how this might be achieved.

In the tête-à-tête between the Dutch correspondent Peter d'Hamecourt and Belgian artist Ives Maes, the realisation of the pressures of history on the kinds of conversations that can be had and the images that can be shared led to a discussion on disinformation and self-representation. Over lunch, the Dutchman had already drawn attention to the Russian notion of a white lie. In English a white lie is a minor untruth, a harmless fib to spare someone's feelings or to avoid conflict. The kind of white lie that d'Hamecourt spoke about also has to do with diplomacy but just as much with self-preservation as with consideration of the other. Such a fabrication is hardly a deception as it is assumed that the listener is aware of the lie being presented. The speaker knows, the listener knows, and the speaker knows the listener knows. Everyone involved in the exchange is conscious of the falsehood

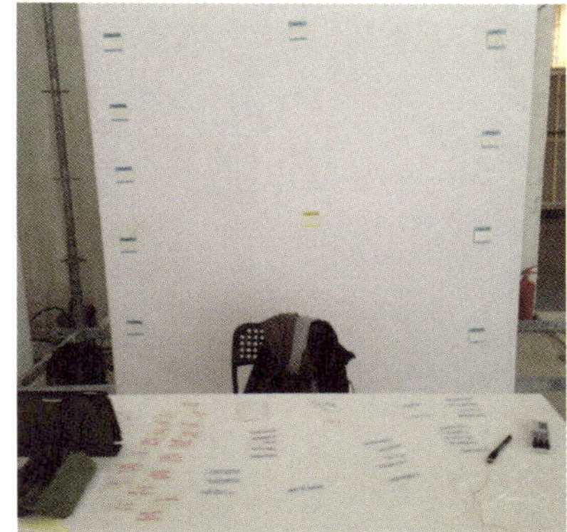

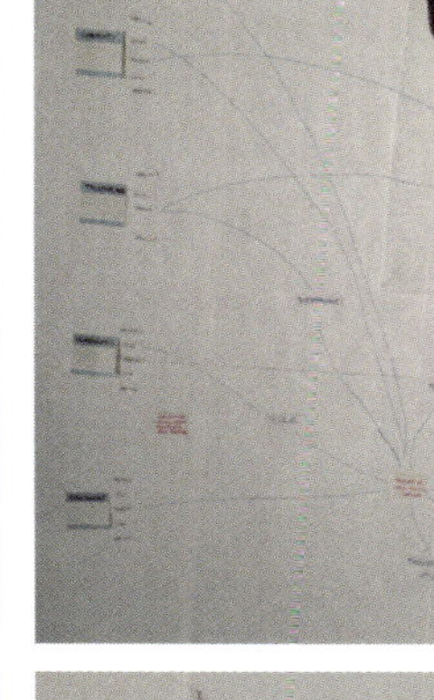

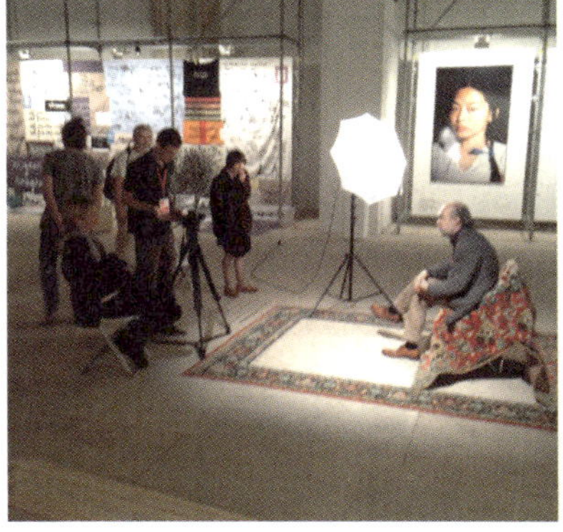

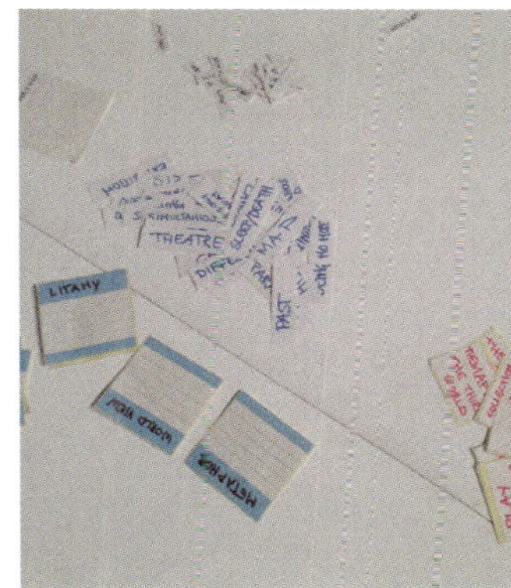
LITANY
THEATRE
PAST

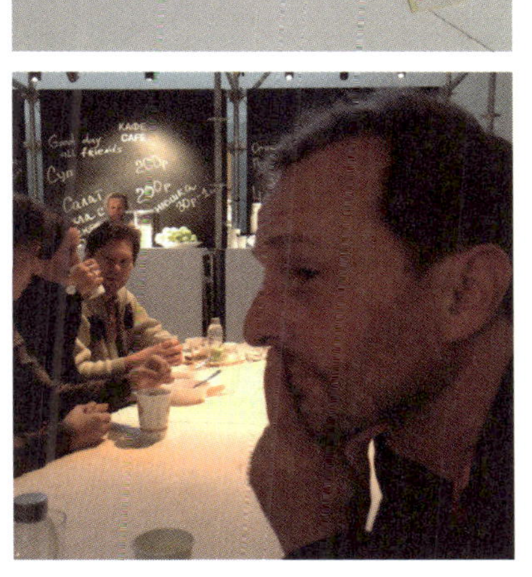
KAFE
CAFE

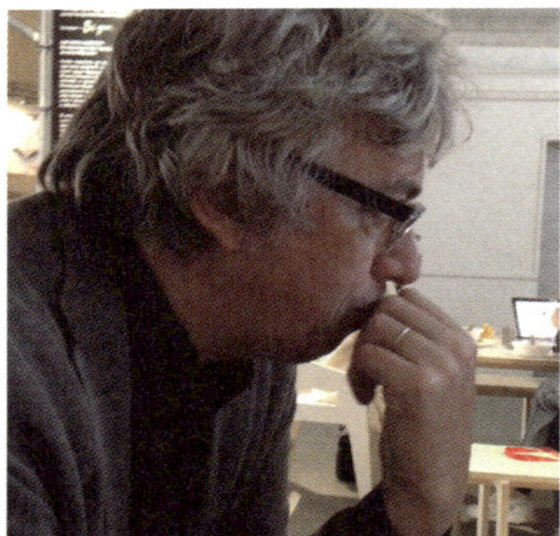

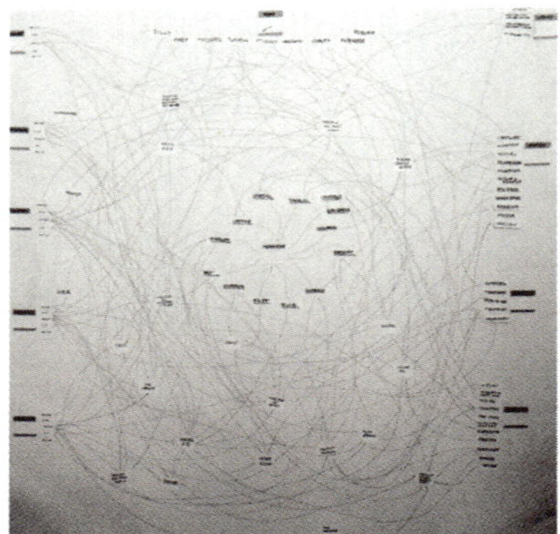

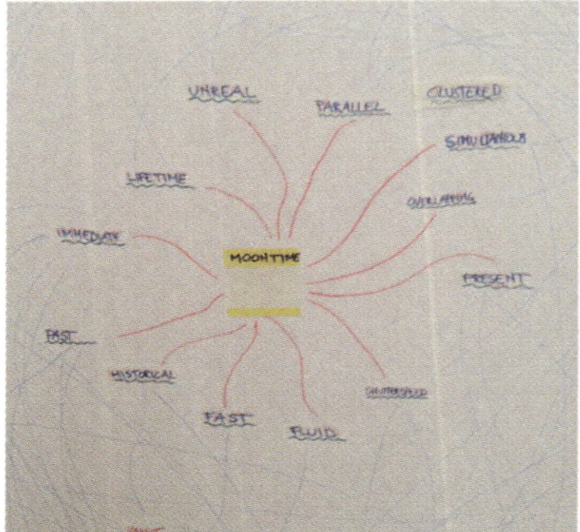

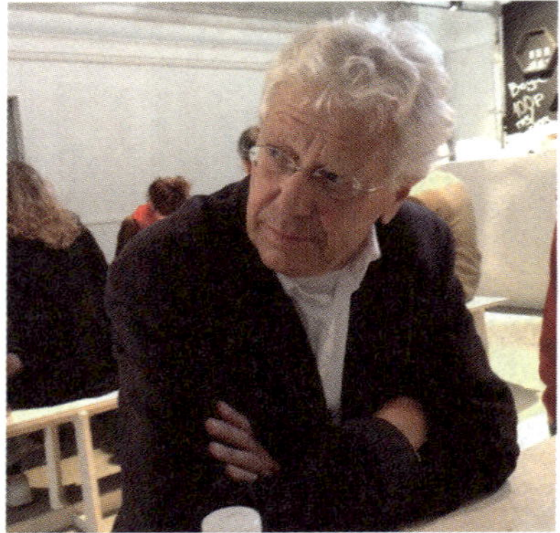

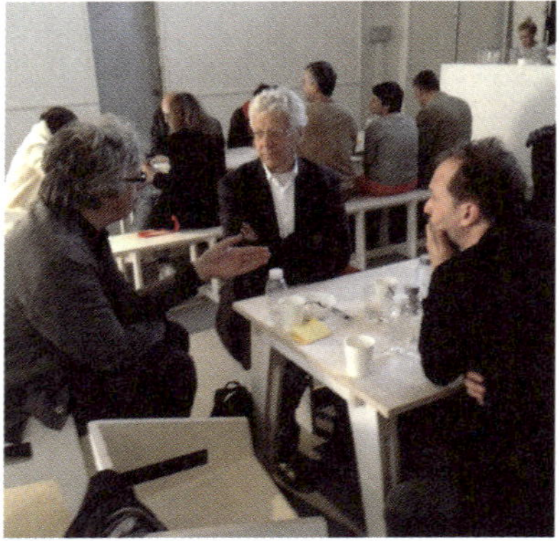

←↑
Maya van Leemput, *Mapping the 6th Moscow Biennale*, September 2015, personal documentation of the process

but nobody calls it. Sometimes it is about not saying everything; sometimes it is more blatant than that. In a climate where a truth can get you killed or imprisoned, the white lie has an important function. It serves to keep things going in conditions that cannot be spoken of.

Among the participants of the biennial there were very few white lies. If spin had a part in what we were doing, it was more in the vein of 'fake it till you make it'. Perhaps we were getting on with things without paying attention to what in actual fact makes them impossible. Beyond this mild denial of the issues surrounding our efforts to answer an impossible question, it seemed we only had to pretend we were gathering and already we were. Leon Kahane just had to show up for his ballet training and he was already performing. The group of elderly and unemployed who carried contradictory slogans in relation to the biennial for Anna Jermolaewa's performance did not need to believe what was written on their banners. Some things are done for effect and as long as the effect is true, there is honesty. However, it is not certain that white lies did not lie at the heart of what made the biennial possible to begin with. Even now they defy being spoken of or written down.

MODELLING MOON TIME

In a constellation that includes the possibility of white lies, what people say becomes less meaningful than what they do or make. This had to be where to look to figure out if our moon time was true. With the dedicated database tool of M HKA's Ensembles[10] in hand, I attempted an overview of the artworks that came together in Pavilion No. 1. Thirty eight of the pieces and performances were represented in the collection and examined for evidence of moon time.

Classifying and labelling artwork is a highly specialised business, an endeavour commonly reserved for art critics, theoreticians and historians, if not just for artists themselves. The categories and concepts used are particular and problematised within an already established cultural discourse. The tags and labels developed for the works of the biennial, however, were meant to identify very different qualities. The questions asked of the pieces and performances addressed their application of moon time and their positions on gathering.

The use of a database held a clear and present risk of reductionism but also provided an opportunity to gather insight into possible approaches to the problem of gathering. Of course, the work of the artists could offer no clearly delineated solutions. Their creations might, however, provide tentative suggestions of potential. Most of the works did not even exist on the first day and I had the honour and the pleasure to see them come into being. The tags used in the database relate as much to these processes as to their end results. Similarly, only a handful of the categories taken into account for the database were ready to use at the outset. The tags and words used to discover the qualities and capacities of moon time developed together with the artefacts and moments they described.

I used eleven categories to think about the artworks that were part of the biennial collection, starting with only four, identifying additional qualities related to 'gathering' over the course of the ten days at VDNKh. For building the final set of categories, I relied on the topics and keywords of the daily key-note lectures and the generous pointers from artists and curators following my progress with the database.

The four categories for labelling I arrived with in Moscow were borrowed from Sohail Inayatullah's *Causal Layered Analysis* (CLA): litany, system, world view and metaphor. This approach is proclaimed for creating transformative spaces for the creation of alternative futures. It seemed that it might also be useful for understanding and hatching parallel time. In the category of Litanies appeared simple surface descriptions of the content of the item. This included statements such as "Bad behaviours can die," (Donna Kukama's *Cemetery of Bad Behaviours*), "World fairs aren't what they used to be," (Ives Maes' photographs) and "It is what it is," (Vaast Colson's daily performances). Amongst others, the systems that were referred to at the second level of CLA were history, exhibition, religion, migration, archaeology, politics, everyday life and language. World views of transcendence, inevitability, tolerance, theatricality and change were discerned. Clearly the subject matter of the Biennale touched upon an inexhaustibly wide range of domains. We concluded that 'everything in the world' is needed for gathering. In discussions with the artists and visitors, it further became evident that linguistic metaphors to match the content of the pieces and performances listed in the database were always going to be interpretations of what point they were able to make or of how they were able to make it, but never a fitting representation of both the what and the how.

Two categories that were derived directly from two keynote speeches (by Michelangelo Pistoletto and Goran Petrović) turned out to have a strong connection to the focus of post-normal theory on uncertainty and contradiction. The first was 'certainty', with the majority of items in the database labelled as having low certainty. The second gave a slightly lower but still impressive count for high 'contrariness'. Further, the labels for 'generosity' were not limited to low, medium or high levels but had to include more precise wording such as 'contained' or 'measured' for adequate description. Overall, the items in the Ensembles bank showed a high degree of generousness and an only slightly lower degree of 'togetherness'. The choice of these two categories was based plainly on artists' expressions of their experiences of the Biennale in informal exchanges. It is not surprising that these particular qualities put forward by the participants themselves did have a high incidence in the overview of their work.

The two most telling sets of labels turned out to be those that addressed the dimension of 'time' in the works and those that addressed their 'mood'. Both were addressed using free tagging and the resulting labels for each of the pieces discussed with the artists for fine-tuning. These were clearly the labels that they showed most interest in and wanted to have a say in.

The inspiration for categorising the moods of the works in the Biennale came from a lunch time foray into the Situation Lab's game called *The Thing From the Future*[11] and ensuing discussions with the curators, the coordinator and the two other academics taking part in the biennial as witnesses. 'Mood' attracted everyone's attention. In a production modus that relies very much on the spirit of its participants, this was not unexpected. While we gathered and considered the different manners in which gathering at different scales might be made possible, much depended on each participant's particular frame of mind and motivation. The atmosphere of our gathering was made up by our combined moods, and our individual moods in turn were tuned by the general atmosphere. Labels for the moods of the items in Ensemble included: friendly, cynical, melodic, investigative, contemplative, playful, committed, observing, inquisitive, balanced, silly, stubborn…

The most important set of labels, focussed on time, included tags such as: immediate, history, parallel, unreal, looking back, day-by-day, parallel, lifetime, shutter speed, simultaneity, preamble, past, present, future, daily, pendulum, simultaneous, fluid, and overlapping. None other than such non-exhaustive, non-exclusive categories and hardly systematic tags could have served. In relation to time, each of the items was unique and specific and it would not have been right to create larger sub-sets that would deny the exceptional nature of each individual work of art.

The labels identified moon time as non-discrete as far as actual time is concerned. No clock would be able to tell if now is moon time or whether tomorrow might be. Moon time is not actual time, it cannot be caught, only imagined or lived. That is precisely what those who gathered in Moscow did. We lived the contradictory times expressed in our work and created another time composed of all the unique moments that passed, one after the other, to create an intangible experience of togetherness and never-ness. This approach and the resulting production at Pavilion No. 1 of VDNKh were labelled 'chaotic' by some outside observers. It defied expectations of what a biennial is and what it can do, and confirmed the event's post-normal nature.

1
Screenshot of ensembles bank Moscow items overview.

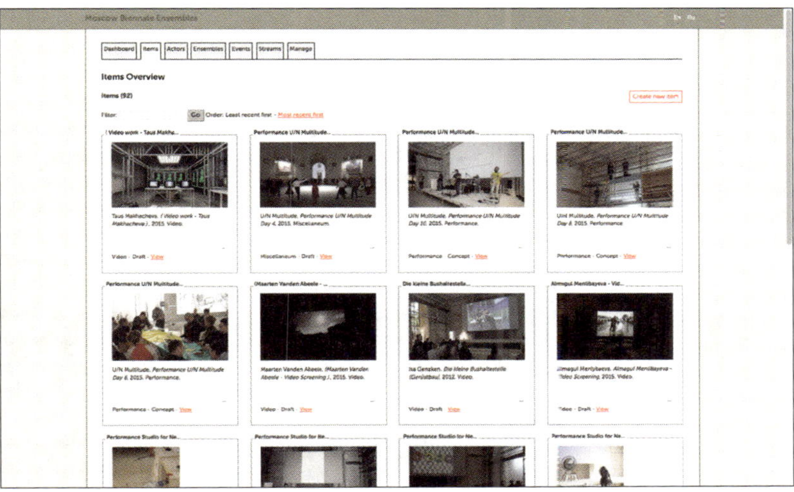

2
Maya van Leemput. *Moon Time*, in: *How to Gather? Acting in a Center in a City in the Heart of the Island of Eurasia. 6th Moscow Biennale for Contemporary Art*. Moscow. 2015, pp. 67–82.

3
Ziauddin Sardar, *Welcome to postnormal times*, in: *Futures* 42 (5) (2010), pp. 435–444. http://ziauddinsardar.com/2011/03/welcome-to-postnormal-times/

4
Jerome R. Ravetz and Silvio Funtowicz, *Post-Normal Science — an insight now maturing*, in: *Futures* 31 (7) (1999), pp. 641–646. https://www.researchgate.net/publication/278600551_Post-Normal_Science_-_an_insight_now_maturing

5
Maya van Leemput. *Moon Time*, in: *How to Gather? Acting in a Centre in a City in the Heart of the Island of Eurasia. 6th Moscow Biennale for Contemporary Art*. Moscow. 2015, pp. 67–82.

6
Ayas, D. De Baere, B., Schafhausen, N. *The biennale as urgency*, in: *How to Gather? Acting in a Centre in a City in the Heart of the Island of Eurasia. 6th Moscow Biennale for Contemporary Art*. Moscow. 2015. pp. 39–66.

7
Ziauddin Sardar, *Welcome to postnormal times*, in: *Futures* 42 (5) (2010), pp. 435–444.

8
Stephen Healy. *Extended peer communities and the ascendance of post-normal politics*, in: *Futures* 31, Elsevier (1999), pp. 656.

9
Stephen Healy. *Extended peer communities and the ascendance of post-normal politics*, in: *Futures* 31, Elsevier (1999), pp. 655.

10
Ensembles is a web tool used by M HKA for the sustainable digital organisation of information and insights. At this moment it contains multi-media information on over 7,000 works of art by more than 2,000 artists.

11
http://situationlab.org/projects/the-thing-from-the-future/

Katja Novitskova — From Social Housing to Mars / Из спального района на Марс

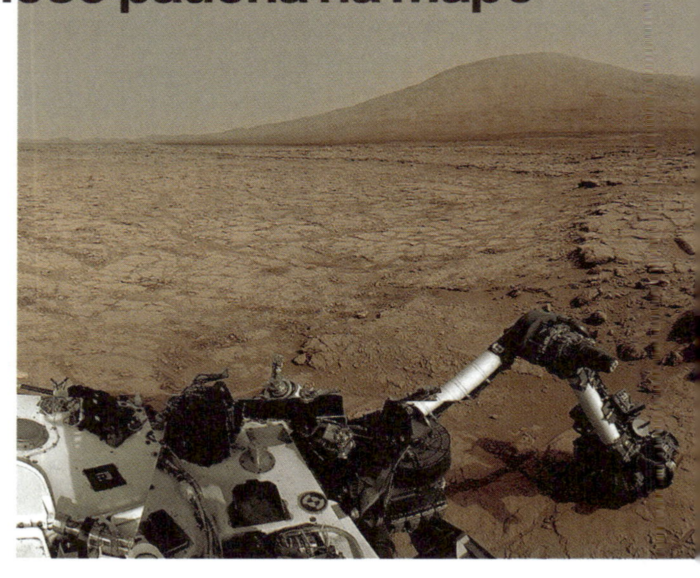

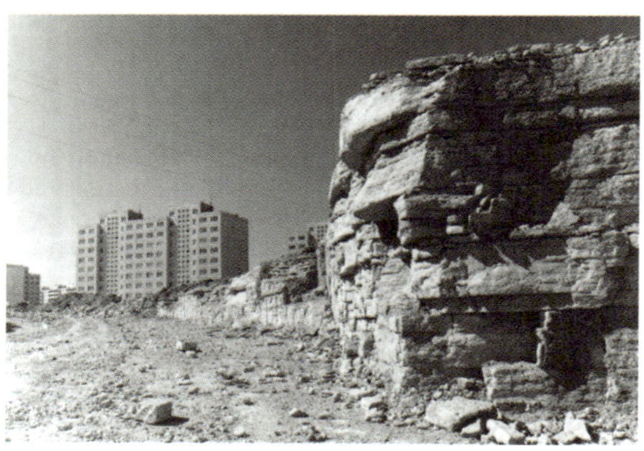

Lasnamäe housing district in Tallinn, Estonia, during construction. Seen from the main thoroughfare, Laagna Road, a trench carved into limestone, in the mid-1980s

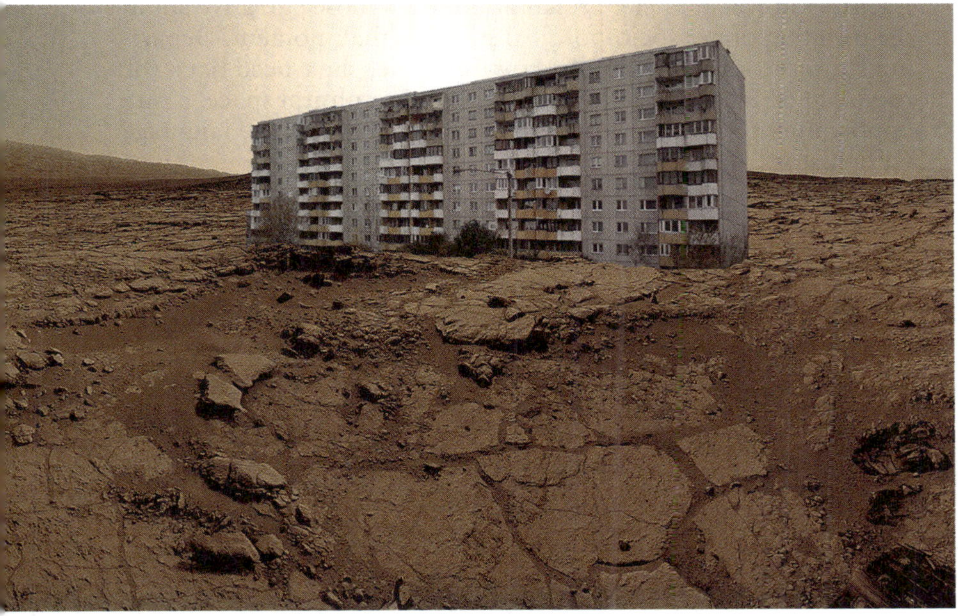

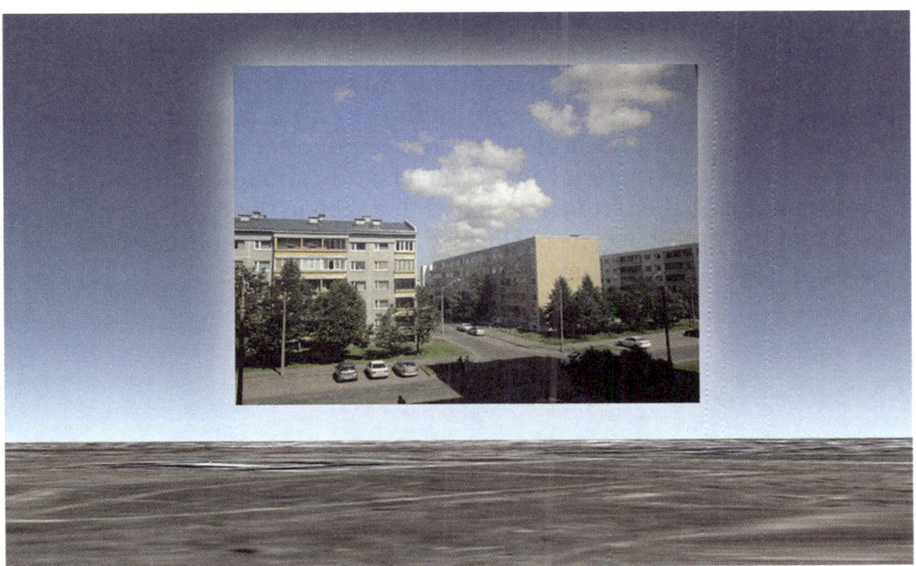

Katya Novitskova, *Social Housing on Mars*, Moscow Biennale 2015, presentation slides

Estonian artist Katja Novitskova spoke about her work in both English and Russian. Her presentation was a loose narrative about the meaning of her socio-political status at that moment. Departing from the setup of the Moscow Biennale, she traced back the roots of her artistic practice in a post-Soviet cultural space, a rare opportunity to truly discuss these impacts in her native language with visitors on site.

Following a trajectory of growing up in a Soviet social housing neighbourhood, Katja described a somewhat abstract and empty place with hardly any cultural life. From today's perspective, it may be compared to a 3D software setting for a computer game or animation—empty land stretching out to the horizon with grey block buildings placed in it... When she was growing up in the 1990s, this setting already felt foreign to the artist. When combined with the sudden poverty and existential fears of the time, she started looking at it from a meta-position.

In Moscow, she read this experience through the lens of escapism, which Katja is investigating as a form of coping. She developed an interest and attraction to all things alien; including Western. Aesthetics of dystopian emptiness, her interest in astronomy, in UFOs and the archaeology of ancient worlds, in art and music—in MTV as a form of escapism from the post-Soviet reality—all led to a contemporary art practice.

In a combination of an artist's talk and a speculative thought experiment, Katja Novitskova showed how this strategy not only applies to her, but resonates through the cultural sphere from various angles. The session ended in more unclear territory with speculative visual material and a conversation about the on-going colonisation of alien frontiers such as that seen in the Arctic, deep-sea mining, and space, as performed by states and multinational corporations. [Marie Egger]

Alexander Ugay — Earth and Shape

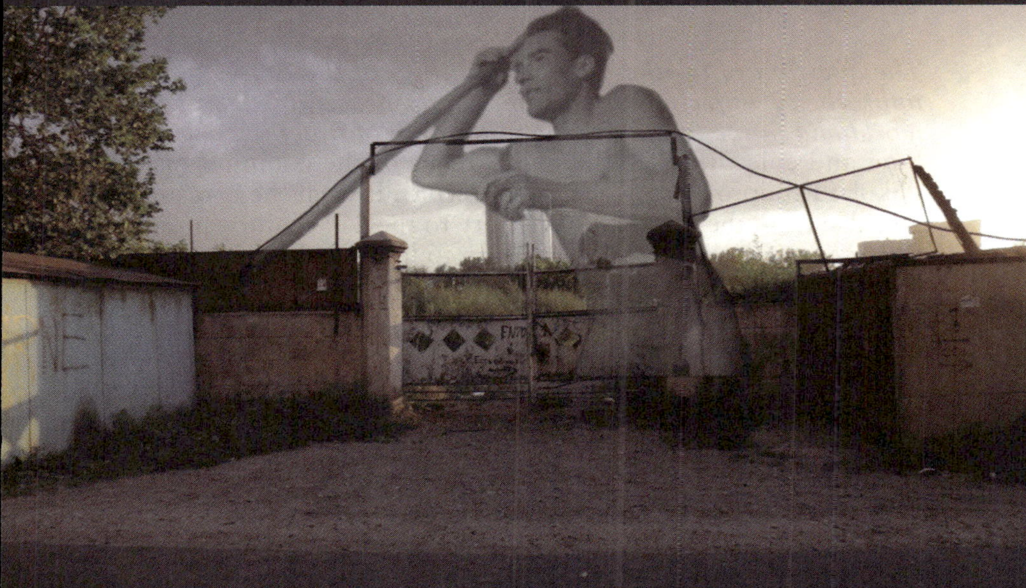

Alexander Ugay, *Earth and Shape*, 2013–2015, video, 17 mins., still

Alexander Ugay's video portrays human life on Earth: A rural environment, birds chirping, a soft wind blowing into the microphone, buildings, small cities, deserted towns, people in everyday life, an old couple in a half-hearted quarrel, street workers on a construction site, children in an odd indoor carousel… filmed in Kazakhstan, Russia, Austria, Korea, Turkey and Bulgaria.

Overlaying these images are athletes launching a discus, throwing a hammer, jumping high and long. These were captured by Leni Riefenstahl.

The video raises doubt in the codes of history and memory until it melts into an ambiguous narration that disconnects geography from history. The individual and their stories vs. the holistic anywhere at any time — Alexander Ugay spans this arc as a reply to the question How to Gather? [Marie Egger]

Anastasya Gacheva — How Can We Learn to Live Together? Nikolai Fyodorov's Answer

The question of brotherhood, or kinship, of the causes of the unbrotherly, unfeeling of kinship, i.e. un-peaceful, state of the world and of the means for the restoration of fraternity—is the long and epic title that the philosopher of the common task, Nikolai Fyodorov, used for his main work. It seems he is casting a bridge from the distant 19th century to the 21st century, posing the same question: How can we learn to live together? He posed this question at a time of growing sense of impending catastrophe worldwide, when every other contemporary event seemed to take swinging blows at the faith in people's ability to order their earthly affairs in accord and happiness, without enmity or killing.

Fyodorov's research leads to the following answer: The root of human disconnection is to be found in *human mortality*. It is precisely mortality, poisoning the individual with the toxins of *fear*, *anxiety*, *desperation* and malignant *cynicism*, that negates hope in a harmonic structuring of life. Mortality is irretrievably connected in the natural order with the law of replacement and the struggle for survival. It is the ontological, as well as simply psychological, soil in which non-fraternity germinates.

The history of today (history as fact) is one of mutual annihilation. Nations rise up against one another, kingdoms against kingdoms, enmity quickens, dies down, and flares up once more. Clashes take on a local character here or a grander scale there. Fyodorov set forth a vision of *a brotherly condition of humanity* and of a path towards this along the idea of the overcoming of death. He conceptualised this surmounting in a radical fashion: mankind must overcome the mortal order of nature—founded on discord and breeding discord—to reach immortality in full muster, returning life to all who have ever lived on earth.

Such a prospect seems utopian. But for Fyodorov utopian folly was something else entirely: to try to establish concord in a world where the grim reaper presides over the ball; to take shelter from inexorable mortal reality by means of ideology, party programmes, or successful business projects. It is utopian to hope to overcome wars and enmity, unless the main root of discord is ripped up. The *issue of wealth and want* that is knocking on doors, giving rise to wars, revolutions, local and general conflicts, exacerbating social divisions, will not, according to Fydorov, be resolved unless it is subjugated to another all-encompassing question: The question of life and death; of the fundamental, natural poverty of man who inexorably ages, weakens, sickens and dies. Fyodorov loads the shoulders of mankind with a burden that is totally inconceivable: The *regulation of nature*, the *conquest of space*, as well as *immortality* and *resurrection*. Each of these tasks has a general and truly universal scope. The regulation of nature begins with the countering of natural disasters and cataclysms and ends in the transformation of the very laws of nature themselves: that the birth of new beings not displace those already born, that people achieve autotrophy and no longer live off other life forms for their sustenance, that life becomes the fraternal assembly of all creatures. The conquest of the cosmos begins with breaking free from earth's orbit, continuing with the colonisation of the moon and the planets of our solar system—to culminate in the scattering of the resurrected generations across an entire universe, transformed by the creative genius of humans as artists.Meanwhile, humanity is pushed on in its development precisely by the drive to do the impossible. The impetus of invention and discovery produce Icaruses, straining for the sun in spite of all the madness and deadly peril of the flight. At the basis of civilisation's scientific and technological breakthroughs lies a dream—a thought, fantasy, or fairy tale, as Konstantin Tsiolkovsky defined this first stage of creative activity in the world, without forgetting at the same time about the scientific calculation that serves as the basis for any dream, or the achievement that crowns the thought.[1]

Andrei Platonov, for whom Fyodorov's *Philosophy of the Common Task* was an indispensible guide, wrote: "One has to love that Universe, which could be, and not the one that is. The impossible is the bride of humanity, and our souls fly towards her..."[2] That such words were uttered by an artist is quite unsurprising. Art is, by its very nature, connected with the building of an ideal, not hesitating to depict and design the future, permanently one step ahead of its age and daring to see what is distant from the present moment in history. Nikolai Fyodorov regarded humans, their memory, labour and culture, to be the force that fights with entropy to save the universe from a burning death, bringing into it the principle of harmony, creating the so-called *noosphere* by opening up a new, consciously creative phase in the evolution of life. The world, in his view, gathers around humans, who have become the lords of creatures, and victory over death is the condition sine qua non of this gathering.Art, science, and religion stand in the vanguard of Fyodorov's struggle with entropy. Religion reveals the aim of this action. Science provides the means. And art lends it beautiful form. The soldiers of this enlightened warrior-host of life are artists and scholars.

The 20th century began with the desire of art to grow beyond the boundaries of the creation of lifeless copies, of an aesthetic reality that had towered haughtily over the real course of life, which this refined and pure art had no connection with, leading to the daring attempts of the Avantgarde to pour out into the flow of history and to transform life. "Art acquires its wings where the call for creativity is simultaneously a call for creativity in life"[3], declared Andrei Bely. And the architects and artists of the Avantgarde set out as their field of action not just the worlds of imagination or fantasy, but the entire cosmos.The aspiration towards brotherhood in a world riven by division and death is a characteristic trait of art in ages when humanity begins to realise its *planetary nature*. In situations of worldly decline, artists in particular begin its convocation. Following the Russian Revolution, the Civil War, famine and the turning of brother against brother and sons against fathers, Vasily Chekrygin put the collapsing world back on its feet in the grandiose artistic intention of his *Cathedral of the Resurrected Museum*, calling on his artist brethren to take part in the fraternal, collective act of painting its walls, announcing that the highest, most perfect art could only be the transformation of the cosmos, the building of paradise. Andrei Platonov, having elevated orphanhood into an ethical and metaphysical category and seeing in it a bitter antithesis to kinship, urged in the spirit of Fyodorov for the restoration of a single chain and, recalling the Gospel's injunction to become as little children, put into the mouths of his young heroes dreams of universal brotherhood and the vanquishing of death.

The artists of the 21st century are likewise reflecting on the overriding of discord, on how to learn to live together, having assembled together in the centre of the Eurasian landmass at the 6th Moscow Biennale for Contemporary Art. Through the language of art, unafraid of experiments, creating above political, national and religious barriers, they aim to reconcile the truth of the individual with that of community, building projects where these truths are not in conflict, but in which they can grow, each within the other.

But where lies the secret of the first step? According to Fyodorov, without victory over death, human unity is impossible. Victory over death, however, is impossible without the unification of mankind. The achievement of one is the necessary condition for the other. Can this vicious circle be broken?

Fyodorov breaks it through love. Through love that connects people in the bosom of the family, that extends to those who stand beyond the boundaries of kinship. This love does not attain its fullest expression in the love of parents for children or of two halves for one another. A love in whose depths is concealed the natural instinct for the preservation of the species, but rather in the love of children for their fathers and mothers, stretching out further along the ladder of the generations to their grandmothers, grandfathers, and great grandparents, all the way to those who we know nothing of in personal terms, who passed on before our birth and who yet nevertheless recorded a particle of themselves in their descendants.

This is a love that is elevated, above the natural, and has nothing of the stimulus of the instinct to preserve the species and raise offspring. It is precisely this love that, for Fyodorov, is the measure of the humanity of man. "The secret of brotherhood is concealed in the fathers", he says. Through love for ancestors, for those who "gave us, or more accurately, handed over to us their life", people, as Fyodorov had it, will also become as brothers.

For this thinker there was no division into "us" and "them". All are related.

1
Tsiolkovsky, K.E. "Foreword", in Tsiolkovsky, K.E. *Exploration of the Spaces of the World by means of Rocket-Propelled Craft* (A reprint of works from 1903 and 1911 with some changes and additions). Kaluga, 1926. p. 3.

2
Platonov, A.P. *Collected Works: In 3 volumes.* Vol. 3. Moscow, 1985. p. 534.

3
Bely, A. "Theatre and Contemporary Drama", in Bely, A. *Symbolism as a World View*. Moscow, 1994. p. 154

Bart De Baere, Anton Vidokle and Arseny Zhilyaev — Society and an Indivisible Whole

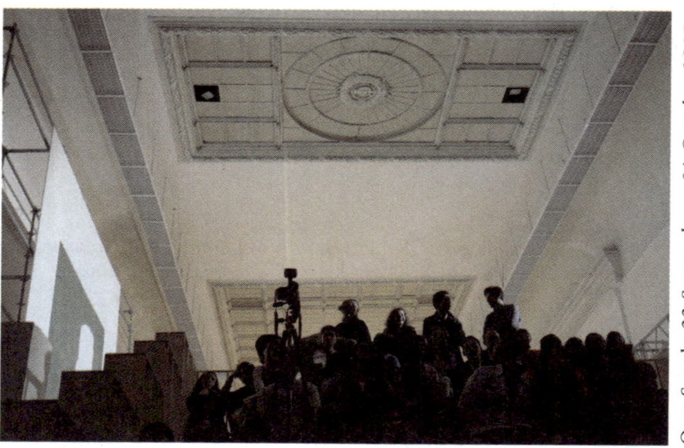

Otto Snoek, 22 *September* – 01 *October* 2015

BART DE BAERE: Anton and Arseny, you were both very present for me during the 6th Moscow Biennale. Anton by avant-premiering *The Communist Revolution Was Caused By the Sun* with the main actor reading her passages live on stage, and also by entering into a discussion with Anastasia Gacheva on cosmism; and Arseny *in absentio*, in a project addressing the future that had been announced for the Cosmonautics Memorial Museum at the entrance of VDNKh, but which was rescheduled. You speak of a long-term cooperation between the two of you. This seems to be not so much a conclusion of a past trajectory as a declaration of a future intent. What is it based upon? Can it be seen in terms of what the German language calls *Wahlverwantschaft* ['elective affinity']? If so, what are the basic aspirations you share?

ANTON VIDOKLE: I first met Arseny in the summer of 2012, albeit very briefly. At that time I was in Moscow working on Time/Bank—an e-flux project, which was basically a network where people in the arts could exchange labour using a certain type of time-based currency that we issued.[1] To jump start this time-based economy, we set up a temporary restaurant in a gallery, where it was possible to pay for food with time, and we organised a series of daily lectures, discussions and presentations at this restaurant, with numerous artists and theorists from Moscow and beyond. At the same time, Arseny was doing his Pedagogical Poem project,[2] which was also an artwork in the form of a discursive structure at the Krasnaya Presnya Museum. Many people told me that I should go and see his project, but because we were so busy cooking for people every day it was impossible for me to get away from the kitchen. In the end we briefly met up with some other friends, but didn't really manage to speak much. Nevertheless I was very intrigued with his activity.

A year or so later we were reintroduced by a mutual friend, and Arseny told me about his idea for a book about avant-garde museology, which was to include writings by Nikolai Fyodorov, the founder of cosmism. Having just made my first film that dealt with Fyodorov's ideas, I was immediately fascinated by Arseny's research into this topic and proposed that e-flux publish this book as the first title in our new series of largely historical books on aesthetic theory. What was very interesting to me, in addition to the actual content, was the fact that an artist was doing some serious historical and editorial work, which is something rare in our field these days. So I really wanted to support this. The collaboration of this book, which is now in print, led to many conversations and exchanges with Arseny, which, in turn, produced more ideas for new projects, such as a new film we are now planning to jointly make based on the writings of Alexander Svyatogor — the futurist poet, anarchist, and founder of bio-cosmism and a radical new religion: the Free Labour Church.[3]

ARSENY ZHILYAEV: Naturally, I had seen a number of projects Anton was somehow engaged in even before we met in person… I guess the first time was in 2007 or so, when I moved from Voronezh to Moscow. It was at a conference where Keti Chukhrov mentioned e-flux several times and spoke about the project of the trial of art, showing specific screenshots of this process. For someone who had just moved from a small Russian town with no trace of contemporary art life, those stories sounded like something happening on another planet.

Much later, I met Anton in Moscow. I knew he had been working on Russian cosmism for a year or two by then, but no specifics. The last thing I had seen at that time was Time/Bank at Documenta in Kassel, a project that was not directly relevant to cosmism but which was already in line with its basic instincts. Later on, when I went deeper into the history of what Anton had created, I realised the cosmic impetus had been there all the time. I am tempted to say "the utopian impetus", but that wouldn't be absolutely correct. Just like any cosmist or historical avant-gardist, Anton holds a very constructivist attitude to art. His approach may seem too radical, impossible in the current context, but always seeking for realisation, always implying a materialist, critical and even pragmatic perspective of his own prospects. And I feel totally comfortable with such an attitude to the common goal.

In my case, the interest in cosmism came from my research on the museum and its role in the transformation of life. Originally, my projects were inspired, in particular, by Marxist museology and possible speculations on the future of this institution. At some point, I realised that the museum in Russian cosmism was the quintessence of the hopes that the avant-garde pinned on the arts. What's more, Fyodorov's project was going beyond that, being more drastic than the then-accepted limit of art's ambitions. Actually, the situation has not changed too much over the last 100+ years. Anyway, by the day we met, I had been preparing a collection of works on avant-garde museology for publication and had already been involved in the project on Fyodorov's curatorship, linked by the funny twist of his life with my home city of Voronezh.

Then there was the long period of joint work on the book—and it took off from there. I think we are both positively disposed by our nature to engage in joint projects. In our case, the deep interest in Russian cosmism boosted this disposition with a lot of energy. I watch Anton's creative intuition with a keen interest. We have initiated a number of joint projects so far, and I hope this is just the beginning.

BDB: An unexpected question that emerged from the Biennale was the notion of the dual. Some of the most fruitful gatherings were gatherings of two people. Europeans have a tendency to approach dualism negatively, in a Manichaean way. A basic operation of European culture is the use of polarising antagonism as a productive combustion engine, through the thesis/antithesis/synthesis triad. Several languages, though, such as Arabic or Slovenian, have two plurals, one of which expresses 'us, the two of us'. And cultures may, as apparently many Amazon cultures do, think of 'two (man/woman)' as the basis to address the world, not the individual. Do you feel the dual to be preferable over the singular? If so, why?

AZ: Yes, indeed, the prevailing Western model of bourgeois democracy based on rivalry and competition is probably opposed by Russian democratic traditions and individual philosophical ideas which aim to eliminate oppositions and establish unity in their place. For instance, the theory of 'rational egoism' is elaborated in *What Is to Be Done?* by Nikolai Chernyshevsky, a pivotal book for Leninism and free thinking in Russia.[4] The theory implies that people inherently act in their own self-interest, but their personal wellbeing begins to depend on the common interest at some point. This principle lies behind the famous 'prisoner's dilemma', which was used by Jacques Lacan, among others. That is, we cannot maximise our profit without regard for the common interest even if we are mathematically guided solely by our own self-interest. Rational egoism is an egoism that considers and supports others.

Interestingly and unexpectedly, this story gets an American spinoff. Ayn Rand[5] developed her theory largely using Chernyshevsky as a negative example. She refused to agree that rational egoism should consider the common interests, and described a strike of the ruling class who could not afford to support the submerged tenth any longer, etc. Strong people should go all the way and stop at no end. In fact, this libertarian viewpoint predetermined the excesses of neoliberalism of the late 20th to early 21st centuries.

Russian cosmism makes this logic ultimate by outlining the horizons of a prospective unity between mankind and the Universe in their spatial and temporal coordinates.

AV: I am not sure that the dialectical method always has to be antagonistic, and I am also not sure antagonism is always productive. Some people seem to think that antagonism is a prerequisite for democracy, but I really hesitate to agree with this. Another model is the Divine Family: the Holy Trinity, in which there is no antagonism and no disagreement between the Father, Son and the Holy Spirit, who are individuated entities yet remain a kind of a singularity. I am not a Christian, but I think that this is a very interesting and inspiring model of how to be together. Nor do I think that the communist society will have such antagonism: while religions tend to identify love as the means of co-existence, similarly in communism it's the emancipated quality of life without alienation, and thus no externality from which such antagonism may arise. It's interesting to think about this…

Regarding Ayn Rand, when I was an art student in New York, one of my teachers—a kind of post-modern, neoclassical sculptor—invited me to attend a small reading group in his studio, dedicated to the discussion of her ideas. It was a sign of appreciation apparently: he thought I was a promising student, so he invited me to join his cult… I have to say that this was a rather pathetic gathering of people as mediocre as Rand's simplistic writing. That's why I was so enormously surprised when I learned much later just how much influence her books had on American political and economic elite: the novels are basically written on the level of teenage heroic fantasies of omnipotence and are full of resentment. So it's still pretty incredible to me that such mediocre writing had this toxic effect on several generations of people who came to occupy key corporate and government positions. It's as though the president of the USA were being secretly guided by Tolkien's *Lord of the Rings* (which is arguably a far better book than *The Fountainhead*.)

I would note that Rand's cult of selfishness is antithetical to Fyodorov's ideas, who specifically implored that one should live with and for everyone. There is no ethical possibility in his thinking to abandon the weak, the old, even those who have already died. His project of the Common Task is all-inclusive.

BDB: Michelangelo Pistoletto sees a third paradise emerging in the focussing point in the midst of the ∞ of barely connected circles. How do you envisage a third paradise?

AV: When I was working on *The Communist Revolution Was Caused By The Sun*, I had a very interesting conversation with the man who fabricated the aero-ionification dish we used in the film. He is essentially a fairly typical post-Soviet entrepreneur: a former high school physics teacher turned businessman, who has a small experimental factory to develop and produce ionising air purifiers for industrial chimneys. He told me that he imagines his device being used by all factories on the planet and removing all

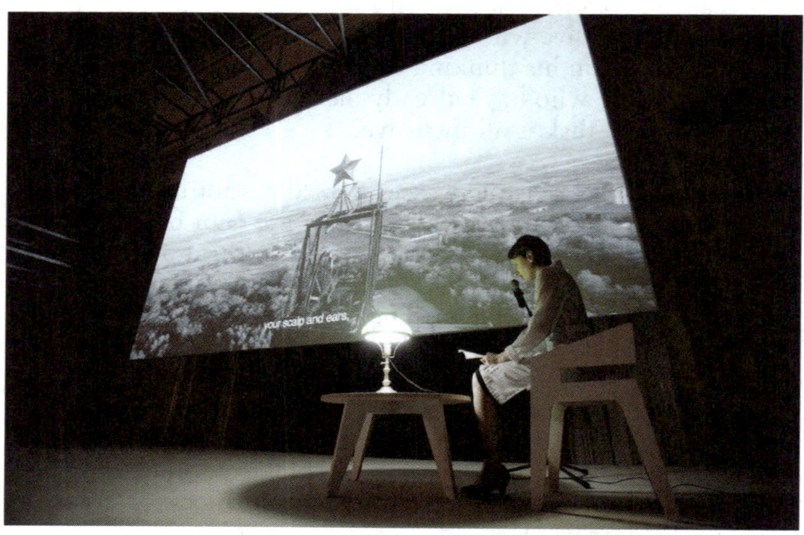

Anton Vidokle, *The Communist Revolution Was Caused By The Sun*, performance, 2015

the carbon that is polluting the atmosphere. I asked him, if he succeeded, what would happen next and he basically described a return to Paradise: as the environment is cleaned of all the waste human civilisation has produced, the climate of our planet would return to its previous condition. Ancient spores of extinct plants would come back to life and Earth will become a garden of primordial trees bearing fruits: we will no longer need to work to feed ourselves. The climate will become very mild, we will not require clothes and will walk around naked. Social relations will change completely in accordance with this new condition and humanity will essentially return to the Garden of Eden. In theology, such a return also implies becoming immortal again. We will be free of death.

Right now he is lobbying the president of Kazakhstan to include his devices in the world fair that is supposed to take place there next year, to be marketed to various industries. He is also trying to convince cosmonauts in the Russian space programme to photograph his devices from orbit, to document the translucent domes of clean air he claims they produce. So here is someone who is actually working towards the production of a second Paradise. I am not sure what a third Paradise might be…

BDB: Fabrice Hyber and Honoré δ'O experimented with telepathic drawing during the 6th Moscow Biennale, with remarkable effects, which they documented. Do you feel telepathy is a future potential?

AZ: We can never be absolutely sure something is impossible. Many of the inventions, familiar to us today—like telephone, radio, TV, let alone the Internet, 3D printers or space flights—are pure magic as seen by previous generations. I guess the first application of telepathy will be military cyborgs interconnected by a wireless network. I'm pretty sure the relevant prototypes have already been created.

AV: Depends on what you mean by telepathy. I was just reading an article about the first transmission of thoughts and images between two people in different parts of the world via computer encoded brain waves. Apparently it was a successful scientific experiment and a transfer of information actually took place. This was several months ago. So technologically speaking, some type of telepathy does actually seem possible. If you mean magical telepathy, I really don't know.

Vladimir Vernadsky, who was one of the scientists associated with cosmism, developed a notion of the *Noosphere*, a kind of an informational, telepathic sphere of reason which, according to him, is emerging around our planet, like the existing geosphere, biosphere, atmosphere, stratosphere, ionosphere etc. He was already writing about this in the 1940s. He felt that the emergence of the noosphere will transform this planet. Some people feel that such a phenomenon is already starting to happen with the invention of the Internet, wireless communications and so forth. A digital telepathy.

BDB: Historically, Eurasianism had a tense relation with cosmism. When focussing on the origin of Eurasianism in the *interbellum*, and especially the desperately refined attempts of Prince Nikolai Trubetzkoy to think up an alternative for his space of origin to both the Tsarist and Bolshevik empires, the question arises as to whether there is an alternative conceivable that might cultivate a localised diversity and yet transcend national borders. Is this where we should go? Can cosmism help us?

AV: Well, you remember my reservations about Eurasianism. It's not much of an ideology in my opinion, and has more dangers than benefits. I think we should just leapfrog over the issues of national boundaries and aim for the Cosmos. The Universe is immeasurable and we are all in it, so it's a bit absurd to conceive of territoriality and geopolitics based on a sliver of surface on one small planet.

AZ: I agree with Anton here. Eurasianism today is an instance of radical proto-fascism, which, besides, has already been successfully appropriated by the Russian government. Working with things like this requires a lot of delicacy and only has an indirect connection with cosmism. In its extreme, cosmism proceeds from overcoming the problem of territory and national states as such, since the size of the Universe makes any territorial dispute solvable.

BDB: The Irish thinker Edmund Burke had an extended view on constituencies: everyone who ever lived, everyone who is now living, and everyone who will ever live. Even the government is, in this case, only a caretaker of its institutions. The upcoming film *Immortality and Resurrection for All* evokes the task of the museum as the resurrection by the living of the fathers, with reason not as an abstraction but as a seeking out of the fathers. Cosmism may be a project about future life, but is future life itself not excluded from this equation?

AV: For Fyodorov, the past is the future. It's a very interesting perspective. Most thinkers see the past and history as a ruin, a pile of rubble, a series of failures, etc. Because basically every project, every construction, every organism, empire, ideology—everything appears to have been destroyed by time. Benjamin's Angel of History looks backwards and sees only death and destruction. It's scary. It's genocide. What is very unique about Fyodorov is that he looks back and sees a field of potential: nothing has failed yet and nobody has truly died until we have exhausted all possible means available to reason, science, technology, art, social organisation and every other conceivable tool to bring back the past, to bring back our ancestors. In this sense they are not dead, but merely wounded, and for Fyodorov it is our responsibility to not leave them behind. So in this sense it's not about production of the new but about a rescue of all that has been laid waste by time.

AZ: Yes, Fyodorov has a very interesting understanding of history, somehow close to that of Walter Benjamin, who believed that history only began with revolution. Revolution, in its turn, is sort of an emergency brake of progress, a locomotive rushing backwards. Similar patterns can be found in Fyodorov's philosophy, which is an overwhelming mix of radical techno-utopianism and conservatism. We shouldn't forget that Russian cosmism was largely inspired by the theory of evolution and the faith in the endless transformational capabilities of human beings. The way to the future life will open up when mankind admits that evolution does not stop here and will continue. Before we achieve the universal resurrection, we have to solve a heap of problems, which are not restricted to overcoming the social and corporal conflicts within our species, which was already pointed out by Fyodorov. If the Cosmos becomes the place for settling the resurrected generations, a key question is: What will be the ratio of these generations? Will each planet be confined to a historical period of its own? What will happen to plants and animals, which obviously contributed to the evolution of Homo sapiens? And, most importantly, how will the people of the past with their corporal inhibitions match up with the people of the future, who will be bodiless or maybe have light-powered phallic pupils, as envisaged by the cosmist Gorsky? Thus, there is plenty of space for the future life with all of its contingencies in Russian cosmism, and this is also true in terms of contemporary art. The mechanism of resurrection is unable to evolve without artistic or, if you prefer, curator's vision. This was described, in particular, by Boris Groys. On the whole, Fyodorov's ideas seem more optimistic to me than the existing inhumanistic theories, at least when it comes to the human being.

BDB: When Alevtina Kakhidze interviewed the curators of the biennial during her present news broadcast, she asked whether animals and plants had also been invited. Should they be included in the notion of constituencies and if so, why and how?

AV: Absolutely. As soon as we learn to be self-feeding, we will stop consuming other forms of life for energy. Plankton already does that: it generates the energy it needs for its life processes directly from sunlight. We should learn from the plankton.

AZ: I would add that if we implement Fyodorov's resurrection project consistently, it should be extended to involve animals, plants, bacteria and other molecular compounds, too. We should definitely raise the question of the evolution of technical equipment, software, computer viruses, etc. Ideally, the time and the history of the whole Universe will be resurrected, including gods, beginning with those who were partly human in nature. This is also about the logic of resurrection, although it has never been articulated clearly before. If we talk about Christianity, mankind should be able to pay its debt to Christ and redeem his sacrifice by resurrecting him and bringing him back to the mundane world.

BDB: In the recent interview of Arseny with Anton, the ethos behind cosmism was formulated as "the desire to contribute directly and literally to the impossibly difficult project of immortality and resurrection for all, by any means possible, including art." Anton's upcoming film, featuring Arseny, states that "There is no art that does not produce a certain action, a certain transformation of life." Should all matter be included into the notion of constituencies, or is it rather the human world, as Hannah Arendt calls it, that should be empowered again?

AV: Yes. This is precisely the eschatology of cosmism. Once we achieve immortality, resurrect all who ever lived and learn to live in the Cosmos, our activity will consist in making all the matter that makes up the Universe conscious: teaching it ways to feel, think, perceive, etc. For Fyodorov this is also the main role and function of art, so as immortal beings we will all be artists with the Cosmos as our artwork. And when the entirety of the Universe becomes conscious, we will be self-same to God. It's a very ambitious project that he came up with…

BDB: In his book *After Nature*, Jedediah Purdy points to how linked up visions of nature and political setups have been, for a long time. Which political preferences does cosmism suggest? And might an orientation towards the future prefer certain political forms over others?

AV: Cosmism is a materialist philosophy that is essentially anti-capitalist, primarily because of the wasteful nature of the market economy, the unfairness of uneven distribution of resources, the triviality of consumer commodity production and so forth. In this sense it echoes the Marxist critique of capitalism. On the other hand, Fyodorov was expressly critical of socialism, primarily because he saw it as godless and not based on love. It can be argued that despite this, Fyodorov is a true Socialist because he deeply believes in radical social equality that extends even to the dead.

AZ: There is an opinion that Fyodorov was "a Marx for the poor", meaning the impetus that was later boosted in liberation theology. However, as Anton has already mentioned, Fyodorov did not accept Marxism because of its revolutionary violence, despite all his anti-capitalist orientation. The philosopher believed that real social transformations could only be achieved through love, respect for the ancestors, enlightenment and hard work towards a common goal. Fyodorov had plenty of contradictions regarding what concerned the authorities of his time, whether religious or secular. Yet, I have no doubt that if he were living today, he would find himself very soon in Snowden's position. The father of cosmism advocated the freedom of knowledge and information distribution. There was nothing less appalling for him than to see an archive like present-day big data being used to make money and hold on to power instead of pursuing the common goal of resurrection and social development.

Ives Maes — A Three-Dimensional Experience On The Spot

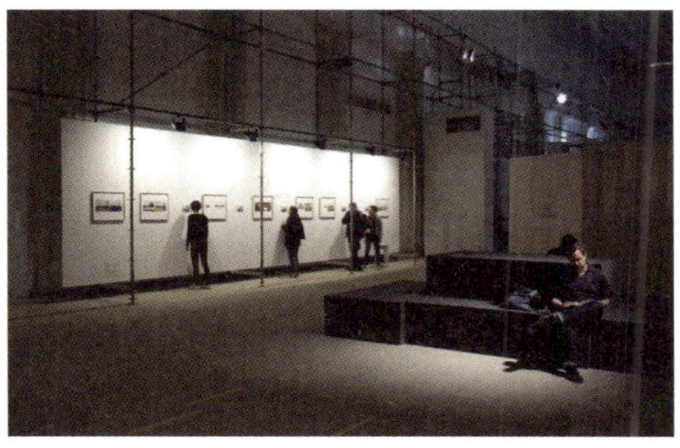

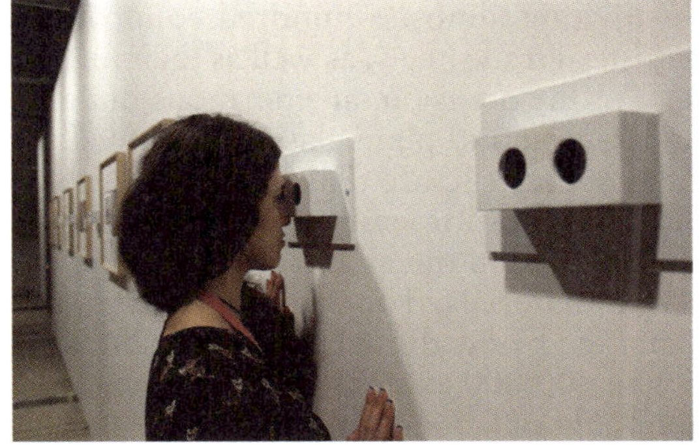

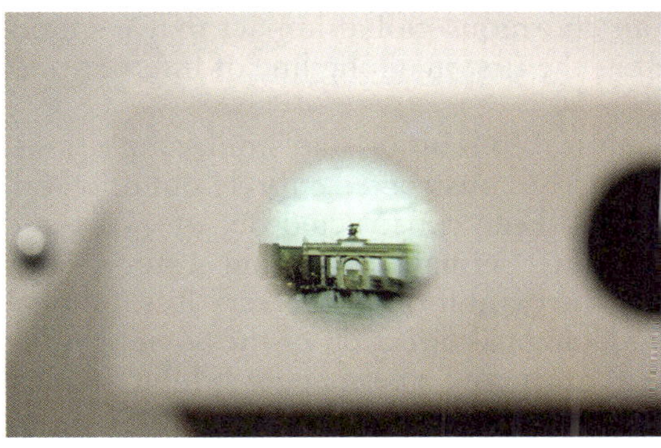

Ives Maes, *Soviet Stereographs*, installation view at Moscow Biennale for Contemporary Art, 2015

It is remarkable when a biennial returns to a former World Exhibition site. It seems to be revisiting its own origins; to contemplate, find guidance or criticise. As if the Venice Biennale were to take place on the former location of the Great Exhibition in London's Hyde Park. It becomes even more peculiar, to make this conundrum even more elusive, when a recurring temporary event such as a biennial settles on a location where a temporary International Exhibition solidified as a permanent structure.

The 6th Moscow Biennale has revisited the former location of the All-Union Agricultural Exhibition that had opened on August 1, 1939. This exhibition, commissioned by Stalin, was to display and celebrate the agricultural achievements of the USSR and to strengthen the hegemony between the international states of the Union.

In doing so, it stepped into a relatively long tradition of International Exhibitions and World Fairs, which started with the Great Exhibition of All Nations and Industries in 1851. This temporary event, lasting almost six months, was the first international exhibition of its kind — inviting almost a hundred countries to display their national industrial trade items, as well as their highest achievements in culture. For the occasion, an enormous building was constructed out of cast iron and plate glass, nicknamed the Crystal Palace: a modular superstructure that was disassembled after the event. The Great Exhibition embodied a synthesis of new industries and arts, reflected in the architectural design and its innovative construction materials. The event's extravaganza was its disappearance, marked by the dismantling of the building and the return of more than 100,000 exhibits. Its transient nature emphasised an extreme amount of labour, study and logistics. This ephemeral formula of good intentions, cultural bravery and pure propaganda had such an enormous global impact that it immediately established itself as the first in a long line of International Exhibitions.

The All-Union Agricultural Exhibition had similar ambitions. At first, its pavilions were to be constructed entirely out of wood. Most world exhibitions had been constructed out of wood and plaster, except for an occasional permanent building in stone. Then Stalin decided to solidify the exhibition in the very last moment since it did not suit the ideological direction of the Soviet Union. It was considered too temporary, and a permanent exhibition park in stone and cement rose from the ground. The exhibition closed later that year on the 25th October, only to reopen indefinitely a few months later.

Between 1939 and 1989 the site had accumulated 82 pavilions on an exhibition area of 700,000 square metres and been renamed the Exhibition of Achievements of the National Economy. There was nothing temporary about this permanent exhibition park, except for its continuously expanding size. The dichotomy of permanent and transitional instalments was widened by an implementation of leftovers from former world exhibitions: One of the first structures to appear on site was Vera Mukhina's famous *Worker and Kolkhoz Woman* sculpture that had crowned the Soviet Pavilion at the *Exposition Internationale des Arts et Techniques dans la Vie Moderne de Paris* in 1937, where it stood in defiance of the Nazi German pavilion. Also, the Soviet Pavilion of the Montreal Expo 1967 was relocated to the site, forming a sort of time capsule of Expo monuments.

After the collapse of the Soviet Union, the site lost its initial meaning, overrun by poverty and ruination. But it was precisely this stage that made the site prey to the ephemeral existence it should have had from the beginning. Through its decay, its primary function was finally activated.

2015 was precisely the right timing to return and mediate the site's lifespan and aftermath. But to hold a biennial at such a location means opening a large can of worms. It comes with an endless amount of meanings, social undertones and political overtones, regardless of the ephemeral complexities or time inconsistencies. Moreover, the current legislature in Moscow had very recently decided to restore the site. Moscow had filed a bid to the *Bureau International des Expositions* to host the 2010 World Expo and the Russian Expo would have taken place on the same site. But this was awarded to the city of Shanghai instead. A slow process of restoration started. The original Soviet Pavilion of the 1937 exposition in Paris was reconstructed in 2012 and once again crowned with the statue by Vera Mukhina — turning it into a shrewd national propaganda tool. In the same fashion, the Cosmos Pavilion and Yuri Gagarin's *Vostok* rocket were restored. Today, Soviet music resonates over the long lanes and all Soviet symbols have received a new coat of red paint. Each former republic of the USSR was invited to reoccupy its national pavilion, restored as in the old days, while the Ukrainian pavilion still stands desolate. And finally, the main Pavilion No. 1 was prepped to host the 6th

Moscow Biennale. Only a few years before it had hosted innumerable trinkets shops and a sloppy wax museum displaying statues of Stalin, Hitler, Napoleon, Shrek and Putin.

So it is remarkable when a biennial returns to a former Expo site, because every Expo site has its specific history to deal with. It is a return to the origins of the biennial system, however tainted it might be by war or colonialism. It cannot be anything other than a moment of reflection, of pause or critique. When the 6th Moscow Biennale visited the site of the All-Union Agricultural Exhibition, it not only needed to reflect that history, but also to mediate its current position, which places it right in the middle of a propaganda episode.

Over centuries, world exhibitions have provided us with countless new frameworks of futures to come. They have structured archaeological treasures in museological systems, popularised the latest discoveries in technology and displayed grand temporary architecture. They have hosted diplomatic assemblies and symposiums and have been responsible for the first exhibitions of contemporary art open to a general and international audience. In its sublime essence, the world exhibition creates a momentum where the world gathers in peace and presents itself as a didactic architectural décor in which the contemporary experts of the humanities, technology, architecture and art manifest their ideas for a nearby future in order to resolve current malfunctions.

With the opening up of global unlimited borders through the advent of radio, television and internet, the end of colonial wealth and decline of Cold War, propaganda consolidates, and alongside the separation of the arts into biennials and art fairs, the world exhibition today seems to have lost all meaning. Proof of this hollowness is easily found in the most recent Expos. Their younger and poorer sibling, the biennial, has partially inherited that power.

The 6th Moscow Biennale made an exciting attempt at hosting a ten-day event during which performances and political lectures passed by and art works created on the spot appeared only to disappear after a few days. The organisers were not afraid to leave the isolation and safety of the white cube and manifest on a location that screamed all sorts of historical connotations and confronted the current political crisis head on. In its ephemeral existence, it fully honoured the sublime legacy of the world fairs with a formula of good intentions, cultural bravery and pure propaganda.

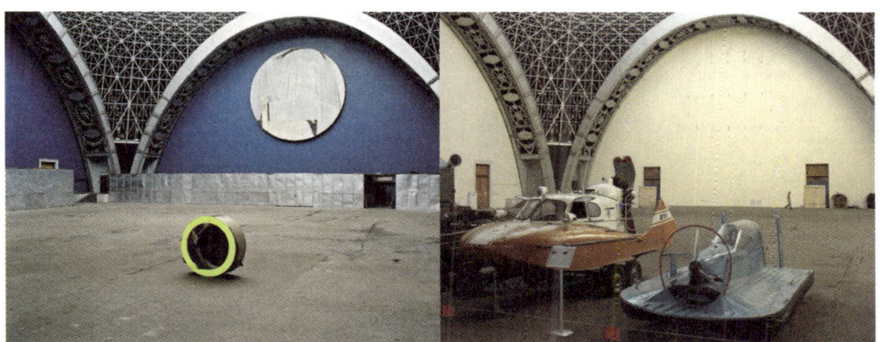

Ives Maes, *Cosmos Pavilion* from the *Soviet Stereographs* series, 2015

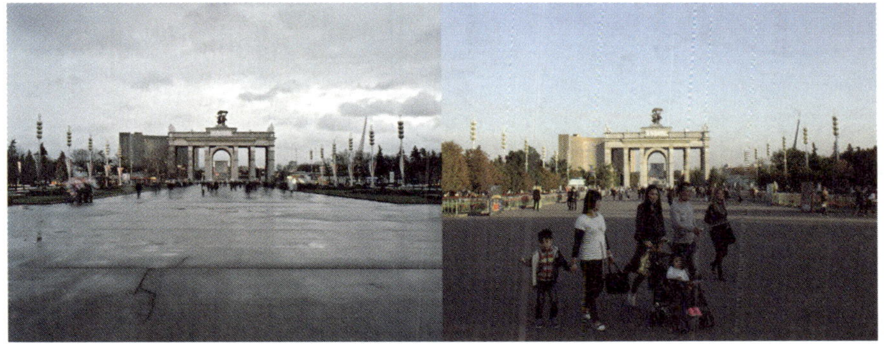

Ives Maes, *Entrance Gate* from the *Soviet Stereographs* series, 2015

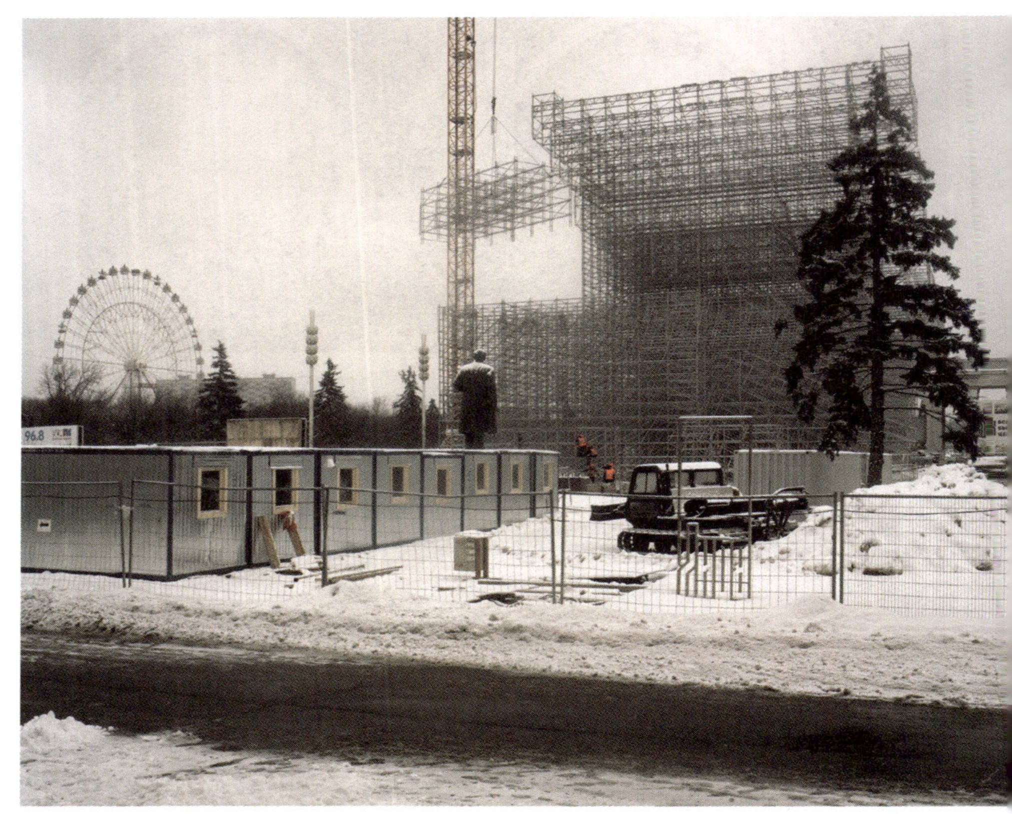

Ives Maes, *Lenin Sculpture* from the *Soviet Stereographs* series, 2015

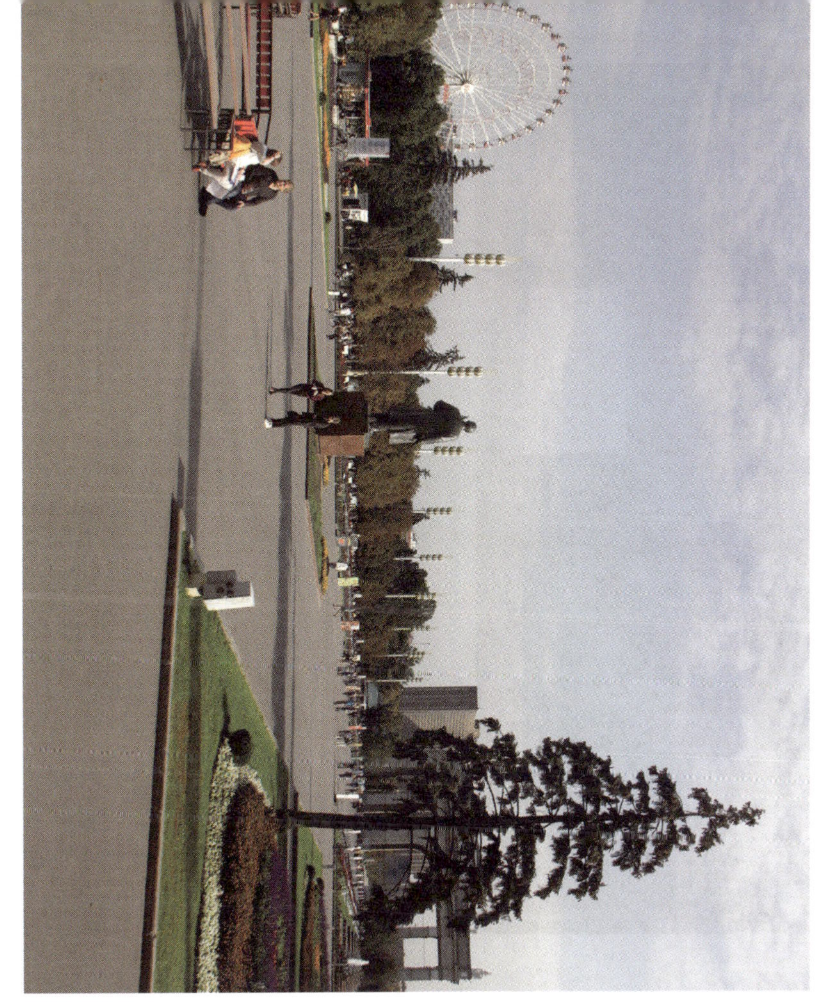

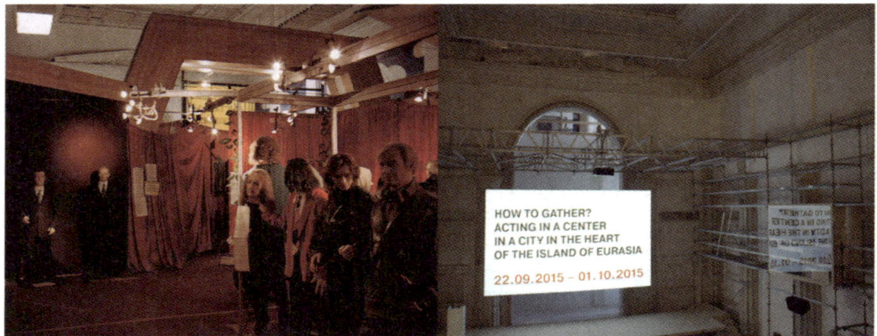

Ives Maes, *Pavilion No. 1* from the *Soviet Stereographs* series, 2015

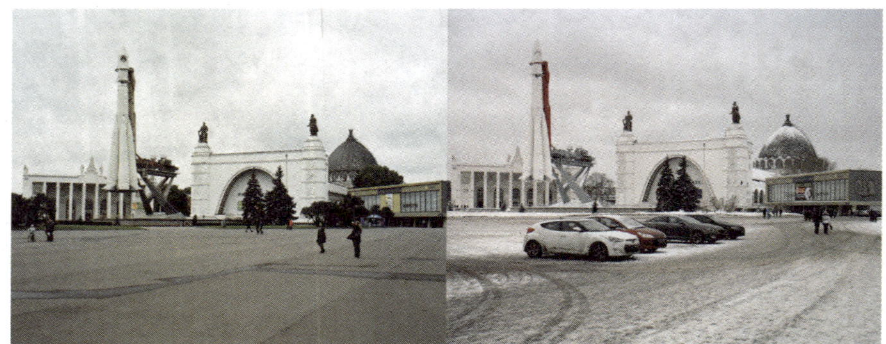

Ives Maes, *Vostok Rocket* from the *Soviet Stereographs* series, 2015

What is essential in the biennial's aftermath is its disclosure of documentation: It is no coincidence that the curators invited photographers to work on site and employed even more photographers, writers and a film crew to document and stream the countless performances, lectures and shifting art works. Instead of propaganda, it transmitted democratic mixed feelings over mixed drinks, and tried to be the voice of reason while being surrounded by noise. A 0% propaganda policy is propaganda as well. The communication of what happened during those ten days is essential to the project.

> "Photography will [...] greatly enrich us with authentic records of works, that would otherwise pass away without a single detaining effort from the hand of the artist, owing to their being of too transient a nature to admit of the accuracy and detail necessary to give it value in future ages. [...] Great is its usefulness as applied to transitory scenes of the above kind, and incalculable will be the advantage posterity is sure to reap from the ever increasing collection of such truly graphic representations; and great service, too, will the plain and truthful records of photography afford to the historian of future ages."[1]
>
> (Sir David Brewster, jury member of the Great Exhibition)

Coming back to the template of great exhibitions, it can easily be argued that the format evolved because of the invention of photography. The temporary nature of the Crystal Palace vitally needed photography to record its short life span. *Ex negativo*, the ephemeral building was only constructed because there was the possibility of candidly recording proof of its transitory existence. "Photography, in addition to all the other uses it served, here served as a means of endowing the fair with the lasting permanence that it couldn't otherwise have."[2] William Henry Fox Talbot photographed the grand hall, as well as Baron J.-B. Louis Gros, Benjamin Brecknell Turner and Robert Bingham. Prince Albert and Queen Victoria valued the medium's unification of science, art and education. They were particularly fond of the most recent invention of stereography, evoking an actual three-dimensional experience on the spot through the looking glass. Claudet, Beard, Mayall and Williams at once began taking stereoscopic views of the interior of the Crystal Palace and of the exhibits. This process resulted in the four volumes of the *Official Descriptive and Illustrative Catalogue of the Great Exhibition*, containing 155 original photographs of the building and its exhibits. These books, with their unprecedented amount of photographs, had a print run of 250,000, with versions published in French and German, abbreviated editions and short guides, in a chain production process never before seen. In 1852, this unbiased record was sent to all the dignitaries of the participating countries, and planted in libraries across the world. In order to remember — long after the rare and curious content of the Crystal Palace had been scattered over the planet and grass had grown over the site — that something extraordinary had happened here at one point in history.

The illustrative catalogue is the only palpable result to remain from the Great Exhibition, just as this record is the only leftover of the 6th Moscow Biennale. Where the Great Exhibition used photography (then a new invention for the masses) to communicate the importance of the event, the 6th Moscow Biennale continuously streamed virtual documents, hours of filmed performances, lectures and interviews, as well as hundreds of photographs and installation views — accessible online everywhere and by everyone. This is the legacy of the 6th Moscow Biennale.

The document you hold in your hands *is* the 6th Moscow Biennale.

1
See Henry Cole, *Official Descriptive and Illustrated Catalogue of the Great Exhibition of the Work of Industry of All Nations*, London, 1852.

2
Elena Filipovic, *After-images*, in: *The Future of Yesterday* — Ives Maes, Antwerp, 2013, p. 7.

Lu Yang — Wrathful King Kong Core & Moving Gods

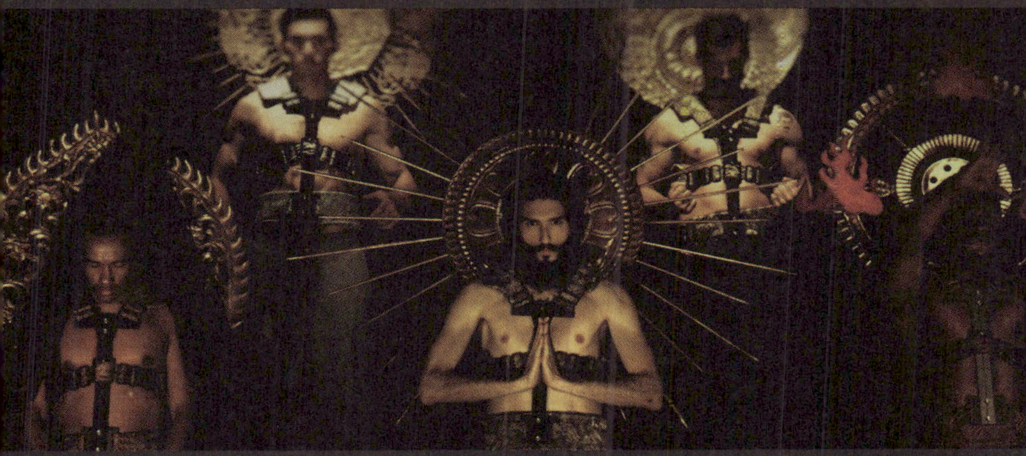

Lu Yang, *Moving Gods*, single channel video, 2015, 4 mins., still

Lu Yang was invited to the Moscow Biennale for her take on concepts of the future and the ancient. Her animated films combine videogame aesthetics with neuroscience, religion and parapsychology. The selection of videos for the biennial programme included *Wrathful King Kong Core* (2011) and *Moving Gods* (2015). In both, Lu Yang investigates iconic religious symbols and transfers them to a present she sees as closely associated with science and technology.

Wrathful King Kong Core portrays Yamantaka, a Buddhist deity with the power to help escape the cycle of rebirth. Yamantaka overcomes the evil and karma of previous lives, which makes the deity one of true enlightenment, for whom anger originates in the goal to destroy death. Lu Yang contrasts this with an analysis of human anger that originates in the brain and may be read from facial expressions.

In *Moving Gods*, a group of men is shown posing in a set of wearable haloes created by Lu Yang. The divide between the divine and the human is revoked. The nimbus as a universal religious symbol normally distinguishes gods from human beings. But with today's technology — do humans bear the potential to become what they once worshipped as gods?

Detecting universal religious symbols, archaic human feelings and expressions, as well as a technological reality that not too long ago was narrated as science fiction, Lu Yang delivers the means to pose questions on the universality of religion and humankind, on the possibility of transient existence, and ultimately, on the relationships between religious belief systems and socio-political conditions such as, for example, fanaticism. [Marie Egger]

Ricardo Brey — Parallel Universes

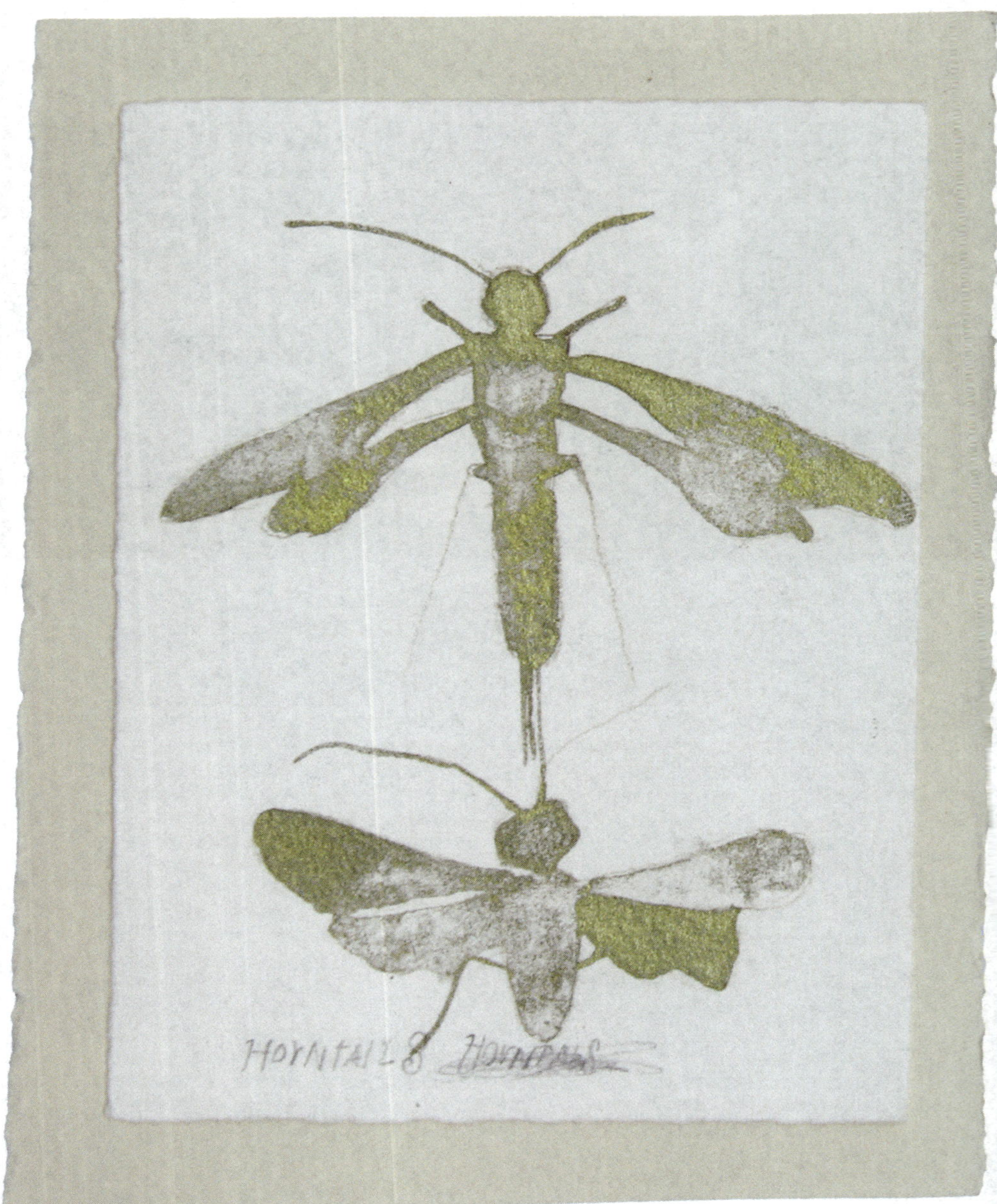

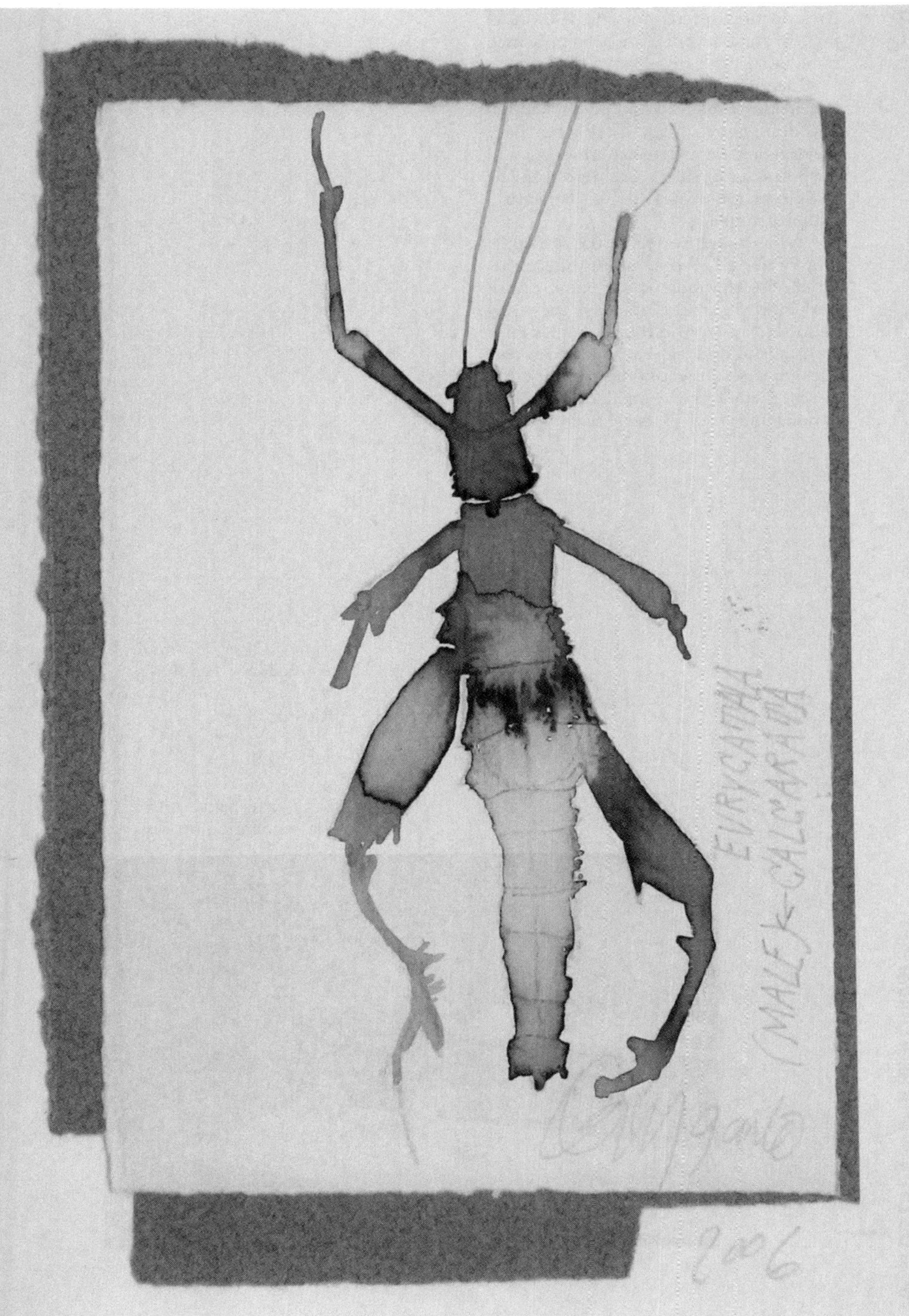
EURYCANTHA
(MALE)-CALCARATA
2006

Ricardo Brey offered to send 100 drawings that had never before been presented publicly.

Biennale production manager Katya Savchenko unpacked and positioned ten new drawings each day. That is the space the drawings aspired to realise, silent and unspectacular. They were placed in the middle of the central dome, beneath a Stalinist cupola.

When asked which of the drawings they preferred, people did not necessarily choose the most spectacular, lavish drawings. As artistic offerings they may be looked at from different angles and, according to Brey, can each be seen as parallel universes. It was in this capacity that he sent them to the biennial; one hundred parallel universes. [Bart De Baere]

←←
Ricardo Brey, *Horntails*, 2006, 135 x 105 mm
←
Ricardo Brey, *In the kitchen*, 2006, 159 x 120 mm
↓
Katya Savchenko during the installation process

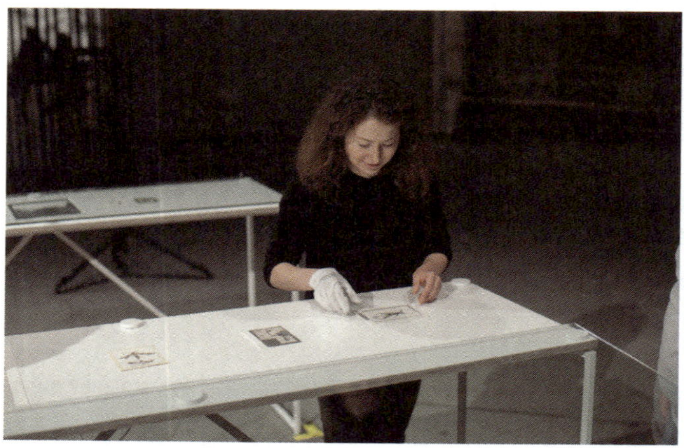

Anne-Mie van Kerckhoven — Madonna and Leviathan

The Biennale asked four artists for an image, that might also be a capacity and focus of artists, defined as such, rather than a generic 'artwork'. Anne-Mie van Kerckhoven was one of the four.

She offered an image based on the baroque Peter Paul Rubens altar piece *The Mystic Wedding of Saint Catherine*, originating from the Church of Saint Augustine in Antwerp where she used to go to Mass as a child. It struck her then that, in the chiaroscuro of the church, the lower part of the body of the Madonna became a black square. She let this Rubens image fall apart, so that it became rather a field of energies with the evocation of a black square in the middle. She complemented it on its right-hand side with a Rorschach shape, the kind of image that is supposed to be a projection field for the imagination.

The title of the resulting proposal, *Madonna and Leviathan*, indicates how images are not merely iconographical facts, but also carriers of a capacity to structure the world. The adoration of the Holy Family is a key reference in this sense within the Catholic tradition, and found in Rubens a unique capacity; a painter that could render any content proposal credible. The Rorschach shape might be seen as its counterpart but in the end both parts of this visual equation prove both their capacity and their limits. [Bart De Baere]

Ieva Epnere — Renunciation

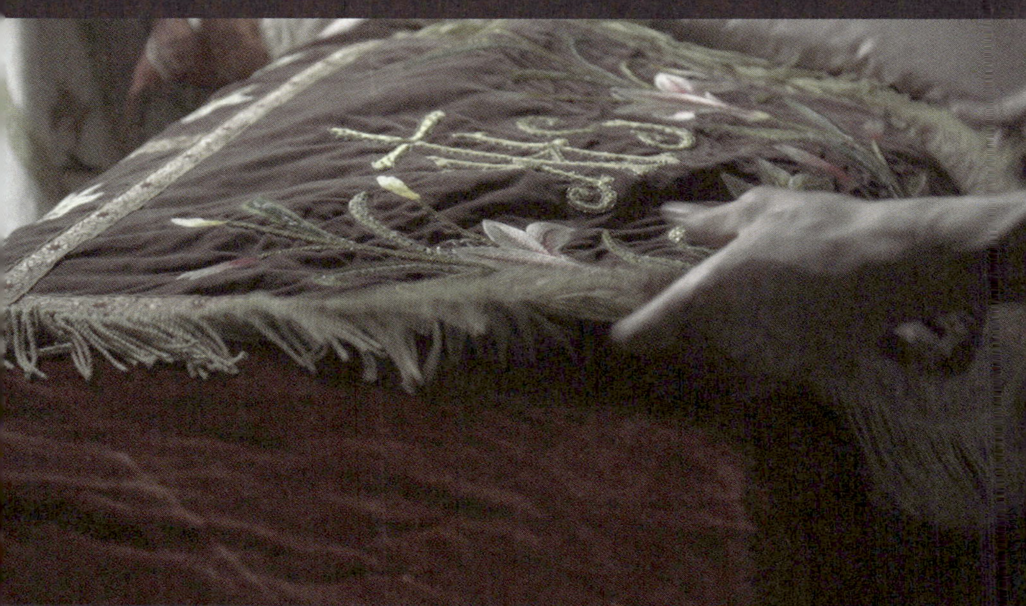

Ieva Epnere, *Renunciation*, video, 2014, 20 mins., still

Renunciation from the World

Renunciation is a 20-minute short film about a Catholic priest and his modest, lonely life as appropriate to his status. The first scene shows a typical Baltic landscape: a steel-coloured sea, dense fog and shore bushes torn apart by the wind. A lonely figure appears in this austere landscape.

The shots are intentionally picturesque and framed in perfect geometry. Similar to the formal language of Russian director Andrey Zvyagintsev, Ieva Epnere works with a mix of landscapes and close ups, with the silent brutality of nature and harsh Northern charm which audiences of *The Return* and *Leviathan* might recognise.

While watching the film, one gets to discover one's own internal voyeur. This reversed peeping effect is achieved through a sincere focus on barely visible details: a heavy knitted sweater, the narrow buttonholes of a shirt, a trembling pencil… The priest is trying to draw. Then he looks through a catalogue with pictures of Baltic beauties wearing traditional outfits. It is an ordinary catalogue that would be read in a moment of leisure. Seemingly, the film is an ordinary documentation of daily life. But there is something else to it, something breaking through the shots; an elusive feeling of concern. Every gesture of the priest shows his inner tension; and the fact that holding back this tension demands a lot of effort.

The priest lays out ritual fabrics with golden patterns, putting them one on one: red velvet on purple brocade and so forth. This process appears to bring him real pleasure. These layered fabrics become a metaphor for our sensual, intellectual, even religious interaction with art: Piety is both a ritual of creation/admiration, and the enchantment by creation/admiration. It is an obsessive desire to see mystery and the inexplicable power in it. Feeling small and fragile in the face of something great and astonishing is the religious experience of awe. The priest seems aware that humans, according to how the Creator made them, are to engage in creation themselves. But in order to create it is necessary to abandon one's feelings of awe and humility, feelings crucial to his eternal service.[1]

Marina Simakova

1 This text appeared in full on the Moscow Biennale Blog: http://moscowbiennale.syg.ma/renunciation-from-the-world

Luc Tuymans — The Worshipper

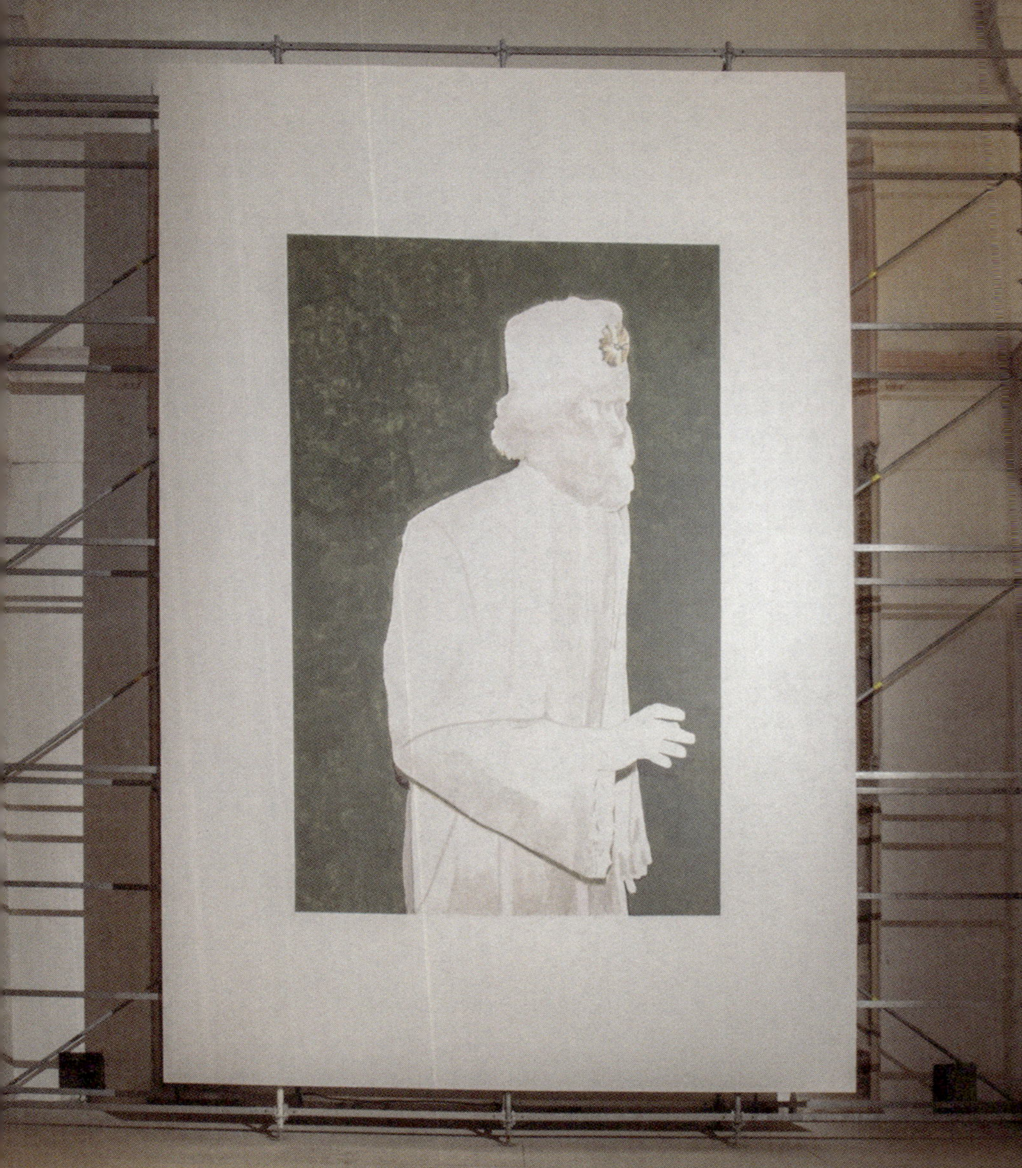

Luc Tuymans, *The Worshipper*, installation view during the Moscow Biennale, 2015

For his large-scale in-situ wall paintings, Luc Tuymans has a specific way of engaging assistants. Many artists, also painters, work with studio assistants who execute (part of) the work. The Antwerp baroque painter Peter Paul Rubens even had four different price categories depending on the amount of work he himself invested in it. In the case of Tuymans, the artist is the only one who is painting, but the role of his assistants — accomplished artists in their own right — is no less important. They function as the artist's additional eyes. They may give indications from their respective positions, so that the work ends up being made under the scrutiny of different perspectives and distances. The challenges that are addressed in this way are of pictorial nature, such as the degree of differentiation and sameness of different zones in the green background of the painting, or the play of the purple hues in the dress of the figure.

As always with Tuymans, the focus is not on how much more might be done but rather on how less being done may strengthen the work. The central element is the hand. It remains in the white of the primary layer, the mere outlines of a shape that seems to be trying to express something, an uncannily ambiguous gesture.

Tuymans is an artist who continuously researches the intertwining of representation and presence. He does not invent images but interprets and positions them in such a way that they get a proper capacity, in between thematic and pictorial meaning. The images that were the starting point are often first unbalanced by an intermediary image. For some time he took Polaroid photos of the images he wanted to work with, and based his work on those, the deviations of their shabby quality informing him as much as the initial starting point.

Here, the foundation was a bad quality reproduction of a painting he had done himself in 2004, *The Worshipper*, that had earlier also been turned into a silkscreen, realised on the occasion of the appearance of a special edition of his monograph with Phaidon Press. The work in Moscow is cropped in relation to the earlier ones: the Christmas tree that was previously visible on the right has been left out. The proportions of the image are not standard, and the painting is a bit narrower — or proportionally higher — than would usually be the case. Because of this, the format may remind one of the main altar painting in a Catholic church.

The figure of a priest of unspecified faith now stands isolated, a figure in a luminous state of fading out within his frame, with a hand that stretches to the whiteness of the surrounding wall, or the wider world. Initially, before entering the hall through its vast entrance arch, visitors only see the bottom part of the body with the hand. As one moves, the head and the shoulders of the figure hovering over the theatre and the tent-like pavilion that houses Kostya Zvezdochotov's Egyptian Museum become visible.

Even if it is obviously possible to connect the subject matter of *The Worshipper* to the primacy of the Russian Orthodox Church and its Patriarch, the work can also be connected to religion in an entirely different way: not to the dominant presence of the Church, but to the spiritual as related to transience and disappearance.

When I shared with Daria Likhovitskaya — one of the volunteers at the Biennale — my sense that this painting generates a strong sense of location, reminiscent of a figurative Kazimir Malevich painting that used to feel like the centre of Paris to me in the former collection hanging of the Centre Pompidou, she responded by saying that this is because this painting allows visitors to have a personalised experience; that's why people will remember it. This is true; the work can be experienced only as an embodied painting. When one approaches the lower part of the figure, it opens itself up as grounded in precise and quite decisive brush strokes.

The impression of a relation to Malevich may also be an outcome of the character of the brush strokes. In both of these artistic spaces, that of Malevich and that of Tuymans, the brush strokes do not testify to an artist realising an art work; they are the witnesses of detachment as an expression of commitment, commitment to an image that needed to be realised. [Bart De Baere]

Alevtina Kakhidze — Unstable Systems

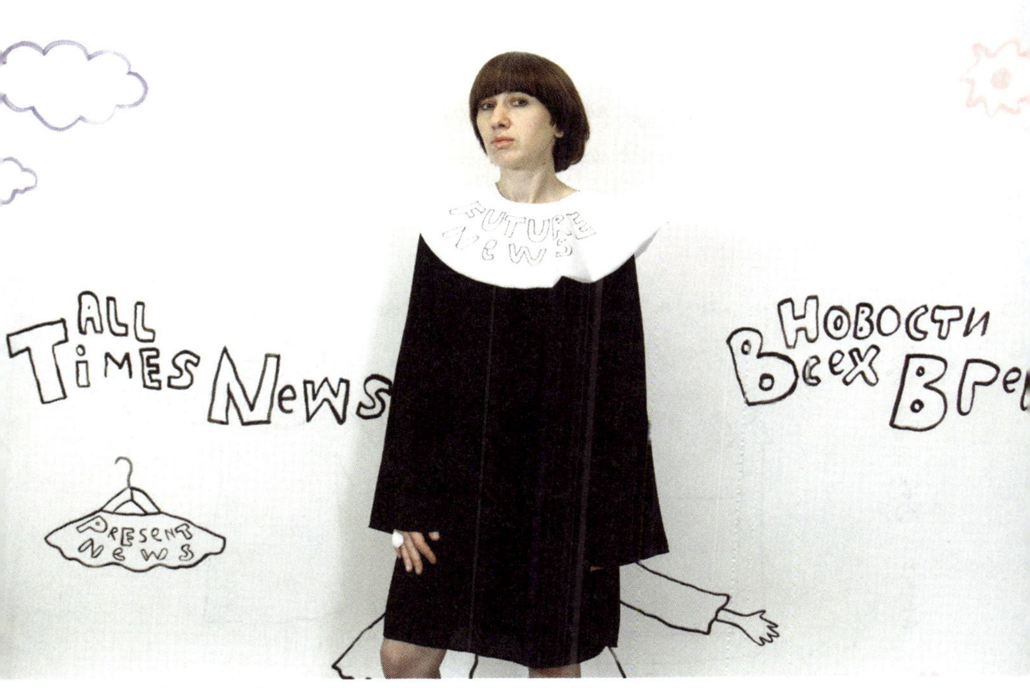

Alevtina Kakhidze, *All Times News*, Moscow Biennale 2015

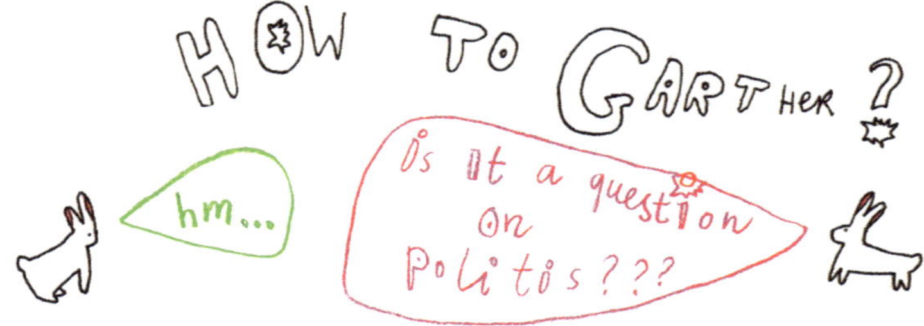

6th Moscow Biennale
6-я Московская биеннале 2015

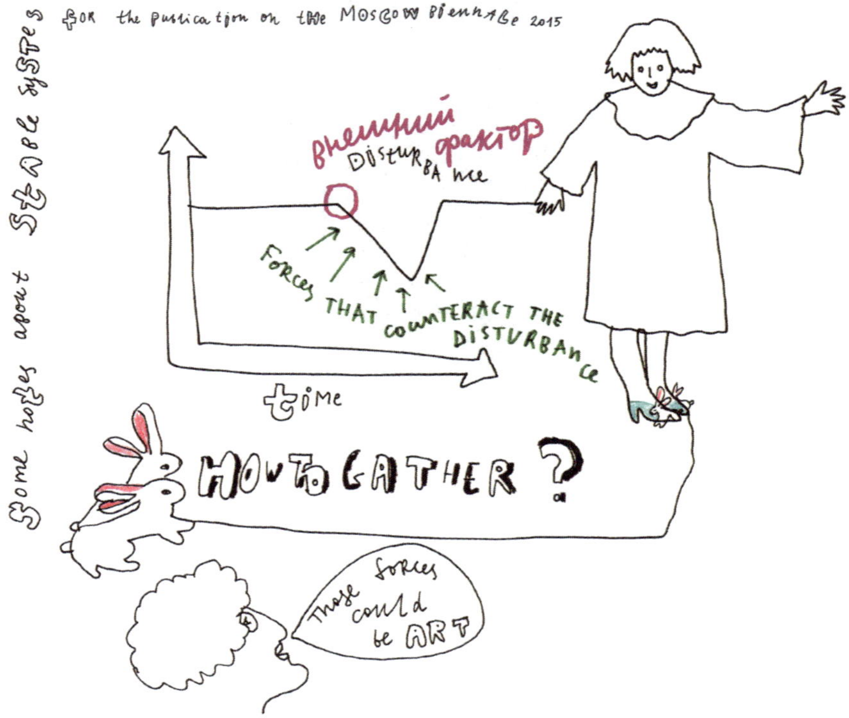

Some notes about stable systems for the publication on the Moscow Biennale 2015

внешний фактор
DISTURBANCE
FORCES THAT COUNTERACT THE DISTURBANCE
time
HOW TO GATHER ?
Those forces could be ART

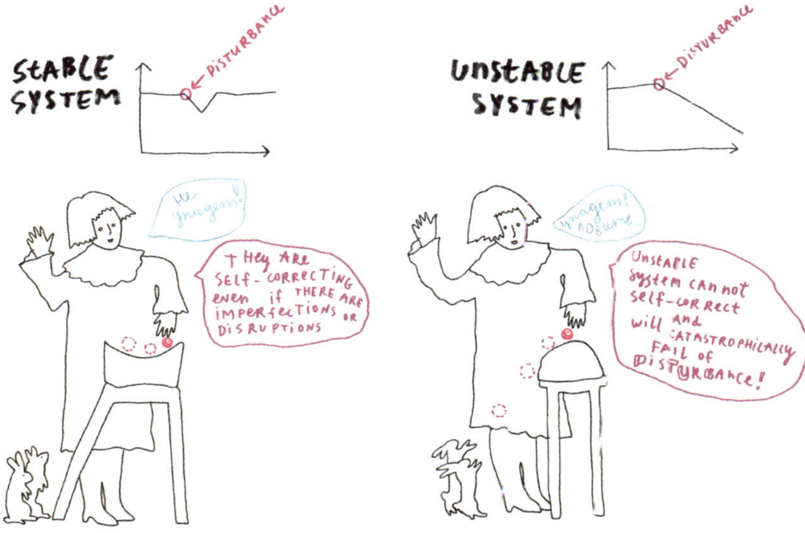
STABLE SYSTEM
DISTURBANCE
не упадет!
† Hey ARE SELF-CORRECTING even if THERE ARE imperfections OR DISRUPTIONS
UNSTABLE SYSTEM
DISTURBANCE
упадет! ловите...
Unstable system can not self-correct and will catastrophically FAIL of DISTURBANCE!

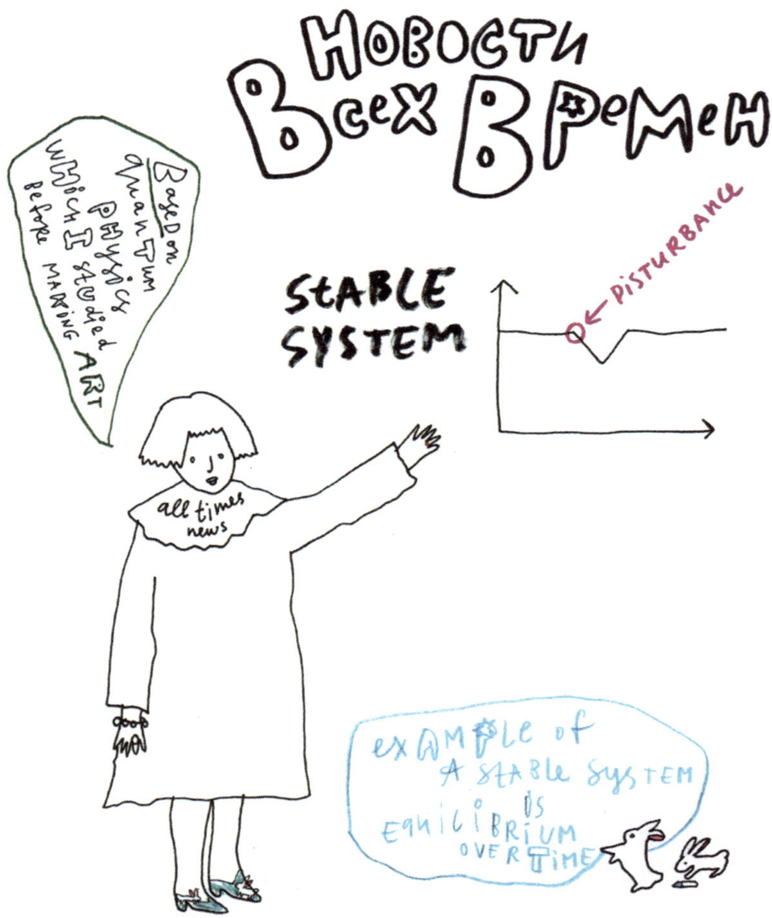
Новости Всех Времен
Based on quantum physics which I studied before making ART
STABLE SYSTEM
DISTURBANCE
all times news
example of a stable system is equilibrium over time

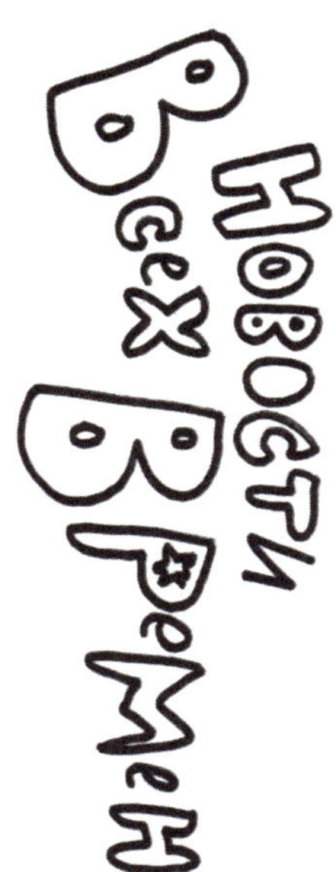
НОВОСТИ
ВСЕХ ВРЕМЕН

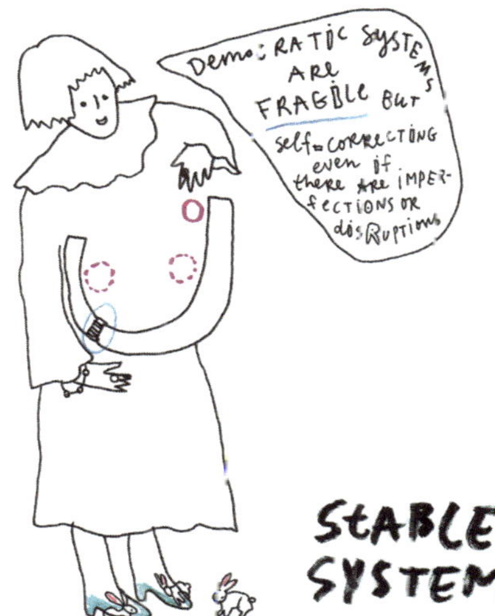
DemocRATIC SYSTEMS ARE FRAGILE BUT self-CORRECTING even if there are IMPERFECTIONS OR disRUPTIONS
STABLE SYSTEM

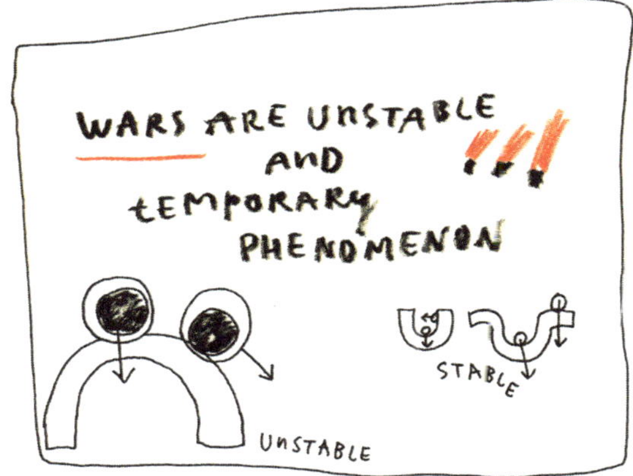
WARS ARE UNSTABLE AND TEMPORARY PHENOMENON
UNSTABLE
STABLE

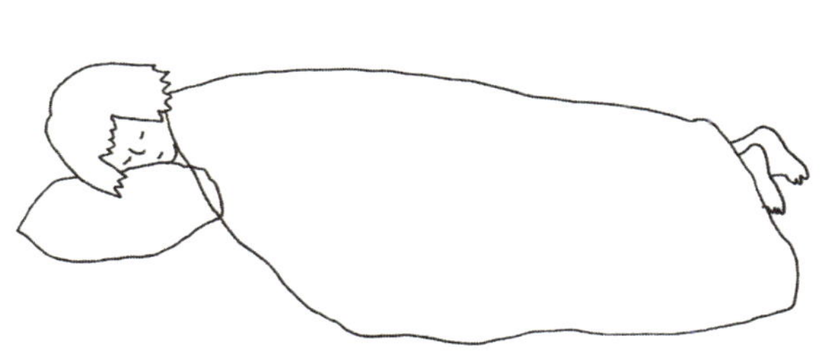

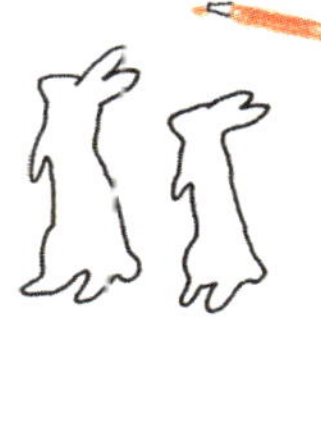

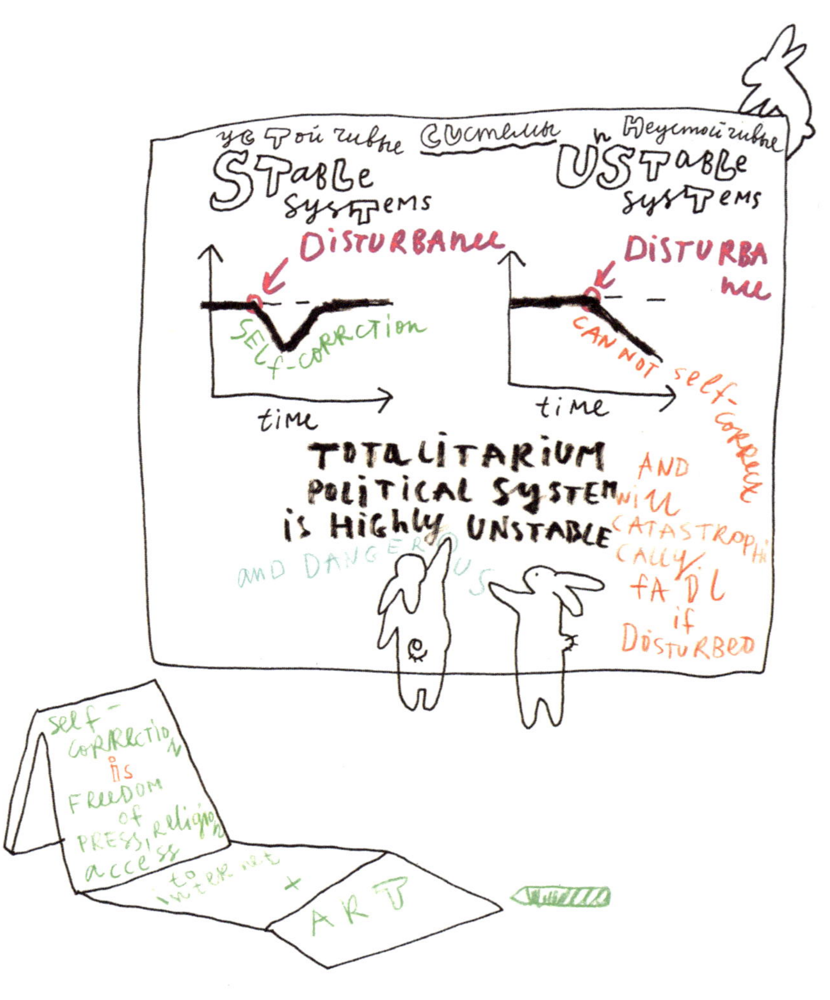

устойчивые системы и неустойчивые
STABLE SYSTEMS
USTABLE SYSTEMS
DISTURBANCE
SELF-CORRECTION
time
DISTURBANCE
CAN NOT self-correct
time
TOTALITARIUM POLITICAL SYSTEM is HIGHLY UNSTABLE
AND DANGEROUS
AND WILL CATASTROPHICALLY FAIL if DISTURBED
self-CORRECTION is FREEDOM of PRESS, religion, access to internet + ART

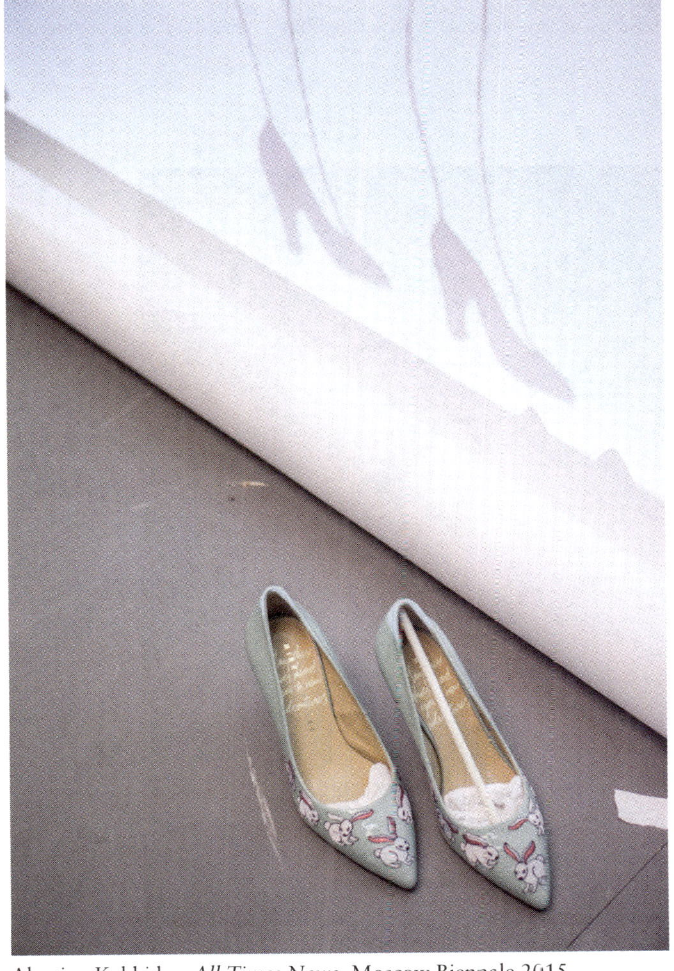

Alevtina Kakhidze, *All Times News*, Moscow Biennale 2015

Suchan Kinoshita — Chaos Pendulum

Suchan Kinoshita was unable to attend the Biennale personally, because of an earlier commitment in Italy. Her various contributions started from the notion 'to whom it may concern'. The most crucial one was not realised. Kinoshita proposed that a chaos pendulum be suspended somewhere in the Biennale space: "This is an item known in physics, so some of the university labs might have one they could lend us. It is a pendulum which is built up out of two or three pendulums which help to prolong the moments of instability. Moments of instability being those which make the connections between circumstances. So the question is how to maintain that condition of instability."

Though the pendulum regrettably was not installed for real, it was there as a mental image. It reminded Alevtina Kakhidze of the laws of unstable systems and her days as an engineer. [Bart De Baere]

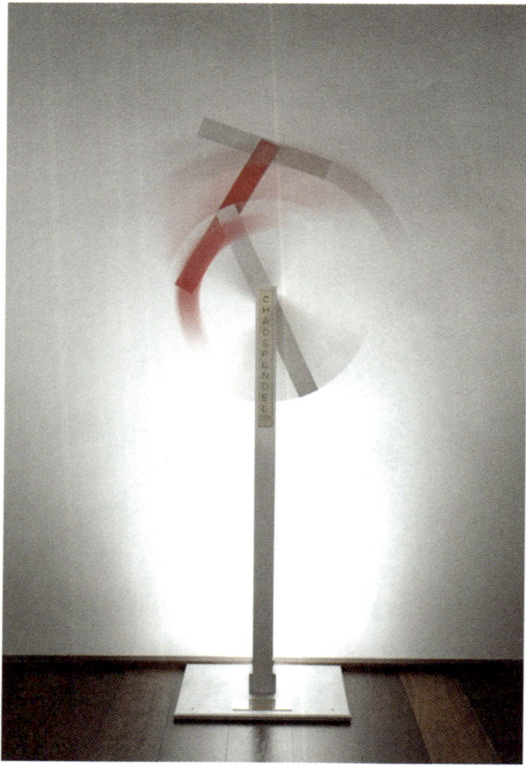

Chaos Pendulum

Elena Kholkina — Dreams of the Pavilion

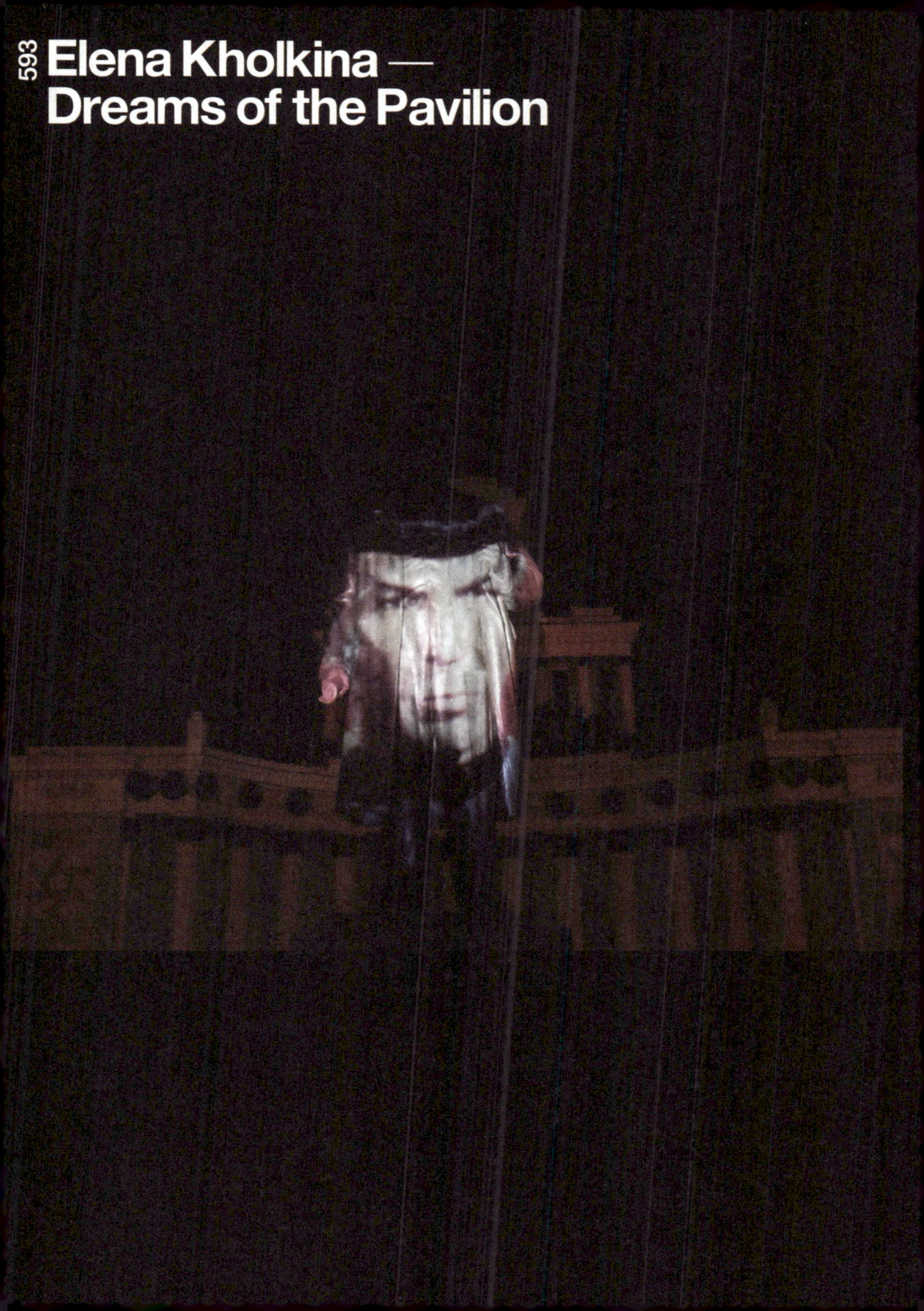

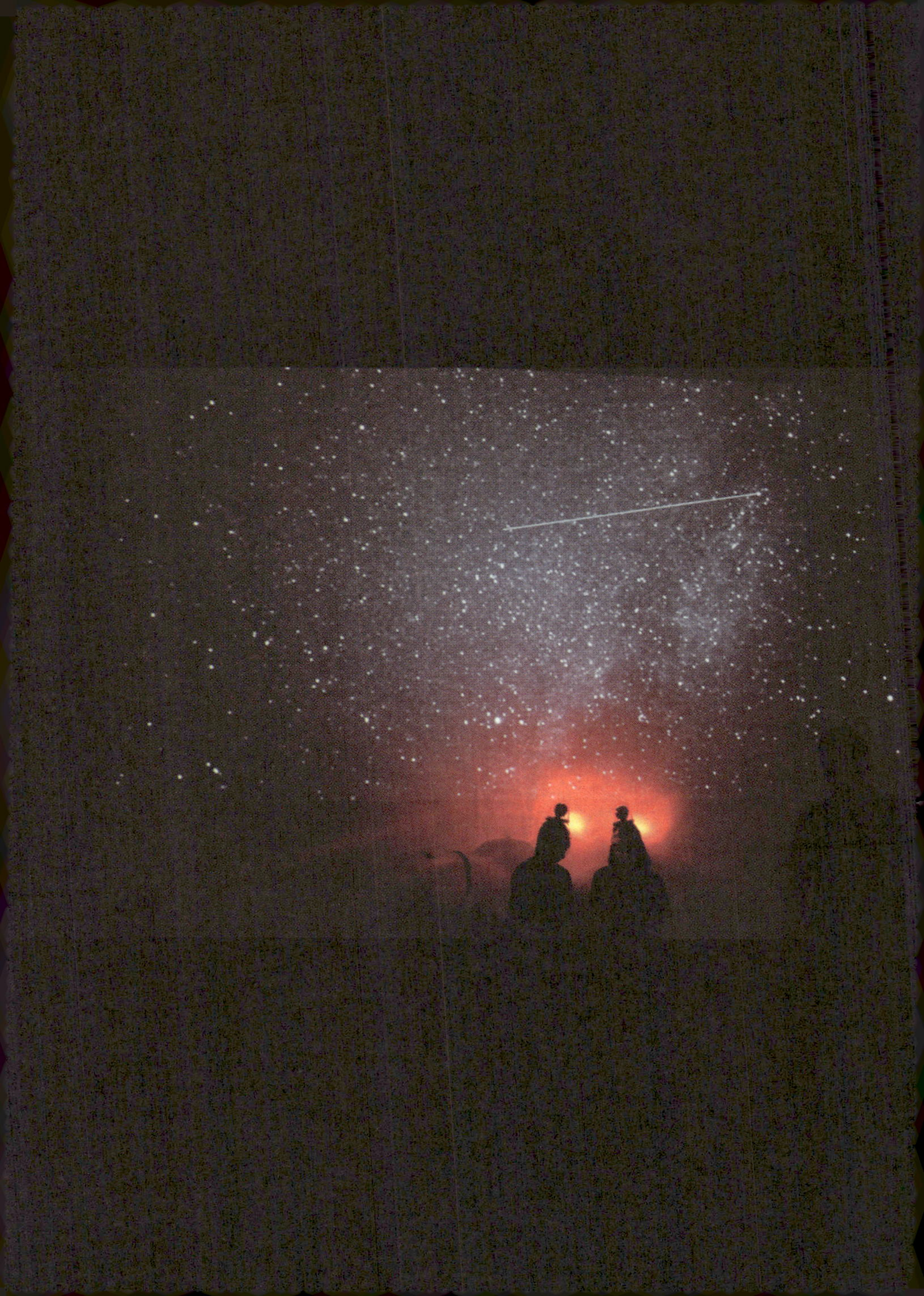

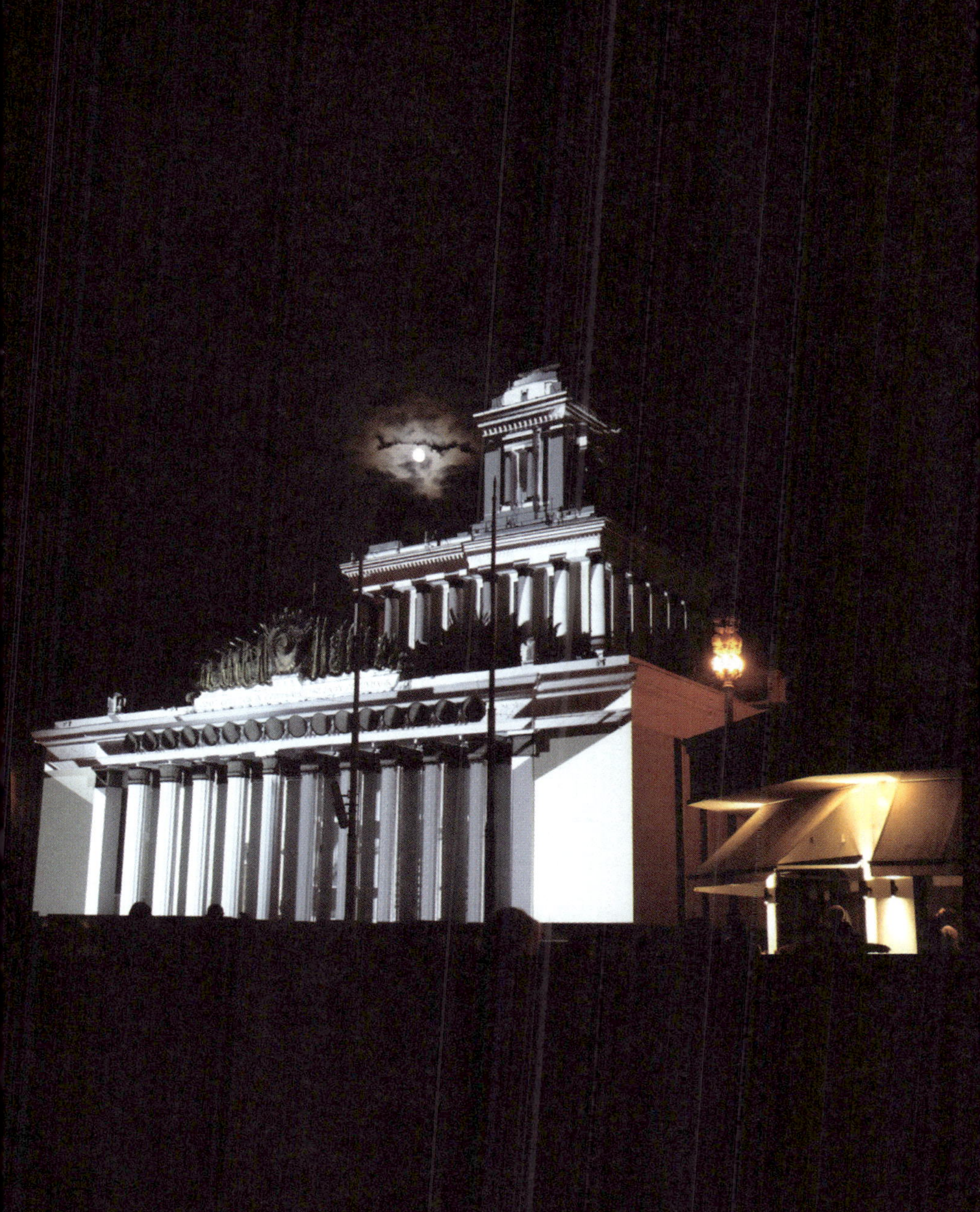

Detached from the basement it sets off as a spaceship and floates somewhere and then moves freely on a near-something orbit. Not near the Earth, but near-something, around a planet of some sort, where a lot of pavilions float in free rotation.

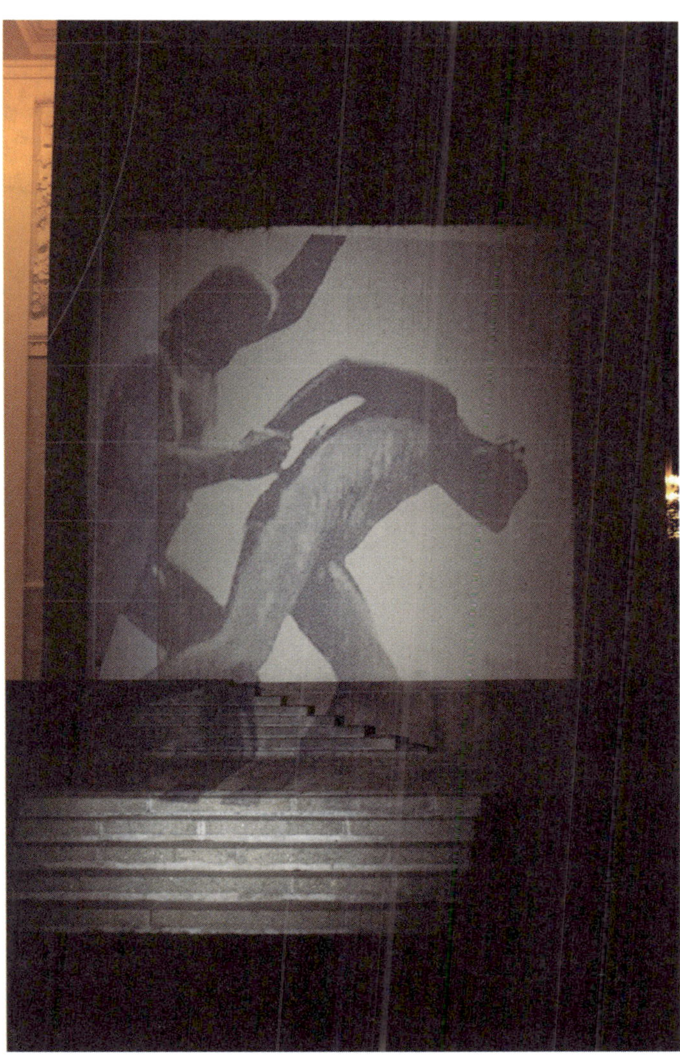

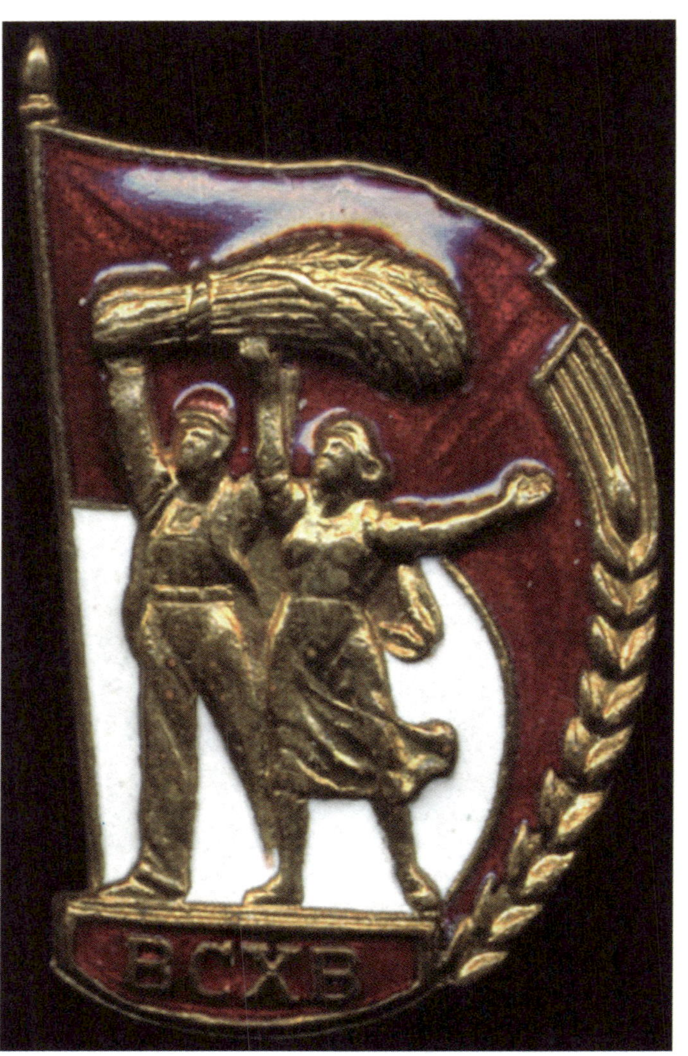
ВСХВ

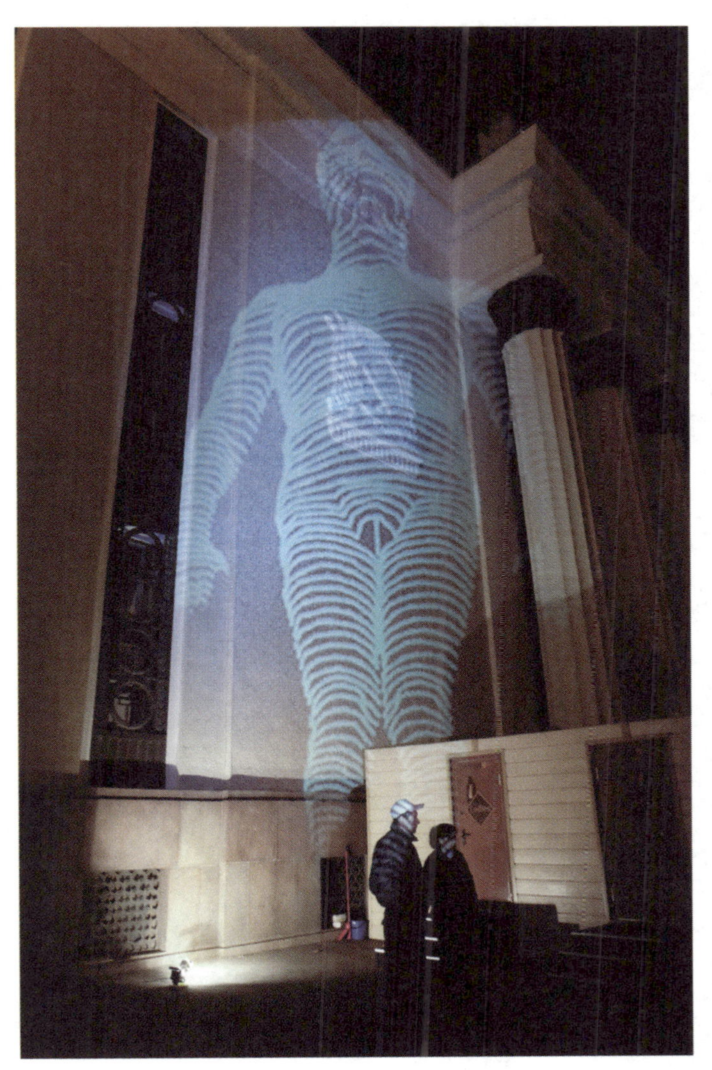

We manufacture the new man.

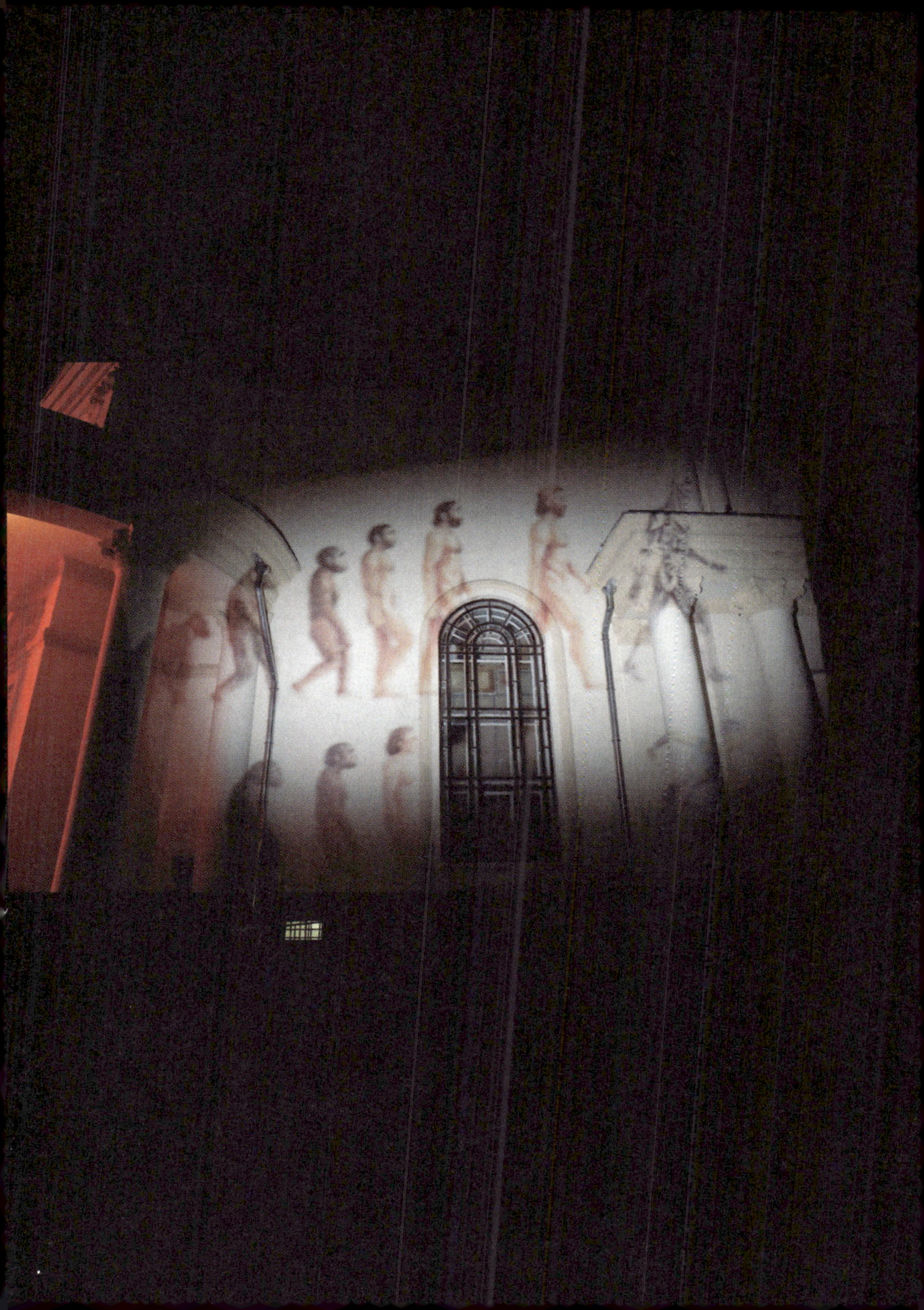

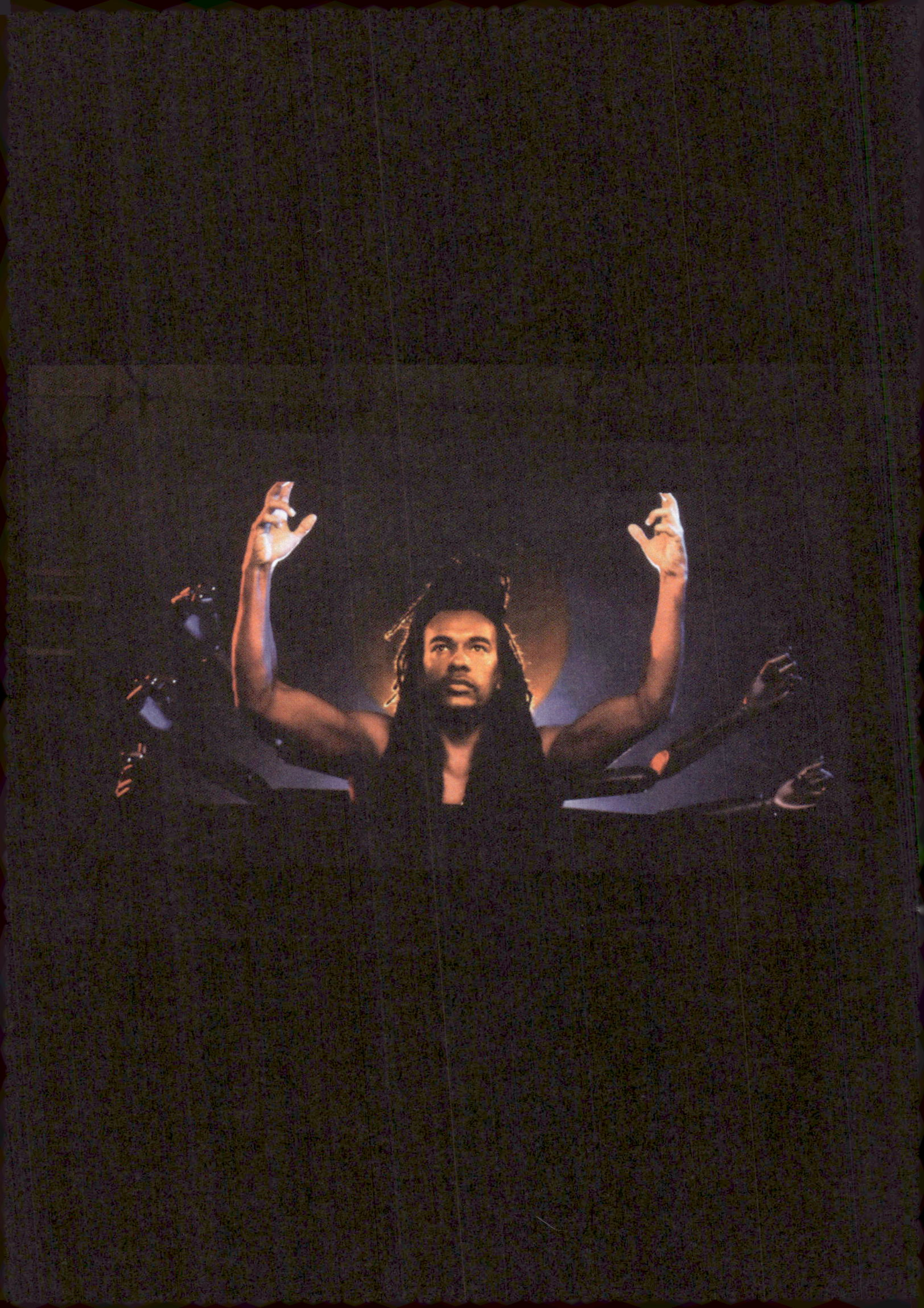

Perhaps the greatest artist is the one

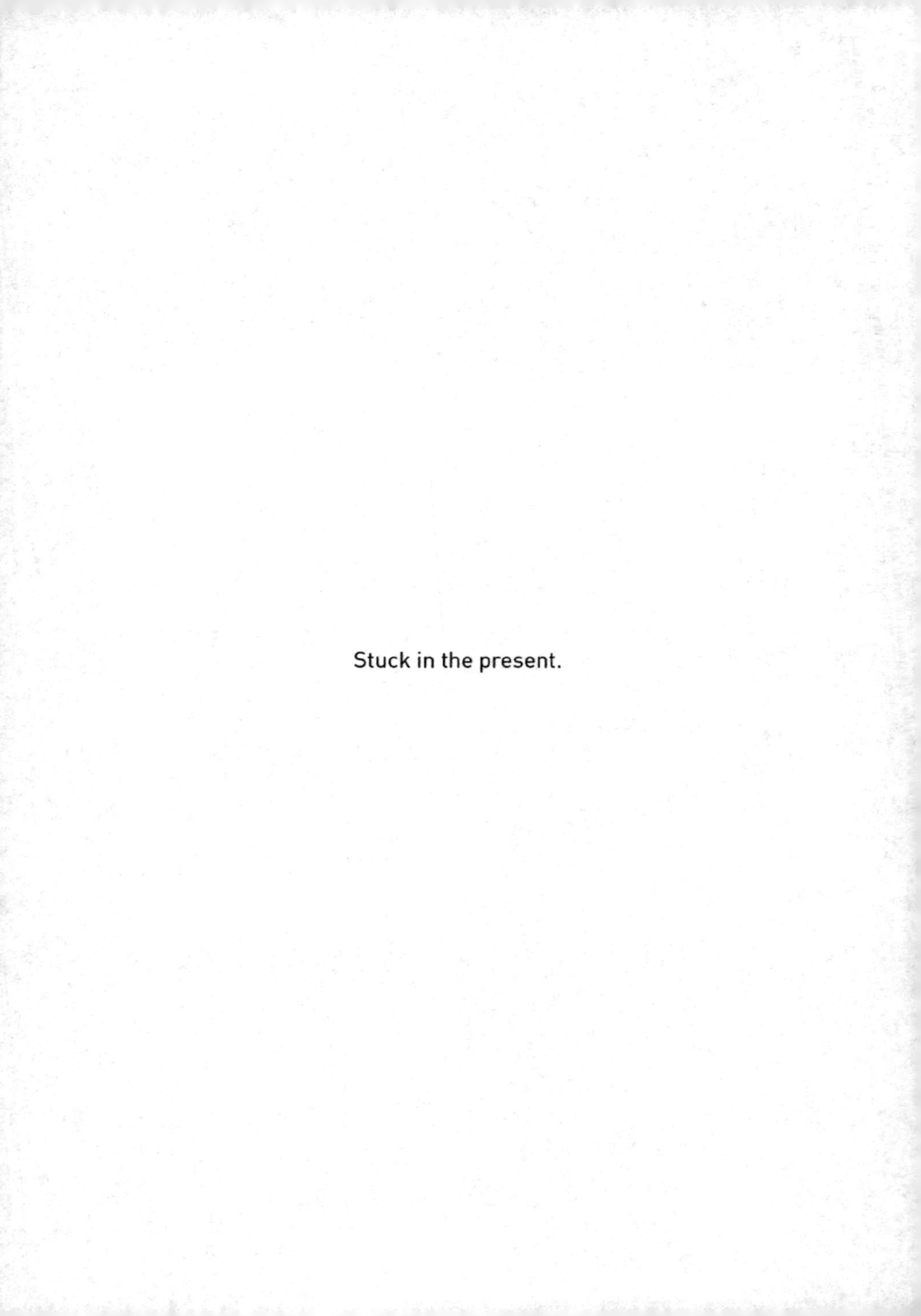
Stuck in the present.

Biographies

ACKBAR ABBAS [1942, CN] teaches comparative literature at the University of California, Irvine and is an honorary professor at Hong Kong University. His research interests include Hong Kong, Chinese culture, architecture and cinema, as well as critical theory, globalisation and post-colonialism.

SAÂDANE AFIF's [1970, FR] works are alterations. In performances, in objects rather than sculptures, in texts, poems, or posters, he deals with cultural production and presentation. He likes to re-interpret and change common formats of exhibitions, plays, dances, writing or other disciplines.

MARIA THERESA ALVES [1961, BR] was born in Brazil and moved to New York at a young age. She has worked for the International Indian Treaty Council in New York City and was the founder of the Brazilian Information Centre, working in defence of the human rights of indigenous people. In 1981, she co-founded the *Partido Verde* (Green Party) in São Paulo, Brazil. She has exhibited her artworks worldwide and often collaborates with Jimmie Durham.

BURAK ARIKAN [1976, TR] works with complex networks. He takes social, economic, and political issues as input and runs them through an abstract machinery which generates network maps and algorithmic interfaces, resulting in performances, and procreates predictions to render inherent power relationships visible and discussable. Arikan is the founder of *Graph Commons*, a collaborative network mapping platform.

DEFNE AYAS [1976, TR] is the Director of the Witte de With Center for Contemporary Art in Rotterdam. She co-founded Arthub Asia in 2007 — an Asia-wide active research and production initiative. Since 2005, she has been a curator of PERFORMA, the biennial of visual art performance in New York. In September 2012, Ayas co-curated the 11th Baltic Triennale as well as the Istanbul and Bandung City pavilions at the 9th Shanghai Biennale. In 2015, Ayas curated the Pavilion of Turkey at the Venice Biennale.

JOSEPH BACKSTEIN [1945, RU] is the commissioner of the Moscow Biennale for Contemporary Art and is director of the Institute of Contemporary Art, Moscow (ICA, Moscow). He is a member of the International Association of Art Critics (AICA), an honorary doctor of Gothenburg University, Sweden, and has been a member of the Russian Academy of Art since 2007.

BABI BADALOV [1959, AZ] is an Azeri artist and poet. After finishing art college in his native country, he left for Saint Petersburg in 1980, where he soon became an influential underground artist and a member of the unofficial Association of Experimental Visual Art (TEII). He expresses his ideas through art objects, paintings, installations and live performances. He also experiments with words and writes improvisational poetry, mixing languages and images of different cultures.

GLEB BERG [1986, RU] is creative director and managing partner of N3Design — an award-winning interactive agency based in Moscow. In 2010, he started work as a writer, collaborating with Vice, W-O-S and others. His prose is dedicated to problems of intercultural dialogue in Russia, as well as the ethics of the Northern Caucasus and the diaspora world of Moscow.

BIRDHEAD [Fc. 2004, SHANGHAI] is a photographic collective founded in 2004, consisting of Ji Weiyu (1980, CN) and Song Tao (1979, CN). Both artists graduated from the Shanghai Arts and Crafts School in 2000. Ji also studied at Central Saint Martins College of Art and Design in London.

SERGEY BRATKOV [1960, UA] conceives most of his photo works in a serial manner. This aesthetic conception or consideration distances Bratkov's work from the tradition of straightforward documentary to which it nonetheless seems inclined. Bratkov's imagery slyly comments upon the double problem of propaganda in contemporary Russian society, both in the residual reflexes of the old Soviet culture and in the cynical celebration of the free market economy.

RICARDO BREY [1955, CU] is a visual artist and graduate from the San Alejandro School of Art and the Cuban National School of Art. His artistic roots lie in the 1970s and 1980s when he was an active member of the group *Volumen I*. Brey moved to Ghent in 1990 and continues to live and work there. In 1997, he was awarded a Guggenheim Fellowship for Installation Art and Sculpture and also received the Culture Prize for Visual Art from the Flemish government.

ILYA BUDRAITSKIS [1981, RU] is a historian and activist in Moscow. Currently he is a post-graduate student at the Russian Academy of Science's Institute for World History. He was a participant in Avdey Ter-Oganyan's project School of Contemporary Art, and in Anatoly Osmolovsky's seminars on critical theory. Since 2005 he has been collaborating with David Ter-Oganyan and Alexandra Galkina in collective art-projects and exhibitions. He has been a political activist since 1997 and is currently the spokesperson for the socialist movement Forward. Budraitskis is a member of the editorial boards of *Moscow Art Magazine* and *Left Politics*.

PARK CHAN-KYONG [1965, KR] is a media artist, filmmaker and curator based in Seoul. His subjects have extended from the Cold War to traditional Korean religious culture, from media-oriented memory to regional utopian imaginations. His films have been shown in several renowned international art institutions and, in 2014, he served as artistic director for the international media art biennial Media City Seoul.

VAAST COLSON [1977, BE] belongs to the younger generation of Antwerp artists asking questions that concern the transformative potential of art in contemporary society. He seeks to define the role and status of the artist in this process of transformation.

KEREN CYTTER [1977, IL] lives and works in New York. She is a recipient of the Baloise Art Prize 2006 and has held solo exhibitions at the Stedelijk Museum in Amsterdam, the Kunsthalle Zürich, Frankfurter Kunstverein and Kunst-Werke in Berlin. Keren Cytter is a professor at Kunstakademie Düsseldorf.

BART DE BAERE [1960, BE] studied archaeology and the history of art. He became director of M HKA in 2002. From 1999 to 2001 he was advisor for cultural heritage and contemporary art to the Flemish Minister of Culture. From 1986 to 2001, Bart De Baere was curator in the Museum of Contemporary Art in Ghent. He has organised and curated events for several venues abroad, including *Documenta IX* in Kassel. He has been involved in establishing a biennial in South Africa and was a member of the International Advisory Council for the network of Soros Centres for Contemporary Art in Eastern Europe.

SIMON DENNY [1982, NZ] explores aspects of media economy, technological evolution, corporate and neoliberal culture, national identity, tech-industry culture and the Internet through his research-based art projects. He represented New Zealand at the 2015 Venice Biennale and has had a solo exhibition at MoMA PS1 in New York.

ELS DIETVORST [1964, BE] is predominantly known as a video-artist, thematising the existential conditions of loneliness and the relations between human beings and their environment. She started out as a drawer and sculptor and has realised impressive figurative works in loam.

BORIS DOLGIN [1971, RU] graduated from the Russian State University for the Humanities in 1993 and has since collaborated with various media. Since 2003, he has been working at *polit.ru*, where he holds the position of science editor and columnist.

JIMMIE DURHAM 1940, US is an internationally known artist, performer, poet and essayist. After 1969 he left the US to study at the École de Beaux Arts in Geneva. Four years later he returned to become an organiser in the American Indian Movement. Durham has lived in Europe since 1994. His artistic practice reflects his political activism and his Native American heritage.

MARIE EGGER 1987, DE is a curator and editor. She was assistant curator at the Kunsthalle Wien and has worked as a researcher and lecturer of contemporary art at Humboldt-University and the Freie Universität Berlin where she studied Cultural Theory, Art History, Iconic Studies and Arts Administration. She was part of the curatorial teams of the Moscow Biennale (2015), the Biennial of the Americas Denver (2013), and the Marrakech Biennale (2012).

IEVA EPNERE's 1977, LV works include photography, video and film. She is interested in relationships between people and their behaviour towards one another. Besides observing and analysing people and their social surroundings, she also often collaborates on photography projects. Personal and private stories oftentimes become a starting point for Ieva Epnere's artistic reflections on identity, tradition, and ritual.

ANASTASIA GACHEVA 1966, RU is director of the *Nikolay Fydorov Museum Library*. Together with Svetlana Semenova she has edited Fyodorov's collected works in a collection of four volumes with extensive notes and commentary. Anastasia Gacheva frequently writes and publishes works on Nikolay Fyodorov as well as related thinkers and writers. She regularly holds seminars, workshops and lectures all over the world and it is due to her work, Fedorov and other cosmists internationally won both academic and popular respect.

ISA GENZKEN 1948, DE assembles various found materials with which she creates sculptures and installations. The artist's interest in the combination of materials, in surfaces and superficialities becomes apparent in colourful, bizarre or conceptual works in different media. Isa Genzken is one of today's most renowned female artists, whose work meanders between severity and eccentric.

PASCAL GIELEN 1970, NL is a professor of Sociology of Art and Cultural Politics at Groningen University's Arts and Society research centre in the Netherlands. He is the editor-in-chief of the book series *Arts in Society*. His research focuses on creative labour, the institutional context of the arts, and on cultural politics.

LIAM GILLICK 1964, GB deploys multiple forms to expose the new ideological control systems that emerged at the beginning of the 1990s. He has developed a number of key narratives that often form the engine for a body of work. Gillick's work exposes the dysfunctional aspects of the modernist legacy in terms of abstraction and architecture when framed within a globalised, neoliberal consensus. His work extends into structural rethinking of the exhibition as a form.

EVGENY GONTMAKHER 1953, RU is an economist. He graduated with a degree in geography from Moscow State University and holds a PhD in Economics. Gontmakher is deputy director of the RAS Institute of World Economy and International Relations, a board member of the Institute for Contemporary Development (INSOR), and deputy director of the Kudrin Foundation for the Support of Civil Initiatives.

NADIA GOROKHOVA 1896, RU is a musician and video artist. She founded the independent publishing house *haec* based in St. Petersburg that releases sound editions and artist books.

EVGENY GRANILSHCHIKOV 1985, RU is an artist and independent film director. A graduate of the Rodchenko Moscow School of Photography and Multimedia, where he studied literature and animation. He works in different media, occasionally combining them into multipart projects. His films deal with the influence of political and social situations on individuals who are trying to work out their historical heritage or the way their background infects their private life.

ULRIKE GUÉROT 1964, DE is a political scientist. She is the founder and director of the European Democracy Lab and teaches at the European School of Governance and at Europa Universität Viadrina. Through former positions at the European Council on Foreign Relations, the Open Society Initiative for Europe, and the German Marshall Fund, she has been involved in the European think tank community.

FLAKA HALITI 1982, RKS is not interested in the recent debate on the political per se. Her credo is more on the lines of 'less political to be more political'. She understands the sensitive and complex nature of setting herself apart from a previous, male-dominated generation in Kosovo, which primarily aimed for European integration in the sense of a deep and somewhat ironic longing for the West.

RANA HAMADEH 1983, LB is a performance and visual artist. Interested in the curatorial approach within her artistic practice, she works on long term discursive research projects that operate as umbrellas for growing series of performances, choreographic / cartographic works, installations as stage sets, and writing projects. Her work stems from an extended investigation into specific concepts and terms, treating the field of theory as fiction.

HO TZU-NYEN 1976, SGP works primarily in film, video, and performance, and has recently developed environmental multimedia installations. He has also written extensively on art. Ho Tzu-Nyen appropriates the structures of epic myths, invoking their grandeur while revealing them to be not merely stories, but discursive tools.

HONORÉ δ'O's 1961, BE oeuvre consists of sculptures, assemblages and chain-reactions. The artist was born in 1961 as Raf Van Ommeslaege and reborn in 1984 in Ghent as Honoré δ'O. This rebirth and choice of name is connected to the artist's take on art and life which, he believes, are interchangeable. His works are dynamic and know no definitive form — they are always in movement. The everyday objects and materials that he uses continually change, split and multiply in an endless variety of ways.

FABRICE HYBER 1961, FR likes to invoke what he calls "the enormous reservoir of the possible." His interests revolve primarily around the power of art to give rise, shape and form to a potentially endless network of relationships between concepts, ideas, images, objects, signs, and thoughts — art as one particular form of materialising the immaterial.

ANNA JERMOLAEWA 1970, RU was born in Saint Petersburg, Russia, and has been based in Vienna, Austria since 1989. In her videos, photographs, and installations, she analyses social interrelations and political circumstances as they appear in everyday life. The subtle humour of her works reveals the effects of history and power manifested in the individual's experience.

LEON KAHANE 1985, DE grew up in the settings of the former GDR. His artistic practice is closely linked to his family history which is one of Jewish Holocaust survivors who came back to Germany. Experiences of migration, of belonging to a minority, and of social and political incapabilities to properly deal with such issues are what led to his interest in the relations between a global, cosmopolitan world and its individual, historical, private microcosms.

ALEVTINA KAKHIDZE 1973, UA has lived in Kiev and in Muzychi (Central Ukraine) since 1995, with the exception of a two-year research term at the

Jan Van Eyck Academy in Maastricht (2004-2006). Kakhidze's works are based on personal experiences and imagination, talking about consumer culture, gender, love, the culture of protest, experience of war, plants, and dogs.

ELENA KHOLKINA RU is a Moscow based photographer who studied at the Institute of Contemporary Art. She creates books and zines where she combines her intimate memories with archive materials, allowing her to remix and change the meaning of photographs, as well as to create new narratives. Her book *Did we ever meet?* won the Rock Your Dummy contest in Paris in 2013 and has since been exhibited all over Russia and Europe.

SUCHAN KINOSHITA 1960, JP worked in the theatre as an actress, director and set builder. These experiences informed her artistic views on the role of the spectator as an active observer. Kinoshita's works of art unfold in the course of time as dynamic processes in which a personal relationship between the spectator and the work takes shape. The place and time of the presentation play an important part. As far as she is concerned, static depictions and representations of 'something else' are only a distraction.

ALEKSANDER KOMAROV BY is an artist, filmmaker and author. He studied at the Academy of Visual Arts, Poznan, PL, and Rijksacademy, Amsterdam, NL. He has published filmic and written essays concerning questions of migrating identities, (cultural) globalisation, the condition of contemporary art and its relation to broader economic contexts.

MARIA KOTLYACHKOVA 1986, RU is a curator and writer currently working at Pikene på Broen in Kirkenes. For her B.A. in psychology, she specialised in intercultural communications. She also holds M.A. degrees in Cultural Management and Curating.

MARIA KRAMAR 1986, RU studied at the Rodchenko Art School in Moscow, at MediaArtLab's Open School Manège, and at Kingston University London where she specialised in Aesthetics and Art Theory. Her main research interests lie in the field of the politics of memory.

DONNA KUKAMA's 1981, ZA works unfold as performances, videos, texts and sound installations. In the shape of laboratories for creative research, they aim at a fictionalisation of reality. Donna Kukama occupies existing canons by using performance as a strategy to invent and apply methods to evoke the unexpected. For her, performance can be "a medium of resistance against already established 'ways of doing'."

ANDREY KUZKIN 1979, RU realises conceptual performances and installations inspired by Russian conceptualism but which bear within them a certain melancholy and brutalism. The artist's drawings and objects are sometimes transformed in the course of an exhibition or encounter. Usually, Andrey Kuzkin is physically involved in his performances, leaving the direction of the project up to the visitors.

GABRIEL LESTER 1972, NL "Trust me, I'm an Artist." — Gabriel Lester

LI MU 1974, CN lives and works in Feng County and Suzhou, China. Li Mu creates works in different genres, for example video, photography, installations and performance. Everyday life plays an important role in Li Mu's works, which succeed in blurring the borders between art and life: At times, Li Mu's life experiences become his works.

HANNE LIPPARD 1984, GB/NO is an artist whose works are based on text and sound. The human voice, often her own, is her main tool and means of creation. Based on stereotypes of everyday language, Lippard creates compositions of words, repetition and alienations. In her performances, the voice becomes a conductor to tell stories of accumulated speech — consisting of quotes, slogans, text messages, advertisements and melodic abstractions.

MADEIN Fd. 2009, CN is a cultural production company created by the Shanghai-based artist Xu Zhen in 2009. Its playful and provocative works span different genres and media including performance, sculpture, video, photography, Internet art, and painting.

IVES MAES 1976, BE has been working for several years around the notion of a 'Recyclable Refugee Camp', a biodegradable living unit following the regulations of the UNHCR, researching with a healthy dose of irony the capacity of art to intervene in the world. Over the last few years, his research has been focused on the relics of World Fairs, often dilapidated remnants of out-dated utopias.

TAUS MAKHACHEVA 1983, RU studied at Goldsmiths College and the Royal College of Art, London. She has developed a performance-based practice that questions cultural and gender norms. Working with video and photography, Makhacheva adopts a humorous criticality to everyday life in an attempt to reconcile the contemporary with the nostalgic, the local with the global, and tradition with progress.

JULIETTE MALOT 1989, FR received her MA at Sciences Po and a BA in Art History at the Sorbonne in Paris. She is a cultural producer and assisted Fabrice Hyber at the 6th Moscow Biennale 2015.

MARIANA MAZZUCATO 1968, IT holds the RM Phillips chair in the Economics of Innovation at the University of Sussex's Science Policy Research Unit (SPRU). She advises policy makers around the world on innovation-led growth and is a member of the Scottish Government's Council of Economic Advisors, a member of the World Economic Forum's Council on the Economics of Innovation, and a permanent member of the European Commission's expert group on Innovation for Growth (RISE).

TOM MCDONOUGH 1969, US is a writer and critic whose work addresses the intersections of art and political struggle in the post-war era, with a special emphasis on France. He is widely known for his books on the Situationist International and is currently Associate Professor of Art History at Binghamton University, State University of New York.

ROBERT MENASSE 1954, AT is a writer. He studied in Vienna, Salzburg and Messina, and completed his PhD on "The outsider phenotype within literature". Menasse is a frequent writer of essays, most recently on the future of Europe and the European Union. Since 2011, Robert Menasse has been curating a writer-in-residence programme for the One World Foundation in Sri Lanka.

ALMAGUL MENLIBAYEVA 1969, KZ studied at the Academy of Art and Theatre in Almaty, Kazakhstan. Her work has been the subject of numerous international solo and group exhibitions, such as the Sydney Biennial of Contemporary Art and the Venice Biennale. In her work, Menlibayeva combines an interest in regional traditions with a critique of official identity politics. She bases this criticism on the idea of nomadic pastoralism, the traditional way of life that distinguishes the history and culture of the Central Asian peoples.

MIÁN MIÁN 1970, CN has published books on Chinese youth and pop culture since the 1990s. After working as a DJ and promoter she also acted in the film version of her book *We Are Panic*. Her novels are internationally recognised and widely translated. Parts of her work have been censored in China.

NÁSTIO MOSQUITO 1981, AGO started out in musical training, and moved from this to film production. He has worked in various capacities for television in his native Angola for some time, but his deviations from entertainment formats formed the basis for what was to become his future life. Mosquito is first of all a performer, translating this into audiovisual representations and installations.

VANESSA JOAN MÜLLER 1968, DE is an art historian and curator. She has edited and contributed to numerous publications on contemporary art. Müller was a curator at the Frankfurter Kunstverein, and director of the Kunstverein für die Rheinlande und Westfalen in Düsseldorf. Since 2013, she has been head of dramaturgy at the Kunsthalle Wien. Müller is a Board Member of IKT — the International Association of Curators of Contemporary Art. In 2017, she curated the Albanian Pavilion at the Venice Biennale.

KATJA NOVITSKOVA 1984, EE is an installation artist whose work focuses on issues of technology, evolutionary processes, digital imagery and corporate aesthetics. Novitskova is interested in investigating how media actively redefines the world and culture. In 2017, she represented Estonia in the Venice Biennale.

ANATOLY OSMOLOVSKY 1969, RU is an artist, curator and teacher based in Moscow. He began his career as a writer, and was a member of the literary group *Vertep* before 1989. Between 1990 and 1992, he was the leader of the ETI (Art Territory Expropriation) movement, and participated in a series of street performances / provocations. In 1995, Osmolovsky founded *Radek Magazine*, which sought to create a space for radical politics under the current atmosphere of official suppression. In the 1990s, he was known as an active member of the Moscow Actionism movement. In 2011, together with Svetlana Baskova, he founded the BAZA Institute — a research and education platform for artists and art-critics.

MICHELANGELO PISTOLETTO 1933, IT has been associated with *arte povera*, defining a new kind of monumentality with his 1960s sculptures juxtaposing rags and other 'worthless' materials with the forms of classical antiquity. Since 1962, he has used mirrors and metals such as gold, silver or copper as reflective backgrounds for 'cut-out' life-sized photographic human figures. These super-impositions fuse the present and the past into a single image, challenging the very idea of representation.

DAVID POLZIN 1982, DE collects objects, reassembling or analysing them to invent spatial interventions. He creates situations that potentially distance the viewer from the artwork they expect to see by putting them right into its centre. A main source of inspiration is his hometown of Velten in Brandenburg, Germany, in the former GDR where he grew up in the 1980s and 1990s.

QIU ZHIJIE 1969, CN lives in Beijing as a full time artist, as well as an art critic and curator. As an artist, Qiu is known for his calligraphy, photography and video-installation works.

JON RAFMAN 1981, CA is an artist, filmmaker, and essayist. He holds an MFA from the School of the Art Institute of Chicago and a BA in Philosophy and Literature from McGill University. He studies the impact of technology on contemporary consciousness.

MEGGY RUSTAMOVA 1985, BE emigrated from Georgia with her mother, first to the Netherlands and then to Brussels. She creates interdisciplinary works which include videos, installations, and performances. Human actions are amongst her favourite subjects. Rustamova explores the way in which everything unfolds in life, how things happen, how to define the essence of the human being and the significance of art therein.

SASKIA SASSEN 1949, NL is the Robert S. Lynd Professor of Sociology and chair of the Committee on Global Thought at Columbia University (www.saskiasassen.com). She is the author of several books and the recipient of diverse awards and mentions, ranging from multiple *honoris causa* doctorates to named lectures and being selected for various honours lists. Her current book is *Expulsions: Brutal-*

ity and Complexity in the Global Economy (Harvard University Press 2014).

NICOLAUS SCHAFHAUSEN 1965, DE is the director of the Kunsthalle Wien. He studied art history in Berlin and Munich and worked as an artist before starting his career as a curator. He was the founding director of the European Kunsthalle. From 2006 to 2012, he headed the Witte de With Center for Contemporary Art in Rotterdam. Nicolaus Schafhausen was curator of the German Pavilion for the 52nd and 53rd Venice Biennales in 2007 and 2009. He has curated several international festivals and exhibitions, including Media City Seoul 2010 and Expo 2010 in Shanghai. Nicolaus Schafhausen is Strategic Director of Fogo Island Arts.

AUGUSTAS SERAPINAS 1990, LT is based in Vilnius, Lithuania, but works frequently in other locations where he realises context-based installations on site. His practice is developed around the alteration and manipulation of architectural spaces by contem plating their contexts and current or former purposes. With his interventions, Serapinas questions what is presented as reality.

ANDREY SHENTAL 1988, RU is an art critic, curator and artist based in Moscow. He received a BA in Art Criticism at Moscow State University and an MA in Critical Theory at the Centre for Research in Modern European Philosophy at Kingston University, London. Currently he works as a senior editor at *Moscow Art Magazine* and foreign correspondent for *Flash Art*.

MARINA SIMAKOVA 1985, RU is a cultural critic and social researcher with a background in Continental philosophy. Her essays cover a wide range of themes related to the problems of ideology and contemporary culture. She is particularly interested in the ways in which culture and politics intersect, and the social effects of these intersections.

OTTO SNOEK 1966, NL engages in photographic investigation of the differences and similarities of different communities. He spent years photographing his fellow citizens shopping and partying together, focusing on the people of his home town, Rotterdam, the 'gateway of Europe', before turning his attention to the wider continent.

STUDIO FOR NEW MUSIC ENSEMBLE Fd. 1993, RU is a leading contemporary music group in Russia. The ensemble was founded by composer Vladimir Tarnopolsky and conductor Igor Dronov in 1993. Every year the ensemble performs about 50 programmes in Moscow and throughout the country, and is a frequent guest at many Western contemporary music festivals.

LUC TUYMANS 1958, BE had his first exhibition in 1988. The selective vagueness of our memories in part determines the stylistic characteristics of his paintings. They are usually of modest format, oftentimes with pale, muted, sparse colours and a strongly simplified figuration bereft of visual 'detail'. Both individual as well as collective memory and past are important sources of inspiration for Tuymans, principally with respect to wartime.

ALEXANDER UGAY 1978, KZ founded the creative group *Bronepoezd* in partnership with Roman Maskalev. The group produces cinema-objects in the form of short experimental film-parables and film-performances recorded on 16 mm film by old cameras manufactured in the Soviet period. Ugay's main topic is time—how the past affects the future and vice versa, and how reality is transformed under the pressure of these streams.

THE UNBOUND is an anonymous art collective formed in 2015 to run the Caucasus Pavilion at the 6th Moscow Biennale for Contemporary Art. The group consists of several members, some of which are strongly connected to global art society, while others are not. The Unbound were nominated for an Innovation Award as the best curatorial project of 2015. No luck though.

U/N MULTITUDE is a community of artists and music historians whose practice is linked to performative and public activities. They refer to their works as "political scores", where music offers a space for understanding social and historical conflicts through immediate experiences.

V-A-C YOUNG CURATORS WORKSHOP is an education programme conceived by V-A-C Foundation — a Moscow-based institution dedicated to the development and international presentation of Russian contemporary culture. The workshop was organised in spring 2016 by Maria Mkrtycheva, head of education at the V-A-C Foundation. Through a series of meetings, it served as a discursive platform to reflect on the notion of togetherness. The participants were previously involved in the Moscow Curatorial Summer School.

ANNE-MIE VAN KERCKHOVEN 1951, BE combines different, seemingly disparate media to create complex installations. She creates drawings, paintings, performances, computer animations and video installations. Recurring themes are the relationships between man and animal, intelligence and intuition, and human creativity and artificial intelligence. For Anne-Mie van Kerckhoven, art functions as a tool of social critique. She questions existing power structures in the art world and in society in general.

MAYA VAN LEEMPUT BE earned a PhD from the University of Westminster in 2001. She combines research and consultancy with a creative multimedia practice. In 2015, she started working as senior researcher at the Erasmushogeschool, setting up the Knowledge Centre for Applied Futures Research — Open Time. Her activities gravitate towards the themes of media, culture, arts, (cross-cultural) communication, development, science and technology in society and urban environments. Her work is based in critical theory on alternative futures with experimental, creative and participatory approaches.

JOHANNA VAN OVERMEIR 1983, BE conveys her ideas to her audience through performances, installations and videos, as well as mixed media. She is the servant of her art; she abandons herself, her ego, during the processes and becomes the subject of her well-prepared actions. Johanna obtained her Master's degree at the KASK, Royal Academy of Fine Arts in Ghent.

MAARTEN VANDEN ABEELE 1970, BE mainly concentrates on photography, but also makes video art and installations. He displays his photographs in series without any apparent basis in narrative or chronology. For the artist, the mutual connection becomes clearer the more photographs he takes. In making each individual image, Vanden Abeele is led by his intuition. He considers photographs as frozen images comprising a memory's materialisation.

YANIS VAROUFAKIS 1961, GR is an economist, academic and politician, who served as the Greek Minister of Finance from January to July 2015, when he resigned. Varoufakis was also Syriza Member of the Hellenic Parliament for Athens B from January to September 2015. He is a member of DiEM25, a pan-European, cross-border movement of democrats.

DMITRY VENKOV 1980, RU is an artist based in Moscow. He graduated from the Rodchenko Art School in Moscow and holds an MA in Film Studies from the University of Oregon, Eugene. His works appeal to artistic, film and academic institutional contexts.

ANTON VIDOKLE 1965, RU/US is an artist and co-founder of e-flux. He has written a number of articles and has produced such projects as *The Next Documenta Should Be Curated by an Artist* (curated by Jens Hoffmann),

Do it (curated by Hans-Ulrich Obrist), and *Utopia Station* (poster project). Vidokle also organised *An Image Bank for Everyday Revolutionary Life* (based on the image archive of David Alfaro Siqueiros) and the Martha Rosler Library.

PETER WÄCHTLER's [1979, DE] works are characterised by dramaturgic components such as melancholy, pathos, ironic or satiric humour, romance and so on. Wächtler's video works, sculptures and texts do not always follow traditional rules of storylines and structures — ever so often doubts may befall the viewer on whether the works are fictitious or based on reality.

EYAL WEIZMAN [1970, IL] is an intellectual and architect. He holds positions as Professor of Spatial and Visual Cultures at Goldsmiths, University of London and Director of the Centre for Research Architecture within the Department of Visual Cultures. His research interests include the place of architecture in international humanitarian law as part of the *Forensic Architecture* project, and political theory on case studies such as Palestinian and Israeli geography and architecture.

INES WEIZMAN [1973, DE] completed her PhD in Architecture History and Theory at the Architectural Association after studying architecture in Weimar, Paris and Cambridge. She is a frequent writer and published the book *Architecture and the Paradox of Dissidence* in 2014. Since 2013, she has taught at Bauhaus Universität in Weimar and is co-director of the Institute for History and Theory of Architecture and Planning.

LEE WENG-CHOY [1963, MY] is an art critic. He studied physics, philosophy and literature before moving to Singapore. His writing on contemporary art has been widely published. In his lectures on cultural studies, essays and talks, he focuses on Asia and Asian art in the global realm as well as current strategies of cultural practice.

LU YANG [1984, CN] is a graduate of the China Academy of Art in the Master of Arts New Media department. She studied new media under Zhang Peili — commonly known as the father of video art in China. She uses biological and technological art to challenge the boundaries of art with her anti-humanistic approach.

ANASTASIYA YAROVENKO [1983, RU] recently graduated from the Akademie für Bildende Künste, Vienna. Her works are based on a definition of the human being as a social actor. She realised a project together with artist Anna Khodorkovskaya and gallery owner Hans Knoll in 2014; a series of exhibitions and lectures focusing on the current situation in different countries, including Russia and Ukraine — allowing for an open dialogue and intercultural exchange.

VASILY ZHARKOV [1974, RU] is head of the Political Science Department at the Moscow School of Social and Economic Sciences. He holds a PhD in Historical Sciences.

ARSENY ZHILYAEV [1984, RU] lives and works in Moscow and Voronezh. Using artistic, political, scientific, and museological histories to uncover and propose potential futures, Zhilyaev explores the productive space between fiction and non-fiction. In his recent projects, the artist casts a revisionist lens on the heritage of Soviet museology and meaning of the museum in Russian cosmism.

KONSTANTIN ZVEZDOCHOTOV [1957, RU] has long been one of the main representatives of the post-Perestroika Russian arts scene, and is a well-regarded key figure among a generation of artists who came of age in an artistic landscape formerly dominated by the likes of Ilya Kabakov. His work is characterised by carnivalesque humour and mixes many different geographic and historical styles.

Image Credits

p. 8
Nicolaus Schafhausen and Defne Ayas in conversation with visitors during Moscow Biennale for Contemporary Art 2015. Photo: Almagul Menlibayeva, 2015. Courtesy of the artist, Moscow Biennale and M HKA.

p. 9
Photo: Otto Snoek, 2015. Courtesy of the artist.

p. 24
Photo: Ivan Erofeev, 2015. Courtesy of the Moscow Biennale and M HKA.

pp. 26–32
Sergey Bratkov, *Predictions on the Moon*, 2015. Courtesy of the artist.

p. 43
Scan: Courtesy of the Moscow Biennale and M HKA, 2015.

pp. 44–45
Contract between Li Mu and the Moscow Biennale Art Foundation, 2015. Courtesy of the artist.

pp. 46–49
Li Mu, *The Labourer*, 2015, diary. Courtesy of the artist.

p. 62
Photo: Otto Snoek, 2015. Courtesy of the artist.

pp. 63–76
Ho Tzu-Nyen, *Curation is also a Form of Transportation*, 2015, video stills. Courtesy of the artist.

pp. 82–83
Meggy Rustamova, *Waiting for the Secret*, 2014, video still. Courtesy of the artist.

pp. 85–86
Johanna van Overmeir, *Janus*, personal notes, 2015. Courtesy of the artist.

p. 87
Photo: Natalya Kogan, 2015. Courtesy of the Moscow Biennale and M HKA.

pp. 89 and 97
Photos: Ivan Erofeev, 2015. Courtesy of the Moscow Biennale and M HKA.

pp. 109–112
Donna Kukama, *The Cemetery for Bad Behaviour*, 2015, scans of testimonies. Courtesy of the artist.

p. 113
Photo: Ivan Erofeev, 2015. Courtesy of the Moscow Biennale and M HKA.

p. 119
Photo: Otto Snoek, 2015. Courtesy of the artist.

pp. 132–133
Photos: Mireille Besnard, 2015. Courtesy of the artists.

pp. 134–136
Fabrice Hyber and Honoré δ'O, *Telepathic Experiment*, 2015, video stills. Courtesy of the artists.

p. 137
Photo: Otto Snoek, 2015. Courtesy of the artist.

pp. 133–139
Qiu Zhijie, *The Map of the Third World*, 2015. Courtesy of the Moscow Biennale and M HKA.

p. 140
Photo: Augustas Serapinas, 2015. Courtesy of the artist.

p. 148
Anastasiya Yarovenko, *The Trap of Habit*, 2015, personal notes. Courtesy of the artist.

p. 151
Photo: Otto Snoek, 2015. Courtesy of the artist. Photo: Yan Linn, 2015. Courtesy of the Moscow Biennale and M HKA.

pp. 154–157
Photos: Daniil Kolchanov, 2015. Courtesy of the artist.

pp. 164, 168 and 175
Photos: Natalya Kogan, 2015. Courtesy of the Moscow Biennale and M HKA.

pp. 175 and 179
Photos: Bart De Baere, 2015. Courtesy of the Moscow Biennale and M HKA.

pp. 180–181
Photo: Maria Anaskina, 2015. Courtesy of the Moscow Biennale and M HKA.

pp. 182–185
Inventing Ritual, instructions for the performance, 2015. Courtesy of the artists.

pp. 186–187
Gabriel Lester, *MurMure*, 2015. Photo: Yan Linn, 2015. Courtesy of the Moscow Biennale and M HKA.

pp. 188–189
Photo: Alexey Sapronenkov, 2015. Courtesy of the Moscow Biennale and M HKA.

p. 190
Photo: Ivan Erofeev, 2015. Courtesy of the Moscow Biennale and M HKA.

pp. 195–213
Honoré δ'O, *The Ten Commandments*, 2015. Courtesy of the artist.

p. 215
Séance I, 22nd September 2015. Photo: Bart De Baere, 2015. Courtesy of the Moscow Biennale and M HKA.
Séance II, 23rd September 2015. Photo: Otto Snoek, 2015. Courtesy of the artist.
How to Produce a Wishing Well, 24th September 2015. Courtesy of the Moscow Biennale and M HKA.

p. 216
500 times White Space, 25th September 2015. Scan: Courtesy of the Moscow Biennale.
Eventually Melons hit the floor, 26th September 2015. Photo: Maria Anaskina, 2015. Courtesy of the Moscow Biennale and M HKA.

p. 217
First Orbit, 27th September 2015. Photo: Almagul Menlibayeva, 2015. Courtesy of the Moscow Biennale and M HKA.
Falling in Love With Elvis, 28th September 2015. Photo: Ivan Erofeev, 2015. Courtesy of the Moscow Biennale and M HKA.
Onstageoffstagededicatingsongsdilemma revisited, 29th September 2015. Courtesy of the Moscow Biennale and M HKA.

p. 218
I Feel Your Pain, 30th September 2015. Photo: Ivan Erofeev, 2015. Courtesy of the Moscow Biennale and M HKA.
Euro Chair—Ruble Chair, 1st October 2015. Photo: Maria Anaskina, 2015. Courtesy of the Moscow Biennale and M HKA.

p. 219
Andrey Kuzkin, *Balloons and Nails*, 2015. Photo: Alexey Sapronenkov, 2015. Courtesy of the Moscow Biennale and M HKA.

p. 220
Isa Genzken, *Die kleine Bushaltestelle (Gerüstbau)*, 2012, installation view. Photo: Bart De Baere, 2015. Courtesy of the Moscow Biennale and M HKA.

p. 225
Photo: Otto Snoek, 2015. Courtesy of the Moscow Biennale and M HKA.

pp. 230–231
Photo: Ivan Erofeev, 2015. Courtesy of the Moscow Biennale and M HKA.

p. 236
Photo: Natalya Kogan, 2015. Courtesy of the Moscow Biennale and M HKA.
Photo: Alexey Sapronenkov, 2015. Courtesy of the Moscow Biennale and M HKA.

p. 238
Leon Kahane, *Fantasia*, 2015, video still. Courtesy of the artist.

pp. 240–241
Photo: Natalya Kogan, 2015. Courtesy of the Moscow Biennale and M HKA.

p. 243
Photo: Ivan Erofeev, 2015. Courtesy of the Moscow Biennale and M HKA.

p. 246
Poster and instructions for Saâdane Afif, *Play Opposite*, 2015. Courtesy of the artist.

pp. 247–249
Saâdane Afif, *Play Opposite*, 2015. Photos: Lilas Duvernois Guevara, 2015. Courtesy of the artist.

p. 258
Photo: Almagul Menlibayeva, 2015. Courtesy of the Moscow Biennale and M HKA.

p. 261
Taus Makhacheva, *On the Benefits of Pyramids in Cultural Education, Strengthening of National Consciousness, and the Formation of Moral and Ethical Guideposts*, 2015. Photo: Otto Snoek, 2015. Courtesy of the artist.

pp. 264–281
Photo: Ivan Erofeev, 2015. Courtesy of the Moscow Biennale and M HKA.

p. 292
Photo: Alexey Sapronenkov, 2015. Courtesy of the Moscow Biennale and M HKA.

p. 307
Photo: Natalya Kogan, 2015. Courtesy of the Moscow Biennale and M HKA.

pp. 308–314
Alevtina Kakhidze, *All Times News*, 2015. Courtesy of Alevtina Kakhidze.

p. 322
Almagul Menlibayeva, 2016. Courtesy of the artist.

pp. 328 and 330
Simon Denny, *DLD—All You need Is Data*, 2013, Kunstverein München. Photo: Ulrich Gebert. Courtesy of the artist.

pp. 331 and 333
Simon Denny, *Disruptive Berlin*, 2014, installation view, Galerie Buchholz, Berlin. Courtesy of Galerie Buchholz, Berlin/Cologne.

p. 335
Courtesy of the artist.

p. 337
Simon Denny, *The Personal Effects of Kim Dotcom*, 2014, installation view at Adam Art Gallery Wellington. Photo: Shaun Waugh. Courtesy of the artist and Adam Art Gallery Wellington.

p.339
Simon Denny, *TEDx Vaduz*, 2013. Courtesy of the artist.

p. 342
Simon Denny, *Secret Power*, 2015 installation views. Photos: Jens Ziehe. Courtesy of the artist.

p. 345
Photo: Otto Snoek. Courtesy of the artist.

pp. 356–359
Aleksander Komarov, *Estate*, 2010/2015, HD video, 20 mins., video stills. Courtesy of the artist.

p. 360
Photo: Otto Snoek. Courtesy of the artist.

p. 373
Almagul Menlibayeva, *Center of Eurasia*, 2014. Photo: Yan Linn, 2015. Courtesy of the Moscow Biennale and M HKA.

p. 374
Park Chan-kyong, *Anyang, Paradise City*, video still. Courtesy of the artist.

p. 380
Almagul Menlibayeva, 2016. Courtesy of the artist.

p. 384
Courtesy of the Moscow Biennale and M HKA.

p. 401
Marcel Duchamp, *Monte Carlo Bond*, 1938. Harvard Art Museums / Fogg Museum, Gift of Peter G. and Elizabeth S. Neumann, 2009.189 (c) Artists Rights Society (ARS), New York / ADAGP, Paris / Estate of Marcel Duchamp, Photo: Imaging Department (c) President and Fellows of Harvard College.

pp. 410–411
Almagul Menlibayeva, 2016. Courtesy of the artist.

p. 423
Photo: Otto Snoek, 2015. Courtesy of the artist.

pp. 424–426
Almagul Menlibayeva, *Green, Yellow, Red and Green Again*, video stills, 2015. Courtesy of the artist.

pp. 435–440
Moscow Biennale for Contemporary Art 2015, installation views. Courtesy of Moscow Biennale, M HKA and Studio MEL.

p. 443
Photo: Ivan Erofeev, 2015. Courtesy of the Moscow Biennale and M HKA.

p. 444
Photo: Babi Badalov, 2015. Courtesy of the artist.

pp. 447 and 449
Maria Thereza Alves, *Tchám Krai Kytõm Pandã Grét (Male Display Among European Populations)*, video, 2:25 mins., 2008, stills. Courtesy of the artist.

pp. 450–451
Fabrice Hyber, *Montmartre Spirit* in Moscow, 2015. Photo: Otto Snoek, 2015. Courtesy of the artist.
p. 452
Photo: Alexey Sapronenkov, 2015. Courtesy of the Moscow Biennale and M HKA.

pp. 456–457
David Polzin, *Department for Information Exchange*, 2015. Courtesy of the artist.

pp. 458–464
Evgeny Granilshchikov, *Unfinished Film*, video, 27 mins., 2014, stills. Courtesy of the artist.

p. 467
Jon Rafman, *Erysichthon*, 2015, still. Courtesy of the artist and Feuer/Mesler, New York.

p. 471
Photo: Ivan Erofeev, 2015. Courtesy of the Moscow Biennale and M HKA.

pp. 472–473
Photo: Ivan Erofeev, 2015. Courtesy of the Moscow Biennale and M HKA.

pp. 474–475
Photos: Bart de Baere, Ivan Erofeev and Yan Linn, 2015. Courtesy of the Moscow Biennale and M HKA.

p. 478
Photo: Alexey Sapronenkov, 2015. Courtesy of the Moscow Biennale and M HKA.
Photo: Yan Linn, 2015. Courtesy of the Moscow Biennale and M HKA.

pp. 490–491
Photo: Maria Anaskina, 2015. Courtesy of the Moscow Biennale and M HKA.

p. 493
Photo: Maria Anaskina, 2015. Courtesy of the Moscow Biennale and M HKA.

p. 495
Photos: Maria Anaskina, 2015. Courtesy of the Moscow Biennale and M HKA.

p. 496
Photo: Otto Snoek, 2015. Courtesy of the artist.

pp. 498–509
Photos: Maarten Vanden Abeele, 2015. Courtesy of the artist.

p. 510
Photo: Otto Snoek, 2015. Courtesy of the artist.

pp. 511–512
Photos: Maria Anaskina, 2015. Courtesy of the Moscow Biennale and M HKA.

p. 513
Courtesy of the Mayakovsky State Museum, Moscow.

p. 516
Photo: Yan Linn, 2015. Courtesy of the Moscow Biennale and M HKA.

p. 519
Installation of Els Dietvorst, *Skull*, 2015. Photo: Yan Linn, 2015. Courtesy of the Moscow Biennale and M HKA.

pp. 522–523
Photo: Otto Snoek, 2015. Courtesy of the artist.

pp. 527–528
Sergey Bratkov, *Eclipse*, 2015. Courtesy of the artist.

pp. 532–533 and 537–538
Courtesy of Maya van Leemput.

pp. 544–545
Photos: Katya Novitskova and Museum of Estonian Architecture.

p. 547
Alexander Ugay, *Earth and Shape*, 2013–2015, video still. Courtesy of the artist.

p. 552
Audience of Moscow Biennale 2015. Photo: Otto Snoek, 2015. Courtesy of the artist.

p. 558
Photo: Alexey Sapronenkov, 2015. Courtesy of the Moscow Biennale and M HKA.

pp. 565–572
Photos: Ives Maes, 2015. Courtesy of the artist.

p. 575
Lu Yang, *Moving Gods*, 2015, video still. Courtesy of the artist.

p. 576
Ricardo Brey, *Horntails*, 2006, 135 x 105 mm. Photo: Isabel Brey. Courtesy of the artist.

p. 577
Ricardo Brey, *In the kitchen*, 2006, 159 x 120 mm. Photo: Isabel Brey. Courtesy of the artist.

p. 578
Photo: Yan Linn, 2015. Courtesy of the Moscow Biennale and M HKA.

p. 579
Anne Mie van Kerckhoven, *Madonna and Leviathan*, 2015. Photo: Maria Anaskina, 2015. Courtesy of the Moscow Biennale and M HKA.

p. 580
Ieva Epnere, *Renunciation*, video still. Courtesy of the artist.

p. 582
Photo: Ivan Erofeev, 2015. Courtesy of the Moscow Biennale and M HKA.

p. 585
Photo: Ksenia Kolesnikova, 2015. Courtesy of the Moscow Biennale and M HKA.

p. 591
Photo: Natalya Kogan, 2015. Courtesy of the Moscow Biennale and M HKA.

p. 592
Photo: Alexander Prokop, 2010. Courtesy Alexander Prokop.

pp. 593–604
Elena Kholkina, *Dreams of the Pavilion*, 2015. Courtesy of the artist.

Colophon

HOW TO GATHER
Acting Relations,
Mapping Positions

This publication is an outcome of the 6th Moscow Biennale for Contemporary Art, presented at VDNKh, Moscow, from 22nd September to 1st October 2015.

Editors:
Bart De Baere, Defne Ayas, Nicolaus Schafhausen, and Marie Egger

Contributors & Participants:
Ackbar Abbas, Saâdane Afif, Maria Theresa Alves, Burak Arikan, Defne Ayas, Joseph Backstein, Babi Badalov, Gleb Berg, Birdhead, Sergey Bratkov, Ricardo Brey, Ilya Budraitskis, Park Chan-kyong, Vaast Colson, Keren Cytter, Bart De Baere, Simon Denny, Els Dietvorst, Boris Dolgin, Igor Doshlygin, Fedor Dubinnikov, Jimmie Durham, Marie Egger, Ieva Epnere, Anastasya Gacheva, Isa Genzken, Pascal Gielen, Liam Gillick, Evgeny Gontmakher, Nadia Gorokhova, Evgeny Granilshchikov, Ulrike Guérot, Flaka Haliti, Rana Hamadeh, Ho Tzu-Nyen, Honoré δ'O, Fabrice Hyber, Ivan Isaev, Anna Jermolaewa, Leon Kahane, Alevtina Kakhidze, Elena Kholkina, Suchan Kinoshita, Daniil Kolchanov, Aleksander Komarov, Maria Kotlyachkova, Maria Kramar, Donna Kukama, Andrey Kuzkin, Gabriel Lester, Li Mu, Hanne Lippard, MadeIn, Ives Maes, Taus Makhacheva, Juliette Malot, Mariana Mazzucato, Tom McDonough, Robert Menasse, Almagul Menlibayeva, Mián Mián, Nástio Mosquito, Maria Mkrtycheva, Vanessa Joan Müller, Katja Novitskova, Anatoly Osmolovsky, Goran Petrovic, Lu Pingyuan, Michelangelo Pistoletto, David Polzin, Qiu Zhijie, Jon Rafman, Meggy Rustamova, Saskia Sassen, Ekaterina Savchenko, Nicolaus Schafhausen, Augustas Serapinas, Andrey Shental, Marina Simakova, Otto Snoek, Sona Stepanyan, Maria Stepkina, Studio for New Music Ensemble, Luc Tuymans, Alexander Ugay, The Unbound, u/n multitude, Anne-Mie van Kerckhoven, Maya van Leemput, Johanna van Overmeir, Maarten Vanden Abeele, Yanis Varoufakis, Dmitry Venkov, Anton Vidokle, Eyal Weizman, Lee Weng-Choy, Ines Weizman, Peter Wächtler, Lu Yang, Zhao Yao, Anastasiya Yarovenko, Vasily Zharkov, Arseny Zhilyaev, Alexander Zhuravlev, Anna Zhurba, Konstantin Zvezdochotov

Managing Editor:
Marie Egger

Associate Editor & Publication Coordinator:
Maria-Louiza Ouranou

Content Management V-A-C Foundation:
Maria Mkrtycheva, Daria Kalugina

Content Management M KHA, Antwerp:
Evi Bert, Pablo Martinez Fraga, Ekaterina Savchenko

V-A-C Young Curators Workshop, Moscow:
Maria Mkrtycheva

Copy-Editors:
Ben McGarr (English)
Evgenia Shestova (Russian)

Translators:
Dina Akhmadeeva, Thomas Clark, Ben McGarr, Ksenia Poluektova-Krimer, Kirill Medvedev, Gerda Maria Newhoner, Alexander Pisarev, Anna Pronina, Maria Pronina, Thomas Reynolds, Andrey Shental, Katya Taylor

Transcriptions:
Sabine Herrygers, Eleanor Taylor, Alexander Pisarev

Design & Layout:
Ayumi Higuchi

Front Cover Design:
Roman Gornitsky

Printed & Bound at:
Tallinn Book Printers

Print-Run:
1500 copies

Published by:
Kunsthalle Wien, Vienna; M HKA, Museum van Hedendaagse Kunst Antwerpen; Witte de With Center for Contemporary Art, Rotterdam, and V-A-C Foundation, Moscow

ISBN 978-5-9906255-7-0

All rights reserved.
© the artists, authors and institutions, 2017.

Published with the support of:
V-A-C Foundation, Moscow

Distribution:
D.A.P. Inc., New York (US only)
Cornerhouse, Manchester (UK and Ireland only)
Idea Books, Amsterdam (The Netherlands and all other EU countries)

Thanks to:
Caroline Cooper, Sophie De Beukelaer, Rosa de Graaf, Polina Demidova, Jan De Vree, Isabella Donadio (Harvard Art Museum), Igor Doshlygin, Fedor Dubinnikov, Ivan Erofeev, Jarmo Kauge (Museum of Estonian Architecture), Teresa Iarocci Mavica, Jayne Miller (TeleGeography), Anna-Lisa Scherfose, Nico Schmidt, Nina Schreckenbach, Nina Shundik (Mayakovsky State Museum, Moscow), Anastasia Skvortsova, Maria Terekhova, Helen Weaver, Stephen Williams (Indiana University Press), Tianyang Wu, and the volunteers and artist assistants of the 6th Moscow Biennale for Contemporary Art: Tatiana Alexanenkova, Mariam Ambartsumyan, Natalya Andrianova, Asya Ashman, Anna Barysheva, Evfrosiniya Bumazhnova, Irina Demiyanets, Elena Ditskova, Sofya Dmitrieva, Lilas Duvernois Guevara, Daria Egorova, Varvara Ganicheva, Elizaveta Golovina, Umrat Kabylova, Alisa Kerr, Polina Klebanova, Daniil Kolchanov, Ekaterina Konyashina, Elena Konyushikhina, Marina Kopytova, Yulia Korobova, Anastasia Kozhukhova, Ivan Kuleshov, Polina Kuprina, Maria Kupriyanova, Inga Kurilova, Valeria Lavrova, Yongxiang Li, Daria Likhovitskaya, Yan Linn, Anna Lopatina, Natalia Lukatskaya, Olga Lyubartovich, Natalya Maximova, Anna Milovanova, Elizaveta Milyukhina, Aisylu Mutigullina, Anna Novikova, Natalia Polyanskaya, Alina Ponomareva, Vera Raskina, Taisiya Reznichenko, Anna Ryavina, Julietta Sarkisyan, Ekaterina Savina, Elizaveta Semenova, Nadezhda Semykina, Natalya Simbireva, Yulia Simpanen, Ekaterina Smolyakova, Julie Syropaeva, Nina Tishina, Natalya Trudolyubova, Anna Trusova, Daria Uryadova, Anastasia Volynova, Ekaterina Vorontsova, Faina Yunusova, Daria Zhdan